The Garbage Collection Handbook

Published in 1996, Richard Jones's *Garbage Collection* was a milestone in the area of automatic memory management. Its widely acclaimed successor, *The Garbage Collection Handbook: The Art of Automatic Memory Management*, captured the state of the field in 2012. Modern technology developments have made memory management more challenging, interesting and important than ever. This second edition updates the handbook, bringing together a wealth of knowledge gathered by automatic memory management researchers and developers over the past sixty years. The authors compare the most important approaches and state-of-the-art techniques in a single, accessible framework.

The book addresses new challenges to garbage collection made by recent advances in hardware and software. It explores the consequences of these changes for designers and implementers of high performance garbage collectors. Along with simple and traditional algorithms, the book covers state-of-the-art parallel, incremental, concurrent and real-time garbage collection. Algorithms and concepts are often described with pseudocode and illustrations.

The Garbage Collection Handbook

The Art of Automatic Memory Management

Richard Jones, Antony Hosking and Eliot Moss

CRC Press
Taylor & Francis Group
Boca Raton London New York

CRC Press is an imprint of the
Taylor & Francis Group, an **informa** business

A CHAPMAN & HALL BOOK

Second edition published 2023
by CRC Press
6000 Broken Sound Parkway NW, Suite 300, Boca Raton, FL 33487-2742

and by CRC Press
4 Park Square, Milton Park, Abingdon, Oxon, OX14 4RN

CRC Press is an imprint of Taylor & Francis Group, LLC

Library of Congress Cataloging-in-Publication Data

Names: Jones, Richard, author. | Hosking, Antony, 1964- author. |
  Moss, J. Eliot B., author.
Title: The Garbage Collection handbook : the art of automatic memory
  management / Richard E. Jones, University of Kent, Antony Hosking,
  The Australian National University, J. Eliot B. Moss, University of
  Massachusetts Amherst.
Description: Second edition. | Boca Raton : CRC Press, 2023. | Includes
  bibliographical references and index.
Identifiers: LCCN 2022055284 (print) | LCCN 2022055285 (ebook) | ISBN
  9781032218038 (hardback) | ISBN 9781032231785 (paperback) | ISBN
  9781003276142 (ebook)
Subjects: LCSH: Memory management (Computer science)
Classification: LCC QA76.9.M45 J66 2023 (print) | LCC QA76.9.M45 (ebook)
  | DDC 005.4/3--dc23/eng/20221117
LC record available at https://lccn.loc.gov/2022055284
LC ebook record available at https://lccn.loc.gov/2022055285

ISBN: 978-1-032-21803-8 (hbk)
ISBN: 978-1-032-23178-5 (pbk)
ISBN: 978-1-003-27614-2 (ebk)

DOI: 10.1201/9781003276142

Typeset in URW PalladioL-Roma font
by KnowledgeWorks Global Ltd.

Publisher's note: This book has been prepared from camera-ready copy provided by the authors.

To
Robbie, Helen, Kate and William
Mandi, Ben, Matt, Jory, Katja and Rowan
Hannah, Natalie and Cas

Contents

List of Algorithms

List of Figures

List of Tables

Preface

This is the second edition of *The Garbage Collection Handbook*. How is it that, more than sixty years after the introduction of garbage collection in 1958 and exactly thirty years[1] since the first *International Workshop on Memory Management* (the forerunner of the *International Symposium on Memory Management*) in 1992, garbage collection in particular and memory management more generally remain such vital topics of research and development?

Garbage collection was born in the Lisp programming language. McCarthy [1978] recollects that the first online demonstration was to an MIT Industrial Liaison Symposium. It was important to make a good impression but, unfortunately, midway through the demonstration, the IBM 704[2] exhausted (all of!) its 32k words of memory — McCarthy's team had omitted to refresh the Lisp core image from a previous rehearsal — and its Flexowriter printed, at ten characters per second,

```
THE GARBAGE COLLECTOR HAS BEEN CALLED. SOME INTERESTING
STATISTICS ARE AS FOLLOWS:
```

and so on at great length, taking all the time remaining for the demonstration. McCarthy and the audience collapsed in laughter. Over sixty years on now, garbage collection is no joke but an essential component of modern programming language implementations. Indeed, Rust (first released in 2012) and Visual Basic (introduced in 1991) are probably the only widely used languages developed since 1990 not to adopt automatic memory management of some kind, yet Rust provides a reference counted smart pointer and VB.NET (2002), a modern incarnation of Visual Basic, relies on the garbage collector in Microsoft's Common Language Runtime.

Garbage collection continues to be a vibrant area of research and is far from a solved problem. In Blackburn's words [2022], "Seismic technology shifts, unprecedented scale, concerns for energy efficiency and security, a diversity of programming languages and above all, ubiquity, have conspired to make memory management more challenging, interesting, and important than ever." Memory management sits at the crucial interface between the hardware and the programming language. It presents deep problems and challenges, both theoretical and engineering. Garbage collection is probably more important and affects more people than ever before. It is in their phones and their browsers; it is in the servers in the cloud on which so much of modern life depends. Despite the growth in capacity on every device from the smallest one in your pocket to the largest systems in enterprise-scale warehouses, memory is not free and efficient access is vital. For example,

---

[1] By yet another curious chronological coincidence, we started writing the first edition on the tenth anniversary of the *First International Symposium on Memory Management*, held in October 1998, itself almost exactly forty years after the implementation of Lisp started in 1958.

[2] The IBM 704's legacy to the Lisp world includes the terms car and cdr. The 704's 36-bit words included two 15-bit parts, the address and decrement parts. Lisp's list or cons cells stored pointers in these two parts. The head of the list, the car, could be obtained using the 704's `car` 'Contents of the Address part of Register' macro instruction, and the tail, the cdr, with its `cdr` 'Contents of the Decrement part of Register' macro instruction.

recently Hunter *et al.* [2021] found (and then recovered) 26% of memory that was wasted due to fragmentation in Google's warehouse-scale computers: a significant cost in both financial and energy terms.

The advantages that garbage collected languages offer to software development are legion. Garbage collection eliminates whole classes of bugs, such as attempting to follow dangling pointers that still refer to memory that has been reclaimed or worse, reused in another context. Thus, it helps reduce memory vulnerabilities, by far the most pressing security concern today. It makes it no longer possible to free memory that has already been freed. It reduces the chances of programs leaking memory, although it cannot cure all errors of this kind. It greatly simplifies the construction and use of concurrent data structures [Herlihy and Shavit, 2008]. Above all, the abstraction offered by garbage collection provides for better software engineering practice. It simplifies user interfaces and leads to code that is easier to understand and to maintain, and hence more reliable. By removing memory management worries from interfaces, it leads to code that is easier to reuse.

The memory management field has developed at an ever-increasing rate in recent years, in terms of both software and hardware. In 1996, a typical Intel Pentium processor had a clock speed of 120 MHz although high-end workstations based on Digital's Alpha chips could run as fast as 266 MHz! Today's top-end processors commonly run at over 3 GHz — Intel's recently announced Core i9-12900KS can even run at up to 5.5 GHz! Multicore chips are ubiquitous. The size of main memory deployed has similarly increased nearly 1000-fold, from a few megabytes to multiple gigabytes being common in desktop machines today, and terabytes in servers. Nevertheless, the advances made in the performance of DRAM memory continue to lag well behind those of processors. At that time, in his first book, *Garbage Collection: Algorithms for Automatic Dynamic Memory Management*, (Wiley, 1996), Richard did not argue that "garbage collection is a panacea for all memory management problems," and in particular pointed out that "the problem of garbage collection for hard real-time programming [where deadlines must be met without fail] has yet to be solved." Yet by the time of the first edition of this book (2012), hard real-time collectors had moved out of the research laboratory and into commercially deployed systems. Nevertheless, although many problems have been solved by modern garbage collector implementations, new hardware, new environments and new applications continue to throw up new research challenges for memory management.

As Blackburn says, we live in interesting times!

The audience

In this book we have tried to bring together the wealth of experience gathered by automatic memory management researchers and developers over the past fifty years. The literature is huge — our online bibliography contains over 3,400 entries at the time of writing. We discuss and compare the most important approaches and state-of-the-art techniques in a single, accessible framework. We have taken care to present algorithms and concepts using a consistent style and terminology. These are described in detail, often with pseudocode and illustrations. Where it is critical to performance, we pay attention to low level details, such as the choice of primitive operations for synchronisation or how hardware components such as caches influence algorithm design.

In particular, we address the new challenges presented to garbage collection by advances in hardware and software over the last couple of decades. The gap in performance between processors and memory has by and large continued to widen. Processor clock speeds have increased, more and more cores are being placed on each die and configurations with multiple processor modules are common. This book focuses strongly on the consequences of these changes for designers and implementers of high performance garbage collectors. Their algorithms must take locality into account since cache performance is critical. Increasing numbers of application programs are multithreaded and run on multicore processors. Memory managers must be designed to avoid becoming a sequential bottleneck. On the other hand, the garbage collector itself should be designed to take advantage of the parallelism provided by new hardware. Richard did not consider at all how to run multiple collector threads in parallel [Jones, 1996]. He devoted but a single chapter to incremental and concurrent collection, which seemed exotic then.

We are sensitive throughout this book to the opportunities and limitations provided by modern hardware. We address locality issues throughout. From the outset, we assume that application programs may be multithreaded. Although we cover many of the more simple and traditional algorithms, we also devote nearly half of the book to discussing parallel, incremental, concurrent and real-time garbage collection.

We hope that this survey will help postgraduate students, researchers and developers who are interested in the implementation of programming languages. The book should also be useful to undergraduates taking advanced courses in programming languages, compiler construction, software engineering or operating systems. Furthermore, we hope that it will give professional programmers better insight into the issues that the garbage collector faces and how different collectors work and that, armed with this knowledge, they will be better able to select and configure the choice of collectors that many languages offer. The almost universal adoption of garbage collection by modern programming languages makes a thorough understanding of this topic essential for any programmer.

Structure of the book

Chapter 1 starts by considering why automatic storage reclamation is desirable, and briefly introduces the ways in which different garbage collection strategies can be compared. It ends with a description of the abstractions and pseudocode notation used throughout the rest of the book.

Chapters 2 to 5 discuss the classical garbage collection building blocks in detail. We look at mark-sweep, mark-compact and copying collection, followed by reference counting. These strategies are covered in depth, with particular focus on their implementation on modern hardware. Readers looking for a gentler introduction might also consult Richard's earlier book *Garbage Collection: Algorithms for Automatic Dynamic Memory Management*. Chapter 6 compares the strategies and algorithms covered in those chapters in depth, assessing their strengths, weaknesses and applicability to different contexts.

How storage is reclaimed depends on how it is allocated. Chapter 7 considers different techniques for allocating memory and examines the extent to which automatic garbage collection leads to allocator policies that are different from those of explicit `malloc/free` memory management.

The first seven chapters make the implicit assumption that all objects in the heap are managed in the same way. However, there are many reasons why that would be a poor design. Chapters 8 to 10 consider why we might want to partition the heap into different spaces, and how we might manage those spaces. We look at generational garbage collection, one of the most successful strategies for managing objects, how to handle large objects and many other partitioned schemes.

The interface with the rest of the run-time system is one of the trickiest aspects of building a collector.[3] We devote Chapter 11 to the run-time interface, including finding pointers,

---

[3]And one that Jones [1996] skipped over!

safe points at which to collect, and read and write barriers, and Chapter 12 to language-specific concerns such as finalisation and weak references.

Next we turn our attention to concurrency. We set the scene in Chapter 13 by examining what modern hardware presents to the garbage collection implementer, and looking at algorithms for synchronisation, progress, termination and consensus. In Chapter 14 we see how we can execute multiple collector threads in parallel while all the application threads are halted. In Chapters 15 to 18, we consider a wide range of concurrent collectors, in which we relax this 'stop-the-world' requirement in order to allow collection to take place with only the briefest, if any, interruptions to the user program. Chapter 19 takes this to its most challenging extreme, garbage collection for hard real-time systems. Chapters 20 and 21 are completely new to this second edition, addressing energy-aware collection and collection of persistent systems.

At the end of each chapter, we offer a summary of issues to consider. These are intended to provoke the reader into asking what requirements their system has and how they can be met. What questions need to be answered about the behaviour of the client program, their operating system or the underlying hardware? These summaries are not intended as a substitute for reading the chapter. Above all, they are not intended as canned solutions, but we hope that they will provide a focus for further analysis.

Finally, what is missing from the book? We have only considered *automatic* techniques for memory management embedded in the run-time system. Thus, even when a language specification mandates garbage collection, we have not discussed in much depth other mechanisms for memory management that it may also support. The most obvious example is the use of 'regions' [Tofte and Talpin, 1994], most prominently used in the Real-Time Specification for Java. We only pay attention briefly to questions of region inferencing or stack allocation and very little at all to other compile-time analyses intended to replace, or at least assist, garbage collection. Neither do we address how best to use techniques such as reference counting in the client program, although this is popular in languages like C++. Finally, the last two decades have seen little new research on distributed garbage collection. In many ways, this is a shame since we expect lessons learnt in that field also to be useful to those developing collectors for the next generation of machines with heterogeneous collections of highly non-uniform memory architectures. Nevertheless, we do not discuss distributed garbage collection here.

e-book

The book is available either in print or as an e-book. The e-book has a number of enhancements over the print version. In particular, it is heavily hyperlinked. There are clickable links from every reference to its target (chapter, section, algorithm, figure, table and so on). Clicking on a citation will take the reader to its entry in the bibliography, many of which have a digital object identifier ('doi'), in turn a link to the original paper. Each entry in the bibliography also includes a list of pages from which it was cited; these are links back to the referring citations. Similarly, entries in the index contain links to the pages where the entry was mentioned. Finally, technical terms in the text have been linked to their entries in the glossary.

Online resources

The web page accompanying the book can be found at

http://www.gchandbook.org

It includes a number of resources including our comprehensive bibliography. The bibliography at the end of this book contains over 600 references. However, our comprehensive online database contains over 3,400 garbage collection related publications. This database can be searched online or downloaded as BIBTEX or PDF. As well as details of the article, papers, books, theses and so on, the bibliography also contains abstracts for some entries and URLs or DOIs for most of the electronically available ones.

We continually strive to keep this bibliography up to date as a service to the community. Richard (R.E.Jones@kent.ac.uk) would be very grateful to receive further entries (or corrections).

Updates in the second edition

This second edition is testament to the continued progress in garbage collection both academically and in major deployed systems. We aimed to include significant work within our scope up through the first half of 2022. While all chapters have seen some revision and refinement, the more significant changes include: considerable revision of the discussions of finalisation and weak references, plus managing changing object layout needed for dynamic languages in Chapter 12; collection on GPUs in Chapter 14; expanded discussion of barriers including load barriers in Chapter 15; expanded discussion of the Garbage-First (G1) collector in Chapter 16 and Chapter 17; discussion of new collectors including Collie, Transactional Sapphire, Platinum, ZGC and Shenandoah, and updated discussion of Pauseless and C4 in Chapter 17; and discussion of the high-performance reference counter, LXR, in Chapter 18. We have added entirely new chapters on energy-aware collection (Chapter 20) and collection of persistent systems based on byte-addressable non-volatile memory (Chapter 21). The glossary and bibliography expanded substantially as has the index. While memory management continues to be a dynamic field of work, we believe this new edition captures the most important developments of the last decade, maintaining the utility and relevance of this handbook.

Acknowledgements

We thank our many colleagues for their support for the original and this new edition. It is certain that without their encouragement (and pressure), this work would not have reached completion. In particular, we thank David Bacon, Steve Blackburn, Hans Boehm, Cliff Click, David Detlefs, Daniel Frampton, Robin Garner, Barry Hayes, Laurence Hellyer, Maurice Herlihy, Martin Hirzel, Abhinav Jangda, Tomáš Kalibera, Roman Kennke, Doug Lea, Simon Marlow, Alan Mycroft, Rupesh Nasre, Cosmin Oancea, Erik Österlund, Erez Petrank, Fil Pizlo, Tony Printezis, John Reppy, Thomas Schatzl, Peter Sewell, David Siegwart, Gil Tene, Tomoharu Ugawa and Mario Wolczko, all of whom have answered our many questions or given us excellent feedback on early drafts. We thank others whose keen eyes have spotted errors in the first edition, including Roberto Cometti, Neil Dhar, Raffaello Giulietti, Tsuneyasu Komiya, Atusi Maeda, Hayley Patton and Carl Shapiro. We also pay tribute to the many computer scientists who have worked on automatic memory management since 1958: without them there would be nothing to write about. In particular, we acknowledge Tomoharu Ugawa and Carl Ritson, co-authors with Richard, of the works on Transactional Sapphire [Ritson et al., 2014; Ugawa et al., 2014, 2018], and Albert Yang and Tobias Wrigstad for their deep dive into ZGC [Yang and Wrigstad, 2022] on which we draw heavily in Section 17.4 and Section 17.5, respectively. We are extremely grateful to Thomas Schatzl, Erik Österlund and Roman Kennke for patiently explaining to us the nitty-gritty details of the Garbage-First (G1) (Section 10.4 and Section 16.5), ZGC and Shenandoah (Section 17.5) collectors.

We are very grateful to Randi Cohen (now Slate), our long-suffering editor at Taylor & Francis, for her support and patience. She has always been quick to offer help and slow to chide us for our tardiness. Dare we recall Douglas Adams, "I love deadlines. I like the whooshing sound they make as they fly by"? We also thank Elizabeth Haylett and Kate Pool from the Society of Authors[4] for their advice, which we recommend highly.

Richard Jones, Antony Hosking, Eliot Moss

Above all, I am grateful to Robbie. How she has borne the stress of another edition of this book, whose writing has yet again stretched well beyond the planned deadline, I will never know. I owe you everything! I also doubt whether this book would have seen the light of day without the inexhaustible enthusiasm of my co-authors. Tony, Eliot, it has been a pleasure and an honour writing with knowledgeable and diligent colleagues.

Richard Jones

In the summer of 2002, Richard and I hatched plans to write a follow-up to his 1996 book. There had been lots of new work on GC in those six years, and it seemed there was

---

[4]http://www.societyofauthors.org.

demand for an update. Little did we know then that it would be another nine years before the current volume would appear. Richard, your patience is much appreciated. As conception turned into concrete planning, Eliot's offer to pitch in was gratefully accepted; without his sharing the load we would still be labouring anxiously. Much of the early planning and writing was carried out while I was on sabbatical with Richard in 2008, with funding from the United Kingdom's Engineering and Physical Sciences Research Council and the United States' National Science Foundation whose support we gratefully acknowledge. Mandi, without your encouragement and willingness to live out our own Canterbury Tale this project would not have been possible.

Antony Hosking

Thank you to my co-authors for inviting me into their project, already largely conceived and being proposed for publication. You were a pleasure to work with (as always) and tolerant of my sometimes idiosyncratic writing style. A formal thank you is also due to the Royal Academy of Engineering, who supported my visit to the UK in November 2009, which greatly advanced the book. Other funding agencies supported the work indirectly by helping us attend conferences and meetings at which we could gain some face-to-face working time for the book as well. And most of all, many thanks to my 'girls,' who endured my absences, physical and otherwise. Your support was essential and is deeply appreciated!

For the second edition: Thanks are again due to my family, especially for their tolerance of my work on the book during what was supposed to be vacation, and to Robbie Jones for hosting me for three weeks in Canterbury as we kicked off the second edition revisions.

Eliot Moss

Authors

Richard Jones is Emeritus Professor of Computer Systems at the School of Computing, University of Kent, Canterbury. He received a BA in Mathematics from Oxford University in 1976. He spent a few years teaching before returning to higher education at the University of Kent, where he has remained ever since, receiving an MSc in Computer Science in 1989. In 1998, he co-founded the International Symposium on Memory Management, of which he was the inaugural Programme Chair. He has published numerous papers on garbage collection, heap visualisation and electronic publishing, and he regularly sits on the programme committees of leading international conferences. He was made an Honorary Fellow of the University of Glasgow in 2005 in recognition of his research and scholarship in dynamic memory management. He was named a Distinguished Scientist of the Association for Computing Machinery in 2006, and in 2014 made a Fellow of the British Computer Society, a Fellow of the RSA and a member of AITO. He is married, with three children, and in his spare time he cycles and sails, including racing a Dart 18 catamaran.

Antony Hosking is Professor in the School of Computing at the Australian National University. He received a BSc in Mathematical Sciences from the University of Adelaide, Australia, in 1985 and an MSc in Computer Science from the University of Waikato, New Zealand, in 1987. He continued his graduate studies at the University of Massachusetts Amherst, receiving a PhD in Computer Science in 1995. His work is in the area of programming language design and implementation, with specific interests in database and persistent programming languages, object-oriented database systems, dynamic memory management, compiler optimisations and architectural support for programming languages and applications. He was named a Distinguished Scientist of the Association for Computing Machinery in 2012, a member of AITO in 2013 and is a Member of the Institute of Electrical and Electronics Engineers. He regularly serves on programme and steering committees of major conferences, mostly focused on programming language design and implementation. He is married, with five children. When the opportunity arises, he most enjoys sitting somewhere behind the bowler's arm on the first day of any Test match at the Adelaide Oval.

Eliot Moss is Professor Emeritus in the Manning College of Information and Computer Sciences at the University of Massachusetts Amherst. He received a BSEE in 1975, MSEE in 1978 and PhD in Computer Science in 1981, all from the Massachusetts Institute of Technology, Cambridge. After four years of military service, he joined the Computer Science faculty at the University of Massachusetts Amherst. He works in the area of programming languages and their implementation and has built garbage collectors since 1978. In addition to his research on automatic memory management, he is known for his work on persistent programming languages, virtual machine implementation, transactional programming and transactional memory. He worked with IBM researchers to license the

Jikes RVM Java virtual machine for academic research, which eventually led to its release as an open source project. In 2007 he was named a Fellow of the Association for Computing Machinery and in 2009 a Fellow of the Institute of Electrical and Electronics Engineers. In 2012 he was co-recipient of the Edsger W. Dijkstra Prize in Distributed Computing for work on transactional memory. He served for four years as Secretary of the Association for Computing Machinery's Special Interest Group on Programming Languages and has served on many programme and steering committees of the significant venues related to his areas of research. Ordained a priest of the Episcopal Church in 2005, he is now retired from that vocation as well. He is married, with two adult children. He enjoys listening to recorded books, movie-going and the company of cats and has been known to play the harp.

Chapter 1

Introduction

Developers are increasingly turning to *managed languages* and *run-time systems* for the many virtues they offer, from the increased security they bestow to code to the flexibility they provide by abstracting away from operating system and architecture. The benefits of *managed code* are widely accepted [Butters, 2007]. Because many services are provided by the virtual machine, programmers have less code to write. Code is safer if it is type-safe and if the run-time system verifies code as it is loaded, checks for resource access violations and the bounds of arrays and other collections, and manages memory automatically. Deployment costs are lower since it is easier to deploy applications to different platforms, even if the mantra 'write once, run anywhere' is over-optimistic. Consequently, programmers can spend a greater proportion of development time on the logic of their application.

Almost all modern programming languages make use of *dynamic memory allocation*. This allows objects to be allocated and deallocated even if their total size was not known at the time that the program was compiled, and if their lifetime may exceed that of the subroutine activation[1] that allocated them. A dynamically allocated object is stored in a *heap*, rather than on the *stack* (in the *activation record* or *stack frame* of the procedure that allocated it) or *statically* (whereby the name of an object is bound to a storage location known at compile or link time). Heap allocation is particularly important because it allows the programmer to:

- choose dynamically the size of new objects (thus avoiding program failure through exceeding hard-coded limits on arrays);

- define and use recursive data structures such as lists, trees and maps;

- return newly created objects to the parent procedure (allowing, for example, factory methods);

- return a function as the result of another function (for example, *closures* or *suspensions* in functional languages, or *futures* or *streams* in concurrent ones).

Heap allocated objects are accessed through references. Typically, a *reference* is a *pointer* to the object (that is, the address in memory of the object). However, a reference may alternatively refer to an object only indirectly, for instance through a *handle* which in turn points to the object. Handles offer the advantage of allowing an object to be relocated (updating its handle) without having to change every reference to that object/handle throughout the program's memory.

---

[1]We tend to use the terms *method, function, procedure* and *subroutine* interchangeably.

1

Figure 1.1: Premature deletion of an object may lead to errors. Here B has been freed. The live object A now contains a dangling pointer. The space occupied by C has leaked: C is not reachable but it cannot be freed.

1.1 Explicit deallocation

Any non-trivial program, running in a finite amount of memory, will need from time to time to recover the storage used by objects that are no longer needed by the computation. Memory used by heap objects can be reclaimed using *explicit deallocation* (for example, with C's `free` or C++'s `delete` operator) or automatically by the run-time system, using reference counting [Collins, 1960] or a tracing garbage collector [McCarthy, 1960]. Manual reclamation risks programming errors; these may arise in two ways.

Memory may be freed prematurely, while there are still references to it. Such a reference is called a *dangling pointer* (see Figure 1.1). If the program subsequently follows a dangling pointer, the result is unpredictable. The application programmer has no control over what happens to deallocated memory, so the run-time system may choose, among other options, to clear (fill with zeroes) the space used by the deleted object, to allocate a new object in that space or to return that memory to the operating system. The best that the programmer can hope for is that the program crashes immediately. However, it is more likely that it will continue for millions of cycles before crashing (making debugging difficult) or simply run to completion but produce incorrect results (which might not even be easy to detect). One way to detect dangling references is to use *fat pointers*. These can be used to hold the version number of their target as well as the pointer itself. Operations such as dereferencing must then check that the version number stored in the pointer matches that stored in the object. However, this approach is mostly restricted to use with debugging tools because of its overhead, and it is not completely reliable.[2]

The second kind of error is that the programmer may fail to free an object no longer required by the program, leading to a *memory leak*. In small programs, leaks may be benign but in large programs they are likely to lead either to substantial performance degradation (as the memory manager struggles to satisfy new allocation requests) or to failure (if the program runs out of memory). Often a single incorrect deallocation may lead to both dangling pointers and memory leaks (as in Figure 1.1).

Programming errors of this kind are particularly prevalent in the presence of sharing, when two or more subroutines may hold references to an object. This is even more problematic for concurrent programming when two or more threads may reference an object. With the increasing ubiquity of multicore processors, considerable effort has gone into the construction of libraries of data structures that are thread-safe. Algorithms that access these structures need to guard against a number of problems, including deadlock, livelock and ABA errors.[3] Automatic memory management eases the construction of concurrent algorithms significantly (for example, by eliminating certain ABA problems). Without this, programming solutions are much more complicated [Herlihy and Shavit, 2008].

The issue is more fundamental than simply being a matter of programmers' needing to take more care. Difficulties of correct memory management are often inherent to the pro-

---

[2]Tools such as the `memcheck` leak detector used with the `valgrind` open source instrumentation framework (see `http://valgrind.org`) are more reliable, but even slower. There are also a number of commercially available programs for helping to debug memory issues.

[3]ABA error: a memory location is written (*A*), overwritten (*B*) and then overwritten again with the previous value *A* (see Chapter 13).

gramming problem in question.[4] More generally, safe deallocation of an object is complex because, as Wilson [1994] points out, "liveness is a *global* property," whereas the decision to call free on a variable is a local one.

So how do programmers cope in languages not supported by automatic dynamic memory management? Considerable effort has been invested in resolving this dilemma. The key advice has been to be consistent in the way that they manage the *ownership* of objects [Belotsky, 2003; Cline and Lomow, 1995]. Belotsky [2003] and others offer several possible strategies for C++. First, programmers should avoid heap allocation altogether, wherever possible. For example, objects can be allocated on the stack instead. When the objects' creating method returns, the popping of the stack will free these objects automatically. Secondly, programmers should pass and return objects by value, by copying the full contents of a parameter/result rather than by passing references. Clearly both of these approaches remove all allocation/deallocation errors, but they do so at the cost of both increased memory pressure and the loss of sharing. In some circumstances it may be appropriate to use custom allocators, for example, that manage a pool of objects. At the end of a program phase, the entire pool can be freed as a whole.

C++ has seen several attempts to use special pointer classes and templates to improve memory management. These overload normal pointer operations in order to provide safe storage reclamation. However, such *smart pointers* do have several limitations. The auto_ptr class template cannot be used with the Standard Template Library [Boehm and Spertus, 2009], and was removed in the C++17 standard. It was replaced by an improved unique_ptr that provides strict ownership semantics that allow the target object to be deleted when the unique pointer is. The C++11 standard also introduced reference counted shared_ptr. Rust provides analogous library types, perhaps with more safety enforced automatically when used by multiple threads. Reference counted pointers are unable to manage self-referential (cyclic) data structures. Most smart pointers are provided as libraries, which restricts their applicability if efficiency is a concern. Possibly, they are most appropriately used to manage very large blocks, references to which are rarely assigned or passed, in which case they might be significantly cheaper than tracing collection. On the other hand, without the cooperation of the compiler and run-time system, reference counted pointers are not an efficient, general purpose solution to the management of small objects, especially if pointer manipulation is to be thread-safe.

Despite years of effort, memory safety remains a problem. The Chromium Project's web page reports that 70% of all Chrome's 912 high or critical security bugs are memory safety problems, of which more than half are 'use after free' bugs.[5] They considered that just running more processes in their own restricted environments ('sandboxes') would not solve this problem. Speaking at a security conference in February 2019, a Microsoft engineer said that around 70% of all security updates released for Microsoft products over the past twelve years were fixes for memory safety vulnerabilities.[6] Again 'use after free' was a major vector for attacks. Microsoft was able to substantially reduce this vulnerability[7] with *MemGC*, a conservative garbage collector for the Document Object Model (DOM) in Internet Explorer and Edge. Other projects are looking at languages such as Rust that provide compile-time safety checks. However, the memory safety features of such languages are demonstrably harder to use compared with garbage collection [Coblenz *et al.*, 2022].

---

[4]"When C++ is your hammer, everything looks like a thumb," Steven M. Haflich, Chair of the NCITS/J13 technical committee for ANSI standard for Common Lisp.

[5]https://www.chromium.org/Home/chromium-security/memory-safety/

[6]https://www.zdnet.com/article/chrome-70-of-all-security-bugs-are-memory-safety-issues/

[7]https://www.zdnet.com/article/microsoft-were-creating-a-new-rust-based-programming-language-for-secure-coding/

The plethora of strategies for safe manual memory management throws up yet another problem. If it is essential for the programmer to manage object ownership consistently, which approach should she adopt? This is particularly problematic when using library code. Which approach does the library take? Do all the libraries used by the program follow the same approach?

1.2 Automatic dynamic memory management

Automatic dynamic memory management resolves many of these issues. *Garbage collection* (GC) prevents creation of dangling pointers: an object is only reclaimed when there is no pointer to it from a reachable object. Conversely, in principle all garbage is guaranteed to be freed — any object that is unreachable will eventually be reclaimed by the collector — with two caveats. The first is that *tracing collection* uses a definition of 'garbage' that is decidable and may not include all objects that will never be accessed again. The second is that in practice, as we shall see in later chapters, garbage collector implementations may choose for efficiency reasons not to reclaim some objects. Only the collector releases objects so the double-freeing problem cannot arise. All reclamation decisions are deferred to the collector, which has global knowledge of the structure of objects in the heap and the threads that can access them. The problems of explicit deallocation were largely due to the difficulty of making a global decision in a local context. Automatic dynamic memory management simply finesses this problem.

Above all, memory management is a software engineering issue. Well-designed programs are built from components (in the loosest sense of the term) that are highly cohesive and loosely coupled. Increasing the cohesion of modules makes programs easier to maintain. Ideally, a programmer should be able to understand the behaviour of a module from the code of that module alone, or at worst a few closely related modules. Reducing the coupling between modules means that the behaviour of one module is not dependent on the implementation of another module. As far as correct memory management is concerned, this means that modules should not have to know the rules of the memory management game played by other modules. In contrast, explicit memory management goes against sound software engineering principles of minimal communication between components; it clutters interfaces, either explicitly through additional parameters to communicate ownership rights, or implicitly by requiring programmers to conform to particular idioms. Requiring code to understand the rules of engagement limits the reusability of components and complicated interfaces.

The key argument in favour of garbage collection is not just that it simplifies coding — which it does — but that it uncouples the problem of memory management from interfaces, rather than scattering it throughout the code. It improves reusability. This is why garbage collection, in one form or another, has been a requirement of almost all modern languages (see Table 1.1). There is substantial evidence that managed code, including automatic memory management, reduces development costs [Butters, 2007]. Unfortunately, most of this evidence is anecdotal or compares development in different languages and systems (hence comparing more than just memory management strategies), and few detailed comparative studies have been performed. A notable exception is that of Coblenz *et al.* [2022], comparing coding in Rust with and without garbage collection support. They found that garbage collection indeed dramatically reduced coding time, at least for novice programmers. One author has suggested as long ago as 1985 that memory management should be the *prime* concern in the design of software for complex systems [Nagle, 1995]. Rovner [1985] estimated that 40% of development time for Xerox's Mesa system was spent on getting memory management correct. Possibly the strongest corroboration of the case

ActionScript (2000)	Algol-68 (1965)	APL (1964)
AppleScript (1993)	AspectJ (2001)	Awk (1977)
Beta (1983)	C# (1999)	Cyclone (2006)
Managed C++ (2002)	Cecil (1992)	Cedar (1983)
Clean (1984)	CLU (1974)	D (2007)
Dart (2011)	Dylan (1992)	Dynace (1993)
E (1997)	Eiffel (1986)	Elasti-C (1997)
Emerald (1988)	Erlang (1990)	Euphoria (1993)
F# (2005)	Fortress (2006)	Green (1998)
Go (2010)	Groovy (2004)	Haskell (1990)
Hope (1978)	Icon (1977)	Java (1994)
JavaScript (1994)	Liana (1991)	Limbo (1996)
Lingo (1991)	Lisp (1958)	LotusScript (1995)
Lua (1994)	Mathematica (1987)	MATLAB (1970s)
Mercury (1993)	Miranda (1985)	ML (1990)
Modula-3 (1988)	Oberon (1985)	Objective-C (2007–)
Obliq (1993)	Perl (1986)	Pike (1996)
PHP (1995)	Pliant (1999)	POP-2 (1970)
PostScript (1982)	Prolog (1972)	Python (1991)
R (1993)	Rexx (1979)	Ruby (1993)
Sather (1990)	Scala (2003)	Scheme (1975)
Self (1986)	SETL (1969)	Simula (1964)
SISAL (1983)	Smalltalk (1972)	SNOBOL (1962)
Squeak (1996)	Swift (2014)	Tcl (1990)
Theta (1994)	VB.NET (2001)	VBScript (1996)
Visual Basic (1991)	VHDL (1987)	X10 (2004)
YAFL (1993)		

Table 1.1: A selection of languages that rely on garbage collection

Online sources: Dictionary of Programming Languages, Wikipedia and Google

for automatic dynamic memory management is an indirect, economic one: the continued existence of a wide variety of vendors and tools for detection of memory errors.

We do not claim that garbage collection is a silver bullet that will eradicate all memory-related programming errors or that it is applicable in all situations. Memory leaks are one of the most prevalent kinds of memory error. Although garbage collection tends to reduce the chance of memory leaks, it does not guarantee to eliminate them. If an object structure becomes unreachable to the rest of the program (for example, through any chain of pointers from the known roots), then the garbage collector will reclaim it. Since this is the only way that an object can be deleted, dangling pointers cannot arise. Furthermore, if deletion of an object causes its children to become unreachable, they too will be reclaimed. Thus, neither of the scenarios of Figure 1.1 is possible. However, garbage collection cannot guarantee the absence of space leaks. It has no answer to the problem of a data structure that *is* still reachable, but grows without limit (for example, if a programmer repeatedly adds data to a cache but never removes objects from that cache), or that is reachable and simply never accessed again.

Automatic dynamic memory management is designed to do just what it says. Some critics of garbage collection have complained that it is unable to provide general resource management, for example, to close files or windows promptly after their last use. However, this is unfair. Garbage collection is not a universal panacea. It attacks and solves a specific question: the management of memory resources. Nevertheless, the problem of general resource management in a garbage collected language is a substantial one. With explicitly managed systems there is a straightforward and natural coupling between memory reclamation and the disposal of other resources. Automatic memory management introduces the problem of how to structure resource management in the absence of a natural coupling. However, it is interesting to observe that many resource release scenarios require something akin to a collector in order to detect whether the resource is still in use (reachable) from the rest of the program.

1.3   Comparing garbage collection algorithms

In this book we discuss a wide range of collectors, each designed with different workloads, hardware contexts and performance requirements in mind. Unfortunately, it is never possible to identify a 'best' collector for all configurations. For example, Fitzgerald and Tarditi [2000] found in a study of 20 benchmarks and six collectors that for every collector there was at least one benchmark that would run at least 15% faster with a more appropriate collector. Singer *et al.* [2007b] applied machine learning techniques to predict the best collector configuration for a particular program. Others have explored allowing Java virtual machines to switch collectors as they run if they believe that the characteristics of the workload being run would benefit from a different collector [Printezis, 2001; Soman *et al.*, 2004]. In this section, we examine the metrics by which collectors can be compared. Nevertheless, such comparisons are difficult in both principle and practice. Details of implementation, *locality* and the practical significance of the constants in algorithmic complexity formulae make them less than perfect guides to practice. Moreover, the metrics are not independent variables. Not only does the performance of an algorithm depend on the topology and volume of objects in the heap, but also on the access patterns of the application. Worse, the tuning options in production virtual machines are interconnected. Variation of one parameter to achieve a particular goal may lead to other, contradictory effects.

Safety

The prime consideration is that garbage collection should be *safe*: the collector must never reclaim the storage of live objects. However, safety comes with a cost, particularly for concurrent collectors (see Chapter 15). The safety of *conservative collection*, which receives no assistance from the compiler or run-time system, may in principle be vulnerable to certain compiler optimisations that disguise pointers [Jones, 1996, Chapter 9].

Throughput and cycles consumed

A common goal for end users is that their programs should run faster. However, there are several aspects to this. One is that the overall time spent in garbage collection should be as low as possible. This is commonly referred to in the literature as the *mark/cons ratio*, comparing the early Lisp activities of the collector ('marking' live objects) and the mutator (creating or 'consing' new list cells). However, the user is most likely to want the application as a whole (mutator *plus* collector) to execute in as little time as possible. In most well-designed configurations, much more CPU time is spent in the mutator than the collector. Therefore, it may be worthwhile trading some collector performance for increased mutator throughput. For example, systems managed by mark-sweep collection occasionally perform more expensive compacting phases in order to reduce fragmentation so as to improve mutator allocation performance (and possibly mutator performance more generally). Throughput and wall-clock time may not be the only metrics on interest here, especially in the context of parallel and concurrent collectors which devote several threads to garbage collection. Different collectors may consume very different numbers of CPU cycles that could otherwise be used by other applications on the same host, be it a personal computer or a shared server [Cai *et al.*, 2022].

Completeness and promptness

Ideally, garbage collection should be *complete*: eventually, all garbage in the heap should be reclaimed. However, this is not always possible nor even desirable. Pure reference counting collectors, for example, are unable to reclaim cyclic garbage (self-referential structures). For performance reasons, it may be desirable not to collect the whole heap at every collection cycle. For example, generational collectors segregate objects by their age into two or more regions called generations (we discuss generational garbage collection in Chapter 9). By concentrating effort on the youngest generation, generational collectors can both improve total collection time and reduce the average *pause time* for individual collections.

Concurrent collectors interleave the execution of mutators and collectors; the goal of such collectors is to avoid, or at least bound, interruptions to the user program. One consequence is that objects that become garbage after a collection cycle has started may not be reclaimed until the end of the next cycle; such objects are called *floating garbage*. Hence, in a concurrent setting it may be more appropriate to define completeness as *eventual* reclamation of all garbage, as opposed to reclamation within one cycle. Different collection algorithms may vary in their *promptness* of reclamation, again leading to time/space trade-offs.

Pause time and latency

On the other hand, an important requirement may be to minimise the collector's intrusion on program execution. Many collectors introduce pauses into a program's execution because they stop all mutator threads while collecting garbage. It is clearly desirable to make these pauses as short as possible. This might be particularly important for interactive applications or servers handling transactions (when failure to meet a deadline might lead to the transaction being retried, thus building up a backlog of work). However, mechanisms for limiting pause times may have side effects, as we shall see in more detail in later chapters. For example, generational collectors address this goal by frequently and quickly collecting a small nursery region, and only occasionally collecting larger, older generations. Clearly, when tuning a generational collector, there is a balance to be struck between the sizes of the generations, and hence not only the pause times required to collect different generations but also the frequency of collections. However, because the sources of some inter-generational pointers must be recorded, generational collection imposes a small tax on pointer write operations by the mutator.

Parallel collectors stop the world to collect but reduce pause times by employing multiple threads. Concurrent and incremental collectors aim to reduce pause times still further by occasionally performing a small quantum of collection work interleaved or in parallel with mutator actions. This too requires taxation of the mutator in order to ensure correct synchronisation between mutators and collectors. As we shall see in Chapter 15, there are different ways to handle this synchronisation. The choice of mechanism affects both space and time costs. It also affects termination of a garbage collection cycle. The cost of the taxation on mutator time depends on how and which manipulations of the heap by the mutator (loads or stores) are recorded. The costs on space, and also collector termination, depends on how much floating garbage (see below) a system tolerates. Multiple mutator and collector threads add to the complexity. In any case, decreasing pause time will tend to increase overall processing time (decrease processing rate).

Maximum or average pause times on their own are not adequate measures. Low pause times do not necessarily translate to low application latency [Cai *et al.*, 2022]. It is also important that the mutator makes progress. The distribution of pause times is therefore also of interest. There are a number of ways that pause time distributions may be reported. The simplest might be a measure of variation such as standard deviation or a graphical representation of the distribution. More interesting measures include *minimum mutator utilisation* (MMU) and *bounded mutator utilisation* (BMU). Both the MMU [Cheng and Blelloch, 2001] and BMU [Sachindran *et al.*, 2004] measures seek to display concisely the (minimum) fraction of time spent in the mutator, for any given time window. The x-axis of Figure 1.2 represents time, from 0 to total execution time, and its y-axis the fraction of CPU time spent in the mutator (utilisation). Thus, not only do MMU and BMU curves show total garbage collection time as a fraction of overall execution time (the y-intercept, at the top right of the curves is the mutators' overall share of processor time), but they also show the maximum pause time (the longest window for which the mutator's CPU utilisation is zero) as the x-intercept. In general, curves that are higher and more to the left are preferable since they tend towards a higher mutator utilisation for a smaller maximum pause. Note that the MMU is the *minimum* mutator utilisation (y) in any time window (x). As a consequence, it is possible for a larger window to have a lower MMU than a smaller window, leading to dips in the curve. In contrast, BMU curves give the MMU in that time window or *any larger* one. Monotonically increasing BMU curves are perhaps more intuitive than MMU.

However, measuring MMU is problematic. It is often difficult to disentangle overhead due to the garbage collector from mutator activity. For example, concurrent collectors may inject synchronisation code (barriers) around mutator read or write operations. A collector that requires an expensive barrier may therefore lead to a higher mutator utilisation than one using a cheaper barrier. For latency-sensitive workloads, query-time percentiles may be a more appropriate metric.

Space overhead

The goal of memory management is safe and efficient use of space. Different memory managers, both explicit and automatic, impose different space overheads. Some garbage collectors may impose per-object space costs (for example, to store reference counts); others may be able to smuggle these overheads into objects' existing layouts (for example, a mark bit can often be hidden in a header word, or a forwarding pointer may be written over user data). Collectors may have a per-heap space overhead. For example, copying collectors divide the heap into two semispaces. Only one semispace is available to the mutator at any time; the other is held as a copy reserve into which the collector will evacuate live objects at collection time. Collectors may require auxiliary data structures. Tracing collectors need mark stacks to guide the traversal of the pointer graph in the heap; they may also store mark bits in separate bitmap tables rather than in the objects themselves. Concurrent collectors, or collectors that divide the heap into independently collected regions, require remembered sets that record where the mutator has changed the value of pointers, or the locations of pointers that span regions, respectively.

Energy use

As discussed further in Chapter 20, energy consumed by computing devices is in many cases a first-order concern. While reducing execution time will tend to reduce energy consumption, many factors come into play, particularly in concurrent systems. There are two

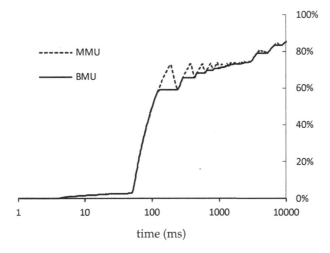

Figure 1.2: Minimum mutator utilisation and bounded mutator utilisation curves display concisely the (minimum) fraction of time spent in the mutator, for any given time window. MMU is the *minimum* mutator utilisation (y) in any time window (x) whereas BMU is the minimum mutator utilisation in that time window or *any larger* one. In both cases, the x-intercept gives the maximum pause time and the y-intercept is the overall fraction of processor time used by the mutator.

primary metrics that have been used with respect to energy consumption. The first is just energy consumed, which is simply power integrated over time. However, promptness of computation is often also important, so a blended metric, *energy-delay product*, can be more appropriate. This product simply multiplies the time needed by a computation by the energy it consumes.

Both energy and energy-delay product can be affected by choice of memory management technique and by a variety of other system parameters such as the number of mutator and collector threads and processor clock speeds. Garbage collection by its nature tends to do many memory accesses and often exhibits less locality than does application code. Because memory accesses are both time- and energy-consuming, how a system collects therefore makes a difference in how it consumes energy.

Optimisations for specific languages

Garbage collection algorithms can also be characterised by their applicability to different language paradigms. Functional languages in particular have offered a rich vein for optimisations related to memory management. Some languages, such as ML, distinguish mutable from immutable data. Pure functional languages, such as Haskell, go further and do not allow the user to modify any values (programs are *referentially transparent*). Internally, however, they typically update data structures at most once (from a 'thunk' to weak head normal formal); this gives multi-generation collectors opportunities to promote fully evaluated data structures eagerly (see Chapter 9). Authors have also suggested complete mechanisms for handling cyclic data structures with reference counting. Declarative languages may also allow other mechanisms for efficient management of heap spaces. Any data created in a logic language after a 'choice point' becomes unreachable after the program backtracks to that point. With a memory manager that keeps objects laid out in the heap in their order of allocation, memory allocated after the choice point can be reclaimed in constant time. Conversely, different language definitions may make specific requirements of the collector. The most notable are the ability to deal with a variety of pointer strengths and the need for the collector to cause dead objects to be finalised.

Scalability and portability

The final metrics we identify here are scalability and portability. With the prevalence of multicore hardware on the desktop, laptops and even portable devices such as tablets and mobile phones (rather than just in large servers), it is becoming increasingly important that garbage collection can take advantage of the parallel hardware on offer. Furthermore, parallel hardware is increasing in scale (number of cores and sockets) and heterogeneous processors have become common. The demands on servers are also increasing, as heap sizes move into the hundreds of gigabytes or even terabytes and as transaction loads increase. A number of collection algorithms depend on support from the operating system or hardware (for instance, by protecting pages or by double mapping virtual memory space, or on the availability of certain atomic operations on the processor). Such techniques are not necessarily portable.

1.4   A performance disadvantage?

We conclude the discussion of the comparative merits of automatic and manual dynamic memory management by asking if automatic memory management must be at a performance disadvantage compared with manual techniques. In general, the cost of automatic dynamic memory management is highly dependent on application behaviour and even hardware, making it impossible to offer simple estimates of overhead. Nevertheless, a long-running criticism of garbage collection has been that it is slow compared to explicit memory management and imposes unacceptable overheads, both in terms of overall throughput and in pauses for garbage collection. While it is true that automatic memory management does impose a performance penalty on the program, it is not as much as is commonly assumed. Furthermore, explicit operations like `malloc` and `free` also impose a significant cost. Hertz *et al.* [2005] measured the true cost of garbage collection for a variety of Java benchmarks and collection algorithms. They instrumented a Java virtual machine to discover precisely when objects became unreachable, and then used the reachability trace as an oracle to drive a simulator, measuring cycles and cache misses. They compared a wide variety of garbage collector configurations against different implementations of `malloc`/`free`: the simulator invoked `free` at the point where the trace indicated that an object had become garbage. Although, as expected, results varied between both collectors and explicit allocators, Hertz *et al.* found that garbage collectors could match the execution time performance of explicit allocation provided they were given a somewhat larger heap (25% to 56% more than the minimum required). Sareen and Blackburn [2022] found similar results — 15% to 27% for the immix collector depending on the explicit allocator with which it is compared.[8]

More recently, Cai *et al.* [2022] developed a method to identify a lower bound for the overhead of garbage collection. For a given application, they distil out explicit garbage collection costs (such as costs during stop-the-world pauses), and repeat this to find the minimum distilled cost from running the application with different collectors. The lower

---

[8]It is often cited that Hertz *et al.* [2005] found that garbage collectors require a heap two to five times larger that explicit allocators to offer comparable performance, but that compares two different explicit allocators. See footnote 5 of Sareen and Blackburn [2022].

bound overhead is then the total cost of running the application less the minimum distilled cost. Usefully, this methodology is run-time and algorithm independent: it can be applied to different metrics, such as throughput, cycles executed, cache misses and so on. On the DaCapo[9] suite of medium-sized benchmarks for Java, they found throughput overheads from 3% to 94%, depending on the algorithm and the size of the heap provided.

1.5 Experimental methodology

One of the most welcome changes over the past two decades or so has been the improvement in experimental methodology reported in the literature on memory management. Nevertheless, it remains clear that reporting standards in computer science have some way to go before they match the quality of the very best practice in the natural or social sciences. Mytkowicz *et al.* [2008] find measurement bias to be "significant and commonplace."

In a study of a large number of papers on garbage collection, Georges *et al.* [2007] found the experimental methodology, even where reported, to be inadequately rigorous in many cases. Many reported performance improvements were sufficiently small, and the reports lacking in statistical analysis, to raise questions of whether any confidence could be placed in the results. Errors introduced may be systematic or random. Systematic errors are largely due to poor experimental practice and can often be reduced by more careful design of experiments. Random errors are typically due to non-determinism in the system under measurement. By their nature, these are unpredictable and often outside the experimenter's control; they should be addressed statistically.

The use of synthetic or small scale, 'toy', benchmarks has long been criticised as inadequate [Zorn, 1989]. Such benchmarks risk introducing systematic errors because they do not reflect the interactions in memory allocation that occur in real programs, or because their working sets are sufficiently small that they exhibit locality effects that real programs would not. Wilson *et al.* [1995a] provide an excellent critique of such practices. Fortunately, other than for stress testing, synthetic and toy benchmarks have been largely abandoned in favour of larger scale benchmark suites, consisting of widely used programs that are believed to represent a wide range of typical behaviour (for example, the DaCapo suite for Java). However, the availability of and access to benchmark sets that represent enterprise-scale applications remains problematic.

Experiments with benchmark suites that contain a large number of realistic programs can introduce systematic bias. Managed run-times, in particular, offer several opportunities for the introduction of systematic errors. Experimenters need to take care to distinguish the context that they are trying to examine: are they interested in start-up costs (important, for example, for short-lived programs) or in the steady state? For the latter, it is important to exclude system warm-up effects such as class loading and dynamic code optimisation. In both cases, it is probably important to disregard cold-start effects such as latency caused by loading the necessary files into the disk cache: thus Georges *et al.* [2007] advocate running several invocations of the virtual machine and benchmark and discarding the first.

Dynamic (or run-time) compilation is a major source of non-determinism and is particularly difficult to deal with when comparing alternative algorithms. One solution is to remove it. *Compiler replay* [Blackburn *et al.*, 2006a] allows the user to record which methods are optimised, and to which level, in a preparatory run of the benchmark. This record can then be used by the virtual machine to ensure the same level of optimisation in subsequent, performance runs. However, a problem with this approach is that alternative implemen-

---

[9]https://dacapobench.org [Blackburn *et al.*, 2006a]

tations typically execute different methods, particularly in the component under test. It is not clear which compilation record should be used. Two separate ones? Their intersection?

Sound experimental practice requires that outcomes are valid even in the presence of bias (for example, random errors). This requires repetitions of the experiment and statistical comparison of the results. To be able to state with confidence that one approach is superior to another requires that, first, a confidence level is stated and, second, confidence intervals for each alternative are derived from the results and that these intervals are found not to overlap. Georges *et al.* [2007] offer a statistically rigorous methodology to address non-deterministic and unpredictable errors (including the effects of dynamic compilation). They advocate invoking one instance of the virtual machine and executing a benchmark many times until it reaches a steady state (that is, when the coefficient of variation[10] for the last k benchmark iterations falls below some preset threshold). These k iterations can then be used to compute a mean for the benchmark under steady state. By repeating this process, an overall mean and a confidence interval can be computed. Better, the whole distribution (or at least more than one or two moments of it) should be reported.

Garbage collection research needs thorough performance reports. A single 'spot' figure, even if decorated with a confidence interval, is not sufficient. The reason is that memory management involves space and time trade-offs. In most circumstances, one way to reduce collection times is to increase the size of the heap (up to a certain point — after that locality effects typically cause execution times to deteriorate). Thus, no experiment that reports a figure for just a single heap size can be taken seriously. It is vital, therefore, that environments allow the user to control the size of heaps (and spaces within those heaps) in order to understand fully the performance characteristics of a particular memory management algorithm. We firmly advocate this even for production virtual machines which may automatically adapt sizes for optimal performance; while automatic adaptation might be appropriate for end users, researchers and developers need more insight.

The chaotic nature of garbage collection reinforces this requirement. By calling garbage collection chaotic, we mean that small changes in configuration can, and commonly do, lead to large changes in behaviour. One example is the scheduling of collections. Even a small change to the point at which a garbage collection occurs may mean that a large data structure either remains reachable or becomes garbage. This can have large effects not only on the cost of the current collection but also on how soon the next collection will occur, thus making such variation self-amplifying. By providing results for a range of heap sizes (often expressed in terms of multiples of the smallest heap size in which a program will run to completion), such 'jitter' is made readily apparent.

1.6   Terminology and notation

We conclude this chapter by explaining the notation used in the rest of the book. We also give more precise definitions of some of the terms used earlier.

First, a note about units of storage. We adopt the convention that a byte comprises 8 bits. Similarly, we use the terms *kilobyte* (KB), *megabyte* (MB), *gigabyte* (GB) and *terabyte* (TB) to mean a corresponding power-of-two multiple of the unit byte (2^{10}, 2^{20}, 2^{30}, 2^{40}, respectively), in flagrant disregard for the standard definitions of the SI decimal prefixes. A *word* is a sequence of contiguous bytes large enough to contain a memory address (pointer), typically 32 or 64 bits, and often required to be aligned on a particular byte boundary (4 or 8 bytes).

---

[10]The coefficient of variation is the standard deviation divided by the mean.

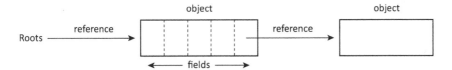

Figure 1.3: Roots, heap cells and references. Objects, denoted by rectangles, may be divided into a number of fields, delineated by dashed lines. References are shown as solid arrows.

The heap

The heap is either a contiguous array of memory words or organised into a set of discontiguous blocks of contiguous words. A *granule* is the smallest unit of allocation, typically a word or double-word, depending on *alignment* requirements. A *chunk* is a large contiguous group of granules. A *cell* is a generally smaller contiguous group of granules and may be allocated or free, or even wasted or unusable for some reason.

An *object* is a cell allocated for use by the application. An object is usually assumed to be a contiguous array of addressable bytes or words, divided into *slots* or *fields*, as in Figure 1.3 (although some memory managers for real-time or embedded systems may construct an individual large object as a pointer structure, this structure is not revealed to the user program). A field may contain a reference or some other *scalar* non-reference value such as an integer. A *reference* is either a pointer to a heap object or the distinguished value null.[11] A reference will be the *canonical pointer* to the object, usually to its head (that is, its first address), or it may point to some offset from the head. An object will sometimes also have a *header* field which stores metadata used by the run-time system, commonly (but not always) stored at the head of an object. A *derived pointer* is a pointer obtained by adding an offset to an object's canonical pointer. An *interior pointer* is a derived pointer to an internal object field.

A *block* is an aligned chunk of a particular size, usually a power of two. For completeness, we mention also that a *frame* (when not referring to a *stack frame*) means a large 2^k sized portion of address space, and a space is a possibly discontiguous collection of chunks, or even objects, that receive similar treatment by the system. A *page* is as defined by the hardware and operating system's virtual memory mechanism, and a *cache line* (or *cache block*) is as defined by its *cache*. A *card* is a 2^k aligned chunk, smaller than a page, related to some schemes for remembering cross-space pointers (Section 11.8).

The heap is often characterised as an *object graph*, which is a *directed graph* whose *nodes* are heap objects and whose directed edges are the references to heap objects stored in their fields. An edge is a reference from a *source* node or a *root* (see below) to a *destination* node.

The mutator and the collector

Following Dijkstra *et al.* [1976, 1978], a garbage-collected program is divided into two semi-independent parts.

- The *mutator* executes application code, which allocates new objects and mutates the object graph by changing reference fields so that they refer to different destination objects. These reference fields may be contained in heap objects as well as other places known as *roots*, such as static variables, thread stacks and so on. As a result of

---

[11]Note that some of the algorithms we present later assume that the numeric value of null is less than the numeric value of any other reference. Since the numeric value of null is typically 0, this usually holds, but those algorithms may require adjustment if a particular implementation uses some other distinguished value for null.

such reference updates, any object can end up disconnected from the roots, that is, *unreachable* by following any sequence of edges from the roots.

- The *collector* executes garbage collection code, which discovers unreachable objects and reclaims their storage.

A program may have more than one mutator *thread*, but these threads together can usually be thought of as a single actor over the heap. Equally, there may be one or more collector threads running in parallel.

The mutator roots

Separately from the heap memory, we assume some finite set of mutator roots, representing pointers held in storage that is *directly* accessible to the mutator without going through other objects. By extension, objects in the heap referred to directly by the roots are called *root objects*. The mutator visits objects in the graph by loading pointers from the current set of root objects (adding new roots as it goes). The mutator can also *discard* a root by overwriting the root pointer's storage with some other reference (that is, null or a pointer to another object). We denote the set of (addresses of) the roots by Roots.

In practice, the roots usually comprise static/global storage and thread-local storage (such as thread stacks) containing pointers through which mutator threads can directly manipulate heap objects. As mutator threads execute over time, their state (and so their roots) will change.

In a type-safe programming language, once an object becomes unreachable in the heap, and the mutator has discarded all root pointers to that object, then there is no way for the mutator to reacquire a pointer to the object. The mutator cannot 'rediscover' the object arbitrarily (without interaction with the run-time system) — there is no pointer the mutator can traverse to it and arithmetic construction of new pointers is prohibited. A variety of languages support *finalisation* of at least some objects. These appear to the mutator to be 'resurrected' by the run-time system. Our point is that the mutator cannot gain access to any arbitrary unreachable object by its efforts alone.

References, fields and addresses

In general, we shall refer to a heap node N by using its memory address (though this need not necessarily be the initial word of an object, but may be to some appropriate standard point in the layout of the object's data and metadata, which we call the *canonical* pointer). Given an object (at address) N, we can refer to arbitrary fields of the object — which may or may not contain pointers — by treating the object as an array of fields: the ith field of an object N will be denoted $N[i]$, counting fields from 0; the number of fields of N is written $|N|$. We write the usual C syntax for dereferencing a (non-null) pointer p as $*p$. Similarly, we use & to obtain the address of a field. Thus, we write $\&N[i]$ for the address of the ith field of N. Given an object (at address) N the set Pointers(N) denotes the set of (addresses of) *pointer fields* of N. More formally:

$$\text{Pointers}(N) = \{a \mid a = \&N[i], \forall i : 0 \leq i < |N| \text{ where } N[i] \text{ is a pointer}\}$$

For convenience, we write Pointers to denote the set of all pointer fields of all objects in the heap. Similarly, Nodes denotes the set of all (allocated) objects in the heap. For convenience, we will also treat the set Roots as a pseudo-object (separate from the heap), and define Pointers(Roots)=Roots synonymously. By implication, this allows us to write Roots[i] to refer to the ith root field.

Liveness, correctness and reachability

An object is said to be *live* if it will be accessed at some time in the future execution of the mutator. A garbage collector is correct only if it never reclaims live objects. Unfortunately, *liveness* is an *undecidable* property of programs: there is no way to decide for an arbitrary program whether it will ever access a particular heap object or not.[12] Just because a program continues to hold a pointer to an object does not mean it will access it. Fortunately, we can approximate liveness by a property that is decidable: *pointer reachability*. An object N is *reachable* from an object M if N can be reached by following a chain of pointers, starting from some field f of M. By extension, an object is only usable by a mutator if there is a chain of pointers from one of the mutator's roots to the object.

More formally (in the mathematical sense that allows reasoning about reachability), we can define the immediate 'points-to' relation $\rightarrow_f$ as follows. For any two heap nodes M, N in Nodes, $M \rightarrow_f N$ if and only if there is some field location $f = \& M[i]$ in Pointers(M) such that $*f = N$. Similarly, Roots $\rightarrow_f N$ if and only if there is some field f in Roots such that $*f = N$. We say that N is *directly reachable* from M, written $M \rightarrow N$, if there is some field f in Pointers(M) such that $M \rightarrow_f N$ (that is, some field f of M points to N). Then, the set of reachable objects in the heap is the transitive referential closure from the set of Roots under the $\rightarrow$ relation, that is, the least set

$$reachable = \{N \in \text{Nodes} \mid (\exists r \in \text{Roots} : r \rightarrow N) \lor (\exists M \in reachable : M \rightarrow N)\} \quad (1.1)$$

An object that is unreachable in the heap, and not pointed to by any mutator root, can never be accessed by a type-safe mutator. Conversely, any object reachable from the roots may be accessed by the mutator. Thus, liveness is more profitably defined for garbage collectors by reachability. Unreachable objects are certainly dead and can safely be reclaimed. But any reachable object may still be live and must be retained. Although we realise that doing so is not strictly accurate, we will tend to use *live* and *dead* interchangeably with *reachable* and *unreachable*, and *garbage* as synonymous with unreachable.

Pseudocode

We use a common pseudocode to describe garbage collection algorithms. We offer these algorithm fragments as illustrative rather than definitive, preferring to resolve ambiguities informally in the text rather than formally in the pseudocode. Our goal is a concise and representative description of each algorithm rather than a fully fledged implementation.

Indentation denotes the extent of procedure bodies and the scope of control statements. The assignment operator is $\leftarrow$ and the equality operator is $=$. Otherwise, we use C-style symbols for the other logical and relational operators, such as $\|$ (conditional or), && (conditional and), $\leq, \geq, \neq, \%$ (modulus) and so on.

The allocator

The heap *allocator* can be thought of as functionally orthogonal to the collector, though in practice some pairings of allocator and collector implementation strategies make more sense than others. The allocator supports two operations: `allocate`, which reserves the underlying memory storage for an object, and `free` which returns that storage to the allocator for subsequent reuse. The size of the storage reserved by `allocate` is passed as an optional parameter; when omitted, the allocation is of a fixed-size object, or the size of the object is not necessary for understanding of the algorithm. Where necessary, we may pass

---

[12]The undecidability of liveness is a corollary of the halting problem.

further arguments to allocate, for example to distinguish arrays from other objects, or arrays of pointers from those that do not contain pointers, or to include other information necessary to initialise object headers.

Mutator read and write operations

As they execute, mutator threads perform several operations of interest to the collector: New, Read and Write. We adopt the convention of naming mutator operations with a leading upper-case letter, as opposed to lower-case for collector operations. Generally, these operations have the expected behaviour: allocating a new object, reading an object field or writing an object field. Specific memory managers may augment these basic operations with additional functionality that turns the operation into a *barrier*: an action that results in synchronous or asynchronous communication with the collector. We distinguish *read barriers* and *write barriers*.

New(). The New operation obtains a new heap object from the heap allocator which returns the address of the first word of the newly allocated object. The mechanism for actual allocation may vary from one heap implementation to another, but collectors usually need to be informed that a given object has been allocated in order to initialise metadata for that object, and before it can be manipulated by the mutator. The trivial default definition of New simply allocates.

```
New():
    return allocate()
```

Read(**src**,**i**). The Read operation accesses an object field in memory (which may hold a scalar or a pointer) and returns the value stored at that location. Read generalises memory loads and takes two arguments: (a pointer to) the object and the (index of its) field being accessed. We allow src=Roots if the field src[i] is a root (that is, &src[i]∈Roots). The default, trivial definition of Read simply returns the contents of the field.

```
Read(src, i):
    return src[i]
```

Write(**src**,**i**,**val**). The Write operation modifies a particular location in memory. It generalises memory stores and takes three arguments: (a pointer to) the source object and the (index of its) field to be modified, plus the (scalar or pointer) value to be stored. Again, if src=Roots, then the field src[i] is a root (that is, &src[i]∈Roots). The default, trivial definition of Write simply updates the field.

```
Write(src, i, val):
    src[i] ← val
```

Atomic operations

In the face of concurrency among mutator threads, among collector threads, and between the mutator and collector, all collector algorithms require that certain code sequences appear to execute *atomically*. For example, stopping mutator threads makes the task of garbage collection appear to occur atomically: the mutator threads will never access the heap in the middle of garbage collection. Moreover, when running the collector concurrently with the mutator, the `New`, `Read` and `Write` operations may need to appear to execute atomically with respect to the collector and/or other mutator threads. To simplify the exposition of collector algorithms we will usually leave implicit the precise mechanism by which atomicity of operations is achieved, simply marking them with the keyword `atomic`. The meaning is clear: all the steps of an atomic operation must appear to execute indivisibly and instantaneously with respect to other operations. That is, other operations will appear to execute either before or after the atomic operation, but never interleaved between any of the steps that constitute the atomic operation. For discussion of different techniques to achieve atomicity as desired, see Chapter 11 and Chapter 13.

Sets, multisets, sequences and tuples

We use abstract data structures where this clarifies the discussion of an algorithm. We use mathematical notation where it is appropriate but does not obscure simpler concepts. For the most part, we will be interested in sets and tuples, and simple operations over them to add, remove or detect elements.

We use the usual definition of a *set* as a collection of distinct (that is, unique) elements. The *cardinality* of a set S, written $|S|$, is the number of its elements.

In addition to the standard set notation, we also make use of *multisets*. A multiset's elements may have repeated membership in the multiset. The cardinality of a multiset is the total number of its elements, including repeated memberships. The number of times an element appears is its *multiplicity*. We adopt the following notation:

- $[\,]$ denotes the empty multiset

- $[a, a, b]$ denotes the multiset containing two as and one b

- $[a, b] + [a] = [a, a, b]$ denotes multiset union

- $[a, a, b] - [a] = [a, b]$ denotes multiset subtraction

A *sequence* is an ordered list of elements. Unlike a set (or multiset), order matters. Like a multiset, the same element can appear multiple times at different positions in the sequence. We adopt the following notation:

- $(\,)$ denotes the empty sequence

- (a, a, b) denotes the sequence containing two as followed by a b

- $(a, b) \cdot (a) = (a, b, a)$ denotes appending of the sequence (a) to (a, b)

While a *tuple* of length k can be thought of as being equivalent to a sequence of the same length, we sometimes find it convenient to use a different notation to emphasise the fixed length of a tuple as opposed to the variable length of a sequence, and so on. We adopt the notation below for tuples; we use only tuples of length two or more.

- $\langle a_1, ..., a_k \rangle$ denotes the k-tuple whose ith member is a_i, for $1 \leq i \leq k$

Chapter 2

Mark-sweep garbage collection

All garbage collection schemes are based on one of four fundamental approaches: *mark-sweep collection, copying collection, mark-compact collection, reference counting* or some combination of these. Different collectors may combine these approaches in different ways, for example, by collecting one region of the heap with one method and another part of the heap with a second method. The next four chapters focus on these four basic styles of collection. In Chapter 6 we compare their characteristics.

For now we shall assume that the mutator is running one or more threads, but that there is a single collector thread. All mutator threads are stopped while the collector thread runs. For most systems, it is not safe to interrupt a mutator at any point in its execution in order to perform a garbage collection. A collection can only be started at a point where (i) the collector is guaranteed to be able to find all live objects (for instance, it must be able to find all roots), and (ii) the mutator is guaranteed to be able to resume correctly after the collection (which, in some algorithms, may have moved objects). The points where these requirements hold are called *GC safe-points*. Mutators will check whether a collection is needed at several points in the code. These must include object allocation sites and points at which a thread may suspend, but may include other places in the code such as loop back-edges. These points are called *GC check-points*. A GC check-point must be a GC safe-point. We look at the details of GC safe-points in Section 11.6.

This stop-the-world approach simplifies the construction of collectors considerably. From the perspective of the mutator threads, collection appears to execute atomically: no mutator thread will see any intermediate state of the collector, and the collector will not see interference with its task by the mutator threads. We can assume that each mutator thread is stopped at a point where it is safe to examine its roots. Stopping the world provides a snapshot of the heap, so we do not have to worry about mutators rearranging the topology of objects in the heap while the collector is trying to determine which objects are live. This also means that there is no need to synchronise the collector thread with other collector threads as it returns free space or with the allocator as it tries to acquire space. We avoid the question of how multiple mutator threads can acquire fresh memory until Chapter 7. There are more complex run-time systems that employ parallel collector threads or allow mutator and collector threads to execute concurrently; we discuss them in later chapters.

We encourage readers to familiarise themselves with the collectors in the next four chapters before progressing to the more advanced collectors covered in later chapters. Experienced readers may wish to skip the descriptions of the basic algorithms, although we hope that the accounts of more sophisticated ways to implement these collectors will prove of interest. We refer readers who find some of the material in these four chapters rather too compressed to Chapters 2 to 6 of Jones [1996], where the classical algorithms are covered in greater detail with more examples.

The goal of an ideal garbage collector is to reclaim the space used by every object that will no longer be used by the program. Any automatic memory management system has three tasks:

1. to allocate space for new objects;

2. to identify live objects;[1]; and

3. to reclaim the space occupied by dead objects.

These tasks are not independent. In particular, the way space is reclaimed affects how fresh space is allocated. As we noted in Chapter 1, true liveness is an undecidable problem. Instead, we turn to an over-approximation of the set of live objects: pointer reachability (defined on page 15). We accept an object as live if and only if it can be reached by following a chain of references from a set of known roots. By extension, an object is dead, and its space can be reclaimed, if it cannot be reached though any such chain of pointers. This is a safe estimate. Although some objects in the live set may never be accessed again, all those in the dead set are certainly dead.

The first algorithm that we look at is *mark-sweep collection* [McCarthy, 1960]. It is a straightforward embodiment of the recursive definition of pointer reachability. Collection operates in two phases. In the first, the collector traverses the graph of objects, starting from the roots (registers, thread stacks, global variables) through which the program might immediately access objects, and then following pointers and *marking* each object that it finds. Such a traversal is called *tracing*. In the second, *sweeping* phase, the collector examines every object in the heap: any unmarked object is deemed to be garbage and its space reclaimed.

Mark-sweep is an *indirect collection* algorithm. It does not detect garbage per se, but rather identifies all the live objects and then concludes that anything else must be garbage. Note that it needs to recalculate its estimate of the set of live objects at each invocation. Not all garbage collection algorithms behave like this. Chapter 5 examines a *direct collection* method, *reference counting*. Unlike indirect methods, direct algorithms determine the liveness of an object from the object alone, without recourse to tracing.

2.1 The mark-sweep algorithm

From the viewpoint of the garbage collector, mutator threads perform just three operations of interest, New, Read and Write, which each collection algorithm must redefine appropriately (the default definitions were given in Chapter 1 on page 16). The mark-sweep interface with the mutator is very simple. If a thread is unable to allocate a new object, the collector is called and the allocation request is retried (Algorithm 2.1). To emphasise that the collector operates in stop-the-world mode, without concurrent execution of the mutator threads, we mark the collect routine with the atomic keyword. If there is still insufficient memory available to meet the allocation request, then heap memory is exhausted. Often this is a fatal error. However, in some languages, New may raise an exception in this circumstance that the programmer may be able to catch. If memory can be released by deleting references (for example, to cached data structures which could be recreated later if necessary), then the allocation request could be repeated.

Before traversing the object graph, the collector must first prime the marker's work list with starting points for the traversal (markFromRoots in Algorithm 2.2). Each root object is marked and then added to the work list (we defer discussion of how to find

---

[1]Or, more or less equivalently, to identify dead ones.

Algorithm 2.1: Mark-sweep: allocation

```
1  New():
2      ref ← allocate()
3      if ref = null                          /* Heap is full */
4          collect()
5          ref ← allocate()
6          if ref = null                      /* Heap is still full */
7              error "Out of memory"
8      return ref
9
10 atomic collect():
11     markFromRoots()
12     sweep(HeapStart, HeapEnd)
```

Algorithm 2.2: Mark-sweep: marking

```
1  markFromRoots():
2      initialise(worklist)
3      for each fld in Roots
4          ref ← *fld
5          if ref ≠ null && not isMarked(ref)
6              setMarked(ref)
7              add(worklist, ref)
8              mark()
9
10 initialise(worklist):
11     worklist ← empty
12
13 mark():
14     while not isEmpty(worklist)
15         ref ← remove(worklist)              /* ref is marked */
16         for each fld in Pointers(ref)
17             child ← *fld
18             if child ≠ null && not isMarked(child)
19                 setMarked(child)
20                 add(worklist, child)
```

Algorithm 2.3: Mark-sweep: sweeping

```
1  sweep(start, end):
2      scan ← start
3      while scan < end
4          if isMarked(scan)
5              unsetMarked(scan)
6          else free(scan)
7          scan ← nextObject(scan) ·
```

roots to Chapter 11). An object can be marked by setting a bit (or a byte), either in the object's header or in a side table. If an object cannot contain pointers, then because it has no children there is no need to add it to the work list. Of course the object itself must still be marked. In order to minimise the size of the work list, markFromRoots calls mark immediately. Alternatively, it may be desirable to complete scanning the roots of each thread as quickly as possible. For instance, a concurrent collector might wish to stop each thread only briefly to scan its stack and then traverse the graph while the mutator is running. In this case, mark (line 8) could be moved outside the loop.

For a single-threaded collector, the work list could be implemented as a stack. This leads to a *depth-first traversal* of the graph. If mark bits are co-located with objects, it has the advantage that the elements that are processed next are those that have been marked most recently, and hence are likely to still be in the hardware cache. As we shall see repeatedly, it is essential to pay attention to cache behaviour if the collector is not to sacrifice performance. Later we discuss techniques for improving locality.

Marking the graph of live objects is straightforward. References are removed from the work list, and the targets of their fields marked, until the work list is empty. Note that in this version of mark, every item in the work list has its mark bit set. If a field contains a null pointer or a pointer to an object that has already been marked, there is no work to do; otherwise, the target is marked and added to the work list.

Termination of the marking phase is enforced by not adding already marked objects to the work list, so that eventually the list will become empty. At this point, every object reachable from the roots will have been visited and its mark bit will have been set. Any unmarked object is therefore garbage.

The sweep phase returns unmarked nodes to the allocator (Algorithm 2.3). Typically, the collector sweeps the heap linearly, starting from the bottom, freeing unmarked nodes and resetting the mark bits of marked nodes in preparation for the next collection cycle. Note that we can avoid the cost of resetting the mark bit of live objects if the sense of the bit is switched between one collection and the next.

We will not discuss the implementation of allocate and free until Chapter 7, but note that the mark-sweep collector imposes constraints upon the heap layout. First, this collector does not move objects. The memory manager must therefore be careful to try to reduce the chance that the heap becomes so fragmented that the allocator finds it difficult to meet new requests, which would lead to the collector being called too frequently, or in the worst case, preventing the allocation of new memory at all. Second, the sweeper must be able to find each node in the heap. In practice, given a node, sweep must be able to find the next node even in the presence of *padding* introduced between objects in order to observe alignment requirements. Thus, nextObject may have to parse the heap instead of simply adding the size of the object to its address (line 7 in Algorithm 2.3); we also discuss heap parsability in Chapter 7.

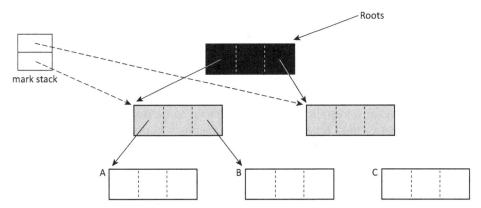

Figure 2.1: Marking with the tricolour abstraction. Black objects and their children have been processed by the collector. The collector knows of grey objects but has not finished processing them. White objects have not yet been visited by the collector (and some will never be).

2.2 The tricolour abstraction

It is very convenient to have a concise way to describe the state of objects during a collection (have they been marked, are they in the work list, and so on). The *tricolour abstraction* [Dijkstra *et al.*, 1976, 1978] is a useful characterisation of tracing collectors that permits reasoning about collector correctness in terms of invariants that the collector must preserve. Under the tricolour abstraction, tracing collection partitions the object graph into *black* (presumed live) and *white* (possibly dead) objects. Initially, every node is white; when a node is first encountered during tracing, it is shaded *grey*; when it has been scanned and its children identified, it is coloured black. Conceptually, an object is black if the collector has finished processing it, and grey if the collector knows about it but has not yet finished processing it (or needs to process it again). We use the term shading to mean colouring a white object grey; shading a grey or black object has no effect. By analogy with object colour, fields can also be given a colour: grey when the collector first encounters them, and black once traced by the collector. Some collectors even add these colours to pointers explicitly. This analogy also allows reasoning about the mutator roots as if the mutator were an object [Pirinen, 1998]. A grey mutator has roots that have not yet been scanned by the collector. A black mutator has roots that have already been scanned by the collector (and do not need to be scanned again). Tracing makes progress through the heap by moving the collector *wavefront* (the grey objects) separating black objects from white objects until all reachable objects have been traced black.

Objects are coloured by mark-sweep collection as follows. Figure 2.1 shows a simple object graph and a mark stack (implementing the work list), mid-way through the mark phase. Any objects held on the mark stack will be visited again, and so are grey. Any object that has been marked, and is not on the stack, is black (the root of the graph in the figure). All other objects are white (currently, A, B and C). However, once mark has completed its traversal of the graph, the mark stack will be empty (no grey nodes), only C will remain white (garbage), and all other nodes will have been marked (black).

The algorithm preserves an important invariant: at the end of each iteration of the marking loop, there are no references from black to white objects. Thus any white object that is reachable must be reachable from a grey object. If this invariant were to be broken, then a live descendant of a black object might not be marked (and hence would be freed incorrectly) since the collector does not process black nodes further. The tricolour view of the state of garbage collection is particularly useful when algorithms for concurrent garbage collection are considered, where mutator threads run concurrently with the collector.

2.3   Improving mark-sweep

It is not uncommon for an application's performance to be dominated by its cache behaviour. The latency to load a value from main memory is possibly hundreds of clock cycles, whereas the latency for Level 1 caches may be only three or four cycles. Caches improve performance because applications typically exhibit good *temporal locality*: if a memory location has been accessed recently, it is likely that it will be accessed again soon, and so it is worth caching its value. Applications may also exhibit good *spatial locality*: if a location is accessed, it is likely that adjacent locations will also be accessed soon. Modern hardware can take advantage of this property in two ways. Rather than transferring single words between a cache and lower levels of memory, each entry in the cache (a cache line or cache block) holds a fixed number of bytes, typically 32 to 128 bytes. Secondly, processors may use hardware *prefetching*. For example, many modern micro-architectures can detect a regular stride in the memory access pattern and fetch streams of data in advance. Explicit prefetching instructions are also commonly available for program-directed prefetching.

Unfortunately, garbage collectors do not behave like typical applications. The temporal locality of mark-sweep collection is poor. In the mark phase, the collector typically reads and writes an object's header just once, since most objects are not shared (that is, they are referenced by just one pointer), although a small number of objects may be very popular [Printezis and Garthwaite, 2002]. The mark bit is read, and set if the object has not already been marked: it is unlikely to be accessed again in this phase. Typically, the header also contains a pointer to type information (possibly also an object itself), needed so that the collector can find the reference fields in this object. This information may contain either a descriptor identifying these fields, or it may be code that will mark and push the object's descendants onto the mark stack. Because programs only use a limited number of types, and their frequency distribution is heavily skewed in favour of a small number of heavily used types, type information may be a good candidate for caching. But, otherwise, objects tend to be touched just once in this phase. Hardware prefetching is not tuned for this kind of pointer chasing.

We now consider ways to improve the performance of a mark-sweep collector.

2.4   Bitmap marking

Space for a mark bit can usually be found in an object header word. Alternatively, mark bits can be stored in a separate bitmap table to the side of the heap, with a bit associated with every address at which an object might be allocated. The space needed for the bitmap depends on the object alignment requirements of the virtual machine. Either a single bitmap can be used or, in a block-structured heap (treated in Chapter 7), a separate bitmap can be used for each block. The latter organisation has the advantage that no space is wasted if the heap is not contiguous. Per-block bitmaps might be stored in the blocks. However, placing the bitmap at a fixed position in each block risks degrading performance. This is because the bitmaps will contend for the same sets in a set-associative cache. Also, accessing the bitmap implies touching the page. Thus it may be better to use more instructions to access the bit rather than to incur locality overheads due to paging and cache associativity. To avoid the cache associativity issue, the position of the bitmap in the block can be varied by computing some simple hash of the block's address to determine an offset for the bit map. Alternatively, the bitmap can be stored to the side [Boehm and Weiser, 1988], but using a table that is somehow indexed by block, perhaps by hashing. This avoids both paging and cache conflicts.

Bitmaps suffice if there is only a single marking thread. Otherwise, setting a bit in a bitmap is vulnerable to losing updates to races, whereas setting a bit in an object header only risks setting the same bit twice: the operation is idempotent. Instead of a bitmap, byte maps are commonly used (at the cost of an eight-fold increase in space), thereby making marking races benign. Alternatively, a bitmap must use a synchronised operation, such as compare-and-swap or atomic fetch-and-or, to set a bit. In practice, matters are often more complicated for header bits in systems that allow marking concurrently with mutators, since header words are typically shared with mutator data such as locks or hash codes. With care, it may be possible to place this data and mark bits in different bytes of a header word. Otherwise, even mark bits in headers must be set atomically.

Mark bitmaps have a number of potential advantages. We identify these now, and then examine whether they materialise in practice on modern hardware. A bitmap stores marks much more densely than if they are stored in object headers. Consider how mark-sweep behaves with a mark bitmap. With a bitmap, marking will not modify any object, but will only read pointer fields of live objects. Other than loading the type descriptor field, no other part of pointer-free objects will be accessed. Sweeping will not read or write to any live object although it may overwrite fields of garbage objects as part of freeing them (for example to link them into a free-list). Thus bitmap marking is likely to modify fewer words, and to dirty fewer cache lines so less data needs to be written back to memory.

Bitmap marking dates to at least Lisp 1.5 but was adopted for a conservative collector designed to provide automatic memory management for uncooperative languages like C [Boehm and Weiser, 1988]. *Type-accurate* systems can precisely identify every slot that contains a pointer, whether it is in an object, the stack frame of a thread or some other root. Conservative collectors, on the other hand, do not receive this level of support from the compiler or run-time system and so have to make conservative decisions on pointer identity. If the value held in a slot looks sufficiently like an object reference, it is assumed to be one. We discuss the problems of pointer finding in more detail in Chapter 11. *Conservative collection* may interpret a slot as a pointer when it is not; this has two consequences for safety. First, the collector must not alter the value stored in any location owned by the mutator (including objects and roots). This rules out all algorithms that move objects since this would require updating every reference to a moved object. It also rules out storing mark bits in object headers since the 'object' in question might not be an object if it was reached by following a false pointer. Setting or clearing a bit might destroy user data. Second, it is very useful to minimise the chance of the mutator interfering with the collector's data. Adding a header word for the collector's use, contiguous to every object, is riskier than keeping collector metadata such as mark bits in a separate data structure.

Bitmap marking was also motivated by the concern to minimise the amount of paging caused by the collector [Boehm, 2000]. However, in modern systems, any paging at all due to the collector is generally considered unacceptable. The question for today is whether bitmap marking can improve cache performance. There is considerable evidence that objects tend to live and die in clusters [Hayes, 1991; Jones and Ryder, 2008]. Many allocators will tend to allocate these objects close to each other. Sweeping with a bitmap has two advantages. It allows the mark bits of clusters of objects to be tested and cleared in groups as the common case will be that either every bit/byte is set or every bit/byte is clear in a map word. A corollary is that it is simple from the bitmap to determine whether a complete block of objects is garbage, thus allowing the whole block to be returned to the allocator.

Many memory managers use a block-structured heap (for example, Boehm and Weiser [1988]; see Chapter 7). A straightforward implementation might reserve a prefix of each

Algorithm 2.4: Printezis and Detlefs bitmap marking

```
1  mark():
2      cur ← nextInBitmap()
3      while cur < HeapEnd              /* marked ref is black if and only if ref < cur */
4          add(worklist, cur)
5          markStep(cur)
6          cur ← nextInBitmap()
7
8  markStep(start):
9      while not isEmpty(worklist)
10         ref ← remove(worklist)                                  /* ref is marked */
11         for each fld in Pointers(ref)
12             child ← *fld
13             if child ≠ null && not isMarked(child)
14                 setMarked(child)
15                 if child < start
16                     add(worklist, child)
```

block for its bitmap. As previously discussed, this leads to unnecessary cache conflicts and page accesses, so collectors tend to store bitmaps separately from user data blocks.

Garner *et al.* [2007] adopt a hybrid approach, associating each block in a segregated fits allocator's data structure with a byte in a map, as well as marking a bit in object headers. The byte is set if and only if the corresponding block contains at least one object. The byte map of used/unused blocks thus allows the sweeper to determine easily which blocks are completely empty (of live objects) and can be recycled as a whole. This has two advantages. Both the bit in the object header and the byte in the byte map, corresponding to the block in which the object resides, can be set without using synchronised operations. Furthermore, there are no data dependencies on either write (which might lead to cache stalls), and writing the byte in the byte map is unconditional.

Printezis and Detlefs [2000] use bitmaps to reduce the amount of space used for mark stacks in a mostly-concurrent, generational collector. First, as usual, mutator roots are marked by setting a bit in the map. Then, the marking thread linearly searches this bitmap, looking for live objects. Algorithm 2.4 strives to maintain the invariant that marked objects below the current 'finger', cur in the mark routine, are black and those above it are grey. When the next live (marked) object cur is found, it is pushed onto the stack and we enter the usual marking loop to restore the invariant: objects are popped from the stack and their children marked recursively until the mark stack is empty. If an item is below cur in the heap, it is pushed onto the mark stack; otherwise, its processing is deferred to later in the linear search. The main difference between this algorithm and Algorithm 2.1 is its conditional insertion of children onto the stack at line 15. Objects are only marked recursively (thus consuming mark stack space) if they are behind the black wavefront which moves linearly through the heap. Although the complexity of this algorithm is proportional to the size of the space being collected, in practice searching a bitmap is cheap.

A similar approach can be used to deal with mark stack overflow. When the stack overflows, this is noted and the object is marked but not pushed onto the stack. Marking continues until the stack is exhausted. Now we must find those marked objects that could

Algorithm 2.5: Lazy sweeping with a block-structured heap

```
 1  atomic collect():
 2     markFromRoots()
 3     for each block in Blocks
 4        if not isMarked(block)          /* no objects marked in this block? */
 5           add(blockAllocator, block)    /* return block to block allocator */
 6        else
 7           add(reclaimList, block)        /* queue block for lazy sweeping */

 9  atomic allocate(sz):
10     result ← remove(sz)                /* allocate from size class for sz */
11     if result = null                   /* if no free slots for this size... */
12        lazySweep(sz)                            /* sweep a little */
13        result ← remove(sz)
14     return result                          /* if still null, collect */

16  lazySweep(sz):
17     repeat
18        block ← nextBlock(reclaimList, sz)
19        if block ≠ null
20           sweep(start(block), end(block))
21           if spaceFound(block)
22              return
23     until block = null      /* reclaim list for this size class is empty */
24     allocSlow(sz)                           /* get an empty block */

26  allocSlow(sz):                              /* allocation slow path */
27     block ← allocateBlock()                 /* from the block allocator */
28     if block ≠ null
29        initialise(block, sz)
```

not be added to the stack. The collector searches the heap, looking for any marked objects with one or more unmarked children and continues the trace from these children. The most straightforward way to do this is with a linear sweep of the heap. Sweeping a bitmap will be more efficient than examining a bit in the header of each object in the heap.

2.5   Lazy sweeping

The complexity of the mark phase is $O(L)$, where L is the size of the live data in the heap; the complexity of the sweep phase is $O(H)$ where H is the size of the heap. Since $H > L$, at first sight it might seem that the mark-sweep algorithm is dominated by the cost of sweeping. However, in practice, this is not the case. Chasing pointers in the mark phase leads to unpredictable memory access patterns, whereas sweep behaviour is more predictable. Further, the cost of sweeping an object tends to be much less than the cost of tracing it. One way to improve the cache behaviour of the sweep phase is to prefetch objects. In order to avoid fragmentation, allocators supporting mark-sweep collectors typically lay out objects of the same size consecutively (see Chapter 7 on page 98) leading to a fixed stride as a block of same-sized objects is swept. Not only does this pattern allow software prefetching, but it is also ideal for the hardware prefetching mechanisms found in modern processors.

Can the time for which the mutators are stopped during the sweep phase be reduced or even eliminated? We observe two properties of objects and their mark bits. First, once an object is garbage, it remains garbage: it can neither be seen nor be resurrected by a mutator.[2] Second, mutators cannot access mark bits. Thus, the sweeper can be executed in parallel with mutator threads, modifying mark bits and even overwriting fields of garbage objects to link them into allocator structures. The sweeper (or sweepers) could be executed as separate threads, running concurrently with the mutator threads, but a simple solution is to use *lazy sweeping* [Hughes, 1982]. Lazy sweeping amortises the cost of sweeping by having the *allocator* perform the sweep. Rather than a separate sweep phase, the responsibility for finding free space is devolved to `allocate`. At its simplest, `allocate` advances the sweep pointer until it finds sufficient space in a sequence of unmarked objects. However, it is more practical to sweep a block of several objects at a time.

Algorithm 2.5 shows a lazy sweeper that operates on a block of memory at a time. It is common for allocators to place objects of the same *size class* into a block (we discuss this in detail in Chapter 7). Each size class will have one or more current blocks from which it can allocate and a *reclaim list* of blocks not yet swept. As usual the collector will mark all live objects in the heap, but instead of eagerly sweeping the whole heap, `collect` will simply return any completely empty blocks to the block level allocator (line 5). All other blocks are added to the reclaim queue for their size class. Once the stop-the-world phase of the collection cycle is complete, the mutators are restarted. The `allocate` method first attempts to acquire a free slot of the required size from an appropriate size class (in the same way as Algorithm 7.7 would). If that fails, the lazy sweeper is called to sweep one or more remaining blocks of this size class, but only until the request can be satisfied (line 12). However, it may be the case that no blocks remain to be swept or that none of the blocks swept contained any free slots. In this case, the sweeper attempts to acquire a whole fresh block from a lower level block allocator. This fresh block is initialised by setting up its metadata — for example, threading a free-list through its slots or creating a mark byte map. However, if no fresh blocks are available, the collector must be called.

There is a subtle issue that arises from lazy sweeping a block-structured heap such as one that allocates from different size classes. Hughes [1982] worked with a contiguous heap and thus guaranteed that the allocator would sweep every node before it ran out of space and invoked the garbage collector again. However, lazily sweeping separate size classes does not make this guarantee since it is almost certain that the allocator will exhaust one size class (and all the empty blocks) before it has swept every block in every other size class. This leads to two problems. First, garbage objects in unswept blocks will not be reclaimed, leading to a memory leak. If the block also contains a truly live object, this leak is harmless since these slots would not have been recycled anyway until the mutator made a request for an object of this size class. Second, if all the objects in the unswept block subsequently become garbage, we have lost the opportunity to reclaim the whole block and recycle it to more heavily used size classes.

The simplest solution is to complete sweeping all blocks in the heap before starting to mark. However, it might be preferable to give a block more opportunities to be lazily swept. Garner *et al.* [2007] trade some leakage for avoiding some sweeps. They achieve this for the Jikes RVM Java virtual machine with the MMTk memory management toolkit [Blackburn *et al.*, 2004b] by marking objects with a bounded integer rather than a bit. This

---

[2]Some finalisation schemes can resurrect objects, but that is done by the collector, not the mutator.

does not usually add space costs since there is often room to use more than one bit if marks are stored in object headers, and separate mark tables often mark with bytes rather than bits. Each collection cycle increments modulo 2^K the value used as the mark representing 'live', where K is the number of mark bits used, thus rolling the mark back to zero on overflow. In this way, the collector can distinguish between an object marked in this cycle and one marked in a previous cycle. Only marks equal to the current mark value are considered to be set. Marking value wrap-around is safe because, immediately before the wrap-around, any live object in the heap is either unmarked (allocated since the last collection) or has the maximum mark bit value. Any object with a mark equal to the next value to be used must have been marked last some multiple of 2^K collections ago. Therefore, it must be floating garbage and will not be visited by the marker. This potential leak is addressed somewhat by block marking. Whenever the MMTk collector marks an object, it also marks its block. If none of the objects in a block has been marked with the current value, then the block will not have been marked either and so will be reclaimed as a whole at line 5 in Algorithm 2.5. Given the tendency for objects to live and die in clumps, this is an effective tactic.

Lazy sweeping offers a number of benefits. It has good locality: object slots tend to be used soon after they are swept. It reduces the algorithmic complexity of mark-sweep to be proportional to the size of the live data in the heap, the same as semispace copying collection, which we discuss in Chapter 4. In particular, Boehm [1995] suggests that mark and lazy sweep will perform best in the same circumstance that copying performs best: when most of the heap is empty, as the lazy sweep's search for unmarked objects will terminate quickly. In practice, the mutator's cost of initialising objects is likely to dominate the cost of sweeping and allocation.

2.6 Cache misses in the marking loop

We have seen how prefetching can improve the performance of the sweep phase. We now examine how it can also be employed to advantage in the mark phase. For example, by densely packing mark bits into a bitmap, the number of cache misses incurred by testing and setting marks can be reduced. However, cache misses will be incurred as the fields of an unmarked object are read as part of the traversal. Thus, much of the potential cache advantage of using mark bitmaps in the mark phase will be lost as object fields are loaded.

If an object is pointer-free, it is not necessary to load any of its fields. Although matters will vary by language and by application, it is likely that the heap may contain a significant volume of objects with no user-defined pointer fields. Whether or not an object contains pointers is an aspect of its type. One way that this can be determined is from the type information slot in an object's header. However, it is also possible to obtain information about an object from its *address*, for example if objects with similar characteristics are located together. Lisp systems have often used a *big bag of pages allocation* (BiBoP) technique, allocating objects of only one type (such as `cons` cells) on a page, thus allowing type information to be compactly associated with the page rather than each object [Foderaro *et al.*, 1985]. Similarly, pointer-full and pointer-free objects can be segregated. Pointers themselves can also encode type information [Steenkiste, 1987; Steenkiste and Hennessy, 1988].

Boehm [2000] observes that marking dominates collection time, with the cost of fetching the first pointer from an object accounting for a third of the time spent marking on an Intel Pentium III system. He suggests *prefetching on grey*: fetching the first cache line of an object as that object is greyed (added to the mark stack, line 20 of Algorithm 2.2), and prefetching a modest number of cache lines ahead as very large objects are scanned.

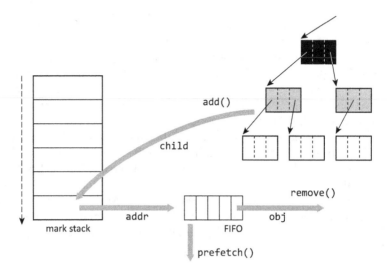

Figure 2.2: Marking with a FIFO prefetch buffer. As usual, references are added to the work list by being pushed onto the mark stack. However, to remove an item from the work list, the oldest item is removed from the FIFO buffer and the entry at the top of the stack is inserted into it. The object to which this entry refers is prefetched so that it should be in the cache by the time this entry leaves the buffer.

Algorithm 2.6: Marking with a FIFO prefetch buffer

```
1   add(worklist, item):
2       markStack ← getStack(worklist)
3       push(markStack, item)
4
5   remove(worklist):
6       markStack ← getStack(worklist)
7       addr ← pop(markStack)
8       prefetch(addr)
9       fifo ← getFifo(worklist)
10      prepend(fifo, addr)
11      return remove(fifo)
```

However, this technique relies on the timing of the prefetch. If the cache line is prefetched too soon, it may be evicted from the cache before it is used. If it is fetched too late, then the cache miss will occur anyway.

Cher *et al.* [2004] observe that the fundamental problem is that cache lines are fetched in a *breadth-first, first-in, first-out* (FIFO), order but the mark-sweep algorithm traverses the graph *depth-first, last-in, first-out* (LIFO). Their solution is to insert a first-in, first-out queue in front of the mark stack (Figure 2.2 and Algorithm 2.6). As usual, when mark adds an object to its work list, a reference to the object is pushed onto a mark stack. However, when mark wants to acquire an object from the work list, a reference is popped from the mark stack but inserted into the queue, and the oldest item in the queue is returned to mark. The reference popped from the stack is also prefetched, the length of the queue determining the prefetch distance. Prefetching a few lines beyond the popped reference will help to ensure that sufficient fields of the object to be scanned are loaded without cache misses.

Algorithm 2.7: Marking graph edges rather than nodes

```
1  mark():
2      while not isEmpty(worklist)
3          obj ← remove(worklist)
4          if not isMarked(obj)
5              setMarked(obj)
6              for each fld in Pointers(obj)
7                  child ← *fld
8                  if child ≠ null
9                      add(worklist, child)
```

Prefetching the object to be marked through the first-in, first-out queue enables `mark` to load the object to be scanned without cache misses (lines 16–17 in Algorithm 2.2). However, testing and setting the mark of the child nodes will incur a cache miss (line 18). Garner *et al.* [2007] realised that `mark`'s tracing loop can be restructured to offer greater opportunities for prefetching. Algorithm 2.2 added each *node* of the live object graph to the work list exactly once; an alternative would be to traverse and add each *edge* exactly once. Instead of adding children to the work list only if they are unmarked, this algorithm inserts the children of unmarked objects unconditionally (Algorithm 2.7). Edge enqueuing requires more instructions to be executed and leads to larger work lists than node enqueuing since graphs must contain more edges than nodes (Garner *et al.* suggest that typical Java applications have about 40% more edges than nodes). However, if the cost of adding and removing these additional work list entries is sufficiently small then the gains from reducing cache misses will outweigh the cost of this extra work. Algorithm 2.7 hoists marking out of the inner loop. The actions that might lead to cache misses, `isMarked` and `Pointers`, now operate on the same object `obj`, which has been prefetched through the first-in, first-out queue, rather than on different objects, `obj` and its children, as previously. Garner *et al.* observe that tracing edges rather than nodes can improve performance even without software prefetching, speculating that the structure of the loop and the first-in, first-out queue enables more aggressive hardware speculation through more predictable access patterns.

2.7 Issues to consider

Despite its antiquity as the first algorithm developed for garbage collection [McCarthy, 1960], there are many reasons why mark-sweep collection remains an attractive option for developers and users today.

Mutator overhead

Mark-sweep in its simplest form imposes no overhead on mutator read and write operations. In contrast, reference counting (which we introduce in Chapter 5) imposes a significant overhead on the mutator. However, note that mark-sweep is also commonly used as a base algorithm for more sophisticated collectors which do require some synchronisation between mutator and collector. Both generational collectors (Chapter 9), and concurrent and incremental collectors (Chapter 15), require the mutator to inform the collector when they modify pointers. However, the overhead of doing so is typically small, a few percent of overall execution time.

Throughput

Combined with lazy sweeping, mark-sweep offers good throughput. The mark phase is cheap compared to other collection methods, and is dominated by the cost of pointer chasing. It simply needs to set a bit or byte for each live object discovered, in contrast to algorithms like semispace copying collection (Chapter 4) or mark-compact (Chapter 3) which must copy or move objects. On the other hand, like all the tracing collectors in these initial chapters, mark-sweep requires that all mutators be stopped while the collector runs. The pause time for collection depends on the program being run and its input, but can easily extend to several seconds or worse for large systems.

Space usage

Mark-sweep has significantly better space usage than approaches based on semispace copying. It also potentially has better space usage than reference counting algorithms. Mark bits can often be stored at no cost in spare bits in object headers. Alternatively, if a side bitmap table is used, the space overhead depends on object alignment requirements; it will be no worse than 1/alignment of the heap ($\frac{1}{32}$ or $\frac{1}{64}$ of the heap, depending on architecture), and possibly better depending on alignment restrictions. Reference counting, on the other hand, requires a full slot in each object header to store counts (although this can be reduced if a limit is placed on the maximum reference count stored). Copying collectors make even worse use of available memory, dividing the available heap into two equally sized semispaces, only one of which is used by the mutator at any time. On the debit side, non-compacting collectors, like mark-sweep and reference counting, require more complex allocators, such as segregated fits free-lists. The structures needed to support such collectors impose a further, non-negligible overhead. Furthermore, non-compacting collectors can suffer from fragmentation, thus increasing their effective space usage.

However, mark-sweep is a tracing algorithm. Like other tracing algorithms, it must identify all live objects in a space before it can reclaim the memory used by any dead objects. This is an expensive operation and so should be done infrequently. This means that tracing collectors must be given some headroom in which to operate in the heap. If the live objects occupy too large a proportion of the heap, and the allocators allocate too fast, then a mark-sweep collector will be called too often: it will thrash. For moderate to large heaps, the headroom necessary may be between 20% and 50% of the heap [Jones, 1996] though Hertz and Berger [2005] and Sareen and Blackburn [2022] show that, in order to provide the same throughput, Java programs managed by mark-sweep collection may need a heap about 25% to 50% larger than if it were to be managed by explicit deallocation.

To move or not to move?

Not moving objects has both advantages and disadvantages. Its benefit is that it makes mark-sweep a suitable candidate for use in uncooperative environments where there is no communication between language compiler and garbage collector (see Chapter 11). Without *type-accurate* information about the mutators' roots and the fields of objects, they cannot be updated with the new locations of moved objects — the putative 'root' might not be a pointer but other user data. In some cases, hybrid *mostly-copying collection* is possible [Bartlett, 1988a; Hosking, 2006]. Here, a program's roots must be treated conservatively (if it looks like a pointer, assume it is a pointer), so the collector cannot move their referents. However, type-accurate information about the layout of objects is available to the collector so it can move others that are not otherwise pinned to their location.

Safety in uncooperative systems managed by a conservative collector precludes the collector's modifying user data, including object headers. It also encourages placing collector metadata separate from user or other run-time system data, to reduce the risk of modification by the mutator. For both reasons, it is desirable to store mark bits in bitmaps rather than object headers.

The problem with not moving objects is that, in long-running applications, the heap tends to become fragmented. Non-moving memory allocators require space $O(\log \frac{max}{min})$ larger than the minimum possible, where *min* and *max* are the smallest and largest possible object sizes [Robson, 1971, 1974]. Thus a non-compacting collector may have to be called more frequently than one that compacts. Note that all tracing collectors need sufficient headroom (say, 20% to 50%) in the heap in order to avoid thrashing the collector.

To avoid having performance suffer due to excessive fragmentation, many production collectors that use mark-sweep to manage a portion of the heap also periodically use another algorithm such as mark-compact to defragment it. This is particularly true if the application does not maintain fairly constant ratios of object sizes or allocates many very large objects. If the application allocates more large objects than it previously did, the result may be many small holes in the heap no longer being reused for new allocations of objects of the same size. Conversely, if the application begins to allocate smaller objects than before, these smaller objects might be allocated in gaps previously occupied by larger objects, with the remaining space in each gap being wasted. However, careful heap management can reduce the tendency to fragment by taking advantage of objects' tendency to live and die in clumps [Dimpsey *et al.*, 2000; Blackburn and McKinley, 2008]. Allocation with segregated-fits can also reduce the need to compact. For instance, the Riptide collector [Pizlo, 2017] for the WebKit browser engine, used by the Safari browser and many other applications, does not move objects.

Chapter 3

Mark-compact garbage collection

Fragmentation[1] can be a problem for non-moving collectors. Although there may be space available in the heap, either there may be no contiguous chunk of free space sufficiently large to handle an allocation request, or the time taken to allocate may become excessive as the memory manager has to search for suitable free space. Allocators may alleviate this problem by storing small objects of the same size together in blocks [Boehm and Weiser, 1988] especially, as we noted earlier, for applications that do not allocate many very large objects and whose sets of different objects sizes do not change much. However, many long-running applications, when managed by non-moving collectors, will fragment the heap and performance will suffer.

In this and the next chapter we discuss two strategies for *compacting* live objects in the heap in order to eliminate *external fragmentation*. The major benefit of a compacted heap is that it allows very fast sequential allocation simply by testing against a heap limit and 'bumping' a free pointer, thus often called a *bump pointer*, by the size of the allocation request (we discuss allocation mechanisms further in Chapter 7). The strategy we consider in this chapter is in-place compaction[2] of objects into one end of the same region. In the next chapter we discuss a second strategy, *copying collection* — the evacuation of live objects from one region to another (for example, between semispaces).

Mark-compact algorithms operate in a number of phases. The first phase is always a *marking* phase, which we discussed in the previous chapter. Then, further *compacting* phases compact the live data by relocating objects and updating the pointer values of all live references to objects that have moved. The number of passes over the heap, the order in which these are executed and the way in which objects are relocated varies from algorithm to algorithm. The *compaction order* has locality implications. Any moving collector may rearrange objects in the heap in one of three ways.

Arbitrary: objects are relocated without regard for their original order or whether they point to one another.

Linearising: objects are relocated so that they are adjacent to related objects, such as ones to which they refer, which refer to them, which are siblings in a data structure, and so on, as far as this is possible.

Sliding: objects are slid to one end of the heap, squeezing out garbage, thereby maintaining their order of placement in the heap.

---

[1]We discuss fragmentation in more detail in Section 7.3.
[2]Often called *compactifying* in older papers.

Most compacting collectors of which we are aware use arbitrary or sliding orders. Arbitrary order compactors are simple to implement and fast to execute, particularly if all nodes are of a fixed size, but lead to poor spatial locality for the mutator because related objects may be dispersed to different cache lines or virtual memory pages. All modern mark-compact collectors implement sliding compaction, which does not interfere with mutator locality by changing the relative order of object placement. Copying collectors can even improve mutator locality by varying the order in which objects are laid out by placing them close to their parents or siblings. Conversely, experiments with a collector that compacts in an arbitrary order confirm that its rearrangement of objects' layout can lead to drastic reductions in application throughput [Abuaiadh *et al.*, 2004].

Compaction algorithms may impose further constraints. Arbitrary order algorithms handle objects of only a single size or compact objects of different sizes separately. Compaction may require two or three passes through the heap. It may be necessary to provide an extra slot in object headers to hold relocation information; such an overhead is likely to be significant for a general purpose memory manager. Compaction algorithms may impose restrictions on pointers. For example, in which direction may references point? Are interior pointers allowed? We discuss the issues they present in Chapter 11.

We examine several styles of compaction algorithm. First, we introduce Edwards's Two-Finger collector [Saunders, 1974]. Although this algorithm is simple to implement and fast to execute, it disturbs the layout of objects in the heap. The second compacting collector is a widely used sliding collector, the Lisp 2 algorithm. However, unlike the Two-Finger algorithm, it requires an additional slot in each object's header to store its *forwarding address*, the location to which it will be moved. Our third example, Jonkers's threaded compaction [1979], slides objects without any space overhead. However, it makes two passes over the heap, both of which tend to be expensive. The final class of compacting algorithms that we consider are fast, modern sliding collectors that similarly require no per-object storage overhead. Instead, they compute forwarding addresses on the fly. All compaction algorithms are invoked as follows:

```
atomic collect():
    markFromRoots()
    compact()
```

3.1   Two-finger compaction

Edwards's *Two-Finger* algorithm [Saunders, 1974] is a two-pass, arbitrary order algorithm, designed to compact regions containing objects of a fixed size. The idea is simple: given the volume of live data in the region to be compacted, we know where the high-water mark of the region will be after compaction. Live objects above this threshold are moved into gaps below the threshold. Algorithm 3.1 starts with two pointers or 'fingers', free which points to the start of the region of fixed-size slots and scan which starts at the end of the region. The first pass repeatedly advances the free pointer until it finds a gap (an unmarked object) in the heap, and retreats the scan pointer until it finds a live object. If the free and scan fingers pass each other, the phase is complete. Otherwise, the object at scan is moved into the gap at free, overwriting a field of the old copy (at scan) with a forwarding address, and the process continues. This is illustrated in Figure 3.1, where object A has been moved to its new location A' and some slot of A (say, the first slot) has been overwritten with the address A'. Note that the quality of compaction depends on the size of the gap at free closely matching the size of the live object at scan. Unless this algorithm is used on fixed-size objects, the degree of defragmentation might be very poor

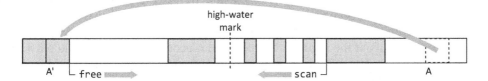

Figure 3.1: Edwards's Two-Finger algorithm. Live objects at the top of the heap are moved into free gaps at the bottom of the heap. Here, the object at A has been moved to A'. The algorithm terminates when the `free` and `scan` pointers meet.

Algorithm 3.1: The Two-Finger compaction algorithm

```
1   compact():
2      relocate(HeapStart, HeapEnd, slotSize)
3      updateReferences(HeapStart, free, slotSize)
4
5   relocate(start, end, slotSize):
6      free ← start
7      scan ← end
8
9      while free < scan
10         while isMarked(free)
11            unsetMarked(free)
12            free ← free + slotSize              /* find next hole */
13
14         while not isMarked(scan) && scan > free
15            scan ← scan − slotSize              /* find previous live object */
16
17         if scan > free
18            unsetMarked(scan)
19            move(scan, free)
20            *scan ← free              /* leave forwarding address (destructively) */
21            free ← free + slotSize
22            scan ← scan − slotSize
23
24   updateReferences(start, end, slotSize):
25      for each fld in Roots          /* update roots that pointed to moved objects */
26         ref ← *fld
27         if ref ≥ end
28            *fld ← *ref              /* use the forwarding address left in first pass */
29
30      scan ← start
31      while scan < end                      /* update fields in live region */
32         for each fld in Pointers(scan)
33            ref ← *fld
34            if ref ≥ end
35               *fld ← *ref          /* use the forwarding address left in first pass */
36         scan ← scan + slotSize                         /* next object */
```

indeed, since the algorithm would leave holes where the next free gap is smaller than the size of the object to move, or in the worst case, might not compact the region at all if there is no gap sufficiently large to accommodate the first object to be moved. At the end of this phase, free points at the high-water mark. The second pass updates the old values of pointers that referred to locations beyond the high-water mark with the forwarding addresses found in those locations, that is, with the objects' new locations.

The benefits of this algorithm are that it is simple and fast, doing minimal work at each iteration. It has no memory overhead, since forwarding addresses are written into slots above the high-water mark only after the live object at that location has been relocated: no information is destroyed. The algorithm supports interior pointers. Its memory access patterns are predictable, and hence provide opportunities for prefetching (by either hardware or software) which should lead to good cache behaviour in the collector. The scan pointer movement in relocate requires that the heap (or at least the live objects) can be parsed 'backwards', which is not a problem as objects are fixed-size here. Unfortunately, the order of objects in the heap that results from this style of compaction is arbitrary, and this tends to harm the mutator's locality. Nevertheless, it is easy to imagine how mutator locality might be improved somewhat. Since related objects tend to live and die together in clumps, rather than moving individual objects, we could move groups of consecutive live objects into large gaps. In the remainder of this chapter, we look at sliding collectors which maintain the layout order of the mutator.

3.2   The Lisp 2 algorithm

The *Lisp 2* collector (Algorithm 3.2) is widely used, either in its original form or adapted for parallel collection [Flood *et al.*, 2001]. It can be used with objects of varying sizes and, although it makes three passes over the heap, each iteration does little work (compared, for example, with threaded compactors). Although all mark-compact collectors have relatively poor throughput, a complexity study by Cohen and Nicolau [1983] found the Lisp 2 compactor to be the fastest of the compaction algorithms they studied. However, they did not take cache or paging behaviour into account, which is an important factor as we have seen before. The chief drawback of the Lisp 2 algorithm is that it requires an additional full-slot field in every object header to store the address to which the object is to be moved; this field can also be used for the mark bit.

The first pass over the heap (after marking) computes the location to which each live object will be moved, and stores this address in the object's forwardingAddress field (Algorithm 3.2). The computeLocations routine takes three arguments: the addresses of the start and the end of the region of the heap to be compacted, and the start of the region into which the compacted objects are to be moved. Typically the destination region will be the same as the region being compacted, but parallel compactor threads may use their own distinct source and destination regions. The computeLocations procedure moves two 'fingers' through the heap: scan iterates through each object (live or dead) in the source region, and free points to the next free location in the destination region. If the object discovered by scan is live, it will (eventually) be moved to the location pointed to by free so free is written into its forwardingAddress field, and is then incremented by the size of the object (plus any alignment padding). If the object is dead, it is ignored.

The second pass (updateReferences in Algorithm 3.2) updates the roots of mutator threads and references in marked objects so that they refer to the new locations of their targets, using the forwarding address stored in each about-to-be-relocated object's header by the first pass. Finally, in the third pass, relocate moves each live (marked) object in a region to its new destination.

Algorithm 3.2: The Lisp 2 compaction algorithm

```
1  compact():
2      computeLocations(HeapStart, HeapEnd, HeapStart)
3      updateReferences(HeapStart, HeapEnd)
4      relocate(HeapStart, HeapEnd)
5
6  computeLocations(start, end, toRegion):
7      scan ← start
8      free ← toRegion
9      while scan < end
10         if isMarked(scan)
11             forwardingAddress(scan) ← free
12             free ← align(free + size(scan))
13         scan ← nextObject(scan)
14
15 updateReferences(start, end):
16     for each fld in Roots                              /* update roots */
17         ref ← *fld
18         if ref ≠ null
19             *fld ← forwardingAddress(ref)
20
21     scan ← start                                       /* update fields */
22     while scan < end
23         if isMarked(scan)
24             for each fld in Pointers(scan)
25                 if *fld ≠ null
26                     *fld ← forwardingAddress(*fld)
27         scan ← nextObject(scan)
28
29 relocate(start, end):
30     scan ← start
31     while scan < end
32         if isMarked(scan)
33             dest ← forwardingAddress(scan)
34             move(scan, dest)
35             unsetMarked(dest)
36         scan ← nextObject(scan)
```

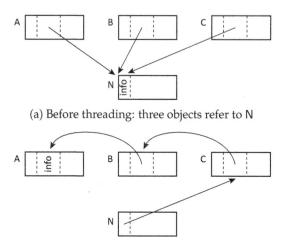

(a) Before threading: three objects refer to N

(b) After threading: all pointers to N have been 'threaded' so that the objects that previously referred to N can now be found from N. The value previously stored in the header word of N, which is now used to store the threading pointer, has been (temporarily) moved to the first field (in A) that referred to N.

Figure 3.2: Threading pointers

Notice that the direction of the passes (upward, from lower to higher addresses in our code) is opposite to the direction in which the objects will move (downward, from higher to lower addresses). This guarantees that when the third pass copies an object, it is to a location that has already been vacated. Some parallel compactors that divide the heap into blocks slide the contents of alternating blocks in opposite directions. This results in larger 'clumps', and hence larger free gaps, than sliding each block's contents in the same direction [Flood *et al.*, 2001]. An example is shown in Figure 14.8.

This algorithm can be improved in several ways. Data can be prefetched in similar ways as for the sweep phase of mark-sweep collectors. Adjacent garbage can be merged after line 10 of computeLocations in order to improve the speed of subsequent passes.

3.3   Threaded compaction

The most immediate drawbacks of the Lisp 2 algorithm are (i) that it requires three complete passes over the heap, and (ii) that space is added to each object for a forwarding address. The one is the consequence of the other. Sliding compacting garbage collection is a destructive operation which overwrites old copies of live data with new copies of other live data. It is essential to preserve forwarding address information until all objects have been moved and all references updated. The Lisp 2 algorithm is non-destructive at the cost of requiring an extra slot in the object header to store the forwarding address. The Two-Finger algorithm is non-destructive because the forwarding addresses are written beyond the live data high-water mark into objects that have already been moved, but it reorders objects arbitrarily which is undesirable.

Fisher [1974] solved the pointer update problem with a different technique, *threading*, that requires no extra storage yet supports sliding compaction. Threading needs there to be sufficient room in object headers to store an address (if necessary overwriting other data), which is not an onerous requirement, and that pointers can be distinguished from other

Algorithm 3.3: Jonkers's threaded compactor

```
 1  compact():
 2      updateForwardReferences()
 3      updateBackwardReferences()
 4
 5  thread(ref):                                          /* thread a reference */
 6      if *ref ≠ null
 7          *ref, **ref ← **ref, ref
 8
 9  update(ref, addr):              /* unthread all references, replacing with addr */
10      tmp ← *ref
11      while isReference(tmp)
12          *tmp, tmp ← addr, *tmp
13      *ref ← tmp
14
15  updateForwardReferences():
16      for each fld in Roots
17          thread(*fld)
18
19      free ← HeapStart
20      scan ← HeapStart
21      while scan ≤ HeapEnd
22          if isMarked(scan)
23              update(scan, free)                /* forward refs to scan set to free */
24              for each fld in Pointers(scan)
25                  thread(fld)
26              free ← free + size(scan)
27          scan ← scan + size(scan)
28
29  updateBackwardReferences():
30      free ← HeapStart
31      scan ← HeapStart
32      while scan ≤ HeapEnd
33          if isMarked(scan)
34              update(scan, free)                /* backward refs to scan set to free */
35              move(scan, free)                  /* slide scan back to free */
36              free ← free + size(scan)
37          scan ← scan + size(scan)
```

values, which may be harder. The best known threading is probably that due to Morris [1978, 1979, 1982] but Jonkers [1979] imposes fewer restrictions (for example, on the direction of pointers). The goal of threading is to allow all references to a node N to be found from N. It does so by temporarily reversing the direction of pointers. Figure 3.2 shows how fields previously referring to N can be found by following the threaded pointers from N. Notice that, after threading as in Figure 3.2b, the contents info of N's header has been written into a pointer field of A. When the collector chases the pointers to unthread and update them, it must be able to recognise that this field does not hold a threaded pointer.

Jonkers requires two passes over the heap, the first to thread references that point forward in the heap, and the second to thread backward pointers (see Algorithm 3.3). The first pass starts by threading the roots. It then sweeps through the heap, start to finish, computing a new address free for each live object encountered, determined by summing the volume of live data encountered so far. It is easiest to understand this algorithm by considering a single marked (live) node N. When the first pass reaches A, it will thread the reference to N. By the time that the pass reaches N, all the *forward* pointers to N will have been threaded (see Figure 3.2b). This pass can then update all the forward references to N by following this chain and writing the value of free, the address of the location to which N will be moved, into each previously referring slot. When it reaches the end of the chain, the collector will restore N's info header word. The next step on this pass is to increment free and thread N's children. By the end of this pass, all forward references will have been updated to point to their new locations and all backward pointers will have been threaded. The second pass similarly updates references to N, this time by following the chain of *backward* pointers. This pass also moves N.

The chief advantage of this algorithm is that it does not require any additional space, although object headers must be large enough to hold a pointer (which must be distinguishable from a normal value). However, threading algorithms suffer a number of disadvantages. They modify each pointer field of live objects twice, once to thread and once to unthread and update references. Threading requires chasing pointers so is just as cache unfriendly as marking but has to chase pointers three times (marking, threading and unthreading) in Jonkers's algorithm. Martin [1982] claimed that combining the mark phase with the first compaction pass improved collection time by a third, but this is a testament to the cost of pointer chasing and modifying pointer fields. Because Jonkers modifies pointers in a destructive way, it is inherently sequential and so cannot be used for concurrent compaction. For instance, in Figure 3.2b, once the references to N have been threaded, there is no way to discover that the first pointer field of B held a reference to N (unless that pointer is stored at the end of the chain as an extra slot in A's header, defeating the goal of avoiding additional storage overhead). Threading is also problematic for heaps that mingle ordinary and meta-objects because reversing pointers means that the collector cannot obtain the object layout information stored in those meta-objects. One solution is to segregate meta-objects in a separate heap, but Onozawa *et al.* [2021] solve this by placing ordinary objects at one end of a monolithic heap and meta-objects at the other; their algorithm threads pointers in ordinary objects before those in the meta-objects (which have a fixed layout) and then slides ordinary objects towards one end of the heap and meta-objects towards the other. Finally, Jonkers does not support interior pointers, which may be an important concern for some environments. However, the threaded compactor from Morris [1982] can accommodate interior pointers at the cost of an additional tag bit per field, and the restriction that the second compaction pass must be in the opposite direction to the first (adding to the problem of heap parsability).

3.4   One-pass algorithms

If we are to reduce the number of passes a sliding collector makes over the heap to two (one to mark and one to slide objects), and avoid the expense of threading, then we must store forwarding addresses in a side table that is preserved throughout compaction. Abuaiadh *et al.* [2004] and Kermany and Petrank [2006] both designed high performance mark-compact algorithms for multiprocessors that do precisely this. The former is a parallel stop-the-world algorithm (it employs multiple compaction threads); the latter, the *Com-*

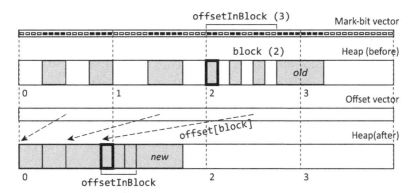

Figure 3.3: The heap (before and after compaction) and metadata used by Compressor [Kermany and Petrank, 2006]. Bits in the mark bit vector indicate the start and end of each live object. Words in the offset vector hold the address to which the first live object that starts in their corresponding block will be moved. Forwarding addresses are not stored but are calculated when needed from the offset and mark bit vectors.

pressor, can also be configured to be concurrent (allowing mutator threads to run alongside collector threads) and incremental (periodically suspending a mutator thread briefly to perform a small quantum of compaction work). We discuss the parallel, concurrent and incremental aspects of these algorithms in later chapters. Here, we focus on the core compaction algorithms in a stop-the-world setting.

Both algorithms use a number of side tables or vectors. Common to many collectors, marking uses a bitmap with one bit for each granule (say, a word). Marking sets the bits corresponding to all (or, more efficiently, the first and the last) granules of each live object. For example, bits 44–51 are set for the object marked *old* in Figure 3.3. By scrutinising the mark bitmap in the compaction phase, the collector can calculate the size of any contiguous run of live objects.

Second, a table is used to store forwarding addresses. It would be prohibitively expensive to do this for every object (especially if we assume that objects are word-aligned) so both these algorithms divide the heap into small, equal-sized blocks (256 or 512 bytes, respectively). The `offset` table stores the forwarding address of the first live object in each block. The new locations of the other live objects in a block can be computed on the fly from the offset and mark bit vectors. Similarly, given a reference to any object, we can compute its block number and thus derive its forwarding address from the entry in the offset table and the mark bits for that block. This allows the algorithms to replace multiple passes over the full heap to relocate objects and to update pointers with a single pass over the mark bit vector to construct the offset vector and a single pass over the heap (after marking) to move objects and update references by consulting these summary vectors. Reducing the number of heap passes has consequent advantages for locality. Let us consider the details as they appear in Algorithm 3.4.

After marking is complete, the `computeLocations` routine passes over the mark bit vector to produce the `offset` vector. Essentially, it performs the same calculation as in Lisp 2 (Algorithm 3.2) but does not need to touch any object in the heap. For example, consider the first marked object in block 2, shown with a bold border in Figure 3.3. Bits 4–7 and 12–15 are set in the first block, and bits 6–11 in the second (in this example, each block comprises 16 slots). This represents 14 granules (words) that are marked in the bitmap

Algorithm 3.4: Compressor

```
 1  compact():
 2      computeLocations(HeapStart, HeapEnd, HeapStart)
 3      updateReferencesRelocate(HeapStart, HeapEnd)
 4
 5  computeLocations(start, end, toRegion):
 6      loc ← toRegion
 7      block ← getBlockNum(start)
 8      for b ← 0 to numBits(start, end)−1
 9          if b % BITS_IN_BLOCK = 0                /* crossed block boundary? */
10              offset[block] ← loc                /* first object will be moved to loc */
11              block ← block + 1
12          if bitmap[b] = MARKED
13              loc ← loc + BYTES_PER_BIT          /* advance by size of live objects */
14
15  newAddress(old):
16      block ← getBlockNum(old)
17      return offset[block] + offsetInBlock(old)
18
19  updateReferencesRelocate(start, end):
20      for each fld in Roots
21          ref ← *fld
22          if ref ≠ null
23              *fld ← newAddress(ref)
24      scan ← start
25      while scan < end
26          scan ← nextMarkedObject(scan)          /* use the bitmap */
27          for each fld in Pointers(scan)          /* update references */
28              ref ← *fld
29              if ref ≠ null
30                  *fld ← newAddress(ref)
31          dest ← newAddress(scan)
32          move(scan, dest)
```

---

before this object. Thus the first live object in block 2 will be relocated to the 14th slot in the heap. This address is recorded in the offset vector for the block (see the dashed arrow marked offset[block] in the figure).

Once the offset vector has been calculated, the roots and live fields are updated to reflect the new locations. The Lisp 2 algorithm had to separate the updating of references and moving of objects because relocation information was held in the heap and object movement destroyed this information as relocated objects are slid over old objects. In contrast, Compressor-type algorithms relocate objects and update references in a single pass, updateReferencesRelocate in Algorithm 3.4. This is possible because new addresses can be calculated reasonably quickly from the mark bitmap and the offset vector on the fly: Compressor does not have to store forwarding addresses in the heap. Given the address of any object in the heap, newAddress obtains its block number (through shift and mask operations) and uses this as an index into the offset vector. The offset vector gives the forwarding address of the *first* object in that block. Compressor must then consult the bitmap for that block to discover how much live data precedes this object in its block, and therefore how much to add to the offset. This can be done in constant time by a table lookup. For example, the `old` object in the figure has an offset of 6 marked slots in its block so it is moved to slot 20: `offset[block]=14` plus `offsetInBlock(old)=6`.

3.5 Issues to consider

Is compaction necessary?

Mark-sweep garbage collection uses less memory than other techniques such as copying collection (which we discuss in the next chapter). Furthermore, since it does not move objects, a mark-sweep collector only needs to identify (a superset of) the roots of the collection; it does not need to modify them. Both of these considerations may be important in environments where memory is tight or where the run-time system cannot provide type-accurate identification of references (see Section 11.2).

Being a non-moving collector, mark-sweep is vulnerable to fragmentation. Using a parsimonious allocation strategy like segregated-fits (see Section 7.4) reduces the likelihood of fragmentation becoming a problem, provided that the application does not allocate very many large objects and that the set of object sizes does not change much. However, fragmentation is certainly likely to be a problem if a general-purpose, non-moving allocator is used to allocate a wide variety of objects in a long-running application. For this reason, most production Java virtual machines use moving collectors that can compact the heap.

Throughput costs of compaction

Sequential allocation in a compacted heap is fast. If the heap size is large compared to the amount of memory available, mark-compact is an appropriate moving collection strategy since it has half the memory requirements of copying collectors. Algorithms like Compressor are also easier to use with multiple collector threads than many copying algorithms (as we shall see in Chapter 14). There is, of course, a price to be paid. Mark-compact collection is likely to be slower than either mark-sweep or copying collection. Furthermore, many compaction algorithms incur additional overheads or place restrictions on the mutator.

Mark-compact algorithms offer worse throughput than mark-sweep or copying collection largely because they tend to make more passes over objects in the heap; Compressor and other region-evacuating algorithms are exceptions. Each pass tends to be expensive, not least because many require access to type information and object pointer fields, and these are the costs that tend to dominate after 'pointer chasing', as we saw in Chapter 2. A common solution is to run with mark-sweep collection for as long as possible, switching to mark-compact collection only when fragmentation metrics suggest that this be profitable [Printezis, 2001; Soman *et al.*, 2004].

Long-lived data

It is not uncommon for long-lived or even immortal data to accumulate near the beginning of the heap in moving collectors. Copying collectors handle such objects poorly, repeatedly copying them from one semispace to another. On the other hand, generational collectors (which we examine in Chapter 9) deal with these well, by moving them to a different space which is only collected infrequently. However, a generational solution might not be acceptable if heap space is tight. It is also obviously not a solution if the space being collected is the oldest generation of a generational collector! Mark-compact, however, can simply elect not to compact objects in this 'sediment'. Hanson [1977] was the first to observe that these objects tended to accumulate at the bottom of the 'transient object area' in his SITBOL system. His solution was to track the height of this 'sediment' dynamically, and simply avoid collecting it unless absolutely necessary, at the expense of a small amount of fragmentation. Sun Microsystems' HotSpot Java virtual machine used mark-compact as the default collector for its old generation. It too avoids compacting objects in the user-configurable 'dense prefix' of the heap [Sun Microsystems, 2006]. If bitmap marking is used, the extent of a live prefix of desired density can be determined simply by examining the bitmap.

Locality

Mark-compact collectors may preserve the allocation order of objects in the heap or they may rearrange them arbitrarily. Although arbitrary order collectors may be faster than other mark-compact collectors and impose no space overheads, the mutator's locality is likely to suffer from an arbitrary scrambling of object order. Sliding compaction has a further benefit for some systems: the space occupied by all objects allocated after a certain point can be reclaimed in constant time, just by retreating the free space pointer.

Limitations of mark-compact algorithms

A wide variety of mark-compact collection algorithms has been proposed. A fuller account of many older compaction strategies can be found in Chapter 5 of Jones [1996]. Many of these have properties that may be undesirable or unacceptable. The issues to consider include what space overheads may be incurred to store forwarding pointers (although this cost will be lower than that of a copying collector); *break table* methods smuggle this overhead into the gaps between objects as they are being compacted but come with significant time overheads [Haddon and Waite, 1967; Fitch and Norman, 1978; Strandh, 2014]. Some compaction algorithms place restrictions on the mutator. Simple compactors like the Two-Finger algorithm can only manage fixed-size objects. It is certainly possible to segregate objects by size class, but in this case, to what extent is compaction necessary? Threaded compaction requires that it be possible to distinguish pointers from non-pointer values temporarily stored in pointer fields. Threading is also incompatible with concurrent collection because it (temporarily) destroys information in pointer fields. Morris's [1978,1979,1982] threaded algorithm also restricts the direction in which references may point. Finally, most compaction algorithms preclude the use of interior pointers: the Two-Finger algorithm is an exception.

Chapter 4

Copying garbage collection

So far we have seen that mark-sweep has comparatively cheap collection costs but may suffer from fragmentation. Given that garbage collection should only account for a small proportion of overall execution time in any well-configured system, it is essential that overheads on the mutator are kept to a minimum and, in particular, that allocation is fast, since mutator costs dominate those of the collector. Mark-compact collectors eliminate fragmentation and support very fast, 'bump pointer' allocation (see Chapter 7) but require multiple passes over live objects, and can significantly increase collection times. In this chapter, we discuss a third style of tracing garbage collection, *semispace copying* [Fenichel and Yochelson, 1969; Cheney, 1970]. Copying compacts the heap, thus allowing fast allocation, yet only requires a single pass over the live objects in the heap. Its chief disadvantage is that it reduces the size of the available heap by half. It also requires processing *all* the bytes of each object rather than only the pointers.

4.1 Semispace copying collection

Basic copying collectors divide the heap into two equally sized *semispaces*, called *fromspace* and *tospace*. For simplicity, Algorithm 4.1 assumes that the heap is one contiguous region of memory, but this is not essential. New objects are allocated in tospace by incrementing the value of a `free` pointer if there is sufficient room.[1] Otherwise, the role of the two semispaces is *flipped* (line 2 in Algorithm 4.2) before the collector copies all live objects from what is now the fromspace to the tospace. This collector simply picks out — *evacuating* or *scavenging* — live objects from the old semispace. At the end of the collection, all live objects will have been placed in a dense prefix of tospace. The collector simply abandons fromspace (and the objects it contains) until the next collection. In practice, however, many collectors will zero that space for safety during the initialisation of the next collection cycle (see Chapter 11 where we discuss the interface with the run-time system).

After initialisation, semispace copying collectors populate their work list by copying the root objects into tospace (line 4). Copied but not yet scanned objects are grey. Each pointer field of a grey object will hold either null or a reference to a fromspace object. The copying scan traces each grey field, updating it to point to the tospace replica of its target. When the trace visits a fromspace object, `forward` checks whether it has been evacuated (forwarded) yet. If not, the object is copied now to the location in tospace to which `free` points, and the `free` pointer is incremented by the size of the object (as for allocation).

---

[1]Note: our `allocate` and `copy` routines ignore issues of alignment and padding, and also the possibility that a copied object may have a different format, such as an explicit rather than an implicit hash code for Java objects.

Algorithm 4.1: Semispace copying garbage collection: initialisation and allocation. For simplicity this assumes that the heap is a single contiguous region.

```
 1  createSemispaces():
 2      tospace ← HeapStart
 3      extent ← (HeapEnd − HeapStart) / 2          /* size of a semispace */
 4      top ← fromspace ← HeapStart + extent
 5      free ← tospace
 6
 7  atomic allocate(size):
 8      result ← free
 9      newfree ← result + size
10      if newfree > top
11          return null                             /* signal 'Memory exhausted' */
12      free ← newfree
13      return result
```

It is essential that collectors preserve the topology of live objects in the tospace copy of the heap. This is achieved by storing the address of each tospace object as a forwarding address in its old fromspace replica when the object is copied (line 34). The forward routine, tracing from a tospace field, uses this forwarding address to update the field, regardless of whether the copy was made in this tracing step or a previous one (line 22). Collection is complete when all tospace objects have been scanned.

Unlike most mark-compact collectors, semispace copying does not require any extra space in object headers. Any slot in a fromspace object can be used for the forwarding address (at least, in stop-the-world implementations), since that copy of the object is not used after the collection. This makes copying collection suitable even for header-less objects.

Work-list implementations

Like all tracing collectors, semispace copying needs a work list of objects to process. The work list can be implemented in different ways, leading to different orders of traversing the object graph and different space requirements. Fenichel and Yochelson [1969] implemented the work list as a simple auxiliary stack, just like the mark-sweep collectors described in Chapter 2 did. Copying is complete when the stack is empty.

The elegant *Cheney scanning* algorithm [Cheney, 1970] uses the grey objects in tospace as a first-in, first-out queue. It requires no additional storage other than a single pointer, scan, which points to the next unscanned object. When the semispaces are flipped, both the free and scan pointers are set to point to (the start of) tospace (see initialise in Algorithm 4.3). After the root objects are copied, the work list — the set of grey objects — comprises precisely those (copied but unscanned) objects between scan and free. This invariant is maintained throughout the collection. The scan pointer is advanced as tospace fields are scanned and updated (line 9). Collection is complete when the work list is empty: when the scan pointer catches up with the free pointer. Thus, the actions of this implementation are very simple. To check termination, isEmpty does no more than compare the scan and free pointers; remove just returns the scan pointer; and no action is required to add work to the work list.

Algorithm 4.2: Semispace copying garbage collection

```
 1  atomic collect():
 2      flip()
 3      initialise(worklist)                                    /* empty */
 4      for each fld in Roots                             /* copy the roots */
 5          process(fld)
 6      while not isEmpty(worklist)              /* copy transitive closure */
 7          ref ← remove(worklist)
 8          scan(ref)
 9
10  flip():                                           /* switch semispaces */
11      fromspace, tospace ← tospace, fromspace
12      top ← tospace + extent
13      free ← tospace
14
15  scan(ref):
16      for each fld in Pointers(ref)
17          process(fld)
18
19  process(fld):                   /* update field with reference to tospace replica */
20      fromRef ← *fld
21      if fromRef ≠ null
22          *fld ← forward(fromRef)             /* update with tospace reference */
23
24  forward(fromRef):
25      toRef ← forwardingAddress(fromRef)
26      if toRef = null                              /* not copied (not marked) */
27          toRef ← copy(fromRef)
28      return toRef
29
30  copy(fromRef):                      /* copy object and return forwarding address */
31      toRef ← free
32      free ← free + size(fromRef)
33      move(fromRef, toRef)
34      forwardingAddress(fromRef) ← toRef                         /* mark */
35      add(worklist, toRef)
36      return toRef
```

Algorithm 4.3: Copying with Cheney's work list

```
 1   initialise(worklist):
 2       scan ← free
 3
 4   isEmpty(worklist):
 5       return scan = free
 6
 7   remove(worklist):
 8       ref ← scan
 9       scan ← scan + size(scan)
10       return ref
11
12   add(worklist, ref):
13       /* nop */
```

An example

Figure 4.1 shows an example of how a Cheney scan would copy L, a linked list structure with pointers to the head and tail of the list. Figure 4.1a shows fromspace before the collection starts. At the start of the collection, the roles of the semispaces are flipped and L, which we assume is directly reachable from the roots, is copied to tospace (advancing the free pointer) and a forwarding reference to the new location L′ is written into L (for instance, over the first field). The scan pointer points to the first object in tospace (Figure 4.1b). The collector is now ready to start copying the transitive closure of the roots. The scan pointer points to the first object to process. L′ holds references to A and E in fromspace, so these objects are evacuated to the location pointed at by free in tospace (advancing free), the references in L′ are updated to point to the new locations A′ and E′ (Figure 4.1c), and scan is advanced to the next grey object. Note that the collector is finished with L′ so it is conceptually black, whereas the next objects to scan, A′ and E′, are grey. This process is repeated for each tospace object until the scan and free pointers meet (Figure 4.1f). Observe that, in Figure 4.1e, D′ holds a reference to E, which has already been copied. The referring field in D′ is therefore updated with the forwarding address stored in E, thereby preserving the shape of the graph. As with other tracing algorithms, copying garbage collection can cope with all shapes of graphs, including cyclic data structures, preserving sharing properly.

4.2   Traversal order and locality

Mutator and collector locality can have a significant impact on program performance. As we saw in the previous chapter, the collector can harm the mutator's locality, and hence its performance, if it moves objects to arbitrary new locations without regard for either pointer relationships or the original allocation order [Abuaiadh *et al.*, 2004]. However, there is a performance trade-off between locality benefits for the mutator, and for the collector and the frequency of collections. Compare mark-sweep and copying collection. Mark-sweep collectors have twice as much usable heap space available as do copying collectors, and hence will perform half as many collections, all other things being equal. Consequently, we might expect that mark-sweep collection offers better overall performance. Blackburn *et al.* [2004a] found that this was indeed the case for collection in tight heaps, where they used a segregated-fits allocator for the non-moving collector. Conversely, in large heaps

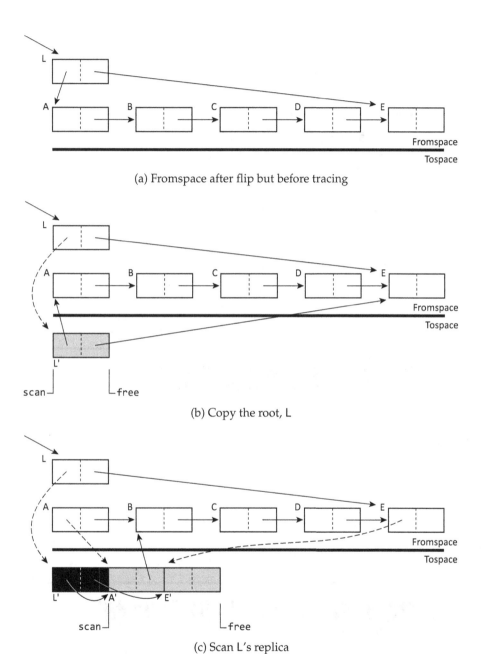

(a) Fromspace after flip but before tracing

(b) Copy the root, L

(c) Scan L's replica

Figure 4.1: Cheney copying garbage collection: an example

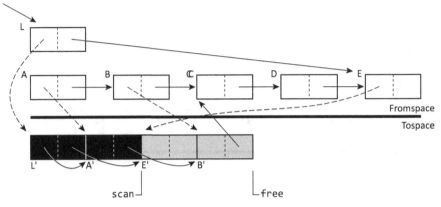

(d) Scan A's replica, and so on...

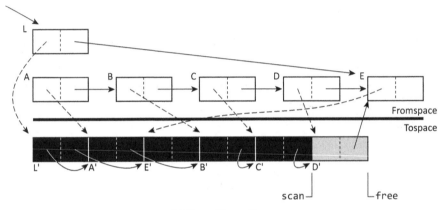

(e) Scan C's replica.

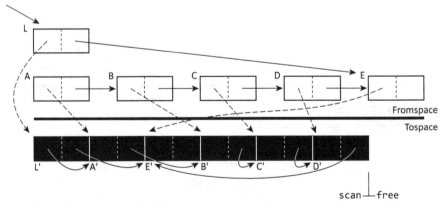

(f) Scan D's replica. scan=free so collection is complete.

Figure 4.1 (continued): Cheney copying garbage collection: an example

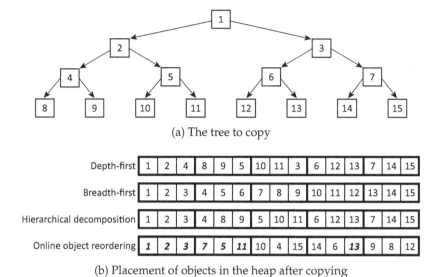

(a) The tree to copy

Depth-first	1	2	4	8	9	5	10	11	3	6	12	13	7	14	15
Breadth-first	1	2	3	4	5	6	7	8	9	10	11	12	13	14	15
Hierarchical decomposition	1	2	3	4	8	9	5	10	11	6	12	13	7	14	15
Online object reordering	*1*	*2*	*3*	*7*	*5*	*11*	10	4	15	14	6	*13*	9	8	12

(b) Placement of objects in the heap after copying

Figure 4.2: Copying a tree with different traversal orders. Each row shows how a traversal order lays out objects in tospace, assuming that three objects can be placed on a page (indicated by the thick borders). For *online object reordering*, prime numbered (bold italic) fields are considered to be hot.

the locality benefits to the mutator of sequential allocation outweighed the space efficiency of mark-sweep collection, leading to better miss rates at all levels of the cache hierarchy. This was particularly true for newly allocated objects which tend to experience higher mutation rates than older objects [Blackburn and McKinley, 2003].

The Blackburn *et al.* [2004a] study did object copying depth-first. In contrast, Cheney's copying collector traverses the graph breadth-first. Although this is implemented by a linear scan of — and hence predictable access to — the work list of grey tospace objects, breadth-first copying adversely affects mutator locality because it tends to separate parents and children. The table in Figure 4.2b compares the effect of different traversal orders on object layout, given the tree in Figure 4.2a. Each row shows where different tracing orders would place objects in tospace. If we examine row 2, we see that breadth-first traversal only places objects 2 and 3 near their parent. In this section we look more closely at traversal order and its consequences for locality.

White [1980] suggested long ago that the garbage collector could be used to *improve* the performance of the mutator. Both copying and compacting garbage collectors move objects, thus potentially affecting the mutators' locality patterns. Sliding is generally considered to be best order for mark-compact algorithms since it preserves the order of layout of objects established by the allocator. This is a safe, conservative policy, but can we do better? Mark-compact algorithms condense the heap in place, either by moving objects into holes (arbitrary order compactors) or by sliding live data (only overwriting garbage or objects that have already been moved), and thus have no opportunity for more locality-aware reorganisation. However, any collector that evacuates live objects to a fresh region of the heap without destroying the original data can rearrange their layout so as to improve the performance of the mutator.

Unfortunately, there are two reasons why we cannot find an optimal layout of objects which minimises the number of cache misses suffered by the program. First of all, the collector cannot know what the pattern of future accesses to objects will be. But worse,

Algorithm 4.4: Approximately depth-first copying [Moon, 1984] (we assume that objects do not span pages)

```
 1  initialise(worklist):
 2      scan ← free
 3      partialScan ← free
 4
 5  isEmpty(worklist):                                          /* as per Cheney */
 6      return scan = free
 7
 8  remove(worklist):
 9      if (partialScan < free)
10          ref ← partialScan                           /* prefer secondary scan */
11          partialScan ← partialScan + size(partialScan)
12      else
13          ref ← scan                                         /* primary scan */
14          scan ← scan + size(scan)
15      return ref
16
17  add(worklist, ref):        /* secondary scan on the most recently allocated page */
18      partialScan ← max(partialScan, startOfPage(ref))
```

Petrank and Rawitz [2002] show that the placement problem is NP-complete: even given perfect knowledge of future accesses, there is no efficient algorithm to compute an optimal placement. The only practical solution is to use heuristics. One possibility is to use past behaviour as a predictor of future behaviour. Some researchers have used either profiling, on the assumption that programs behave similarly for different inputs [Calder *et al.*, 1998], or online sampling, assuming that behaviour remains unchanged from one period to the next [Chilimbi *et al.*, 1999]. Another heuristic is to preserve allocation order, as sliding compaction does. A third strategy is to try to place children close to one of their parents, since the only way to access a child is by loading a reference from one of its parents. Cheney's algorithm uses breadth-first traversal, but its unfortunate consequence is that it separates related data, tending to co-locate distant cousins rather than parents and children. Depth-first traversal (row one), on the other hand, tends to place children closer to their parents.

Early studies of the locality benefits of different copying orders focused on trying to minimise page faults: the goal was to place related items on the same page. Stamos found that simulations of Smalltalk systems suggested that depth-first ordering gave a modest improvement over breadth-first ordering but worse paging behaviour than the original object creation order [Stamos, 1982; Blau, 1983; Stamos, 1984]. However, Wilson *et al.* [1991] argue that these simulations ignore the topology of real Lisp and Smalltalk programs which tended to create wide but shallow trees, rooted in hash tables, designed to spread their keys in order to avoid clashes.

If we are prepared to pay the cost of an auxiliary last-in, first-out marking stack, then the Fenichel and Yochelson algorithm leads to a depth-first traversal. However, it is possible to obtain a pseudo-depth-first traversal without paying the space costs that come from using a stack. Moon [1984] modified Cheney's algorithm to make it *'approximately depth-first'*. He added a second, partialScan pointer in addition to the primary scan pointer (see Figure 4.3). Whenever an object is copied, Moon's algorithm starts a secondary scan from the last page of tospace that has not been completely scanned. Once the last tospace

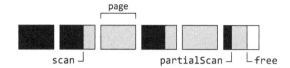

Figure 4.3: Moon's approximately depth-first copying. Each block represents a page. As usual, scanned fields are black, and copied but not yet scanned ones are grey. Free space is shown in white.

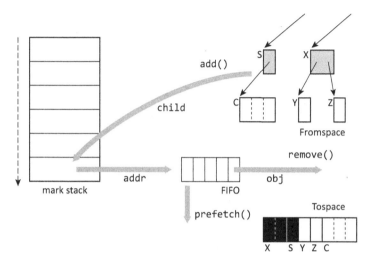

Figure 4.4: A FIFO prefetch buffer (discussed in Chapter 2) does not improve locality with copying as distant cousins (C, Y, Z), rather than parents and children, tend to be placed together.

page has been scanned, the primary scan continues from the first incompletely scanned page (Algorithm 4.4). In effect, the work list is implemented as a *pair* of Cheney queues. The advantage of this *hierarchical decomposition* scheme is that it is more effective than pure breadth-first search at depositing parents on the same page as their children. The hierarchical decomposition line of Figure 4.2b shows how this algorithm would copy the tree, assuming a page size of three objects.

The disadvantage of Moon's algorithm is that objects may be scanned twice since he records only a pair of scan pointers, thus forgetting blocks between scan and free that have already been partially scanned; indeed, Wilson *et al.* [1991] suggest that around 30% may be rescanned. They modified this algorithm to provide each page with its own scan and free pointers, making the work list now a *list* of partially scanned blocks to complete. This means that the primary scan does not have to revisit objects on pages already processed by a secondary scan.

When we discussed how to improve the marking loop of a mark-sweep collector in Section 2.6, we mentioned that Cher *et al.* [2004] argued that using a stack to guide tracing leads to a depth-first traversal of the graph but cache lines are fetched breadth-first. A natural question to ask is: can we combine stack-based, depth-first copying with the first-in, first-out prefetch queue suggested by Cher *et al.* [2004]? Unfortunately it seems not, because although first-in, first-out helps the copying loop avoid cache miss stalls, it separates parents from children since it visits an object to follow its references only when

Algorithm 4.5: Online object reordering

```
 1  atomic collect():
 2      flip()
 3      initialise(hotList, coldList)
 4      for each fld in Roots
 5          adviceProcess(fld)
 6      repeat
 7          while not isEmpty(hotList)
 8              adviceScan(remove(hotList))
 9          while not isEmpty(coldList)
10              adviceProcess(remove(coldList))
11      until isEmpty(hotList)
12
13  initialise(hotList, coldList):
14      hotList ← empty
15      coldList ← empty
16
17  adviceProcess(fld):
18      fromRef ← *fld
19      if fromRef ≠ null
20          *fld ← forward(fromRef)
21
22  adviceScan(obj):
23      for each fld in Pointers(obj)
24          if isHot(fld)
25              adviceProcess(fld)
26          else
27              add(coldList, fld)
```

it is removed from the queue, not from the stack.[2] Imagine that a string object S is popped from the stack. Desirably, S should be placed adjacent to its associated character array C in tospace, as the depth-first algorithm would do. Using the first-in, first-out queue, after S is popped from the stack, it is added to the queue. Suppose that the queue is full, so the oldest entry X is removed, copied and its references Y and Z pushed on the stack, as illustrated in Figure 4.4. Unfortunately, Y and Z will be removed from the queue and copied after S but *before* C.

The reorganisations above are static: the algorithms pay no attention to the behaviour of individual applications. However, it is clear that the benefits of layout-reordering schemes depend on the behaviour of the mutator. Lam *et al.* [1992] found that both algorithms were sensitive to the mix and shape of program data structures, giving disappointing performance for structures that were not tree-like. Siegwart and Hirzel [2006] also observed that a parallel hierarchical decomposition collector led to benefits for some benchmarks but little improvement overall for others. Huang *et al.* [2004] address this by dynamically profiling the application and trying to copy 'hot' fields of objects alongside their parent. Their *online object-reordering* scheme and its effect are shown in Algorithm 4.5 and the last row of Figure 4.2b. The main scanning loop of their algorithm (line 6) processes all hot fields in its work lists before any cold fields. Piggybacking on the method sampling mechanism of

---

[2]Tony Printezis, personal communication.

an adaptive dynamic compiler allows these fields to be identified comparatively cheaply (Huang *et al.* report less than 2% of total execution time). Their implementation also accommodates changes of behaviour in different program phases by allowing the 'heat' of fields to decay and be resampled. They find that the performance of their system matches or improves that of static reorderings such as breadth-first.

Chilimbi and Larus [1998] and Chen *et al.* [2006] invoke the collector somewhat eagerly to improve locality in a generational collector. Their mechanism is expensive so it is not always turned on. Instead, they use changes in allocation rates as their primary trigger to collection in order to improve locality; changes in data translation lookaside buffer or Level 2 cache miss rates are used as a secondary trigger. They record object accesses in a fixed-size, circular buffer (they argue that profiling at the node level rather than the field level leads to overheads of less than 5%, since most nodes in object-oriented programs are smaller than 32 bytes). An expensive (but aggressively optimised) read barrier[3] operates during bursty sampling phases to identify hot objects as the mutators load references to them. Their collector copies hot objects in two phases. First, contemporaneously accessed objects are copied to a temporary buffer. Then, to improve paging, the collector appends hot objects to this buffer, using hierarchical decomposition [Wilson *et al.*, 1991]. The original locations of copied objects are marked free, and the rearranged group of objects is moved from the temporary buffer to one end of the heap. The scheme aims to improve both cache performance and paging behaviour: the benefit of combining both optimisations was found to be greater than the sum of either applied on its own, and gave an average improvement in execution time for a range of large C# applications. Although it is possible that some garbage objects may be preserved, in practice the volume is very small.

Other authors have also suggested custom, static reordering by object type [Wilson *et al.*, 1991; Lam *et al.*, 1992], particularly for system data structures. By allowing the order in which fields are copied to be specified, Novark *et al.* [2006] reduce the cache miss rate significantly for certain data structures. Shuf *et al.* [2002] use off-line profiling to identify *prolific types*. The allocator is modified so that, when a parent is created, adjacent space is left for its children, thus both improving locality and encouraging clustering of objects with similar lifetimes. This approach may address to some extent the problem identified on page 55 of combining a first-in, first-out prefetch queue with depth-first copying.

4.3 Issues to consider

Copying collection offers two immediately attractive advantages over non-moving garbage collectors like mark-sweep: it provides fast allocation and elimination of fragmentation (other than to satisfy alignment requirements). Simple copying collectors are also easier to implement than mark-sweep or mark-compact collectors. The trade-off is that copying collection uses twice as much virtual memory as other collectors in order to match their frequency of collections.

Allocation

Allocation in a compacted heap is fast because it is simple. In the common case, it only requires a test against a heap or block limit and that a free pointer be incremented. If a block-structured rather than a contiguous heap is used, occasionally the test will fail and a new block must be acquired. The slow path frequency will depend on the ratio of the average size of objects allocated and the block size. Sequential allocation also works well with multithreaded applications since each mutator can be given its own local allocation buffer

---

[3]We discuss barriers in Chapter 11.

in which to allocate without needing to synchronise with other threads. This arrangement is simpler and requires little metadata, in contrast with local allocation schemes for non-moving collectors where each thread might need its own size class data structures for segregated-fits allocation.

The code sequence for such bump pointer allocation is short but, even better, it is well behaved with respect to the cache as allocation advances linearly through the heap. Although the combination of sequential allocation, typically short object lifetimes and semispaces means that the next location to be allocated is likely to be the one least recently used, the prefetching abilities of modern processors are likely to hide the latency that might otherwise result. If this behaviour conflicts with the operating system's least recently used (LRU) page eviction policy to the extent that paging becomes a problem, it is time to reconsider the configuration of the system. Either it requires more physical memory to run the application satisfactorily, or another collection policy — maybe one of the generational collectors we discuss in Chapter 9 — should be used.

Blackburn *et al.* [2004a] found that although sequential allocation had an 11% advantage over free-list allocation in a micro-benchmark limit study, allocation itself accounted for less than 10% of overall running time in real applications. Thus, the difference in cost between bump pointer allocation and free-list allocation may not be significant. However, allocation is only part of the picture for the mutator since the cost of creating a new object is likely to be dominated by its initialisation, certainly in systems that distinguish these actions. Furthermore, objects share similar life-cycles in many applications. The mutator creates some semantically related objects at around the same time, uses them, and finally tends to abandon them all at once. Here, compacted heaps offer good spatial locality, with related objects typically allocated on the same page and maybe in the same cache line if they are small. Such a layout is likely to lead to fewer cache misses than if related objects are allocated from different free-lists.

Space and locality

The immediate disadvantage of semispace copying is the need to maintain a second semispace, sometimes called a *copy reserve*. For a given memory budget and ignoring the data structures needed by the collector itself, semispace copying provides only half the heap space of that offered by other whole heap collectors. The consequence is that copying collectors will perform more garbage collection cycles than other collectors. Whether or not this translates into better or worse performance depends on trade-offs between the mutator and the collector, the characteristics of the application program and the volume of heap space available.

Simple asymptotic complexity analyses might prefer copying over mark-sweep collection. Let M be the total size of the heap and L be the volume of live data. Semispace collectors must copy, scan and update pointers in live data. Mark-sweep collectors must similarly trace all the live objects but then sweep the whole heap. Jones [1996] defines the time complexities for copying and mark-sweep collection as, respectively:

$$t_{Copy} = cL \qquad\qquad\qquad\qquad t_{MS} = mL + sM$$

The amount of memory reclaimed by each collector is:

$$m_{Copy} = M/2 - L \qquad\qquad\qquad m_{MS} = M - L$$

Let $r = L/M$ be the proportion of live memory, which we assume to be constant. The efficiency of an algorithm can be described by its *mark/cons ratio*, e, the amount of work done by the collector per unit allocated. The efficiency of these two algorithms is therefore:

$$e_{Copy} = \frac{2cr}{1 - 2r} \qquad\qquad\qquad e_{MS} = \frac{mr + s}{1 - r}$$

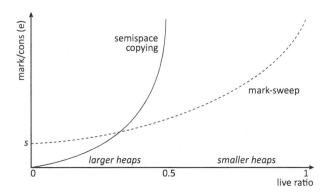

Figure 4.5: Mark/cons ratios for mark-sweep and copying collection (lower is better)

The mark/cons ratio curves presented in Figure 4.5 show that copying collection can be made more efficient than mark-sweep collection, provided that the heap is large enough and r is small enough. However, such a simple analysis ignores several matters. Modern mark-sweep collectors are likely to use lazy sweeping, thus reducing the constant s and lowering mark-sweep's mark/cons ratio. Complexity analyses need to be treated with some caution since they ignore implementation details, although Hertz and Berger [2005] confirm experimentally the general shape of the curves (for example, that the cost of mark-sweep collection is inversely proportional to the size of the heap). However, pragmatic details are important for real collectors. These are not captured by complexity analyses. One example is the locality benefit of sequential allocation [Blackburn *et al.*, 2004a].

So, sequential allocation tends to lay out contemporaneously accessed objects contiguously, which helps to improve the mutator's cache miss rate. But copying collection then reorders surviving objects in the heap. Although Cheney-style collectors need no auxiliary stack to guide the trace, their breadth-first traversal tends to separate parents and children. Hierarchical decomposition offers a compromise between paying the costs of a tracing stack and improving the layout of objects in the heap. However, although careful reordering has benefits for some programs, it often has negligible effects. Why is this? Most objects have short lifetimes and do not survive a collection. Moreover, many applications concentrate accesses, and especially writes, on these young objects [Blackburn and McKinley, 2003]. Collector traversal policies cannot affect the locality properties of objects that are never moved.

Printezis has also pointed out that whether parallel collector threads are used or not will influence the choice of copying mechanism. It may be simpler to do very fine-grained load-balancing by work stealing from per-thread stacks as opposed to using a Cheney queue.[4] We discuss these issues in depth in Chapter 14.

Moving objects

Choosing whether to use a copying collector will depend in part on whether it is possible to move objects and the cost of doing so. In some environments objects cannot be moved. One reason is that lack of type accuracy means that it would not be safe to modify the slot holding a reference to a putative object. Another is that a reference to the object has been passed to unmanaged code (perhaps, as an argument in a system call) that does not expect the reference to change. Furthermore, the problem of pointer finding can often be simpler in a mark-sweep context than that of a moving collector: it suffices to find at least

---

[4]Tony Printezis, personal communication.

one reference to a live object with a non-moving collector. On the other hand, a moving collector must find and update *all* references to an evacuated object. As we will see in Chapter 17, this also makes the problem of concurrent moving collection much harder than concurrent non-moving collection since all the references to an object must appear to be updated atomically.

It is expensive to copy some objects. Although copying even a small object is likely to be more expensive than marking it, the cost and latency of doing so is often absorbed by the costs of chasing pointers and discovering type information. On the other hand, repeatedly copying large, pointer-free objects will lead to poor performance. One solution is simply not to copy them but instead devolve the management of large objects to a non-moving collector. Another is to copy them virtually but not physically. This can be done either by holding such objects on a linked list maintained by the collector, or by allocating large objects on their own virtual memory pages which can be remapped. We consider such techniques in Chapters 8 to 10.

Chapter 5

Reference counting

The algorithms considered so far have all been indirect. Each has traced the graph of live objects from a set of known roots to identify all live objects. In this chapter, we consider the last class of fundamental algorithms, *reference counting* [Collins, 1960]. Rather than tracing reachable objects and then inferring that all unvisited objects must be garbage, reference counting operates directly on objects as references are created or destroyed.

Reference counting maintains a simple invariant: an object is presumed to be live if and only if the number of references to that object is greater than zero.[1] Reference counting therefore associates a *reference count* with each object managed; typically this count is stored as an additional slot in the object's header. In its most naive implementation, shown in Algorithm 5.1, reference counts are incremented or decremented as references to objects are created or destroyed. Procedure Write increments the reference count of the new target and then decrements the count of the old target. Note that it is called even for updates of local variables. We also assume it is called to write null into local variables before each procedure returns. The operations addReference and deleteReference increment and decrement, respectively, the reference counts of their object argument. Note that it is essential that the reference counts are adjusted in this order (lines 9–10) to prevent premature reclamation of the target in the case when the old and the new targets of the pointer are the same, that is, src[i]=ref. Once a reference count is zero (line 20), the object can be freed and the reference counts of all its children decremented, which may in turn lead to their reclamation and so on recursively.

The Write method in Algorithm 5.1 is an example of a *write barrier*. For these, the compiler emits a short code sequence around the actual pointer write. As we shall see later in this book, mutators are required to execute barriers in many systems. More precisely, they are required whenever collectors do not consider the liveness of the *entire* object graph *atomically* with respect to the mutator. Such collectors may execute concurrently, either in lock-step with the mutator as for reference counting or asynchronously in another thread. Alternatively, the collector may process different regions of the heap at different frequencies, as do generational collectors. In all these cases, mutator barriers must be executed in order to preserve the invariants of the collector algorithm.

---

[1]*Reference listing* algorithms, commonly used by distributed systems such as Java's RMI libraries, modify this invariant so that an object is deemed to be live if and only if the *set* of clients believed to be holding a reference to the object is non-empty. This offers certain fault tolerance benefits, for example, set insertion or deletion is idempotent, unlike counter arithmetic.

5.1   Advantages and disadvantages of reference counting

There are a number of reasons why reference counting might be an attractive option. Memory management costs are distributed throughout the computation. Potentially, reference counting can recycle memory as soon as an object becomes garbage (but we shall see below why this may not always be desirable). Consequently, it may continue to operate satisfactorily in a nearly full heap, unlike tracing collectors which need some headroom. Since reference counting operates directly on the sources and targets of pointers, the locality of a reference counting algorithm may be no worse than that of its client program. Client programs can use destructive updates rather than copying objects if they can prove that an object is not shared. Reference counting can reclaim some memory even if parts of the system are unavailable: this is particularly useful in distributed systems [Rodrigues and Jones, 1998]. Simple reference counting can be implemented fairly easily without assistance from or knowledge of the run-time system. In particular, it is not necessary to know the roots of the program. Reference counting may also facilitate prompt, in-place reuse of memory (see, for example, Vießmann *et al.* [2018], Reinking *et al.* [2021] or Lorenzen and Leijen [2022]). However, implementing high performance reference counting in the presence of concurrent mutator threads and cyclic data structures is more complex. Because high-performance systems depend on high-performance garbage collection, Jibaja *et al.* [2011] argue that support for high-performance memory management requires pervasive changes throughout a virtual machine implementation but that this discipline is less burdensome when followed from the beginning rather than trying to retrofit it later.

For these reasons, reference counting has been adopted for many systems including language implementations (for example, early versions of Smalltalk and Lisp; Objective-C and Swift; AWK, Perl, PHP and Python); applications such as Photoshop, Real Networks' Rhapsody Music Service, Océ printers, scanners and document management systems; as well as operating systems' file managers. Libraries to support safe reclamation of objects are widely available for languages like C++ (`unique_ptr` and `shared_ptr`) and Rust (`Box`, `Rc` and `Arc`) that do not require automatic memory management. Such libraries may use *smart pointers* to access objects. Smart pointers typically override constructors and operators such as assignment, either to enforce unique ownership of objects or to provide reference counting. *Unique pointers* (such as `unique_ptr` in C++) ensure that an object has a single 'owner'. When this owner is destroyed, the object also can be destroyed. Rust's ownership concept is based on this principle, adding the notion of being able to pass ownership on and also to borrow it temporarily. In Rust, pointers are unique by default, with `Box` supporting unique pointers to dynamically allocated objects. Many C++ programmers use smart pointers to provide reference counting to manage memory automatically. In the past, libraries such as Boost[2] were popular, but as of C++11 `unique_ptr` and `shared_ptr` are part of the standard library, with `shared_ptr` offering reference counting semantics. Edelson [1992] argued that smart pointers are sufficiently different from ordinary pointers to be problematic, or at least non-transparent, replacements for them. C++11's `unique_ptr` and `shared_ptr` almost entirely overcome such differences and are intended to replace raw pointers, giving reference counted semantics.

Unfortunately, there are also a number of disadvantages to reference counting. First, it imposes a time overhead on the mutator. In contrast to the tracing algorithms we considered in earlier chapters, Algorithm 5.1 redefines all pointer `Read` and `Write` operations in order to manipulate reference counts. Even non-destructive operations such as iteration require the reference counts of each element in the list to be incremented and then decremented as a pointer moves across a data structure such as a list. From a performance point of view, it is particularly undesirable to add overhead to operations that manipulate

---

[2]The Boost libraries for C++, www.boost.org.

Algorithm 5.1: Simple reference counting

```
 1   New():
 2       ref ← allocate()
 3       if ref = null
 4           error "Out of memory"
 5       rc(ref) ← 0
 6       return ref
 7
 8   atomic Write(src, i, ref):
 9       addReference(ref)
10       deleteReference(src[i])
11       src[i] ← ref
12
13   addReference(ref):
14       if ref ≠ null
15           rc(ref) ← rc(ref) + 1
16
17   deleteReference(ref):
18       if ref ≠ null
19           rc(ref) ← rc(ref) − 1
20           if rc(ref) = 0
21               for each fld in Pointers(ref)
22                   deleteReference(*fld)
23               free(ref)
```

registers or thread stack slots. For this reason alone, this naive algorithm is impractical for use as a general purpose, high volume, high performance memory manager. Fortunately, as we shall see, the cost of reference counted pointer manipulations can be reduced substantially, even to become competitive with high performance tracing collectors.

Second, both the reference count manipulations and the pointer load or store must be a single atomic action in order to prevent races between mutator threads which would risk premature reclamation of objects. It is insufficient to protect the integrity of the reference count operation alone. For now, we simply assert that actions are atomic, without explaining how this might be achieved. We reconsider this in Chapter 18 when we examine reference counting and concurrency in detail. Some smart pointer libraries that provide reference counting require careful use by the programmer if races are to be avoided. For example, in the Boost library, concurrent threads can read the same shared_ptr instance simultaneously, or can modify different shared_ptr instances simultaneously, but the library enforces atomicity only upon reference count manipulations. The combination of pointer read or write and reference count increment is *not* a single atomic action. Thus, the application programmer must take care to prevent races to update a pointer slot, which might lead to undefined behaviour.

Third, naive reference counting turns read-only operations into ones requiring stores to memory (to update reference counts). Similarly, it requires reading and writing the old referent of a pointer field when changing that field to refer to a different object. These writes 'pollute' the cache and induce extra memory traffic.

Fourth, reference counting cannot reclaim cyclic data structures (that is, data structures that contain references to themselves). Even if such a structure is isolated from the rest of the object graph — it is unreachable — the reference counts of its components will never drop to zero. Unfortunately, self-referential structures are common (doubly linked lists, trees whose nodes hold a back pointer to the root, and so on), although their frequency varies widely between applications [Bacon and Rajan, 2001]. While it is possible to use reference counting in ways that break cycles or ignore back-links, these techniques are not a general purpose solution and must be used with care.

Fifth, in the worst case, the number of references to an object could be equal to the number of objects in the heap. This means that the reference count field must be pointer sized, that is, a whole slot. Given that the average size of nodes in object-oriented languages is small (for example, Java instance objects are typically 20 to 64 bytes long [Dieckmann and Hölzle, 1999, 2001; Blackburn *et al.*, 2006b], and Lisp cons cells usually fit into two or three slots), this overhead can be significant.

Finally, reference counting may still induce pauses. When the last reference to the head of a large pointer structure is deleted, reference counting must recursively delete each descendant of the root. Boehm [2004] suggests that thread-safe implementations of reference counting may even lead to longer maximum pause times than tracing collectors. Weizenbaum [1969] suggested *lazy reference counting*: rather than immediately freeing garbage pointer structures, deleteReference adds an object with a zero reference count to a *to-be-freed* list, without destroying its contents. When the object is later acquired by the allocator, its children can be processed similarly, without recursive freeing. Unfortunately, this technique allows large garbage structures to be hidden by smaller ones, and hence increases overall space requirements [Boehm, 2004].

Let us now see the extent to which we can resolve two of the major problems facing reference counting: the cost of reference count manipulations and collecting cyclic garbage. It turns out that common solutions to both of these problems involve a stop-the-world pause. We mention these here but examine how this requirement can be relaxed in Chapter 18.

5.2   Improving efficiency

Programs may spend a significant amount of execution time on reference counting operations, especially if those need to be synchronised. For example, Choi *et al.* [2018] report that Swift client (respectively, server) programs spend 42% (respectively, 15%) of their execution time on reference counting operations despite compiler optimisations intended to remove unnecessary ones. There are a number of ways in which an optimiser may statically remove reference counting operations or replace synchronised operations with cheaper, unsynchronised ones. It can remove paired increments and decrements [Cann and Oldehoeft, 1988]. It can eliminate reference count operations on a reference whose lifetime is completely nested within the lifetime of another reference to the same object. It can replace synchronised modifications to an object's reference count with unsynchronised ones if an escape analysis proves that the object is not shared with other threads. However, it may be difficult to optimise away reference count operations. Gottesman [2019] observes that common compiler optimisations may easily defeat an optimiser's attempt to reconstruct ownership relations from a soup of reference count increments and decrements resulting in mis-compiles and semantic disagreements in between optimiser and front-end. To address this, the mid-level representation was changed in Swift 5 to use *Ownership SSA* (Static Single Assignment) form which imbues def-use edges with ownership information. By default, Swift 5.7 uses Ownership SSA to discard all automatic reference counting operations emitted by the compiler front-end and then re-infer in the back-end the minimal set of reference counted operations needed by the program, taking care only to shrink lifetimes aggressively when it is certain that no references can escape (for example if a managed class value is converted to a raw pointer).

In contrast to static approaches to optimising reference counting, Blackburn and McKinley [2003] define a useful taxonomy of dynamic solutions.

Deferral *Deferred reference counting* trades fine grained incrementality (the immediate recovery of all garbage) for efficiency. The identification of some garbage objects is deferred to a reclamation phase at the end of some period. These schemes eliminate some barrier operations.

Coalescing Many reference count adjustments are temporary and hence 'unnecessary'; programmers often remove them by hand. In some special cases, this can also be done by the compiler. However, it is also possible to do this more generally at run time by tracking only the state of an object at the beginning and end of some period. This *coalesced reference counting* ignores all but the first modification to a field of an object in each period.

Buffering *Buffered reference counting* also defers identification of garbage. However, unlike deferred or coalesced reference counting, it buffers *all* reference count increments and decrements for later processing. Only the collector thread is allowed to apply reference count modifications. Buffering considers *when* to apply reference count modifications, not *whether* to.

One fundamental obstacle to efficiency is that object reference counts are part of the global state of the program, but operations on (thread) local state are usually more efficient. The three classes of solution above share a common approach to this problem: they divide execution into periods or *epochs*. Within an epoch, some or all synchronised reference counting operations can be either eliminated or replaced by unsynchronised writes (to thread-local buffers). Identification of garbage is only performed at the end of an epoch, either with mutator threads halted, or concurrently by a separate collector thread (or threads). In all cases, changes to local reference count state are not revealed (that is, applied to the global state using an atomic action) until an epoch boundary.

In this chapter, we consider two sequential approaches, deferred and coalesced reference counting. Here, collection epochs are separated by stop-the-world pauses to repair reference counts. In Chapter 18, we shall see first how buffered reference counting devolves responsibility for reference count manipulations to a concurrent thread, and then how we can coalesce reference counts concurrently.

5.3 Deferred reference counting

Manipulating all reference counts is expensive compared with the cost to the mutator of simple tracing algorithms. Although, as we shall see in later chapters, generational and concurrent algorithms also impose a small overhead on the mutator, these are much lower than the overhead of safely manipulating reference counts. To overwrite a pointer, `Write` in Algorithm 5.1 executes a dozen or so instructions (though in some cases the compiler can statically elide some tests). The reference count adjustments must be atomic operations and be kept consistent with pointer updates. Furthermore, `Write` modifies both the old and new targets of the field in question, possibly polluting the cache with dirty words that will not be reused soon.

Most high-performance reference counting systems (for example, those of Shahriyar *et al.* [2013] or Zhao *et al.* [2022a,b]) use *deferred reference counting*. The overwhelming majority of pointer loads are to local and temporary variables, that is, to registers or stack slots. Long ago, Deutsch and Bobrow [1976] showed how to remove reference count manipulations from these operations by adjusting counts only when pointers are stored into

Algorithm 5.2: Deferred reference counting

```
1   New():
2       ref ← allocate()
3       if ref = null
4           collect()
5           ref ← allocate()
6           if ref = null
7               error "Out of memory"
8       rc(ref) ← 0
9       add(zct, ref)
10      return ref
11
12  Write(src, i, ref):
13      if src = Roots
14          src[i] ← ref
15      else
16          atomic
17              addReference(ref)
18              remove(zct, ref)
19              deleteReferenceToZCT(src[i])
20              src[i] ← ref
21
22  deleteReferenceToZCT(ref):
23      if ref ≠ null
24          rc(ref) ← rc(ref) − 1
25          if rc(ref) = 0
26              add(zct, ref)                          /* defer freeing */
27
28  atomic collect():
29      for each fld in Roots                          /* mark the stacks */
30          addReference(*fld)
31      sweepZCT()
32      for each fld in Roots                          /* unmark the stacks */
33          deleteReferenceToZCT(*fld)
34
35  sweepZCT():
36      while not isEmpty(zct)
37          ref ← remove(zct)
38          if rc(ref) = 0                             /* now reclaim garbage */
39              for each fld in Pointers(ref)
40                  deleteReference(*fld)
41              free(ref)
```

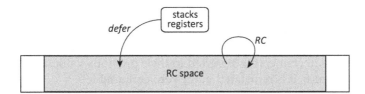

Figure 5.1: Deferred reference counting schematic, showing whether reference counting operations on pointer loads or stores should be deferred or be performed eagerly. The arrows indicate the source and target of pointers loaded or stored.

Blackburn and McKinley [2003], doi: 10.1145/949305.949336

heap objects. Figure 5.1 shows an abstract view of deferred reference counting in which operations on heap objects are performed immediately but those involving stacks or registers are deferred. There is, of course, a cost to pay. If reference count manipulations on local variables are ignored, then counts will no longer be accurate. It is therefore no longer safe to reclaim an object just because its reference count is zero. In order to reclaim any garbage, deferred reference counting must periodically correct counts during stop-the-world pauses. Fortunately, these pauses are likely to be short compared with those of tracing collectors, such as mark-sweep [Ungar, 1984].

Algorithm 5.2 loads object references using the simple, unbarriered implementation of Read from Chapter 1. Similarly, references can also be written to roots using an unbarriered store (line 14). In contrast, writes to heap objects must be barriered. In this case, the reference count of the new target is incremented as usual (line 17). However, if decrementing the reference count of the old target causes it to drop to zero, the Write barrier adds the object whose reference count is zero to a *zero count table* (ZCT) rather than immediately reclaiming it (line 26). The zero count table can be implemented in a variety of ways, for example with a bitmap [Baden, 1983] or a hash table [Deutsch and Bobrow, 1976]. An object with a reference count of zero cannot be reclaimed at this point because there might be an uncounted reference to it from the program stack. Conceptually, the zero count table contains objects whose reference counts are zero but may be live. Depending on the implementation of the zero count table and whether it is desirable to limit its size, we can also choose to remove the new target from the zero count table when writing a reference into a heap object, as its true reference count must be positive (line 19).

However, at some point garbage objects must be collected if the program is not to run out of memory. Periodically, for example when the allocator fails to return memory to New, all threads are stopped while each object in the zero count table is scrutinised to determine whether its true reference count should be zero. An object in the zero count table with reference count zero can only be live if there are one or more references to it from the roots. The simplest way to discover this is to scan the roots and 'mark' any objects found. Just as with a tracing collector, this requires either cooperation from the compiler to provide an accurate stack map of addresses that the collector should consider to be references to objects, or that the call stack be scanned conservatively (we discuss this further in Section 11.2); in constrast, simple reference counting requires no compiler support. The reference counts (line 29) of any objects found in the roots scan are incremented. After this, no object referenced from the stack can have a reference count of zero, so any object with a zero count must be garbage. We could now sweep the entire heap, as with mark-sweep collection (for example, Algorithm 2.3), looking for and reclaiming 'unmarked' objects with zero reference counts. However, it is sufficient to confine this search to the zero count table. The entries in the zero count table are scanned and any objects with zero counts are immediately processed and freed, in the same way as in the simple Algorithm 5.1. Finally, the 'mark' operations must be reversed: the stack is scanned again and the reference counts of any objects found are decremented (reverted to their previous value). If an object's reference count becomes zero, it is reinstated in the zero count table.

Deferred reference counting removes the cost of manipulating reference counts on local variables from the mutator. Several, older, studies have suggested that it can reduce the cost of pointer manipulations by 80% or more [Ungar, 1984; Baden, 1983]. Given the increased importance of locality, we can speculate that its performance advantage over naive reference counting will be even larger on modern hardware. However, reference count adjustments due to object field updates must still be performed eagerly rather than deferred, and must be atomic. Next, we explore how to replace expensive atomic reference count manipulations caused by updates to objects' fields with simple instructions, and how to reduce the number of modifications necessary.

5.4   Coalesced reference counting

Deferred reference counting addresses the problem of the cost of applying reference count operations to local variables. This leaves the question of how to reduce the reference counting overhead of writing to objects' pointer fields. Levanoni and Petrank [1999] observed that, in any period and for any object field, only the values of the field at the start and the end of the period need be considered; intermediate operations can be ignored. Thus several states of the object can be *coalesced* to just these two. For example, suppose an object X has a field f which originally refers to object O_0, and that this field is repeatedly modified to refer to objects $O_1, O_2, \ldots, O_n$. This would incur the reference counting operations

$$\texttt{rc}(O_0)\texttt{--,}\; \boxed{\texttt{rc}(O_1)\texttt{++, rc}(O_1)\texttt{--}}\;,\; \boxed{\texttt{rc}(O_2)\texttt{++,}\ldots}\;,\; \texttt{rc}(O_n)\texttt{++.}$$

The pairs of intermediate operations (shown boxed) cancel each other and can be omitted. Levanoni and Petrank eliminate them by copying objects to a local log before their first modification in an epoch. When a pointer slot of a clean object is updated, Algorithm 5.3 logs the object by saving its address and the values of its pointer fields to a local update buffer (line 5). The modified object is marked as *dirty*. Note that an initialising store need not be logged, as the object's reference fields will be null. Instead, we only need to record the object as dirty.

The log procedure attempts to avoid duplicating entries in the thread's local log by first appending the original values of the object's pointer fields to the log (line 11). Next it checks that src is still not dirty, and only then is the entry committed by writing src to the log (appendAndCommit), tagged so that it can be recognised as an object entry rather than a field entry, and the log's internal cursor is advanced (line 13). The object is marked dirty by writing a pointer to this log entry in its header. Note that even if a race leads to records being created in more than one thread's local buffer, the algorithm guarantees that all these records will contain identical information, so it does not matter to which log's entry the header points. Depending on the processor's memory consistency model, this write barrier may not require any synchronisation operations. This algorithm logs all fields of the object; it is also possible to log individual fields as they are modified, as done by LXR [Zhao *et al.*, 2022a,b].

Later, we will discuss how coalesced reference counts can be processed concurrently with mutator threads, but here we simply stop the world periodically to process the logs. At the start of each collection cycle, Algorithm 5.4 halts every thread, transfers their update buffers to the collector's log, and allocates fresh ones. As we noted above, race con-

Algorithm 5.3: Coalesced reference counting: write barrier

```
1   me ← myThreadId
2
3   Write(src, i, ref):
4       if not dirty(src)
5           log(src)
6       src[i] ← ref
7
8   log(src):
9       for each fld in Pointers(src)
10          if *fld ≠ null
11              append(updates[me], *fld)
12      if not dirty(src)
13          slot ← appendAndCommit(updates[me], src)
14          setDirty(src, slot)
15
16  dirty(src):
17      return logPointer(src) ≠ CLEAN
18
19  setDirty(src, slot)
20      logPointer(src) ← slot          /* address of entry for src in updates[me] */
```

ditions mean that an entry for an object may appear in more than one thread's update buffer. This is harmless provided the collector only processes each dirty object once. The processReferenceCounts procedure tests whether an object is still dirty before updating the reference counts. The counts of the children of an object at the time of the collection are incremented, and then those of its children before its first modification in this epoch are decremented (the increments are applied before the decrements in order to avoid adding unnecessary entries to the zero count table). In a simple system, any object whose reference count drops to zero could be freed recursively. However, if reference counting on local variables is deferred, or if for efficiency the algorithm does not guarantee to process all increments before decrements, we simply remember any object whose count has dropped to zero. The algorithm cleans the object so that it will not be processed again in this cycle. Pointers to an object's previous children can be found directly from the log entry. Its current children can be found from the object itself (recall that the log contains a reference to that object). Notice that there is opportunity for prefetching objects or reference count fields in both the increment and decrement loops [Paz and Petrank, 2007].

Let us look at the example in Figure 5.2. Suppose that A was modified in the previous epoch to swing its pointer from C to D. The old values of the object's fields (B and C) will have been recorded in a log which has been passed to the collector (shown on the left of the figure). The collector will therefore increment those of B and D and decrement the reference counts of B and C. This retains the original value of B's reference count since the pointer from A to B was never modified.

Thus, through a combination of deferred reference counting and coalescing, much of reference counting's overhead on the mutator has been removed. In particular, we have removed any necessity for mutator threads to employ expensive synchronisation operations. However, this benefit has come at some cost. We have reintroduced pauses for garbage collection although we expect these to be shorter than those required for tracing

Algorithm 5.4: Coalesced reference counting: update reference counts

```
 1  atomic collect():
 2      collectBuffers()
 3      processReferenceCounts()
 4      sweepZCT()
 5
 6  collectBuffers():
 7      collectorLog ← []
 8      for each t in Threads
 9          collectorLog ← collectorLog + updates[t]
10
11  processReferenceCounts():
12      for each entry in collectorLog
13          obj ← objFromLog(entry)
14          if dirty(obj)                          /* Do not process duplicates */
15              logPointer(obj) ← CLEAN
16              incrementNew(obj)
17              decrementOld(entry)
18
19  decrementOld(entry):
20      for each fld in Pointers(entry)    /* use the values in the collector's log */
21          child ← *fld
22          if child ≠ null
23              rc(child) ← rc(child) − 1
24              if rc(child) = 0
25                  add(zct, child)
26
27  incrementNew(obj):
28      for each fld in Pointers(obj)              /* use the values in the object */
29          child ← *fld
30          if child ≠ null
31              rc(child) ← rc(child) + 1
```

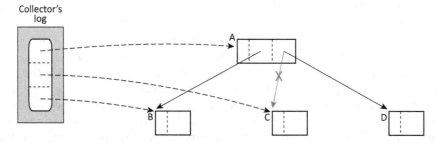

Figure 5.2: Coalesced reference counting: if A was modified in the previous epoch, for example by overwriting the reference to C with a reference to D, A's reference fields will have been copied to the log. The old referent C can be found in the collector's log and the most recent new referent D can be found directly from A.

collection. We have reduced the promptness of collection (since no object is reclaimed until the end of an epoch) and added space overheads for the buffers and zero count table. Coalesced reference counting may also require the collector to decrement and then increment the same children of unmodified slots.

5.5 Cyclic reference counting

Because the reference counts of objects making up a cyclic data structure must necessarily be at least one, reference counting on its own cannot reclaim such structures. However, cycles are common, created both by application programmers and by the run-time system. Applications often use doubly linked lists and circular buffers. Object-relation mapping systems may require that databases know their tables and vice versa. Some real-world structures are naturally cyclic, such as roads in geographical information systems. Lazy functional language implementations commonly use cycles to express recursion [Turner, 1979, the Y combinator]. A number of techniques have been proposed to solve the cycle problem; we review some of these now.

The simplest approach is to combine reference counting with occasional, backup tracing collection. The hope is that most objects will not be reachable from cycles and hence will be reclaimed promptly by reference counting; the remaining cyclic structures will be handled by the tracing collector. This simply reduces the frequency of full, tracing collections. At the language level, Friedman and Wise [1979] observed that cycles can only be created in pure functional languages by recursive definitions, and hence can be treated specially provided certain restrictions are observed. Bobrow [1980] required the programmer to identify reference counted groups of cells, which are then collected *en masse*.

Several authors have suggested distinguishing writes of pointers that close cycles from those of other pointers [Friedman and Wise, 1979; Brownbridge, 1985; Salkild, 1987; Pepels *et al.*, 1988; Axford, 1990]. Normal references are denoted *strong* and others *weak*. Some languages offer support for different reference strengths either directly (as in Swift which provides weak and unowned as well as normal, strong references) or indirectly using special weak objects to hold weak references (such as Java's Reference types). Weak references have several uses (discussed in Chapter 12) but one is to close cycles. The intention is that a weak reference on its own will not cause its target to be retained. If strong references are never allowed to form a cycle, then the strong-pointer graph will be amenable to standard reference counting. However, weak reference systems are fragile and need to be used with extreme care, especially when managed by reference counting. Programmers using weak references must at all times retain a clear understanding of the relative lifetimes of referring objects and their referents, and ensure that the pointer types used, strong or weak, always reflect this accurately. Incorrect usage may lead to either cycles that cannot be reclaimed or premature reclamation of live objects.

Although Brownbridge's algorithm has been widely cited as an automatic technique for managing cycles with reference counting, it is unsafe and may reclaim objects prematurely: see Salkild's counter-example [Jones, 1996, Chapter 6.5]. In brief, Brownbridge gives each object a strong and a weak reference count. The write barrier checks the strength of pointers and targets, and weakens any pointer that would close a cycle. Reference deletion may require the strength of pointers to be modified in order to preserve the invariants that all reachable objects are strongly reachable without creating any cycles of strong references. Salkild [1987] amended the algorithm to make it safe but at the cost of nontermination in some cases. Pepels *et al.* [1988] provided a very complex solution but it is expensive both in terms of space, with double the space overheads of normal reference counting, and in terms of performance, having twice the cost of standard reference counting in most cases and being exponential in the worst case.

The most widely adopted automatic mechanisms for handling cycles through reference counting use a technique called *trial deletion*. The key observation is that it is not necessary for a backup tracing collector to visit the whole live object graph. Hence, its attention can be confined to those parts of the graph where a pointer deletion might have created a garbage cycle. Note that:

- in any garbage pointer structure, all reference counts must be due to internal pointers (that is, pointers between objects within the structure);

- garbage cycles can only arise from a pointer deletion that leaves a reference count greater than zero.

Partial tracing algorithms take advantage of these observations by tracing the subgraph rooted at an object suspected of being garbage. These algorithms trial-delete each reference encountered by temporarily decrementing reference counts, in effect removing the contribution of these internal pointers. If the reference count of any object remains non-zero, it must be because there is a pointer to the object from outside the subgraph, and hence neither the object nor its transitive closure is garbage.

The *Recycler* [Bacon *et al.*, 2001; Bacon and Rajan, 2001; Paz *et al.*, 2007] supports concurrent, cyclic, deferred reference counting. In Algorithm 5.5 we show the simpler, synchronous, version deferring the asynchronous collector to Chapter 15. However, we note for now that the single collector is the only thread that modifies objects' reference count fields. Instead, for any object whose reference count should be incremented or decremented, the mutator adds the object's address and the operation (increment or decrement) to mutator-local buffers, which are periodically turned over to the collector thread. Objects are allocated with a reference count of 1, with a corresponding decrement operation immediately written into the mutation buffer; in this manner, temporary objects never referenced from the heap can be collected quickly. The cycle collection algorithm operates in three phases.

1. The collector traces partial graphs, starting from objects identified as possible members of garbage cycles, decrementing reference counts due to internal pointers (mark-Candidates). Objects visited are coloured grey.

2. The reference count of each object in these subgraphs is checked: if it is non-zero, the object must be live due to a reference external to the subgraph being traced, and so the effect of the first phase must be undone (scan), recolouring live grey objects black. Other grey objects are coloured white.

3. Finally, any members of the subgraph that are still white must be garbage and are reclaimed (collectCandidates).

In its synchronous mode, the Recycler uses five colours to identify objects. As usual, black means live (or free) and white is garbage. Grey is now a possible member of a garbage cycle, and we add the colour *purple* to indicate objects that are candidates for roots of garbage cycles.

Deleting any reference other than the last to an object may isolate a garbage cycle. In this case, Algorithm 5.5 colours the object purple and adds it to a set of candidate members of garbage cycles (line 22). Otherwise, the object is garbage and its reference count must be zero. Procedure release resets the object's colour to black, processes its children recursively and, if it is not a candidate, frees the object. The reclamation of any objects in the candidates set is postponed to the markCandidates phase. For example, in Figure 5.3a, some reference to object A has been deleted. A's reference count was non-zero, so it has been added to the candidates set.

Algorithm 5.5: The Recycler

```
1   New():
2       ref ← allocate()
3       if ref = null
4           collect()                               /* the cycle collector */
5           ref ← allocate()
6           if ref = null
7               error "Out of memory"
8       rc(ref) ← 0
9       return ref
10
11  addReference(ref):
12      if ref ≠ null
13          rc(ref) ← rc(ref) + 1
14          colour(ref) ← black                     /* cannot be in a garbage cycle */
15
16  deleteReference(ref):
17      if ref ≠ null
18          rc(ref) ← rc(ref) − 1
19          if rc(ref) = 0
20              release(ref)
21          else
22              candidate(ref)                      /* might isolate a garbage cycle */
23
24  release(ref):
25      for each fld in Pointers(ref)
26          deleteReference(fld)
27      colour(ref) ← black                         /* objects on the free–list are black */
28      if not ref in candidates                    /* deal with candidates later */
29          free(ref)
30
31  candidate(ref):                                 /* colour as a candidate and add to the set */
32      if colour(ref) ≠ purple
33          colour(ref) ← purple
34          candidates ← candidates ∪ {ref}
35
36  atomic collect():
37      markCandidates()
38      for each ref in candidates
39          scan(ref)
40      collectCandidates()
```

Algorithm 5.5 (continued): The Recycler

```
41  markCandidates():
42      for ref in candidates
43          if colour(ref) = purple
44              markGrey(ref)
45          else
46              remove(candidates, ref)
47              if colour(ref) = black && rc(ref) = 0
48                  free(ref)
49
50  markGrey(ref):
51      if colour(ref) ≠ grey
52          colour(ref) ← grey
53          for each fld in Pointers(ref)
54              child ← *fld
55              if child ≠ null
56                  rc(child) ← rc(child) − 1            /* trial deletion */
57              markGrey(child)
58
59  scan(ref):
60      if colour(ref) = grey
61          if rc(ref) > 0
62              scanBlack(ref)                  /* there must be an external reference */
63          else
64              colour(ref) ← white                         /* looks like garbage... */
65              for each fld in Pointers(ref)                    /* ...so continue */
66                  child ← *fld
67                  if child ≠ null
68                      scan(child)
69
70  scanBlack(ref):                          /* repair the reference counts of live data */
71      colour(ref) ← black
72      for each fld in Pointers(ref)
73          child ← *fld
74          if child ≠ null
75              rc(child) ← rc(child) + 1                 /* undo the trial deletion */
76              if colour(child) ≠ black
77                  scanBlack(child)
```

Algorithm 5.5 (continued): The Recycler

```
78  collectCandidates():
79      while not isEmpty(candidates)
80          ref ← remove(candidates)
81          collectWhite(ref)
82
83  collectWhite(ref):
84      if colour(ref) = white && not ref in candidates
85          colour(ref) ← black                    /* free–list objects are black */
86          for each fld in Pointers(ref)
87              child ← *fld
88              if child ≠ null
89                  collectWhite(child)
90          free(ref)
```

In the first phase of collecting cycles, the `markCandidates` procedure establishes the extent of possible garbage structures and removes the effect of internal references from the counts. It considers every object in the set of garbage `candidates`. If the object is still purple (hence, no references to the object have been added since it was added to the set), its transitive closure is marked grey. Otherwise, it is removed from the set and, if it is a black object with reference count zero, it is freed. As `markGrey` traces a reference, the reference count of its target is decremented. Thus, in Figure 5.3b, the subgraph rooted at A has been marked grey and the contribution of references internal to the subgraph has been removed from the reference counts.

In the second phase of collection, each candidate and its grey transitive closure is scanned for external references. If a reference count is non-zero, it can only be because there is a reference to this object from outside the grey subgraph. In this case, the effect of `markGrey` is undone by `scanBlack`: reference counts are incremented and objects are reverted to black. On the other hand, if the reference count is zero, the object is coloured white and the scan continues to its children. Note that at this point we cannot say that a white object is definitely garbage, as it might be revisited later by `scanBlack` starting from another object in the subgraph. For example, in Figure 5.3b, objects Y and Z have zero reference counts but are externally reachable via X. When `scan` reaches X, which has a non-zero reference count, it will invoke `scanBlack` on the grey transitive closure of X, restoring reference counts, leaving the graph in the state shown in Figure 5.3c.

Finally, the third, `collectWhite` phase reclaims white (garbage) objects. The set of `candidates` is emptied and the colour of each object inspected. Each white object found is freed (its colour reset to black) and its children inspected recursively. Note that the algorithm does not process child objects found to be in the candidates set but defers reclaiming these to a subsequent iteration of the inner loop of `collectCandidates` in this cycle.

The asynchronous Recycler algorithm improves over earlier trial deletion algorithms, such as that of Martinez *et al.* [1990], which performed the trial deletion eagerly as soon as a candidate was discovered. Lins [1992] also processed candidates lazily like the Recycler in the hope that candidates will be eliminated by later mutator actions, which might either remove the last reference so that the object can be freed immediately or add a fresh

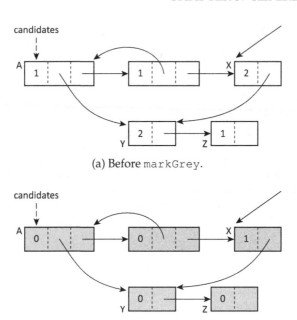

(a) Before `markGrey`.

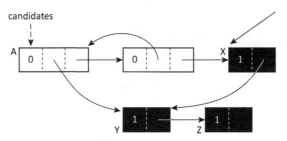

(b) After `markGrey`, all objects reachable from a candidate object have been marked grey and the effect of references internal to this grey subgraph have been removed. Note that X, which is still reachable, has a non-zero reference count.

(c) After `scan`, all reachable objects are black and their reference counts have been corrected to reflect live references.

Figure 5.3: Cyclic reference counting. The first field of each object is its reference count.

reference to it. Unfortunately, he performed all three phases of the collection cycle separately on each object, which led to complexity quadratic in the size of the graph in the worst case. In contrast, the complexity of the Recycler is $O(N + E)$, where N is the number of nodes and E the number of edges. This seemingly small change made a substantial difference to performance, reducing the garbage collection time for moderately sized Java programs from minutes (Lins) to a maximum of a few milliseconds (Recycler).

Further improvements can be gained by recognising statically that certain classes of objects, including but not limited to those objects that contain no pointers, can never be members of cyclic data structures. The Recycler allocates objects of these types as *green* rather than black, and never adds them to the candidate set nor traces through them. Bacon and Rajan [2001] found that this reduced the size of the candidate set by an order of magnitude. Figure 5.4 illustrates the full state transition system of the synchronous Recycler, including green objects.

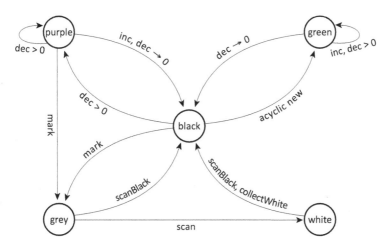

Figure 5.4: The synchronous Recycler state transition diagram, showing mutator and collector operations and the colours of objects

With kind permission from Springer Science+Business Media: Bacon and Rajan [2001], figure 3, page 214

5.6 Limited-field reference counting

The remaining concern is the space overhead incurred by storing reference counts in object headers. In theory, the reference count field of an object should be large enough to hold a pointer-sized value since an object may be referenced by every other object in the heap. An additional field of this size represents a significant overhead to small objects. However, only contrived applications will cause counts to grow so large; in practice most objects have small reference counts. Indeed, most objects are not shared at all and so the space they use could be reused immediately the pointer to them is deleted [Clark and Green, 1977; Stoye *et al.*, 1984; Hartel, 1988]. In functional languages, this allows objects such as arrays to be updated in place rather than having to modify a copy of the object. Given *a priori* knowledge of the upper bound on reference counts, it would be possible to use a smaller field for the reference count. Unfortunately, it is common for some objects to be very popular [Printezis and Garthwaite, 2002].

However, it is still possible to limit the size of the reference count field provided that some backup mechanism is occasionally invoked to deal with reference count overflow. Once a reference count has been incremented to the maximum permissible value, it becomes a *sticky reference count*, not changed by any subsequent pointer updates. The most extreme option is to use a single bit for the reference count, thus concentrating reference counting on the common case of objects that are not shared. The bit can either be stored in the object itself [Wise and Friedman, 1977] or in the pointer [Stoye *et al.*, 1984]. The corollary of limited-field reference counts is that once objects become stuck they can no longer be reclaimed by reference counting. A backup tracing collector is needed to handle such objects. As the tracing collector traverses each pointer, it can restore the correct reference counts (wherever this is no greater than the sticky value); Wise [1993a] shows that, with some effort, a mark-compact or copying collector can also restore uniqueness information. Such a backup tracing collector would be needed to reclaim garbage cycles in any case.

Griffin *et al.* [2005] devised a scheme to tag pointers in the stack to avoid incrementing reference counts more than once for objects with multiple references in the stack. See Chapter 20 on page 467 for details.

5.7   Issues to consider

Reference counting is attractive for the promptness with which it reclaims garbage objects and its good locality properties. Simple reference counting can reclaim the space occupied by an object as soon as the last pointer to that object is removed. Its operation only involves the targets of old and new pointers read or written, unlike tracing collection which visits every live object in the heap. However, these strengths are also the weaknesses of simple reference counting. Because it cannot reclaim an object until the last pointer to that object has been removed, it cannot reclaim cycles of garbage. Reference counting taxes every pointer read and write operation and thus imposes a much larger tax on throughput than tracing does. Furthermore, multithreaded applications require the manipulation of reference counts and updating of pointers to be expensively synchronised. This tight coupling of mutator actions and memory manager risks some fragility, especially if 'unnecessary' reference count updates are optimised away by hand. Finally, reference counts increase the sizes of objects.

The environment

Despite these concerns, it would be wrong to dismiss reference counting without further thought. Certainly, its drawbacks make simple reference counting uncompetitive as a general purpose memory management component of a virtual machine, especially if the majority of objects managed are small, cycles are common and the rate of pointer mutation is high. However, there are environments which are favourable to reference counting. Reference counting can play well in a mixed ecology where the lifetimes of most objects are sufficiently simple to be managed explicitly. It can be restricted to managing a smaller number of resources with more complex owner relationships. Often such resources will be large, in which case the overhead for an additional reference count field in the header will be negligible. Data such as bitmaps for images and so on will not contain any pointers, so the problem of reclaiming cyclic structures does not arise. Furthermore, reference counting can be implemented as part of a library rather than being baked into the language's run-time system. It can therefore give the programmer complete control over its use, allowing her to make the decision between performance overhead and guarantees of safety. Nevertheless, it is essential that reference counting be used carefully. In particular, the programmer must ensure that races between pointer modifications and reference count updates are avoided. If reference counting is implemented through smart pointers, he must also be aware that the semantics of pointers and smart pointers differ. As Edelson [1992] wrote, "They are smart, but they are not pointers."

Advanced solutions

Sophisticated reference counting algorithms can offer solutions to many of the problems faced by naive reference counting but, paradoxically, these algorithms often introduce behaviours similar to those of stop-the-world tracing collectors. We examine this duality further in the next chapter.

Garbage cycles can be reclaimed by a backup, tracing collector or by using the trial deletion algorithms we discussed in Section 5.5. In both cases, this requires mutator threads to be suspended while we reclaim cyclic data (although we show how these stop-the-world pauses can be removed in later chapters).

Although the worst case requires reference count fields to be almost as large as pointer fields, most applications only hold a few references to most objects. Often, it is possible for the reference count to hijack a few bits from an existing header word (for example, one used for object hashing or for locks). However, it is common for a very few objects to be heavily referenced. If limited-field reference counting is used, these objects will either leak — which may not be a serious problem if they are few in number or have very long lifetimes — or must be reclaimed by a backup tracing collector. Note, however, that in comparing the space overhead of reference counting and, say, mark-sweep collection it is not sufficient simply to measure the cost of the reference count fields. In order not to thrash, tracing collectors require some headroom in the heap. If the application is given a heap of, say, 20% larger than its maximum volume of live data, then at least 10% of the heap will be 'wasted' on average. This fraction may be similar to the overhead of reference counting (depending on the average size of objects it manages).

The throughput overhead of reference counting can be addressed by omitting to count some pointer manipulations and by reducing the cost of others. Deferred reference counting ignores mutator operations on local variables. This allows the counts of objects reachable from roots to be lower than their true value, and hence it prevents their prompt reclamation (since a reference count of zero no longer necessarily means that the object is garbage). Coalesced reference counting accounts for the state of an object only at the beginning and end of an epoch: it ignores pointer manipulations in between. In one sense, this automates the behaviour of programmers who often optimise away temporary adjustments to reference counts (for example, to an iterator as it traverses a list). However, once again, one consequence of deferred and coalesced reference counting is to reintroduce stop-the-world pauses during which reference counts are corrected. The overall effect is somewhat similar to generational collection, discussed in Chapter 9.

As well as removing some reference counting operations, both deferred and coalesced reference counting reduce the synchronisation cost of other operations. Deferred reference counting does so simply by omitting to manipulate reference counts on local variables. Coalesced reference counting does not need synchronisation because races are benign: at worst, the same values might be written to the logs of two different threads. However, both solutions add space overhead to the cost of reference counting, either to store the zero count table or to store update logs.

Shahriyar et al. [2012] combine several of these optimisations in a reference counting system for Java that is competitive with a high-performance mark-sweep collector. Because an extra 32-bit header word would increase space consumption and hence incur a time overhead both for garbage collection and overall, they steal bits in an existing header word for a sticky reference count. In a detailed study of reference counting options, they found that 3 bits was sufficient for the vast majority of objects: the reference count fields of only 0.65% of objects from the DaCapo benchmarks overflow, although overflowed objects were popular, attracting 23% of reference count increments and decrements. Overflowed reference counts that become stuck with a limited-field reference count were either ignored or restored by occasional backup tracing collections: both techniques improved on standard reference counting.

It is common for the overwhelming majority of new objects to have short lifetimes. We discuss this further in Chapter 9. Shahriyar et al. take advantage of this to avoid a significant fraction of expensive freeing operations in their deferred, coalescing reference counter. First, unlike the Recycler [Bacon and Rajan, 2001], they do not log new objects but set a 'new' bit in the object's header. The object will only be added to a modification buffer if it is encountered when the collector processes increments. Second, they allocate new objects as dead, thus removing the need for a decrement when freeing short-lived objects. Overall, the combination of limited bits for the reference count, lazy modification buffer insertions and allocating new objects as dead reduced the average execution time of their benchmarks by 24% compared with an already optimised reference counting scheme Blackburn and McKinley [2003] (which we discuss in Chapter 10). Zhao et al. [2022a,b]

extend these ideas in their high performance reference counting collector, LXR , which has been shown to offer excellent throughput and latency, especially in constrained heaps, and lower total CPU cycles than some concurrent tracing collectors. We discuss LXR in Chapter 18.

A further attraction of these advanced reference counting techniques is that they scale well with large heaps. Their cost is only proportional to the number of pointer writes made, and not to the volume of live data. As we shall see in Chapter 10, hybrid collectors are possible, combining tracing collection for short-lived, heavily mutated data with reference counting for longer-lived, more stable data.

In the next chapter, we compare all four forms of collection we have examined so far: mark-sweep, mark-compact, copying and reference counting. We then consider a remarkable abstraction of tracing and advanced reference counting collection that reveals that they are surprisingly similar in many ways.

Chapter 6

Comparing garbage collectors

In the preceding chapters, we presented four different styles of garbage collection. In this chapter, we compare them in more detail. We examine the collectors in two different ways. First, we consider criteria by which we may assess the algorithms, and the strengths and weaknesses of the different approaches in different circumstances. We then present abstractions of tracing and reference counting algorithms due to Bacon *et al.* [2004]. These abstractions reveal that while the algorithms exhibit superficial differences they also bear a deep and remarkable similarity.

It is common to ask: which is the best garbage collector to use? However, the temptation to provide a simple answer needs to be resisted. First, what does 'best' mean? Do we want the collector that provides the application with the best throughput, or do we want the shortest latencies? Is space utilisation important? Or is a compromise that combines these desirable properties required? Second, it is clear that, even if a single metric is chosen, the ranking of different collectors will vary between different applications. For example, in a study of twenty Java benchmarks and six different collectors, Fitzgerald and Tarditi [2000] found that for each collector there was at least one benchmark that would have been at least 15% faster with a more appropriate collector. And furthermore, not only do programs tend to run faster given larger heaps, but also the relative performance of collectors varies according to the amount of heap space available. To complicate matters yet further, excessively large heaps may disperse temporally related objects, leading to worsened locality that may slow down applications.

6.1 Throughput

The first item on many users' wish lists is likely to be overall application throughput. This might be the primary goal for a 'batch' application or for a web server where pauses might be tolerable or obscured by aspects of the system such as network delays. Although it is important that garbage collector actions be performed as quickly as possible, employing a faster collector does not necessarily mean that a computation will execute faster. In a well-configured system, garbage collection should only account for a small fraction of overall execution time. If the price to be paid for faster collection is a larger tax on mutator operations, then it is quite possible for the application's execution time to become longer rather than shorter. The cost to the mutator may be explicit or implicit. Explicit actions include read and write barrier actions, such as those that reference counting requires. However, the performance of the mutator may also be affected implicitly, for example because a copying collector has rearranged objects in such a way as to affect cache behaviour adversely, or because a reference count decrement has touched a cold object. It is also important to avoid wherever possible any need to synchronise operations. Unfortunately, reference count modifications must be synchronised in order not to miss updates. Deferred and coalesced reference counting can eliminate much of these synchronisation costs.

One can consider the algorithmic complexity of different algorithms. For mark-sweep collection, we would need to include the cost of the tracing (mark) and the sweep phases, whereas the cost of copying collection only depends on tracing. Tracing requires visiting every *live* object, whereas sweeping requires visiting every object (live and dead). It is tempting to assume that the cost of mark-sweep collection must therefore necessarily be greater than copying collection. However, the number of instructions executed to visit an object for mark-sweep tracing is fewer than those for copying tracing. Locality plays a significant part here as well. We saw in Section 2.6 how prefetching techniques could be used to hide cache misses. However, it is an open question as to whether such techniques can be applied to copying collection without losing the benefits to the mutator of depth-first copying. In either of these tracing collectors, the cost of chasing pointers is likely to dominate. Furthermore, if marking is combined with lazy sweeping, we obtain the greatest benefit in the same circumstances that copying performs best: when the proportion of live data in the heap is small.

6.2 Pause time and latency

The next item for many users is the extent to which garbage collection interrupts program execution. Low pause times are important but insufficient on their own, as many very short pauses clustered together may still be disruptive. Interactive applications and others such as transaction processors need to avoid delays that may cause backlogs of work to build up. For such applications, latency is likely to be a better metric. The tracing collectors considered so far have all been stop-the-world: all mutator threads must be brought to a halt before the collector runs to completion. Garbage collection pause times in early systems were legendary but, even on modern hardware, stop-the-world collectors may pause very large applications for over a second. The immediate attraction of reference counting is that it should avoid such pauses, instead distributing the costs of memory management throughout the program. However, as we have seen, this benefit is not realised in high performance reference counting systems. First, the removal of the last reference to a large pointer structure leads to recursive reference count modifications and freeing of components. Fortunately, reference count modifications on garbage objects are not contended, though they may cause contention on the cache lines containing the objects. More importantly, we saw that deferred and coalesced reference counting, the most effective ways to improve reference counting performance, both reintroduce a stop-the-world pause to reconcile reference counts and reclaim garbage objects in the zero count table. They also delay reclaiming objects, reducing promptness. As we shall see in Section 6.6, high performance reference counting and tracing schemes are not so different as they might first appear.

6.3 Space

Memory footprint is important if there are tight physical constraints on memory, if applications are very large, or in order to allow applications to scale well. All garbage collection algorithms incur space overheads. Several factors contribute to this overhead. Algorithms may pay a per-object penalty, for example for reference count fields. Semispace copying collectors need additional heap space for a copy reserve; to be safe, this needs to be as large as the volume of data currently allocated, unless a fall-back mechanism is used (for example, mark-compact collection). Non-moving collectors face the problem of fragmentation, reducing the amount of heap usable to the application. It is important not to ignore the costs of non-heap, metadata space. Tracing collectors may require marking stacks, mark bitmaps or other auxiliary data structures. Any non-compacting memory manager, including explicit managers, will use space for their own data structures, such as segregated free-lists and so on. Finally, if a tracing or a deferred reference counting collector is not to thrash by collecting too frequently, it requires sufficient room for garbage in the heap. Systems are typically configured to use a heap anything from 30% to 200% or 300% larger than the minimum required by the program. Many systems also allow the heap to expand when necessary, for example in order to avoid thrashing the collector. Sareen and Blackburn [2022] suggest that a garbage collected heap about 25% to 50% larger than that required by an explicitly managed heap is needed to achieve comparable application performance, corroborating earlier results of Hertz *et al.* [2005].

In contrast, simple reference counting frees objects as soon as they become unlinked from the graph of live objects. Apart from the obvious advantage of preventing the accumulation of garbage in the heap, this may offer other potential benefits. Space is likely to be reused shortly after it is freed, which may improve cache performance. It may also be possible in some circumstances for the compiler to detect when an object becomes free, and to reuse it immediately, without recycling it through the memory manager.

It is desirable for collectors to be not only complete (to reclaim all dead objects *eventually*) but also to be prompt, that is, to reclaim all dead objects *at each collection cycle*. The basic tracing collectors presented in earlier chapters achieve this, but at the cost of tracing all live objects at every collection. However, modern high-performance garbage collectors typically trade promptness for performance, allowing some garbage to float in the heap from one collection to a subsequent one. Reference counting faces the additional problem of being incomplete; specifically, it is unable to reclaim cyclic garbage structures without recourse to tracing.

6.4 Implementation

Garbage collection algorithms are difficult to implement correctly, and concurrent algorithms notoriously so. The interface between the collector and the compiler is critical. Errors made by the collector often manifest themselves long afterwards (maybe many collections afterwards), and then typically as a mutator attempts to follow a reference that is no longer valid. It is important, therefore, that garbage collectors be constructed to be robust as well as fast. Blackburn *et al.* [2004a] have shown that this performance-critical system component can be designed with respect for good software engineering practices of modularity and composability, leading to maintainable code. Model checking is also a useful and easy to adopt technique that, while it may not prove the correctness of an *implementation*, helps increase confidence in an algorithm (see, for example, Vechev [2007], Ugawa *et al.* [2017, 2018], Xu *et al.* [2022] or Yang and Wrigstad [2022]).

One advantage of simple tracing collectors is that the interface between the collector and the mutator is simple: when the allocator exhausts memory, the collector is called. The chief source of complexity in this interface is determining the roots of collection, including global variables, and references held in registers and stack slots. We discuss this in more detail in Chapter 11. However, we note here that the task facing copying and compacting collectors is more complex than that facing non-moving collectors. A moving collector must identify *every* root and update the reference accordingly, whereas a non-moving collector need only identify *at least one* reference to each live object, and never needs to change the value of a pointer. So-called *conservative* collectors [Boehm and Weiser, 1988] can reclaim memory without accurate knowledge of mutator stack or indeed object layouts. Instead, they make intelligent (but safe, conservative) guesses about whether a value really is a reference. Because non-moving collectors do not update references, the risk of misidentifying a value as a heap pointer is confined to introducing a space leak: the value itself will not be corrupted. A full discussion of conservative garbage collection can be found in Jones [1996, Chapters 9 and 10].

Reference counting has both the advantages and disadvantages of being tightly coupled to the mutator. The advantages are that reference counting can be implemented in a library, making it possible for the programmer to decide selectively which objects should be managed by reference counting and which should be managed explicitly. The disadvantages are that this coupling introduces the processing overheads discussed above and that it is essential that all reference count manipulations are correct.

The performance of any modern language that makes heavy use of dynamically allocated data is heavily dependent on the memory manager. The critical actions typically include allocation, mutator updates including barriers, and the garbage collector's inner loops. Wherever possible, the code sequences for these critical actions need to be inlined, but this has to be done carefully to avoid exploding the size of the generated code. If the processor's instruction cache is sufficiently large and the code expansion is sufficiently small (in older systems with much smaller caches, Steenkiste [1989] suggested less than 30%), this blowup may have negligible effect on performance. Otherwise, it will be necessary to distinguish in these actions the common case which needs to be small enough to be inlined (the 'fast path'), whilst calling out to a procedure for the less common 'slow path' [Blackburn and McKinley, 2002]. There are two lessons to be learnt here. The output from the compiler matters and it is essential to examine the assembler code produced. The effect on the caches also has a major impact on performance.

6.5   Adaptive systems

Commercial systems often offer the user a choice of garbage collectors, each of which comes with a large number of tuning options. To complicate matters further, the tuning knobs provided with these collectors tend not to be independent of one another. A number of researchers have suggested having systems adapt to the environment at hand. The Java run-time developed by Soman *et al.* [2004] adapts dynamically by switching collectors at run time, according to heap size available. Their system either requires off-line profiling runs to annotate programs with the best collector/heap-size combination, or it can switch based on comparing the current space usage of the program with the maximum heap available. Singer *et al.* [2007a], in contrast, apply machine learning techniques to predict the best collector from static properties of the program (and thus only require a single training run). *Ergonomic tuning*[1] attempts to tune the HotSpot collector's performance against user-supplied throughput and maximum pause time goals, adjusting the size of spaces within the heap accordingly.

The best, and possibly the only, advice that we can suggest to developers is, know your application. Measure its behaviour, and the size and lifetime distributions of the objects it uses. Then experiment with the different collector configurations that are on offer. Unfortunately, this needs to be done with real data sets. While synthetic and toy benchmarks can assist the development of new collectors by making it easier to understand the detailed effect of changes and algorithms, they may also mislead.

---

[1]https://docs.oracle.com/en/java/javase/18/gctuning/ergonomics.html

6.6 A unified theory of garbage collection

In the preceding chapters, we considered two styles of collection: direct, reference counting and indirect, tracing collection. Bacon *et al.* [2004] show that these collectors share remarkable similarities. Their abstract framework allows us to express a wide variety of different collectors in a way that highlights precisely where they are similar and where they differ.

Abstract garbage collection

In place of concrete data structures, the following abstract framework makes use of simple abstract data structures whose implementations can vary. We start by observing that garbage collection can be expressed as a fixed-point computation that assigns reference counts $\rho(n)$ to nodes $n \in$ Nodes. Reference counts include contributions from the root set and incoming edges from nodes with non-zero reference counts:

$$
\begin{aligned}
\forall \texttt{ref} \in \texttt{Nodes}: \\
\rho(\texttt{ref}) \quad = \quad & \left| \{ \texttt{fld} \in \texttt{Roots} : *\texttt{fld} = \texttt{ref} \} \right| \\
+ \quad & \left| \{ \texttt{fld} \in \texttt{Pointers(n)} : \texttt{n} \in \texttt{Nodes} \wedge \rho(\texttt{n}) > 0 \wedge *\texttt{fld} = \texttt{ref} \} \right|
\end{aligned}
\tag{6.1}
$$

Having assigned reference counts, nodes with a non-zero count are retained and the rest should be reclaimed. Reference counts need not be precise, but may simply be a safe approximation of the true value. Abstract garbage collection algorithms compute such fixed-points using a work list W of objects to be processed. When W is empty, these algorithms terminate. In the following, W is a multiset, since every entry in W represents a distinct source for each reference.

Tracing garbage collection

The abstraction casts tracing collection as a form of reference counting. Abstract tracing collection is illustrated by Algorithm 6.1, which starts with the reference counts of all nodes being zero. At the end of each collection cycle, sweepTracing resets the count of all nodes to zero, and New initialises new nodes with a zero reference count. The collectTracing procedure accumulates all non-null root pointers using rootsTracing and passes them to scanTracing as the work list W.

Collection proceeds as we would expect by tracing the object graph to discover all the nodes reachable from the roots. The procedure scanTracing accomplishes this by tracing elements from the work list, reconstructing the reference count of each node, by incrementing its reference count each time it is encountered (recall how we suggested in Section 5.6 that a tracing collector could be used to correct sticky reference counts). When a reachable node src is discovered for the first time (when $\rho(\texttt{src})$ is set to 1, line 11), the collector recurses through all the out-edges of src by *scanning* its fields and adding the (pointers to) child nodes found in those fields to the work list W.[2]

Termination of the while loop yields all the live nodes, each of which has a non-zero reference count equal to the number of its in-edges. The sweepTracing procedure then frees unused nodes and resets the reference counts for the next round of collection. Note that a practical implementation of tracing can use a single-bit value for each node's reference count, in other words a mark bit rather than a full-sized reference count, to record

---

[2]Alternatively, the object could be added to the log in order to trade the size of the log for improved cache performance in the tracing loop (see Section 2.6), but this does not match so well the reference counting abstraction of Algorithm 6.2.

Algorithm 6.1: Abstract tracing garbage collection

```
 1   atomic collectTracing():
 2       W ← []
 3       rootsTracing(W)
 4       scanTracing(W)
 5       sweepTracing()
 6
 7   scanTracing(W):
 8       while not isEmpty(W)
 9           src ← remove(W)
10           ρ(src) ← ρ(src) + 1                           /* shade src */
11           if ρ(src) = 1                            /* src was white, now grey */
12               for each fld in Pointers(src)
13                   ref ← *fld
14                   if ref ≠ null
15                       W ← W + [ref]
16
17   sweepTracing():
18       for each node in Nodes
19           if ρ(node) = 0                                /* node is white */
20               free(node)
21           else                                          /* node is black */
22               ρ(node) ← 0                           /* reset node to white */
23
24   New():
25       ref ← allocate()
26       if ref = null
27           collectTracing()
28           ref ← allocate()
29           if ref = null
30               error "Out of memory"
31       ρ(ref) ← 0                                        /* node is white */
32       return ref
33
34   rootsTracing(R):
35       for each fld in Roots
36           ref ← *fld
37           if ref ≠ null
38               R ← R + [ref]
```

whether the node has already been visited. The mark bit is thus a coarse approximation of the true reference count.

The tracing collector computes the *least* fixed-point solution to Equation 6.1: the reference counts on the nodes are the lowest counts that satisfy it.

We can interpret garbage collection algorithms in terms of the tricolour abstraction discussed in Section 2.2. In Algorithm 6.1, nodes with reference count 0 are white, while nodes with non-zero reference count are black. The transition of a node from white via grey to black occurs as that node is first traced and then scanned. Thus, we can recast the abstract tracing algorithm as partitioning the nodes into two sets, black being reachable and white being garbage.

Reference counting garbage collection

The abstract reference counting collection Algorithm 6.2 shows reference count operations being *buffered* by the mutator's inc and dec procedures rather than performed immediately, in order to highlight the similarity with tracing. This buffering technique turns out to be very practical for multithreaded applications; we consider it further in Chapter 18. This logging of actions also shares similarities with coalesced reference counting, discussed in Section 5.4. The garbage collector, collectCounting, performs the deferred increments I with applyIncrements and the deferred decrements D with scanCounting.

Mutation, using the Write procedure, stores a new destination reference dst into a field src[i]. In doing so, it buffers an increment for the new destination, inc(dst) and a decrement for the old referent, dec(src[i]), before storing the new destination to the field, src[i]←dst.

Each collection begins by applying all deferred increments to bring them up to date. The deferred decrements are applied in the next phase. The scanCounting procedure begins with reference counts that over-estimate the true counts. Thus, it must decrement the counts of nodes in the work list as it encounters them. Any source node whose count, $\rho(src)$, is decremented to zero in this phase is treated as garbage, and its child nodes are added to the work list. Finally, the procedure sweepCounting frees the garbage nodes.

The tracing and reference counting algorithms are identical but for minor differences. Each has a scan procedure: the scanTracing collector uses reference count increments whereas the scanCounting collector uses decrements. In both cases the recursion condition checks for a zero reference count. Each has a sweep procedure that frees the space occupied by garbage nodes. In fact, the outline structures of the first 32 lines in Algorithm 6.1 and Algorithm 6.2 are identical. Deferred reference counting, which defers counting references from the roots, is similarly captured by this framework (see Algorithm 6.3).

Finally, we noted earlier that computing reference counts is tricky when it comes to cycles in the object graph. The trivial object graph in Figure 6.1 shows a simple isolated cycle, where assuming A has reference count zero allows B also to have reference count zero (since only source nodes with a non-zero count contribute to the reference counts of their destinations). But there is a chicken-and-egg problem here, since the reference counts of A and B are mutually dependent. It is just as feasible for us to claim that A has reference count 1, because of its reference from B, leading us to claim that B also has reference count 1.

This seeming anomaly arises generally for fixed-point computations, where there may be several different feasible solutions. In Figure 6.1 we have the case that Nodes = $\{A, B\}$ and Roots = $\{\}$. There are two fixed-point solutions of Equation 6.1 for this simple graph: a least fixed-point $\rho(A) = \rho(B) = 0$ and a greatest fixed-point $\rho(A) = \rho(B) = 1$. Tracing collectors compute the least fixed-point, whereas reference counting collectors compute the greatest, so they cannot (by themselves) reclaim cyclic garbage. The difference between these two solutions is precisely the set of objects reachable only from garbage cycles. We saw in Section 5.5 that reference counting algorithms can use partial tracing to reclaim garbage cycles. They do so by starting from the greatest fixed-point solution and contracting the set of unreclaimed objects to the least fixed-point solution.

Algorithm 6.2: Abstract reference counting garbage collection

```
 1   initialise():
 2       I ← []
 3       D ← []
 4
 5   atomic collectCounting(I,D):
 6       applyIncrements(I)
 7       scanCounting(D)
 8       sweepCounting()
 9
10   scanCounting(W):
11       while not isEmpty(W)
12           src ← remove(W)
13           ρ(src) ← ρ(src) − 1
14           if ρ(src) = 0
15               for each fld in Pointers(src)
16                   ref ← *fld
17                   if ref ≠ null
18                       W ← W + [ref]
19
20   sweepCounting():
21       for each node in Nodes
22           if ρ(node) = 0
23               free(node)
24
25   New():
26       ref ← allocate()
27       if ref = null
28           collectCounting(I,D)
29           ref ← allocate()
30           if ref = null
31               error "Out of memory"
32       ρ(ref) ← 0
33       return ref
34
35   dec(ref):
36       if ref ≠ null
37           D ← D + [ref]
38
39   inc(ref):
40       if ref ≠ null
41           I ← I + [ref]
42
43   atomic Write(src, i, dst):
44       inc(dst)
45       dec(src[i])
46       src[i] ← dst
47
48   applyIncrements(I):
49       while not isEmpty(I)
50           ref ← remove(I)
51           ρ(ref) ← ρ(ref) + 1
```

Algorithm 6.3: Abstract deferred reference counting garbage collection

```
1   initialise():
2       I ← []
3       D ← []
4
5   atomic collectDrc(I,D):
6       rootsTracing(I)
7       applyIncrements(I)
8       scanCounting(D)
9       sweepCounting()
10      rootsTracing(D)
11      applyDecrements(D)
12
13  New():
14      ref ← allocate()
15      if ref = null
16          collectDrc(I, D)
17          ref ← allocate()
18          if ref = null
19              error "Out of memory"
20      ρ(ref) ← 0
21      return ref
22
23  atomic Write(src, i, dst):
24      if src ≠ Roots
25          inc(dst)
26          dec(src[i])
27      src[i] ← dst
28
29  applyDecrements(D):
30      while not isEmpty(D)
31          ref ← remove(D)
32          ρ(ref) ← ρ(ref) − 1
```

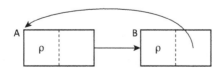

Figure 6.1: A simple cycle

Chapter 7

Allocation

There are three aspects to a memory management system: (i) allocation of memory in the first place, (ii) identification of live (or dead) objects and (iii) reclamation for future use of memory previously allocated but currently occupied by dead objects. Garbage collectors address these issues differently than do explicit memory managers, and different automatic memory managers use different algorithms to manage these actions. However, in all cases allocation and reclamation of memory are tightly linked: how memory is reclaimed places constraints on how it is allocated.

The problem of allocating and freeing memory dynamically under program control has been addressed since the 1950s. Most of the techniques devised over the decades are of potential relevance to allocating in garbage collected systems, but there are several key differences between automatic and explicit freeing that have an impact on desirable allocation strategies and performance.

- Garbage collected systems tend to free space all at once rather than one object at a time. Furthermore, some garbage collection algorithms (those that copy or compact) free large contiguous regions at one time.

- Many systems that use garbage collection have more information available when allocating, such as static knowledge of the size and type of object being allocated.

- Because of the availability of garbage collection, users will write programs in a different style and are likely to use heap allocation more often.

We proceed by describing key allocation mechanisms according to a taxonomy similar to that of Standish [1980], and later return to discuss how the points above affect the choices a designer might make in constructing the allocators for a garbage collected system.

There are two fundamental strategies, *sequential allocation* and *free-list allocation*. We then take up the more complex case of allocation from *multiple free-lists*. After that, we describe a range of additional, more practical, considerations, before summarising the factors to take into account in choosing an allocation scheme.

7.1 Sequential allocation

Sequential allocation uses a large free chunk of memory. Given a request for n bytes, it allocates that much from one end of the free chunk. The data structure for sequential allocation is quite simple, consisting of a *free pointer* and a *limit pointer*. Algorithm 7.1 shows

Algorithm 7.1: Sequential allocation

```
1  sequentialAllocate(n):
2      result ← free
3      newFree ← result + n
4      if newFree > limit
5          return null                    /* signal 'Memory exhausted' */
6      free ← newFree
7      return result
```

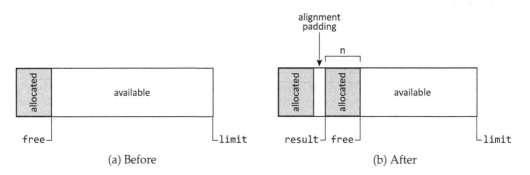

(a) Before   (b) After

Figure 7.1: Sequential allocation: a call to `sequentialAllocate(n)` which advances the `free` pointer by the size of the allocation request, n, plus any padding necessary for proper alignment.

pseudocode for allocation that proceeds from lower addresses to higher ones, and Figure 7.1 illustrates the technique. Sequential allocation is colloquially called *bump pointer allocation* because of the way it 'bumps' the free pointer. It is also sometimes called *linear allocation* because the sequence of addresses allocated is linear for a given chunk. See Section 7.6 and Algorithm 7.8 for details concerning any necessary *alignment* and padding when allocating. The properties of sequential allocation include the following.

- It is simple.

- It is efficient, although Blackburn *et al.* [2004a] have shown that the fundamental performance difference between sequential allocation and segregated-fits free-list allocation (see Section 7.4) for a Java system is on the order of 1% of total execution time.

- It appears to result in better cache locality than does free-list allocation, especially for initial allocation of objects in moving collectors [Blackburn *et al.*, 2004a].

- It may be less suitable than free-list allocation for non-moving collectors, if uncollected objects break up larger chunks of space into smaller ones, resulting in many small sequential allocation chunks as opposed to one or a small number of large ones.[1]

---

[1]But see, for example, the immix collector Blackburn and McKinley [2008] described in Chapter 10.

7.2 Free-list allocation

The alternative to sequential allocation is *free-list allocation*. In free-list allocation, a data structure records the location and size of free cells of memory. Strictly speaking, the data structure describes a *set* of free cells, and some organisations are in fact not list-like, but we will use the traditional term 'free-list' for them anyway. One can think of sequential allocation as a degenerate case of free-list allocation, but its special properties and simple implementation distinguish it in practice.

We consider first the case of organising the set as a single *list* of free cells. The allocator considers each free cell in turn, and according to some policy, chooses one to allocate. This general approach is called *sequential fits allocation*, since the algorithm searches sequentially for a cell into which the request will fit. The classical versions of sequential fits are *first-fit*, *next-fit* and *best-fit* [Knuth, 1973, Section 2.5], which we now describe in turn.

First-fit allocation

When trying to satisfy an allocation request, a *first-fit* allocator will use the first cell it finds that can satisfy the request. If the cell is larger than required, the allocator may *split* the cell and return the remainder to the free-list. However, if the remainder is too small (allocation data structures and algorithms usually constrain the smallest allocatable cell size), then the allocator cannot split the cell. Further, the allocator may follow a policy of not splitting unless the remainder is larger than some absolute or percentage size threshold. Algorithm 7.2 gives code for first-fit. Notice that it assumes that each free cell has room to record its own size and the address of the next free cell. It maintains a single global variable `head` that refers to the first free cell in the list.

A variation that leads to simpler code in the splitting case is to return the portion at the *end* of the cell being split, illustrated in Algorithm 7.3. A possible disadvantage of this approach is the different alignment of objects, but this could cut either way. First-fit tends to exhibit the following characteristics [Wilson *et al.*, 1995a, page 31].

- Small remainder cells accumulate near the front of the list, slowing down allocation.

- In terms of space utilisation, it may behave rather similarly to best-fit since cells in the free-list end up roughly sorted from smallest to largest.

An interesting issue with first-fit is the order of cells in the list. When supporting explicit freeing, there are a number of options for where in the list to enter a newly freed cell. For example, the allocator can insert the cell at the head, at the tail, or according to some order such as by address or size. When supporting garbage collection with a single free-list, it is usually more natural to build the list in address order, which is what a mark-sweep collector does.

Next-fit allocation

Next-fit is a variation of first-fit that starts the search for a cell of suitable size from the point in the list where the last search succeeded [Knuth, 1973]. This is the variable `prev` in the code sketched by Algorithm 7.4. When it reaches the end of the list, it starts over from the beginning, and so is sometimes called *circular first-fit allocation*. The idea is to reduce the need to iterate repeatedly past the small cells at the head of the list. While next-fit is intuitively appealing, in practice it exhibits drawbacks.

Algorithm 7.2: First-fit allocation

```
 1  firstFitAllocate(n):
 2      prev ← addressOf(head)
 3      loop
 4          curr ← next(prev)
 5          if curr = null
 6              return null                    /* signal 'Memory exhausted' */
 7          else if size(curr) < n
 8              prev ← curr
 9          else
10              return listAllocate(prev, curr, n)
11
12  listAllocate(prev, curr, n):
13      result ← curr
14      if shouldSplit(size(curr), n)
15          remainder ← result + n
16          next(remainder) ← next(curr)
17          size(remainder) ← size(curr) − n
18          next(prev) ← remainder
19      else
20          next(prev) ← next(curr)
21      return result
```

Algorithm 7.3: First-fit allocation: an alternative way to split a cell

```
 1  listAllocateAlt(prev, curr, n):
 2      if shouldSplit(size(curr), n)
 3          size(curr) ← size(curr) − n;
 4          result ← curr + size(curr)
 5      else
 6          next(prev) ← next(curr)
 7          result ← curr
 8      return result
```

- Objects from different phases of mutator execution become mixed together. Because they become unreachable at different times, this can affect fragmentation (see Section 7.3).

- Accesses through the roving pointer have poor locality because the pointer cycles through all the free cells.

- The allocated objects may also exhibit poor locality, being spread out through memory and interspersed with objects allocated by previous mutator phases.

Best-fit allocation

Best-fit allocation finds the cell whose size most closely matches the request. The idea is to minimise waste, as well as to avoid splitting large cells unnecessarily. Algorithm 7.5

Algorithm 7.4: Next-fit allocation

```
 1  nextFitAllocate(n):
 2      start ← prev
 3      loop
 4          curr ← next(prev)
 5          if curr = null
 6              prev ← addressOf(head)  /* restart from the beginning of the free–list */
 7              curr ← next(prev)
 8          if prev = start
 9              return null                        /* signal 'Memory exhausted' */
10          else if size(curr) < n
11              prev ← curr
12          else
13              return listAllocate(prev, curr, n)
```

---

sketches the code. In practice best-fit seems to perform well for most programs, giving relatively low wasted space in spite of its bad worst-case performance [Robson, 1977]. Though such measurements were for explicit freeing, we would expect the space utilisation to remain high for garbage collected systems as well.

Speeding free-list allocation

Allocating from a single sequential list may not scale very well to large memories. Therefore researchers have devised a number of more sophisticated organisations of the set of free cells to speed free-list allocation according to various policies. One obvious choice is to use a balanced binary tree of the free cells. These might be sorted by size (for best-fit) or by address (for first-fit or next-fit). When sorting by size, it saves time to enter only one cell of each size into the tree, and to chain the rest of the cells of that size from that tree node. Not only does the search complete faster, but the tree needs reorganisation less frequently since this only happens when adding a new size or removing the last cell of a given size.

To use balanced trees for first-fit or next-fit, one needs to use a Cartesian tree [Vuillemin, 1980]. This indexes by both address (primary key) and size (secondary key). It is totally ordered on addresses, but organised as a 'heap' for the sizes, which allows quick search for the first or next fit that will satisfy a given size request. This technique is also known as *fast-fits allocation* [Tadman, 1978; Standish, 1980; Stephenson, 1983]. A node in the Cartesian tree must record the address and size of the free cell, the pointers to the left and right child, and the maximum of the sizes of all cells in its subtree. It is easy to compute this maximum from the maximum values recorded in the node's children and it own size. Hence, the minimum possible size for a node is larger than for simple list-based schemes. While we omit code for inserting and removing nodes from the tree, to clarify the approach we give sample code for searching under the first-fit policy in Algorithm 7.6. The code uses the single global variable root, which refers to the root of the binary tree. Each node n maintains a value max(n) that gives the maximum size of any nodes in that node's subtree. Next-fit is only slightly more complicated than first-fit. Balanced binary trees improve worst-case behaviour from linear to logarithmic in the number of free cells. Self-adjusting (*splay*) trees [Sleator and Tarjan, 1985] have similar (amortised time) benefits.

Another useful approach to address-ordered first-fit or next-fit allocation is *bitmapped-fits allocation*. A bitmap on the side has one bit for each granule of the allocatable heap.

Algorithm 7.5: Best-fit allocation

```
 1  bestFitAllocate(n):
 2      best ← null
 3      bestSize ← ∞
 4      prev ← addressOf(head)
 5      loop
 6          curr ← next(prev)
 7          if curr = null || size(curr) = n
 8              if curr ≠ null
 9                  bestPrev ← prev
10                  best ← curr
11              else if best = null
12                  return null              /* signal 'Memory exhausted' */
13              return listAllocate(bestPrev, best, n)
14          else if size(curr) < n || bestSize < size(curr)
15              prev ← curr
16          else
17              best ← curr
18              bestPrev ← prev
19              bestSize ← size(curr)
```

Algorithm 7.6: Searching in Cartesian trees

```
 1  firstFitAllocateCartesian(n):
 2      parent ← null
 3      curr ← root
 4      loop
 5          if left(curr) ≠ null && max(left(curr)) ≥ n
 6              parent ← curr
 7              curr ← left(curr)
 8          else if prev < curr && size(curr) ≥ n
 9              prev ← curr
10              return treeAllocate(curr, parent, n)
11          else if right(curr) ≠ null && max(right(curr)) ≥ n
12              parent ← curr
13              curr ← right(curr)
14          else
15              return null                  /* signal 'Memory exhausted' */
```

Rather than scanning the heap itself, we scan the bitmap. We can scan a byte at a time by using the byte value to index pre-calculated tables giving the size of the largest run of free granules within the eight-granule unit represented by the byte, or a word at a time with a little more calculation. The bitmap can also be augmented with run-length information that speeds calculating the size of larger free or allocated cells, in order to skip over them more quickly.

Another approach to finding free granules quickly is hierarchical bitmaps, used, for example, by Ueno *et al.* [2011]. The bottom level of the hierarchy records information for each granule. The next level records summary information for each group of k granules, where k is typically the number of bits in a machine word. For finding free granules quickly, this level would have a 1 if the group of k has *any* free granules, that is, it is the logical or of the group of k free bits. The third level summarizes groups of second-level bits and so on, to whatever depth is useful. This kind of hierarchical bitmap goes back at least to Kudoh *et al.* [1995]. However, Wilmore [1980] describes a more general scheme that is useful to finding both free and allocated granules. In Wilmore's approach, the higher levels use *two* bits for each group of k items in the next lower level, with 00 meaning all the lower level bits are 0, 11 meaning that they are all 1, and 10 meaning there is a mix of 1s and 0s. Ueno *et al.* use hierarchical bitmaps in their allocation manager for a non-moving, generational collector (Chapter 9). They assumed that objects allocated close together share similar lifetimes and so the bits in the lowest level bitmap are more likely to be all set or all unset. They support objects in different generations by using multiple bitmaps, one for each generation. Note that hierarchical bitmaps have been used for other sets in a memory manager, such as remembered sets or card tables, where this might be viewed as a card summarisation technique [Detlefs *et al.*, 2002a]. Bitmaps have several virtues:

- They are 'on the side' and thus less vulnerable to corruption. This is especially important for less safe languages such as C and C++, but also helpful in improving the reliability and debuggability of collectors for other, more safe, languages.

- They do not require information to be recorded in the free and allocated cells, and thus minimise constraints on cell size. This effect can more than pay back the 3% (respectively, 1.5%) storage overhead of one bit per 32-bit (respectively, 64-bit) word. However, other considerations may require headers in objects, so this does not always hold.

- They are compact, so scanning them causes few cache misses, thereby improving locality.

7.3 Fragmentation

At the beginning an allocation system generally has one, or a small number, of large cells of contiguous free memory. As a program runs, allocating and freeing cells, it typically produces a larger number of free cells, which can individually be small. This dispersal of free memory across a possibly large number of small free cells is called *fragmentation*. Fragmentation has at least two negative effects in an allocation system:

- It can prevent allocation from succeeding. There can be enough free memory, in total, to satisfy a request, but not enough in any particular free cell. In non-garbage collected systems this generally forces a program to terminate. In a garbage collected system, it may trigger collection sooner than would otherwise be necessary.

- Even if there is enough memory to satisfy a request, fragmentation may cause a program to use more address space, more resident pages and more cache lines than it would otherwise.

It is impractical to avoid fragmentation altogether. For one thing, the allocator usually cannot know what the future request sequence will be. For another, even given a known request sequence, optimal allocation — that is, using the smallest amount of space necessary for an entire sequence of allocate and free requests to succeed — is NP-hard [Robson, 1980]. However, some approaches tend to be better than others; while we cannot *eliminate* fragmentation, we have some hope of *managing* it. Generally speaking, we should expect a rough trade-off between allocation speed and fragmentation, while also expecting that fragmentation is quite difficult to predict in any given case.

For example, best-fit intuitively seems good with respect to fragmentation, but it can lead to a number of quite small fragments scattered through the heap. First-fit can also lead to a large number of small fragments, which tend to cluster near the beginning of the free-list. Next-fit will tend to distribute small fragments more evenly across the heap, but that is not necessarily better. The only total solution to fragmentation is compaction or copying collection.

7.4   Segregated-fits allocation

Much of the time consumed by a basic free-list allocator is spent searching for a free cell of appropriate size. Hence, using multiple free-lists whose members are segregated by size can speed allocation [Comfort, 1964]. In Chapter 9 we describe collectors that manage multiple *spaces*. While multiple spaces will almost always be managed using multiple allocators, when we speak of *segregated-fits* we mean multiple *lists* being used for allocating for the *same* (logical) space. The distinction is not always precise. For example, some collectors segregate large objects, or large objects that contain no outgoing references (such as images or other binary data). They do this partly for performance reasons, and perhaps also partly because such objects have different lifetime characteristics. The large objects may be in a different space, receiving different treatment during collection. Alternatively, each space may have a segregated set of large objects. The latter is more like segregated-fits, though smaller objects might be allocated sequentially rather than from a free-list. There are many ways to combine approaches.

The basic idea behind segregated-fits is that there is some number k of size values, $s_0 < s_1 < \cdots < s_{k-1}$. The number k might vary, but is often fixed. There are $k + 1$ free-lists, $f_0, \ldots, f_k$. The size b of a free cell on list f_i is constrained by $s_{i-1} < b \leq s_i$, where we set $s_{-1} = 0$ and $s_k = +\infty$. Since the point is to avoid searching for a cell of suitable size, we restrict the condition further: the size of a free cell on list f_i must be *exactly* s_i. The one exception is f_k, which holds all cells larger than s_{k-1}, the largest size of the single-size lists. Thus, when requesting a cell of size $b \leq s_{k-1}$, the allocator rounds the request size up to the smallest s_i such that $b \leq s_i$. The sizes s_i are called *size classes*, and the size class for cell size b is therefore that s_i such that $s_{i-1} < b \leq s_i$.

List f_k, for cells larger than s_{k-1}, is organised to use one of the basic single-list algorithms we previously presented. In this case, a Cartesian tree or other data structure with good expected-time performance is probably a good choice. For one thing, larger objects are usually allocated less frequently. Even if that is not the case, just initialising them takes the application longer, so if the per-cell overheads are a bit higher for these larger cells than for allocating from the one-size lists, it will still not impact total execution time much as a percentage.

Algorithm 7.7: Segregated-fits allocation

```
1  segregatedFitAllocate(j):                    /* j is the index of a size class sⱼ */
2      result ← remove(freeLists[j])
3      if result = null
4          large ← allocateBlock()
5          if large = null
6              return null                       /* signal 'Memory exhausted' */
7          initialise(large, sizes[j])
8          result ← remove(freeLists[j])
9      return result
```

There are a variety of ways to speed the calculation of the size class s_i when given the desired object size b. For example, size classes s_0 through s_{k-1} might be evenly spaced, that is, $s_i = s_0 + c \cdot i$, for some suitable $c > 0$. Then the size class is s_k if $b > s_{k-1}$ and otherwise s_j where $j = \lfloor (b - s_0 + c - 1)/c \rfloor$ (using linear fit, where adding $c - 1$ does the appropriate rounding up). For example, an allocation scheme might have $s_0 = 8$, $c = 8$ and $k = 16$, giving size classes as multiples of eight from 8 to 128, and using a general free-list algorithm for $b > 128$. The typical unit here is one byte, which makes sense for byte-addressed machines, as would a unit of one word for word-addressed machines. Still, even when bytes are the unit for describing size, a *granule* is more likely to be the size of a word, or even larger. Having c be a power of two speeds the division in the formula by allowing substitution of a shift for the generally slower division operation.

In addition to a very dense range of small size classes, a system might provide one or more ranges of somewhat larger sizes, less densely packed, as opposed to switching immediately to a general free-list mechanism. For example, the Boehm-Demers-Weiser collector has separate lists for each size from the minimum up to eight words, and then for even numbers of words up to 16, and for multiples of four words up to 32 [Boehm and Weiser, 1988]. Above that size, it determines size classes somewhat dynamically, filling in an array that maps requested size (in bytes) to allocated size (in words). It then directly indexes an array of free-lists using the allocated size. Only those sizes used will be populated.

If the set of size classes is built into a system (that is, fixed at system build time), then a compiler can in principle determine the appropriate free-list in advance for any allocation call whose size is known at compile time. This can substantially improve the common case cost for most allocations.

To sum up concerning the time required to allocate a cell, schemes with single free-lists may search sequentially (first-fit, best-fit, and so on), which can take a long time to find a cell satisfying a given request. They may also use a balanced tree to attain worst-case or amortised logarithmic time. The particular advantage of segregated-fits is that for size classes other than s_k, the allocation fast path typically requires constant time, as shown in Algorithm 7.7; see also the lazy sweeping variant in Algorithm 2.5.

Fragmentation

In the simpler free-list allocators we discussed previously, there was only one kind of fragmentation: free cells that were too small to satisfy a request. This is known as *external fragmentation*, because it is unusable space *outside* any allocated cell. When we introduce size classes, if the sizes are at all spread out, then there is also *internal fragmentation*, where space is wasted *inside* an individual cell because the requested size was rounded up. The need for specific alignment may introduce fragmentation in a similar way, although strictly speaking it is external fragmentation (between allocated cells). Segregated-fits introduces a trade-off between internal fragmentation and the number of size classes.

Populating size classes

It should now be reasonably clear how segregated-fits allocation works, except for the important consideration of how to populate each free-list. We discuss two approaches: dedicating whole blocks to particular sizes, also called *big bag of pages* (BiBoP), and *splitting*.

Big bag of pages block-based allocation. In this approach, we choose some *block* size B, a power of two. We provide an allocator for blocks, designed also to support requests for objects larger than one block by allocating multiple contiguous blocks. For a size class $s < B$, when we need more cells of size s we allocate a block and then immediately slice it into cells of size s, putting them on that free-list. Typically we also associate with the block the fact that it is dedicated to cells of size s. While that information might be stored in the block itself, along with other metadata such as mark bits for the cells in the block, Boehm and Weiser [1988] suggest that it is better to store this information in a separate area. Using a separate area results in fewer translation lookaside buffer misses or page faults when consulting or updating only the metadata, and it also avoids aligning every block's metadata so that they compete for the same cache sets.

When we discussed lazy sweeping in Section 2.5, we described basic block-based allocation. Block-based allocation complicates the issue of fragmentation. Because we dedicate a whole block to cells of a given size, we will waste (on average) half a block, and we could waste up to the fraction $(B-s)/B$ of the storage for a given size (if we have exactly one cell used in each block). However, we reduce the per-cell metadata. There is also some space waste if there is an unused portion of size less than s at the end of the block.[2] Whether we call these cases of unusable space internal or external fragmentation depends on our point of view: they are internal to a block but external to cells.

In some systems the metadata associated with a cell includes not just the size s but also the *type* of object allocated into the cell. While such segregation of types can result in greater fragmentation (since two types might be of the same size, but we must allocate them from separate blocks and maintain separate free-lists for them), for small objects the savings (by not having to record type information in each object) can be great. Examples include Lisp cons cells.

Beyond the combining of small cells' metadata across an entire block, block-based allocation has the virtue of making the recombining of free cells particularly simple and efficient: it does not recombine unless all cells in a block are free, and then it returns the block to the block pool. Its common case for allocation, grabbing an available cell from a known list, is quite efficient and, if the list is empty, populating it is straightforward. Its primary disadvantage is its worst-case fragmentation.

Splitting. We have already seen cell *splitting* as a way to obtain cells of a given size s: the various simple free-list schemes will split a larger cell if that is the only way to satisfy a request. If we use a fairly dense collection of size classes, then when we split a cell, we will be likely to have a suitable free-list to receive the portion not allocated. There are some particular organisations of less dense size classes that also have that property. One

---

[2]Boehm and Weiser [1988] place this portion at the *start* of the block rather than its end, presumably to reduce competition for cache lines near the beginning of blocks. This helps more for small cache lines, since it is only effective for (some) cell sizes larger than a cache line.

such scheme is the *buddy system*, which uses sizes that are powers of two [Knowlton, 1965; Peterson and Norman, 1977]. It is clear that we can split a cell of size 2^{i+1} into two cells of size 2^i. We can also recombine (or *coalesce*) two adjacent cells of size 2^i into one cell of size 2^{i+1}. A buddy system will recombine that way only if the cells were split from the *same* cell of size 2^{i+1} originally. Hence cells of size 2^i come in pairs, that is, are buddies. Given the high internal fragmentation of this approach (its average is 25% for arbitrarily chosen allocation requests), it is now largely of historical as opposed to practical interest.

A variation of the 2^i buddy system is the *Fibonacci buddy system* [Hirschberg, 1973; Burton, 1976; Peterson and Norman, 1977], in which the size classes form a Fibonacci sequence: $s_{i+2} = s_{i+1} + s_i$, with a suitable s_0 and s_1 to start. Because the ratio of adjacent sizes is smaller than in the power-of-two buddy system, the average internal fragmentation will be lower (as a percentage of allocated memory). However, locating adjacent cells for recombining free cells after collection is slightly more complicated, since a buddy can have the next size larger or smaller depending on which member of a buddy pair is under consideration. Other variations on the buddy system have been described by Wise [1978], Page and Hagins [1986] and Wilson *et al.* [1995b].

7.5 Combining segregated-fits with first-, best- and next-fit

We can use segregated-fits as an accelerating front end to the schemes that use a single free-list. In this case, we place a cell that falls into a given size class onto the list for that class. If a request finds that the free-list for its size class is empty, we can implement best-fit by searching the larger size classes in order of increasing size looking for a non-empty free-list. Having a segregated-fits front end modifies first- and next-fit, leading to a design choice of what to do when the free-list for the desired size class is empty. But in any case, if we end up searching list f_k, the list of all cells of size greater than s_{k-1}, then we apply the single-list scheme (first-fit, best-fit or next-fit).

Another way of seeing this is that we really have a segregated-fits scheme and are simply deciding how we are going to manage f_k. To summarise, we can manage it in these ways:

- as a single free-list, using first-fit, best-fit, next-fit or one of the variations on them previously discussed, including Cartesian trees or other data structures that reduce search time;

- using block-based allocation;

- using a buddy system.

7.6 Additional considerations

Actual allocators often must take into account some additional considerations. We now discuss these: alignment, size constraints, boundary tags, heap parsability, locality, wilderness preservation and crossing maps.

Alignment

Depending on constraints of the underlying machine and its instruction set, or for better packing and improved memory hierarchy performance (cache, translation lookaside buffer or paging), an allocated object may require special *alignment*. For example, consider a

Algorithm 7.8: Incorporating alignment requirements

```
1  fits(n, a, m, blk):
2      /* need n bytes, alignment a modulo m, m a power of 2. Can blk satisfy this request? */
3      z ← blk − a                                              /* back up */
4      z ← (z + m − 1) & ~(m − 1)                              /* round up */
5      z ← z + a                                              /* go forward */
6      pad ← z − blk
7      return n + pad ≤ size(curr)
```

Java array of `double`. On some machines, the double-word floating point values must be aligned on double-word boundaries, that is, their addresses must be 0 modulo 8 (with the three low bits of the address equal to zero). One way to address the overall problem is to make double-words the granule of allocation. In that case, all allocated and free cells are a multiple of eight bytes in size, and are aligned on an eight-byte boundary. This is simple, but perhaps slightly wasteful. Further, when allocating an array of `double`, there is still some special work that might be required. Suppose that the Java heap design requires two header words for scalar (non-array) objects, one to refer to the object's class information (for virtual method dispatch, type determination and so on) and one for the object's hash code and Java synchronisation (locking). This is a typical design. Array objects require a third word, giving the number of elements in the array. If we store these three header words at the start of the allocated space and follow them immediately by the array elements, the elements will be aligned on an odd word boundary, not an even one as required. If we use double-words as the granule, then we simply use four words (two double-words) for the three-word header and waste a word.

But suppose our granule is one word and we wish to avoid wasting a word whenever we can. In that case, if a free cell we are considering is aligned on an odd word boundary (that is, its address is 4 modulo 8), we can simply use the cell as is, putting the three header words first, immediately followed by the array element, which will be double-word aligned as required. If the cell starts on an even word boundary, we have to skip a word to get the proper alignment. Notice that this complicates our determination of whether a request will fit in a given cell: it may or may not fit, depending on the required and actual alignment — see Algorithm 7.8.

Size constraints

Some collection schemes require a minimum amount of space in each object (cell) for managing the collection process. For example, basic compacting collection needs room for the new address in each object. Some collectors may need two words, such as a lock/status word plus a forwarding pointer. This implies that even if the language only needs one word, the allocator will still need to allocate two words. In fact, if a program allocates some objects that contain no data and only serve as distinct unique identifiers, for some languages they could in principle consume no storage at all! In practice this does not work since the address of the object forms its unique identity (or else you must calculate a unique value and store it in the object), so the object *must* consume at least one byte.

Boundary tags

In order to support recombination when freeing objects, many allocate-free systems associate an additional header or *boundary tag* with each cell, outside the storage available to the program [Knuth, 1973]. The boundary tag indicates the size of the cell and whether it is allocated or free. It may also indicate the size of the previous cell, making it easier to find its flag indicating whether it is free, and its free-list chaining pointers if it is free. Thus, a boundary tag may be two words long, though with additional effort and possibly more overhead in the allocation and freeing routines, it may be possible to pack it into one word.

Using bitmaps on the side to indicate which granules are allocated or free avoids the need for boundary tags, and may be more robust as we previously observed. Which approach uses less storage depends on the average object size and the allocation granularity.

We further observe that because garbage collection frees objects all at once, a given algorithm may not need boundary tags, or may need less information in them. Further, in managed languages we will generally know the size of a cell by examining its type and so do not need to record that information separately.

Heap parsability

The sweeping phase of a mark-sweep collector must be able to advance from cell to cell in the heap. This capability is what we call *heap parsability*. Other kinds of collectors may not *require* parsability, but it can be a great help in debugging collectors so it is good to support parsability if possible and the cost is not too high.

Generally we only need parsability in one direction, most commonly in order of increasing address. A typical language will use one or two words to record an object's type and other necessary information. We call this the object's *header*. For example, many Java implementations use one word to record what amounts to a type (a pointer to type information, including a vector of addresses of methods of the object's class) and one word for a hash code, synchronisation information, garbage collection mark bit and so on. In order to make indexing into arrays efficient on most machines, it helps if the object reference refers to the first element of the array, with successive elements at successively higher addresses. Since the language run-time and the collector need to find the type of an object in a uniform way given a reference to the object, we place the header immediately before the object data. Thus, the object reference points not to the first allocated byte, but into the middle of the allocated cell, after the header. Having the header come before the object contents therefore facilitates upward parsing of the heap. This is an example of the canonical pointer to an object being different from the address of the object's first byte.

Again using a Java system as an example, array instances need to record the length of the individual array. For easy parsability, it helps if the `length` field comes *after* the two-word object header. Therefore, the first array element falls at the third word of the allocated cell, the `length` is at word -1 and the rest of the header is at words -2 and -3. A scalar (non-array) object needs to place its header at words -2 and -3 as well. This would appear to leave word -1 as a 'hole', but in fact there is no problem placing the first (scalar) field of the object there (assuming that the machine can index by a small negative constant just as well as by a small positive one, and most can). Further, if the object has no additional fields, there is still no problem: the header of the next object can legally appear at the address to which the object reference points! We illustrate all this in Figure 7.2.

A particular issue arises when an implementation over-writes one object with another (necessarily smaller) one, as some functional language implementations do in replacing a closure with its evaluated value. With no further action, a scan that parses the heap may land in the middle of 'unformatted' bits and get quite confused. Non-Stop Haskell and other collectors solve this problem by inserting *filler objects* [Cheadle *et al.*, 2004]. In the usual case they only need to insert a reference to metadata indicating a pointer-free object of the appropriate size; they pre-construct metadata for sizes from one to eight words. Larger fillers are quite rare but would require creating metadata dynamically.[3]

---

[3]They do not offer details, but it seems reasonable to us to place the metadata *in the filler* in that case, thus avoiding any run-time allocation to restore heap parsability.

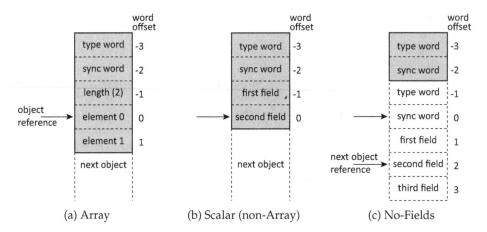

Figure 7.2: A Java object header design for heap parsability. Grey indicates the words forming the referent object. Neighbouring objects are shown with dashed lines.

One final consideration arises from alignment requirements. If an individual object needs to be shifted one or more words from the beginning of its cell for proper alignment, we need to record something in the gap so that in heap parsing we will know to skip. If ordinary object headers cannot begin with an all-zero word, and if we zero all free space in advance, then when parsing we can simply skip words whose value is zero. A simple alternative is to devise a distinct range of values to write at the start of gap, identifying it as a gap and giving its length. For example, Sun (now Oracle) have long used what they call a 'self-parsing' heap. When they free an object (in a non-moving space), they overwrite its memory with a filler object, which includes a field giving its size (think of it as an array of words). This is particularly useful for skipping ahead to the next real object when sweeping the heap.

A bitmap on the side, indicating where each object starts, makes heap parsing easy and simplifies the design constraints on object header formats. However, such bits consume additional space and require additional time to set during allocation. Allocation bitmaps are useful in many collectors, especially parallel and concurrent ones. Some concurrent collectors, such as OpenJDK's Garbage-First (G1), avoid some of the cost to sequential allocation of setting these bits by deeming any object above a high-water mark address determined at the start of a collection to be implicitly live.

Similar considerations apply to languages other than Java. Furthermore, block-based allocation offers simple parsing for small cells, and it is also easy to handle large blocks. For improved cache performance, the location of a large object inside a sequence of one or more blocks is something we might randomise, that is, we randomise how much of the wasted space comes before, and how much after, the application object. It is easy to record at the start of the block where the object is, in order to support parsability.

Locality

Locality issues come up several ways in allocation. There is locality of the allocation process itself, and of freeing. Other things being equal, an address-ordered free-list may improve locality of allocator memory accesses. Sequential allocation also leads naturally to sequential accesses with good locality. In fact, software prefetching a bit ahead of the allocator can help [Appel, 1994], though for certain hardware that is unnecessary [Diwan *et al.*, 1994]. But there is an entirely different notion of locality that is also useful to consider: objects that may become unreachable at about the same time. If some objects become unreachable at the same time, and they are allocated adjacent to one another, then after collection their space will coalesce into a single free chunk, thus minimising fragmentation. Empirically, objects allocated at about the same time often become unreachable at about the same time. This makes non-moving systems less problematic than might be presumed [Hayes, 1991; Dimpsey *et al.*, 2000; Blackburn and McKinley, 2008]. It also suggests applying a heuristic of trying to allocate next to, or at least near, the most recently allocated object. Specifically, if the previous allocation request was satisfied by splitting a larger chunk, then it can help reduce fragmentation to prefer splitting the same chunk for requests in the near future, if the future request cannot be satisfied directly from a free-list for objects of the appropriate size.

Wilderness preservation

A typical heap organisation consists of a large contiguous part of the machine's address space, often bounded at the low end by the program's static code and data areas. The other end is often not occupied, but rather is open for expansion. This boundary in Unix systems is called the 'break', and the `sbrk` call can grow (or shrink) the available space by adjusting the boundary. Space beyond the boundary may not even be in the virtual memory map. The last free chunk in the heap is thus expandable. Since it begins what could be called 'unoccupied territory', it is called the *wilderness*, and Korn and Vo [1985] found that *wilderness preservation* — allocating from the wilderness only as a last resort — helped reduce fragmentation. It also has the salutary effect of tending to defer the need to grow the heap, and thus conserves overall system resources.

Crossing maps

Some collection schemes, or their write barriers, require the allocator to fill in a *crossing map*. This map indicates, for each aligned segment of the heap of size 2^k for some suitable k, the address (or offset within the 2^k segment) of the last object that begins in that segment. Combined with heap parsability, this allows a barrier or collector to determine fairly quickly, from an address within an object, the start of the object, and thus to access the object's headers, and so on. We discuss crossing maps in more detail in Section 11.8.

7.7 Allocation in concurrent systems

If multiple threads attempt to allocate simultaneously, then since most steps in allocation need to be atomic to preserve the integrity of the allocation data structures, they will need to use atomic operations or locks. Allocation can thus become a serial bottleneck. The basic solution is to give each thread its own allocation area. If a thread runs out, it can obtain another chunk of free space in which to allocate from a global pool. Only interactions with the global pool need to be atomic. Individual threads may vary in their allocation rates, so to improve both time and space performance it can help to employ an adaptive algorithm to adjust the size of the free space chunks handed out to each thread — a slowly allocating thread might receive a small chunk while a rapidly allocating one gets a large chunk. Dimpsey *et al.* [2000] noted substantial performance improvement in a multiprocessor Java system using a suitably organised *local allocation buffer* (LAB) for each thread.[4] They further note that since the local allocation buffers absorb almost all allocation of small objects, it was beneficial to retune the global free-list-based allocator since its typical request was for a new local allocation buffer chunk.

Garthwaite *et al.* [2005] discussed adaptive sizing of local allocation buffers and found benefit from associating them with *processors* rather than *threads*. They describe the original mechanism for sizing per-thread local allocation buffers, as follows. Initially, a thread requests a 24-word (96-byte) local allocation buffer. Each time it requests another local allocation buffer, it multiplies the size by 1.5. However, when the collector runs, it decays each thread's local allocation buffer size by dividing by two. The scheme also involves adjustment to the young generation's size according to the number of different threads allocating. The per-processor local allocation buffer scheme relies on multiprocessor restartable critical sections, which Garthwaite *et al.* introduced. This mechanism allows a thread to determine whether it has been preempted and rescheduled, which implies that it may be running on a different processor. By having such preemption modify a register used in addressing the per-processor data, they can cause stores after preemption to produce a trap, and the trap handler can restart the interrupted allocation. Even though per-processor local allocation buffers involve more instructions, their latency was the same, and they required less sophisticated sizing mechanisms to work well. They also found that for small numbers of threads, per-thread local allocation buffers were better (consider especially the case where there are fewer threads than processors), and per-processor local allocation buffers were better when there are many allocating threads. Therefore, they designed their system to support switching between the two approaches dynamically.

A typical local allocation buffer is used for sequential allocation. Another design is for each thread (or processor) to maintain its own set of segregated free-lists, in conjunction with incremental sweeping. When a thread sweeps a block incrementally during allocation, it puts the free cells into its own free-lists. This design has certain problems that arise when it is used for explicit storage management, as addressed by Berger *et al.* [2000]. For example, if the application uses a producer-consumer model, then the producer allocates message buffers and the consumer frees them, leading to a net transfer of buffers from one to the other. In the garbage collected world, the collection process may return buffers to a global pool. However, incremental sweeping that places free cells on the sweeper's free-lists naturally returns free buffers to threads that allocate them most frequently.

7.8   Issues to consider

There are some particular issues to consider when designing an allocator for a garbage collected system: Allocation cannot be considered independently of the collection algorithm. In particular, non-moving collectors such as mark-sweep more or less demand a free-list approach as opposed to sequential allocation — but see Section 10.3 for contrary views on this, and some local allocation buffer approaches also use sequential allocation in conjunction with mark-sweep collection. Conversely, sequential allocation makes the most sense for copying and compacting collectors, because it is fast and simple. It is not necessarily much faster than segregated-fits free-list allocation, but its simplicity may offer better overall reliability.

If a collector uses mark-sweep but offers occasional or emergency compaction to eliminate fragmentation, then it needs to provide for updating the allocation data structures to reflect the state of the world after compaction.

---

[4]Some authors use the term 'thread-local heap'. We use local allocation buffer when the point is separate *allocation*, and reserve use of 'thread-local heap' for the case where the local areas are *collected* separately. Thus, while a 'thread-local heap' is almost certainly a local allocation buffer, the reverse need not be true.

Bitmaps on the side for recording free/allocated granules and where cells or objects start add robustness and simplify object header design. They can also speed collector operations and improve the collector's memory hierarchy performance. Their space cost is modest, but they do add some time cost during allocation, even in the common case.

Block-based allocation can reduce per-object overheads, both for the language implementation (for example, if a block is dedicated to objects of a single type) and for collector metadata. This may be offset by the space consumed by unallocated cells and the unusable space within some blocks. Block-based allocation may also fit well with organisations that support multiple spaces with different allocation and collection techniques.

Segregated-fits is generally faster than single free-list schemes. This is of greater importance in a garbage collected context since programs coded assuming garbage collection tend to do more allocation than ones coded using explicit freeing.

Because a collector frees objects in batches, the techniques designed for recombining free cells for explicit freeing systems are less relevant. The sweep phase of mark-sweep can rebuild a free-list efficiently from scratch. In the case of compacting collectors, in the end there is usually just one large free chunk appropriate for sequential allocation. Copying similarly frees whole semispaces without needing to free each individual cell.

Chapter 8

Partitioning the heap

So far we have assumed a monolithic approach to garbage collection: all objects are managed by the same collection algorithm and all are collected at the same time. However, there is no reason why this should be so, and substantial performance benefits accrue from a more discriminating treatment of objects. The best known example is *generational collection* [Lieberman and Hewitt, 1983; Ungar, 1984], which segregates objects by age and preferentially collects younger objects. There are many reasons why it might be beneficial to treat different categories of object in different ways. Some but not all of these reasons are related to the collector technology that might be used to manage them. As we saw in earlier chapters, objects can be managed either by a direct algorithm (such as reference counting) or by an indirect, tracing algorithm. Tracing algorithms may move objects (mark-compact or copying) or not (mark-sweep). We might therefore consider whether or not we wish to have the collector move different categories of object and, if so, how we might wish to move them. We might wish to distinguish, quickly by their address, which collection or allocation algorithm to apply to different objects. Most commonly, we might wish to distinguish when we collect different categories of object.

8.1 Terminology

It is useful to distinguish the sets of objects to which we want to apply certain memory management *policies* from the *mechanisms* that are used to implement those policies efficiently. We shall use the term *space* to indicate a logical set of objects that receive similar treatment. A space may use one or more chunks of address space. *Chunks* are contiguous and often power-of-two sized and aligned.

8.2 Why to partition

It is often effective to split the heap into partitions, each managed under a different policy or with a different mechanism. These ideas were first explored in Bishop's influential thesis [1977]. These reasons include object mobility, size, lower space overheads, easier identification of object properties, improved garbage collection yield, reduced pause time, better locality and so on. We examine these motivations now, before considering particular models of garbage collection and object management that take advantage of heap partitioning.

Partitioning by mobility

In a hybrid collector it may be necessary to distinguish objects that can be moved from those that either cannot be moved or are costly to move. It may be impossible to move objects due to lack of communication between the run-time system and the compiler, or because an object is passed to unmanaged code including the operating system (for example, to an I/O buffer). Chase [1987, 1988] suggests that asynchronous movement may also be particularly detrimental to compiler optimisations. In order to move an object, we must be able to discover *every* reference to that object so that each can be updated to point to the object's new location. In contrast, if collection is non-moving, it suffices that a tracing collector finds at least one reference. Thus, objects cannot be moved if a reference has been passed to a library (for example, through the Java Native Interface) that does not expect garbage collection. Either such objects must be *pinned* or we must ensure that garbage collection is not enabled for that space while the object is accessible to the library.[1]

The references that must be updated in order to move objects include the root set. Determining an *accurate* map of root references is one of the more challenging parts of building the interface between a managed language and its run-time. We discuss this in detail in Chapter 11. One commonly chosen route, sometimes to an initial implementation, is to scan roots (thread stacks and registers) conservatively rather than construct a *type-accurate* map of which stack frame slots and so on contain object references. This tactic is inevitable if the compiler does not provide type-accurate information (for example, compilers for languages like C and C++). *Conservative stack scanning* [Boehm and Weiser, 1988] treats every slot in every stack frame as a potential reference, applying tests to discard those values found that cannot be pointers (for example, because they 'point' outside the range of the heap or to a location in the heap at which no object has been allocated). Since conservative stack scanning identifies a superset of the true pointer slots in the stack, it is not possible to change the values of any of these (since we might inadvertently change an integer that just happened to look like a pointer). Thus, conservative collection cannot move any object directly referenced by the roots. However, if appropriate information (which need not be full type information) is provided for objects in the heap, then a mostly-copying collector can safely move any object except for one which appears to be directly referenced from *ambiguous roots* [Bartlett, 1988a].

Partitioning by size

It may also be undesirable (rather than impossible) to move some objects. For example, the cost of moving large objects may outweigh the fragmentation costs of not moving them. A common strategy is to allocate objects larger than a certain threshold into a separate *large object space* (LOS). We have already seen how segregated-fits allocators treat large and small objects differently. Large objects are typically placed on separate pages (so a minimum size might be half a page), and are managed by a non-moving collector such as mark-sweep. Notice that, by placing an object on its own page, it can also be 'copied' virtually, either by Baker's Treadmill [1992a] or by remapping virtual memory pages [Withington, 1991].

Partitioning for space

It may be useful to segregate objects in order to reduce overall heap space requirements. It is desirable to create objects in a space managed by a strategy that supports fast allocation and offers good spatial locality (as a sequence of objects is allocated and initialised).

---

[1]An alternative to passing a direct object reference into the library is to pass an indirect reference (or *handle*), which can be registered with the collector for updating as necessary. This is typical for the Java Native Interface.

Blackburn *et al.* [2004a] showed that the difference in cost between sequential and free-list allocation is small (accounting for only 1% of total execution time) and is dominated by the second-order effect of improved locality, particularly for young objects which benefit from being laid out in allocation order.

Both copying and sliding collectors eliminate fragmentation and allow sequential allocation. However, copying collectors require twice the address space of non-moving collectors and mark-compact collection is comparatively slow. It is therefore often useful to segregate objects so that different spaces can be managed by different memory managers. Those objects that are expected to live for some time, and for which fragmentation is not likely to be an immediate concern, can be kept in a space that is primarily non-moving but visited by occasional compaction passes. Those objects with higher rates of allocation and higher expected mortality can be placed in a space managed by a copying collector for fast allocation and cheap collection (proportional to the number of survivors, which is expected to be low). Note that the expense of reserving copy space for large objects is a further reason for managing large object spaces with a non-copying collector.

Partitioning by kind

Physically segregating objects of different categories also allows a particular property, such as type, to be determined simply from the address of the object rather than by retrieving the value of one of its field or, worse, by chasing a pointer. This has several benefits. First, it offers a cache advantage since it removes the necessity to load a further field (particularly if the placement of objects of a particular category is made statically and so the address comparison is against a compile-time constant). Second, segregation by property, whereby all objects sharing the same property are placed in the same contiguous chunk in order to allow a quick address-based identification of the space, allows the property to be associated with the space rather than replicated in each object's header. Third, the kind of the object is significant for some collectors. Objects that do not contain pointers do not need to be scanned by a tracing collector. Large pointer-free objects may benefit from being stored in their own space, whereas the cost of processing a large array of pointers is likely to be dominated by the cost of tracing the pointers rather than, say, the cost of moving the object. Conservative collectors benefit particularly from placing large bitmaps in areas that are never scanned, as they are a frequent source of *false pointers* [Boehm, 1993]. Cycle-collecting tracing collectors can also benefit from segregating inherently acyclic objects which cannot be candidate roots of garbage cycles.

Virtual machines often generate and store code sequences in the heap. Moving and reclaiming code has special problems such as identifying, and keeping consistent, references to code, references within code (which may be embedded within instructions and so on), or determining when code is no longer used and hence can be unloaded. Class reloading is generally not transparent since the class may have state. Code objects also tend to be large and long-lived. For these reasons, it is often desirable not to relocate code objects [Reppy, 1993], and to consider unloading code as an exceptional case particular to certain applications such as application servers and integrated development environments (IDEs).

Partitioning for yield

The best known reason for segregation is to exploit object demographics. It is common for some objects to remain in use from the moment they are allocated to the end of the program while others have very short lives. As long ago as 1976, Deutsch and Bobrow noted that "statistics show that a newly allocated datum is likely to be either 'nailed down' or abandoned within a relatively short time." Indeed, it is even common for a significant fraction of allocation points in Java programs to create objects with a bimodal lifetime distribution [Jones and Ryder, 2008]. Numerous studies have confirmed that the object lifetime behaviour of many (but not all) applications supports the *weak generational hypothesis* that "most objects die young" [Ungar, 1984]. The insight behind a range of strategies, both generational and quasi-generational, is that the best way to reclaim the most storage space for the least effort is to concentrate collection effort on those objects most likely to be garbage.

If the distribution of object lifetimes is sufficiently skewed, then it is worth repeatedly collecting a subset (or subsets) of the heap rather than the entire heap [Baker, 1993]. For example, generational garbage collectors typically collect a single space of the heap (the *young generation* or *nursery*) many times for every time that they collect the entire heap. Note that there is a trade-off here. By not tracing the whole heap at every collection, the collector allows some garbage to go unreclaimed (to *float* in the heap). This means that the space available for the allocation of new objects is smaller than it would have been otherwise, and hence that the collector is invoked more often. Furthermore, as we shall see later, segregating the heap into collected and uncollected spaces imposes more book-keeping effort on both the mutator and the collector. Nevertheless, provided that the space chosen for collection has a sufficiently low survival rate, a partitioned collection strategy can be very effective.

Partitioning for responsiveness

The cost of collection to a tracing collector is largely dependent on the volume of live objects to be traced. If a copying collector is used, the cost of the scavenge only depends on the volume of live objects; even in a mark-sweep collector, the cost of tracing dominates the cost of sweeping. By restricting the size of the *condemned space* that the collector traces, we bound the volume of objects scavenged or marked, and hence the time required for a garbage collection. In a stop-the-world collector, this means shorter pause times and reduced latency. Unfortunately, collecting a subset of the heap only improves expected times. Since collection of a single space may return insufficient free space for computation to continue, it may still be necessary to collect the whole heap. Thus, in general, partitioned collection cannot reduce worst-case pause times or latency.

The extreme case for partitioning is to allow a space to be reclaimed in constant time. If no objects within a condemned region are reachable from outside that region, then there is no tracing work for a collector to do to reclaim the region: the memory occupied by that region can be returned *en masse* to the allocator. Determining that a region is unreachable requires the combination of appropriate object access disciplines and heap structures (such as stacks of scoped regions). The responsibility for correct usage is typically placed entirely on the programmer (as for example with the Real-time Specification for Java). However, given a suitably tractable language, such as ML, regions can also be inferred automatically [Tofte and Talpin, 1994]. The *Cyclone* extension to C reduces the burden on programmers through a complex type system which allows some type and region inferencing [Grossman *et al.*, 2002]. Rust, and the `unique_ptr` and related types of C++11, allow both compile-time and run-time determination of when object lifetimes end, which in the compile-time case may allow reclamation of some objects allocated dynamically during a function call.

Partitioning for locality

The importance of locality for good performance continues to increase as the memory hierarchy becomes more complex (more levels, multiple CPU cores and sockets, and non-uniform memory access). Simple collectors tend to interact poorly with virtual memory and caches. Tracing collectors touch every live object as part of the trace. Mark-sweep collectors may touch dead objects as well. Copying collectors may touch every page of the heap even though only half of it is in use for live objects at any time.

Researchers have long argued that a collector should not be used simply to reclaim garbage but should also be used to improve the locality of the system as a whole [Fenichel and Yochelson, 1969; White, 1980]. We saw in Chapter 4 how the traversal order of copying collectors can be varied in order to improve mutator locality by co-locating parents and children. Generational collectors can obtain further locality improvements for both the collector and the mutator. The collector benefits from concentrating most effort on a subsection of the heap likely to return the most free space for the least effort. The mutator benefits from reducing its working set size, since younger objects typically have higher mutation rates than older ones [Blackburn *et al.*, 2004b].

Partitioning by thread

Garbage collection requires synchronisation between mutator and collector threads. On-the-fly collection, which never pauses more than one mutator thread at a time, may require a complex system of handshakes with the mutator threads but even stop-the-world collection requires synchronisation to bring all mutator threads to a halt. This cost can be reduced if we halt just a single thread at a time and only collect those objects that were allocated by that thread and which cannot have escaped to become reachable by other threads. To achieve this, the collector must be able to distinguish those objects that are only accessible from one thread from those that may be shared, for example by allocating in thread-local heaplets. Thread-local heaplets that cannot contain any cross-references are said to be *disentangled*. A heap structure comprising shared and thread-local heaplets is particularly suitable for functional languages where mutation is rare, and mutable objects are identified by the type system [Doligez and Leroy, 1993; Doligez and Gonthier, 1994; Marlow and Peyton Jones, 2011; Guatto *et al.*, 2018; Arora *et al.*, 2021]. However, thread-local heaplets have also been employed for imperative languages like Java, with support from an escape analysis [Steensgaard, 2000; Jones and King, 2005].

At a larger granularity, it may be desirable to distinguish the objects accessible to particular tasks, where a task comprises a set of cooperating threads. For example, a server may run multiple managed applications, each of which usually requires its own complete virtual machine to be loaded and initialised. In contrast, a *multi-tasking virtual machine* allows many applications (tasks) to run within a single invocation of the multi-tasking virtual machine [Palacz *et al.*, 1994; Soman *et al.*, 2006, 2008; Wegiel and Krintz, 2008]. Care is clearly needed to ensure that different tasks cannot interfere with one another, either directly (by obtaining access to another's data) or indirectly (through denying another task fair access to system resources such as memory, CPU time, and so on). It is particularly desirable to be able to unload all the resources of a task when it has completed without having to disturb other tasks (for example, without having to run the garbage collector). All these matters are simplified by segregating unshared data owned by different threads.

Partitioning by availability

One reason for not wishing to touch objects that are accessible to other threads is to reduce synchronisation overheads. However, we may also wish to partition objects by their usage because their geography leads to different demographic behaviours. Xian *et al.* [2007] observed that remotable objects instantiated as part of client requests in an application server tend to live longer than local objects; extending (then) Sun's HotSpot generational collector to recognise this allowed the server to handle larger workloads. More generally, in a system managed by distributed garbage collection, it will be desirable to manage local and remote objects and references with different policies and mechanisms, since the cost of accessing a remote object will be many orders of magnitude more expensive than accessing a local object.

Distribution is not the only reason why the cost of object access may not be uniform. Earlier we paid particular attention to how tracing collectors might minimise the cost of cache misses. The cost of a cache miss may be a few hundred cycles, whereas accessing an object on a page that is swapped out will incur millions of cycles. Avoiding frequent page misses was a priority for an earlier generation of collectors, whereas today a configuration that leads to heavy paging might be considered irredeemably broken.[2] Physical page organisation (in memory or swapped-out) can be considered to be another form of heap partitioning, and indeed one that can be exploited. The Bookmarking collector [Hertz *et al.*, 2005] cooperates with the virtual memory system in order first of all to improve the choice (from the collector's point of view) of the page to be swapped out and, second, to allow a collector's trace to complete without access to objects on non-resident pages.

Similarly, non-uniform memory access machines have some banks of memory closer to particular processors than others. The HotSpot collector recognises this property and will preferentially allocate objects in 'near' memory to minimise latency on large servers where access times to memory vary significantly.

Partitioning by mutability

Finally, we might wish to partition objects according to their mutability. Recently created objects tend to be modified more frequently (for example, to initialise their fields) than longer-lived objects [Wolczko and Williams, 1992; Bacon and Rajan, 2001; Blackburn and McKinley, 2003; Levanoni and Petrank, 2006]. Memory managers based on simple reference counting tend to incur a high per-update overhead, and thus are less suitable for objects that are modified frequently. On the other hand, in very large heaps, only a comparatively small proportion of objects will be updated in any period but a tracing collector must nevertheless visit all objects that are candidates for garbage. Reference counting might be better suited to this scenario.

Doligez and Gonthier segregate ML objects by mutability (and by thread) in order to allow each thread to have its own space of immutable, unshared objects, as well as a single shared space [Doligez and Leroy, 1993; Doligez and Gonthier, 1994]. Their scheme requires a strong property from references: there must be no pointers to objects inside a thread's local heap from objects outside that local heap (that is, from other threads' local heaps or from the shared space). References into a thread's private heap are prevented from escaping to the shared heap by a copy on write policy; this is semantically transparent since the target of the reference is immutable. Together, these properties allow each thread's private heap to be collected asynchronously. A further advantage of this approach is that, unlike most schemes in which spaces are collected independently, it is not necessary to track pointers that cross spaces (though the mutator must still detect them).

8.3   How to partition

Probably the most obvious, and the most common, way to partition the heap is by dividing it into non-overlapping ranges of addresses. At its simplest, each space occupies a contiguous chunk of heap memory so this mapping is one-to-one. It is more efficient to

---

[2]On the other hand, many current generation netbooks have limited memory, and page thrashing is a concern.

align chunks on power-of-two boundaries. In that case an object's space is encoded into the highest bits of its address and can be found by a shift or mask operation. Once the space identity is known, the collector can decide how to process the object (for example, mark it, copy it, ignore it, and so on). If the layout of the spaces is known at compile time, this test can be particularly efficient — a comparison against a constant. Otherwise, the space can be looked up, using these bits as an index into a table.

However, contiguous areas may not make efficient use of memory in 32-bit systems, as the range of virtual address space they may occupy must be reserved in advance. Although this does not commit physical memory pages, which can be mapped in and out of the contiguous space on demand, contiguous spaces are nevertheless inflexible and may lead to virtual memory exhaustion even though there are sufficient physical pages available. An additional difficulty in many cases is the tendency of the operating system to map code segments for libraries in unpredictable places — sometimes intentionally unpredictable in order to improve security. This makes it difficult to reserve large contiguous ranges of virtual address space. For the most part, these problems can be eliminated in a 64-bit address space.

The alternative is to implement spaces as discontiguous sets of chunks of address space. Typically, a discontiguous space comprises a list of fixed-size *frames* of contiguous virtual address space. As before, operations on frames are more efficient if frames are aligned on 2^n boundaries and are a multiple of the operating system's page size. Again, the disadvantage is that an object's space may need to be looked up in a table.

It is not always necessary to implement spaces by segregating objects physically. Instead, an object's space may be indicated by some bits in its header [Domani *et al.*, 2002]. Although this precludes determining its space through a fast address comparison, this approach nevertheless has some advantages. First, it allows objects to be partitioned according to properties that vary at run time, such as age or thread reachability, even in the case where the collector does not move objects. Second, it may facilitate handling objects that need to be pinned temporarily, for example because they are accessible to code that is not collector aware. Finally, run-time partitioning may be more accurate than choices made statically. For example, static *escape analyses* only provide a conservative estimate of whether an object may be shared. Static analyses do not yet scale to the very largest programs, and the presence of dynamic class loading commonly necessitates excessively conservative analysis, although Jones and King [2005] show how to obtain a more accurate static estimate of escapement in the context of thread-local allocation. If object escapement is tracked dynamically, then the distinction is between objects that are currently thread-local and those that are (or have been) accessible to more than one thread.[3] The downside of dynamic segregation is that it imposes more work on the write barrier. Whenever a pointer update causes its referent to become potentially shared, then the referent and its transitive closure must be marked as shared.

Finally in this section, we note that only collecting a subset of the partitions of the heap necessarily leads to a collector that is incomplete: it cannot reclaim any garbage in partitions that are not collected. Even if the collector takes care to scavenge every partition at some time, say on a round-robin basis, garbage cycles that span partitions will not be collected. In order to ensure completeness, some discipline must be imposed on the order in which partitions are collected and the destination partition to which unreclaimed objects are moved. A simple, and widely used, solution is to collect the entire heap when other tactics fail. However, more sophisticated strategies are possible as we shall see when we consider Mature Object Space collection (the 'Train' collector) [Hudson and Moss, 1992].

---

[3]We do not know of any system that reverts objects that were once shared, but are no longer, back to local.

8.4   When to partition

Partitioning decisions can be made statically (at compile time) or dynamically — when an object is allocated, at collection time or by the mutator as it accesses objects.

The best known partitioning scheme is generational, whereby objects are segregated by age, but this is just one form of age-related partitioning. Age-related collectors segregate objects by their age into a number of spaces. In this case, partitioning is performed dynamically, by the collector. As an object's age increases beyond some threshold, it is *promoted* (moved physically or logically) into the next space.

Objects may also be segregated by the *collector* because of constraints on moving objects. For example, mostly-copying collectors may not be able to move some objects while they are considered pinned — accessible by code that is not aware that objects' locations may change.

Partitioning decisions may be also made by the *allocator*. Most commonly, allocators determine from the size of an allocation request whether the object should be allocated in a large object space. In systems supporting explicit memory regions visible to the programmer or inferred by the compiler (such as scoped regions), the allocator or compiler can place objects in a particular region. Allocators in thread-local systems place objects in a heaplet of the executing thread unless they are directed that the object is shared. Some generational systems may attempt to co-locate a new object in the same region as one that will point to it, on the grounds that eventually it will be promoted there anyway [Guyer and McKinley, 2004].

An object's space may also be decided statically, by its type, because it is code, or through some other analysis. If it is known *a priori* that all objects of a particular kind share a common property, such as immortality, then the compiler can determine the space in which these objects should be allocated, and generate the appropriate code sequence. Generational collectors normally allocate in a nursery region set aside for new objects; later, the collector may decide to promote some of these objects to an older generation. However, if the compiler 'knows' that certain objects (for instance, those allocated at a particular point in the code) will usually be promoted, then it can *pretenure* these objects by allocating them directly into that generation [Cheng *et al.*, 1998; Blackburn *et al.*, 2001, 2007; Marion *et al.*, 2007]. Bruno *et al.* [2017] describe an object lifetime profiling tool and programmer controlled pretenuring support.

Finally, objects may be repartitioned by the mutator as it runs if the heap is managed by a concurrent collector (Chapter 15). Mutator access to objects may be mediated by *read* or *write barriers*, each of which may cause one or more objects to be moved or marked. The colouring of objects (black, grey, white) and the old/new space holding the object may be thought of as a partitioning. The mutator can also dynamically discriminate objects according to other properties. As we saw above, the write barrier used by Domani *et al.* [2002] logically segregates objects as they escape their allocating thread. Collaboration between the run-time system and the operating system can repartition objects as pages are swapped in and out [Hertz *et al.*, 2005].

In the next two chapters, we investigate a variety of partitioned garbage collectors. Chapter 9 looks at generational collectors in detail, while Chapter 10 examines a wide variety of other schemes, including both those based on different ways of exploiting object's ages and those based on non-temporal properties.

Chapter 9

Generational garbage collection

The goal of a collector is to reclaim the space occupied by dead objects. Tracing collectors (and copying collectors in particular) are most efficient if the space they manage contains few live objects. On the other hand, long-lived objects are handled poorly if the collector processes them repeatedly, either marking and sweeping, or copying them again and again from one semispace to another. We noted in Chapter 3 that long-lived objects tend to accumulate in the bottom of a heap managed by a mark-compact collector, and that some collectors avoid compacting this dense prefix. While this eliminates the cost of relocating these objects, they must still be traced and all references they contain must be updated.

Generational collectors extend this idea by not considering the oldest objects whenever possible. By concentrating reclamation effort on the youngest objects in order to exploit the *weak generational hypothesis* that most objects die young, they hope to maximise yield (recovered space) while minimising effort. Generational collectors segregate objects by age into *generations*, typically physically distinct areas of the heap. Younger generations are collected in preference to older ones, and objects that survive long enough are *promoted* (or *tenured*) from the generation being collected to an older one.

Most generational collectors manage younger generations by copying. If, as expected, few objects are live in the generation being collected, then the mark/cons ratio between the volume of data processed by the collector and the volume allocated for that collection will be low. The time taken to collect the youngest generation (or *nursery*) will in general depend on its size. By tuning its size, we can control the expected pause times for collection of a generation. Young generation pause times for a well-configured collector (running an application that conforms to the weak generational hypothesis) are typically of the order of tens to hundreds of microseconds on current hardware. Provided the interval between collections is sufficient, such a collector will be unobtrusive to many applications.

Occasionally a generational collector must collect the whole heap, for example when the allocator runs out of space and the collector estimates that insufficient space would be recovered by collecting only the younger generations. Generational collection therefore only improves expected pause times, not the worst case. On its own, it is not sufficient for real-time systems. We consider the requirements for garbage collection in a hard real-time environment and how to achieve them in Chapter 19.

Generational collection can also improve throughput by avoiding repeatedly processing long-lived objects. However, there are costs to pay. No garbage in an old generation can be reclaimed by collection of younger generations only: collection of long-lived objects that become garbage is not prompt. In order to be able to collect one generation without collecting others, generational collectors impose a bookkeeping overhead on mutators in order to track references that span generations, an overhead hoped to be small compared to

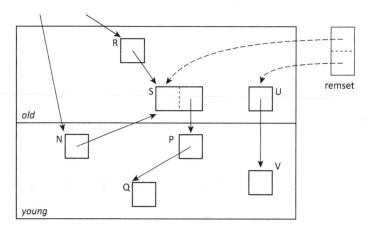

Figure 9.1: Inter-generational pointers. If live objects in the young generation are to be preserved without tracing the whole heap, a mechanism and a data structure are needed to remember objects S and U in the old generation that hold references to objects in the young generation.

the benefits of generational collection. Tuning generational collectors to meet throughput and pause-time goals simultaneously is a subtle art.

9.1 Example

Figure 9.1 shows a simple example of generational collection. This collector is using two generations. Objects are created in the young generation. At each *minor collection* (or nursery collection), objects in the young generation are promoted to the old generation if they are sufficiently old. Before the first collection, the young generation in this example contains four objects, N, P, Q and V, and the old generation three objects, R, S and U. R and N are reachable from outside the generational space; maybe some roots point to them. The collector is about to collect the young generation. Suppose that N, P and V were allocated some time ago but Q was only created shortly before the collector was invoked. The question of which objects should be promoted raises important issues.

A generational collector will promote objects it discovers from the young generation to the old one, provided they are old enough. This decision requires that it has a way of *measuring time* and *a mechanism for recording ages*. In our example, no objects in the young generation other than N are referenced by the roots, but P and Q are also clearly live since they are reachable from the roots via R and S. Most generational collectors do not examine the whole heap, but only trace the generation(s) being collected. Since the old generation is not to be traced here, a generational system must *record inter-generational pointers* such as the one from S to P in order that the collector may discover P and Q.

Such inter-generational pointers can arise in two ways. First, the mutator creates a pointer that requires tracking whenever it writes a pointer to an object in a generation G_1 into a field of an object in a generation G_2 that will be collected later than G_1. Second, the collector itself may create inter-generational pointers when it promotes an object. In the example, the collector will create such a pointer if it promotes P but not Q. In both cases, the inter-generational pointer can be detected with a write barrier. The mutator requires a *barrier* on pointer writes that records whether a pointer between generations has been written. A generational collector needs a similar copy write barrier to detect any inter-generational references created by promotion. In the example, the *remembered set* (remset) records the location of any objects (or fields) that may contain an inter-generational pointer of interest to the garbage collector, in this case S and U.

Unfortunately, treating the source of inter-generational pointers as roots for a minor collection exacerbates the problem of floating garbage. Minor collections are frequent but do not reclaim garbage in the old generation, such as U. Worse, U holds an inter-generational pointer so must be considered a root for the young generation. This *nepotism* will lead to the young garbage child V of the old garbage object U being promoted rather than reclaimed, thus further reducing the space available for live objects in the older generation.

9.2 Measuring time

Before objects can be segregated by their age, we need to decide how time is to be measured. There are two choices: bytes allocated or seconds elapsed. Wall-clock time is useful for understanding a system's external behaviour. How long does it run? What are the pause times for garbage collection and how are they distributed? Answers to these questions determine whether a system is fit for purpose: will it complete its task in sufficient time and will it be sufficiently responsive? One requirement might be that it does not disturb an interactive human user. Another requirement might be to meet a hard real-time guarantee (say, in an embedded system) or a soft one (where occasionally missing a deadline is not disastrous but missing many is). On the other hand, internally, object lifetimes are better measured by the number of bytes of heap space allocated between their birth and their death. Space-allocated is a largely machine-independent measure, although clearly a system with 64-bit addresses or integers will use more space than a 32-bit one. Bytes-allocated also directly measures the pressure placed upon the memory manager; it is closely related to the frequency with which the collector must be called.

Unfortunately, measuring time in terms of bytes allocated is tricky in multithreaded systems (where there are multiple application or system threads). A simple global measure of the volume of allocation may inflate the lifetime of an object, since the counter will include allocation by threads unrelated to the object in question [Jones and Ryder, 2008].

In practice generational collectors often measure time in terms of how many collections an object has survived, because this is more convenient to record and requires fewer bits, but the collections survived is appropriately considered to be an approximate proxy for actual age in terms of bytes allocated.

9.3 Generational hypotheses

The *weak generational hypothesis*, that most objects die young, appears to be widely valid, regardless of programming paradigm or implementation language. Foderaro and Fateman [1981] found that, for a computer algebra system written in MacLisp, 98% of the volume of data recovered by a collection had been allocated since the previous one. Zorn [1989] reported that between 50% and 90% of Common Lisp objects survive less than 10 kilobytes of allocation. The story is similar for functional languages. For Haskell, between 75% and 95% of heap data died before they were 10 kilobytes old and only 5% lived longer than 1 megabyte [Sansom and Peyton Jones, 1993]. Appel [1992] observed that Standard ML/NJ reclaimed 98% of any given generation at each collection, and Stefanović and Moss [1994] found that only 2% to 8% of allocated data survived the 100-kilobyte threshold.

It also holds for many programs written in object-oriented languages. Ungar [1986] found that less than 7% of Smalltalk objects lived beyond 140 kilobytes. Dieckmann and

Hölzle [1999] reported that the volume of Java objects in the SPECjvm98 benchmark suite surviving 100 kilobytes varied between 1% and 40%, and that less than 21% lived beyond 1 megabyte although the proportion varied significantly from one application to another. Blackburn *et al.* [2006b] found that on average less than 9% of objects allocated by the SPECjvm98 and DaCapo benchmark suites escaped from a 4-megabyte nursery, although there was wide variation between benchmarks; note that this is an upper bound on the volume of objects living longer than 4 megabytes since some escapees may only have been allocated shortly before the nursery was collected. Jones and Ryder [2008] found bimodal lifetime distributions common in Java applications; between 65% and 96% of DaCapo objects survived no longer than 64 kilobytes, with 3% to 16% being immortal or living longer than 4 megabytes. Even in imperative languages without automatic memory management support, the lifetimes of many objects are short. Barrett and Zorn [1993] reported that more than 50% of allocated data died within 10 kilobytes and less than 10% survived 32 kilobytes in allocation-intensive C programs.

On the other hand, there is much less evidence for the *strong generational hypothesis* that, even for objects that are not newly created, younger objects will have a lower survival rate than older ones [Hayes, 1991]. Simple models like the weak generational hypothesis account adequately in many programs for the behaviour of objects overall. However, once the shortest-lived objects are discounted, objects' demographics over a longer timescale are more complex. Object lifetimes are not random. They commonly live in clumps and die all at the same time, because programs operate in phases [Dieckmann and Hölzle, 1999; Jones and Ryder, 2008]. A significant number of objects may never die. The lifetime of objects may be correlated with their size, although opinion has differed on this [Caudill and Wirfs-Brock, 1986; Ungar and Jackson, 1988; Barrett and Zorn, 1993]. However, as we saw above, there are other reasons why we might want to treat large objects specially.

9.4   Generations and heap layout

A wide variety of strategies have been used to organise generations. Collectors may use two or more generations, which may be segregated physically or logically. Each generation may be bounded in size, or the size of one space may be traded against that of another. The structure within a generation may be flat or it may comprise a number of *age-based* subspaces, called *steps* or *buckets*. Generations may also hold their own large object subspaces. Each generation may be managed by a different algorithm.

The primary goals of generational garbage collection are reduced pause times and improved throughput. Assuming that the youngest generation is processed by copying collection, expected pause times depend largely on the volume of data that survives a minor collection of that generation, which in turn depends on the size of the generation. However, if the size of the nursery is too small, collection will be fast but little memory will be reclaimed as the objects in the nursery will have had insufficient time to die. This will have many undesirable consequences.

First, young generation collections will be too frequent. As well as its copying cost proportional to the volume of surviving objects — which will be higher since objects have had less time to die — each collection must also bear the cost of stopping threads and scanning their stacks.

Second, the older generation will fill too fast and then it too will have to be collected. High promotion rates will cause time-consuming older generation or full heap collections to take place too frequently. In addition, premature promotion will increase the incidence of nepotism, as 'tenured' garbage objects in the old generation preserve their offspring in the young generation, artificially inflating the survival rate as those dead children will also be promoted.

Third, there is considerable evidence that newly created objects are modified more frequently than older ones. If these young objects are promoted prematurely, their high mutation rate will put further pressure on the mutator's write barrier; this is particularly undesirable if the cost of the write barrier is high. Any transfer of overheads between mutator and collector needs careful evaluation with realistic workloads. Typically, the collector will account for a much smaller proportion of execution time than the mutator in any well configured system. For example, suppose a write barrier comprises just a few instructions in its fast path yet accounts for 5% of overall execution time; suppose further that the collector accounts for 10% of overall running time. It would be quite easy for an alternative write barrier implementation to double the cost of the barrier, thus adding 5% to overall execution time. To recover this, garbage collection time must be reduced by 50%, which would be hard to do.

Finally, by promoting objects the program's working set may be diluted. Generational organisation is a balancing act between keeping minor collections as short as possible, minimising the number of minor and the much more expensive full, *major collections*, and avoiding passing too much of the cost of memory management to the mutator. We now look at how this can be achieved.

9.5 Multiple generations

Adding further generations is one solution to the dilemma of how to preserve short pause times for nursery collections without incurring excessively frequent full heap collections, because the oldest generation has filled too soon. The role of the intermediate generations is to filter out any objects that have survived collection of the youngest generation but do not live much longer. If a garbage collector promotes all live objects *en masse* from the youngest generation, the survivors will include the most recently allocated objects despite the expectation that most of these will die very soon. By using multiple generations, the size of the youngest generation can be kept small enough to meet expected pause time requirements without increasing the volume of objects dying in the oldest generation shortly after their promotion.

Using multiple generations has a number of drawbacks. Most systems will collect all younger generations when any older generation is collected. This offers the benefit that pointers need to be tracked in only one direction: old to young, which occur less frequently than young to old. Although the time taken to collect an intermediate generation will be less than that required to collect the full heap, pause times will be longer than those for nursery collections. Multiple generation collectors are also more complex to implement and may introduce additional overheads to the collector's tracing loop, as this performance critical code must now distinguish between multiple generations rather than just two (which can often be accomplished with a single check against an address, maybe a compile-time constant). Increasing the number of generations will tend to increase the number of inter-generational pointers created, which in turn may increase the pressure on the mutator's write barrier, depending on implementation. It will also increase the size of the root set for younger generations since objects have been promoted that would not have been if some of the space used for the intermediate generations had been used to increase the size of the young generation.

Although many early generational collectors for Smalltalk and Lisp offered multiple generations, most modern generational collectors for object-oriented systems provide just two. Even where collectors provide more than two generations, such as those for functional languages where allocation and death rates are prodigiously high, often only two generations are used by default [Marlow *et al.*, 2008]. Instead, mechanisms within generations, especially the youngest generation, can be used to control promotion rates.

9.6   Age recording

En masse promotion

Age recording and promotion policy are tightly coupled. Multiple generations provide an imprecise way of recording objects' ages. Figure 9.2 shows four ways in which a young generation can be structured to control object promotion. We discuss each of these in turn. The simplest arrangement is for each generation except the oldest to be implemented as a single semispace (see Figure 9.2a). When that generation is collected, all surviving objects are promoted *en masse* to the next. This structure has the advantages of simplicity and optimal utilisation of the memory devoted to the young generation. There is neither any need to record per-object ages nor is there any necessity for copy reserve space in each generation (except for the last if indeed it is managed by copying). The generational collectors used by the MMTk memory manager in the Jikes RVM Java virtual machine use *en masse* promotion in this way [Blackburn *et al.*, 2004b]. Both the Android Runtime (ART) and Webkit's *Riptide* [Pizlo, 2017] use variations of *en masse* promotion for generational mark-sweep collection that use *sticky mark bits* (originally introduced for a conservative generational collector [Demers *et al.*, 1990]). Here, minor collections simply leave the mark bits set. Thus a marked object is implicitly also an old one, and the write barrier records a marked object into the remembered set the first time it is updated to refer to an unmarked (and thus young) object. A major collection simply resets the mark bits and discards the remembered set before starting to mark. However, Zorn [1993] has suggested that *en masse* promotion of every live object (in a Lisp system) may lead to promotion rates 50% to 100% higher than can be achieved by requiring objects to survive more than one minor collection before they are promoted.

Figure 9.3, due to Wilson and Moher [1989b], illustrates the survival rates from the youngest generation that might be obtained by delaying promotion for one or two collections. The curves show the fraction of objects that survive a future scavenge if they were allocated at time t, assuming that most objects die young. The closer an object is born to a collection, the more likely it is to survive that collection. Let us focus on the area of the graph between scavenges n and $n + 1$. Curve (b) shows the proportion of objects that will survive one scavenge: most objects will die before the next collection (the data in the light grey area). The data in the black area below curve (c) will survive two scavenges. If the policy is to promote *en masse* all objects that survive the collection, then the data in the dark grey and black areas below curve (b) will be promoted. However, if promotion is restricted to those objects that survive two collections, then only the data in the black area below curve (c) will be tenured. By requiring a copy count greater than one, the very youngest objects (which we can expect to die soon) are denied tenure, and the promotion rate is substantially reduced. In principal, increasing the copy count for promotion is likely to pay diminishing returns [Ungar, 1984; Shaw, 1988; Ungar and Jackson, 1988]; Wilson [1989] suggested that it may be necessary to increase the count by a factor of four or more to reduce the number of remaining survivors by half. However, the user-configurable tenuring thresholds for the HotSpot Java virtual machine's modern collectors typically lie between 7 and 15 copies.

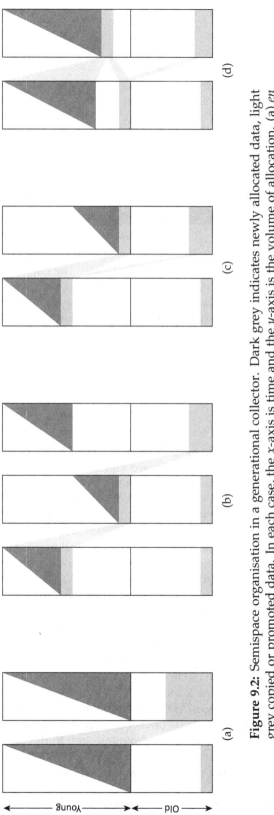

Figure 9.2: Semispace organisation in a generational collector. Dark grey indicates newly allocated data, light grey copied or promoted data. In each case, the *x*-axis is time and the *y*-axis is the volume of allocation. (a) *en masse* promotion; (b) aging semispaces (records per space age); (c) aging semispaces (records per object age); (d) survivor spaces promotion (records per object age).

Jones [1996]. Reprinted by permission.

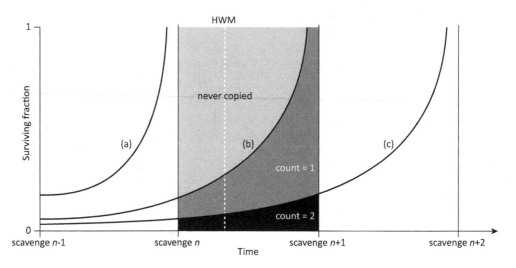

Figure 9.3: Survival rates with a copy count of 1 or 2. The curves show the fraction of objects that will survive a future collection if they were born at time x. Curve (b) shows the proportion that will survive one collection and curve (c) the proportion that will survive two. The coloured areas show the proportions of objects that will not be copied or will be promoted (copied) under different copy count regimes.

Wilson and Moher [1989b], doi: 10.1145/74877.74882
© 1989 Association for Computing Machinery, Inc. Reprinted by permission.

Aging semispaces

Promotion can be delayed by structuring a generation into two or more *aging spaces*. This allows objects to be copied between the fromspace and tospace an arbitrary number of times within the generation before they are promoted. In the orignal Lieberman and Hewitt generational collector [1983], a generation is collected several times before all survivors are eventually promoted *en masse*. In terms of the aging semispaces of Figure 9.2b, either all live objects in fromspace are evacuated to tospace within this generation or all are promoted to the next generation, depending on the age of the generation as a whole. While this arrangement allows the older members of the generation time to die, the very youngest will still be promoted, possibly prematurely.

Sun's *ExactVM*[1] also implemented the younger of two generations as a pair of semispaces (see Figure 9.2c) but controlled promotion of an individual object by stealing five bits from one of two header words to record its age. In this case, individual live objects can either be evacuated to tospace or promoted to the next generation. While this throttles the promotion of the youngest objects, it adds a test and an addition operation to the work done to process live objects in the young generation.

Bucket brigade and *step* systems allow a somewhat finer discrimination between object ages without maintaining per-object ages. Here, a generation is divided into a number of subspaces and objects are advanced from one bucket or step to the next at each collection. Some step systems advance all surviving objects from one step to the next at each collection: live objects from the oldest step are promoted to the next generation. Here, an *n*-step system guarantees that objects will not reach the next generation until they have survived

---

[1]Later called the Sun Microsystems Laboratories *Virtual Machine for Research*; for details see White and Garthwaite [1998].

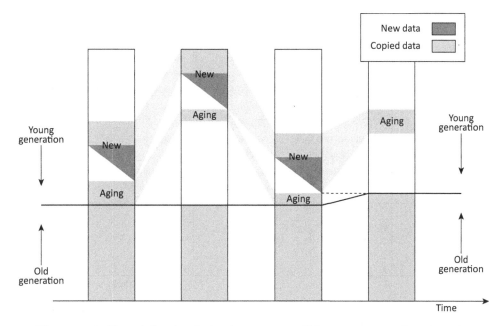

Figure 9.4: Shaw's bucket brigade system. Objects are copied within the young generation from a creation space to an aging semispace. By placing the aging semispace adjacent to the old generation at even numbered collections, objects can be promoted to the old generation simply by moving the boundary between generations.

Jones [1996]. Reprinted by permission.

n scavenges. Glasgow Haskell allows an arbitrary number of steps in each generation (although the default is two in the young generation and one in others), as did the *UMass GC Toolkit* [Hudson *et al.*, 1991]. Shaw [1988] further divides each step into a pair of semispaces in his bucket brigade scheme. Survivors are copied between each pair of semispaces b times before advancing to the next step. Thus, the two-bucket scheme guarantees that objects will not reach the next generation until they have survived between $2b$ and $2b - 1$ scavenges. Shaw arranged his scheme to simplify promotion. Figure 9.4 shows an instance of his scheme with two buckets: $n = 3$ so objects are copied up to three times within a bucket before being evacuated to the aging bucket or promoted. Because Shaw's generations are contiguous, he can merge the aging bucket with the old generation by delaying the promotion step until the oldest bucket's tospace is adjacent to the old generation. At this point the bucket is promoted by adjusting the boundary between the generations. The aging spaces of Figure 9.2c have some similarities with a two-bucket scheme but pay the cost of manipulating age bits in the headers of survivors.

It is important to understand the differences between steps and generations. Both segregate objects by age, but different generations are collected at different frequencies whereas all the steps of a generation are collected at the same time. Generations also differ in how pointers that span spaces are treated. Because one generation may be collected later than another, it is essential to track pointers from an older generation to a younger one. On the other hand, there is no need to track inter-step pointers. By using steps in the youngest generation (where most mutation occurs), and by reducing premature collection, the load on the write barrier can be reduced while also controlling promotion, without need for per-object age records.

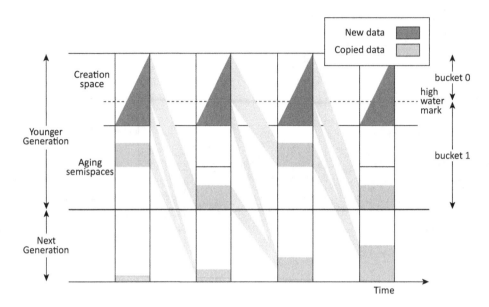

Figure 9.5: High water marks. Objects are copied from a fixed creation space to an aging semispace within a younger generation and then promoted to an older generation. Although all survivors in an aging semispace are promoted, by adjusting a 'high water mark', we can choose to copy or promote an object in the creation space simply through an address comparison.

Wilson and Moher [1989b], doi: 10.1145/74877.74882
© 1989 Association for Computing Machinery, Inc. Reprinted by permission.

Survivor spaces and flexibility

All the semispace organisations described above are wasteful of space since they reserve half the space in the generation for copying. Ungar [1984] organised the young generation as one large *creation space* (often called *eden*) and two smaller buckets or *survivor semispaces* (see Figure 9.2d). As usual, objects are allocated in eden, which is scavenged alongside the survivor fromspace at each minor collection. All live eden objects are promoted to the survivor tospace. Live objects in survivor fromspace are either evacuated to tospace within the young generation or promoted to the next generation, depending on their age. This organisation can improve space utilisation because the eden region is very much larger than the two semispaces. For example, the HotSpot Java virtual machine has a default eden versus survivor space ratio of 8:1, thus using a copy reserve of 6.25% of the young generation. HotSpot's Ergonomics promotion policy does not impose a fixed age limit for promotion but instead attempts to keep the survivor space half empty. In contrast, the other semispace schemes waste half of the nursery space on copy reserve.

The *Opportunistic* garbage collector [Wilson and Moher, 1989b] used a bucket brigade system with the space parsimony of survivor spaces and some flexibility in promotion age. The age at which objects are promoted can be varied down to the granularity of an individual object without the overhead of having to store or manipulate each object's age. As before, the young generation is divided into a creation space and a pair of aging spaces. The aging spaces are not semispaces but simply act as steps. At each minor collection, survivors from the creation space are evacuated to one of the aging spaces; survivors of the other aging space are promoted. With just this organisation, promoted objects would have a copy count of two. However, Wilson and Moher observe that objects are placed in the creation space in allocation order. By drawing a *high water mark* across creation space, younger objects (above the line in Figure 9.5) can be distinguished from older ones by a simple address comparison. Younger members of the creation space are treated as members of bucket 0. Older members and all of the aging space become bucket 1; survivors of this bucket are promoted.

This scheme limits the promotion age to a maximum of two minor collections, and so does not offer as wide a range of promotion age as those that explicitly store ages in objects or associate them with spaces (such as the semispace organisations we considered earlier). However, any non-integral promotion threshold between one and two can be selected, and modified at any time, including during scavenges. We can see the effect in Figure 9.3. Any data in the dark grey or black regions to the left of the dashed white high water mark line will be promoted at their first collection. Those to the right of the high water mark line will be promoted if they are in the black area below curve (c), or evacuated to die later in the aging space if they are in the grey area above the curve. Wilson and Moher used this scheme with three generations for the byte-coded Scheme-48; it was also used in Standard ML with up to 14 generations [Reppy, 1993].

9.7 Adapting to program behaviour

The Opportunistic collector is an example of a garbage collector that can adapt its promotion policy as a program runs. It provides a particularly fine-grained and simple mechanism. Adaptation is needed because objects' lifetime demographics are neither random nor stationary. Instead, real programs (unlike toy ones or synthetic benchmarks) tend to operate in phases. There are a wide range of common patterns of behaviour. A set of live objects may gradually accumulate and then die all at once. Alternatively, its size may reach a plateau after which the objects live for a long time. Ungar and Jackson [1988] cite the example of objects born in a clump that slowly diminishes, "rather like a pig that has been swallowed by a python." Demographics that do not adhere strictly to the weak generational hypothesis can cause problems for generational collectors. If a large volume of data lives for sufficient time to reach an older generation and then dies, performance will suffer. To deal with this, Ungar and Jackson have argued for flexible mechanisms that control tenuring [1988; 1992].

It is useful to be able to adapt garbage collectors in general to the mutator's behaviour, for example to reduce expected pause time or to improve overall throughput. The simplest scheduling mechanism is to invoke the collector only when the allocator runs out of space, but a generational memory manager can control pause times by adjusting the size of the youngest generation: smaller nurseries reduce the volume of objects that must be scavenged by young generation collection. The size of the space also affects the rate of promotion from one generation to another. If a space is too small to give young objects sufficient time to die, then the promotion rate will be higher. Conversely, if the nursery is very large, the interval between collections will be greater and a smaller fraction of objects will survive to reach the older generation.

Appel-style garbage collection

Appel [1989a] introduced an adaptive generational layout for Standard ML that gives as much room as possible to the young generation for a given memory budget, rather than using fixed-size spaces. This scheme is designed for environments where infant mortality is high: typically only 2% of ML's young generation survived a collection. The heap is divided into three regions: the old generation, a copy reserve and the young generation

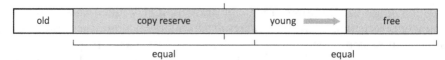

(a) Before a minor collection, the copy reserve must be at least as large as the young generation.

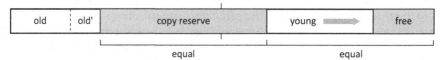

(b) At a minor collection, survivors are copied into the copy reserve, extending the old generation. The copy reserve and young generation are reduced but still of equal size.

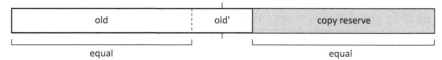

(c) After a minor collection and before a major collection. Only objects in the oldest region, old, will be evacuated into the copy reserve. After the evacuation, all live old objects can be moved to the beginning of the heap.

Figure 9.6: Appel's simple generational collector. Grey areas are empty.

(see Figure 9.6a). Nursery collections promote all young survivors *en masse* to the end of the old generation (Figure 9.6b). After the collection, any space not needed for old generation objects is split equally to create the copy reserve and a new young generation. If the space allocatable to the young generation falls below some threshold, the full heap is collected.

As in any scheme managed by copying, Appel must ensure that the copy reserve is sufficient to accommodate the worst case, that all old and young objects are live. The most conservative way is to ensure that $old + young \leq reserve$. However, Appel can initiate full heap collections less frequently, only requiring that $old \leq reserve \wedge young \leq reserve$ for safety, arguing as follows. Before a minor collection, the reserve is sufficient even if all *young* objects survive. Immediately after a minor collection, all newly promoted objects in old' are live: they do not need to be moved. The reserve is sufficient to accommodate all previously promoted objects in *old* (Figure 9.6c). Following the scavenge of *old*, all surviving data (now at the top of the heap) can be block moved to the bottom of the heap. We note that in this collect-twice approach any cycle of dead objects that lies partly in the nursery and partly in the old generation will be preserved. However, it will be reclaimed during the next full collection since it is then contained entirely in the old generation.

The entire generational universe in Appel was contiguous, but Appel-style collectors can also be implemented in block-structured heaps, which avoids the necessity of sliding the live data to the start of the heap after a major collection. Shrinking nurseries can also be used in conjunction with an old generation managed by a non-moving algorithm, such as mark-sweep.

The advantage of Appel-style collection is that by dynamically adapting the size of the copy reserve it offers good memory utilisation and reduces the number of collections needed compared with configurations that use *en masse* promotion and fix the size of the young generation. However, some caution is necessary to avoid thrashing the collector.

Benchmarks that have high allocation rates but promote little data from the young generation are common: indeed this was one of the motivations for Appel's design. This can lead
to the situation where the space allotted to the nursery shrinks to become so small that it
leads to overly frequent minor collections but never enough data is promoted to trigger
a major collection. To combat this, the old generation should be collected whenever the
young generation's size falls below a minimum.

Feedback-controlled promotion

Other schemes for controlling promotion rate are more directly related to pause time goals.
Demographic feedback-mediated tenuring [Ungar and Jackson, 1988, 1992] attempts to smooth
out long pauses incurred by bursts of promotion of objects that die soon after promotion.
The volume of objects promoted at one collection is used as a predictor for the length
of the next collection, and to throttle or accelerate promotion. The excess of survivors
above a desired maximum becomes an index into a table indicating the age threshold for
promotion that should be used at the next collection. Although this mechanism can control
promotion rates, it cannot demote objects from an older to a younger generation. Barrett
and Zorn [1995] vary a *threatening boundary* between two generations in both directions.
The cost is that they must track more pointers as they cannot predict where the inter-
generational boundary will lie.

The HotSpot family of collectors introduced *Ergonomics,*[2] an adaptive mechanism for
resizing generations based on user provided goals, in JDK 1.5.0. Ergonomics configures a
collector to preferentially meet one of two soft goals — maximum pause time and throughput — rather than attempting to provide hard real-time guarantees. Once the preferred
goal is met, the collector will target the other. In order to achieve the pause time goal, the
collector measures the average pause times so far, weighted towards more recent pauses.
If this average plus its variance is greater that the maximum pause time goal specified, the
collector will adjust heap and space sizes in order to try to meet this goal. The collector
monitors the throughput goal by considering the time spent inside and outside collecting
garbage. If the ratio of collection time to mutator time is exceeded, the collector may increase the size of the heap and the generations, the latter in proportion to the time taken to
collect each generation. Once it has met the pause time and throughput goals, the collector
will start to reduce sizes until one of the goals cannot be met (invariably the throughput
goal). By default, sizes are increased more aggressively than they are decreased.

Vengerov [2009] offers an analytical model for the throughput of HotSpot. From this
model he derives a practical algorithm for tuning the collector by adjusting the relative
sizes of HotSpot's two generations and the promotion threshold, the number of collections
that a young object must survive before it is promoted. He makes an important observation that it is insufficient to consider whether to adjust the promotion threshold simply on
the basis of whether it would reduce the number of objects promoted. Instead, it is essential also to consider the ratio of free space in the old generation after a major collection to
the volume promoted into it at each minor collection. His *ThruMax* algorithm provides
a co-evolutionary framework for alternately adjusting the size of the young generation
and the promotion threshold. In brief, ThruMax is invoked after the first major collection
and once the volume of data in HotSpot's survivor spaces reaches a steady state (between
75% and 90% of the young generation's survivor space for two consecutive minor collections). ThruMax first increases the nursery size S until it reaches the neighbourhood of
an optimum value (discovered by observing that S has been decreased and so it is probably oscillating around this value). Then, ThruMax adjusts the tenuring threshold until the

---

[2]https://docs.oracle.com/en/java/javase/18/gctuning/ergonomics.html

model shows that a further change would decrease throughput. After this, a new episode of adjustments is begun provided that there is no pressure to decrease S and sufficient minor collections are expected before the next major collection.

Overall, sophisticated collectors like HotSpot present the user with a large number of tuning knobs, which are likely to be interdependent.

9.8   Inter-generational pointers

A generation's roots must be discovered before it can be collected. As we saw in the example in Figure 9.1, the roots for a generation consist not only of pointer values held in registers, stacks and globals but also any references to objects in this generation from objects in other parts of the heap that are not being collected at the same time. These typically include older generations and spaces outside the generational heap, such as large object spaces and spaces that are never collected, including those for immortal objects and possibly code. As we noted above, inter-generational pointers are created in just three ways, by initialising writes as an object is created, by other mutator updates to pointer slots and when objects are moved to different generations. In general such pointers must be detected as they are created and recorded so that they can be used as roots when a generation is collected. We shall call any pointer that must be recorded an *interesting* pointer.

An interesting case of objects outside the generational heap are objects in the *boot image*: those objects present when the system starts. A generational system can handle them in at least three ways: it can *trace* through the boot image objects, which has the benefit of not retaining objects only reachable from boot image objects that have become unreachable; it can *scan* the boot image objects to find references from them into the generational heap; or it can *remember* the interesting pointers that reside in boot image objects. Tracing can be expensive, and might only be applied during full collections. Thus it would be applied in conjunction with scanning or remembered sets. Scanning has the virtue of not requiring a write barrier on updates to boot image objects, but the down side that the collector must consider more fields to find the interesting pointers. If used in conjunction with tracing, then after a trace the collector should zero the fields of unreachable boot image objects, to prevent misinterpretation of pointers that may refer to old garbage now reclaimed. Remembered sets have their usual virtues and costs, and also do not require zeroing of unreachable boot image objects' fields.

Remembered sets

The data structure used to record inter-generational pointers is called a *remembered set* (remset).[3] Remembered sets record the location of possible *sources* of pointers (for example, U and the second slot of S in the example) from one space of the heap to another. The source rather than the target of an interesting pointer is recorded for two reasons. It allows a moving collector to update the source field with the new address of an object that has been copied or promoted. A source field may be updated more than once between successive collections, so remembering the source ensures that the collector only processes the object that is referenced by the field at the time of the collection, and not the targets of any obsolete pointers. Thus, the remembered set for any generation holds those locations at which a potentially interesting pointer to an object in this generation has been stored. Remembered set implementations vary in the precision with which they record these locations. The choice of precision is a trade-off between overhead on the mutator, space for

---

[3]Our terminology differs from that of Jones [1996] who distinguished card table schemes from other remembered set implementations.

the remembered sets and the collector's cost of processing them. Note that the term remembered 'set' is sometimes a misnomer because an implementation may allow duplicate entries (and hence be a multiset).

Clearly, it is important to detect and record as few pointers as possible. Pointer writes by the collector as it moves objects are easily identified. Pointer stores by the mutator can be detected by a software write barrier, emitted by the compiler at each pointer store. This may not be possible if an uncooperative compiler is used. In this case, the locations where writes have occurred can often be determined from the operating system's virtual memory manager.

The prevalence of pointer stores will vary between different programming languages and their implementations. From a static analysis of a suite of SPUR Lisp programs, Zorn [1990] found the frequency of pointer stores to be 13% to 15%, although Appel found a lower static frequency of 3% for Lisp [1987] and a dynamic, run-time frequency of 1% for ML [1989a]. State-based languages can be expected to have a higher incidence of destructive pointer writes. Java programs vary widely in terms of the frequency of pointer stores: for example, Dieckmann and Hölzle [1999] found that between 6% and 70% of heap accesses were stores (the latter was an outlier, the next highest was 46%). But even in pure functional languages like Haskell, the lazy evaluation mechanism will destructively update a very great number of thunks.

Pointer direction

Fortunately, not all stores need to be detected or recorded. Some languages (such as implementations of ML) store procedure activation records in the heap. If these frames are scanned as part of the root set at every collection, the pointer slots they contain can be discovered by the techniques we discuss later in Chapter 11. If stack writes can be identified as such by the compiler, then no barrier need be emitted on writes to these stack frames. Furthermore, many stores will refer to objects in the same partition. Although such stores will probably be detected, the pointers are not interesting from a generational point of view and need not be recorded.

If we impose a discipline on the order in which generations are collected, then the number of inter-generational pointers that need to be recorded can be reduced further. By guaranteeing that younger generations will be collected whenever an older one is, young-to-old pointers need not be recorded (for example, the pointer in N in Figure 9.1). Many pointer writes are initialising stores to newly created objects — Zorn [1990] estimated that 90% to 95% of Lisp pointer stores were initialising (and that of the remaining non-initialising stores two-thirds were to objects in the young generation). By definition, these pointers must refer to older objects. Unfortunately, many languages separate the allocation of objects from the initialisation of their fields, making it hard to separate the non-initialising stores that may create old-young pointers. Other languages provide more support for the compiler to identify pointer stores that do not require a write barrier. For example, the majority of pointer writes in a pure, lazy functional language like Haskell will refer to older objects; old-new pointers can only arise when a thunk (a function applied to its arguments) is evaluated and overwritten with a pointer value. ML, a strict language with side effects, requires the programmer to annotate mutable variables explicitly; writes to these objects are the only source of old-to-young references.

Object-oriented languages like Java present a more complex scene. Here the programming paradigm centres on updating objects' states, which naturally leads to old-young pointers being more frequent. Nevertheless, many programmers write in a somewhat functional style, eschewing side effects, and for many applications the overwhelming majority of pointer stores will be to initialise objects in the young generation. However, Blackburn *et al.* [2006b] demonstrate that there is considerable variation in behaviour not only between applications but also within individual ones. Their report strikingly contrasts pointer stores — in terms of their direction and distance (between the time the source and target objects were created) — and pointers discovered in the graph. One cause of these differences is that there may be many writes to the same location: this has implications for how remembered sets are implemented.

Different pointer filtering will be necessary in heaps with multiple independently collected spaces. For example, a collector may apply heuristics to decide which space to scavenge with the intention of prioritising those spaces containing the smallest volume of live objects. In this case, the write barrier must remember pointers in both directions, although if the policy decision is made always to collect the young generation at the same time, we can ignore writes to the nursery (which we expect to be prevalent). Because this design is likely to increase the number of pointers to be remembered, it is best used with an implementation where the size of the remembered set does not depend on the number of pointers remembered. We discuss implementation of write barriers and remembered sets in Chapter 11.

9.9 Space management

Young generations are usually managed by evacuation, either copying surviving objects to a fresh semispace in the same generation or to a space in an older generation. Young generation collections are expected to be frequent and brief, on the assumption of few survivors and hence little to trace. Collections of older generations, on the other hand, are expected to be infrequent, but when they do occur, they are expensive as all younger generations must also be collected unless we are willing to pay the cost of a bidirectional write barrier. Commonly, a collection of the oldest generation will also collect all other spaces in the heap except any immortal spaces or the boot image, although references held in these spaces must be used as roots and may be updated. A full heap collection will not use remembered sets (except for locations in the immortal space or boot image, and even these are unnecessary if those spaces are scanned).

A wider range of strategies can be used to manage the oldest generation. One possibility is semispace copying, but this may not be the best choice. It requires a copy reserve of half the generational heap, and so limits the room available for its own fromspace and to younger generations, thus increasing the frequency of collections at all levels. It also leads to long-lived data being moved repeatedly. Mark-sweep collection offers better utilisation of memory, especially in small heaps [Blackburn *et al.*, 2004a]. The argument against free-list allocation has been that it is slower than sequential allocation and its locality is not so predictable. But this is more a problem for object creation, where allocation rates are high, allocation order provides good spatial locality for young objects [Blackburn *et al.*, 2004a]. The drawback of mark-sweep collection is that it is non-moving and may eventually degrade as the old generation fragments. The solution is to run an additional compacting pass over the old generation, not necessarily every time but certainly when fragmentation is damaging performance. Compaction can also treat very long-lived data specially. As we noted in Chapter 3, these will tend to end up compacted into a 'dense prefix' at the bottom of the old generation. The HotSpot mark-compact collector, for example, avoids moving this sediment at the cost of some (user-specified) degree of fragmentation.

Generational collectors almost always distinguish generations by physical segregation. This requires younger generations to be managed by copying collection. A copying collector such as Appel's conservatively requires copy reserve space equal to the size of generation being collected as all objects may survive in the worst case. However, in practice most

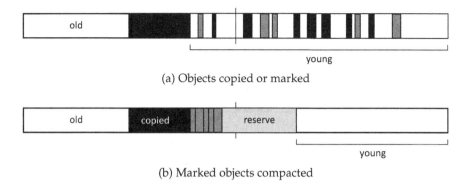

(a) Objects copied or marked

(b) Marked objects compacted

Figure 9.7: Switching between copying and marking the young generation. (a) The copy reserve is full. Black objects from the young generation have been copied into the old generation. Grey objects have been marked but not copied. All other new objects are dead. (b) The compaction pass has slid the grey objects into the old generation.

objects do not survive a young generation collection. However, some collectors do not segregate generations. We mentioned above that the Android Runtime (ART) and Webkit's Riptide [Pizlo, 2017] collectors manage all objects in-place, with mark-sweep collection.

Better space utilisation can be obtained with a smaller copy reserve and switching from copying to compacting collection whenever the reserve is too small [McGachey and Hosking, 2006]. Here, the collector must be able to switch between copying and marking on the fly because it will discover that the copy reserve is too small only during a collection. Figure 9.7a shows the state of the heap once all survivors have been identified: copied objects are shown in black and the remaining live young objects are marked grey. The next step is to compact the marked objects to one end of the nursery (Figure 9.7b); as usual, this takes several passes. Unfortunately, compaction will destroy the forwarding addresses left in the black objects in the young generation. McGachey and Hosking solve this problem by requiring the first pass over the grey young generation objects to fix up references to copied objects. Next, they move the marked objects with Jonkers's sliding compactor (see Section 3.3 in Chapter 3) because this threaded algorithm does not require additional space in object headers. A better solution might be to adapt Compressor for this purpose (discussed in Section 3.4), since it neither requires extra space in object headers nor overwrites any part of live objects. With a copy reserve of 10% of the heap, they gained improvements in performance of 4% on average — but sometimes up to 20% — over MMTk collectors that manage the old generation by either copying or mark-sweep collection.

9.10 Older-first garbage collection

Generational garbage collection has proved to be a highly effective way of managing short-lived objects for a wide range of applications. However, as we saw in Section 9.7, longer-lived objects may be more problematic. Generational collectors operate by collecting a youngest prefix of the set of objects in the heap and ignoring other objects. This prefix may be one or more generations depending on whether a collection is a nursery collection, an intermediate collection (in a configuration that uses more than two generations) or a full heap collection. Adaptive techniques that control the promotion of objects can be thought of as ways of varying the age boundary of the young (to be collected) prefix in order to give young objects more time to die. However, generational garbage collection is but one

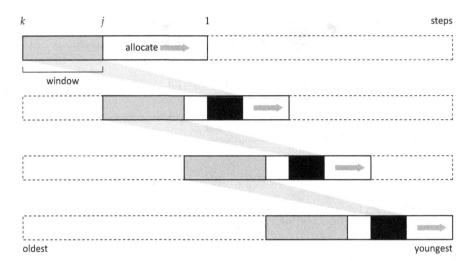

Figure 9.8: Renewal-Older-First garbage collection. At each collection, the objects least recently collected are scavenged and survivors are placed after the youngest objects.

design that avoids collecting the whole heap (we look at schemes outside an age-based context in the next chapter). Possibilities for age-based collection include the following.

Youngest-only (generational) collection: Here, the collector condemns only the *youngest* objects in the heap.

Oldest-only collection: Similarly, we could imagine a collector that only considered the *oldest* objects in the heap, that is, those that have had the longest opportunity to die. However, it is unlikely that such a strategy would be effective as it would spend much of its time repeatedly processing immortal or very long-lived objects. We noted earlier that some collectors deliberately avoid processing this ancient sediment for precisely this reason.

Older-first collection: The collector aims to focus effort on *middle-aged* objects. It gives the youngest objects sufficient time to die but reduces the time spent considering very long-lived objects (although these are examined from time to time).

Older-first collection presents two challenges: how to identify those objects considered to be 'older' and the increased complexity of managing pointers into the condemned set since interesting pointers may point in either direction (oldest to older, or youngest to older). In the rest of this section, we consider two different solutions to these problems.

Renewal-Older-First garbage collection. One approach is to consider the 'age' of an object to be the time since it was created or last collected, whichever is most recent [Clinger and Hansen, 1997; Hansen, 2000; Hansen and Clinger, 2002]. *Renewal-Older-First* always collects the 'oldest' prefix of the heap. To simplify remembered set management, the heap is divided into k equally sized steps. Allocation is always into the lowest-numbered empty step. When the heap is full, the oldest $k - j$ steps (the grey window in Figure 9.8) are condemned, and any survivors are evacuated to a copy reserve at the youngest end of the heap (the black region in the figure). Thus, survivors are 're-newed' and the youngest steps j to 1 are now the oldest. In the figure, the heap advances rightwards through virtual address space. This simplifies the write barrier: only pointers from right to left in the figure, and

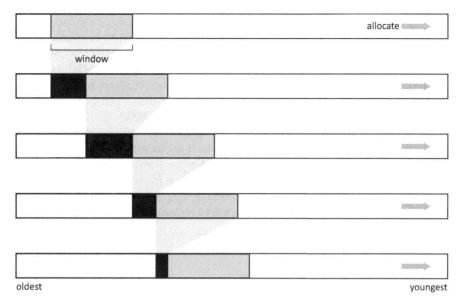

Figure 9.9: Deferred-Older-First garbage collection. A middle-aged window of the heap is selected for collection. Survivors are placed after the survivors of the previous collection. The goal is that the collector will discover a sweet spot, where the survival rate is very low and the window advances very slowly.

whose source is an address larger than j, need to be remembered by the mutator. Although this arrangement might be feasible for some programs in a 64-bit address space, it would soon exhaust a 32-bit address space. In this case, Renewal-Older-First must renumber all the steps in preparation for the next cycle, and its write barrier must filter pointers by comparing the step numbers of the source and targets; this requires table lookups rather than simple address comparisons. A second potential disadvantage of Renewal-Older-First is that it does not preserve the order of objects in the heap by their true ages but irreversibly mixes them. Although Hansen filters out many pointers in the Larceny implementation of Scheme by adding a standard generational nursery (and using Renewal-Older-First only to manage the old generation), his remembered sets are large.

Deferred-Older-First garbage collection. The alternative does preserve the true age order of objects in the heap [Stefanović, 1999; Stefanović *et al.*, 1999]. *Deferred-Older-First* slides a fixed-size collection window (the grey region in Figure 9.9) from the oldest to the youngest end of the heap. When the heap is full, the window is collected, ignoring any older or younger objects (the white regions). Any survivors (the black region) are moved to immediately after the oldest region of the heap, and any space freed is added to the youngest (rightmost) end of the heap. The next collection window is immediately to the right (younger end) of the survivors. The intuition behind Deferred-Older-First is that it will seek out a sweet spot in the heap where the collection window finds few survivors. At this point, the collector's mark/cons ratio will be low and the window will only move very slowly (as in the lower rows of the figure). However, at some point the window will reach the youngest end of the heap, where the collector must reset it to the oldest end of the heap. Although objects are stored in true-age order, Deferred-Older-First requires a more complicated write barrier. The mutator's write barrier must remember all pointers from the oldest region into either the collection window or the youngest region and all young-old pointers (except those whose source is in the condemned window). Similarly, the collector's copy write barrier must remember all pointers from survivors to other regions and all young survivor-old survivor pointers. Once again, Deferred-Older-First collectors typically divide the heap into blocks; they associate a 'time of death' with each block (ensuring that blocks older than the collection window have a higher time of death than younger ones). Barriers can be implemented through block time-of-death comparisons and care is needed to handle time-of-death overflow [Stefanović *et al.*, 2002].

Although Deferred-Older-First was found to improve over other generational schemes on maximum pause time, like Renewal-Older-First it too needed to track more pointers. It appears that in smaller address spaces older-first algorithms have difficulty competing with the best of other schemes because of the cost of the more complex write barrier for remembering in older-first heap layouts. However, in larger address spaces, such as for 64 bits, its write barrier is much simplified and it may be more competitive.

9.11 Beltway

In this chapter we have looked at a wide range of designs for age-based collection. Five key insights have shaped most of these.

- "Most objects die young": the weak generational hypothesis [Ungar, 1984].

- As a corollary, generational collectors avoid repeatedly collecting old objects.

- Response times have been improved by exploiting incrementality. Generational collectors commonly use small nurseries; other techniques such as the Mature Object Space (often called the 'Train') collector [Hudson and Moss, 1992] also bound the size of spaces collected.

- Small nurseries managed by sequential allocators improve data locality [Blackburn *et al.*, 2004a].

- Objects need sufficient time to die.

The *Beltway* garbage collection framework [Blackburn *et al.*, 2002] combines all these insights. It can be configured to behave as any other region-based copying collector. The Beltway unit of collection is called an *increment*. Increments can be grouped into queues, called *belts*. In Figure 9.10 each row represents a belt with increments shown as 'trays' on each belt. Increments on a belt are collected independently first-in, first-out, as also are belts, although typically the increment selected for collection is the oldest non-empty increment on the youngest belt. A promotion policy dictates the destination of objects that survive a collection: they may be copied to another increment on the same belt or they may be promoted to an increment on a higher belt. Note that Beltway is not just another generational collector and belts are not generations. A generational collector would collect *all* increments on a belt; Beltway collects each increment independently.

Figure 9.10 shows examples of existing and new collectors. A simple semispace collector comprises a single belt with two increments (Figure 9.10a): each increment is half of the heap. All survivors from the first increment (fromspace) on the belt are copied to the second (tospace) increment. Generational collectors use a belt per generation. Fixed-size nursery collectors limit the size of belt 0 increment (Figure 9.10b) whereas Appel-style collectors allow both increments to grow to consume all usable memory (Figure 9.10c). Aging semispaces can be modelled by increasing the number of increments on belt 0 (Figure 9.10d). However, unlike the aging semispace discussed in Section 9.6, this design trades increased space for reduced collection time: unreachable objects in the second

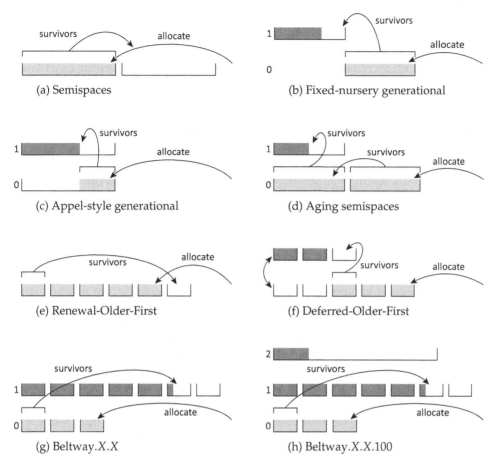

Figure 9.10: Beltway can be configured as any copying collector. Each figure shows the increment used for allocation, the increment to be collected and the increment to which survivors will be copied for each configuration.

Blackburn *et al.* [2002], doi: 10.1145/512529.512548
© 2002 Association for Computing Machinery, Inc. Reprinted by permission.

increment are not reclaimed in this collection cycle. Renewal-Older-First and Deferred-Older-First can also be modelled. Figure 9.10e shows clearly how objects of different ages are mixed by Renewal-Older-First collectors. Deferred-Older-First collectors use two belts, whose roles are flipped when the collection window reaches the youngest end of the first belt. Blackburn *et al.* also used the Beltway framework to introduce new copying collection algorithms. *Beltway.X.X* (Figure 9.10g) adds incrementality to an Appel-style collector: when belt 1 is full, it collects only the first increment. In this configuration X is the maximum size of the increment as a fraction of usable memory: thus, Beltway.100.100 corresponds to a standard Appel-style generational collector. If $X < 100$, Beltway.X.X is not guaranteed to be complete since garbage cycles may span belt 1 increments. Beltway.X.X.100 provides completeness by adding a third belt that contains only one increment, which is allowed to grow sufficiently large to hold the whole heap.

Assuming that every configuration collects only oldest increments on youngest belts implies that Beltway's write barrier needs to remember references from older to younger belts and younger to older increments on the same belt. If we number belts upwards from 0 (youngest) and increments in each belt in the order in which they are created, an increment can be identified by the pair $\langle b, i \rangle$ where b is its belt number and i its creation order in belt b. In that numbering a pointer from $\langle b_i, i \rangle$ to $\langle b_j, j \rangle$ is interesting in the case when $b_j < b_i \lor (b_j = b_i \land i < j$. However, the collector can associate a unique small number n_i with each increment i such that a pointer from i to j is interesting exactly when $n_j < n_i$. It may need to renumber occasionally, such as when fresh increments are added to belts. A typical implementation breaks up the address space using frames, assigning each increment a disjoint set of frames. In a large address space it may be possible to lay increments out such that direct address comparisons work rather than having to map to increment numbers first, similar to such layouts for older-first algorithms.

The performance of Beltway collectors is sensitive to their configuration. The layout of belts in the heap and the implementation of write barriers is crucially important, not only to determine whether pointers need to be remembered but also to decide whether objects need to be copied and if so, where to.

9.12   Analytic support for generational collection

Generational collectors handle short-lived objects well but most do not manage longer-lived ones optimally. There are two problems. First, collection of garbage in older generations is almost never prompt. The mostly reference counting *LXR* collector [Zhao *et al.*, 2022a,b] is the only collector of which we are aware that promptly reclaims (non-cyclic) garbage in the old generation. We discuss LXR in Chapter 18. No tracing collectors as yet schedule old generation collection as soon as possible after the death of significant volumes of old objects. Second, long-lived objects must be copied from the young generation to the old generation. Most collectors that are concerned about objects dying soon after they reach an older generation require objects to have been copied several times before they are promoted. This copying is wasted work: it would be better if long-lived objects were directly allocated or *pretenured* into the generation that they will eventually reach.

Several researchers have tackled this problem by analysing the lifetime distributions of objects allocated by particular points in a program. Sometimes this can be done by the virtual machine implementer who may know that certain virtual machine data structures are permanent, or that certain libraries or code objects cannot or at least are unlikely to be unloaded. Pretenuring of these objects can be baked into the virtual machine.

Researchers have also used profiling to identify longevity. Cheng *et al.* [1998] recorded which allocation sites consistently created objects that were promoted. Blackburn *et al.* [2001; 2007] used lifetime metrics that compared the longevity of objects allocated at a particular program point with some fraction of the program's largest heap footprint in order to discriminate between short-lived, long-lived and immortal objects. Both techniques necessitated the time-consuming gathering of off-line traces. This information was then used to optimise the code so that new objects were allocated in the most appropriate generation or the immortal space. Some pretenuring decisions may be specific to a single program, although Blackburn *et al.* computed generic advice for allocation sites used by all programs (that is, those in the boot image or library code). The effectiveness of such generic advice makes the necessary profiling more reasonable.

In contrast, the approach used by Marion *et al.* [2007] is generic and provides true prediction rather than self-prediction: they obtain pretenuring advice by syntactic comparison of programs' *micro-patterns* [Gil and Maman, 2005] against a pre-existing knowledge bank (derived by using machine learning techniques on a large set of program traces to predict lifetimes from micro-patterns). Harris [2000] and Jump *et al.* [2004] obtain modest performance improvements by pretenuring through online sampling. All these approaches obtained most benefit from the identification of those program points which allocated objects that tended to be immortal rather than those that were simply long-lived. Gains for medium-lived objects were modest.

Guyer and McKinley [2004] sought to co-locate connected objects, on the basis that they are likely to share similar lifetimes. They combined a compiler analysis which identifies the object to which a new object might be connected with a specialised allocator which places the new object in the same space as the connectee. The analysis is neither required to be sound nor did it rely on a site tending to allocate objects with similar lifetimes. As well as reducing copying and obtaining significant reductions in collection time, co-location also reduced pressure on the write barrier.

Generational collectors for lazy functional languages require write barriers only on updates to suspended computations (or thunks) as all other stores must refer to younger objects. Thunks are updated at most once; all other objects are immutable. In a step-based generational collector, Marlow *et al.* [2008] take advantage of this observation to promote an object eagerly to the same generation or step as an object referring to it: ideally this would be to the oldest from which the target is reachable. Even for mutable objects, no write to a newly created object can be interesting. Zee and Rinard [2002] used a static analysis for Java to eliminate write barriers on these objects, obtaining small improvements in overall execution time for some programs.

9.13 Issues to consider

Generational garbage collection has proved to be a highly effective organisation, offering significant performance improvements for a wide range of applications. By limiting the size of the youngest generation, and concentrating collection effort on that generation, expected pause times can be reduced to a point where they are usually unnoticeable in many environments. This tactic can also increase overall throughput in two ways. First, it reduces the frequency with which long-lived data is processed, and thereby not only reduces processing effort but also gives older objects more time to die (so that they need not be traced at all). Second, generational collectors usually allocate young objects sequentially in a nursery area. Sequential allocation obtains cache locality benefits because the memory consumption pattern is predictable and, furthermore, with generational collectors most writes are made to the youngest objects.

Generational collection is not a universal panacea, however. Its effectiveness depends strongly on the lifetime demographics of the application program. The cost of more frequent collections of the nursery and of write barriers must be amortised by obtaining a much better than average pay-back from collecting young generations. If object mortality statistics are not heavily skewed in favour of the young generation — in other words, if the overwhelming majority of objects do not die young — then generational collection will not be an appropriate solution.

Furthermore, generational collection only improves *expected* pause times; eventually the collector must collect the full heap, and generational collection on its own cannot solve the problem of the *worst-case* pause time, which may be excessive for large heaps. Consequently, generational collection cannot provide the guarantees required for hard real-time collection where deadlines must always be met.

It is simpler to implement generational collection if the collector can move objects in order to segregate young and old objects. Physical segregation not only offers the locality benefits noted above, but can also offer more efficient space tests, needed by the write barrier or while tracing a young generation. Nevertheless, objects can also be segregated virtually, maybe by the value of a bit in their header or in a bitmap.

Generational collectors raise many tuning questions, both for the implementer and for the end user. Not only are there a wide variety of design choices but also any given generational collector needs careful configuration to match a given application. Generational collectors offer many more tuning parameters than the simple choice of heap size.

The first implementation decision is likely to be whether to offer more than two generations. The choice depends largely upon the anticipated lifetime distributions of the applications that the collector is expected to support. If a significant fraction of objects are expected to survive the young generation but to die shortly after promotion to an older generation, then the addition of intermediate generations may be worthwhile. However, in our experience, most systems offer only two generations plus an immortal generation, at least as the default configuration. The problem that the use of multiple generations seeks to solve is that of premature promotion, and there are other ways to deal with this.

In the first place, promotion rate depends on the size of the young generation: larger nurseries allow objects more time to die. Some generational collectors may allow the user to set a fixed size for the youngest generation. Others allow the young generation to expand on demand until it fills all of the heap except that required by other spaces (including the old generation and any necessary reserve for copying). More sophisticated collectors may vary the young generation size in order to meet particular throughput of pause time goals, making resizing decisions based on profiling the collector's behaviour.

Second, promotion can be limited by controlling the age at which objects are tenured. One approach is *en masse* promotion in which all survivors of the generation being collected are evacuated to an older generation. This is the simplest promotion to implement, since the remembered set for the young generation can be discarded after collection. Alternatively, a collector may require an object to survive more than one collection before being promoted. In this case, we need a mechanism to record object ages. Either some bits in the header of each object in the younger generations must be used to hold its age, or the generation must be divided into subspaces each of which holds objects of a particular age, or both. Common configurations include step-based schemes and eden plus survivor semispaces. In all cases, the subspaces of a generation are collected together.

Finally, it is often possible to avoid having to promote certain objects. Many collectors reserve an immortal space for objects that will survive until the end of the program. Often these objects can be recognised either at the time the collector is built or by the compiler. Such objects might include the collector's own data structures or objects representing the code being executed (assuming that it will not be necessary to unload code).

Promotion rates may also affect the cost of the write barrier and size of remembered sets. Higher rates may lead to more inter-generational pointers that must be recorded. Whether or not this affects the performance of the write barrier depends on its implementation, a subject considered in more detail in Section 11.8. Write barriers may record pointer writes unconditionally or they may filter out writes of no interest to the collector. The space requirements for card tables are independent of the number of writes recorded, in contrast to remembered sets implemented as sequential store buffers or hash tables.

The frequency with which write barriers are invoked also depends on whether generations can be collected independently. Independent collection requires *all* inter-generational pointers to be recorded. However, if we are prepared to give up this flexibility in favour of collecting all younger generations whenever an older one is collected, then the write barrier only needs to record old-young pointers, which we can expect to be far fewer. The number of pointers recorded also depends on whether we record the *field* or the *object* into which a pointer is written. For card tables, the choice is likely to be irrelevant. However,

Algorithm 9.1: Abstract generational garbage collection: collector routines

```
1   atomic collectNursery(I):
2       rootsNursery(I)
3       scanNursery(I)
4       sweepNursery()
5
6   scanNursery(W):
7       while not isEmpty(W)
8           src ← remove(W)
9           ρ(src) ← ρ(src) + 1                        /* shade src */
10          if ρ(src) = 1                               /* src was white, now grey */
11              for each fld in Pointers(src)
12                  ref ← *fld
13                  if ref in Nursery
14                      W ← W + [ref]
15
16  sweepNursery():
17      while not isEmpty(Nursery)
18          node ← remove(Nursery)                      /* en masse promotion */
19          if ρ(node) = 0                              /* node is white */
20              free(node)
21
22  rootsNursery(I):
23      for each fld ∈ Roots
24          ref ← *fld
25          if ref ≠ null && ref ∈ Nursery
26              I ← I + [ref]
```

by noting in the object whether it has already been recorded as a possible source of an inter-generational pointer, we can reduce the size of the remembered set if we use object remembering rather than field remembering.

The different mechanisms used by the mutator to record the possible sources of inter-generational pointers affect the cost of collection. Although less precise recording mechanisms may reduce the cost of the write barrier, they are likely to increase the amount of work done by the collector. Field-recording with sequential store buffers may be the most precise mechanism, although the buffer may contain duplicate entries. Both object-recording and card tables require the collector to scan the object or card to find any inter-generational pointers.

In conclusion, generations are but one way of partitioning the heap to improve garbage collection. In the next chapter, we look at other partitioning methods.

9.14 Abstract generational garbage collection

Finally, let us see how the abstract collection framework we introduced in Section 6.6 can be applied to generational collection. Recall that Bacon *et al.* [2004] cast abstract tracing as a form of reference counting, incrementing the count of each object as it is marked. An abstract representation of a conventional, two-generation, *en masse* promotion, nursery collection algorithm is shown in Algorithm 9.1.

Algorithm 9.1 (continued): Abstract generational garbage collection: mutator routines

---

```
27  New():
28      ref ← allocate()
29      if ref = null
30          collectNursery(I)
31          ref ← allocate()
32          if ref = null
33              collect()                           /* tracing, counting, or other full–heap GC */
34              ref ← allocate()
35              if ref = null
36                  error "Out of memory"
37      ρ(ref) ← 0                                                          /* node is black */
38      Nursery ← Nursery ∪ {ref}                                     /* allocate in nursery */
39      return ref
40
41  incNursery(node):
42      if node in Nursery
43          I ← I + [node]
44
45  decNursery(node):
46      if node in Nursery
47          I ← I − [node]
48
49  Write(src, i, ref):
50      if src ≠ Roots && src ∉ Nursery
51          incNursery(ref)
52          decNursery(src[i])
53      src[i] ← ref
```

For analogy to the previous abstract collection algorithms, this algorithm maintains a multiset I of 'deferred' reference count increments to nursery objects. Recall that a remembered set is a set of fields that together include all references from the older generation(s) to the nursery. The multiset I contains exactly the nursery references from those locations, which is why decNursery removes elements from the multiset: a (possibly) remembered slot is being overwritten. The result is that if a nursery object n appears in I, then n will be retained by the generational collector. The number of times n appears in I is n's reference count, not counting references from the nursery or roots. A tracing algorithm summarises in a single mark bit the truth of $n \in I$.

When collectNursery is invoked, multiset I is the set of non-zero reference counts, restricted to the nursery, only counting references from old objects. It is the complement of deferred reference counting's zero count table. After adding references from roots to the nursery (rootsNursery), the nursery is traced from I (scanNursery) and is then swept, removing survivors from Nursery, which implicitly adds them to the older generation, and freeing unreachable nursery objects, that is, those whose abstract reference count is zero. Note that the statement in line 18 performs *en masse* promotion of all the live nursery objects: it would be straightforward to modify this to model other promotion policies.

Chapter 10

Other partitioned schemes

In the previous chapter we looked at generational and other age-based collection schemes. Those algorithms partitioned objects by their age and chose a partition to collect based on some age-related property. For example, generational collectors preferentially collect the youngest partition (or generation). Although this strategy in particular is highly effective for a wide range of applications, it does not address all the problems facing the collector. In this chapter we examine schemes outside the age-based collection framework but still based on partitioning the heap.

We start by considering one of the commonest forms of segregation, allocating large objects in a separate space. We then examine collectors that partition the heap based on the topology of the object graph, before looking at possibilities for allocation on thread stacks or into scoped regions. We conclude by discussing hybrid algorithms that partition the heap and collect different spaces at different times or use different algorithms, or both.

10.1 Large object spaces

Large object spaces are one of the most common ways to partition the heap. The definition of 'large' can be chosen on the basis of either the absolute size of an object (say, greater than 1024 bytes [Ungar and Jackson, 1988]), its size relative to that of the blocks used by the allocator [Boehm and Weiser, 1988] or its size relative to the heap [Hosking *et al.*, 1992]. Large objects meet several of the criteria for segregation that we identified in Chapter 8. They are more expensive to allocate and more likely to induce fragmentation, both internal and external. It is therefore worthwhile to use policies and mechanisms to manage them that would be inefficient if applied to smaller ones. Allocating objects in a copying space is particularly expensive since additional space must also be reserved so that they can be copied. Performing the copy may also be expensive, although that cost is likely to be dominated by the cost of updating the object's fields and processing any child pointers, especially if the object is a large array of pointers. For these reasons, large object spaces are often managed by collectors that usually do not physically move their objects, although the trade-off between the performance advantages of not moving objects and the costs of fragmentation make it likely that even large objects may need to be compacted occasionally [Lang and Dupont, 1987; Hudson and Moss, 1992].

There are a number of ways in which large object spaces might be implemented and managed. The simplest is to use one of the free-list allocators described in Chapter 7 and to reclaim objects with a mark-sweep collector. It is also possible to combine a non-moving large object space with a wider range of algorithms including copying. Several implemen-

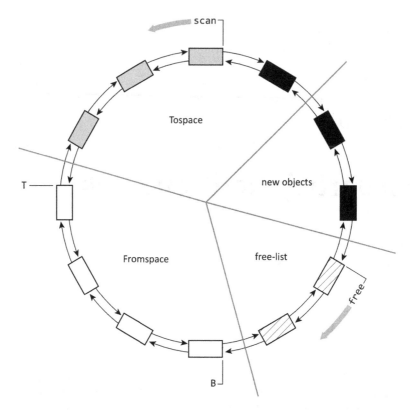

Figure 10.1: The Treadmill collector: objects are held on a double-linked list. Each of the four segments holds objects of a different colour, so that the colour of an object can be changed by 'unsnapping' it from one segment and 'snapping' it into another. The pointers controlling the Treadmill are the same as for other incremental copying collectors [Baker, 1978]: scanning is complete when `scan` meets `T`, and memory is exhausted when `free` meets `B`.

Jones [1996]. Reprinted by permission.

tations have separated large objects into a small (possibly fixed-size) header and a body [Caudill and Wirfs-Brock, 1986; Ungar and Jackson, 1988, 1992; Hosking *et al.*, 1992]. The body is kept in a non-moving area, but the header is managed in the same way as other small objects. It may also be handled by a generational garbage collector; opinions differ on whether large object headers should be promoted by the collector [Hudson *et al.*, 1991] or not (so that the large amount of space that they occupy can be reclaimed as soon as possible after the object's death [Ungar and Jackson, 1992]). Other Java virtual machines and collectors, including HotSpot's Garbage-First (G1), do not use a separate space but allocate large objects directly into the old generation. Since large objects are by their nature likely to survive for some time, this approach saves copying them from the young generation.

The Treadmill garbage collector

It is also possible to copy or move objects logically without moving them physically. In this section we discuss the *Treadmill*; in the next section we consider how to move objects with operating system support. In terms of the tricolour abstraction, a tracing garbage collector partitions heap objects into four sets: black (scanned), grey (visited but not fully scanned), white (not yet visited) and free; it processes the grey set until it is empty. Each collection algorithm provides a different way to represent these sets. The Treadmill [Baker, 1992a] provides some of the advantages of semispace copying algorithms but in a non-moving collector. Although it was intended as an incremental collector its virtues have also led it to be used in stop-the-world configurations for managing large objects.

The Treadmill is organised as a cyclic, double-linked list of objects (Figure 10.1) so that, considered anticlockwise, the black segment is followed by the grey one, then the white one and finally the free one. The black and grey segments comprise the tospace, and the white segment the fromspace of the heap. Four pointers are used to operate the Treadmill. Just as with Cheney's algorithm, `scan` points to the start of the grey segment which it divides from the black one. `B` and `T` point to the bottom and top of the white fromspace list, respectively, and `free` divides the free segment from the black segment.

Before a stop-the-world collection, all objects are black and in tospace. An object is allocated by advancing the `free` pointer clockwise, thus removing it from the free segment and adding it to the start of the black segment. When the `free` pointer meets the `B` pointer at the bottom of fromspace, free memory is exhausted and it is time to flip. At this point, the Treadmill contains at most two colours, black and white. The black segment is reinterpreted as white, and the `T` and `B` pointers are swapped. The collector then behaves much as any semispace copying collector. As grey objects are scanned, the `scan` pointer is moved anticlockwise to add the object to the end of the black segment. When a white object in fromspace is visited by the collector, it is evacuated to tospace by unsnapping it from the white segment and snapping it into the grey segment. When the `scan` pointer meets the `T` pointer, the grey segment is empty and the collection is complete.

The Treadmill has several benefits. Allocation and 'copying' are fairly fast. A concurrent Treadmill can allocate objects of any colour simply by snapping them into the appropriate segment. As objects are not moved physically by snapping, allocation and 'copying' are constant time operations not dependent on the size of the object. Snapping simplifies the choice of traversal order compared with other techniques discussed in Chapter 4. Snapping objects to the end of the grey segment (before the `T` pointer) gives breadth-first traversal. Snapping objects at the start of the segment (at the `scan` pointer) gives depth-first traversal without needing an explicit auxiliary stack, although effectively a stack is embedded in the links of the Treadmill for all traversal orders.

One disadvantage of the Treadmill for general purpose collection is the per-object overhead of the two links. However, for copying collection, this overhead is offset by removing the need for any copy reserve as the Treadmill does not physically copy objects. Another issue for the Treadmill is how to accommodate objects of different sizes (see [Brent, 1989; White, 1990; Baker *et al.*, 1985]). One solution is to use separate Treadmills for each size class [Wilson and Johnstone, 1993]. However, these disadvantages are less of an issue for large objects. Large object Treadmills (for example, as used in MMTk memory management framecwork) keep each object on its own page (or sequences of pages). If links are kept in the pages themselves, they may simply consume some of the space otherwise wasted when rounding up the size to an integral number of pages. Alternatively, the links can be stored together, outside the pages. The best reason for keeping links separate from user data is to reduce the risk of rogue code corrupting the collector's metadata, but doing so may also reduce cache and paging overheads.

Moving objects with operating system support

It is also possible to 'copy' or 'compact' large objects without physically moving them, using support from the operating system. In this case, each large object must again be allocated to its own set of pages. Instead of copying the object word by word, its pages can be remapped to fresh virtual memory addresses [Withington, 1991]. It is also possible to use operating system support to initialise large objects incrementally. Rather than zero the space for the whole object in one step, the object's pages can be memory protected. Any attempt to access uninitialised sections of the object will spring this trap, at which point the page in question can be zeroed and unprotected; see also zeroing in Section 11.1.

Pointer-free objects

There are good reasons for segregating typically large objects not directly related to their size. If an object does not contain any pointers, it is unnecessary to scan it. Segregation allows knowledge of whether the object is pointer-free to be derived from its address. If the mark bit for the object is kept in a side table, then it is not necessary to touch the object at all. Allocating large bitmaps and strings in their own area, managed by a specialised scanner, can lead to significant performance improvements, even if the size of the area is modest. For example, Ungar and Jackson [1988] obtained a fourfold pause time reduction by using a separate space of only 330 kilobytes, tiny by today's standards.

10.2   Topological collectors

One way of arranging objects in the heap is to relate their placement to the topology of pointer structures in the heap. This arrangement offers opportunities for new garbage collection algorithms, which we consider in this section.

Mature Object Space garbage collection

One of the goals of generational garbage collection is to reduce pause times. By and large, the pause to collect the youngest generation can be bounded by controlling the size of the youngest generation. However, the amount of work done to collect the oldest generation is limited only by the volume of live data in the heap. As we saw in Chapter 9, the Beltway.$X.X$ generational configuration [Blackburn *et al.*, 2002] attempted to address this by collecting each belt in fixed-size increments. However, this approach trades one problem for another: cycles of garbage too large to be accommodated in a single increment cannot be reclaimed. Both Bishop [1977] and Beltway.$X.X.100$ add a further area/increment of unlimited size to provide a collector that is complete but that no longer bounds the work done in each collection cycle.

Hudson and Moss [1992] seek to manage a *mature object space* (MOS) outside an age-based scheme, as the oldest generation of a generational system. They too divide this space into a number of fixed-size areas. At each collection, a single area is condemned and any survivors are copied to other areas. Hudson and Moss resolve the cycle problem by structuring the areas, which they call *cars*, into a number of first-in, first-out lists called *trains*: hence, the algorithm is colloquially known as the 'Train' collector. As might be expected, at each collection they condemn a single car but they also impose a discipline on the destination cars to which they copy any survivors. This ensures that a garbage cycle will eventually be copied to a train of its own, all of which can be reclaimed in isolation from other trains. The algorithm proceeds as follows.

1. If there are no root references to the lowest numbered train t and if t's remembered set is empty, then reclaim train t as a whole as its contents are unreachable. Otherwise...

2. Select the lowest numbered car c of the lowest numbered train t as the from-car.

3. Copy any object in c that is referenced by a root to a to-car c' in a higher numbered train t', possibly a fresh one.

4. Recursively copy objects in c that are reachable from to-car c' to that car; if c' is full, append a fresh car to t'.

5. Move any object promoted from the generational scheme to a train holding a reference to it.

6. Scan the remembered set of from-car c. If an object o in c is reachable from another train, copy it to that train.

7. Copy any other object reachable from other cars in this train t to the last car of t, appending a new car if necessary.

Step 1 reclaims whole trains that contain only garbage, even if this includes pointer structures (such as cycles) that span several cars of the train. As the train's remembered set is empty, there can be no references to it from any other train. Steps 3 and 4 move into a different train all objects in the from-car that are reachable from roots via reference chains contained in this car. These objects are certainly live, and this step segregates them from any possibly-garbage objects in the current train. For example, in Figure 10.2, objects A and B in car C1, train T1 are copied to the first car of a new train T3. The last two steps start to disentangle linked garbage structures from other live structures. Step 6 removes objects from this train if they are reachable from another one: in this example, P is moved to train 2, car 2. Finally, Step 7 moves the remaining potentially live objects in this car (for example, X) to the end of its train. It is essential that these steps are done in this order since a single object may be reachable from more than one train. Following Step 7, any objects remaining in car c are unreachable from outside it and so this from-car is discarded, just as a semispace collector would do.

The Train algorithm has a number of virtues. It is incremental and bounds the amount of copying done at each collection cycle to the size of a single car. Furthermore, it attempts to co-locate objects with those that refer to them. Because of the discipline imposed on the order in which trains and cars are collected, it only requires references from high to low numbered trains/cars to be remembered. If it is used with a young generation collector so that all spaces outside the mature object space are collected at each cycle, no references from outside mature object space need be remembered.

Unfortunately, the Train collector can be challenged by several common mutator behaviours.[1] Isolating a garbage structure into its own train may require a number of garbage collection cycles quadratic in the number of cars over which the structure is distributed. As presented above, the algorithm may fail to make progress in certain conditions. Consider the example in Figure 10.3a where there is insufficient room for both objects (or pointer structures) to fit in a single car. Object A will be moved to a fresh car at the end of the current train when the first car is collected. Provided that none of the pointers in this example are modified, the next collection will find an external reference to the leading car, so B will be evacuated to a higher numbered train. Similarly, the third collection will find a reference to A from B's train and so move A there. There are no cars left in this train, so we can dispose of it. The next cycle will collect the first car of the next train, as desired. However, now suppose that, after each collection cycle, the mutator switches the external reference to the object in the second car, as in Figure 10.3b. The Train collector never discovers an external reference to the object in the leading car, and so the object will forever be

---

[1]It was superseded as the 'low pause' collector in Sun Microsystems' JDK after Java 5 in favour of a concurrent collector.

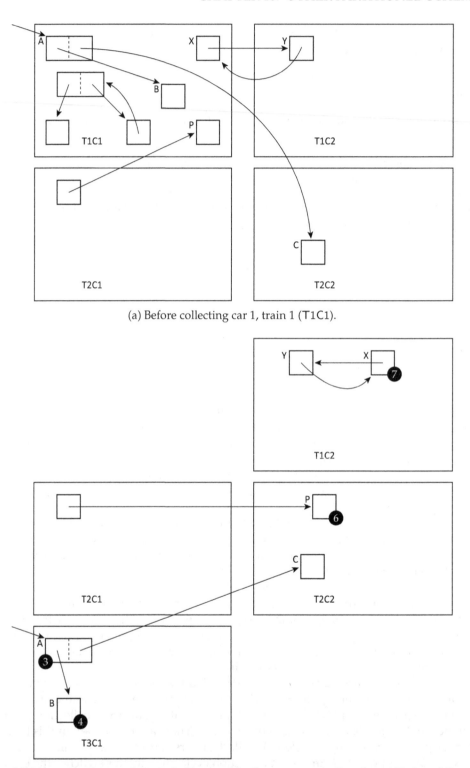

(a) Before collecting car 1, train 1 (T1C1).

(b) After collecting car 1, train 1. X moved to the same car as its referent Y, A and B to a fresh train T3. The next collection cycle will isolate T2 and reclaim it wholesale. Numbered labels show the copies made in each algorithm step.

Figure 10.2: The Train copying collector

Jones [1996]. Reprinted by permission.

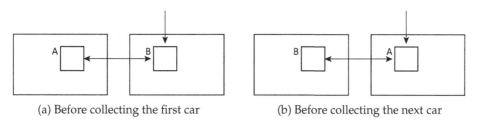

(a) Before collecting the first car   (b) Before collecting the next car

Figure 10.3: A 'futile' collection. After a collection which moves A to a fresh car, the external reference is updated to refer to A rather than B. This presents the same situation to the collector as before, so no progress can be made.

moved to the last car of the current train, which will never empty. The collector can never progress to collect other trains. Seligmann and Grarup [1995] called these 'futile' collections. They solve the problem by remembering external pointers further down the train and using these in futile collections, thereby forcing progress by eventually evacuating the whole train.

The Train bounds the amount of copying done in each collection cycle but does not bound other work, such as remembered set scanning and updating references. Any 'popular', highly referenced objects will induce large remembered sets and require many referring fields to be updated when they are moved to another car. Hudson and Moss suggest dealing with such objects by moving them to the end of the newest train, into their own car, which can be moved logically rather than physically in future collections without need to update references. Unfortunately, this will not always segregate a garbage cycle that spans popular cars. Even if a popular car is allowed to contain more than one popular item, it may still be necessary to disentangle these to separate cars unless they are part of the same structure. Both Seligmann and Grarup [1995] and Printezis and Garthwaite [2002] found popular objects to be common in practice. The latter address this by allowing remembered sets to expand up to some threshold (say 4,096 entries) after which they *coarsen* a set by rehashing its entries into a set of the same size but using a coarser hashing function. Seligmann and Grarup tune the frequency of train collections by tracking a running estimate of the garbage collected (a low estimate allows the collection frequency to be reduced). But Printezis and Garthwaite found it to be common for an application to have a few very long trains of long-lived data; this defeats such a tuning mechanism.

Connectivity-based garbage collection

Management of remembered sets can contribute significantly to the time and space costs of collectors such as the Train and G1 algorithms. The performance of these collectors would be improved if the number of inter-partition pointers that need to be remembered could be reduced or even eliminated. In the previous chapter, we saw how Guyer and McKinley [2004] used a static analysis to place new objects in the same generation as the object to which they would be connected, and Zee and Rinard [2002] eliminated write barriers for the initialisation of the newest object in a generational collector. Hirzel *et al.* [2003] explored connectivity-based allocation and collection further. They observed that the lifetimes of Java objects are strongly correlated with their connectivity. Those reachable only from the stack tend to be short-lived whereas those reachable from globals tend to live for most of the execution of the program (and they note that this property is largely independent of the precise definition of short- or long-lived). Furthermore, objects connected by a chain of pointers tend to die at the same time.

Based on this observation, they proposed a new model of *connectivity-based collection* [Hirzel *et al.*, 2003]. Their model has four components. A conservative pointer analysis divides the object graph into stable partitions: if an object a may point to an object b, then either a and b share a partition or there is an edge from a's partition to b's partition in the directed acyclic graph of partitions. Although new partitions may be added (for example, as classes are loaded), partitions are never split. The collector can then choose any partition (or set of partitions) to collect provided it also collects all its predecessor partitions in the graph. Partitions in the condemned set are collected in topological order. This approach has two benefits. The collector requires neither write barriers nor remembered sets. Partitions can be reclaimed early. By collecting in topological order, as soon as the collector has finished tracing objects in a partition, any unvisited (white) objects in that partition or earlier ones must be unreachable and so can be reclaimed. Note that this also allows popular child partitions to be ignored.

Hirzel *et al.* suggest that the performance of connectivity-based garbage collectors depends strongly on the quality of partitioning, their estimate of the survivor volume of each partition and their choice of partitions to collect. However, they obtained disappointing results (from simulation) for a configuration based on partitioning by the declared types of objects and their fields, estimating a partition's chance of survival from its global or stack reachability, moderated by a partition age based decay function, and using a greedy algorithm to choose partitions to collect. Although mark/cons ratios were somewhat better than those of a semispace copying collector, they were much worse than those of an Appel-style generational collector. On the other hand, worst-case pause times were always better. Comparison with an oracular collector, that received perfect advice on the choice of partition, suggested that there was a performance gap that might be exploited by a better configuration. Dynamic partitioning based on allocation site also improved performance of the collector at the cost of re-introducing a write barrier to combine partitions.

Thread-local garbage collection

One way to reduce garbage collection pause times is to run the collector concurrently with the mutator threads. A variation on this is to perform collection work incrementally, interleaving the mutator and collector. Both approaches increase the complexity of implementations, chiefly by requiring greater synchronisation between collectors and mutators; we defer discussion of incremental and concurrent garbage collection to later chapters. However, if we can prove that a set of objects can only ever be accessed by a single thread, and if these objects are stored in their own thread-local heaplet, then these heaplets can be managed without synchronisation: the problem is reduced to stop-the-world collection for each thread. In this section, we investigate different designs for thread-local collection. Of course, thread-local approaches cannot deal with objects that may be shared; they must still be dealt with by halting all mutator threads during collection or by more complex concurrent or incremental techniques.

The key to thread-local collection is to segregate objects that can be reached by just one thread from those that are potentially shared. In its simplest configuration, heaps configured for thread-local collection use a single shared space and a set of per-thread *heaplets*. More generally, implementations may deploy a tree of heaplets. This requires strict regulation on the direction of pointers. A hierarchy of heaplets is said to be *disentangled* if an object in a thread-local heaplet may only point to another object in the same heaplet or to a potentially shared object in an ancestor heaplet. Objects in ancestor heaplets may not hold *down-pointers* to objects in descendent heaplets, nor may an object hold a *cross-pointer* to an object in another unrelated heaplet, such as a sibling heaplet. The segregation of

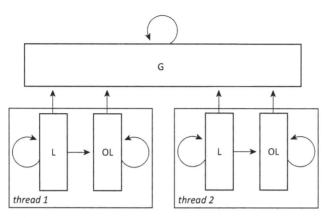

Figure 10.4: Thread-local heaplet organisation, indicating permitted pointer directions between purely local (L), optimistically-local (OL) and shared heaplets (G) [Jones and King, 2005]

objects may be made statically, using a pointer analysis, or it may be dynamic, requiring infringements of the pointer direction rule to be detected at run time. Note that any organisation can be used within a heaplet (for example, a flat arrangement or with generations). However, it is also possible to mark objects as shared on an object by object basis.

Steensgaard [2000] used a fast but conservative pointer analysis similar to that of Ruf [2000] to identify Java objects potentially reachable from a global variable and by more than one thread. The goal of his flow-insensitive, context-sensitive escape analysis is to allow methods that create objects to be specialised in order to allocate the object in either the thread's local heaplet or the shared heaplet. Each heaplet comprises an old and a young generation. His collector is only mostly thread-local. Because Steensgaard treats all static fields as roots for a local heaplet, each collection requires a global rendezvous. A single thread scans the globals and *all* thread stacks in order to copy any directly referenced objects, before Cheney-scanning the shared heaplet. The local threads are released only after the shared scan is complete in order to finish independent collections of their own heaplets. These threads may encounter uncopied objects in the shared heaplet: if so, a global lock must be acquired before the object is copied.

Static disentanglement of shared and thread-local objects requires a whole program analysis. This is a problem for any language that permits classes to be loaded dynamically, since polymorphic methods in subclasses loaded after the analysis is complete may 'leak' references to local objects by writing references into fields of globally reachable ones. Jones and King address this problem and provide a design for a truly thread-local collector [King, 2004; Jones and King, 2005]. Their escape analysis builds on Steensgaard's but is compositional: it supports Java's dynamic class loading, dealing safely with classes loaded after the analysis is complete. Designed for long-running Java applications, the analysis was sufficiently fast to be deployed at run time in a background thread, with Sun's ExactVM Java virtual machine running on a multiprocessor under Solaris. They provide each thread with two local heaplets: one for objects that are guaranteed to be reachable by only the thread that allocated them, no matter what further classes may be loaded, and one for *optimistically-local* objects: those that are accessible by no more than one thread at the time of the analysis but which may become shared if an antagonistic class is loaded. Purely thread-local objects turn out to be comparatively rare: these are mostly objects that do not escape their allocating method. Optimistically-local objects are fairly common, however. The rules for pointer directionality are extended. Local objects may also point to optimistically-local ones, but not vice versa; optimistically-local objects may refer to global ones. A schematic of permissible pointers is shown in Figure 10.4. Jones and King collect each thread independently, with no global rendezvous. Both a thread's local and optimistically-local heaplets are collected together, provided no classes have been loaded that compromise the analysis. Whenever a class is loaded dynamically, it is analysed both to specialise its methods, and to discover whether it extends a class already loaded and whether any of its methods potentially cause an allocation site marked optimistically-local to become shared. If so — and such 'non-conforming' methods are very rare — the optimistically-local heaplets of all threads that may use this method are marked shared and no longer collected thread-locally, but instead are collected alongside the shared heap.

Steensgaard disentangle objects statically, at the cost of a global rendezvous; Jones and King also use a static escape analysis but collect purely thread-locally, with a dynamic class loading check to handle non-conforming methods. However, it is also possible to detect objects dynamically as they escape from their allocating thread. Domani *et al.* [2002] create objects in thread-local allocation buffers but detect escape *precisely*, using a write barrier (see Section 15.2). Because shared and local objects are intermingled in the heap, each object is associated with a *global* bit (held in a separate bitmap) which is set by the write barrier just before a thread creates a reference to an object it did not allocate. The barrier must also set this bit for every object in the transitive closure of the target object. The Domani *et al.* parallel mark-sweep collector collects threads independently. It stops all threads only if it is unable to allocate a large object or a fresh allocation buffer. They also allocate objects known to be always global (such as thread and class objects or those identified as global by off-line profiling) into a separate shared region. Co-existence of global and local collections requires some synchronisation to ensure that a global collection is not initiated while a local one is in progress; we discuss the handshakes necessary in later chapters.

Collecting thread-locally is simpler if all objects are immutable. Erlang [Armstrong *et al.*, 1996] is a strict, dynamically typed, functional programming language. Erlang programs typically use very large numbers of extremely light-weight processes which communicate with each other through asynchronous message passing. The original Erlang/OTP run-time system was process-centric, with each process managing its own private memory area. Because Erlang does not allow destructive assignment, message passing uses copying semantics and thread-local heaps can be collected independently. The costs of this design are that message passing is an $O(n)$ operation (where n is the size of the message) and message data are replicated between processes.

Sagonas and Wilhelmsson add to this architecture a shared area for messages and one for binaries, in order to reduce the cost of message passing [Johansson *et al.*, 2002; Sagonas and Wilhelmsson, 2004; Wilhelmsson, 2005; Sagonas and Wilhelmsson, 2006]. They impose the usual restrictions on pointer direction between the process-local areas and the shared messages area. Their shared message area does not contain any cyclic data and the binaries do not contain references. A static message analysis guides allocation: data that is likely to be part of a message is allocated speculatively on the shared heap and otherwise in a process's local heap. All message operands are wrapped in a copy-on-demand operation that checks that the operand is indeed in the shared heap and otherwise copies it; often this test can be eliminated by the compiler. Note that the copying semantics of Erlang message passing allow the analysis to both over- and under-approximate sharing. Local heaps are managed with a generational, stop-and-copy Cheney-style collector, using generational stack scanning (and *en masse* promotion) to avoid scanning frames that can only point to the old generation [Cheng *et al.*, 1998]. As they contain no cycles, the shared binaries are reference counted. Each process maintains a *remembered list*[2] of pointers to binaries. When a process dies, the reference counts of binaries in this list are decremented. The shared message area is collected by an incremental mark-sweep collector, which requires global synchronisation. We discuss incremental mark-sweep algorithms in Chapter 16.

Doligez and Leroy [1993] (and Doligez and Gonthier [1994]) were the first to introduce the thread-local/shared region memory architecture. In their case, these local/shared heaplets also served as the young/old generations of their collector. Their target was Concurrent Caml Light, ML with concurrency primitives. Unlike Erlang, ML *does* have mutable variables. In order to allow threads to collect their young generations independently, the *Doligez-Leroy-Gonthier* algorithm stores mutable objects in the shared old generation. If a mutable object is updated to refer to an object in a thread-local young generation, then the transitive closure of the young object is *globalised*: it is copied to the old generation. As in the Erlang case, making two copies of the data structure is safe since young objects are guaranteed to be immutable. As well as copying the young objects, the collector updates a forwarding address in each object header to refer to its shared replica. These addresses are used by subsequent thread-local, young generation collections; the mutator write barrier has done some of the collector's work for it. Note that the forwarding pointer must be stored in a reserved slot in the object's header rather than written destructively over user data since the young copy is still in use. This additional header word is stripped from the old generation copy as it is not required by the shared heap's concurrent mark-sweep collector. While this additional word imposes a space overhead in the young generations, this overhead may be acceptable since young generation data will usually occupy a much smaller fraction of total heap size than old generation data. A young generation collection promotes all survivors from a thread-local heaplet to the shared heaplet. Anderson [2010] observed that there may be many more young generation collections with this heap organisation than might be experienced with a more traditional organisation. He noted that after a collection, a thread's stack could not contain any reference to its thread-local heaplet. He was thus able to reduce stack walking overhead by 50% in *TGC*, his Doligez-Leroy-Gonthier-based collector for pH, parallel Haskell, by introducing stack barriers to 'watermark' the highest stack frame below which there could be no references to the thread's local heaplet. A young generation collection therefore need not scan any frame below the watermark for roots. We explain stack barriers in more detail in Section 11.5.

The shared/local heaplet structure can be extended to a tree of heaplets to support nested-parallel computation. In this model, a parent task forks child tasks and suspends until their completion, at which point it resumes. Mirroring the structure of the computation, each task is given its own heaplet in a disentangled tree of heaplets that grows and shrinks as tasks are forked and joined. Typically, heaplets are block-structured, which facilitates joining a heaplet to its parent when a subtask completes. This allows any subtree of the heaplet hierarchy to be collected independently. Guatto *et al.* [2018] suggest a system for nested-parallel ML. Their algorithm is biased towards the common cases of (i) reading immutable fields; and (ii) reading mutable fields or writing non-pointer fields. Their treatment of pointer updates is a natural extension of Doligez-Leroy-Gonthier. Rather than globalising the transitive closure of an object in a descendent heaplet by copying it to a single shared heaplet whenever a down-pointer `ptr` would have been created, the transitive closure is copied to the ancestor heaplet that holds the object whose field is being updated. In the context of nested-parallel ML programs that use destructive updates for efficiency, `ptr` may be written repeatedly into objects held at decreasing depths, and hence the object at `ptr` promoted several times. This leads to the creation of a chain of pointers

---

[2]Not to be confused with *reference lists* used by distributed reference counting systems where the *target* maintains a list of processes that it believes hold references to it.

to a unique, authoritative copy in the shallowest ancestor heaplet, rather than a single forwarding pointer. All accesses to mutable fields are made to the master copy, the last element of this chain. In order to to avoid races when different tasks may be trying to promote (copy) objects, update forwarding pointers, or traverse the chain to find the master copy, their algorithm many need to lock paths of heaplets from the object at ptr to the ancestor heaplet, using a shared lock when searching for the master and an exclusive lock to insert a new forwarding pointer.

Globalising the entire transitive closure of a mutated object is expensive, unless such mutations are rare. However, even in a pure functional language like Haskell, the lazy evaluation mechanism will update a very great number of thunks, and these may be repeatedly mutated; Marlow and Peyton Jones report that having the write barrier naively copy the transitive closure of all mutated objects would add nearly 30% to overall running time. Researchers have therefore considered how to reduce the number of objects that need to be globalised to the shared heap.

Marlow and Peyton Jones [2011] treat thunks and mutable arrays specially in a collector for GHC Haskell that combines thread-local young generation collection with a stop-the-world, parallel, old generation collector. Their system takes advantage of the fact that every pointer dereference in GHC already has a read barrier, in case the target is an unevaluated thunk. They use this read barrier for free to allow some references from the global, old generation heap to thread-local, young generation heaplets, having their write barrier insert *proxy*, indirection objects. A proxy has two fields: a pointer to the local object and an integer identifying the processor that owns the local heap. A proxy looks just like a thunk to the read barrier, so a caller will just jump to its entry code. The current processor will simply continue if it owns the proxy, otherwise it will send a message to owner of the proxy and block until it receives a reply. On receipt of this message, the owner will globalise at least some of data, before overwriting the proxy with a plain indirection to the now global object and sending a wakeup message to the blocked thread. This allows their write barrier (combined with the existing generational write barrier) to maintain the invariant that there are no references from the global heap to a thread-local heaplet except for proxy indirections. It also allows flexibility in deciding whether to globalise all global-local references or to stop at any point and insert a proxy. Their scheme treats immutable, mutable and thunk objects separately. Immutable objects, such as constructors and functions, are copied to the global heap to globalise them, overwriting the header of the local object with a forwarding pointer to its global replica in case there are other references to it. A thunk is globalised by being moved to the global heap, globalising its arguments and overwriting the local object with an indirection. The local object is reclaimed at the next collection. Other mutable objects, such as mutable variables and arrays, are not copied but allocated in an immovable local heaplet called the *sticky heap*, and globalised in a similar way to Domani *et al.* [2002] by flipping a bit in a bitmap (Marlow and Peyton Jones considered this simpler to implement than storing the bit in the object's header). Once globalised, an object can only be reclaimed by a global collection.

Westrick *et al.* [2019] show that programs that are free of determinacy races lead to disentangled heaplets because a cross-pointer can only be created by reading a down-pointer into the heaplet of some concurrently executing task, which is racy because the read conflicts with the write that created the down-pointer. Their *MPL* system for nested-parallel ML programs without determinacy races uses a tree of thread-local heaplets similar to that of Guatto *et al.*, but does not use chains of forwarding pointers or locks. Since programs are race-free, it is possible to delay the promotion of the targets of down-pointers until a heaplet is collected. Instead, each heaplet holds a remembered set of incoming references from its ancestors in the tree of heaplets. When the heaplet is collected, the remembered set is consulted to promote recursively objects reachable from ancestor heaplets: this may require updating some remembered sets in ancestor heaplets. MPL is shown to have significant performance advantages over implementations of nested-parallelism in other managed languages but at the expense of space utilisation: MPL used twice as much space as the sequential MLton implementation. Arora *et al.*'s [2021] *MPL** extends MPL to allow workers to steal tasks. A heaplet's remembered set is updated when another worker steals a task, or by a deletion barrier when a reference from an ancestor heaplet is deleted, as well as when a new down-pointer is created. MPL* offers similar performance to MPL but is significantly more space-efficient.

Stack allocation

Several researchers have proposed allocating objects on the stack rather than in the heap, wherever possible. A wide variety of mechanisms have been suggested, but fewer have been implemented, especially in production systems. Stack allocation has some attractions. It potentially reduces the frequency of garbage collection, and expensive tracing or reference counting is unnecessary for stack allocated data. Thus, stack allocation should in theory be gentler on caches. On the down side, it may prolong the lifetime of objects allocated in frames that persist on the stack for a long time.

The key issue is to ensure that no stack allocated object is reachable from another object with a longer lifetime. This can be determined either conservatively through an escape analysis (for example, [Blanchet, 1999; Gay and Steensgaard, 2000; Corry, 2006]) or by run-time escape detection using a write barrier. Baker [1992b] was the first to suggest (but not implement) stack allocation in the context of an otherwise garbage collected heap. Laying out the stack to grow away from the heap could allow the system to use an efficient address-based write barrier to detect references to objects on the stack from locations that might outlive them. In such a case, the object would be copied ('lazily allocated') into the heap. He also required a read barrier to handle the forwarding addresses that copying introduced. Others have suggested allocating objects in a stack of frames separate from the call stack. Cannarozzi *et al.* [2000] used a write barrier to partition the heap, with each partition associated with the oldest activation record that might refer to it. Unfortunately, the cost (in Sun's handle-based JDK 1.1.8) was large: an extra four 32-bit words per object. Qian and Hendren [2002] allocated frames lazily to avoid allocating any empty ones. They used a write barrier to mark such a frame as global if any of its objects escaped. In this case, the write barrier also marked the site in the method allocating the object as non-local but this requires storing a site identity in the object's header. They shared the lock word for this purpose at the cost of making the frame global if an object is ever locked; unfortunately, library code often contains redundant (that is, local) locking (which is why biased locking is so effective). Corry [2006] used a cheaper intraprocedural escape analysis that associates object frames with loops rather than method invocations and hence works well with dynamic class loading, reflection, factory methods and so on.

Azul Systems' multicore, multiprocessor Java appliances provided hardware-supported object-by-object escape detection. When an object is allocated on the stack, some pointer bits are used to store the frame's depth in the stack. These bits are ignored by pointer loads but checked by stores: storing a reference to an object in a new frame into an object in an old frame causes a trap which moves the object and fixes up references to it (which can only be held by objects in newer frames). The fixup is expensive so needs to be rare. If stack allocating an object would cause the frame to become too large, it is placed in an overflow area to the side. Azul found that they still need occasional thread-local collections to deal with dead stack allocated objects in long-lived frames.

Overall, most of these schemes have not been implemented, are reported with insufficient detail of comparative systems or do not offer significant performance improvements.
While it is likely that for many applications a large fraction of objects might be stack allocatable, most of these are likely to be short-lived. Azul found that over half of all objects
may be stack allocated in large Java applications. However, this scenario is precisely the
one in which generational garbage collection excels. It is not clear that stack allocation
reduces memory management costs sufficiently to make it worthwhile. Another rationale
for stack allocation is that it can reduce memory bandwidth by keeping these objects entirely in the cache, given a sufficiently large cache. One related strategy that is effective is
scalar replacement or *object inlining* whereby an object is replaced by local variables representing its fields [Dolby, 1997; Dolby and Chien, 1998, 2000; Gay and Steensgaard, 2000].
A common application of scalar replacement is for iterators in object-oriented programs.

Region inferencing

Stack allocation is a restricted form of more general region-based memory management.
The key idea behind region-based memory is that objects are allocated into *regions* and that
entire regions are reclaimed as soon as none of their contents is required by the program.
Typically, region reclamation is a constant time operation. The decisions as to when to
create a region, into which region to place an object and when to reclaim a region may
fall to the programmer, the compiler, the run-time system or a combination of these. For
example, the programmer may be required to add explicit instructions or annotations to
create and destroy regions or to indicate the region into which an object must be allocated.
Possibly the best known explicit system is the Real-Time Specification for Java (RTSJ). In
addition to the standard heap, the RTSJ provides an immortal region and scoped regions.
The RTSJ enforces strict rules on pointer directionality: an object in an outer scoped region
cannot refer to one in an inner scope.

Other region-based systems may relax the requirements on pointer direction, allowing
regions to be reclaimed even if there are references into that region from other, live regions.
To be safe, such systems require a guarantee that the mutator will never follow a dangling
pointer into a deallocated region. These systems require compiler support, either for inferring the region into which an object should be allocated and when it is safe to reclaim the
region, or to check programmer annotations (possibly in the form of non-standard type
systems). The best known, fully automatic, region inferencing system is that for Standard
ML [Tofte *et al.*, 2004]. Used with care, these systems can lead to programs that are efficient and use less memory. However, this is very dependent on program style, often
requiring the programmer to have a deep understanding of the inferencing algorithm (although not its implementation). Region inferencing can also make programs harder to
understand and more difficult to maintain as small changes can have significant effects on
the inferencing decisions [Coblenz *et al.*, 2022]. The *ML Kit* inferencing algorithm was also
very expensive for large programs (for example, a 58,000 line program took one and a half
hours to compile). Tofte *et al.* report that it was often best to restrict region inferencing
to well-understood coding patterns and manage other parts of the program by garbage
collection.

More recently, the Rust language includes as part of the language a system similar to
region inferencing, there called *lifetimes*, that is often implicit but that also supports explicit
lifetime parameters and types. As Coblenz *et al.* found, this system appears more difficult
to use than automatic garbage collection, at least for novice programmers.

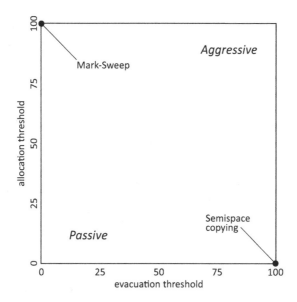

Figure 10.5: A continuum of tracing collectors. Spoonhower *et al.* contrast an evacuation threshold — sufficient live data to make a block a candidate for evacuation — with an *allocation threshold* — the fraction of a block's free space reused for allocation.

Spoonhower *et al.* [2005], doi: 10.1145/1064979.1064989
© 2005 Association for Computing Machinery, Inc. Reprinted by permission.

10.3 Hybrid mark-sweep, copying collectors

When considering how the volume of live objects in a block can be used to make evacuate or mark decisions, Spoonhower *et al.* [2005] contrast an evacuation threshold — whether the block contains sufficiently little live data to make it a candidate for evacuation — with an *allocation threshold* — how much of the block's free space should be reused for allocation. These thresholds determine when and how fragmentation is reduced. For example, a mark-sweep collector has an evacuation threshold of zero (it never copies) but an allocation threshold of 100% (it reuses all free space in a block), whereas a semispace copying collector has an evacuation threshold of 100% but an allocation threshold of zero (fromspace pages are not used for allocation until after the next collection); these two collectors are shown in Figure 10.5. Overly passive memory managers with low evacuation and allocation thresholds can suffer from fragmentation; overly aggressive managers, where both thresholds are high, have high overheads either because they replicate data or because they require more passes to collect the heap.

The performance of a large or long-running application may eventually suffer from fragmentation unless the heap is managed by a compacting collector. Unfortunately, compaction is likely to be expensive in time or space compared with non-moving collection. Semispace copying requires a copy reserve but mark-compact algorithms require several passes over the heap in addition to the cost of moving objects. To address these problems, Lang and Dupont [1987] proposed combining mark-sweep collection with semispace copying to compact the heap incrementally, one region at a time. The heap is divided into $k + 1$ equally sized regions, one of which is empty. At collection time, some region is chosen to be the fromspace and the empty region is used as the tospace. All other regions are managed by a mark-sweep collector. As the collector traces the heap, objects are evacuated

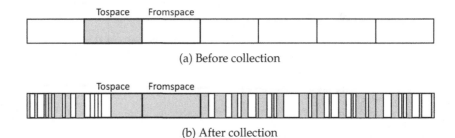

Figure 10.6: Incremental incrementally compacting garbage collection. One space (fromspace) is chosen for evacuation to an empty space (tospace), shown as grey; the other spaces are collected in place. By advancing the two spaces, the whole heap is eventually collected.

Jones [1996]. Reprinted by permission.

to the tospace region if they are in the fromspace region; otherwise they are marked (see Figure 10.6). References in any region to fromspace objects must be updated with their tospace replicas.

By rotating the region chosen to be the fromspace through the heap, Lang and Dupont can compact the whole heap in k collections at a space overhead of $1/k$ of the heap. Unlike mark-compact algorithms, no extra passes or data structures are required. They observe that this algorithm can provide flexibility in tracing order, especially if tospace is managed by a Cheney algorithm. At each tracing step, the collector can choose whether to take the next item from the mark-sweep or the copying work list: Lang and Dupont advocate preferring the mark-sweep collector in order to limit the size of its stack. There is also a locality argument here since mark-sweep tends to have better locality than Cheney copying.

The Spoonhower *et al.* [2005] collector for C# takes a more flexible approach. It uses block residency predictions to decide whether to process a block in place to tospace or to evacuate its contents. Predictions may be static (for example, large object space pages), use fixed evacuation thresholds (generational collectors assume few young objects survive) or dynamic ones (determined by tracing). Spoonhower *et al.* use residency counts from the previous collection to determine whether to evacuate or mark objects in a block (blocks containing pinned objects are processed in place) in order not to need an extra pass at each collection. In a manner similar to Dimpsey *et al.* [2000] (discussed below), they maintain a free-list of gaps, and bump allocate into these.

10.4 Garbage-First: collecting young regions

Garbage-First (G1) [Detlefs *et al.*, 2004] is a sophisticated and complex incrementally compacting algorithm, intended for applications with large heaps and designed to meet a soft real-time performance goal that collection should consume no more than x milliseconds of any y millisecond time slice. Initially introduced as an experimental feature of Sun Microsystems' HotSpot Java virtual machine in JDK 6, G1 was intended as a longer term replacement for a concurrent mark-sweep collector in order to provide compaction with more predictable response times; it has been the default collector since JDK 9. Here we discuss how the forthcoming version of G1 (to appear in JDK 20[3]) treats partitions, focusing

---

[3]Thomas Schatzl's blog provides excellent explanations of G1 policies and mechanisms, https:// tschatzl.github.io.

Algorithm 10.1: Garbage-First remembered set barrier fast path. The deletion barrier for snapshot-at-the-beginning tracing is omitted (see Section 15.1).

```
 1  Write(src, i, ref):
 2      ...                                        /* deletion barrier */
 3      src[i] ← ref                                            $
 4      field ← &src[i]                          /* the address of the field */
 5      if region(field) = region(ref) || ref = null
 6          return
 7      if card(field) = Young
 8          return
 9      StoreLoadFence
10      if card(field) = dirty                                 $
11          return
12      card(field) ← dirty
13      enqueueCard(dirtyCardBuffer, card(field))
```

on 'young only' collections. In line with common usage, we will refer to G1 partitions as 'regions'. We will turn to how G1 concurrently marks old regions in Chapter 16.

G1 uses the same generation structure as other OpenJDK collectors. Its young generation comprises an eden (newly allocated) space and a pair of survivor spaces, and it has a single old generation. Like the Lang and Dupont collector, G1 divides these spaces into equal-sized regions of contiguous virtual memory. Typically, these are in the range of 1 to 32 megabytes although the HotSpot Java virtual machine allows users to configure region sizes up to 512 megabytes. Allocation occurs into a current allocation region in eden, taken from a list of empty regions. To minimise synchronisation between mutator threads, each thread has its own bump pointer local allocation buffer, acquired from the current allocation region with an atomic compare-and-swap operation; larger objects may similarly be allocated directly in the allocation region. 'Humongous' objects, larger than half a region, are allocated in their own sequence of regions.

Unlike Lang and Dupont, G1 allows an arbitrary set of regions to be chosen for collection. It therefore requires the mutator's write barrier to record *any* pointer that it writes which may refer to a region that may be evacuated. Engineering of regions, write barriers and remembered sets is therefore complex and critical. G1 maintains a global card table and, for each region R, a remembered set: a sparse set of cards, each of which corresponds to a configurable range (default, 512 bytes) of addresses that might hold a reference to R (we discuss the implementation of card tables in more detail in Chapter 11). G1 uses the card table for two purposes. Mutators use it as a temporary scratch space to reduce the number of duplicates in their *refinement* buffers (which we describe below); in garbage collection pauses, G1 repurposes the table as a combined remembered set for all the regions to be evacuated.

The G1 filtering write barrier records interesting pointers. Algorithm 10.1 shows the fragment of the post-write barrier to support region evacuation (but omits the pre-write barrier required for concurrent marking). Each mutator thread has a `dirtyCardBuffer`, a local sequential store buffer (array) of recently dirtied cards (default, 256). The write barrier first filters out any writes of `null` or of pointers between objects in the same region, and any writes to young objects. For other writes, it checks if the card corresponding to the overwritten field is dirty and, if not, dirties the card and adds it to the thread's dirtyCardBuffer. When this buffer is full, the barrier appends it to a global queue of filled remembered set buffers.

Concurrent remembered set *refinement threads* wait on a condition variable for the size of this queue to become sufficiently large. The purpose of these threads is to populate the regions' remembered sets. A refinement thread scans each card of a buffer, first setting the card to Clean before examining the pointer fields of the objects whose modification may have dirtied the card. If any interesting inter-region pointer is discovered, the card is inserted into the remembered set of the referenced region. Note that the write barrier in Algorithm 10.1 requires a StoreLoad fence between the pointer update and adding the card to the buffer to prevent reorderings[4] of memory stores and loads that may prevent the refinement thread from seeing the mutator store. G1 fixes the values of cards corresponding to young regions as Young in order to mitigate the performance impact of the StoreLoadFence in the barrier. Some cards may contain fields that are updated frequently. G1 defers processing such cards until the next evacuation pause, placing them in a cache of 'hot' cards; it uses a second card table to record how many times a card has been dirtied since the last evacuation pause.

This organisation gives considerable flexibility in the choice of regions to be evacuated. Regions are compacted in parallel, in evacuation pauses with all mutator threads stopped (see Chapter 14). In general, G1 will choose those regions with low fractions of live data, attempting to meet a soft real-time pause time goal, which can be supplied by the user. It predicts the pause time required to evacuate a condemned set[5] (CS) of regions according to the formula

$$T(CS) = T_{\text{fixed}} + T_{\text{mergeCard}} \times N_{\text{dirtyCard}} + \sum_{r \in CS} \left(T_{\text{mergeRS}} \times rsSize(r) + T_{\text{copy}} \times liveBytes(r) \right)$$

where T_{fixed} represents fixed costs common to all pauses, $T_{\text{mergeCard}}$ the average time to merge a card from the refinement buffer into the combined remembered set, $N_{\text{dirtyCard}}$ the number of dirty cards in the refinement buffer at the start of the collection, T_{mergeRS} the average time to merge a card from a region's remembered set into the condemned set, $rsSize(r)$ the number of cards in r's remembered set, T_{copy} the cost per byte of evacuating (and scanning) a live object and $liveBytes(r)$ an estimate of the number of live bytes in region r.

As implemented in OpenJDK, G1 is a generational collector. It starts in a 'young only' mode, collecting only young generation and humongous regions. In this mode, G1 needs to maintain only the remembered sets belonging to young regions as humongous objects are not moved and old generation regions are not collected. A 'young only' collection starts by halting mutator threads and disconnecting their thread-local allocation buffers. Before evacuation, G1 merges all remembered sets of the current condemned set (here, the young generation), the refinement queues and the hot card cache into a single remembered set (repurposing the card table to represent this). This removes any duplicates from the individual remembered sets that would otherwise need to be filtered out later in a more expensive way. This is straightforward to parallelise as is subsequent iteration over the card table. By recording approximate areas larger than cards with a second-level card table, G1 can avoid scanning all of the card table corresponding to the old generation. In many cases, this results in its only needing to scan a small fraction of the card table (in contrast, for example, to the OpenJDK parallel collector which always needs to scan the entire card table). In the evacuation phase, parallel threads move objects starting from the roots (thread stacks, the unified remembered set, Java virtual machine internal data structures

---

[4]We discuss memory consistency in Section 13.2.

[5]OpenJDK calls a condemned set a 'collection set'.

and code), promoting those in eden regions to survivor regions, and those in survivor regions to old generation regions once they have survived sufficiently many collections. After this phase has finished copying live objects, G1 does any necessary clean-up work, including processing weak references, before restarting the mutators.

Eventually it will become necessary to collect old regions as well. G1 initiates such 'mixed collections', starting by concurrently marking live objects once the old generation occupies a sufficient fraction (adaptively adjusted) of the heap or after a humongous object is allocated. We discuss 'mixed collections' in Chapter 16. Overall, G1 is a complex and delicate collector that relies on its automatic Ergonomics tuning and careful work by its developers over many years.

10.5 Trading space and time

Next, we examine collectors that trade off the space-time costs of mark-sweep collection and fragmentation. Each takes a different approach to the problems of trying to make best use of available heap space, avoiding the need to defragment (whether through evacuation or mark-compact) and reducing time overheads in the collector's loops.

Dimpsey *et al.* [2000] describe a sophisticated parallel mark-sweep (with occasional compaction) collector for IBM's server Java virtual machine, version 1.1.7. Like Sun's 1.1.5 collectors, the IBM server used thread-local allocation buffers.[6] Small objects were bump-allocated within a buffer without synchronisation; synchronised allocation of buffers and other large objects (greater than 0.25 times the buffer size) was performed by searching a free-list. Dimpsey *et al.* found that this architecture on its own led to poor performance. Although most large object requests were for local allocation buffers, free chunks that could not satisfy these requests tended to congregate at the start of the free-list, leading to very long searches. To address this, they introduced two further free-lists, one for objects of exactly the local allocation buffer size (1.5 kilobytes plus header) and one for objects between 512 kilobytes and the buffer size. Whenever the buffer list became empty, a large chunk was obtained from the large object list and split into many buffers. This optimisation substantially improved Java performance on uniprocessors and even more so on multiprocessors.

The IBM server collector marked objects in a side bitmap. Sweeping traversed the bitmap, testing bits a byte or a word at a time. Dimpsey *et al.* optimise their sweep by ignoring short sequences of unused space; a bit in the object header was used to distinguish a large object from a small one followed by garbage, and two tables were used to translate arbitrary byte values in the mark bitmap to counts of leading and trailing zeroes. The consequence of this is that, after a collection, parts of an allocation buffer may be free but not usable for allocation since the server bump-allocates only from fresh buffers. However, not only did this approach reduce sweep time but it also reduced the length of the free-lists, since they no longer contain any small blocks of free space.

The potential cost of this technique is that some free space is not returned to the allocator. However, objects tend to live and die together and Dimpsey *et al.* exploit this property to avoid compaction as much as possible. They follow the advice of Johnstone [1997] by using an address-ordered, first-fit allocator in order to increase the chance of creating holes in the heap large enough to be useful. Furthermore, they allow local allocation blocks to be of *variable* length. If the first item on the local allocation buffer free-list is smaller than a desired size T (they use 6 kilobytes), it is used as is (note that the item must be larger than the minimum size accepted for inclusion in the free-list). If it is between T and $2T$, it is split into two evenly sized buffers. Otherwise, the block is split to yield a buffer of size T.

---

[6]Contrary to our conventions, Dimpsey *et al.* call these 'thread-local heaps'.

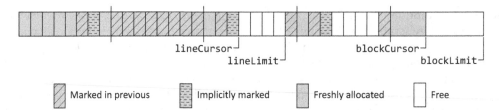

lineCursor⌐   blockCursor⌐
        lineLimit⌐   blockLimit⌐

◹ Marked in previous   ▦ Implicitly marked   ▩ Freshly allocated   □ Free

Figure 10.7: Allocation in immix, showing *blocks* of *lines*. Immix uses bump
pointer allocation within a partially empty block of small objects, advancing lineCursor to lineLimit, before moving onto the next group of unmarked lines. It acquires wholly empty blocks in which to bump-allocate
medium-sized objects. Immix marks both objects and lines. Because a small
object may span two lines (but no more), immix treats the line after any sequence of (explicitly) marked lines as implicitly marked: the allocator will
not use it.
Blackburn and McKinley [2008], doi: 10.1145/1375581.1375586
© 2008 Association for Computing Machinery, Inc. Reprinted by permission.

Dimpsey *et al.* also set aside 5% of the heap beyond the 'wilderness boundary' [Korn and
Vo, 1985], to be used only if insufficient space is available after a collection.

10.6   Mark-region collection: immix

Like the Dimpsey *et al.* IBM server, the *immix* collector [Blackburn and McKinley, 2008]
attempts to avoid fragmentation. It too is a mostly mark-sweep collector, but it eliminates
fragmentation when necessary by copying rather than compacting collection. Immix employs a block-structured heap, just as the other collectors discussed in this section. Its
32-kilobyte blocks are the basis for both thread-local allocation and the units for defragmentation. At collection time, immix chooses whether to mark a block in place or to evacuate its live objects, using liveness estimates gathered from the previous collection cycle (in
the same way as Spoonhower *et al.* but in contrast to Detlefs [2004a], who obtain their estimates from concurrent marking). Both the IBM server and immix use fast bump-pointer
allocation. Whereas Dimpsey *et al.* reduce fragmentation by allocating from variable-sized
buffers, immix can also allocate sequentially into line-sized gaps in partially filled buffers.
Immix *lines* are 128 bytes, chosen to roughly match cache line lengths. Just as Dimpsey
et al. optimise their collector's sweep by ignoring short sequences of unused space, so immix reclaims space in recyclable blocks at the granularity of lines rather than individual
objects. Let us look at the immix collector in detail.

Immix allocates from either completely free or partially filled ('recyclable') blocks. Figure 10.7 shows the structure of recyclable blocks. For the purpose of allocation, immix
distinguishes large objects (which are allocated in a large object space), medium-sized
objects whose size is greater than a line, and small objects; most Java objects are small.
Algorithm 10.2 shows the immix algorithm for small and medium-sized objects. Immix
preferentially allocates into empty line-sized gaps in partially filled blocks using a linear,
next-fit strategy. In the fast path, the allocator attempts to bump-allocate into the current
contiguous sequence of free lines (line 2). If this fails, the search distinguishes between
small and medium-sized allocation requests.

We consider small requests first. In this case, the allocator searches for the next sequence of free lines in the current block (line 11). If this fails, immix tries to allocate from
free lines in the next partially filled block (line 13) or the next empty block (line 15). If

Algorithm 10.2: Allocation in immix

```
 1  alloc(size):
 2      addr ← sequentialAllocate(lines, size)
 3      if addr ≠ null
 4          return addr
 5      if size ≤ LINE_SIZE
 6          return allocSlowHot(size)
 7      else
 8          return overflowAlloc(size)

10  allocSlowHot(size):
11      lines ← getNextLineInBlock()
12      if lines = null
13          lines ← getNextRecyclableBlock()
14          if lines = null
15              lines ← getFreeBlock()
16              if lines = null
17                  return null                          /* Out of memory */
18      return alloc(size)

20  overflowAlloc(size):
21      addr ← sequentialAllocate(overflowBlock, size)
22      if addr ≠ null
23          return addr
24      overflowBlock ← getFreeBlock()
25      if overflowBlock = null
26          return null                                  /* Out of memory */
27      return sequentialAllocate(overflowBlock, size)
```

neither request succeeds, the collector is invoked. Notice that, unlike first-fit allocation, the immix allocator never retreats even though this may mean that some lines are only partially filled.

In most applications, a small number of Java objects are likely to be larger than a line but not 'large'. Blackburn and McKinley found that treating these like the small objects above led to many lines being wasted. To avoid fragmenting recyclable blocks, these medium-sized objects are bump-allocated into empty blocks (`overflowAlloc`). They found that the overwhelming proportion of allocation was into blocks that were either completely free or less than a quarter full. Note that allocation of both small and medium-sized objects is into thread-local blocks; synchronisation is only required to acquire a fresh block (either partially filled or completely empty).

The immix collector marks both objects (to ensure correct termination of the scan) and lines (the authors call this '*mark-region*'). A small object is by definition smaller than a line, but may still span two lines. Immix marks the second line implicitly (and conservatively): the line following any sequence of marked lines is skipped by the allocator (see Figure 10.7) even though, in the worst case, this might waste nearly a line in every gap. Blackburn and McKinley found that tracing performance was improved if a line was marked as an object was *scanned* rather than when it was marked and added to the work list, since the more expensive scanning operation better hid the latency of line marking. Implicit marking improved the performance of the marker considerably. In contrast, medium-sized objects are marked exactly (a bit in their header distinguishes small and medium objects), but omitting the mark for the last line occupied by the object.

Immix compacts opportunistically, depending on fragmentation statistics, and in the same pass as marking. These statistics are recorded at the end of each collection by the sweeper, which operates at the granularity of lines. Immix annotates each block with the number of gaps it contains and constructs histograms mapping the number of marked lines as a function of the number of gaps blocks contain. The collector selects the most-fragmented blocks as candidates for compaction in the next collection cycle. As these statistics can only provide a guide, immix can stop compacting early if there is insufficient room to evacuate objects. In practice, compaction is rare for many benchmarks.

10.7 Copying collection in a constrained memory space

As we have seen, these incremental techniques require a copy reserve of just one block but take many collections to compact the whole heap. Sachindran and Moss [2003] adopt this approach for generational collection in memory constrained environments, dividing the old generation into a sequence of contiguous blocks. Rather than evacuate a single block at each collection, *Mark-Copy* collects the whole heap one block at a time at each full heap collection. Like any other generational collector, objects are allocated into the nursery which is collected frequently, with any survivors being copied to the old generation. If the space remaining drops to a single block, a full heap collection is initiated.

Independent collection of each block requires a remembered set for each one, but this would complicate the generational write barrier since it would have to record not only inter-generational pointers but also inter-block ones. Instead, Mark-Copy's first phase marks all live objects, and also constructs per-block unidirectional remembered sets and counts the volume of live data for each block. Two advantages arise from having the marker rather than the mutator construct the remembered sets: the remembered sets are precise (they only contain those slots that actually hold pointers from higher numbered to lower numbered blocks at the time of collection) and they do not contain any duplicates. G1 similarly has collector threads construct remembered sets for old generation regions. Windows of consecutive blocks are evacuated one at a time, starting with the lowest numbered (to avoid the need for bidirectional remembered sets), copying live data to the free block. Because the marker has counted the volume of live data in each block, the collector can determine how many blocks can be evacuated in each pass. For example, the second pass in Figure 10.8 was able to evacuate a window of three blocks. At the end of each pass, the space consumed by the evacuated blocks is released (unmapped).

By evacuating blocks one at a time if necessary, collectors like Mark-Copy effectively increase the space available compared with a standard semispace collector, which may lead to fewer collections given the same space budget. Mark-Copy may also be incremental, interleaving collections of blocks in the old generation with nursery collections. However, it has disadvantages. Each full collection scans every object twice, once to mark it and once to copy it. Marking requires space for a mark stack and for the remembered sets. Each copying pass may require thread stacks and global data to be rescanned. Still, under some useful range of conditions it performs well compared with copying generational collectors that must reserve more of the available space for copying into.

The MC^2 collector [Sachindran *et al.*, 2004] relaxes Mark-Copy's requirement for blocks to occupy contiguous locations by numbering blocks logically rather than by their (virtual) address. This has several advantages. It removes the need for blocks to be remapped at the end of each pass (and hence the risk of running out of virtual address space in a

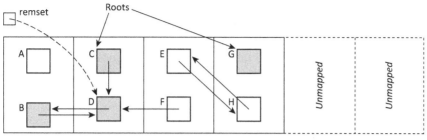

(a) After marking (live objects are shown in grey)

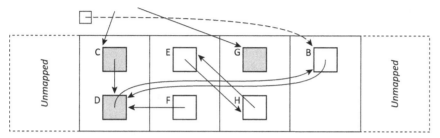

(b) After the first copying pass. B has been evacuated and the first block has been unmapped.

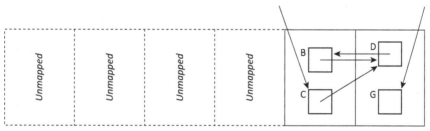

(c) After the second copying pass. Note that there was sufficient room to evacuate three blocks.

Figure 10.8: Mark-Copy divides the space to be collected into blocks. After the mark phase has constructed a remembered set of objects containing pointers that span blocks, the blocks are evacuated and unmapped, one at a time.

Sachindran and Moss [2003], doi: 10.1145/949305.949335

32-bit environment). It also allows blocks to be evacuated logically simply by changing their block number, which is useful if the volume of live data in the block is sufficiently high to outweigh the benefit of copying and compacting it. Numbering the blocks logically also allows the order of collection of blocks to be modified at collection time. Unlike Mark-Copy, MC^2 spreads the passes required to copy old generation blocks over multiple nursery collections; it also marks the old generation incrementally using a Steele insertion barrier (we discuss incremental marking in Chapter 15). Because of its incrementality, it starts collecting the old generation somewhat before space runs out, and adaptively adjusts the amount of work it does in each increment to try to avoid a large pause that might occur if space runs out. Like other approaches discussed in this chapter, MC^2 segregates popular objects into a special block for which it does not maintain a remembered set (thus treating them as immortal although this decision can be reverted). Furthermore, in order to bound the size of remembered sets, it also coarsens the largest ones by converting them from sequential store buffers to card tables (we explain these techniques in Chapter 11). Large arrays are also managed by card tables, in this case by allocating space for their own table at the end of each array. Through careful tuning of its combination of techniques, it achieves high space utilisation, high throughput and well-balanced pauses.

10.8   Bookmarking garbage collection

These incremental compaction techniques have allowed the heap to be compacted (eventually) without the time overhead of traditional mark-compact algorithms or the space overhead of standard semispace collection. Nevertheless, programs will still incur a significant performance penalty if the number of pages occupied by the heap is sufficiently large that either mutator activity or garbage collector tracing leads to paging. The cost of evicting and loading a page is likely to be of the order of millions of cycles, making it worth expending considerable effort to avoid page faults. The *Bookmarking* collector [Hertz *et al.*, 2005] mitigates the total cost of mutator page faults and avoids faults during collection.

The collector cooperates with the operating system's virtual memory manager to guide its page eviction decisions. In the absence of such advice, the manager is likely to make a poor choice of which page to evict. Consider a simple semispace collector and a virtual memory manager which always evicts the least recently used page. Outside collection time, the page chosen will always be an as yet unused but soon to be occupied tospace page. Indeed, if most objects are short-lived, it is quite likely that the least recently used page will be the very next one to be used by the allocator — the worst possible paging scenario from its point of view! A fromspace page would be a much better choice: not only will it not be accessed (and hence reloaded) until the next collection but its contents do not need to be written out to the backing store.

The Bookmarking collector can complete a collection trace without faulting in non-resident pages. The trace conservatively assumes that all objects on a non-resident page are live but it also needs to locate any objects reachable from that page. To support this, if a live page has to be scheduled for eviction, the run-time system scans it, looking for outgoing references, and 'bookmarks' their targets. When this page is reloaded, its bookmarks are removed. These bookmarks are used at collection time to propagate the trace.

The virtual memory manager is modified to send a signal whenever a page is scheduled for eviction. On receipt of a signal, the Bookmarking collector always attempts to choose an empty page. If this is not possible, it calls the collector and then selects a newly emptied page. This choice can be communicated to the virtual memory manager through a system call, for example `madvise` with the `MADV_DONTNEED` flag. Thus Bookmarking attempts to shrink the heap to avoid page faults. It never selects pages in the nursery or those containing its metadata. If Bookmarking cannot find an empty page, it chooses a victim (often the scheduled page) and scans it for outgoing references, setting a bit in their targets' headers. Hertz *et al.* extend the Linux kernel with a new system call allowing user processes to surrender a list of pages.

If the whole heap is not memory resident, full heap collections start by scanning it for bookmarked objects, which are added to the collector's work list. While this is expensive, it is cheaper in a small heap than a single page fault. Occasionally it is necessary to compact the old generation. The marking phase counts the number of live objects of each size class and selects the minimum set of pages needed to hold them. A Cheney pass then moves objects to these pages (objects on the target page are not moved). Bookmarked objects are never moved in order to avoid having to update pointers held in non-resident pages.

10.9 Ulterior reference counting

So far we have seen a number of different partitioned organisations of the heap. Each partitioning scheme allows different spaces of the heap to be managed by different policies or algorithms, collected either at the same or at different times. Segregation has been used to distinguish objects by their expected lifetimes, by their size or in order to improve heap utilisation. In the final section of this chapter, we consider segregation of objects according to the rate at which they are mutated.

There is ample evidence that for a wide range of applications young objects are allocated and die at very high rates; they are also mutated frequently (for example, to initialise them) [Stefanović, 1999]. Evacuation is an effective technique for such objects since it allows fast bump pointer allocation and needs to copy only live data, little of which is expected. Modern applications require increasingly large heaps and live sets. Long-lived objects tend to have lower mortality and update rates. All these factors are inimical to tracing collection: its cost is proportional to the volume of live data and it is undesirable to trace long-lived data repeatedly. On the other hand, reference counting is well suited to such behaviour as its cost is simply proportional to the rate at which objects are mutated. Blackburn and McKinley [2003] argue that each space, young and old, should be managed by a policy appropriate to its size, and to the expected lifetimes and mutation rate of the objects that it contains.

Their *Ulterior reference counting* collector therefore manages young objects by copying and older ones by reference counting. It allocates young objects into a bounded-size nursery space, using bump pointer allocation. Any young objects that survive a nursery collection are copied to a mature space, managed with segregated fits free-lists. The mutator write barrier is responsible both for managing reference counts of objects in the mature space and for remembering pointers from that space to young objects. Reference counting is deferred for operations involving stacks or registers, and the collector coalesces reference count updates made to other heap objects. Whenever a pointer field of an unlogged object is updated, the object is logged. Logging records the address of the object and buffers a decrement for each of the object's referents in the reference counted mature space.[7]

At garbage collection time, the collector moves surviving young objects into the reference counted world, and reclaims unreachable data in both spaces. It increments the count of each reference counted child in the mutation log; any targets in the nursery are marked as live, and added to the nursery collector's work list. As surviving young objects are promoted and scavenged, the collector increments the reference counts of their targets. As with many other implementations of deferred reference counting, the counts of objects referenced by the roots are also incremented temporarily during collection. All the buffered increments are applied before the buffered decrements. Cyclic garbage is handled using the Recycler algorithm [Bacon and Rajan, 2001]. However, rather than invoking it at each collection on all those decremented objects whose count did not reach zero, Blackburn and McKinley trigger cycle detection only if the available heap space falls below a user-defined limit. An abstract view of Ulterior reference counting is shown in Figure 10.9; compare this with standard deferred reference counting shown in Figure 5.1 in Chapter 5.

Goodell *et al.* [2010] adopt a different approach to optimising reference counting heavily contended objects for multithreaded MPI programs in high performance computing, partitioning objects by type. First, they suppress reference counting on predefined objects with immortal lifetimes (those with lifetimes from MPU_Init to MPI_Finalize). Second, they manage heavily contended objects with a mark-sweep collector. The reference

---

[7]In contrast, the write barrier of Levanoni and Petrank [2001] records a snapshot of the mutated object (see Chapter 5).

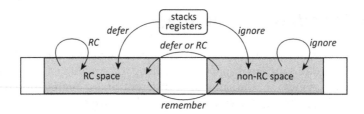

Figure 10.9: Ulterior reference counting schematic: the heap is divided into a space that is managed by reference counting and one that is not. The schematic shows whether reference counting operations on pointer loads or stores should be performed eagerly, deferred or ignored.

Blackburn and McKinley [2003], doi: 10.1145/949305.949336
© 2003 Association for Computing Machinery, Inc. Reprinted by permission.

counts for these objects are not manipulated when a transient object acquires or releases a reference to them. Instead, they are allocated with a reference count of two — the second reference being held by the garbage collector which maintains a set of these objects. At collection time, the collector (i) sweeps its set of collector-managed objects, marking them not live, (ii) traces from its set of allocated transient objects, marking live any collector-managed objects it finds, and finally (iii) sweeps the set of collector-managed objects again, reclaiming any not marked live.

10.10   Issues to consider

As we have seen in this chapter, there are several reasons other than age to segregate objects in the heap. We can partition the set of objects in the heap so that we can manage different partitions or spaces under different policies and with different mechanisms: the policies and mechanisms adopted will be those most appropriate to the properties of the objects in the space. Partitioning by physical segregation can have a number of benefits including fast address-based space membership tests, increased locality, selective defragmentation and reduced management costs.

One of the most common policies is to manage large objects differently from small ones. Large objects are placed in their own space, which is typically a non-moving space in order to avoid the cost of copying or compacting these objects. Large objects are usually allocated to their own sequence of pages, which are not shared with other objects. It can be worthwhile distinguishing objects that do not contain pointers (such as bitmaps representing images) from large arrays of pointers: it is not necessary to trace the former and, if they are marked in a separate bitmap, it is never necessary for the collector to access them, thus avoiding page and cache faults.

Partitioning can also be used to allow the heap to be collected incrementally rather than as a whole. Here, we mean that the collector can choose to collect only a subset of the spaces in the heap in the same way that generational collectors preferentially collect only the nursery generation. The benefit is the same: the collector has a more tightly bounded amount of work to do in any single cycle and hence it is less intrusive.

One approach is to partition the graph by its topology or by the way in which the mutator accesses objects. One reason for doing this is to ensure that large pointer structures are eventually placed in a single partition that can be collected on its own. Unless this is done, garbage cyclic structures that span partitions can never be reclaimed by collecting a single partition on its own. Collectors like the Train algorithm [Hudson and Moss, 1992] or connectivity-based garbage collection [Hirzel *et al.*, 2003] use the topology of objects. The Train algorithm collects a small space at a time and relocates survivors into the same spaces as other objects that refer to them. Connectivity-based collection uses a pointer analysis to place objects into a directed acyclic graph of partitions, which can be collected in topological order. Objects can also be placed into regions that can be reclaimed in constant time, once it is known that all the objects in a region are dead. Placement can either be done explicitly, as for example by the Real-Time Specification for Java, or automatically guided by a region inferencing algorithm [Tofte *et al.*, 2004]. Rust and C++ may also be able to infer (some) dynamically allocated objects that die as a scope is exited.

Pointer analyses have also been used to partition objects into heaplets that are never accessed by more than one thread [Steensgaard, 2000; Jones and King, 2005]. These heaplets can then be collected independently and without stopping other threads. Blackburn and McKinley [2003] exploit the observation that mutators are likely to modify young objects more frequently than old ones. Their Ulterior reference counting collector thus manages young objects by copying and old ones by reference counting. High mutation rates do not impose any overhead on copying collection which is also well suited to spaces with high mortality rates. Reference counting is well suited to very large, stable spaces which would be expensive to trace.

Another common approach is to divide the heap into spaces and apply a different collection policy to each space, chosen dynamically [Lang and Dupont, 1987; Detlefs *et al.*, 2004; Blackburn and McKinley, 2008]. The usual reason for this is to allow the heap to be defragmented incrementally, thus spreading the cost over several collection cycles. At each collection, one or more regions are chosen for defragmentation; typically their survivors are evacuated to another space whereas objects in other spaces are marked in place. Copying live data space by space also reduces the amount of space required to accommodate the survivors compared with standard semispace collection. At the extreme, the Mark-Copy collector [Sachindran and Moss, 2003], designed for collection in restricted heaps, copies the whole of its old generation in a single collection cycle, but does so block-by-block in order to limit the space overhead to a single block. Its successor, MC^2 [Sachindran *et al.*, 2004], offers greater incrementality, working to achieve good utilisation of available memory and CPU resources while also avoiding large or clustered pauses.

Chapter 11

Run-time interface

The heart of an automatic memory management system is the collector and allocator, their algorithms and data structures, but these are of little use without suitable means to access them from a program or if they themselves cannot appropriately access the underlying platform. Furthermore, some algorithms impose requirements on the programming language implementation, for example to provide certain information or to enforce particular invariants. The interfaces between the collector (and allocator) and the rest of the system, both the language and compiler above, and the operating system and libraries beneath, are the focus of this chapter.

We consider in turn allocating new objects; finding and adjusting pointers in objects, global areas and stacks; actions when accessing or updating pointers or objects (barriers); synchronisation between mutators and the collector; managing address space; and using virtual memory.

11.1   Interface to allocation

From the point of view of a programming language, a request for a new object returns an object that is not only allocated, but also initialised to whatever extent the language and its implementation require. Different languages span a large range of requirements. At one end of the spectrum is C, which only requires a freshly allocated cell of storage of the requested size — the values in that cell are arbitrary and initialising the cell is entirely the programmer's responsibility. At the other end of the spectrum lie pure functional languages such as Haskell, where at the language level one must provide values for all the fields of a new object and it is not possible to perceive an uninitialised object. Languages more concerned with type safety require proper initialisation of all fields, either by requiring the programmer to provide (or assign) values or by using safe defaults for each type, or through some combination of these techniques.

For our purposes, we break allocation and initialisation down into three steps, not all of which apply in every language or case.

1. Allocate a cell of the proper size and alignment. This is the job of the allocation subsystem of the memory manager.

2. System initialisation. By this we mean the initialisation of fields that must be properly set before the object is usable in any way. For example, in object-oriented languages this might include setting the method dispatch vector in the new object. It generally also includes setting up any header fields required by the language, the

171

memory manager or both. For Java objects this might include space for a hash code or synchronisation information, and for Java arrays we clearly need to record their length somewhere.

3. Secondary initialisation. By this we mean to set (or update) fields of the new object *after* the new object reference has 'escaped' from the allocation subsystem and has become potentially visible to the rest of the program, other threads and so on.

Consider the three example languages again.

- C: All the work happens in Step 1; the language neither requires nor offers any system or secondary initialisation — the programmer does all the work (or fails to). Notice, though, that allocation may include setting up or modifying a header, outside of the cell returned, used to assist in freeing the object later.

- Java: Steps 1 and 2 together provide an object whose method dispatch vector, hash code and synchronisation information are initialised, and all fields set to a default value (typically all zeroes). For arrays, the length field is also filled in. At this point the object is type safe but 'blank'. This is what the new bytecode returns. Step 3 in Java happens in code provided inside a constructor or static initialiser, or even afterwards, to set fields to non-zero values. Even initialisation of final fields happens in Step 3, so it can be tricky to ensure that other threads do not see those fields change if the object is made public too soon.

- Haskell: The programmer provides the constructor with values for all fields of the requested object, and the compiler and memory manager together guarantee complete initialisation before the new object becomes available to the program. That is, everything happens in Steps 1 and 2, and Step 3 is disallowed. ML works the same way for object creation even though it offers mutable objects as a special case, and Lisp is likewise biased towards functional creation of objects even though it also supports mutation.

If a language requires complete initialisation, like Haskell and ML, then there is a bit of a problem defining the interface to allocation: there is an essentially infinite variety of signatures for allocating, depending on the number of fields and their types. The implementers of Modula-3, which allows functional-style initialisation of new objects but does not require it, solved the problem by passing an *initialising closure* to the allocation subroutine. Allocation then acquires the necessary storage and invokes the initialising closure to fill in the new object. The closure has access to the values to insert and code to copy those values into the object. Given the static scoping of Modula-3, such closures do not themselves require heap allocation, but only a static chain pointer (reference to the enclosing environment's variables) — a good thing, since otherwise there might be an infinite regress. However, if the compiler generates the initialisation code for these languages, whether the initialisation happens 'inside' the allocation routine or outside does not matter.

The Glasgow Haskell Compiler solves the problem in a different way: it inlines all of Steps 1 and 2, calling the collector if memory is exhausted. It uses sequential allocation so obtaining the cell is simple, and initialisation proceeds by setting the header word and the object's fields, whose values were already calculated. This is an example of tight integration of a compiler and a particular approach to allocation (and collection).

Note that functional initialisation has two strong advantages: it helps ensure complete initialisation of objects and, provided that the initialisation code is effectively atomic with respect to possible garbage collection, it allows the initialising stores to avoid some write barriers. In particular one can omit generational write barriers in the functional initialisation case because the object being initialised *must* be younger than any objects to which it refers. In contrast, this is not generally true in Java constructors [Zee and Rinard, 2002].

A language-level request for a new object will eventually translate into a call to an allocation routine, which may sometimes be inlined by a compiler, to accomplish Step 1 and possibly some or all of Step 2. The key property that allocation needs to satisfy is that Steps 1 and 2 are effectively atomic with respect to other threads and to collection. This guarantees that no other component of the system will perceive an object that lacks its system initialisation. However, if we consider the interface to the allocator (Step 1), there remains a range of possibilities depending on the division of labour between Steps 1, 2 and 3. Arguments to an allocation request may include the following.

The size requested, generally in bytes, but possibly in words or some other granule size. When requesting an array, the interface may present the element size and the number of elements separately.

An alignment constraint. Typically there is a default alignment and a way to request an alignment that is more strict. These constraints may consist of only a power-of-two indication (word, double-word, quad-word alignment, and so on) or a power of two and an offset within that modulus (such as aligned on word two of a quad-word).

The kind of object to allocate. For example, managed run-time languages such as Java typically distinguish between array and non-array objects. Some systems distinguish between objects that contain no pointers and ones that may contain pointers [Boehm and Weiser, 1988]; objects containing executable code may also be special. In short, any distinction that requires attention by the allocator needs to appear at the interface.

The specific type of object to allocate, in the sense of programming language types. This is different from 'kind' in that it may not of itself be interesting to the allocator. Rather, the allocator may use it in initialising the object, and so forth. Passing this value in may simplify making Step 2 atomic (by moving the burden to Step 1) and may also reduce code size by avoiding one or more extra instructions at each allocation site.

Which of these arguments we need depends somewhat on the language we are supporting. Furthermore, we may present information somewhat redundantly at the interface to avoid forcing additional computation at run time. While it is possible to provide a single rich allocation function that takes many arguments and handles all cases, for speed and compactness we might provide a number of allocation functions, tailored to different kinds of object. Considering Java as an example, we might break it down into: scalar objects (non-arrays), arrays of `byte`/`boolean` (one-byte elements), arrays of `short`/`char` (two-byte elements), arrays of `int`/`float` (four-byte elements), arrays of references and arrays of `long`/`double` (eight-byte elements). Beyond this there may be internal things such as the objects that represent classes, method dispatch tables, method code and so on, depending on whether they are held in the collected heap. Even if they are not part of the collected heap, one still needs an interface to the explicit-free allocator that creates them.

Here are some of the possibilities for the post-condition that the allocator guarantees at the end of Step 1 if it succeeds.

- The referenced cell has the requested size and alignment, but is not otherwise prepared for use.

- Beyond having correct size and alignment, the cell is zeroed. Zeroing helps to guarantee that the program cannot treat old pointers — or non-pointer bit patterns for that matter — as valid references. Zero is a good value because it typically represents the null pointer and is otherwise a bland and legal value for most types. Some languages, such as Java, require zeroing or something similar for their security and type-safety guarantees. It can also be helpful in debugging a system if non-allocated memory has a specific and easily recognised non-zero bit pattern, such as `0xdeadbeef` or `0xcafebabe`, values we have actually seen.

- The allocated cell appears to be an object of the requested type. This is a case where we present the type to the allocator. The difference between this and the weakest post-condition (the first one in this list) is that the allocator fills in the object header.

- The allocator guarantees a fully type-safe object of the requested type. This involves both zeroing and filling in the object header. This is not quite the same as a fully *initialised* object in that zeroing provides a safe, but bland, default value, while a program will generally initialise at least one field to a non-default value.

- The allocator guarantees a fully initialised object. This may be less common, since the interface must provide for passing the initial value(s). A good example is the `cons` function in Lisp, which we might provide as a separate allocation function because calls to it are so common and need to be fast and simple from the program's side.

What is the most desirable post-condition? Some aspects, such as zeroing, may be dictated by the language semantics. Likewise, some may be dictated by the level of concurrency in the environment, and whether and how objects might 'leak' from an allocating thread and become visible to other threads or the collector. Generally, the more concurrent or leaky the setting, the stronger the post-condition we need.

What happens if the allocator cannot immediately satisfy the request? In most systems we want to trigger collection internally and avoid revealing this case to the caller. There is generally little that a caller can do, and it is wasteful to insert retry loops everywhere the program tries to allocate an object.[1] However, especially in the presence of inlining, we might inline the common (successful) case and call a collect-and-retry function out of line. Of course if we inline Step 1, then there remains little distinction between Steps 1 and 2 — the overall code sequence must be effectively atomic. Later on we discuss handshaking between mutators and collectors, so as to achieve such atomicity. We note that for purposes of atomicity it is generally more appropriate to view allocation as a mutator activity.

Speeding allocation

Since many systems and applications tend to allocate at a high rate relative to the rest of their computation, it is important to tune allocation to be fast. A key technique is to inline the common case code (the *'fast path'*) and call out to *'slow path'* code that handles the rarer, more complex cases. Making good choices here requires careful comparative measurements under suitable workloads.

An apparent virtue of sequential allocation is its simplicity, which leads to a short code sequence for the common case. This is especially true if the target processor provides enough registers to dedicate one to hold the bump pointer, and possibly one more to hold the heap limit. In that case the typical code sequence might be: move the bump pointer to the result register; add-immediate the needed size to the bump pointer; compare the bump

---

[1]In principle a Java program can catch the exception and try nulling some pointers and restarting a computation, but we are not aware of that strategy in real programs. Besides, Java's soft references are an arguably better way to do the same thing.

pointer against the limit; conditionally branch to a slow path call. Notice that putting the bump pointer into a register assumes per-thread sequential allocation areas. Some ML and Haskell implementations further combine multiple allocations in a straight line (basic block) of code into one larger allocation, resulting in just one limit test and branch. The same technique can work for code sequences that are single-entry but multiple-exit by allocating the maximum required along any of the paths, or at least using that as the basis for one limit test on entry to the code sequence. Clifford *et al.* [2014] gave a name to this optimisation of combining multiple allocations into a single one: *allocation folding*. They went on to observe that, because the objects are guaranteed at the time of allocation to reside in the same generation, a compiler can safely remove more write barriers for stores to those objects, at least up to the next garbage collection safe-point (see Section 11.6). They found that these optimisations can offer significant improvements in performance.

It might seem that sequential allocation is necessarily faster than free-list techniques, but segregated-fits can also be quite efficient if partially inlined and optimised. If we know the desired size class statically, and we keep the base pointer to the array of free-list pointers in a dedicated register, the sequence is: load the desired list pointer; compare it with zero; branch if zero to a slow path call; load the next pointer; store the next pointer back to the list head. In a multithreaded system the last step may need to be atomic, say a compare-and-swap with branch back to retry on failure, or we can provide each thread with a separate collection of free-list heads.

Zeroing

Some system designs require that free space contain a distinguished value, often zero, for safety, or perhaps some other value (generally for debugging). Systems offering a weak allocation guarantee, such as C, may not do this,[2] or may only do it as an option for debugging. Systems with a strong guarantee, such as functional languages with complete initialisation, do not need zeroing — though optionally setting free space to a special value may aid in debugging. Java is the typical example of a language that requires zeroing.

How and when might a system zero memory? We could zero each object as we allocate it, but experience suggests that bulk zeroing is more efficient. Also, zeroing with explicit memory writes at that time may cause a number of cache misses, and on some architectures, reads may block until the zeroing writes drain from a hardware write buffer/store queue. Some ML implementations, and also Oracle's HotSpot Java virtual machine, *prefetch* ahead of the (optimised) bump pointer precisely to try to hide the latency of fetching newly allocated words into the cache [Appel, 1994; Gonçalves and Appel, 1995]. Modern processors may also detect this pattern and perform the prefetching in hardware. Diwan *et al.* [1994] found that write-allocate caches that can allocate on a per-word basis offered the best performance, but these do not seem to be common in practice.

From the standpoint of writing an allocator, it is often best to zero whole chunks using a call to a library routine such as `bzero`. These routines are typically well optimised for the target system, and may even use special instructions that zero directly in the cache without fetching from memory, such as `dcbz` (Data Cache Block Zero) on the PowerPC or `dc zva` (Data Cache Zero by Virtual Address) on the ARMv8-A architecture. Notice that direct use of such instructions may be tricky since the cache line size is a model-specific parameter. In any case, a system is likely to obtain best performance if it zeroes large chunks that are power-of-two aligned.

Another technique is to use demand-zero pages in virtual memory. While these are fine for start-up, the overhead of the calls to remap freed pages that we are going to reuse, and of the traps to obtain freshly zeroed real memory from the operating system, may be

---

[2]While `malloc` does not zero memory, `calloc` does.

higher than zeroing pages ourselves. In any case, we should probably remap pages in bulk if we are going to use this technique, to amortise some of the cost of the call.

Another question is *when* to zero. We might zero immediately after collection. This has the obvious disadvantage of lengthening the collection pause and the less obvious disadvantage of dirtying memory long before it will be used. Such freshly zeroed words will likely be flushed from the cache, causing write-backs, and then will need to be reloaded during allocation. Anecdotal experience suggests the best time to zero from the standpoint of performance is somewhat ahead of the allocator, so that the processor has time to fetch the words into the cache before the allocator reads or writes them, but not so far ahead of the allocator that the zeroed words are likely to be flushed. Given modern cache miss times, it is not clear that the prefetching technique that Appel described will work; at least it may need tuning to determine the proper distance ahead of the allocator that we should prefetch. Yang *et al.* [2011] explored the performance issues in some detail, finding the average overhead of zeroing to be 3% to 5%, and up to more than 12%, on a high performance virtual machine. They found that bulk zeroing could benefit from using a hardware feature called *non-temporal stores* (also called *cache bypassing*), that is, stores that do not cause the updated data to be fetched into the cache. They obtained average performance improvement of 3% with their techniques. For purposes of *debugging*, zeroing or writing a special value into memory should be done as soon as we free cells, to maximise the range of time during which we will catch errors.

11.2   Finding pointers

Collectors need to find pointers in order to determine reachability. Some algorithmic tactics require *precise* knowledge of pointers. In particular, safely moving an object at location x to a new location x' and reusing its original cell requires us to update all pointers to x to refer to x'. However, safely reclaiming an object demands certainty that the program will no longer use it, but the converse is not true: it is *safe* to retain an object that the program will never use again, although it is space-inefficient (which admittedly could cause a program to fail for lack of available heap). Thus a collector can *estimate* references to non-moving objects, as long as its estimates are conservative — it may only *over*-estimate the references to an object but not under-estimate them. Reference counting without cycle collection is conservative, but another way conservatism arises in some schemes is because they lack precise knowledge of pointers. Thus they may treat a non-pointer value as if it is a pointer, particularly if it appears to refer to an allocated object. We consider first techniques for conservative pointer finding and then ones for accurately finding pointers in various locations.

Conservative pointer finding

The foundational technique for conservative pointer finding is to treat each contiguous pointer-sized and aligned sequence of bytes as a *possible* pointer value, called an *ambiguous pointer*. Since the collector knows what memory regions compose the heap, and even which parts of those regions are allocated, it can discriminate possible pointers from values that cannot be pointers. For speed, the collector's algorithm for testing a pointer value's 'pointer-ness' needs to be efficient. A typical approach works in two steps. First it filters out values that do not refer to any heap area in memory. It might do this with a range test if the heap is one contiguous area, or by taking the value's upper bits, obtaining a chunk number and looking in a table of heap chunks. The second step is to see if the referenced storage in the heap is actually allocated. It might check that by consulting a

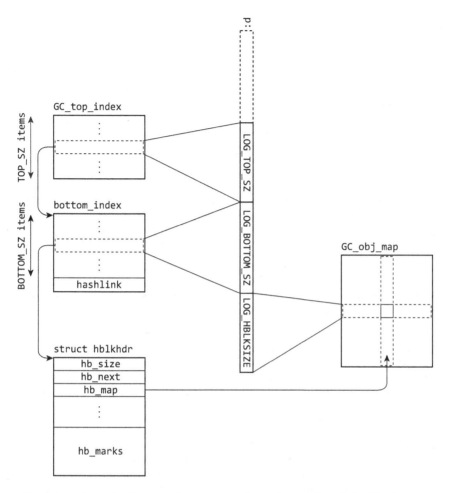

To determine whether a value p is a pointer to an allocated object:

1. Does p point between the lowest and highest plausible heap addresses?

2. Use high-order bits of p as an index into the first-level table to obtain the second-level table. In a 64-bit address space, the top-level table is a chained hash table rather than an array.

3. Use middle-order bits of p as an index into the second-level table to get the block header.

4. Is the offset of the supposed object a multiple of hb_size from the start of the block?

5. Consult the object map for blocks of this size; has the slot corresponding to this object in this block been allocated?

Figure 11.1: Conservative pointer finding. The two-level search tree, block header and map of allocated blocks in the Boehm-Demers-Weiser conservative collector.

Jones [1996]. Reprinted by permission.

bitmap of allocated words. For example, the *Boehm-Demers-Weiser* conservative collector [Boehm and Weiser, 1988] works in terms of blocks, with each block dedicated to cells of a particular size. A block has associated metadata giving the cell size, and also a bitmap indicating allocated versus free cells. After doing a range check using the heap bounds, this algorithm next checks to see if the referenced block is allocated at all, and if the block is allocated it checks whether the particular object is allocated. Only then will it set a mark bit in its marking phase. The whole process, illustrated in Figure 11.1, has a typical path length of about 30 RISC instructions.

Some languages require that pointers refer to the first word of their referent object, or some standard offset into the object, such as after some header words (see Figure 7.2). This allows a conservative collector to ignore possible interior pointer values as opposed to their canonical reference pointer. It is fairly easy to build conservative pointer finding algorithms in both cases; the Boehm-Demers-Weiser collector can be configured either way.[3] One caution concerning conservative collection for C is that it is legal for an 'interior' reference to an array to point one element *beyond the end* of the array. Therefore, conservative collectors for C may need to retain two objects in that case, or else over-allocate arrays by one word to avoid possible ambiguity. An explicit-free system may interpose a header between objects, which also solves the problem. In the presence of compiler optimisations, pointers may be even further 'mangled'; see Section 11.2 for a discussion of this topic.

Since a non-pointer bit pattern *may* cause the collector to retain an object that is in fact not reachable, Boehm [1993] devised a mechanism called *blacklisting*, which tries to avoid using regions of virtual address space as heap when their addresses correspond to these kinds of non-pointer values. In particular, if the collector encounters a possible pointer that refers to memory in a non-allocated block, it blacklists the block, meaning it will not allocate the block. Were it to allocate the block (and an object at that address), future traces would mistakenly recognise the false pointer as a true pointer. The collector also supports blocks used for strictly non-pointer objects, such as bitmaps. Distinguishing this data not only speeds the collector (since it does not need to scan the contents of these objects), but it also prevents excessive blacklisting that can result from the bit patterns of the non-pointer data. The collector further refines its blacklisting by discriminating between invalid pointers that may be interior, and those that cannot be interior, because they are from the heap in the configuration that disallows heap-stored interior pointers. In the possibly interior case, the referenced block is blacklisted from *any* use, while in the other case the collector allows the block to be used for small non-pointer objects (this cannot cause much waste). To initialise the blacklist, the collector does a collection immediately before the first heap allocation. It also avoids using blocks whose address ends in many zeroes, since non-pointer data in the stack often results in such values.

While conservative collection is typically considered to be relevant primarily to languages or implementation strategies that do not admit accurate pointer finding, and thus to be a kind of necessary evil to avoid if accurate pointer finding is possible, Shahriyar *et al.* [2014] (see also [Shahriyar, 2015]) found that conservative pointer finding may be faster. Specifically, for a suite of Java benchmarks they found that conservative deferred reference counting Immix was faster than its accurate counterpart. They also found that the excess retention of objects and the number of objects that had to be pinned (could not be moved) were quite small.

Somewhat conversely, Banerjee *et al.* [2020] explored how to do accurate collection for C programs. Their approach was to track the *provenance* (origin) of pointers through the program. They applied compile-time analyses and optimisations to do much of this tracking

---

[3]In either case it allows interior pointers, but in the more restrictive case it requires that any reachable object have a reachable pointer that is not interior. Thus in that configuration it ignores interior pointers when marking.

Tag	Encoded value
`00`	Pointer
`10`	Object header
`x1`	Integer

Table 11.1: An example of pointer tag encoding

Tag	Encoded value
`00`	Integer
`01`	Pointer
`10`	Other primitive value
`11`	Object header

Table 11.2: Tag encoding for the SPARC architecture

statically, applying dynamic tracking only when necessary. This tracking may introduce an overhead of 16%. However, they found that their sound and accurate collection is 13% faster than conservative collection and reclaims 6% more memory.

Accurate pointer finding using tagged values

Some systems, particularly ones based more on dynamic typing, include a *tag* with each value that indicates its type. There are two basic approaches to tagging: bit stealing and big bags of pages. *Bit stealing* reserves one or more bits, generally at the low or high end of each word, and lays out objects that can contain pointers in a word-oriented fashion.[4] For example, on a byte-addressed machine with a word size of four bytes, we might steal two bits for tags. We force objects to start on a word boundary, so pointers always have their low two bits zero. We choose some other value(s) to indicate (say) integers. Supposing that we give integers word values with a low bit of 1, we end up with 31-bit integers — bit stealing in this way does reduce the range of numbers we can represent easily. We might use a pattern of `10` in the low bits to indicate the start of an object in the heap, for parsability (Section 7.6). Table 11.1 illustrates the sample tag encoding, which is similar to one used in actual Smalltalk implementations.

Dealing with tagged integers efficiently is a bit of a challenge, though arguably the common case on modern pipelined processors might not be that bad — one cache miss might swamp it. Still, in order to support dynamically typed language implementations that use tagged integers, the SPARC architecture included instructions for adding and subtracting tagged integers. These instructions indicate overflow of the operation (there are versions that trap as well) or if either operand's two lowest bits are *not* zero. For this architecture we might use the tag encoding shown in Table 11.2. This encoding does require that we adjust references made from pointers, though in most cases that adjustment can be included in an offset field of a load or store instruction. The exception is in dealing with accesses to arrays, which then require the pointer to the array, the offset computed from the index *and* this additional adjustment. Still, given the hardware support for arithmetic on tagged integers, it seemed a reasonable trade-off. This encoding was previously used with the Motorola MC68000, which has a load instruction that adds an immediate constant, a base register and another register, all to form the effective address, so on the MC68000 there was no big penalty to using the encoding.

---

[4]See Section 15.1 for a different application of bit stealing.

The big bag of pages approach to tagging associates the tag/type information with an entire block. This association is therefore typically dynamic and involves a table lookup. The need for memory references is a disadvantage, but the corresponding advantage is that numeric and other primitive values have their full native length. This tagging approach dedicates whole blocks to hold integers, other blocks to floating point numbers, and so on. Since these are pure values and do not change,[5] when allocating new ones we might use hashing to avoid making new copies of the values already in the table. This technique, also called *hash consing* (from the Lisp `cons` function for allocating new pairs) is quite venerable [Ershov, 1958; Goto, 1974]. In hash consing Lisp pairs, the allocator maintains a hash table of immutable pairs and can avoid allocating a new pair if the requested pair is already in the table. This extends in the obvious way to any immutable heap-allocated objects, such as those of class `Integer` in Java. Notice that this is a case where it might be good to use weak references (Section 12.2) from the hash table to the objects it contains.

Accurate pointer finding in objects

Assuming we are not using tagged values, finding pointers in objects generally requires knowing each object's *type* — at least in the sense of which fields of the object are pointers. In object-oriented languages, that is, those with dynamic method dispatch, where the actual run-time type of an object is not entirely determined by the type of the referring pointer variable or slot, we need type information associated with the particular object. Systems usually accomplish this by adding a header to each object that includes type information. Since object-oriented languages generally have a method dispatch vector for each type, and they generally store a pointer to that vector in the header of each object of that type, they typically store information about the type in, or pointed to by, the dispatch vector. Thus the collector, or any other part of the run-time that uses type information (such as the reflection mechanism in Java), can find the type information quite readily. What the collector needs is a table that indicates where pointer fields lie in objects of the given type. Two typical organisations are a bit vector, similar to a bitmap of mark bits, and a vector of offsets of pointer fields. Huang *et al.* [2004] used a vector of offsets to particular advantage by permuting the *order* of the entries to obtain different tracing orders, and thus different orders of objects in a copying collector, improving cache performance. With care, they did this while the system was running (in a stop-the-world collector).

A way to identify pointers in objects that is simpler in some respects than using a table is to *partition* the pointer and non-pointer data. This is straightforward for some languages and system designs[6] but problematic for others. For example, in ML objects can be polymorphic. If the system generates a single piece of code for all polymorphic versions, and the objects need to use the same field for a pointer in some cases and a non-pointer in others, then segregation fails. In object-oriented systems that desire to apply superclass code to subclass objects, fields added in subclasses need to come after those of superclasses, again leading to mixing of pointer and non-pointer fields. One way around that is to place pointer fields in one direction from the reference point in the object (say at negative offsets) and non-pointer fields in the other direction (positive offsets), which has been called *bidirectional object layout*. On byte-addressed machines with word-aligned objects, the system can maintain heap parsability by ensuring that the first header word has its low bit set — preceding words contain pointers, whose two low bits will always be zero (see US Patent 5,900,001). In practice the tabular approach does not seem to be a problem, and as Huang *et al.* [2004] showed, it can actually be advantageous.

---

[5]This is a property of the representational approach, *not* of the language: in using this form of tagging, the designer made a choice to represent integers (floats, and so on) as tagged pointers to their full (untagged) values.

[6]Bartlett [1989b] takes this approach for a Scheme implementation done by translating to C, and Cheadle *et al.* [2000] take this approach in Non-Stop Haskell.

Some systems actually generate object-oriented style *methods* for tracing, copying and so on [Thomas, 1993; Thomas and Jones, 1994; Thomas, 1995a,b]. One can view the table approach as being like an interpreter and the method approach as the corresponding compiled code strategy. An interesting idea in Thomas's line of work is the system's ability, when copying a closure, to create a tailored version of the closure's environment that omits elements of the environment that the particular function does not use. This saves space in copied environment objects, and perhaps more significantly, avoids copying unused parts of the environment. Cheadle *et al.* [2004] also developed collection code specialised for each type of closure. Bartlett [1989a] applied the idea of methods for collection to C++ by requiring the user to write a pointer-enumerating method for each collected C++ class.

A managed language can use object-oriented indirect function calls in other ways related to collection. In particular, Cheadle *et al.* [2008] dynamically change an object's function pointer so as to offer a self-erasing read barrier in a copying collector, similar to the approach Cheadle *et al.* [2000] used for the Glasgow Haskell Compiler (GHC). That system also used a version of stack barriers (see Section 11.5), implemented in a similar way, and it used the same trick again to provide a generational write barrier when updating thunks. A fine point of systems that update closure environments is that, since they can shrink an existing object, in order to maintain heap parsability they may need to insert a 'fake' object in the heap after the one that shrank. Conversely, they may also need to expand an object: here the old version is overwritten with an indirection node, holding a reference to the new version. Later collections can short-circuit the indirection node. Collectors can also perform other computation on behalf of the mutator such as eager evaluation of applications of 'well-known' functions to arguments already partially evaluated: a common example is the function that returns the head of a list.

In principle, statically typed languages can avoid object headers and save space. Appel [1989b] and Goldberg [1991] explain how to do this for ML, starting from type information provided only for roots (we have to start somewhere). Later, Goldberg and Gloger [1992] observe that this might require full type inference during collection, depending on how the program uses polymorphic types; see also [Goldberg, 1992].

While languages such as C are generally considered as not admitting accurate pointer finding because they permit arbitrary type casting and so on, see the discussion of accurate pointer finding for C at the end of the section on conservative pointer finding, above.

Now that we have described various strategies for accurate pointer finding in objects, how does their performance compare? Garner *et al.* [2011] considered this question across four hardware architectures with a suite of 18 benchmark programs. They found that choice of mechanism made a difference — 16% in collection time on average, with a 2.5% impact on total running time. They saw variation across architectures, but three techniques showed consistent advantage: layout of pointer fields within objects, specialisation, and encoding metadata in object headers. In particular, bidirectional layout sped pointer finding both because of its simplicity and because more user-level types map to the same layout, reducing the variety of cases presented to the collector. (We note that they found its advantages were lost for large heaps.) Specialisation was important in that a few cases can handle 90% of the objects, using code requiring less dispatching and call overhead. This can be characterised as following a policy of inlining the common cases. Lastly, using three bits in the object header to encode those most common cases supports rapid branching to the specialised code for those cases, avoiding memory references to tables describing an object's layout.

Accurate pointer finding in global roots

Finding pointers in global roots is relatively easy by applying almost any of the techniques mentioned for finding pointers in objects. Languages differ primarily in whether the set of global roots is entirely static or whether it can grow dynamically. Such dynamic growth can result from dynamic code loading. Some systems start with a base collection of objects. For example, Smalltalk, some Lisp and some Java systems start with a base system 'image', also called the boot image, that includes a number of classes/functions and instances, particularly if they start with an interactive programming environment. A running program might modify parts of the system image — usually tables of one kind or another — causing image objects to refer to newer objects. A system might therefore treat pointer fields in the image as roots. Notice, though, that image objects can become garbage, so it may be a good idea sometimes to trace through the image to find what remains actually reachable. This is all tied into whether we are using generational collection, in which case we may treat the image as a particularly old generation.

Accurate pointer finding in stacks and registers

One way to deal with call stacks is to heap allocate activation records, as advocated by Appel [1987], for example. See also [Appel and Shao, 1994, 1996] and a counter-argument by Miller and Rozas [1994]. Some language implementations manage to make stack frames look like heap objects and thus kill two birds with one stone. Examples include the Non-Stop Haskell [Cheadle *et al.*, 2000] and its later optimisation [Cheadle *et al.*, 2004]. It is also possible to give the collector specific guidance about the contents of the stack, for example as Henderson [2002] does with custom-generated C code for implementing the Mercury language, and which Baker *et al.* [2009] improved upon for a real-time Java implementation.

However, most languages treat stack frames specially because of the need for a variety of efficiencies in order to obtain best performance. There are three issues we consider:

1. Finding frames (activation records) within the stack.

2. Finding pointers within each frame.

3. Dealing with conventions concerning passing values as arguments, returning them, and saving and restoring values in registers.

In most systems it is not just the collector that needs to find frames in the stack. Mechanisms such as exception handling and continuations may need to 'parse' the stack, not to mention the tremendous value of stack examination in debugging and its requirement in some systems, such as Smalltalk. Of course the view given to the programmer may be one very cleaned up from the typically more optimised and 'raw' layout in the actual frames. Because stack parsing is generally useful, frame layout conventions generally provide for it. For example, many designs include a *dynamic chain* field in each frame, which points to the previous frame. Various other fields generally lie at fixed offsets from the reference point of the frame (the address to which the frame pointer or dynamic chain refers). These might include the return address, the static chain and so on. Systems also generally provide a map to determine from a return address the function within which the address lies. In non-collected systems this might only occur in debugger symbol tables, but many managed systems access this table from the program, so it may be part of the loaded or generated information about code, rather than just in auxiliary debugger tables.

To find pointers within a frame, a system might explicitly add *stack map* information to each frame to help the collector. This metadata might consist of a bitmap indicating which frame fields contain pointers, or the system might partition a frame into pointer-containing and non-pointer portions, with metadata giving the size of each. Notice that there are likely to be some initial instructions of each function during which the new frame exists but is not yet entirely initialised. Collecting during this time might be problematic; see our later discussion of garbage collection safe-points and mutator handshaking in Section 11.6. Alternatively, we might get by with careful collector analysis of the initial code sequence, with careful use of push instructions on a machine that supports them or some other custom-designed approach. Obviously frame scanning is simpler if the compiler uses any given frame field always as a pointer or always as a non-pointer. That way the whole function needs only one map.

However, the single-map approach is not always possible. For example, at least two language features make it difficult:

- generic/polymorphic functions.

- the Java virtual machine jsr instruction.

We previously observed that a polymorphic function may use the same code for pointer and non-pointer arguments. Since a straightforward stack map cannot distinguish the cases, the system needs some additional source of information. Fortunately, the caller 'knows' more about the specific call, but it too may be a polymorphic function. So the caller may need to 'pass the buck' to its caller. However, this is guaranteed to bottom out, at the main function invocation in the worst case. The situation is analogous to typing objects from roots [Appel, 1989b; Goldberg, 1991; Goldberg and Gloger, 1992].

In the Java virtual machine, the jsr instruction performs a local call, which does not create a new frame but rather has access to the same local variables as the caller. It was designed to be used to implement the try-finally feature of the Java language, using a single piece of code to implement the finally block by calling it using jsr in both the normal and the exceptional case. The problem is that during the jsr call, some local variables' types are ambiguous, in the sense that, depending on which jsr called the finally block, a particular variable, not used in the finally block but used later, might contain a pointer from one call site and a non-pointer from another. There are two solution approaches to this problem. One is to refer these cases to the calling site for disambiguation. In this approach rather than have each stack map entry be just 'pointer' or 'non-pointer' (that is, a single bit), we need an additional case that means 'refer to jsr caller'. In addition, we need to be able to find the jsr return address, which requires some analysis of the Java bytecode to track where it stored that value. An alternative, more popular in modern systems, is to transform the bytecode, or dynamically compile code, simply to duplicate the finally block. Whilst in pathological cases that might cause exponential blowup in code size, it substantially simplifies this part of the system. Anecdotal evidence suggests that generating Java stack maps for dynamically compiled code has been a significant source of subtle bugs, so managing system complexity here may be important. We note that some systems defer generating a stack map until the collector needs it, saving space and time in the normal case but perhaps increasing collector pause time.

Another reason that a system might choose not to use a single map per frame is that it further restricts the register allocator: it must use a given register consistently as a pointer or non-pointer. This is particularly undesirable on machines with few registers.

Notice that whether we have one map per function, or different ones for different parts of a function, the compiler must propagate type information far through the back end. This may not be overly difficult if we understand the requirement before we write the compiler, but revising existing compilers to do it can be quite difficult.

Optimising stack scanning. Griffin *et al.* [2005] developed two methods to reduce the typical effort needed to scan a stack. One used tags in stack frames to avoid creating stack maps for a frame over and over (see Chapter 20 on page 466) and incorporated stack barriers (see Section 11.5). The other tagged pointers in frames to avoid processing the same pointer multiple times during each stack scan (see page 467). This latter optimisation may be of most use with a non-moving collector and can help avoid reference count overflows when reference counting.

Finding pointers in registers. To this point we have ignored the issue of pointers in machine registers. There are several reasons why handling registers is more difficult than dealing with stack contents.

- As we pointed out previously, even if each stack frame field is fixed as a pointer or a non-pointer for a whole function, it is less convenient to impose that rule on registers — or to be even further restrictive and require that pointers, and only pointers, reside in a particular subset of the registers. It is probably practical only on machines that provide a large number of registers. Thus most systems will have more than one register map per function.

- Even when guaranteeing that no pointer stored in a global root, heap object or local variable is an interior or derived pointer (see pages 193–194 of this section), efficient local code sequences may result in a register holding such an 'untidy' pointer.

- Calling conventions often provide that some registers follow a *caller-save* protocol, in which the caller must save and restore a register if it wants the value to survive across a call, and that some other registers follow a *callee-save* protocol, in which the callee must save and restore a register, on behalf of callers deeper in the stack, before the callee can use the register. Caller-save registers are not a problem since the caller knows what kind of value is in them, but callee-save registers have contents known only to some caller up the stack (if any). Thus a callee cannot indicate in a register map whether or not an unsaved callee-save register contains a pointer. Likewise, if a callee saves a callee-save register to a frame field, the callee cannot say whether that field contains a pointer.

A number of systems require a callee-save stack unwinding mechanism as a matter of course, in order to reconstruct the frame structure of the stack and call chain, especially for systems that do not designate a 'previous frame' register and the like.

We now introduce an approach to the callee-save registers problem. First, we add metadata that indicates for each function which callee-save registers it saves, and where in its frame it saves them. We assume the more common design where a function saves in one go, near the beginning of the function, all the callee-save registers that it will use. If the compiler is more sophisticated and this information varies from place to place within a function, then the compiler will need to emit per-location callee-save information.

Starting with the top frame, we reconstruct the register state for each frame by 'unsaving' a callee's saved callee-save registers to obtain the register state of the caller at the point of call. As we go, we record which registers we 'unsaved' and the value that the callee had in them, for use as we come back up the stack. When we reach the base of the stack, we can ignore any saved callee-save register contents since there is no caller. Therefore, for that frame we can produce any pointers for the collector, and allow it to update them.

As we walk back up the stack, we re-save the callee-save registers. Notice that if the collector updated a pointer, then this will update the saved value appropriately. We get from our side memory the value that the callee had in the register. Once we have done this for all callee-save registers saved by the callee, we produce pointers for the callee, and allow the collector to update them as necessary. However, we should skip any registers

Algorithm 11.1: Callee-save stack walking

```
1   processStack(thread, func):
2       Regs ← getRegisters(thread)              /* register contents thread would see */
3       Done ← empty                             /* no registers processed yet */
4       Top ← topFrame(thread)
5       processFrame(Top, Regs, Done, func)
6       setRegisters(thread, Regs)      /* get corrected register contents back to thread */
7
8   processFrame(Frame, Regs, Done, func):
9       IP ← getIP(Frame)                        /* current instruction pointer (IP) */
10      Caller ← getCallerFrame(Frame)
11
12      if Caller ≠ null
13          Restore ← empty                      /* holds info to restore after doing caller */
14
15          /* Update Regs to Caller's view at point of call */
16          for each ⟨reg,slot⟩ in calleeSavedRegs(IP)
17              add(Restore, ⟨reg, Regs[reg]⟩)
18              Regs[reg] ← getSlotContents(Frame, slot)
19          processFrame(Caller, Regs, Done, func)
20
21          /* Write updated saved callee–save register value back to slots */
22          for each ⟨reg, slot⟩ in calleeSavedRegs(IP)
23              setSlotContents(Frame, slot, Regs[reg])
24
25          /* Update Regs to our view, adjusting Done */
26          for each ⟨reg, value⟩ in Restore
27              Regs[reg] ← value
28              remove(Done, reg)
29
30      /* process our frame's pointer slots */
31      for each slot in pointerSlots(IP)
32          func(getSlotAddress(Frame, slot))
33
34      /* process our frame's pointers in registers */
35      for each reg in pointerRegs(IP)
36          if reg ∉ Done
37              func(getAddress(Regs[reg]))
38              add(Done, reg)
```

---

whose contents we processed in the caller, to avoid processing them a second time. In some collectors, processing the same root more than once is not harmful; mark-sweep is an example since marking twice is not a problem. However, in a copying collector it is natural to assume that any unforwarded referent is in fromspace. If the collector processes the same root twice (not two different roots referring to the same object), then it would make an extra copy of the tospace copy of the object, which would be bad.

We offer details of this process in Algorithm 11.1, and now proceed to describe the example illustrated in Figure 11.2. In the algorithm, *func* is the function applied to each

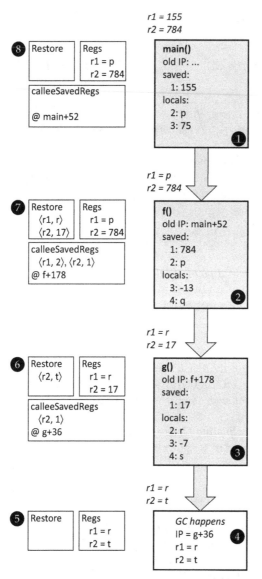

(a) Stack scanning: walking from the top

Figure 11.2: Stack scanning

frame slot and register, for example the body of the for each loop in markFromRoots of Algorithm 2.2 (Mark-Sweep, Mark-Compact) or the body of the root scanning loop in collect of Algorithm 4.2 (Copying).

Considering Figure 11.2a, notice first the call stack, which appears shaded on the right. The sequence of actions leading to that stack is as follows.

1. Execution begins at main with r1 containing 155 and r2 containing 784. Whatever effectively called main is outside the scope of the collected system, so it cannot refer to heap allocated objects and those register contents therefore cannot be references. Likewise we are not interested in the return address oldIP. As it executed, main saved

r1 in slot 1 and set local 2 to refer to object p and local 3 to hold 75. It then called f with r1 containing p, r2 containing 784 and a return address of main + 52.

2. Function f saved the return address, saved r2 in slot 1 and r1 in slot 2, and set local 3 to −13 and local 4 to refer to object q. It then called g with r1 containing a reference to object r, r2 holding 17 and a return address of f + 178.

3. Function g saved the return address, saved r2 in slot 1, and set local 2 to refer to object r, local 3 to hold −7 and local 4 to refer to object s.

The register contents above each frame's box indicate the values as execution entered the function in question, and the contents below the frame's box the values when that frame suspended execution. These are the values that our unwinding procedure should attempt to recover.

We now assume that a garbage collection occurs in the middle of g.

4. Garbage collection occurs at location g + 36 in g, when register r1 contains a reference to object r and r2 a reference to object t. One can think of the IP and register values as being stored in a suspended thread data structure or perhaps in an actual frame for the garbage collection routine.

At some point, garbage collection calls processStack on this thread stack, with *func* being the copy function of a copying collector. This is the most interesting case, since the collector will generally update object references because the target object moved. The boxes to the left in Figure 11.2a show the values of Regs and Restore as we proceed to examine the frames in the order g, f, main. We show numbered snapshots of Restore and Regs on the left in the figure, labelled with the numbers corresponding to these comments:

5. Here processStack has retrieved registers from the thread state into Regs and initialised Restore. Execution is at line 15 in Algorithm 11.1 for the frame for g.

6. Here we have updated Regs and saved information into Restore for later use. Execution is at line 19 for g's frame. Since g had saved r2 into slot 1, the proper value for f to see is 17. We save into Restore the fact that g's view of r2 should be t, when we get back to handling g after the recursive call of processFrame. We show the pairs returned by calleeSavedRegs for g's IP value in a box to the left of g's frame.

7. Execution is at line 19 for f's frame. We 'un-saved' both r1 and r2 in this case, from slots 2 and 1, respectively.

8. Execution is at line 19 for main's frame. Here we assume that Caller is null, so we do not 'un-save' any callee-saved registers — they cannot contain pointers since their values come from outside the managed universe.

Having reconstructed the register contents that held just as main called f, we can proceed to process the frame and registers for main, and likewise handle f and g. Turning to Figure 11.2b, we illustrate two states for each frame: first the state at line 35 of Algorithm 11.1 and then the state after line 38. The frames themselves show the state at line 35. Those values that are written, though their value is not necessarily *changed*, are in boldface; those not written are in grey.

9. Regs holds the register values at the point main called f; as yet, Done is empty.

10. Register r1 was updated by *func* (because r1 is in pointerRegs for main + 52). Done indicates that r1 refers to a (possibly) new location of its referent object.

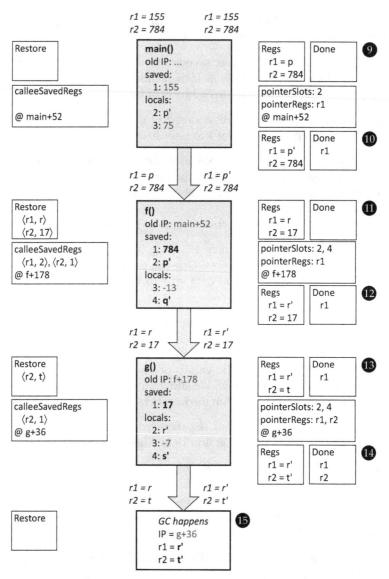

(b) Stack scanning: walking back to the top

Figure 11.2 (continued): Stack scanning

11. `Regs` holds the register values at the point where f called g. Notice that the values of r1 and r2 are saved into slots 2 and 1 of f's frame, and their values in `Regs` have been set from `Restore`.

12. Register r1 was updated by *func* and added to `Done`.

13. `Regs` holds the register values at the point garbage collection occurred in g. Specifically, the value in r2 is saved into slot 1 of g's frame and its value in `Regs` has been set from `Restore`. Since r1 has *not* been set from `Restore`, r1 remains listed in `Done`.

14. Register r1 was skipped (because it was in `Done`), but r2 was updated by *func* and added to `Done`

Algorithm 11.2: Stack walking for non-modifying *func*

```
 1  processStack(thread, func):
 2      Top ← topFrame(thread)
 3      processFrame(Top, func)
 4      Regs ← getRegisters(thread)          /* register contents thread would see */
 5      for each reg in pointerRegs(IP)       /* trace from registers at GC-point */
 6          func(getAddress(Regs[reg]))
 7
 8  processFrame(Frame, func):
 9      Done ← empty
10      loop
11          IP ← getIP(Frame)                 /* current instruction pointer (IP) */
12
13          /* process our frame's pointer slots */
14          for each slot in pointerSlots(IP)
15              func(getSlotAddress(Frame, slot))
16
17          /* process our frame's pointers in registers */
18          for each reg in pointerRegs(IP)
19              if reg ∉ Done
20                  func(getAddress(Regs[reg]))
21                  add(Done, reg)
22
23          Caller ← getCallerFrame(Frame)
24          if Caller = null
25              return
26
27          /* Update Regs to Caller's view at point of call */
28          for each ⟨reg,slot⟩ in calleeSavedRegs(IP)
29              Regs[reg] ← getSlotContents(Frame, slot)
30              remove(Done, reg)
31
32          Frame ← Caller
```

Finally, in step 15 processStack stores the values in Regs back to the thread state.

Variations on Algorithm 11.1. There are a number of reasonable variations on Algorithm 11.1. Here are some of particular interest:

- If *func* will not update its argument, then one can omit the Done data structure, the statements that update it, and the conditional test on line 36, invoking *func* unconditionally on line 37. This simplification applies for non-moving collectors and non-moving phases of moving collectors. It also applies if a moving collector's implementation of *func* works correctly if invoked on the same slot more than once.

- Rather than calling *func* late in processFrame, one can move the two for loops at the end upwards, inserting them after line 9. If combined with variation one, the resulting algorithm needs to process the stack only in one direction, which allows an iterative implementation as opposed to a recursive one, as shown in Algorithm 11.2.

Algorithm 11.3: No callee-save stack walking

```
 1  processStack(thread, func):
 2      Top ← topFrame(thread)
 3      processFrame(Top, func)
 4      Regs ← getRegisters(thread)              /* register contents thread would see */
 5      for each reg in pointerRegs(IP)          /* trace from registers at GC–point */
 6          func(getAddress(Regs[reg]))
 7      setRegisters(thread, Regs)               /* get corrected reg contents back to thread */
 8
 9  processFrame(Frame, func):
10      repeat
11          IP ← getIP(Frame)                    /* current instruction pointer */
12          for each slot in pointerSlots(IP)    /* process frame's pointer slots */
13              func(getSlotAddress(Frame, slot))
14          Frame ← getCallerFrame(Frame)
15      until Frame = null
```

- If the system does not support callee-save registers, and a function desires a register's contents to be preserved across a call, then the function must save and restore the register itself (caller-save). A saved caller-save register value will have a type known in the caller, so one can treat it just like a local or temporary variable. This results in the substantially simplified Algorithm 11.3, which is also iterative.

Compressing stack maps. Experience shows that the space needed to store stack maps can be a considerable fraction of the size of the code in a system. For example, Diwan *et al.* [1992] found their tables for Modula-3 for the VAX to be 16% of the size of code, and Stichnoth *et al.* [1999] reported their tables for Java to be 20% of the size of x86 code. Tarditi [2000] describes techniques for compressing these tables and applies them in the Marmot Java compiler, achieving a compression ratio of 4 to 5 and final table sizes averaging 3.6% of code size. The approach exploits two empirical observations.

- While there may be many garbage collection points (GC-points) needing maps, many of those maps are the same. Thus a system can save space if multiple GC-points share the same map. In the Marmot system, this is particularly true of call sites, which tend to have few pointers live across them. Tarditi [2000] found that this technique cut table space in half.

- If the compiler works to group pointers close together in stack frames, then even more maps tend to be the same. Using live variable analysis and colouring to place pointer variables with disjoint lifetimes into the same slot also increases the number of identical maps. Tarditi [2000] found this to be important for large programs.

The overall flow of Tarditi's scheme is as follows.

1. Map the (sparse) set of return addresses to a (smaller, denser) set of GC-point numbers.[7] In this mapping, if table entry t[i] equals return address ra, then ra maps to GC-point i.

---

[7]Tarditi uses the term 'call site' where we use 'GC-point'.

2. Map the set of GC-point numbers to a (small dense) set of map numbers. This is useful because multiple GC-points often have the same map. Given the GC-point i above, this can be written as map number mn=mapnum[i].

3. Index into a map array using the map number to get the map information. Given mn from the previous step, this can be written as info=map[mn].

In Tarditi's scheme the map information is a 32-bit word. If the information fits in 31 bits, then that word is adequate and its low bit is set to 0; otherwise, the low bit is set to 1 and the remaining bits point to a variable-length record giving the full map. The details probably need to be retuned for different platforms (language, compiler and target architecture), so refer to the paper for the exact encoding.

Tarditi also explored several organisations for mapping IP (instruction pointer) values to GC-point numbers.

- Using the same number for adjacent GC-points whose stack maps are the same, a technique also used by Diwan *et al.* [1992]. This only records the first GC-point, and subsequent ones whose address is less than the next address in the table are treated as being equivalent.

- Using a two-level table to represent what is conceptually a large array of GC-point addresses. This builds a separate table for each 64-kilobyte chunk of code space. Since all GC-points in the chunk have the same upper bits, it needs to record only the low 16 bits in each table entry. In a 32-bit address space this saves essentially half the table space. We also need to know the GC-point number for the first GC-point in a chunk; simply adding this to the index of a return address within the chunk's table will get the GC-point number for the matching IP.

- Using a sparse array of GC-points and interpolating by examining the code near the IP value. This chooses points roughly *k* bytes apart in the code, indicating where these places are, their GC-point number and their map number. It starts from the highest location preceding the IP value and disassembles code forward. As it finds calls (or other garbage collection points), it updates the GC-point number and map number. Notice that it must be able to recognise GC-points by inspection. Tarditi found that even for the x86 the disassembly process for these purposes was not overly complex or slow, though the scheme includes a 16-element cache to reduce repeated computation for the same return address values. It was the most compact of the schemes examined and the disassembly overhead was small.

Stichnoth *et al.* [1999] described a different stack map compression technique, oriented towards producing a map *for every instruction*. Similar to the sparse array of Tarditi [2000], this uses a scheme that records full information for certain reference points in the code, and then disassembles forward from the nearest preceding point to the IP value of interest. Stichnoth *et al.*, though, compute the actual map, as opposed to the GC-point number. The reference points at which it starts are (roughly) the beginning of basic blocks in the code. However, if the map at the end of one block is the same as the map at the beginning of the next one — that is, there was no flow merge that affected the map — then they treat the two blocks as one large block. Working forward from each reference point, they encode the length of the instruction at that point (because the x86 has variable length instructions) and the *delta* to the map caused by the instruction. For example, the instruction might push or pop a value on the stack, load a pointer into a register, and so on. They Huffman code the delta stream to obtain additional compression. Across a suite of benchmarks they get an average map size of about 22% of code size. They argue that, as a fraction of code size, the situation should not be worse for machines with larger register sets — the instructions increase in size too. Also, the overall space used might be somewhat better for machines with fixed-length instructions, since there is still a noticeable overhead for recording instruction lengths, even though (like Tarditi [2000]) they use a disassembler in most cases to avoid recording instruction lengths. They still need a fraction of a bit to mark those places where they cannot legally allow garbage collection, such as in the middle of the sequence for a write barrier. Given that a fixed-length instruction machine probably uses something like 4 bytes for each instruction, and the average instruction length for the x86 may be half that or less, the table size for a fixed-length instruction machine using the techniques of Stichnoth *et al.* may be more in the range of 5% to 10% of code size.

Accurate pointer finding in code

Code may contain embedded references to heap allocated objects, particularly in managed run-time systems that load or generate code dynamically. Even code compiled ahead of time may refer to static/global data, that might lie in an initially loaded heap. There are several difficulties around pointers within code:

- It is not always easy, or even possible, to distinguish code from any data embedded within it.

- As in the case of uncooperative compilers, it is not generally possible to tell embedded pointers from non-pointer data that happen to have a value that looks as if it refers to a location in the heap.

- When embedded in instructions, a pointer may be broken into smaller pieces. For example, on the MIPS processor, loading a 32-bit static pointer value into a register would typically require a load-upper-immediate instruction, which loads a 16-bit immediate field into the upper half of a 32-bit register and zeroes the low 16 bits, and then an or-immediate of another 16-bit value into the lower half of the register. Similar code sequences occur for other instruction sets. This is a particular case of derived pointers.

- An embedded pointer value may not refer directly to its target object; see our discussions of interior (on the facing page) and derived (on page 194) pointers.

In some cases one may be able to disassemble code to find embedded pointers, but going through all the code each time the collector needs to process the roots may have a large overhead. Of course, the program cannot update such embedded pointers, so caching their locations would be effective.

The more general solution is to arrange for the compiler to generate a side table that indicates where embedded pointers lie in the code.

Some systems simply rule out embedded pointers to avoid the issues altogether. The impact on code performance will vary according to target architecture, compilation strategy and statistics of programs' accesses.

Target objects that move. If the target of an embedded reference moves, then the collector must update the embedded reference. One possible difficulty is that for safety or security reasons code areas may be read-only. Thus the collector must either change the permissions temporarily (if possible), which might involve expensive system calls, or the system must disallow embedded references to moving objects. Another difficulty is that updating code in main memory generally does not force updates or invalidations of copies of that code residing in instruction caches. The solution is to require all processors to invalidate the affected instruction cache lines. Some machines may need to follow this by a special synchronisation instruction that guarantees that future instruction fetches occur logically after the invalidations. Furthermore, before invalidating instruction cache lines, one may need to force modified lines in the *data* cache (holding the bytes of code that were updated) to main memory, and synchronise to make sure that the writes are complete. The details are architecture specific.

Code that moves. A particular case of targets that move is code that a collector moves. Not only must this take into account the concerns that we just considered, but it must also fix up return addresses that lie in the stack and registers since they might refer to code that the collector is moving. Further, it must invalidate *all* instruction cache lines corresponding to the new location of the code and perform the careful code writing steps we enumerated above. Clearly it would be more deeply problematic if the code of the collector itself could move. Finally, moving code is particularly difficult in the case of concurrent collectors. Either the collector must stop the world, or arrange that threads can use either the old or the new copy of the code, move them to the new code over a period of time, and reclaim the space of the old code only after it knows all the threads have moved over.

Handling interior pointers

An *interior pointer* is a pointer that refers to some location inside an object, but not necessarily using the standard reference to the object. More precisely, we consider each object to occupy a set of memory locations (addresses), disjoint from those of any other object. An interior pointer to an object refers to one of the object's locations. If we consider Figure 7.2 we see that an object's standard reference may not correspond to any of its interior pointers! Also, the set of locations an object occupies may be larger than just the locations holding its programmer-visible data. For example, C allows pointers one location beyond the end of an array and that reference is still a legal interior pointer to the array.

While it is possible that a system might break a language-level object up into multiple pieces (as done by, for example, Siebert [1999]), for the purpose of handling interior (and derived) pointers we use the term 'object' to mean a contiguous range of locations devoted to representing a particular (language-level) object.

The key problem the collector faces with an interior pointer is determining the object to which the pointer refers, that is, how to compute the standard reference to the object from the value of the interior pointer. Several approaches are possible.

- Provide a table that records the start of each object. A system might maintain an array of object start addresses, perhaps in two-level form as done by Tarditi [2000] for recording GC-point addresses in code (see Section 11.2). Another way is to use a bitmap with one bit per granule (unit of allocation), setting the corresponding bit for granules that are the first granules of objects. This might be useful for the allocator and collector in any case.

- If the system supports heap parsability (Section 7.6), then one can scan the heap to find the object whose locations contain the target of the interior pointer. It would be prohibitively expensive to search from the beginning of the heap every time, so typically a system records the first (or last) object-start position within each k byte chunk of the heap, where k is usually a power of two for convenient and efficient calculation. This allows parsing to start in the chunk to which the interior pointer refers, or the previous chunk as necessary. There is a trade-off between the space used for this side table and the overhead of parsing. For a more detailed discussion, see Section 11.8.

- A big bag of pages organisation can determine object size by looking up the target block's metadata. It can compute the offset of the target within the block (simply mask so as to keep the appropriate lower bits of the address), and round that down using the object size to determine the first location of the object.

We do assume that given knowledge of the set of locations occupied by the target object, the collector can determine the standard reference and work from there. Notice that if the object moves, as in a copying collector, then we need to update the interior pointer, moving it by the same amount, that is, causing it to refer to the same relative position in the moved object as it did in the old copy. Alternatively, the system might support pinning of objects, as discussed in Section 11.4.

The primary objection to dealing with interior pointers is the space and time overhead they can add to processing. If interior pointers are relatively rare and distinguished from *tidy pointers* (those that refer to an object's standard reference point), then the time overhead of dealing with the interior pointers themselves may not be great. However, making provision for them at all may add space cost for tables — though the particular collector design may include the necessary tables or metadata anyway — and add time cost for maintaining the tables. There are also the considerations of programming complexity and software engineering and maintenance costs.

Return addresses are a particular case of interior pointers into code. They present no special difficulty, though for a variety of reasons the tables for looking up the function containing a particular return address may be distinct from the tables the collector uses for other objects.

Handling derived pointers

Diwan *et al.* [1992] identified what they call *derived pointers*, that is, values that are derived from one or more pointers via an arithmetic expression. Interior pointers are a special case where the expression has the simple form $p + i$ or possibly $p + c$ where p is a pointer, i is a dynamically computed integer offset and c is a statically known constant. However, for an interior pointer the resulting expression value must be an address within the set of locations of object p, which leads to the simpler solutions already discussed. Derived pointers can be much more general, for example:

- $upper_k(p)$ or $lower_k(p)$, the upper or lower k bits of the pointer p.

- $p \pm c$ such that the resulting address lies outside of the locations of p.

- $p - q$, the distance between two objects.

In some cases, we can reconstruct a tidy pointer — one that points to the referent's standard reference address — from the derived pointer. An example is $p + c$ where c is a compile-time known constant. In the general case, we must have access to the base expression from which the derived pointer was derived. That expression might itself be a derived pointer, but eventually gets back to tidy pointers.

In a non-moving collector, just having the tidy pointers available as roots is enough. Notice, though, that at a GC-point the tidy pointer may no longer be live in the sense of compiler live variable analysis, even though the derived pointer *is* live. Thus the compiler must keep at least one copy of the tidy pointer(s) for each live derived pointer. An exception to this rule is the $p \pm c$ case since adjusting with a compile-time known value produces the tidy pointer without reference to other run-time data.

For a moving collector, we need additional compiler support: the compiler needs to produce extended stack maps that give, for each derived pointer, the locations of the expressions from which it was derived and the operations needed to reconstruct the derived pointer. Diwan *et al.* [1992] give details on handling derived quantities of the form $\sum_i p_i - \sum_j q_j + E$ where the p_i and q_j are pointers or derived values and E is an expression not involving pointers (and thus not affected if any of the p_i or q_j move). The advantage of this form is that it can subtract out the p_i and add in q_j, forming E before moving any objects; do any moving; then add back the new p_i' and subtract off the new q_j' to produce the correct adjusted derived pointer.

Diwan *et al.* [1992] point out several issues that arise in optimising compilers when trying to handle derived pointers, including dead base variables (which we mentioned above), multiple derivations reaching the same point in code (for which they add more variables to record the path that actually pertains), and indirect references (where they record the value in an intermediate location along the chain of references). Supporting derived pointers sometimes required producing less optimal code, but the impact was slight. They achieved table sizes about 15% the size of code for Modula-3 on the VAX.

11.3 Object tables

For reasons of mutator speed and space consumption, many systems have represented object references as direct pointers to their referent objects. A more general approach is to give each object a unique identifier and to locate its contents via some mapping mechanism. This has been of particular interest when the set of objects is large, and possibly persistent, but the hardware's underlying address space is small in comparison. The focus here is on heaps that fit into the address space. Even in that case, however, some systems have found it helpful to use *object tables*. An object table is a typically dense array of small records, *handles*, which refer to objects. A handle may contain only a pointer to the object's data, or it may also contain additional status information, which might otherwise have been held in the object's header. For speed, an object reference is typically either a direct index into the object table or else a pointer to the handle in the object table. Using an index makes it easier to relocate the table, but requires adding the object table base in order to access an entry — which may not cost additional instructions provided that the system dedicates a register to point to the base of the table.

A significant advantage of object tables is that they permit straightforward compaction, or indeed moving of any object, at any time by simply moving the object(s) and then (atomically) updating its object table entry to reflect its new location. To simplify this, each object should have a hidden self-reference field (or back-pointer to its object table entry), to make it possible to find the table entry from the object's data. With this, a mark-compact collector can proceed by marking as usual (modulo the level of indirection imposed by the object table) and then doing a simple sliding compaction of the object data. Although it is easy to simply chain free object table entries into a free-list, Kalibera and Jones [2011] found this offered very poor performance in *Minuteman*, a framework for experimenting with real-time collection for Java. Instead, they construct the object table as a linked list of blocks of handles. Although they tried different implementations of handles, they found it most effective to place metadata in the handle, including a reference to class and size information but not array size (in order to allow fixed-size handles), instead of in the object header. Careful treatment of freed handles was important. To improve locality, their collector attempted to keep together freed handles from the same handle block as objects/handles tended to die in clumps. They also kept the blocks in address order. Notice that in marking it may be advantageous to keep mark bits in the handles, so as to save a memory reference when checking or setting the mark bit. A side mark bitmap has similar benefits.

Object tables may be problematic, or simply unhelpful, if the language allows interior or derived pointers. If a language disallows interior pointers, then whether or not the implementation uses an object table should not affect semantics of the implementation. However, there is one language feature that more or less *assumes* an object table for its efficient implementation: the Smalltalk `become:` primitive. This operator causes two objects to swap their roles in the object universe. This is easy to do with object tables: the system merely swaps the contents of two table entries. Without an object table a `become:` may require a sweep over the entire heap. If used sparingly (Smalltalk typically uses `become:` to install a new version of something) this may remain acceptable, particularly because direct object reference implementations are generally faster than object table ones.

11.4   References from external code

Some languages and systems support use of heap allocated objects from outside of the managed environment. A typical example is the Java Native Interface, which allows code written in C, C++ or possibly other languages to access objects in the Java heap. More generally, just about every system needs to support input/output, which must somehow move data between the operating system and heap objects. Two difficulties arise in supporting references from external code and data to objects in a managed heap. The first issue is ensuring that the collector continues to treat an object as reachable while external code possesses a reference to the object. This is necessary to prevent the object from being reclaimed before the external code is done with it. Often we need the guarantee only for the duration of a call to external code. We can make that guarantee by ensuring that there is a live reference to the object in the stack of the calling thread.

However, sometimes the object will be used by external code for a period of time that extends beyond an initial call. In that case the usual solution is for the collector to maintain a table of *registered objects*. The external code is required to register an object if the code will use the object after the current call. The external code must also explicitly deregister the object when the code no longer needs the object and will not attempt further use of it. The collector simply treats entries in the registered-object table as additional roots.

The second issue is ensuring that external code knows where an object is. This is only relevant to moving collectors. Some interfaces keep external code at arm's length by requiring all accesses to heap objects to go through collector-provided access routines. This makes it easier to support collectors that move objects. Typically the collector provides to external code a pointer to a handle. The handle contains a reference to the actual heap object, and possibly some other management data. Handles act as registered-object table entries, and thus are roots for collection. The Java Native Interface works this way.

While handles offer a clean separation of the managed heap from the unmanaged world, and they more easily admit collection techniques that move objects, not all external code is prepared to follow the access protocols, notably operating system calls. Thus it may be necessary to prevent externally referenced objects from moving. To support this, a *pinning* interface may offer *pin* and *unpin* operations, with the meaning that an object cannot be moved while it is pinned, and the further implication that pinned objects are reachable and will not be reclaimed.

If we know when allocating an object that it may need to be pinned, then we can allocate the object directly into a non-moving space. This may work for buffers for file stream I/O if the buffered-stream code allocates the buffers itself. However, in general it is difficult to determine in advance which objects will need to be pinned. Thus, some languages support `pin` and `unpin` functions that the programmer can invoke on any object.

Pinning is not a problem for non-moving garbage collectors, but is inconvenient for ones that normally move an object. There are several solutions, each with its own strengths and weaknesses.

- Defer collection, at least of a pinned object's region, while it is pinned. This is simple, but there is no guarantee that it will be unpinned before running out of memory.

- If the application requests pinning an object, and the object is not in a non-moving region, we can immediately collect the object's containing region (and any others required to be collected at the same time) and move the object to a non-moving region. This might be acceptable if pinning is not frequent, and the collector is of a design such as a generational collector with a nursery whose survivors are copied to a non-moving mature space.

- We can extend our collector to tolerate not moving pinned objects, which complicates the collector and may introduce new inefficiencies.

As a simple example of extending a moving collector to support pinning, consider a basic non-generational copying collector. Extending it to support pinned objects requires first of all that the collector can distinguish pinned from unpinned objects. It can copy and forward unpinned objects as usual. It will trace through pinned objects, updating pointers from the pinned object to objects that move, but leaving pinned objects where they are. The collector should also record in a table the pinned objects it encounters. When all survivors have been copied, the collector reclaims only the holes between pinned objects rather than reclaiming all of fromspace. Thus, rather than obtaining a single, large, free region, it may obtain an arbitrary number of smaller ones. The allocator can use each one as a sequential allocation space. This can lead to a degree of fragmentation, but that is unavoidable in the presence of pinning. Notice that a future collection may find that a previously pinned object is no longer pinned, so the fragmentation need not persist. As we saw in Section 10.3, some mostly non-moving collectors take a similar approach, also sequentially allocating in the gaps between surviving objects [Dimpsey *et al.*, 2000; Blackburn and McKinley, 2008].

Another possible difficulty is that, even though an object is pinned, the collector is examining and updating it, which may lead to races with external code that accesses the object at the same time. Thus, we may need to pin not only a given object but also some of the objects to which it refers. Likewise, if, starting from a given object, external code traces through to other objects, or even just examines or copies references to them without examining the objects' contents, those other objects also need to be pinned.

Features of a programming language itself, and its implementation, may require pinning. In particular, if the language allows passing object fields by reference, then there may be stack references to the interior of objects. The implementation can apply the interior pointer techniques described on page 193 in order to support moving the object containing the referent field. However, such support can be complex and the code for handling interior pointers correctly may thus be difficult to maintain. Therefore, an implementation might choose simply to pin such objects. This requires being able to determine fairly easily and efficiently which object contains a given referent. Hence it most readily allows interior pointers but not more general cases of derived pointers (see page 194 above).

11.5 Stack barriers

Earlier we described techniques for finding pointers in stacks, but assumed it was acceptable to scan the whole stack of a thread at once, that is, that the system could pause the thread long enough to process its entire stack. It is not safe to scan a frame in which a thread is actively running, so we must either pause the thread for some period of time or get the thread to scan for us (that is, call a scanning routine, essentially pausing itself) — see Section 11.6 for more discussion of when it is appropriate to scan a thread's registers and stack. It is possible to scan a stack incrementally, however, and also mostly-concurrently, using a technique called *stack barriers*. The idea is to arrange for a thread to be diverted if it tries to return (or throw) beyond a given frame in its stack. Suppose we have placed a barrier in frame F. Then we can asynchronously process the caller of F, its caller, and so on, confident that the running thread will not cut the stack back from under our scanning.

The key step to introduce a stack barrier is to hijack the return address of the frame. In place of the actual return address, we write the address of the stack barrier handler we wish to install. We put the original return address in some standard place that the stack barrier handler can find, such as a thread-local variable. The handler can then remove the barrier, as appropriate. Naturally it must be careful not to disturb any register contents that the caller may examine.

For incremental stack scanning by the thread itself, when it encounters the barrier, the handler scans some number of frames up the stack and sets a new barrier at the limit of its scanning (unless it finished scanning the whole stack). We call this *synchronous* incremental scanning. For *asynchronous* scanning by another thread, the barrier serves to stop the running thread before it overtakes the scanning thread. For its part, the scanning thread can move the barrier down after it scans some number of frames. That way it is possible that the running thread will never hit the barrier. If it does hit the barrier, then it merely has to wait for the scanning thread to advance and unset that barrier; then it can continue.

Cheng and Blelloch [2001] introduced stack barriers in order to bound the collection work done in one increment and to support asynchronous stack scanning. Their design breaks each stack into a collection of fixed-size stacklets that can be scanned one at a time. That is, returning from one stacklet to another is the possible location of what we call a stack barrier. But the idea does not require discontiguous stacklets or predetermination of which frames can have a barrier placed on them.

Stack barriers can also be used in the opposite way from that described above: they can mark the portion of the stack that has not changed, and thus that the collector does not need to reprocess to find new pointers. In collectors that are mostly-concurrent this approach can shorten the 'flip' time at the end of a collection cycle.

Another use for stack barriers is in handling dynamic changes to code, particularly optimised code. For example, consider the situation where routine A calls B, which calls C, and there is a frame on the stack for an optimised version of A that inlined B but did not further inline C. In this situation there is a frame for $A + B$ and another one for C. If the user now edits B, future calls of B should go to the new version. Therefore, when returning from C, the system should deoptimise $A + B$ and create frames for unoptimised versions of A and B, so that when B also returns, the frame for A supports calling the new version of B. It might also be possible to re-optimise and build a new $A + B$. The point here is that returning to $A + B$ triggers the deoptimisation, and the stack barrier is the mechanism that supports the triggering.

Yet another application of stack barriers is in implementing generalized work stealing [Kumar *et al.*, 2014], covered in Section 13.8.

11.6   GC safe-points and mutator suspension

In Section 11.2 we mentioned that a collector needs information about which stack frame slots and which registers contain pointers. We also mentioned that this information can vary according to the specific code location (we will say IP, for instruction pointer) at which garbage collection happens in a function. There are two issues of concern about where garbage collection can happen: whether a given IP is *safe* for garbage collection, and the size of the stack map tables (see Section 11.2 for details on compressing maps), which tend to be large if more IPs are legal for garbage collection.

What might make a given IP unsafe for garbage collection? Most systems have occasional short sequences of code that must be run in their entirety in order to preserve invariants relied on by garbage collection. For example, a typical write barrier needs to do both the underlying write and some recording. If a garbage collection happens between the two steps, some object may be missed by the collector or some pointer not properly updated by it. Systems usually have a number of such short sequences that need to be atomic with respect to garbage collection (though not necessarily atomic with respect to true concurrency). In addition to write barriers other examples include setting up a new stack frame and initialising a new object.

A system is simpler in one way if it can allow garbage collection at any IP — there is no concern about whether a thread is suspended at a point safe for garbage collection, a *GC safe-point* or *GC-point* for short. However, such a system is more complex in that it must support stack maps for every IP, or else employ techniques that do not require them, as for uncooperative C and C++ compilers. If a system allows garbage collection at most IPs, then if it needs to collect and a thread is suspended at an unsafe point, it can either interpret instructions ahead for the suspended thread until it is at a safe-point, or it can wake the thread up for a short time to get it to advance (probabilistically) to a safe-point. Interpretation risks rarely exercised bugs, while nudging a thread only gives a probabilistic guarantee. Such systems may also pay the cost of larger maps [Stichnoth *et al.*, 1999].

Many systems make the opposite choice and only allow garbage collection at certain restricted safe-points, and only produce maps for those points. The minimal set of safe-points needed for correctness includes each allocation (since garbage collection is always a possibility there)[8] and each call of a routine in which there may be allocation or which may cause the thread to suspend in a wait (since if the thread suspends, some other thread may cause a garbage collection).

Beyond the minimal points needed for correctness, a system may wish to allow garbage collection at more locations so as to guarantee that garbage collection can proceed without an unbounded wait for the thread to reach its next safe-point. To make this stronger guarantee, there needs to be a safe-point in each loop; a simple rule is to place a safe-point at each backwards branch in a function. In addition there needs to be a safe-point in each function entry or each return, since otherwise functions, especially recursive ones, could perform many calls and returns before encountering a safe-point. Since these additional safe-points do not do anything that actually can trigger a garbage collection, they need to have an added check for whether garbage collection is needed/requested, so we call them *GC check-points*. This checking adds overhead to the normal operation of mutators, though perhaps not very much, particularly if the compiler takes some simple measures to reduce the overhead. For example, it might omit the checks in methods that are quite short or have no loops or calls. Also, by inserting an additional level of looping it can avoid checking on every iteration of a loop and only check every nth iteration. If the check itself is cheap, then these measures will not be necessary. In any case there is a clear trade-off between the overhead of frequent checks and the latency of infrequent ones.

Agesen [1998] compared two ways of causing a thread to suspend at a GC-point. One is *polling*, alluded to above, where the thread checks a flag that indicates that a collection has been requested. The other technique is *patching*, which involves modifying the code at the next GC-point(s) of the thread so that when the suspended thread is restarted, it will stop

---

[8]Excepting the possibility of checking for adequate thread-private free space before a sequence of allocations.

at the next GC-point. This is similar to placing temporary breakpoints in a debugger. Some processors support a single-step trap mechanism that may be useful here. Agesen found that patching has much lower overhead than polling, but of course it is more difficult to implement, and more problematic in a concurrent system.

In bringing up the idea of GC check-points, notice that we have introduced the notion of a *handshake* mechanism between the collector and a mutator thread. Such handshakes may be necessary even if a system does not include true concurrency but merely multiplexes several mutator threads on one processor — the collector may need to indicate the need for garbage collection and then wake up any suspended thread that is not at a safe-point so that the thread can advance to a safe-point. Some systems allow threads to suspend only at safe-points so as to avoid this additional complexity, but for other reasons a system may not control all aspects of thread scheduling, and so may need this handshake.

For concreteness we mention some particular mechanisms for the handshake. Each thread can maintain a thread-local variable that indicates whether the rest of the system needs that thread's attention at a safe-point. This mechanism can be used for things other than signalling for a garbage collection. At a GC check-point, the thread checks that thread-local variable, and if it is non-zero (say) it calls a system routine that uses the exact value of the variable to determine what action to take. One particular value will indicate 'time to garbage collect'. When the thread notices the request, it sets another thread-local variable to indicate it has noticed, or perhaps decrements a global variable on which a collector thread is waiting. Systems typically arrange for thread-local variables to be cheap to access, so this may be a good approach.

Another possibility is to set a processor condition code in the saved thread state of the suspended thread. A GC check-point can then consist of a very cheap conditional branch over a call to the system routine for responding to the request. This approach only works if the processor has multiple condition code sets (as for the PowerPC) and can be guaranteed not to be in external code when awakened. If the machine has enough registers that one can be dedicated to the signalling, a register can be used almost as cheaply as a condition code flag. If a thread is in external code, the system needs an alternate method of getting attention when the thread comes out of that code (unless it is suspended as a safe-point already). Hijacking the return address (see also Section 11.5) is a way to get attention as the external code completes.

As an alternative to flag setting and return address hijacking, in some cases an operating system-level inter-thread signal, such as those offered by some implementations of POSIX threads, may be a viable alternative. This may be problematic for wide portability, and it may not be very efficient. It can be slow in part because of the relatively long path through the operating system kernel to set up and deliver a signal to a user-level handler. This can be ameliorated if the processor and operating system support user-mode trap delivery. It can also be slow because of the need not only for a low-level processor interrupt but because of the effect on caches and translation lookaside buffers.

In sum, there are two basic approaches: *synchronous* notification, also appropriately called *polling*, and *asynchronous* notification via some kind of signal or interrupt. Each approach has its own overheads, which vary across platforms. Polling may also require a degree of compiler cooperation, depending on the specific technique. Further, asynchronous notification will usually need to be turned into synchronous, since scanning the stack, or whatever action is being requested, may not be possible at every moment. Thus, the signal handler's main goal may be to set a flag local to its thread where the thread is guaranteed to notice the flag soon and act on it.

We further note that in implementing synchronisation between threads to direct scanning of stacks, considerations of concurrent hardware and software crop up, for which we offer general background in Chapter 13. Of particular relevance may be Section 13.7, which discusses coordinating threads to move from phase to phase of collection, which mutator threads may need to do as collection begins and ends.

11.7 Garbage collecting code

While many systems statically compile all code in advance, garbage collection has its roots in implementations of languages like Lisp, which can build and execute code on the fly — originally interpretively but also compiled to native code since early days. Systems that load or construct code dynamically, and that optimise it at run time, are if anything more common now. Loading and generating code dynamically leads logically enough to the desire to reclaim the memory consumed by that code when the code is no longer needed. Straightforward tracing or reference counting techniques often will not work, because code for many functions is accessible through global variables or symbol tables that will never be cleared. In some languages, little can be done if the program does not explicitly remove such entries — and the language may provide no approved way to do that.

Two specific cases deserve further mention. First, closures consist of a function and an environment of bindings to use when the function runs. Naive construction of a closure, say for function g nested within function f, provides g with the full environment of f, possibly sharing a common environment object. Thomas and Jones [1994] described a system that, upon collection, can specialise the environment to just those items that g uses. This may ultimately make some other closure unreachable and thus reclaimable.

The other case is class-based systems, such as Java. One consideration is that in such systems object instances generally refer to their class. It is common to place classes, and the code for their methods, in a non-moving, non-collected area. In that way the collector can ignore the class pointer in every object. But to reclaim classes, the collector will need to trace the class pointer fields — possibly a significant cost in the normal case. It might avoid that cost by tracing through class pointers only when invoked in a special mode.

For Java in particular, a run-time class is actually determined by both the class's code and its class loader. Since loading a Java class has side effects such as initialising static variables, unloading a class is not transparent if the class might be reloaded by the same class loader. The only way to guarantee that a class will not be reloaded by a given class loader is for the class loader itself to be reclaimable. A class loader has a table of the classes it has loaded (to avoid reloading them, reinitialising them, and so on) and a run-time class needs also to mention its class loader (as part of its identity). So, to reclaim a class, there must be no references to its class loader, any class loaded by that class loader, or any instance of one of those classes, from existing threads or global variables (of classes loaded by other class loaders). Furthermore, since the bootstrap class loader is never reclaimed, no class that it loads can be reclaimed. While Java class unloading is something of a special case, certain kinds of programs rely on it or else servers will run out of space.

In addition to user-visible code elements such as methods, functions and closures, a system may generate multiple versions of code to be interpreted or run natively, for example optimised and unoptimised code, or specialised versions of functions. Generating a new version of a function may make old versions unreachable for future invocations of the function. However, invocations still in process may need the old versions. Thus return addresses embedded in the stack or closures may retain old code. In any case, the system may need tracing or reference counting rather than immediately reclaiming old versions. A related technique is *on-stack replacement*, in which a system replaces an in-process invocation's code with new code. While this is commonly done more in order to improve the performance of the still-running invocation, it also helps make old versions reclaimable. See Fink and Qian [2003] and Soman and Krintz [2006] for examples of on-stack replacement approaches and applications for Java. While on-stack replacement is most often directed at optimising code, some applications, such as debugging, requires *de*optimised code, which can have the same effect of helping to make old versions of code reclaimable.

11.8   Read and write barriers

Several classes of garbage collection algorithm require 'interesting' pointers to be detected as mutators run. If a collector only collects part of the heap, then any reference to an object in that region from outside it is of interest to the collector: in the absence of further knowledge, the collector must treat that reference as a root. For example, generational collectors must detect any reference to a younger generation object written into an object in an older generation. As we shall see in Chapter 15, interleaving mutation and collection (whether or not the collector runs in its own thread) presents ample opportunities for the mutator to hide pointers from the collector. If these references are not detected and passed to the collector, then live objects may be reclaimed prematurely. All these cases require the mutator to add references on the fly to the collector's work list. This is achieved through read or write barriers.

Other chapters on specific algorithms address the particular content of read and write barriers as needed by those algorithms. However, here we offer some general observations about how to implement barriers. To abstract from particular needs of a collection algorithm, such as generational or concurrent collectors, we concern ourselves with the detection and recording of 'interesting' pointers. *Detection* is the determination that a particular pointer is 'interesting' while *recording* is noting that fact for later use by the collector. To some extent detection and recording are orthogonal, though some detection methods may lend themselves more to particular recording methods. For example, detection via page protection violations lends itself more to recording the location being modified.

Engineering

A typical barrier involves one or more checks that guard an action. Typical checks include whether a pointer being stored is null and the relationship between the generations of the referring object and its referent, and a typical action is to record an object in a remembered set. The full code for all the checks and the action may be too large to inline entirely, depending on implementation. Even a fairly modest sequence of instructions would create very large compiled code and also risk poor instruction cache performance since much of the code only executes rarely. Therefore, designers often separate the code into what is commonly called 'fast path' and 'slow path' portions. The fast path is inlined for speed, and it calls the slow path part only if necessary; there is one copy of the slow path in order to conserve space and improve instruction cache performance. It is critical that the fast path code include the most common cases and that the slow path part be less common. However, it sometimes helps to apply the same principle to the slow path code. If the barrier involves multiple tests — and they usually do — then it is important to order those tests so that the first one filters out the most cases, the second the next larger set of cases, and so on, modulo the cost of performing the test. In doing this tuning, there is no substitute for trying various arrangements and measuring performance on a range of programs, because so many factors come into play on modern hardware that simple analytical models fail to give adequate guidance. This is exemplified by the study of barrier performance presented by Yang *et al.* [2012], which showed the impact of differences in micro-architectures with same instruction set (Intel 32-bit machines). The increased use of out-of-order micro-architectures with powerful memory subsystems since that work, and the shift to 64-bit machines, may well have caused further performance shifts. Indeed, we have heard of cases where a barrier that does more work actually executes faster.

Another significant factor in barrier performance is speed in accessing any required data structures, such as card tables. It may be a good trade-off to dedicate a machine register to hold a data structure pointer, such as the base of the card table, but this can vary considerably by machine and algorithm.

Also of concern is the software engineering and maintenance of those aspects of the garbage collection algorithm — mostly barriers, GC checks and allocation sequences — that are built into the compiler(s) of a system. If possible, it seems best to arrange for the compiler to inline a routine in which the designer codes the fast path portion of a sequence. That way the compiler does not need to know the details and the designer can change them freely. However, as we noted before, these code sequences may have constraints, such as no garbage collection in the middle of them, that require care on the compiler's part. The compiler may also have to disable some optimisations on these code sequences, such as leaving apparently dead stores that save something useful for the collector and not reordering barrier code or interspersing it with surrounding code. To that end, the compiler might support special pragmas or markers for the designer to use to indicate special properties such as uninterruptible code sequences.

In the remainder of this section we discuss write barriers. We defer the discussion of read barriers to later chapters where we discuss incremental and concurrent collection since this is the context in which they are used. Write barriers are more complex than read barriers since they not only have to detect 'interesting' writes but must also record some information for the garbage collector's later use. In contrast, read barriers typically cause an immediate action, such as copying to tospace the target of the reference just loaded.

Precision of write barriers

Interesting pointers can be remembered using different policies and mechanisms. Policies dictate the precision with which the location of an interesting pointer is recorded in the remembered set. The choice of policy is a trade-off between adding overheads to the mutator or to the collector. In general it is better to favour adding overhead to relatively infrequent collector actions (such as discovering roots) than to very frequent mutator actions (such as heap stores). Without a barrier, pointer stores are normally very fast (although null pointer or array bounds checks are often required by managed languages). Adding a write barrier can increase the instruction count for a pointer write by a factor of two or more, though some of this cost may be masked if the cache locality of the barrier is better than that of the mutator itself (for example, it is probably unnecessary to stall the user code while the write barrier records an interesting pointer). Likewise, the high instruction level parallelism support from many modern microarchitectures will tend to absorb some of these costs. Typically, more precise recording of interesting pointers in the remembered set means less work for the collector to do to find the pointer but more work for the mutator to filter and log it. At one extreme, in a generational collector, not logging any pointer stores transfers all overheads from the mutator to the collector which must scan all other spaces in the heap looking for references to the condemned generation. While this is unlikely to be a generally successful policy, linear scanning has better locality than tracing, and this may be the only way to collect generationally if there is no support for detecting pointer stores from the compiler or operating system [Bartlett, 1989a]. Swanson [1986] and Shaw [1988] have suggested that this can reduce garbage collection costs by two-thirds compared with simple semispace copying.

There are three dimensions to remembered set policy. First, how accurately should pointer writes be recorded? Not all pointers are interesting to a collector, but unconditional logging may impose less overhead on the mutator than filtering out uninteresting pointers. The implementation of the remembered set is key to this cost. Remembered sets with cheap mechanisms for adding an entry, such as simply writing a byte in a fixed-size table, will favour unconditional logging, especially if addition is idempotent. On the other hand, if adding an entry is more expensive or the size of the remembered set is a concern, then it is more likely to be worthwhile to filter out uninteresting pointers. Filtering is essential for concurrent or incremental collectors to ensure that their work lists do eventually empty. For a particular filtering scheme, there is a trade-off between how much filtering to do inline and when to call an out-of-line routine to complete the filtering and possibly add the pointer to a remembered set. The more filtering that is done inline, the fewer instructions that may be executed, but the code size will increase and the larger instruction cache footprint may undermine any performance gains. This requires careful tuning of the order of filter tests and which are done inline.

Second, at what granularity is the location of the pointer to be recorded? The most accurate is to record the address of the *field* into which the pointer was written. However, this will increase the size of the remembered set if many fields of an object, such as an array, are updated. An alternative is to record the address of the *object* containing the field: this also permits duplicates to be filtered, which field remembering does not (since there is generally no room in the field to record that it has been remembered). Object remembering requires the collector to scan every pointer in the object at scavenge time in order to discover those that refer to objects that need to be traced. A hybrid solution might be to object-record arrays and field-record scalars on the assumption that if one slot of an array is updated, then many are likely to be. Conversely, it might be sensible to field-record arrays (to avoid scanning the whole thing) and object-record scalars (since they tend to be smaller). For arrays it may make sense to record only a portion of the array. This is analogous to card marking, but specific to arrays and aligned with the array indices rather than with the addresses of the array's fields in virtual memory. Whether to store the object or one of its slots may also depend on what information the mutator has at hand. If the write action knows the address of the object as well as the field, the barrier can choose to remember either; if only the address of the field is passed to the barrier, then computing the address of the object will incur further overhead. Hosking *et al.* [1992] resolve this dilemma by storing the addresses of both the object and the slot in their sequential store buffer for an interpreted Smalltalk system. Blackburn [2019] presents performance results for a design of field-recording that uses one bit per field to avoid recording a field more than once. These bits are stored adjacent to the object. That work showed that a careful implementation can get the overhead of field-recording as compared to object-recording down to about 1% to 2%.

Card table techniques (which we discuss below) divide the heap logically into small, fixed-size *cards*. Pointer modifications are recorded at the granularity of a card, typically by setting a byte in a card table. Note that the card marked can correspond to either the updated field or object (these may reside on different cards). At scavenge time, the collector must first find any dirty cards corresponding to the condemned generation and then find all the interesting pointers held in that card. The choice of object or field card marking will affect how this search is performed. Coarser than cards, pointer stores can be logged at the granularity of a virtual memory page. With help from the hardware and operating system, this may impose no direct overhead on the mutator but, like cards, increases work for the collector. Unlike cards, marked pages will always correspond to the updated slot not to its containing object since the operating system is oblivious to object layout.

Third, should the remembered set be allowed to contain duplicate entries? The case for duplicates is that not checking eases the burden on the mutator; the case against is that duplicates increase the size of the remembered set and move the cost of handling duplicates to the collector. Card and page marking eliminate duplicates since they typically simply set a bit or a byte in a table. Object recording can also eliminate most duplicates by marking objects as logged, for example by using a bit in their header, regardless of the implementation of the remembered set itself, whereas duplicate elimination is unlikely to be so simple if word-sized fields are recorded (but Zhao *et al.* [2022a,b] achieve good results with a field recording barrier). The cost to the mutator is that this is an additional check which may or may not be absorbed by the reduction in remembered set entries added, and that an additional write is performed. Otherwise, remembered sets must be implemented as true sets rather than multisets if they are not to contain duplicates.

In summary, if a card- or page-based scheme is used, then the collector's scanning cost will depend on the number of dirty cards or pages. Otherwise, the cost will depend on the number of pointer writes if a scheme without duplicate elimination is used. With duplicate elimination, it will depend on the number of different objects modified. In all cases, uninteresting pointer filtering will reduce the collector's root scanning cost. Mechanisms for implementing remembered sets include hash sets, sequential store buffers, card tables, virtual memory mechanisms and hardware support. We consider each of these in turn.

Hash tables

The remembered set must implement a true set if it is to remember slots without duplicating entries. Equally, a set is required for object remembering if there is no room in object headers to mark an object as remembered. A further requirement for a remembered set is that adding entries must be a fast, and preferably constant time, operation. Hash tables meet these requirements.

Hosking *et al.* [1992] implement a remembered set with a circular hash table, using linear hashing in their multiple generation memory management toolkit, for a Smalltalk interpreter that stores stack frames in generation 0, step 0 in the heap. More specifically, a separate remembered set is maintained for each generation. Their remembered sets can store either objects or fields. The tables are implemented as arrays of $2^i + k$ entries (they use $k = 2$). Hence addresses are hashed to obtain i bits (from the middle bits of the address), and the hash is used to index the array. If that entry is empty, the address of the object or field is stored at that index; otherwise, the next k entries are searched (this is not done circularly, which is why the array size is $2^i + k$). If this also fails to find an empty entry, the table is searched circularly.

In order not to increase further the work that must be done by the remembering code, the write barrier filters out all writes to generation 0 objects and all young-young writes. In addition, it adds all interesting pointers to a single *scratch* remembered set rather than to the remembered set for the target generation. Not deciding at mutator time the generation to whose remembered set it should be added might be even more apposite in a multithreaded environment; there per-processor scratch remembered sets could be used to avoid contention as thread-safe hash tables would be too expensive. In all, Hosking *et al.* used 17 inlined MIPS instructions in the fast path of the write barrier, including the call to update the remembered set, making it comparatively expensive even on the MIPS, a register-rich architecture. At scavenge time, the roots for a given generation may reside either in that generation's remembered set or in the scratch remembered set. Duplicates between the remembered sets are removed by hashing the generation's remembered set into the scratch remembered set, and the scratch remembered set is processed: any interesting pointers encountered are added to the appropriate remembered sets. We saw in Section 10.4 that the OpenJDK G1 collector similarly does not decide at mutator time which region's remembered set to update but instead, and only where necessary, its write barrier simply updates a card which it appends to a thread-local sequential store buffer

Algorithm 11.4: Recording stored pointers with a sequential store buffer

---

```
1  Write(src, i, ref):
2      add %src, %i, %fld                          /* fld := &src[i] */
3      st %ref, [%fld]                             /* src[i] := ref */
4      st %fld, [%next]                            /* SSB[next] := fld */
5      add %next, 4, %next                         /* next := next + 1 */
```

(see below); concurrent refinement threads subsequently add the location of any interesting pointers found from these buffers to the remembered set of the appropriate region.

Garthwaite [2005] used hash tables in his implementation of the Train algorithm. The common operations on his tables are insertion and iteration, so he used open addressing. Because it is common to map adjacent addresses, he eschewed linear addressing (address modulo N where N is the size of the hash table) which would tend to map these addresses to neighbouring slots in the table. Instead he used a universal hashing function. He chose a 58-bit prime p and assigned to each remembered set hash table parameters a and b, generated by repeated use of a pseudo-random function [Park and Miller, 1988] so that $0 < a, b < p$. An address r is hashed by the function $((ar + b) \mod p) \mod N$. Open-addressing requires a tactic for probing alternative slots when a collision occurs. Linear and quadratic probing (in which the current slot's index is incremented by an amount d and d is incremented by a constant i) suffer from clustering as subsequent insertions follow the same probing sequence, so he used double hashing in which the increment used in quadratic probing is a function of the key. Given a hash table whose size is a power of two, quadratic probing with any odd increment i applied to the probing step d ensures that the entire table will be visited. This scheme doubles the available set of probing sequences by checking whether d is odd. If so, i is set to zero (linear probing). Otherwise, both d and i are set to $d + 1$. Finally, a hash table may need to be expanded when its load becomes too high. An alternative may be to rebalance the table by modifying the insertion process. At each collision, we must decide whether to continue probing with the item being inserted or whether to place it in the current slot and probe with the contents of that slot. In another implementation, Garthwaite *et al.* [2005] used *robin hood* hashing [Celis *et al.*, 1985]. Each entry is stored in its slot along with its depth in the probing sequence, taking advantage of the fact that the least significant bits of an item (such as the address of a card) will be zero. If a slot already contains an item, its depth is compared with the depth of the new item: we leave the value that is deeper in its probing sequence and continue with the other.

Sequential store buffers

Pointer recording can be made faster by using a simpler *sequential store buffer* (SSB), such as a chain of blocks of slots. A buffer per thread might be used for all generations to save the mutator write barrier from having to select the appropriate one and to eliminate contention between threads.

In the common case, adding an entry requires very few instructions: it is simply necessary to compare a `next` pointer against a limit, store to the next location in the buffer and bump the `next` pointer. The MMTk toolkit [Blackburn *et al.*, 2004b] memory management toolkit implements a sequential store buffer as a chain of blocks. Each block is power-of-two sized and aligned, and filled from high addresses to low. This allows a simple overflow test by comparing the low order bits of the `next` pointer with zero (which is often a fast operation). A number of tricks can be used to eliminate the explicit over-

Algorithm 11.5: Misaligned access boundary check

```
1  atomic insert(fld):
2      *(next − 4) ← fld                      /* add the entry in the previous slot */
3      tmp ← next >> (n−1)
4      tmp ← tmp & 6                           /* tmp = 4 or 6 */
5      next ← next + tmp
```

Example: $n = 4$ (4 word buffers):

```
insert at 32: next=40, next>>(n−1)=4, tmp=4
insert at 36: next=44, next>>(n−1)=5, tmp=4
insert at 40: next=48, next>>(n−1)=5, tmp=4
insert at 44: next=54, next>>(n−1)=6, tmp=6
insert at 50: UTRAP!
```

flow check, in which case the cost of adding an entry to the sequential store buffer can be as low as one or two instructions if a register can be reserved for the next pointer, as in Algorithm 11.4. With a dedicated register this might be as low as one instruction on the PowerPC: stwu fld,4(next).

Appel [1989a], Hudson and Diwan [1990] and Hosking *et al.* [1992] use a write-protected guard page. When the write barrier attempts to add an entry on this page, the trap handler performs the necessary overflow action, which we discuss later. Raising and handling a page protection exception is very expensive, costing hundreds of thousands of instructions. This technique is therefore effective only if traps are very infrequent: the trap cost must be less than the cost of the (many) software tests that would otherwise be performed:

$$\text{cost of page trap} \leq \text{cost of limit test} \times \text{buffer size}$$

Appel ensures that his guard page trap is triggered precisely once per collection by storing the sequential store buffer as a list in the young generation. The guard page is placed at the end of the space reserved for the young generation, thus any allocation — for objects or remembered set entries — may spring the trap and invoke the collector. This technique relies on the young generation's area being contiguous. It might appear that a system can simply place the heap at the end of the data area of the address space and use the brk system call to grow (or shrink) the heap. However, protecting the page beyond the end of the heap interferes with use of brk by malloc, as noted by Reppy [1993], so it may be better to use a higher region of address space and manage it with mmap.

Architecture-specific mechanisms can also be used to eliminate the overflow check. One example is the Solaris UTRAP fault, which is designed to handle misaligned accesses and is about a hundred times faster than the Unix signal handling mechanism. Detlefs *et al.* [2002a] implement their sequential store buffer as a list of 2^n-byte buffers, aligned on 2^{n+1} boundaries but not 2^{n+2} ones, which sacrifices some space. The insertion algorithm is shown in Algorithm 11.5. The next register normally points to 4 bytes beyond the next entry, except when the buffer is full (that is, when next points at the slot before a 2^{n+2}-aligned boundary), in which case the increment on line 5 adds 6, causing a UTRAP on the next access.

Sequential store buffers may be used directly as remembered sets or as a fast logging front-end to hash tables. A simple, two-generation configuration with *en masse* promotion can discard the remembered set at each minor collection since the nursery is emptied: there is no need for more complex remembered set structures (provided the sequential store buffer does not overflow before a collection). However, other configurations require remembered sets to be preserved between collections. If multiple generations are used, the records of pointers spanning older generations must be preserved regardless of whether survivors of the condemned generations are promoted *en masse*. If the generations being collected have steps or other mechanisms for delaying promotion (Section 9.4), then the record of older generation pointers to surviving, but not promoted objects, must be kept.

One solution might be simply to remove entries that are no longer needed from the sequential store buffer. An entry for a field will not be needed if the field's value is null, or refers to an object that is only considered at full heap collections (or never). By extension, an entry for an object can be deleted if the object similarly does not contain any interesting pointers. However, this solution encourages unrestrained growth of the remembered set and leads to the collector processing the same long-lived entries from one collection to the next. A better solution is to move entries that need to be preserved to the remembered set of the appropriate generation. These remembered sets might also be sequential store buffers or the information might be transferred into a hash table as we saw above.

Overflow action

Hash tables and sequential store buffers may overflow; this can be handled in different ways. The MMTk acquires and links a fresh block into the sequential store buffer [Blackburn *et al.*, 2004b]. Hosking *et al.* [1992] fix the size of their sequential store buffer by emptying it into hash tables whenever it overflows. In order to keep their hash tables relatively sparse, they grow a table whenever a pointer cannot be remembered to its natural location in the table or one of the k following slots, or when the occupancy of the table exceeds a threshold (for example, 60%). Tables are grown by incrementing the size of the hash key, effectively doubling the table's size; a corollary is that the key size cannot be a compile-time constant, which may increase the size and cost of the write barrier. As Appel [1989a] stores his sequential store buffer in the heap, overflow triggers garbage collection. The MMTk also invokes the collector whenever the size of its metadata (such as the sequential store buffer) grows too large.

Cards and card tables

Card table (*card marking*) schemes divide the heap conceptually into fixed-size, contiguous areas called *cards* [Sobalvarro, 1988; Wilson and Moher, 1989a,b]. Cards are typically small, between 128 and 512 bytes. The simplest way to implement the card table is as an array of bytes, indexed by the cards. Whenever a pointer is written, the write barrier *dirties* an entry in the card table corresponding to the card containing the source of the pointer (for example, see Figure 11.3). The card's index can be obtained by shifting the address of the updated field. The motivation behind card tables is to permit a small and fast write barrier that can be inlined into mutator code. In addition, card tables cannot overflow, unlike hash tables or sequential store buffers. As always, the trade-off is that more overhead is transferred to the collector. In this case, the collector must search dirtied cards for fields that have been modified and *may* contain an interesting pointer: the cost to the collector is proportional to the number of cards marked (and to card size) rather than the number of (interesting) stores made.

Because they are designed to minimise impact on mutator performance, card marking schemes are often used with an unconditional write barrier. This means that the card table is sufficiently large that all locations that might be modified by Write can be mapped to a slot in it. The size of the table could be reduced if it were guaranteed that no interesting pointers would ever be written to some region of the heap, and a conditional test was used

Algorithm 11.6: Recording stored pointers with a card table on SPARC

1	Write(src, i, ref):
2	add %src, %i, %fld — /* fld := &src[i] */
3	st %ref, [%fld] — /* src[i] := ref */
4	srl %fld, LOG_CARD_SIZE, %idx — /* idx := fld >> *LOG_CARD_SIZE* */
5	stb ZERO, [%BASE+%idx] — /* CT[idx] := *dirty* */

Algorithm 11.7: Recording stored pointers with Hölzle's card table on SPARC

1	Write(src, i, ref):
2	st %ref, [%src + %i]
3	srl %src, LOG_CARD_SIZE, %idx — /* *calculate approximate byte index* */
4	clrb [%BASE + %idx] — /* *clear byte in byte map* */

Algorithm 11.8: Two-level card tables on SPARC

1	Write(src, i, ref):
2	add %src, %i, %fld — /* fld := &src[i] */
3	st %ref, [%fld] — /* *do the write* */
4	srl %fld, LOG_CARD_SIZE, %idx — /* *get the level 1 index* */
5	stb ZERO, [%BASE+%idx] — /* *mark the level 1 card dirty* */
6	srl %fld, LOG_SUPERCARD_SIZE, %idx — /* *get the level 2 index* */
7	stb ZERO, [%BASE+%idx] — /* *mark the level 2 card dirty* */

to filter out such uninteresting pointers. For example, if the area of the heap above some fixed virtual address boundary was reserved for the nursery (which is scavenged at every collection), then it is only necessary to map the area below that boundary.

While the most compact implementation of a card table is an array of bits, this is not the best choice for several reasons. Modern processor instruction sets are not designed to write single bits. Therefore, bit manipulations require more instructions than primitive operations: read a byte, apply a logical operator to set or clear the bit, write the byte back. Worse, this sequence of operations is not atomic: card updates may be lost if threads race to update the same card table entry even though they may not be modifying the same field or object in the heap. Some processors offer atomic instructions to update bits, but they tend to be slow. For these reasons, card tables generally use arrays of bytes. Because processors often have fast instructions for clearing memory, 'dirty' is often represented by 0. For example, using a byte array, the card can be dirtied in just two SPARC instructions [Detlefs *et al.*, 2002a] (most other popular architectures can do the same), as shown in Algorithm 11.6. For clarity, we write ZERO to represent the SPARC register %g0 which always holds 0. A BASE register needs to be set up so that it holds the higher order bits of CT1−(H>>LOG_CARD_SIZE) where CT1 and H are the starting addresses of the card table and the heap, respectively, and both are aligned on a card-size boundary, say 512 bytes. Detlefs *et al.* [2002a] use a SPARC local register for that, set up once on entry to a method that might perform a write, and preserved across calls by the register window mechanism.

Hölzle [1993] further reduced the cost of the write barrier in most cases by reducing the precision with which the modified field is recorded, as in Algorithm 11.7. Suppose that marking byte i in the card table indicated that any card in the range $i \ldots i + L$ may be dirty.

Provided that the offset of the updated word is less than L cards from the beginning of the object, the byte corresponding to the object's address can be marked instead. A leeway of one ($L = 1$) is likely to be sufficient to cover most stores except those into array elements: these must be marked exactly in the usual way. With a 128-byte card, any field of a 32-word object can be handled. Ambiguity arises only when the last object on a card extends into the next card, and in that case the collector also scans that object or the necessary initial portion of it.

The space required for the card table is usually modest, even for small card sizes. For example, a byte array for 128-byte cards occupies less than 1% of the heap. Card size is a compromise between space usage and the collector's root scanning time, since larger cards indicate the locations of modified fields less precisely but occupy smaller tables.

At collection time, the collector must search all dirty cards for interesting pointers. There are two aspects to the search. First, the collector must scan the card table, looking for dirty cards. The search can be sped up by observing that mutator updates tend to have good locality, thus clean and dirty cards will tend to occur in clumps. If bytes are used in the card table, four or eight cards can be checked by comparing whole words in the table.

If a generational collector does not promote all survivors *en masse*, some objects will be retained in the younger generation, while others are promoted. If a promoted object refers to an object not promoted, then the older-to-younger reference leads unavoidably to a dirty card. However, when a promoted object is first copied into the older generation, it may refer to objects in the younger generation, all of which end up being promoted. In that case it would be better *not* to dirty the promoted object's card(s), since doing so will cause needless card scanning during the next collection. Hosking *et al.* [1992] take care to promote objects to clean cards, which are updated as necessary as the cards are scanned using a filtering copy barrier.

Even so, a collector may spend significant time in a very large heap skipping clean cards. Detlefs *et al.* [2002a] observe that the overwhelming majority of cards are clean, whilst cards with more than 16 cross-generational pointers are quite rare. The cost of searching the card table for dirty cards can be reduced at the expense of some additional space for a two-level card table. The second, smaller card table uses more coarsely grained cards, each of which corresponds to 2^n fine-grained cards, thus speeding up scanning of clean cards by the same factor. The write barrier can be made very similar to that of Algorithm 11.6 (just two more instructions are needed) by sacrificing some space in order to ensure that the start of the second level card table CT2 is aligned with the first such that CT1$-$(H>>LOG_CARD_SIZE)=CT2$-$(H>>LOG_SUPERCARD_SIZE), as in Algorithm 11.8.

Crossing maps

As a card table is searched, each dirty card discovered must be processed, which requires finding the modified objects and slots somewhere in the card. This is not straightforward since the start of the card is not necessarily aligned with the start of an object, but in order to scan fields we must start at an object. Worse, the field that caused the card to be dirtied may belong to a large object whose header is several cards earlier (this is another reason for storing large objects separately). In order to be able to find the start of an object, we need a *crossing map* that decodes how objects span cards.

The crossing map holds as many entries as cards. Each entry in the crossing map indicates the offset from the start of the corresponding card to an object starting in that card. Entries in the crossing map corresponding to old generation cards are set by the collector as it promotes objects, or by the allocator in the case of cards for spaces outside the generational world. Notice that the nursery space does not need cards since objects there cannot point to other objects that are younger still — they are the youngest objects in the system.

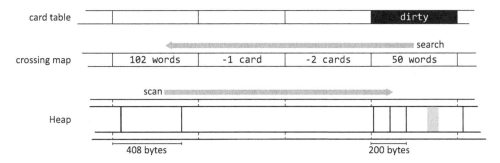

Figure 11.3: Crossing map with slot remembering card table. One card has been dirtied (shown in black). The updated field is shown in grey. The crossing map shows offsets (in words) to the last object in a card.

Algorithm 11.9: Search a crossing map for a slot-recording card table; *trace* is the collector's marking or copying procedure.

```
 1   search(card):
 2       start ← H + (card << LOG_CARD_SIZE)
 3       end ← start + CARD_SIZE                         /* start of next card */
 4       card ← card − 1
 5       offset ← crossingMap[card]
 6       while offset < 0
 7           card ← card + offset                        /* offset is negative: go back */
 8           offset ← crossingMap[card]
 9       next ← H + (card << LOG_CARD_SIZE) + offset
10       repeat
11           trace(next, start, end)                     /* trace the object at next */
12           next ← nextObject(next)
13       until next ≥ end
```

Promotion also requires that the crossing map be updated. The design of the crossing map depends on whether the card table records objects or slots.

Used with a slot-recording write barrier, the crossing map must record the offset to the *last* object in each card, or a negative value if no object starts in a card. Because objects can span cards, the start of the modified object may be several cards earlier than the dirty one. For example, in Figure 11.3, objects are shown as white rectangles in the heap. We assume a 32-bit architecture and 512-byte cards. The last object in the first card starts at an offset of 408 bytes (102 words) from the start of the card, indicated by the entry in the crossing map. This object spans four cards so the next two crossing map entries are negative. A field in the fifth object has been updated (shown as grey) so the corresponding card (card 4) is marked (shown as black). To find the start of this object, the collector consults the crossing map, moving backwards from the dirtied card (to the left) until it finds a non-negative offset (Algorithm 11.9). Note that the negative value indicates a distance to go back — a process that may need to be repeated a number of times if the preceding object is quite large. Alternatively, the system can reserve a single value, such as -1, to mean 'back up,' making backing up slower over a large object.

Old generations are commonly managed by a non-moving collector which mixes used and free blocks in the heap. Parallel collectors are especially likely to create islands of

Entry v	Encoded meaning
$v = 0$	The corresponding card contains no references.
$0 < v \leq 128$	The first object starts v words before the end of this card.
$256 < v \leq 384$	The first $v - 256$ words of this card are a sequence of references at the end of an object.
$v > 384$	Consult the card $v - 384$ entries before.

Table 11.3: The crossing map encoding of Garthwaite *et al.* [2006]

promoted data separated by large areas of free space, as each collector thread will promote to its own heap area in order to avoid contention. To aid heap parsability, each free area can be filled with a self-describing pseudo-object. However, slot-based crossing map algorithms are predicated on the assumption that heap usage is dense. If a very large, say 10 megabyte, free chunk protrudes into a dirty card, the first loop of the `search` algorithm in Algorithm 11.9 will iterate tens of thousands of times to discover the head of the pseudo-object describing this free chunk. One way to reduce this search is to store *logarithmic* backup values when no object starts in the card. Thus, an entry $-k$ would indicate 'go back 2^{k-1} cards and then do what it says there' (and similarly for a linear backup scheme). Note also that if future allocation starts from the beginning of this free block, then only logarithmically many entries (up the 'spine' of this list) have to be changed to restore the crossing table to the correct state.

However, Garthwaite *et al.* [2006] show that a clever encoding of the crossing map can usually eliminate the search loop. The simplest way to consider their scheme is to assume that each crossing map entry v is a 16-bit unsigned integer (two bytes). Table 11.3 shows their scheme. If the value v of a crossing map entry is zero, then no objects in the corresponding card contain any references. A value for v less than `128` indicates the number of words between the start of the *first* object and the end of the card. Notice that this is different from the scheme above which gives the offset to the last word in a card. Finding the first word eliminates the need to search back possibly many cards. Large objects, such as arrays, may span cards. The second encoding deals with the case that such an object spans two or more cards, and that the first $v - 256$ words of the second card are all references and that this sequence terminates the object. The benefit of this encoding is that the references can be found directly, without accessing the object's type information. However, this encoding would not work if the portion of the object overlapping this card contains both references and non-references. In this case, the crossing map entry should be set to a value greater than `384` to indicate that collector should consult the entry $v - 384$ entries earlier. Garthwaite *et al.* also include a scheme in which, if an object completely spans two crossing map slots, then the four bytes of these slots should be treated as the address of the object. In this discussion, we have assumed that a crossing map entry should be two bytes long. However, a single byte suffices if, for example, we use 512-byte cards and 64-bit alignment.

Summarising cards

Some generational collectors do not promote objects *en masse*. Whenever the collector scans a dirty card and finds an interesting pointer but does not promote its referent, the card must be left dirty so that it is found at the next collection and scanned again. It would be preferable to discover interesting pointers directly rather than by searching through cards. Fortunately, it is common for very few dirty cards to contain more than a small number of interesting pointers. Hosking and Hudson [1993] therefore suggest moving interesting pointers to a hash table as a card is cleaned, in the same way as Hosking *et al.* [1992] did with sequential store buffers.

Sun's Java virtual machines optimised card rescanning by having the scavenger summarise dirty cards that retain interesting pointers, taking advantage of card map entries being bytes not bits [Detlefs *et al.*, 2002a]. The state of an old generation card may now be 'clean', 'modified' or 'summarised'. If the scavenger finds up to k interesting pointers in a 'modified' card, it marks the card as 'summarised' and records the offsets of these pointer locations in the corresponding entry of a *summary table*. If the card contains more than k interesting pointers (for example, $k = 2$), it is left 'modified' and the summary entry is recorded as 'overflowed'. The k interesting fields can therefore be processed directly at the next collection (unless the card is dirtied again) rather having to search the card using the crossing map. Alternatively, if cards are reasonably small, each byte-sized entry in the card table itself can store a small number of offsets directly.

Reppy [1993] encodes additional generational information in the card table to save scanning effort. As it cleans cards, his multi-generational collector summarises a dirty card with the lowest generation number of any referent found on it (0 being the nursery). In future, when collecting generation n, cards in the table with values larger than n need not be processed. Used with 256-byte cards, this gave an 80% improvement in garbage collection times in a five-generation Standard ML heap.

Hardware and virtual memory techniques

Some of the earliest generational garbage collectors relied on operating system and hardware support. Tagged pointer architectures allowed pointers and non-pointers to be discriminated, and hardware write barriers could set bits in a page table [Moon, 1984]. However, it is possible to use operating system support to track writes without special purpose hardware. Shaw [1988] modified the HP-UX operating system to use its paging system for this purpose. The virtual memory manager must always record which pages are dirty so that it knows whether to write them back to the swap file when they are evicted. Shaw modified the virtual memory manager to intercept a page's eviction and remember the state of its dirty bit, and added system calls to clear a set of page bits and to return a map of pages modified since the last collection. The benefit of this scheme is that it imposes no normal-case cost on the mutator. A disadvantage is that it overestimates the remembered set since the operating system does not distinguish pages dirtied by writing a pointer or a non-pointer, plus there are the overheads of the traps and operating systems calls.

Boehm *et al.* [1991] avoided the need to modify the operating system by write-protecting pages after a collection. The first write to a page since it was protected leads to a fault; the trap handler sets the dirty bit for the page before unprotecting it to prevent further faults in this collection cycle. Clearly, pages to which objects are promoted should be presumed dirty during collection to avoid incurring traps. Page protection does impose overhead on the mutator but, as for card tables, the cost of the barrier is proportional to the number of pages written rather than the number of writes. However, these schemes incur further expense. Reading dirty page information from the operating system is expensive. Page protection mechanisms are known to incur 'trap storms' as many protection faults are triggered immediately after a collection to unprotect the program's working set [Kermany and Petrank, 2006]. Page protection faults are expensive, particularly if they are referred to user-space handlers. Operating system pages are much larger than cards, so efficient methods of scanning them will be important (perhaps summarising them in the same way that we summarised cards above).

Write barrier mechanisms: in summary

Studies by Hosking *et al.* [1992] and Fitzgerald and Tarditi [2000] found no clear winner amongst the different remembered set mechanisms for generational garbage collectors, although neither study explored Sun-style card summarising. Page-based schemes
performed worst but, if a compiler is uncooperative, they do provide a way to track
where pointers are written. In general, for card table remembered sets, card sizes around
512 bytes performed better than much larger or much smaller cards.

Blackburn and Hosking [2004] examined the overheads of executing different generational barriers alone on a range of platforms. Card marking and four partial barrier mechanisms were studied: a boundary test, a logging test, a frame comparison and a hybrid
barrier. They excluded the costs of inserting an entry into remembered set for the partial barriers. The boundary test checked whether the pointer crossed a space boundary
(a compile-time constant). The logging test checked a 'logged' field in the source of the
pointer's header. The frame barrier compared whether a pointer spanned two 2^n- sized
and aligned areas of the heap by `xor`ing the addresses of its source and target: such barriers can allow more flexibility in the choice of space to be collected [Hudson and Moss,
1992; Blackburn *et al.*, 2002]. Finally, a hybrid test chose statically between the boundary
test for arrays and the logging test for scalars.

They concluded that the costs of the barrier (excluding the remembered set insertion in
the case of the partial techniques) was generally small, less than 2% of execution time. Even
where a write barrier's overhead was much higher, the cost can be more than balanced
by improvements in overall execution time offered by generational collection [Blackburn
et al., 2004a]. However, there was substantial architectural variation between the platforms
used (Intel Pentium 4, AMD Athlon XP and PowerPC 970), especially for the frame and
card barriers. For example, the frame barrier was significantly more expensive than the
others on x86 but among the cheapest on PowerPC; Blackburn and Hosking observed that
`xor` is required to use the `eax` register on x86 which may increase register pressure (this
restriction seems no longer to hold). On the other hand, card marking on the PowerPC
(their compiler generated a longer instruction sequence than the ones shown above) was
very much more expensive than the partial techniques. All of this may be different on
newer microarchitectures. We conclude that, as always, design decisions must be informed
by careful experimentation with realistic benchmarks on a range of hardware platforms,
and for each platform a different technique may be best.

Chunked lists

It is common to find list-like data structures in collectors where an array is attractive because it does not require a linked list pointer or object header for each element, and it
achieves good cache locality, but where the unused part of large arrays, and the possible
need to move and reallocate a growing array, are problematic. A remembered set in a generational collector is such an example. A *chunked list* offers the advantage of high storage
density but without the need to reallocate, and with relatively small waste and overhead.
This data structure consists of a linked-list, possibly linked in both directions for a general
deque, of chunks, where a chunk consists of an array of slots for holding data, plus the one
or two chaining pointers. This is illustrated in Figure 11.4.

A useful refinement of this data structure is to make the size of the chunks a power of
two, say 2^k, and align them on 2^k boundaries in the address space. Then logical pointers
into a chunk, used for scanning, inserting or removing, do not need a separate 'current
chunk' pointer and an index, but can use a single pointer. Algorithm 11.10 shows code
for traversing a bidirectional chunked list in either direction, as a sample of the technique.

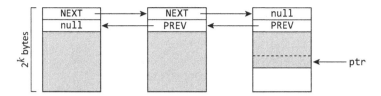

Figure 11.4: A stack implemented as a chunked list. Shaded slots contain data. Each chunk is aligned on a 2^k byte boundary.

Algorithm 11.10: Traversing chunked lists

```
 1   /* Assume chunk is of size 2^k bytes and aligned on a 2^k byte boundary */
 2   /* Assume pointer size and slot size is 4 here */
 3   NEXT = 0 /* byte offset in a chunk of pointer to data of next chunk */
 4   PREV = 4 /* byte offset in a chunk of pointer to end of data of previous chunk */
 5   DATA = 8 /* byte offset in a chunk of first data item */
 6
 7   bumpToNext(ptr):
 8       ptr ← ptr + 4
 9       if (ptr % 2^k) = 0                                  /* went off the end... */
10           ptr ← *(ptr − 2^k + NEXT)        /* ...back up to start of chunk and chain */
11       return ptr
12
13   bumpToPrev(ptr):
14       ptr ← ptr − 4
15       if (ptr % 2^k) < DATA                     /* went off the beginning of the data... */
16           ptr ← *ptr                                               /* ...chain */
17       return ptr
```

The modular arithmetic can be performed with shifting and masking.

An important additional motivation for chunking is related to parallelism. If a chunked list or deque represents a work queue, then individual threads can grab chunks instead of individual items. If the chunk size is large enough, this greatly reduces contention on obtaining work from the queue. Conversely, provided that the chunk size is small enough, this approach still admits good load balancing. Another application for chunking is for local allocation buffers (Section 7.7), though in that case the chunks are just free memory, not a dense representation of a list data structure.

11.9   Managing address space

In other chapters we have described a variety of algorithms and heap layouts, some of which have implications for how a system uses available address space. Some algorithms require, or at least are simpler with, large contiguous regions. In a 32-bit address space it can be difficult to lay out the various spaces statically and have them be large enough for all applications. If that were not problematic enough, on many systems we face the added difficulty that the operating system may have the right to place dynamic link libraries (also called shared object files) anywhere it likes within large swaths of the address space. Furthermore, these libraries may not end up in the same place on each run — for security

Algorithm 11.11: Frame-based generational write barrier

```
1  Write(src, i, ref):
2      ct ← frameTableBase
3      srcFrame ← src >>> LOG_FRAME_SIZE
4      refFrame ← ref >>> LOG_FRAME_SIZE
5      srcGen ← ct[srcFrame]
6      refGen ← ct[refFrame]
7      if srcGen > refGen
8          remember(src, &src[i], ref)
9      src[i] ← ref
```

purposes, the operating system may randomise their placement. Of course one solution is the larger address space of a 64-bit machine. However, the wider pointers needed in a 64-bit system end up increasing the *real memory* requirements of applications.

One of the key reasons for using certain large-space layouts of the address space is to make address-oriented write barriers efficient, that is, to enable a write barrier to work by comparing a pointer to a fixed address or to another pointer rather than requiring a table lookup. For example, if the nursery of a generational system is placed at one end of the address space used for the heap, a single check against a boundary value suffices to distinguish writes of pointers referring to objects in the nursery from other writes.

In building new systems, it may be best not to insist on large contiguous regions of address space for the heap, but to work more on the basis of frames, or at least to allow 'holes' in the middle of otherwise contiguous regions. Unfortunately, this may then require table lookup for write barriers.

Assuming table lookup costs that are acceptable, the system can manage a large logical address space by mapping it down to the available virtual address space. This does not allow larger heaps, but it does give flexibility in that it removes some of the contiguity requirements. To do this, the system deals with memory in power-of-two sized and aligned frames, generally somewhat larger than a virtual memory page. The system maintains a table indexed by frame number (upper bits of virtual address) that gives each frame's logical address. This table then supports the address comparisons used in a variety of address-oriented write barriers. It may lead to even better code to associate a generation number (for a generational write barrier) with each frame. Algorithm 11.11 gives pseudo-code for such a write barrier. Each line can correspond to one instruction on a typical processor, particularly if entries in the frame table are a single byte each, simplifying the array indexing operation. Notice also that the algorithm works even if ref is null — we simply ensure that the entry for null's frame has the highest generation number so the code will always skip the call to remember.

It is further possible to arrange true multiplexing of a large address space into a smaller one — after all, that is what operating systems do in providing virtual memory. One approach would be to use wide addresses and do a check on every access, mimicking in software what the virtual memory hardware accomplishes. This could use the software equivalent of translation lookaside buffers, and so on. The performance penalty might be high. It is possible to avoid that penalty by leveraging the virtual memory hardware, which we discuss in more detail in Section 11.10.

It is good to build into systems from the start the capability to relocate the heap. Many systems have a starting heap or system image that they load as the system initialises. That image assumes it will reside at a particular location in the address space — but what if a dynamic link library lies right in the middle of it? If the image includes a table indicating which words need adjusting when the image is moved, not unlike many code segments, then it is relatively straightforward for the image loader to relocate the image to another place in the address space. Likewise, it might be desirable to support relocating the entire heap, or segments of it, during system operation.

In actually managing virtual memory, we can distinguish between the managed system's notion of address space dedicated to particular uses, which we call *reserving* the space, and actual *allocation* of pages via a call to the operating system. If the operating system might map new dynamic link libraries into the address space on the fly, to guarantee a reservation that the managed system has in mind, it must actually allocate the pages — typically as demand-zero pages. This has relatively low cost, but may involve the operating system in reserving resources such as swap space, and all virtual memory mapping calls tend to be expensive. Allocating pages in advance can also determine earlier that there are not adequate resources for a larger heap. However, operating systems do not always 'charge' for demand-zero pages until they are used, so simply allocating may not give an early failure indication.

11.10 Applications of virtual memory page protection

There are a variety of checks that a system can arrange to happen as part of virtual memory protection checking. Implemented in this way, the checks have little or no normal case overhead and furthermore require no explicit conditional branches. A general consideration is that the overhead of fielding the trap, all the way through the operating system to the collector software and back again, can be quite high. Also, changing page protections can be costly, especially in a multiprocessor system where the operating system may need to stop processes currently executing and update and flush their page mapping information. So sometimes an explicit check is cheaper even when the system could use protection traps [Hosking *et al.*, 1992]. Traps are also useful in dealing with uncooperative code, in which it is not possible to cause barriers or checks in any other way.

A consideration is that there are hardware performance reasons to increase page size. In particular, programs use more memory now than when these techniques were first developed, and systems tend to have more main memory available to map. At the same time, translation lookaside buffer size is not likely to grow because of speed and power concerns. But given that translation lookaside buffer size is more or less fixed, staying with a small page size while programs' memory use increases implies more translation lookaside buffer misses. With larger pages some of the virtual memory 'tricks' may not be as desirable.

We assume a model in which data pages can have their protection set for read-write access, read-only access or no-access. We are not concerned about execute privileges since we are unaware of garbage collection-related exploitation of no-execute protection; it is also less well supported across platforms.

Double mapping

Before considering specific applications, we describe a general technique called *double mapping*, by which the system maps the same page at two different addresses with *different protections*. Consider for example an incremental copying collector with a tospace invariant. To prevent mutators from seeing fromspace pointers in pages not yet processed, the collector can set those pages to no-access, effectively creating a hardware supported read barrier. But how is the collector to process the pages? If the system is concurrent and the collector unprotects the page, some other mutator may see the contents before the collector processes them. However, if the page is mapped a second time in another place, with read-write access, then the collector can process the contents via that second mapping, then unprotect the page and wake up any mutator waiting for it.

In a smaller address space (32 bits is often small now) it may be difficult to double map. A solution to that problem is to fork a child process that holds the second version of the address space with the same pages but different protections. The collector can communicate with the child, requesting the child to process a page, and so forth.

Note also that double mapping is problematic on some systems. One problem arises when caches are indexed by virtual address. In the presence of double mapping, the cache could potentially become incoherent. Typically, the hardware avoids that by preventing aliased entries from residing in the cache at the same time. This can cause extra cache misses. However, in the case at hand it applies only to accesses by the mutator and collector near in time on the same processor. Another problem arises if the system uses inverted page tables. In this scheme, each physical page can have only one virtual address at a time. The operating system can support double mapping by effectively invalidating one of the virtual addresses and then connecting the other one. This may involve cache flushing.

While the relationship between the double mapped addresses may be arbitrary, by employing bit stealing of some high-order bits, the different addresses can function as pointer tags, as discussed in Section 15.1.

Applications of no-access pages

In describing double mapping, we have already given one example of using no-access pages: for an unconditional read barrier. There are at least three more applications for no-access pages in common use. One use is to suspend mutator threads at a GC check-point. When the virtual machine needs to initiate a collection, it makes a well-known page no-access. At GC check-points mutators attempt to access this page and will trap if a collection has been requested.

Another is to detect dereferences of null pointers, which we assume to be represented by the value 0. This works by setting page 0, and possibly a few more pages after it, no-access. If a mutator tries to access a field through a null pointer, it will attempt to read or write the no-access page. Since fielding a null pointer dereference exception is generally not required to be fast, this application can be a good trade-off. In the rare case of an access that has a large offset, the compiler can emit an explicit check. If the object layout places headers or other fields at negative offsets from the object pointer, the technique still works provided that one or more pages with very high addresses are set no-access. Most operating systems reserve the high addresses for their own use anyway.

The other common use for a no-access page is as a *guard page*. For example, the sequential store buffer technique for recording new remembered set entries consists of three steps: ensure there is room in the buffer; write the new element to the buffer; and increment the buffer pointer. The check for room, and the call to the buffer overflow handler routine, can be removed if the system places a no-access guard page immediately after the buffer. Since write barriers can be frequent and their code can be emitted in many places, the guard page technique can speed up mutators and keep their code smaller.

Some systems apply the same idea to detecting stack or heap overflow by placing a guard page at the end of the stack (heap). To detect stack overflow, it is best if a procedure's prologue touches the most remote location of the new stack frame it desires to build. That way the trap happens at a well-defined place in the code. The handler can grow the stack by reallocating it elsewhere, or add a new stack segment, and then restart the mutator with an adjusted stack and frame pointer. Likewise, when using sequential allocation the allocator can touch the most remote word of the desired new object and cause a trap if it falls into the guard page that marks the end of the sequential allocation area.

In either case, if the new stack frame or object is so large that its most remote word might lie *beyond* the guard page, the system needs to use an explicit check. But such large stack frames and objects are rare in many systems, and in any case a large object will take more time to initialise and use, which amortises the cost of the explicit check.

No-access pages can also help in supporting a large logical address space in a smaller virtual address space. An example is the Texas persistent object store [Singhal *et al.*, 1992]. Using the strategy for persistence (maintaining a heap beyond a single program execution) is treated in Chapter 21, but the mechanism is suitable for the non-persistent case as well. In this approach the system works in terms of pages, of the same size as virtual memory pages or some power-of-two multiple of that. The system maintains a table that indicates where each logical page is: either or both of an address in (virtual) memory and a location in an explicitly managed swapping file on disk. A page can be in one of four states.

- Unallocated: Not yet used, empty.

- Resident: In memory and accessible; it may or may not have a disk copy saved yet.

- Non-resident: On disk and not accessible.

- Reserved: On disk and not accessible, but with specific virtual memory reserved.

Initially, a new page starts Resident and has a new logical address, not determined by its virtual memory address. As virtual memory fills, some pages may be evicted to disk, saved according to their logical address. Also, the system converts all pointers in the page to their long logical form, a process called *'unswizzling'* in the literature [Moss, 1992]. Thus the saved form of a page is typically larger than its in-memory form. Also, the system must be able to find all the pointers in a page accurately. After evicting a page, its state is Reserved, and the system sets the virtual memory it occupied to no-access. This guarantees that if the program follows a pointer to an evicted object, there will be a page trap, which alerts the system to fetch the page back.

How can the system free up the Reserved virtual space for reuse? It must determine that there are no longer any Resident pages referring to the Reserved page. It can help make this happen by evicting pages that refer to the Reserved page. At that point the page can become Non-resident and the system can reuse the space. Notice that Resident pages refer to each other and to Reserved pages, but never directly to data in Non-resident pages.

Now consider what happens if the program accesses a Reserved page (and if there are evicted data that are reachable in the object graph, then there must be Reserved pages). The system looks up the page's logical address and fetches it from disk. It then goes through the page's pointers and replaces long logical addresses with short virtual addresses (called pointer *swizzling*). For referents on pages that are Resident or Reserved, this consists of just a table lookup. If the referent is itself on a Non-resident page, then the system must reserve virtual address space for that page, and then replace the long address with a pointer to the newly Reserved page. Acquiring virtual address space for these newly Reserved pages may require evicting other pages so that some page(s) can be made Non-resident and their virtual address space recycled.

Just as an operating system virtual memory manager needs good page replacement policies, so the Texas approach needs a policy, though it can reasonably borrow from the vast store of virtual memory management algorithms.

How does the scheme work in the presence of garbage collection? It is clear that a full heap garbage collection of a heap larger than the virtual address space is probably going to involve significant performance penalties. Collection of persistent stores has its own literature, covered in Chapter 21. However, we can say that partitioned schemes can help and techniques like Mature Object Space collector [Hudson and Moss, 1992] can offer completeness.

Related techniques include the Bookmarking collector [Hertz *et al.*, 2005; Bond and McKinley, 2008]. However, the purpose of bookmarking is more to avoid thrashing real memory — it does not extend the logical address space beyond the physical. Rather it summarises the outgoing pointers of pages evicted by the operating system so that the collector can avoid touching evicted pages and thus remain within the working set, at a possible loss of precision similar to that occasioned by remembered sets and generational collection: the collector may trace from pointers in dead objects of evicted pages.

11.11   Choosing heap size

In Section 9.7, we considered the effect of the size of the young generation on average pause times. In general, a smaller young generation tends to obtain shorter pauses for minor collections at the expense of promoting soon-to-die objects. For this reason, generational collectors usually provide automatic mechanisms that adjust the sizes of the generations, adapting to the behaviour of the running program. HotSpot's Ergonomics is one example of such a mechanism.

Here we focus on heap sizes in general. Other things being equal, larger sizes typically result in higher mutator throughput and lower collection cost. In some cases, a smaller heap size may improve mutator throughput by improving mutator locality by reducing cache or translation lookaside buffer misses. However, too big a heap may lead to a working set larger than can be accommodated in real memory, resulting in thrashing, particularly when the collector is active. Therefore, choosing an appropriate heap size often involves aiming to keep a program's real memory footprint small enough. Knowing how small is small enough typically involves the run-time system and the operating system. We now review a number of schemes that automatic memory managers have used to adjust heap size. Alternative approaches to adjusting the size of the heap include choosing which pages to page out, as in the Bookmarking collector [Hertz *et al.*, 2005; Hertz, 2006], and having the collector save rarely accessed objects to disk [Bond and McKinley, 2008].

Alonso and Appel [1990] devised a scheme where an 'advice server' tracks virtual memory usage using information available from ordinary system calls, `vmstat` in particular. After each full collection (the Appel collector for Standard ML is generational), the collector reports its minimal space need, how much space more than that it is currently using for the heap, how long it has been since the last full collection and how much mutator and collector CPU time it has expended since the last collection. The advice server determines an additional amount of space that appears safe for the process to use, and the process adjusts its heap size accordingly. The aim is to maximise throughput of the managed processes without causing other processes to thrash either.

In contrast to Alonso and Appel, Brecht *et al.* [2001, 2006] control the growth in heap size for Java applications without reference to operating system paging information. Rather, for a system with a given amount of real memory — they considered 64 and 128 megabytes — they give a series of increasing *thresholds*, T_1 to T_k, stated as fractions of the real memory of the system. At any given time, a process uses a heap size of T_i for some i. If collecting at size T_i yields less than $T_{i+1} - T_i$ fraction of the space reclaimed, the system increases the threshold from T_i to T_{i+1}. They considered the Boehm-Demers-Weiser collector [Boehm and Weiser, 1988], which cannot shrink its heap, so their approach only deals with heap growth. The thresholds must be determined empirically, and the approach further assumes that the program in question is the only program of interest running on the system.

Cooper *et al.* [1992] present an approach that aims for a specified working set size for an Appel-style Standard ML collector running under the Mach operating system. They adjust the nursery size to try to stay within the working set size, and they also do two things specific to Mach. One is that they use a large sparse address space and avoid the need to copy tospace to lower addresses in order to avoid hitting the end of the address space. This has little to do with heap sizing, but does reduce collector time. The second thing specific to Mach is having the collector inform the Mach pager that evacuated fromspace pages can be discarded and need not be paged out and, if referenced again, such pages can be offered back to the application with arbitrary contents — the allocator will zero them as necessary. Cooper *et al.* obtain a fourfold improvement in elapsed time for a small benchmark suite, with about half of the improvement coming from the heap size adjustment. However, the target working set size must still be determined by the user.

Yang *et al.* [2004] modify a stock Unix kernel to add a system call whereby an application can obtain advice as to how much it may increase its working set size without thrashing, or how much to decrease it to avoid thrashing. They modify garbage collectors of several kinds to adjust their heap size using this information. They demonstrate the importance of adaptive heap sizing in obtaining the best performance as memory usage by other processes changes. They introduce the notion of the *footprint* of a program, which is the number of pages it needs in memory to avoid increasing the running time by more than a specified fraction t, set to five or ten percent. For a garbage collected program, the footprint depends on the heap size, and for copying collectors, also on the survival rate from full collections, that is, the live size. However, an observation they make, not unlike Alonso and Appel, is that the key relationship is between how the footprint *changes* for a given change in heap size. In particular, the relationship is linear, with the ratio determined by the particular collection algorithm. The ratio is 1 for mark-sweep based collectors, while it is 2 for copying collectors.

Grzegorczyk *et al.* [2007] consider the relative helpfulness of several pieces of information related to paging that can be obtained from a standard Unix kernel. Specifically they look at page outs, the number of pages written to the swap area by the kernel swapping daemon, page faults, the number of pages missing when referenced that had to be fetched from disk, and allocation stalls, the number of times the process had to wait when trying to obtain a fresh page. These counts are all related to the particular executing process in that page outs have to do with the pages of that process, and page faults and allocation stalls occur because of actions of the process. Of these three possible indicators that a system is under so much memory load that shrinking the heap might be wise, they find that the number of allocation stalls is the best indicator to use. When a collection sees no allocation stalls, it will grow the heap by an amount originally set to 2% of the user-specified heap size; values between 2% and 5% gave similar results. If a collection experiences allocation stalls, the collector shrinks the nursery so that the total heap space, including the reserve into which the nursery is copied, fits within the space used the last time that there were no allocation stalls. This leaves the nursery cut by up to 50%. In the absence of memory pressure, the scheme performs similar to a non-adjusting baseline, while in the presence of memory pressure, it performs close to the non-pressure case while the baseline system degrades substantially.

The schemes we have discussed so far concern adjusting individual processes' use of memory dynamically, perhaps in response to general use of memory within a system at any given time. If, on the other hand, the set of programs to be run is known in advance and does not vary, the approach of Hertz *et al.* [2009] aims to indicate the best heap size to give to each program. In this scheme 'best' means 'gives the least overall execution time', which can also be stated as 'give the highest overall throughput'. At run time, their *Poor Richard's Memory Manager* has each process observe its recent page fault counts and resident set size. If the number of page faults observed in one time increment is greater than the number observed in the previous increment by more than a threshold amount, the collector triggers a full collection in order to reduce the working set size. Likewise, it triggers a full collection if the resident set size decreases. The resulting system appears to size competing processes' heaps well to achieve the best throughput.

The dynamic heap sizing mechanism proposed by Zhang *et al.* [2006] is similar in spirit to that of Hertz *et al.*, but has the program itself check the number of page faults at each collection and adjust the target heap size itself, rather than building the mechanism into the collector. Unlike the other mechanisms we have discussed, they assume that the user has somehow identified the phases of the program and inserted code to consider forcing collection at phase changes. They showed that dynamic adaptive heap sizing can substantially improve performance over any single fixed heap size.

11.12   Issues to consider

The allocation interface presents a number of questions that the implementer must answer. Some answers may be dictated by the language semantics or by the level of concurrency in the environment (can objects 'leak' from their allocating thread?). Others may be at the discretion of the implementer and the decisions may be made in order to improve performance or the robustness of the run-time system.

We need to consider what requirements are made of allocation and initialisation. Is the language run-time's job simply to allocate some space of sufficient size, must some header fields be initialised before the object can be usable or must initialising values for all the newly allocated object's fields be provided? What are the alignment requirements for this object? Should the run-time distinguish between different kinds of objects, such as arrays and other objects? Is it beneficial to treat objects that may contain pointers from those that do not? Such a distinction may help to improve tracing since pointer-free objects do not need to be scanned. Avoiding scanning such objects is known to be particularly beneficial for conservative collectors.

Often we will want to consider carefully how much of the allocation code sequence can be inlined. Typically, we might inline a fast path in which an object can be allocated with the least work but not the other slower paths which might involve obtaining space from a lower-level allocator or invoking the collector. However, too much inlining can explode the size of the code and negate the benefit hoped for. Similarly, it might be desirable to dedicate a register to a particular purpose, such as the bump-pointer for sequential allocation. However, doing so may place too much pressure on the register allocator on a register-poor platform.

Depending on the language supported, for safety or for debugging, the run-time may zero memory. Space could be zeroed as objects are allocated but bulk zeroing with a well-optimised library routine is likely to be more efficient. Should memory be zeroed shortly before it is used (for best cache performance) or immediately when it is freed, which may help with debugging (though here writing a special value might be more useful)?

Collectors need to find pointers in order to determine reachability. Should the run-time provide a precise or a conservative estimate to the collector? Or might it provide a conservative estimate of the pointers in program threads and a more precise estimate of pointer locations in the heap? Conservative pointer finding can ease aspects of an implementation, but risks space leaks and may lead to worse performance than type-accurate collection. Finding pointers in the stack, especially if it contains a mixture of frame types (optimised and unoptimised subroutines, native code frames, bridging frames), can be challenging to implement type-accurately. On the other hand, scanning stacks for pointers constrains the choice of collection algorithm as objects directly reachable from stacks cannot be moved.

Systems generally provide stack maps to determine from a return address the function within which the address lies. Polymorphic functions and language constructs such as Java's jsr bytecode complicate their use. The implementer must also decide when stack maps should be generated and when they can be used. Should the maps be generated in advance or should we defer generating until the collector needs one, thereby saving space? Is a map only valid at certain safe points? Stack maps can be large: how can they be compressed, especially if they must be valid at every instruction? Stack scanning also raises the question of whether the stack should be scanned in its entirety, atomically, or incrementally. Incremental stack scanning is more complex but offers two benefits. First, it can bound the amount of work done in an increment (which may be important for real-time collectors). Second, by noting the portion of the stack that has not changed since the last time it was scanned, we can reduce the amount of work that the collector has to do.

Language semantics and compiler optimisations raise further questions. How should interior and derived pointers be handled? Language may allow access to objects from outside the managed environment, typically from code written in C or C++, and every language needs to interact with the operating system for input/output. The run-time must ensure that objects are not reclaimed while they are being used by external code and that external code can find these objects. Typically, this may involve pinning such objects or providing access to them through handles.

Some systems may allow a garbage collection at any point. However, it is usually simpler to restrict where collection can happen to specific GC safe-points. Typically these include allocation, backward branches, and function entry and return. There are alternative ways to cause a thread to suspend at a GC-point. One way is to have threads poll by checking a flag that indicates that a collection has been requested. An alternative is to patch the code of a running thread to roll it forward to the next GC-point. The handshake between collector and mutator thread can be achieved by having threads check a thread-local variable, by setting a processor condition code in the saved thread state of a suspended thread, by hijacking return address or through operating system signals.

Several classes of garbage collection algorithm require 'interesting' pointers to be detected as mutators run. This opens up a wide range of design policies and implementations for the detection and recording of these pointers. As barrier actions are very common, it is essential to minimise any overhead they incur. Barriers may be short sequences of code inserted by the compiler before pointer loads or stores, or they may be provided through operating system support, such as page protection traps. As always, there are trade-offs to be considered. In this case, the trade-offs are between the cost to the mutator and the cost to the collector, between precision of recording and speed of a barrier. In general, it is better to favour adding overhead to relatively infrequent collector actions (such as discovering roots) than to very frequent mutator actions (such as heap stores). Adding a write barrier can increase the instruction count for a pointer write by a factor of two or more, though some of this cost may be masked by cache access times.

How accurately should pointer writes be recorded? Unconditional logging may impose less overhead on the mutator than filtering out uninteresting pointers but the implementation of the remembered set is key to this decision. How much filtering should be inline? Careful tuning is essential here. At what granularity is the location of the pointer to be recorded? Should we record the field overwritten, the object or the card or page on which it resides? Should we allow the remembered set to contain duplicate entries? Should arrays and non-arrays be treated in the same way?

What data structures should be used to record the locations of interesting pointers: hash tables, sequential store buffers, cards or a combination of these? How does this choice vary the overheads between the mutator and the collector? Data structures may overflow: how can this be handled safely and efficiently? Card tables offer an imprecise recording mechanism. At collection time, they must be scanned to find dirty cards and hence objects that may contain interesting pointers. This raises three performance questions. What size should a card be? Card tables are often sparse: how can we speed up the search for dirty cards? Should a two-level card table be used? Can we summarise the state of a card, for example if it contains only one modified field or object? Once a dirty card is found, the collector needs to find the first object on that card, but that object may start on an earlier card. We need a crossing map that decodes how objects span cards. How does card marking interact with multiprocessor cache coherency protocols? If two processors repeatedly write to different objects on the same card, both will want exclusive access to the card's cache line. Is this likely to be a problem in practice?

In systems run with virtual memory, it is important that garbage collected applications fit within available real memory. Unlike non-managed programs, garbage collected ones can adjust their heap size so as to fit better within available memory. What events and counts does the particular operating system provide that a collector might use to adjust heap size appropriately? Which of these events or counts are most effective? What is a good heap growth policy, and an appropriate one for shrinking, if shrinking is possible? How can multiple collected processes cooperate so as to offer good throughput for all?

In summary, many of the details raised here are subtle, but both design choices and implementation details have substantial effect on performance. In later chapters, we shall see how the solutions discussed here can be used by garbage collection algorithms.

Chapter 12

Language-specific concerns

Many programming languages assume the availability of garbage collection. This has led to the development of various means for interacting with the collector in ways that extend the basic semantics of programming language memory management. For example, a program might want to be informed and take some action when a given object is about to be, or has been, reclaimed. We describe such finalisation mechanisms in Section 12.1. Conversely, it is sometimes helpful to support references that do not of themselves force an object to be retained. We consider such weak pointer mechanisms in Section 12.2. Lastly, so far we have considered only the case of objects that do not change their size or type (for garbage collection purposes) after allocation. Languages like JavaScript allow objects' layout to evolve more dynamically; we describe techniques to support changing layouts in Section 12.3.

12.1 Finalisation

Automatic storage reclamation with a garbage collector provides the appropriate semantics for most objects. However, if a managed object refers to some other resource that lies outside the scope or knowledge of the collector, automatic garbage collection does not help, and in fact can lead to resource leaks that are hard to fix. A typical case is open files. The interface to the operating system usually represents each open file with a small integer called a file descriptor, and the interface limits the number of files that a given process may have open at one time. A language implementation will generally have, for each open file, an object that the programmer uses to manage that file stream. Most of the time it is clear when a program has finished with a given file stream, and the program can ask the run-time system to close the stream, which can close the corresponding file descriptor at the operating system interface, allowing the descriptor number to be reused.

But if the file stream is shared across a number of components in a program, it can be difficult to know when they have all finished with the stream. If each component that uses a given stream sets its reference to the stream to null when the component is finished with the stream, then when there are no more references the collector can (eventually) detect that fact. We show such a situation in Figure 12.1. Perhaps we can arrange for the collector somehow to cause the file descriptor to be closed.

To do so, we need the ability to cause some programmer-specified action to happen when a given object becomes no longer reachable — more specifically, when it is no longer reachable by any mutator. This is called *finalisation*. A typical finalisation scheme allows the programmer to indicate a piece of code, called a *finaliser*, that is to be run when the

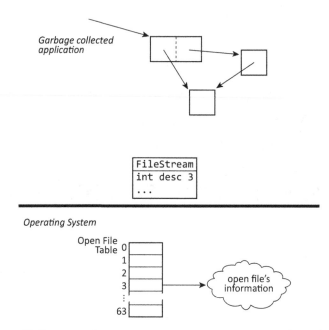

Figure 12.1: Failure to release a resource: a `FileStream` object has become unreachable, but its file descriptor has not been closed.

collector determines that a particular object is no longer mutator reachable. Commonly, the implementation of this has the run-time system maintain a special table of objects for which the programmer has indicated a finaliser. The mutators cannot access this table, but the collector can. We call an object *finaliser-reachable* if it is reachable from this table but not from mutator roots. In Figure 12.2 we show the previous situation but with a finaliser added. The finaliser's call to close the descriptor is conditional, since the application may have already closed the file.

In a reference counting system, before freeing an object the collector checks the finalisation table to see if the object requires finalisation. If it does, then the collector causes the finaliser to run, and removes the object's entry from the table. Similarly, in a tracing system, after the tracing phase the collector checks the finalisation table to see if any untraced object has a finaliser, and if so, the collector causes the finaliser to run, and so on.

There is a range of subtly different ways in which finalisation can work. We now consider some of the possibilities and issues.

When do finalisers run?

At what time do finalisers run? In particular, finalisation might occur during collection, as soon as the collector determines the need for it. However, the situation during collection might not support execution of general user code. For example, it may not be possible for user code to allocate new objects at this time. Therefore most finalisation approaches run finalisers after collection. The collector simply enqueues the finalisers. To avoid the need to allocate space for the queue during collection, the collector can use a linked-list representation for both the table of objects that have a finaliser but have not been enqueued and for the queue of objects to be finalised. When the collector determines an object should be enqueued for finalisation, it simply moves a linked-list node from one list to the other.

In general, finalisers affect shared state; there is little reason to operate only on finalisable objects since they are about to disappear. For example, finalisers may need to access

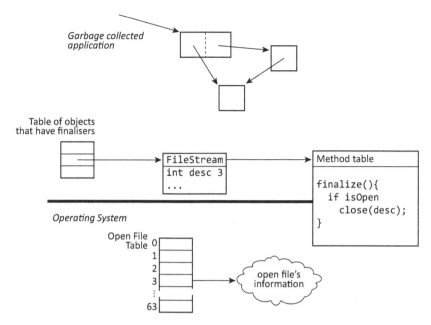

Figure 12.2: Using a finaliser to release a resource: here, an unreachable `FileStream` object has a finaliser to close the descriptor.

some global data to release a shared resource, and so often need to acquire locks. This is another reason not to run finalisers during collection: it could result in a deadlock. Worse, if the run-time system provides re-entrant locks — locks where the same thread can acquire a lock that it already holds — we can have a finaliser run at a time when a critical data structure is in the middle of being changed and its invariants do not hold. Thus we can have absence of deadlock and silent corruption of the state of the application.[1]

Even assuming that finalisers run after collection, there remain several options as to exactly when they run. One possibility is immediately after collection, before mutator thread(s) resume. This improves promptness of finalisation but perhaps to the detriment of mutator pause time. Also, if finalisers communicate with other threads, which remain blocked at this time, or if finalisers compete for locks on global data structures, this policy could lead to communication problems or deadlock.

A last consideration is that it is not desirable for a language's specification of finalisation to constrain the possible collection techniques. In particular, collection on the fly, concurrent with mutation, most naturally leads to running finalisers at arbitrary times, concurrently with mutator execution.

Which thread runs a finaliser?

In a language that permits multiple threads, the most natural approach is to have a background finalisation thread run the enqueued finalisers asynchronously with the mutator threads. In this case, the finalisers may run concurrently with mutators and must therefore be safe for concurrent execution. Of particular concern is the possibility that a finaliser for

---

[1]Java has avoided this by indicating that a finalisation thread will invoke a finaliser with no locks held. Thus the finalisation thread must be one that does not hold a lock on the object being finalised. In practice this pretty much requires finalisation threads to be distinct threads, used only for that purpose. However, finalisation has long been deprecated (since Java 9) and is now scheduled for removal.

an object of type T might run at the same time as the allocation and initialisation code for a new instance of T. Any shared data structures must be synchronised to handle that case.[2]

In a single-threaded language, which thread runs a finaliser is not a question — though it does re-raise the question of *when* finalisers run. Given the difficulties previously mentioned, it appears that the only feasible and safe way, in general, to run finalisers in a single-threaded system is to queue them and have the program run them under explicit control. In a multithreaded system, as previously noted it is best that distinct finalisation threads invoke finalisers, to avoid issues around locks.

Can finalisers run concurrently with each other?

If a large concurrent application uses finalisers, it may need more than one finalisation thread in order to be scalable. Thus, from the standpoint of language design it appears better to allow finalisers to run concurrently with each other, as well as concurrently with mutators. Since, in general, programmers must code finalisers carefully so that they operate correctly in the face of concurrency — because finalisers are essentially asynchronous with respect to mutator operations — there should be no additional problem with running finalisers concurrently with each other.

Can finalisers access the object that became unreachable?

In many cases it is convenient for a finaliser to access the state of the object being reclaimed. In the file stream example, the operating system file descriptor number, a small integer, might most conveniently be stored as a field in the file stream object, as we showed in Figure 12.2. The simplest finaliser can read that field and call on the operating system to close the file (possibly after flushing a buffer of any pending output data). Notice that if the finaliser does not have access to the object, and is provided no additional data but is just a piece of code to run, then finalisation will not be very useful — the finaliser needs some context for its work. In a functional language, this context may be a closure; in an object-oriented language it may be an object. Thus the queuing mechanism needs to provide for the passing of arguments to the finaliser.

On balance it seems more convenient if finalisers can access the object being finalised.[3] Assuming finalisers run after collection, this implies that objects enqueued for finalisation survive the collection cycle in which they are enqueued. So that finalisers have access to everything they might need, the collector must also retain all objects reachable from objects enqueued for finalisation. This implies that tracing collectors need to operate in two passes. The first pass discovers the objects to be finalised, and the second pass traces and preserves objects reachable from the finaliser queue. In a reference counting collector the system can increment the object's reference count as it enqueues it for finalisation, that is, the finalisation queue's reference to the object 'counts'. Once the object is dequeued and its finaliser runs, the reference count will become zero and the object can be reclaimed. Until then, objects reachable from it will not even be considered for reclamation.

---

[2]Java has a special rule to help prevent this: if an object's finaliser can cause synchronisation on the object, then the object is considered mutator reachable whenever its lock is held. This can inhibit removal of synchronisation (because an object otherwise reachable only from the thread that allocated it will now be reachable also from the finalisation thread, though not at the same time).

[3]However, using something like Java's cleaners, which are built using phantom references, avoids the pitfalls of finalisers while not restricting what the programmer can accomplish. See Section 12.2.

When are finalised objects reclaimed?

The fact that finalisers usually hold a reference to the object being finalised means that they might store that reference in a global data structure. This has been called *resurrection*. In a mechanical sense resurrection is not a problem, though it may be surprising to the programmer. Since it is probably difficult to detect stores that resurrect objects, and since setting up an object for future finalisation tends to happen as part of allocation and initialisation, resurrected objects will generally not be re-finalised. Java, for example, guarantees that an object will not be finalised more than once. A language design in which setting up finalisation works more dynamically might allow the programmer to request finalisation for a resurrected object — because it allows such requests for any object.

If a finalised object is not resurrected, then the next collection cycle can reclaim it. In a system with partitioned spaces, such as a generational collector, the finalised object might reside in a space that will not be collected again for a long time, so making it available to the finaliser can substantially extend the object's physical lifetime.

What happens if there is an error in a finaliser?

If finalisation is run synchronously at times known to the application, then programmers can easily wrap finalisation actions with recovery handlers for when a finaliser returns an error or throws an exception. If finalisers run asynchronously, it may be best to catch and log exceptions for later handling by the application at an appropriate time. This is more a concern of software engineering than of the garbage collection algorithm or mechanism.

Is there any guaranteed order to finalisation?

Finalisation order can matter to an application. For example, consider a `BufferedStream` object connected to a `FileStream` that holds an open operating system file descriptor, as shown in Figure 12.3. Both objects may need finalisers, but it is important to flush (write) the buffer of the `BufferedStream` before closing the file descriptor.[4]

Clearly, in a layered design like this, the sensible semantics will finalise from higher layers to lower ones. In this case, because the lower level object is reachable from the higher level one, it is possible for finalisation to occur in the sensible order automatically. Notice that if we impose order on finalisations, ultimate finalisation may be slow, since we only finalise one 'level' in the order at each collection. That is, in a given collection we only finalise those unreached objects that are not themselves reachable from *other* unreached objects.

This proposal has a significant flaw: it does not handle *cycles* of unreachable objects where more than one needs finalisation. Given that such cases appear to be rare, it seems simpler and more helpful to guarantee finalisation in order of reachability; that is, if B is reachable from A, the system should invoke the finaliser for A first.

In the rare case of cycles, the programmer will need to get more involved. Mechanisms such as weak references (see Section 12.2) may help, though using them correctly may be tricky. A general technique is to separate out fields needed for finalisation in such a way as to break the cycle of objects needing finalisation, as suggested by Boehm [2003]. That is, if A and B have finalisers and cross-reference each other as shown in Figure 12.4a, we can split B into B and B′, where B does not have a finaliser but B′ does (see Figure 12.4b). A and B still cross-reference each other, but (importantly) B′ does not refer to A. In this scenario, finalisation in reachability order will finalise A first and then B′.

---

[4]As a more subtle point, note that unless we can guarantee that the `FileStream` is used only by the `BufferedStream`, then the `BufferedStream` should *not* close the `FileStream`. Unfortunately, this implies that it may require *two* collection cycles before the file descriptor is closed.

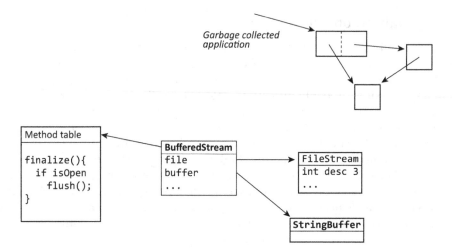

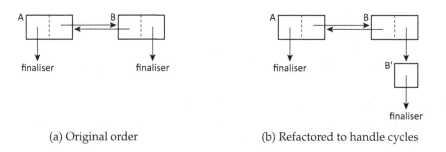

Figure 12.3: Object finalisation order. Unreachable `BufferedStream` and `FileStream` objects, which must be finalised in that order.

(a) Original order   (b) Refactored to handle cycles

Figure 12.4: Restructuring to force finalisation order in cyclic object graphs

The finalisation race problem

Lest we think that finalisation can be used straightforwardly without risk of subtle bugs, even in the case of objects not requiring special finalisation order, there is a subtle kind of race condition that can arise [Boehm, 2003]. Consider the `FileStream` example shown in Figure 12.2. Suppose that the mutator is making its last call to write data to the file. The `writeData` method of `FileStream` may fetch the descriptor, and then as its last action call `write` on the descriptor, passing the data. Significantly, at this point the method's reference to the `FileStream` object is dead, and the compiler may optimise it away. If collection happens during the call to `write`, the finaliser on `FileStream` may run and close the file, *before* `write` actually invokes the operating system to write the data. This is a difficult problem and Boehm's experience is that the bug is pervasive, but rarely triggered because the window of vulnerability is short.

One fix for this is the Java rule mentioned previously that an object must be considered live whenever its lock is held and a finaliser could run that requires synchronisation on the object. A more general way to avoid the race is to force the compiler to retain the reference to the `FileStream` longer. The trick to doing this is to pass the `FileStream` reference in a later call (to a routine that does nothing) that the compiler cannot optimise away. The .NET framework and C# (for example) provide a function for this called `GC.KeepAlive`. Java similarly provides the `Reference.reachabilityFence` method.

Algorithm 12.1: Process finalisation queue

```
 1   process_finalisation_queue():
 2     while not isEmpty(Queue)
 3       do
 4           obj ← remove(Queue)
 5           obj.finalize()
 6       until isEmpty(Queue)
 7       if desired                        /* whatever condition is appropriate */
 8           collect()
```

Finalisers and locks

As noted, for example by Boehm [2003], the purpose of a finaliser is usually to update some global data structure in order to release a resource connected with the object that becomes unreachable. Since such data structures are global, they generally require synchronised access. In cases such as closing open file handles, some other software component (in this case, the operating system) handles the synchronisation implicitly, but for data structures within the program, it must be explicit. The concern is that, from the standpoint of most code in the program, finalisers are asynchronous.

There are two general approaches a programmer can take to the situation. One is to apply synchronisation to all operations on the global data structure — even in the single-threaded case (because a finaliser could run in the middle of a data structure operation otherwise). This counts on the underlying implementation not to elide synchronisation on an apparently private object if that object has a finalisation method. The other approach is to arrange for the collector only to enqueue the object for finalisation, but not to begin the actual finalisation work. Some language implementations offer such queueing mechanisms as built-in features; if a particular implementation does not, then the programmer can code the finalisation method so that all it does is place the object in a programmer-defined queue. In the queueing approach, the programmer will add code to the program, at desirable (that is, safe) points. The code will process any enqueued objects needing finalisation. Since running finalisers can cause other objects to be enqueued for finalisation, such queue-processing code should generally continue processing until the queue is empty, and may want to force collections if it is important to reclaim resources promptly. Suitable pseudocode appears in Algorithm 12.1. As previously noted, the thread that runs this algorithm should not be holding a lock on any object to be finalised, which constrains the places where this processing can proceed safely.

The pain involved in this approach is the need to identify appropriate places in the code at which to empty the finalisation queue. In addition to sprinkling enough invocations throughout the code, the programmer must also take care that invocations do not happen in the middle of other operations on the shared data structures. Locks alone cannot prevent this, since the invoking thread may already hold the lock, and thus can be allowed to proceed. This is the source of the statement in the Java Language Specification that the system will only invoke `finalize` methods while holding no user-visible locks.

Finalisation and weak references

Finalisation and weak references can have complex interactions and require subtle implementation in a collector. This topic is discussed further in Section 12.2.

Finalisation in particular languages

Java. The `Object` class at the top of the Java class hierarchy provides a method named `finalize`, which does nothing. Any subclass can override the method to request finalisation. Java does not guarantee finalisation order, and with respect to concurrency only says that finalisation runs in a context starting with no (user-visible) synchronisation locks held. This pretty much means that finalisation runs in one or more separate threads, even though the specification is not quite worded that way. If `finalize` throws an exception, the Java system ignores it and moves on. If the finalised object is not resurrected, a future collection will reclaim it. Java also provides support for programmer-controlled finalisation through appropriate use of the `java.lang.ref` API, as we describe in Section 12.2. Note that finalisation has been officially deprecated since Java 9 and is now scheduled for removal in a future release.

Lisp. Liquid Common Lisp offers a kind of object called a *finalisation queue*. The programmer can register an ordinary object with one or more finalisation queues. When the registered object becomes otherwise unreachable, the collector enters it into the finalisation queues with which it was registered. The programmer can extract objects from any finalisation queue and do with them what she will. The system guarantees that if objects A and B are both registered and become unreachable in the same collection, and B is reachable from A but not vice versa, then the collector will enter A in the finalisation queue before it enters B. That is, it guarantees order of finalisation for acyclic object graphs. These finalisation queues are similar to the *guardians* described by Dybvig *et al.* [1993].

CLisp offers a simpler mechanism: the programmer can request that the collector call a given function f when it detects that a given object O is no longer reachable. In this case f must not refer to O or else O will remain reachable and the system will never call the finaliser. Since f receives O as an argument, this system permits resurrection. Also, f could register O again, so O can be finalised more than once. A variant of the basic mechanism allows the programmer to specify a *guardian* G in addition to the object O and function f. In this case, when O becomes unreachable the system calls f only if G is still reachable. If at this time G is unreachable, then the system reclaims O but does not call f. This can be used to implement guardians of the kind described by Dybvig *et al.* [1993] — f can add O to the internal queue of G.

C++. The C++ language offers *destructors* to handle disposal of objects, as a converse to constructors which initialise new objects. The primary role of most destructors is to cause explicit freeing of memory and its return to the allocator for reuse. However, since programmers can offer any code they want, C++ destructors can handle the case of closing a file, and so forth. Destructors also provide a hook through which a programmer can support reference counting to reclaim (acyclic) shared data structures. In fact, C++ templates allow a general smart pointer mechanism to drive the reference counting. But this shows again that destructors are mostly about reclaiming memory — a job that a garbage collector already handles. Thus, true finalisation remains relatively rare, even for C++. The memory reclamation aspect of destructors is relatively safe and straightforward, not least because it does not involve user-visible locks. However, as soon as the programmer veers into the realm of 'true' finalisation, all the issues we mention here arise and are dropped into the programmer's lap. This includes dealing with locking, order of invocation of finalisers, and so on. Placing the responsibility for all this on the programmer's shoulders makes it difficult to ensure that it is done correctly.

.NET. The .NET framework adds finalisers to the existing notion of destructors in C, C++, and the other languages supported by the framework. Destructors are called deterministically, starting with compiler-generated code for cleaning up objects as they go out of scope. A destructor may call other objects' destructors, but all destructors are concerned with reclaiming *managed* resources, that is, resources known to the language and .NET runtime system, primarily memory. Finalisers, on the other hand, are for explicitly reclaiming *unmanaged* resources, such as open file handles and the like. If a kind of object needs finalisation, then the destructor should call the finaliser, to cover the case when the object is reclaimed explicitly by compiler-generated code. However, the collector will call the finaliser if the object is being reclaimed implicitly, that is, by the collector. In that case the destructor will not be called. In any case, the finalisation mechanism itself is very similar to that of Java. The end result is a mixture of C++ destructors and something close to Java finalisation, with both synchronous and asynchronous invocation of finalisers possible.

JavaScript Core. JavaScript Core (JSC) is a JavaScript implementation in the WebKit browser. Its heap objects may have destructors that must be called before the storage is reused. These destructors are typically concerned with things like references to items in the browser's DOM (Document Object Model, representation of HTML objects), which may need explicit reclamation when JSC objects are reclaimed. Kim *et al.* [2014] describe a technique to speed up the processing of these destructors. They sweep a block at a time in JSC's lazy sweeping scheme, doing so concurrently with the mutators, invoking the destructors of the dead objects of the block. Note that this finalisation is run entirely by the collector and cannot refer to any other objects in the JSC heap — only the contents of the dead object, which may hold non-JSC references into other spaces such as the DOM. More recently JavaScript added a more typical finalisation scheme similar to Java's phantom references.

For further study

Various languages have supported finalisation for decades and have evolved mechanisms suitable to their contexts. Systematic consideration of the issues and various design approaches across several languages appears more recently in the literature in works such as Hudson [1991] and Hayes [1992]. More careful inspection of the semantics of finalisation and some of the thorny problems at its heart was performed by Boehm [2003], to whom we are indebted as a primary source.

12.2   Weak references

Garbage collection determines which memory to retain and which to reclaim using reachability through chains of pointers. For automatic reclamation this is a sound approach. Still, there are a number of situations in which it is problematic.

For example, in a compiler it can be useful to ensure that every reference to a given variable name, say xyz, uses exactly the same string instance. Then, to compare two variable names for equality, it suffices to compare their pointers. To set this up, the compiler builds a table of all the variable names it has seen so far. The strings in the table are the *canonical* instances of the variable names, and such tables are therefore sometimes called *canonicalisation tables*. But consider what happens if some names fall into disuse as the compiler runs. There are no references to the names from other data structures, but the canonical copy remains. It would be possible to reclaim a string whose only reference is from the table, but the situation is difficult for the program to detect reliably.

Weak references (also called *weak pointers*) address this difficulty. If an object is reachable from a root via a chain consisting only of ordinary *strong references*, we call the object *strongly-reachable*. A *weak* reference continues to refer to its target, also called its referent, as long as the target is strongly-reachable. Conversely, if there is no path from the roots to an object consisting only of strong references, yet the object is reachable from one or more weak references, we call the object weakly-reachable. (This implies that every path from the roots to the object includes at least one weak reference.) The collector may reclaim any weakly-reachable object, and in that case must set any weak references from which the object is strongly-reachable to null. (This is also called *clearing* the weak reference.) As we will see, the collector may also take additional action, such as notifying the mutator that a given weak reference has been cleared.

In the case of the canonicalisation table for variable names, if the reference from the table to the name is a weak reference, then once there are no ordinary references to the string, the collector can reclaim the string and set the table's weak reference to null. Notice that the table design must take this possibility into account, and it may be necessary or helpful for the program to clean up the table from time to time. For example, if the table is organised by hashing with each hash bucket being a linked list, defunct weak references result in linked list entries whose referent is null. We should clean those out of the table from time to time. This also shows why a notification facility might be helpful: we can use it to trigger the cleaning up.

Here is how we can we support weak references in a collector. We consider first the case of tracing collectors. In this case, the collector performs tracing in two passes. In the first pass, the collector does not trace the target of a weak reference. Rather, it records where the weak reference is, for processing in a second pass. Thus, the first tracing pass finds all strongly-reachable objects. In the second pass the collector examines the weak references that it found and noted in the first pass. If a weak reference's target was reached in the first pass, then the collector retains the weak reference, and in copying collectors it updates the weak reference to refer to the new copy. If a weak reference's target is found to be *not* strongly-reachable, then the collector clears the weak reference, thus making the referent no longer reachable (strongly or weakly). At the end of the second pass, the collector can reclaim all unreached objects.

The technique just described requires that the collector be able to identify any weak reference. It may be possible to use a bit in the *reference* to indicate that it is weak. For example, if objects are aligned on word boundaries in a byte-addressed machine, then pointers normally have some low bits that are zero. One of those bits could indicate a weak reference if the bit is set to 1. This approach has the disadvantage that it requires the low bits to be cleared before trying to use a reference that may be weak. That may be acceptable if weak references only arise in certain restricted places in a given language design. Some languages and their implementations may use tagged values anyway, and this simply requires one more possible tag value.

An alternative to using a low bit is to use a high-order bit and double-map the heap. In this case every heap page appears twice in the virtual address space, once in its natural place, lower in the address space, and again at a high memory address. The addresses only differ in the value of a chosen bit near the high-order end of the address. Thus the heap address space is duplicated at a fixed offset from its natural position. This technique avoids the need to mask pointers before using them, and its test for weakness is simple and efficient (test the chosen high-order bit). However, it doubles the use of address space, which may make it undesirable except in large address spaces.

Perhaps the most common implementation approach is to use indirection, so that specially marked weak *objects* hold weak references. The disadvantage of the weak object approach is that it is less transparent to use — it requires an explicit dereferencing operation on the weak object — and it imposes a level of indirection. It also requires allocating a weak object in addition to the object whose reclamation we are trying to control. However, an advantage is that weak objects are only special to the allocator and collector — to all other code they are like ordinary objects. A system can distinguish a weak object from an ordinary one by examining its type, which may have a field reserved for this purpose. An alternative design is to reserve a bit in the object header. A third possibility, if objects have custom-generated tracing methods, is to give weak objects a special one.

An implementation must also provide means for a programmer to obtain a weak reference (weak object) in the first place. In the case of true weak *references*, the system supplies a primitive that, when given a strong reference to object O, returns a weak reference to O. In the case of weak *objects*, the weak object types similarly supply a constructor that, given a strong reference to O, returns a new weak object whose target is O. It is also possible for a system to allow programs to change the referent field in a weak object.

Additional motivations

Canonicalisation tables are but one example of situations where weak references of some kind help solve a programming problem, or solve it more easily or efficiently. Another example is managing a cache whose contents can be retrieved or rebuilt as necessary. Java `SoftReference` objects are intended for this purpose; see below.

Sometimes it is useful to let a program know when an object is weakly-reachable but not strongly-reachable, and to allow it to take some action before the collector reclaims the object. This is a generalisation of finalisation, a topic we took up in Section 12.1. Among other things, suitable arrangements of these sorts of weak references can allow better control of the order in which the program finalises objects.

Weak references in Java: the short story

Java has what is probably the most complex weak reference design to date. To describe it, we start with a simple subset — one arguably sufficient for all the purposes of the full design — and then cover the full design. Our starting point is Java with phantom references, with no other non-strong references and without finalisation. Java uses weak objects, as opposed to weak references. These objects are instances of subclasses of the abstract class `Reference`, a special class known to the allocator and collector. `PhantomReference` is one of those subclasses. Its particular behavior is that you cannot fetch its contained reference. It is possible, however, to test whether it has been *cleared* or still refers to some object. The collector will clear the contained reference when the referent is no longer strongly-reachable.[5]

Another feature of Java weak references is that when a `Reference` object's referent is no longer strongly-reachable, the `Reference` object can be placed on a queue for special processing. These queues are ordinary Java objects, and ordinary Java threads can process `Reference` objects placed in a queue. This makes phantom references more useful — they can accomplish finalisation in a more user-controlled fashion than the built-in finalisation mechanism can. To facilitate this usage pattern, Java now has a `Cleaner` class. A `Cleaner` maintains a collection of *registered objects*, each with an associated *cleaning action*. When the program registers an object O with the cleaner, it provides the cleaning action at the same time. The cleaner then creates a `PhantomReference` to O, and associates that phantom reference with the provided cleaning action. Cleaning actions have a `run()` method and can include any other state needed by the action — but should definitely not include O itself. The cleaner has a `ReferenceQueue` into which its phantom references will be placed

---

[5]In the full model, Phantomly-reachable.

by the collector when the original referents (such as O) are no longer strongly-reachable.[6] The cleaner will then find and run the associated cleaning action, exactly once.

In contrast to Java finalisation, cleaners support application controlled resurrection and re-finalisation, as follows. For a managed object O, the application (i) creates a wrapper object W, which has a reference to O; (ii) registers W with a cleaner, along with an action that has a reference to O; and (iii) only hands out references to W, not to O. When W is no longer reachable, the collector eventually detects that and the cleaner's phantom reference to W is cleared and enqueued. The cleaner will then run the action, which can do whatever it likes with O, including creating and registering another wrapper for O, and so on. The wrapper W will be reclaimed.

This cleaner pattern can support the use cases previously mentioned: canonicalisation tables, caches and finalisation. Cleaners naturally support finalisation in topological order in the object graph, and give the user control over the degree of concurrency of finalisation. Cleaners also avoid direct resurrection, while allowing the application-defined state to be set up for finalisation-like handling again, if that is desirable. Using cleaners for canonicalisation tables and caches may require an additional level of wrapping or indirection in the user objects, but again is a general solution that puts control in the hands of the user rather than the collector.

The Java weak reference model has evolved over time, and may well continue to do so. Finalisation is now deprecated, and cleaners have been added. For simplicity and to guard against future change, future Java code might well restrict itself to cleaners and Phantom references. However, current collector implementers still need to deal with the full model, to which we now turn.

Weak references in Java: the full story

We have endeavoured to explain the Java weak reference and finalisation model correctly as of the time of writing, but note that it may well continue to change. The full model includes three Reference classes: WeakReference, SoftReference and PhantomReference. It also interacts with Java finalisation — objects with a non-empty finalize method can be viewed as referenced by a *finaliser reference* known only to the collector. We describe the semantics and implementation strategy as if finaliser references exist as another kind of Reference object, but they are more likely implemented as just a list or table of all the objects that have non-empty finalize methods.

These four kinds of weak references we will henceforth write as Soft reference, Weak reference, Finaliser reference and Phantom reference, to distinguish the general notion of weak reference from the particlar kinds of references of Java. Each kind of Java weak reference has a different (reachability) *strength*. To define this concept precisely, consider n strengths, $s_1, ..., s_n$, where s_1 is the strongest. Every reference (pointer) has a designated strength. Ordinary pointers are strong references and thus have strength s_1. An object O is *at least s_i-reachable* if there is a sequence of pointers from a root to O each of which has strength s_i or stronger. O is s_i-reachable if it is at least s_i-reachable and it is *not* at least s_{i-1}-reachable.[7]

The Java strengths, in order from strongest to weakest, are: Strong, Soft, Weak, Finaliser and Phantom. In principle, it would seem that up to four passes over the object graph might be needed to determine the level of reachability of each object, but the semantics of the different kinds of weak references simplify this to two: Strongly-reachable and Finaliser-reachable, as we describe below.

---

[6]See footnote 5.

[7]Being 'at least s_1-reachable' is the same as being 's_1-reachable.'

Any Java weak object may have a `ReferenceQueue` associated with it. After it clears the weak object, the collector will add the weak object to the queue. Finaliser references have as their queue the internal finalisation queue of the system.

The differences in semantics between these kinds of weak references are as follows.

Soft: The collector can clear a Soft reference at its discretion, based on current space usage, if the referent is not Strongly-reachable. If a Java collector clears a Soft reference to object O (that is, sets the reference to null), it must at the same time atomically[8] clear all other Soft references from which O is Strongly-reachable. This rule ensures that after the collector clears the references, O will no longer be Softly-reachable.

The recommendation is that collectors clear Soft references based on time, either how recently the reference was created or when it was last accessed.[9] We call this the Soft reference's timestamp. To support the recommendation, a collector can trace through a Soft reference if its timestamp is sufficiently recent, treating the Soft reference as if it is Strong. After tracing, the collector will then clear Soft references whose referent is found to be not Strongly-reachable.

Weak: The collector must clear a Softly-reachable Weak reference if it determines that its referent is Weakly-reachable (and thus not at least Softly-reachable). As with Soft references, if the collector clears a Weak reference to object O, it must simultaneously clear all other at least Softly-reachable Weak references from which O is at least Softly-reachable.

Finaliser: Finaliser references are special in that their implementation is entirely internal to the system, and they enqueue the *referent*, not the reference.

Phantom: Phantom references differ in that they do not allow the program to obtain a reference to their referent. Hence, as previously discussed, they avoid the issues of resurrection of the referent. However, like other Java weak references, they can be enqueued, which is basis for Java cleaners, previously discussed.

We now describe an implementation strategy,[10] followed by an explanation of why it works. This strategy involves using *two* mark bits. One of these records *Strong reachability* and the other records *Finaliser reachability*. The procedure is as follows. Threads that mark from roots trace through all Strong references, plus those Soft references that the collector determines it definitely will not clear. These threads set the Strong mark bit for each object they reach. They also remember all reference objects they encounter. Threads that mark from the internal Finaliser references set the Finaliser mark bit of unmarked objects they encounter. They do not trace through any object with either mark bit set, but should trace through Soft references in the same way the other threads do, and they should also remember reference objects they encounter. When using a single thread, it can do the marking

---

[8]By *atomically* the Java specification seems to mean that no thread can see just some of the references from which a given object is reachable cleared and not others: either all of them are cleared or none are. This can be accomplished by having the reference objects consult a shared flag that indicates whether the referent field should be treated as *possibly* cleared, even if it is not yet set to null. The reference object can itself contain a flag that indicates whether the single global flag should be consulted, that is, whether the reference is being considered for clearing. Doing this safely requires synchronisation in concurrent collectors. On-the-fly collection is particularly complex [Ugawa *et al.*, 2014].

[9]The documentation for the `SoftReference` class in Java SE 18 and JDK 18, 2022, (https://docs.oracle.com/en/java/javase/18/docs/api/java.base/java/lang/ref/SoftReference.html), after noting both the required atomicity of clearing Soft references, and that implementations cannot throw `OutOfMemoryError` unless they first try clearing all Soft references, reads, "Virtual machine implementations are, however, encouraged to bias against clearing recently-created or recently-used soft references."

[10]The ZGC concurrent collector, discussed in Section 17.5, takes this approach, which allows concurrent marking from both roots and Finaliser references.

from roots and then the marking from Finaliser references as two separate passes. In that case it is possible to use a single mark bit, clearing and enqueueing Phantom references after the second pass, but handling the other kinds before the second pass.

After marking, the collector examines the referent of each reference object it encountered. If the referent's Strong mark bit is set, then do not clear the reference.

If neither mark bit is set, this object must be the target of a Soft reference that is not being retained, or it must be the target of a Weak or Phantom reference. Clear the reference and enqueue it as necessary.

If only the Finaliser mark bit is set, then for the target of a Soft or Weak reference, clear the reference and enqueue as necessary. For the target of a Finaliser reference, enqueue the referent for finalisation. For the target of a Phantom reference, leave the reference alone.

Recall that clearing references must be done atomically, as previously discussed, so where we say 'clear the reference' above, we mean that it should be included in the set of references to be cleared atomically.

We now argue that these two marking passes (whether concurrent or sequential) are sufficient, as opposed to the four one might imagine to be necessary. We consider each kind of reference in turn. A Soft reference is only cleared / enqueued if (i) the collector did not choose it as one to keep alive (in that case the referent has its Strong mark bit set because the collector traced through the reference) *and* (ii) it was not otherwise Strongly-reachable. That behaviour matches the specification. A Weak reference is cleared / enqueued if it is not Strongly-reachable. This might seem too eager — what if it were Softly-reachable? We can see that the behaviour is in fact correct if we imagine that the Soft references that will be cleared were *already clear* when the collector started. In that imagined view, a Soft reference that was not cleared causes objects reachable from it to have their Strong mark bit set. Thus the Softly-reachable objects have their Strong mark bit set, as do the Strongly-reachable ones. Concerning Finaliser references, we can make a similar argument, imagining that the appropriate Weak references have already been cleared. Lastly, Phantom references are appropriately sensitive to whether they are Finaliser-reachable because they check the Finaliser mark bit. In fact, it is Phantom references that require the second marking pass.

While we worded the description above in terms of a mark-sweep collector, it works just as well for copying collection, and also generalises to generational collection if one considers older generation objects as Strongly-reachable.

Here is how one might construct a reference counting version of the Java semantics. An object's reference count will record just the number of *strong references* to the object. However, it will have an additional bit to indicate that it is a referent of a weak reference (of any kind). It is also convenient if an object has a separate bit indicating that it has a non-trivial finaliser. We assume that there is a global table that, for each object O that is the referent of at least one `Reference` object, indicates those `Reference` objects that refer to O. We call this the *Reverse Reference Table*.

Before proceeding, we observe that a weakly-reachable cycle of objects connected via strong references will not be reclaimed without special cycle collection techniques, so we ignore that case for the moment. Regardless, if an object's reference count decreases to zero, it is not Strongly-reachable.

Consider what should happen when a reference count goes to zero and the object is a referent of a weak reference or has a finaliser. The collector can handle the situation in order of strength. If the object is the target of any Soft references, then if any of those Soft references should be retained, the object will be retained for now, and handling will be revisited when a weak reference object is reclaimed. If all of the Soft references can be cleared, do so atomically, enqueue the Soft references as necessary, and proceed to the next strength. If there are any Weak references, clear them atomically, enqueue them as necessary, and proceed to the next strength. If there is a finaliser, enqueue the object for finalisation, clear the object's 'I have a finaliser' bit and stop. (Note: the reference from the finalisation queue will count as a strong reference.) If the object's 'I have a finaliser' bit is not set, but there are any Phantom references, clear the Phantom references and enqueue them as necessary. If there was no finaliser and all the weak references were cleared, then the object can be reclaimed. Achieving atomicity of these special reference count adjustments can be tricky, and requires either locking or a technique similar to that described by Ugawa *et al.* [2014].

There are some more cases to note. When we reclaim a `Reference` object, we need to remove it from the Reverse Reference Table. We also need to do that when a `Reference` object is cleared. We further need to check the referent. If its reference count is zero, we need to redo the processing described above since the situation has changed.

A tricky case is when a detector of garbage cycles finds such a cycle. It appears that, before doing anything else, we need to see if *any* of the objects is the referent of a Soft object, and in that case retain them all, but keep checking periodically somehow. If none are Soft referents but some are Weak referents, then we need to clear all those Weak objects atomically, and enqueue any objects requiring finalisation. Finally, if none of the previous cases apply but there are some Phantom referents to the cycle, we need to clear and enqueue all the Phantoms. If no object in the cycle is a Soft or Weak referent, or requires finalisation, we can reclaim the whole cycle.

As perhaps an historical note, we observe that Java[11] defines an object as *"phantomly-reachable* if it is neither strongly-, softly-, nor weakly-reachable, it has been finalized, and some phantom reference refers to it."* This definition is inadequate: consider the following example[12] where F_1 and F_2 are objects with non-trivial finalisers, and P is the referent of a `PhantomReference`. Initially, F_1 holds a reference to P and some root points to F_2 which holds a null reference. Then,

1. F_1's finaliser runs and notionally P's (empty) finaliser runs. F_1 updates F_2 with a strong reference to P. At this point, P has now been finalised and the root points to F_2 which points to P.

2. The root is cleared, making F_2 unreachable. P is now neither strongly, softly or weakly referenced, and it been finalised. Therefore P is phantom-reachable.

3. The `PhantomReference` to P is enqueued, resulting in running a `Cleaner` which maybe deallocates native memory required by P.

4. F_2's finaliser runs and accesses P, which can no longer access the native memory it needs...

The 'has been finalized' check required by `java.lang.ref` is the wrong check; what matters is whether it is *reachable* from a not yet finalised object with a non-trivial finaliser. This requires a reachability analysis such as the one we described above.

Race in weak pointer clearing

We note that, just as certain compiler optimisations can lead to a race that can cause premature finalisation, the same situations can lead to premature clearing of weak pointers. We described the finalisation case in Section 12.1.

---

[11]Java SE 18 and JDK 18, 2022, https://docs.oracle.com/en/java/javase/18/docs/api/java.base/java/lang/ref/package-summary.html
[12]Example due to Hans Boehm.

Weak pointers in other languages

We discussed Java separately because of its multiple strengths of weak references. Other languages offer alternative or additional weak reference features.

Lisp. A number of Lisp implementations support weak arrays and vectors.[13] These are simply multi-entry weak objects: when a referent O is no longer strongly-reachable, the collector sets to `nil` any weak array or vector slots that refer to O.

Some Lisp implementations also support weak hash tables. These often come in three varieties. One offers *weak keys*, in which the keys, but not the values, are weak. In this case, once the key of a given key-value pair is no longer strongly-reachable, the collector removes the entire pair from the hash table. This is useful for things like canonicalisation tables and certain kinds of caches. A second variety offers *weak values*, where the collector removes the key-value pair once the value is no longer strongly-reachable. The third variety supports weak keys *and* values, removing the pair once either the key or the value is no longer strongly-reachable.

Some Lisp implementations support *weak-AND* and *weak-OR* objects. The elements of these objects are potentially weak, but in the following way. A weak-AND will set *all* its elements to `nil` if one or more of them becomes not strongly-reachable. Thus, it is analogous to a Lisp `AND`, which returns `nil` if any argument to `AND` is `nil`. A weak-OR is the converse: it retains all its arguments until none of them are strongly-reachable, and then sets all of its fields to `nil`. We refer readers to the documentation on the Platform Independent Extensions to Common Lisp[14] for more details and further generalisations, including weak associations, weak AND- and OR-mappings, weak association lists and a version of weak hash tables similar to what we discussed above.

Ephemerons. *Ephemerons*[15] [Hayes, 1997] are a particular form of weak key-value pairs useful for maintaining information attached to other objects. Several languages and dialects provide ephemerons, for example GNU Smalltalk and Squeak, .NET languages such as C#, F# and VB.NET, OCaml and the Racket dialect of Lisp. Suppose we wish to associate information I with object O through a side table. We can use an ephemeron with key O and value I. The semantics of an ephemeron are as follows. Its reference to the key is weak. Its reference to the value is strong while the key is non-null, but is weak after the key is set to null. In the example, the reference to the base object O is weak, and initially the reference to the associated information I is strong. Once O is reclaimed and the weak reference to it is set to null, the reference to I is treated as weak. Thus, I is not reclaimable while O is alive, but may become reclaimable once O has gone. A weak-key/strong-value pair with notification (to allow the value reference to be set to null, or to be replaced with a weak reference to the value) more or less simulates an ephemeron. A subtle difference, though, is that it does not 'count' toward reachability of the ephemeron's key if it is reachable from the ephemeron's value. Thus, if I refers to O, as it well might, an ephemeron can still collect O, but the weak-pair approach would prevent O from being reclaimed. The only way around this without ephemerons would seem to be to ensure that any path from I to O includes a weak reference.

Here is a sketch of how to implement ephemerons (ignoring any other forms of weak pointers or other finalisation mechanisms). First, trace through strong pointers from the roots, recording ephemerons but not tracing through them. Iterate over the recorded

---

[13]Arrays may be multi-dimensional while vectors have only one dimension, but the distinction does not affect weak reference semantics.

[14]`https://clisp.cons.org`.

[15]Hayes credits George Bosworth with the invention of ephemerons.

ephemerons repeatedly. If an ephemeron's key has been traced, then trace through the ephemeron's value field and remove the ephemeron from the set of recorded ephemerons. Such tracing may reach other ephemerons' keys and may also find new ephemerons to consider. Eventually we obtain a set, possibly empty, of ephemerons that we have recorded whose keys are not reachable.[16] We clear the key fields of these ephemerons, and the value fields if the value object is not yet traced. Alternatively, we can use a notification mechanism and enqueue the ephemerons, at the risk of possible object resurrection. It may be better to clear the ephemeron's fields and enqueue a new pair that presents the key and the value to a finalisation function.

Swift. The Swift language provides three reference flavours: strong, weak and unowned. Its *Automatic Reference Counting* (ARC) manages strong references in the usual way, retaining an object until its (strong) reference count is zero. The Swift Programming Guide [Apple, 2021] advocates resolving cycles of strong references by including a weak or an unowned reference in the cycle. Weak references are intended for scenarios in which the referent has a shorter lifetime than the referrer. A weak reference does not prevent its target from being reclaimed but instead, when the target is deallocated, Swift's ARC automatically sets the weak reference to nil. For example, a Tenant type may hold a (strong) reference to the apartment they rent, but the Apartment instance should be defined with a weak reference to the tenant. In contrast, an unowned reference is intended to be used when the referent has the same or a longer lifetime than the referrer. An unowned reference is always expected to have a value and is never set to nil by ARC. For instance, a Customer may have an optional credit card property, but a CreditCard would have a (non-optional) unowned customer property, initialised when the CreditCard instance is created. If an unowned reference is marked as optional, it is the programmers's responsibility to ensure that it always refers to a valid object or is set to nil.

It is possible to create strong reference cycles inadvertently. For example, a property of a class may be a closure whose body refers to the instance of the class, self. Swift has two mechanisms to address this. First, the language requires the programmer to write self.someProperty or self.someMethod rather than just someProperty or someMethod as a reminder that it is possible to capture self. Second, Swift allows a closure to provide a 'capture list' defining whether each captured reference is weak or unowned. Captured references should be unowned if both the closure and the instance it captures will be deallocated at the same time, and weak if the reference may become nil.

Other languages. Other languages with weak pointer support, at least in some implementations, include ActionScript, C++ (earlier in the Boost library and now in the standard library), Haskell, JavaScript, OCAML, Python, Rust and Smalltalk. There has also been at least one attempt to give a formal semantics for the feature [Donnelly *et al.*, 2006].

12.3 Changing object layout

In many languages the layout of an object — its number of fields and also usually which of those fields contain pointers — is fixed when the object is allocated and cannot change thereafter. In languages that are more dynamically typed, however, the layout of an object may change over time. If only the type of fields may change, a language may tag values

---

[16]This process is a bit tricky, epecially in a concurrent collection context, and a subtle error in processing ephemerons resulted in a critical defect in the V8 JavaScript engine [Mo, 2021]. The specific setting was the WeakMap built-in object class of JavaScript, which has semantics equivalent to ephemerons.

(see Section 11.2) to allow discrimination of pointers from non-pointers at run time. However, some languages, for example Python and JavaScript, allow objects to change their entire layout and size dynamically.

Clifford *et al.* [2015] describe a design for objects in the V8 implementation of JavaScript. Each object has a *map* (or '*hidden class*') that describes its layout. The map can change as fields are added to and deleted from the object, leading to a transition tree of maps for a particular allocation site. The design separates an object's integer-indexed properties from those indexed by name, with the integer-indexed properties acting like a dynamically adjustable array. For efficiency, arrays that contain only small integers and arrays that contain only numbers (represented as double length floating point numbers) are special cases. A small integer array will transition to a double array if a double is stored into it, and either form of numeric array will transition to a general array, where individual elements are tagged, if a non-numeric value is stored into it. These transitions will never be undone. Further, the design distinguishes between arrays where all elements in a given range are present from ones where elements may have been deleted. The latter are called *holey*, and in them deleted elements are indicated using a distinguished value.

An interesting feature of their system is that it uses instrumentation called *mementos* to collect information on a per allocation site basis to determine the common eventual map for arrays allocated at that site, so as to avoid expensive transitions of array layouts. A memento is a small object that is allocated immediately after an object that the run-time systems wishes to track. The memento refers back to the object, describes the allocation site, and includes whatever other information the run-time system will find useful. The Clifford *et al.* system allocates mementos only for objects allocated in the nursery, and only for allocation sites in unoptimised code. Allocating mementos only for nursery objects keeps the space overhead lower, and allocating them only in unoptimised code keeps the time overhead lower. A nursery collection will detect mementos associated with survivors by checking the object immediately following the survivor in memory (mementos are distinguishable from regular objects), and trigger collection of statistics.

Concerning layout, a memento will trigger recording of the object's layout as of the time of the collection. This is generally long enough after allocation to give good guidance if an allocation site's code is later optimised. Mementos can also be used for optimizations such as pretenuring.

Ugawa *et al.* [2022] similarly aim to identify the maps eventually used by objects allocated at each site, but in the context of the closed world of a JavaScript virtual machine for embedded systems. They use the garbage collector to gather the transitions of each site's map off-line. Using this profile, they are able to eliminate some intermediate maps, biasing chains of transitions to favour the most frequently used cases.

Accomplishing layout changes concurrently with reading and writing fields, without sacrificing too much performance, can be a challenge. Pizlo [2017] describes an obstruction-free scheme for updating object layout metadata that is used in Riptide's JavaScript implementation. Objects in Riptide consist of a *structure id* that identifies the object's layout, a fixed-size area for fields and a pointer to an object extension (initially null). The structure id includes what is effectively a lock bit. A reader of an object, using strongly ordered load instructions, reads the structure id, then data or metadata, and then rereads the structure id. If the two versions of the structure id match and show it to be unlocked, then the reader can trust the data or metadata it read. In the case of an object with immutable structure, the rereading of the structure id is not necessary. A writer of an object first acquires the structure id lock using a compare-and-swap, then updates the information (data or metadata) and releases the lock. Each update of structure information leads to a new structure id value, even if the structure is equivalent to a previous one, which avoids any ABA problem.

Degenbaev *et al.* [2019] describe a different approach to managing layout changes in a concurrent collector. Their objects can be thought of as having a starting address s, an address u of the beginning of a slack (currently unused) area and an address e, of the word beyond the end of the object. Additionally, an object has a map that indicates for addresses a such that $s \leq a < u$ whether the value at that address is *tagged* or *raw*. A tagged value is a reference if the low bit is 1 and a small integer otherwise. The layout of an object consists of the values of s, u and e along with its map, which can be determined from one of the initial fields of the object. A key idea that Degenbaev *et al.* introduce is that some layout changing operations are *safe* with respect to concurrent collection and some are not. The safe operations are ones that cannot lead to confusion as to whether a word read by the collector is tagged or raw. These can proceed with minimal synchronisation, generally needing only acquiring loads and releasing stores. It should be noted that the write barrier is a Dijkstra-style insertion one (we discuss the barriers needed for concurrent collection in Section 15.2) that always ensures that the referent of a stored reference will be marked. Thus races with respect to whether the collector has visited a given field are not an issue. Unsafe layout changes while the collector is running require the mutator to ensure that the object is visited, trying to do so itself if the object is not yet black.

Degenbaev *et al.* consider two ways to process unsafe layout changes. One is for the collector to *snapshot* the object. It does this by using an acquiring load on the object's class word (which implies the object's layout), copying the tagged fields to a private buffer, and doing a releasing compare-and-swap on the mark bits of the object. If the compare-and-swap fails, it knows the mutator is dealing with the object and ignores it. Otherwise, it can correctly use the snapshot. The second way they consider to handle unsafe layout changes is to lock the object (which requires the collector to lock each object as it visits it). They found the snapshot algorithm to be superior to locking, and while concurrent collection unsurprisingly costs a bit more compared with incremental collection, it clearly improved minimum mutator utilisation.

12.4 Issues to consider

While we have termed finalisation and weak pointers 'language-specific' concerns, they are now largely part of the accepted landscape of automatic memory management. Automatic management is a software engineering boon, enabling easier construction of more complex systems that work correctly, but various specific problems motivate finalisation and weak pointers as extensions to language semantics — extensions that have been introduced precisely because of the assumption that memory will be managed automatically.

If the collector and run-time system implementer receive the language being implemented as a given, then many of the design considerations mentioned here have already been decided: the language is what it is. The design questions mentioned earlier, particularly with respect to choices in the design of support for finalisation, are more relevant in the context of designing a new programming language. Likewise, the varieties of weak pointer mechanisms, such as which 'weak' data structures to offer, how many strengths of references to support, and so on, are also more the province of language design.

Where a collector and run-time system implementer has more scope is in the choice and design of allocation and collection techniques. Here are some of the considerations of how those choices relate to the mechanisms discussed in this chapter.

Weak pointers and finalisation tend to require additional tracing 'passes'. These typically complete quickly — their performance is typically not of unusual concern. However, they complicate otherwise basic algorithms and require considerable care in their design. It is best to design in the necessary support from the beginning rather than to attempt to add it on later. Needless to say, it is very important to gain a solid understanding of the semantics of the features and of how proposed implementation strategies enact those semantics.

Some mechanisms, notably some of the 'strengths' of Java's weak references, require that a whole group of related weak references be cleared at the same time. This is relatively easy to accomplish in a stop-the-world collector, but in a more concurrent setting it requires additional mechanism and care. As mentioned earlier, traversing the weak references needs to include a check of a shared flag and possibly some additional synchronisation, to ensure that collector and mutator threads make the same determination as to which weakly referenced objects are live — they need to resolve the race between any mutator thread trying to obtain a strong reference and the collector trying to clear a group of weak references atomically. This race is by no means peculiar to Java's weak reference mechanisms, and is a potentiality in supporting weak pointers in any concurrent setting.

Given the concerns about atomic clearing of sets of weak references and the general complexity of weak pointer and finalisation support, it may be reasonable to handle those features in a stop-the-world phase of an otherwise concurrent collector, or at least to use locks rather than lock-free or wait-free techniques. Chapter 13 discusses these different approaches to controlling concurrent access to data structures.

Java soft references require a collector mechanism to decide whether it is appropriate to clear them during a given collection cycle.

Dynamic languages such as JavaScript may change the layout of objects on the fly. For such languages it can be important to consider common cases, detecting them statically, dynamically or both, to reduce impacts on both the mutator and the collector. Special care must be taken in the presence of concurrency so that layout changes do not confuse the collector into treating a pointer as a non-pointer, vice versa or missing fields entirely.

Chapter 13

Concurrency preliminaries

Concurrent collection algorithms have been studied for a long time, going back at least to the 1970s [Steele, 1975]. For a long time, though, they were relevant to a small minority of users. Now, multiprocessors enjoy widespread commercial availability — even the laptop on which this text was written has an 8-core processor. Moreover, programmers need to deploy multiple cores to cooperate on the same task since that has become the only way to get a job done faster: clock speed increases can no longer deliver the regular performance boost they used to. Therefore, language implementations need to support concurrent programming, and their run-time systems, and their garbage collectors in particular, need to support the concurrent world well. Later chapters explore parallel, concurrent and real-time collection in depth. Here we consider concepts, algorithms and data structures fundamental to collection in presence of logical and physical parallelism, including an introduction to the relevant aspects of hardware, memory consistency models, atomic update primitives, progress guarantees, mutual exclusion algorithms, work sharing and termination detection, concurrent data structures and the emerging model called transactional memory. Concurrency and the number of cores available in processors continues to grow in both scale and relevance.

13.1 Hardware

In order to understand both the correctness and the performance of parallel and concurrent collection, it is necessary first to understand relevant properties of multiprocessor hardware. This section offers definitions and overviews of several key concepts: processors and threads, including the various 'multis', multiprocessor, multicore, multiprogrammed, and multithreaded; interconnect; and memory and caches.[1]

Processors and threads

A *processor* (CPU) is a unit of hardware that executes instructions. A *thread* is a sequential program, that is, an execution of a piece of software. A thread can be *running* (also called scheduled), *ready* to run, or *blocked* awaiting some condition such as arrival of a message, completion of input/output or for a particular time to arrive. A *scheduler*, which is usually an operating system component, chooses which threads to schedule onto which processors at any given time. In general, if a thread is *descheduled* (moved from running to ready or

---

[1]We are indebted to Herlihy and Shavit [2008] for the organisation of our discussion, and recommend that book for additional study.

blocked), when it is next scheduled it may run on a different processor than the one on which it ran previously, though the scheduler may recognise and offer some degree of *affinity* of a thread to a particular processor; this is now offered by most operating systems.

A slight complication in these definitions is that some processor hardware supports more than one logical processor using a single execution pipeline. This is called *simultaneous multithreading* (SMT) or *hyperthreading*, and unfortunately for our terminology, the logical processors are often called *threads*. Here thread will always mean the software entity and SMTs will be viewed as providing multiple (logical) processors, since the logical processors are individually schedulable, and so on.

A *multiprocessor* is a computer that provides more than one processor. A *chip multiprocessor* (CMP), also called a *multicore* or even *many-core processor*, is a multiprocessor that has more than one processor on a single integrated circuit chip. Except in the case of SMT, *multithreaded* refers to software that uses multiple threads, which may run concurrently on a multiprocessor. *Multiprogrammed* refers to software executing multiple processes or threads on a single processor.

Interconnect

What distinguishes a multiprocessor from the general case of cluster, cloud or distributed computing is that it involves shared memory, accessible to each of the processors. This access is mediated by an interconnection network of some kind. The simplest interconnect is a single shared *bus*, through which all messages pass between processors and memory. It is helpful to think of memory accesses as being like the sending of messages between a processor and a memory unit, given how long the accesses take in terms of processor cycles — now in the hundreds of cycles. A single bus can be reasonably fast in terms of its raw speed, but it can obviously be a bottleneck if multiple processors request service at the same time. The highest bandwidth interconnect would provide a private channel between each processor and each memory, but the hardware resources required grow as the product of the number of processor and number of memory units. Note that for better overall bandwidth (number of memory accesses per second across the entire system), splitting the memory into multiple units is a good idea. Also, transfers between processors and memories are usually in terms of whole cache lines (on the next page) or possibly larger units rather than single bytes or words.

In larger CMPs a memory request may need to traverse multiple nodes in an interconnection network, such as a grid, ring or torus connection arrangement. Details lie beyond our scope, but the point is that access time is long and can vary according to where a processor is in the network and where the target memory unit is. Concurrent traffic along the same interconnect paths can introduce more delay.

Note that the bus in single-bus systems generally becomes a bottleneck when the system has more than about eight to sixteen processors. However, buses are generally simpler and cheaper to implement than other interconnects, and they allow each unit to listen to all of the bus traffic (sometimes called *snooping*), which simplifies supporting cache coherence.

If the memory units are separate from the processors, the system is called a *symmetric multiprocessor* (SMP), because processors have equal access times to each memory. It is also possible to associate memory with each processor, giving that processor more rapid access to that portion of the memory, and slower access to other memory. This is called *nonuniform memory access* (NUMA). A system may have both global SMP-style memory and NUMA memory, and processors may also have private memory, though it is the shared-access memory that is most relevant to garbage collection.[2]

---

[2]Private memory is suitable for thread-local heaps if the threads can be bound to processors (only allowed to run on the specific processor where their heap resides). It is also suitable for local copies of immutable data.

The most relevant properties of interconnect are that memory takes a long time to access, that interconnect can be a bottleneck, and that different portions of memory may take relatively longer times to access from different processors.

Memory

From the standpoint of garbage collection, shared memory appears as a single address space of words or bytes, even though it may be physically spread out across multiple memory units or processors. Because memory consists of multiple units accessed concurrently, it is not necessarily possible to describe it as having a single definite global state at any given moment. However, each unit, and thus each word, has a well-defined state at each moment.

Caches

Because memory accesses take so long, modern processors typically add one or more layers of *cache* to hold recently accessed data and thus statistically reduce the number of memory accesses a program requires as it runs. Caches generally operate in terms of *cache lines* (also called *cache blocks*), typically 32 or 64 bytes in size. If an access finds its containing line in the cache, that is a *cache hit*, otherwise the access is a *cache miss*, which requires accessing the next higher level of cache, or memory if this was the highest level. In CMPs it is typical for some processors to share some higher levels of cache. For example, each processor might have its own Level One (L1) cache but share its L2 cache with a neighbour. The line sizes of different levels are usually, but need not be, the same.

When there is a cache miss and there is not room for the new line in the cache, then a line currently in the cache, chosen according to the cache's replacement policy, must be *evicted* before loading the new line. The evicted line is called the *victim*. Some caches are *write-through*, meaning that updates to lines in the cache are passed on to the next level as soon as practicable, while some caches are *write-back*, meaning that a modified line (also called a *dirty* line) is not written to the next higher level until it is evicted, explicitly *flushed* (which requires using a special instruction) or explicitly written back (which also requires a special instruction).

A cache's replacement policy depends substantially on the cache's internal organisation. A *fully associative* cache allows any set of lines, up to the cache size, to reside in the cache together. Its replacement policy can choose to evict any line. At the opposite end of the spectrum are *direct-mapped* caches, where each line must reside in a particular place in the cache, so there is only one possible victim. In between these extremes are *k-way set-associative* caches, where each line is mapped to a set of k lines of cache memory, and the replacement policy can choose any of the k lines as its victim. A variety of other organisations occur, such as *victim caches*, whereby a small number of recent victims are held in a fully associative table on the side of the primary cache, with the primary usually being direct mapped. This gives the hit rate of higher associativity with lower hardware cost.

Another aspect of cache design concerns the relationship between different levels of cache. A design of two adjacent levels of cache is called *(strictly) inclusive* if every line in the lower level *must* be held by the higher level. Conversely, a design is *exclusive* if a line can be held in at most one of the two levels. A design need not be either: it may *allow* a line to reside in both caches, but not require it.

Coherence

Caches hold copies of memory data that is potentially shared. Because not all copies are updated at the same moment, particularly with write-back caches, the various copies in general do not contain the same value for each address. Thus, it may be possible for two processors to disagree on the value at a particular location. This is undesirable, so the underlying hardware generally supports some degree of *cache coherence*. Cache coherence is generally defined to mean that the memory system, including the caches, obeys two properties, namely (i) that writes to a given memory location happen in an order consistent with the order in which writes are executed by each processor, and (ii) all processors see those writes as happening in that order. Note that this says nothing about memory consistency, the order of stores to *different* memory locations, discussed in Section 13.2.

To enforce cache coherence, the hardware enforces a *coherence protocol*. One of the common coherence protocols is MESI, from the initial letters of the names it gives to the possible states of a given line of memory in each cache.

Modified: This cache is the only one holding a copy of the line, and its value has been updated but not yet written back to memory.

Exclusive: This cache is the only one holding a copy of the line, but its value corresponds with that in memory.

Shared: Other caches may hold a copy of this line, but they all have the same value as in memory.

Invalid: This cache does not hold a copy of this line.

What MESI and similar protocols guarantee is that there is only one writer at a time for any given line, and that two caches never hold disagreeing values for the same line. We omit details of the state transitions, but note that in order to modify a line a given processor must first get the line into its cache in the M or E state, which implies that if other caches hold the line, they need to drop it. Following a coherence protocol requires sending low-level messages between processors, caches and memory.

While some experimental processors have tried dispensing with hardware supported cache coherence in favor of explicitly managed software coherence, because hardware coherence can have difficulties scaling to large numbers of processors, so far most multiprocessors provide coherence in hardware.

Cache coherence introduces an issue called *false sharing*. If two processors access and update different data that happen to lie in the same cache line, then they will tend to cause a lot of coherence message traffic on the interconnect and possibly extra reads from memory, as the line 'ping-pongs' between the two processors' caches, since each must acquire it in an exclusive state before updating it. Of course, true sharing can likewise result in considerable coherence traffic.

Cache coherence performance example: spin locks

A typical mutual exclusion *lock* can be implemented with an AtomicExchange primitive, as shown in Algorithm 13.1. We distinguish primitive atomic instructions by starting their name with an upper case letter. We also denote low-level read and write operations by load and store, respectively, in order to avoid any confusion with the interface between the user program and the mutator. The initial value of the lock should be zero, meaning 'unlocked'. This is called a *spin lock* because the processor is said to 'spin' in the while loop. Each invocation of the atomic read-modify-write operation will try to acquire the lock's cache line exclusively. If multiple processors contend for the lock, then the line will ping-pong, even while some other processor holds the lock. And even that processor will need to contend for the line just to unlock! This form of lock is also called a *test-and-set lock*, even though it does not use the TestAndSet primitive, discussed a little later.

Algorithm 13.1: AtomicExchange spin lock

```
1   exchangeLock(x):
2       while AtomicExchange(x, 1) = 1
3           /* do nothing */
4
5   exchangeUnlock(x):
6       *x ← 0
7
8   AtomicExchange(x, v):
9       atomic
10          old ← *x
11          *x ← v
12      return old
```

Algorithm 13.2: Test-and-Test-and-Set AtomicExchange spin lock

```
1   testAndTestAndSetExchangeLock(x):
2       while testAndExchange(x) = 1
3           /* do nothing */
4
5   testAndTestAndSetExchangeUnlock(x):
6       *x ← 0
7
8   testAndExchange(x):
9       while *x = 1
10          /* do nothing */
11      return AtomicExchange(x, 1)
```

Because the code of Algorithm 13.1 can cause extreme cache contention, many programs use a more subtle version that has the same semantics, called a *test-and-test-and-set lock*, shown in Algorithm 13.2. The important difference is in line 9, which does ordinary read accesses *outside* the AtomicExchange. This spins accessing the processor's (coherent) cache, without going to the bus. If the lock is not in cacheable memory, then a thread might want to delay between tests using an idle loop or a hardware idle instruction, possibly using exponential back-off or some similar algorithm so as to consume fewer resources in longer waits. For even longer waits the thread might involve the operating system scheduler, by giving up the rest of its quantum, or moving to wait on an explicit signal, in which case things must be arranged so that the lock holder will send the signal when the lock is released.

While Section 13.3 covers the range of most frequently available atomic hardware primitives, it is edifying to consider test-and-set and test-and-test-and-set locks implemented with a TestAndSet primitive, as shown in Algorithm 13.3. A possible advantage of the TestAndSet primitive is that the overall intent and use of the values 0 and 1 are implicit in its semantics. This implies that a processor can avoid a bus access and avoid requesting the cache line for exclusive access if the value of the lock is 1 in the cache. In principle, hardware could do that same thing for AtomicExchange, but it would require detecting that the old and new values are the same as opposed to looking for the specific value 1.[3]

---

[3]Certain Intel x86 processors do something like this, called *hardware lock elision* (HLE).

Algorithm 13.3: Spin locks implemented with the `TestAndSet` primitive

```
1   testAndSetLock(x):
2       while TestAndSet(x) = 1
3           /* do nothing */
4
5   testAndSetUnlock(x):
6       *x ← 0
7
8   TestAndSet(x):
9       atomic
10          old ← *x
11          if old = 0
12              *x ← 1
13              return 0
14          return 1
15
16  testAndTestAndSetLock(x):
17      while testAndTestAndSet(x) = 1
18          /* do nothing */
19
20  testAndTestAndSet(x):
21      while *x = 1
22          /* do nothing */
23      return TestAndSet(x)
24
25  testAndTestAndSetUnlock(x):
26      testAndSetUnlock(x)
```

13.2 Hardware memory consistency

We assume that shared memory provides coherence as discussed above: all processors perceive writes to the same location as occurring in the same order. This implies that, in the absence of pending incomplete writes, if two processors read the same memory location, they will obtain the same value.[4]

However, a program's view of the order of writes (and reads) to *more than one location* does not necessarily correspond with the order of those actions at caches or memories, and thus as perceived by other processors. That is, *program order* is not necessarily consistent with *memory order*. This raises two questions: why, and what are the implications? To answer the 'why' question, it is a matter of both hardware and software. Broadly, the reasons are tied up with performance: strict consistency requires either more hardware resources, or reduces performance or both. One hardware reason is that many processors contain a *write buffer* (also called a *store buffer*), that receives pending writes to memory. A write buffer is basically a queue of ⟨address, data⟩ pairs. Normally these writes may be performed in order, but if a later write is to an address already in the buffer, the hardware may combine it with the previous pending write. This means the later write can effectively pass an earlier write to a different location and appear in memory sooner. Designers are

---

[4]The Java memory model is looser: if two writes are not otherwise synchronised, then a processor can observe either value on any future read, and thus the value may oscillate.

careful to provide each processor with a consistent view of its own actions. Thus a read of a location that has a pending write in the write buffer will ultimately produce the value in the write buffer, either with a direct hardware path (faster but more costly) or by waiting for the write buffer to empty and then reading the value from cache. Another reason program actions can be reordered at the memory is cache misses. Many processors will continue executing later instructions past a (data) cache miss, and thus reads can pass reads and writes (and so can writes). Further, write-back caches present writes to memory only when dirty lines are evicted or flushed, so writes to different lines can be drastically reordered. This summary of hardware reasons is illustrative but not exhaustive.

Software reasons for reordering mostly come from compilers. For example, if two reads are known to go to the same location and there are no intervening writes that can affect that location, the compiler may just use the value originally fetched. More generally, if the compiler can show that variables are not aliased (do not refer to the same memory location), it can freely reorder reads and writes of the locations, since the same overall result will obtain (on a uniprocessor in the absence of thread switches). Languages allow such reordering and reuse of the results of previous accesses because it leads to more efficient code, and much of the time it does not affect the semantics.[5]

Obviously, from a programmer's standpoint lack of consistency between program and memory order is potentially problematic — but from an implementation perspective it can boost performance and reduce cost.

What are the implications of looser consistency? First, it should be obvious that it can be easy for programmers' intuitions to go completely wrong and for code that works under strict consistency to fail in confusing ways — though perhaps only rarely — under more relaxed models. Second, for techniques such as locks to work, there needs to be some way to guarantee particular ordering between accesses to two different locations when ordering is needed. There are three primary kinds of accesses that an ordering model distinguishes: *reads*, *writes* and *atomic* operations.[6] Atomic operations apply an atomic read-modify-write primitive, often conditionally, such as test-and-set. It can also be useful to consider *dependent loads*, where the program issues a load from address x and then later issues a load from address y where the value y depends on the value returned by loading x. An example is following a pointer chain. There are many different kinds of memory access orderings weaker than strict consistency.

Fences and happens-before

A *memory fence* is an operation on a processor that prevents certain reorderings of memory accesses. In particular it can prevent certain accesses issued before the fence, or certain accesses issued after the fence, or both, from being performed in an order that places them on the other side of the fence. For example, a total read fence requires all reads before the fence to happen before all reads issued after the fence.

This notion of *happens-before* can be formalised, and refers to requirements on the order in which operations occur on memory. Thus, the total read fence imposes a happens-before relationship between each previous read and each later read. Typically, atomic operations imply a total fence on all operations: every earlier read, write and atomic operation must happen-before each later read, write and atomic operation. However, other models are possible, such as *acquire-release*. In that model, an acquiring operation (think of it as being like acquiring a lock) prevents later operations from being performed before the acquire,

---

[5]To force the compiler to emit a load (or store) for each access to a given variable, languages such as C/C++ and Java have a declaration modifier, `volatile`, one can apply to variables.

[6]Some authors use the word 'synchronising' where we use 'atomic', but this conflates the atomicity of these operations with their usual influence on ordering, which is a strictly different notion.

Algorithm 13.4: The `CompareAndSwap` and `CompareAndSet` primitives

```
1   CompareAndSwap(x, old, new):
2       atomic
3           curr ← *x
4           if curr = old
5               *x ← new
6           return curr
7
8   CompareAndSet(x, old, new):
9       atomic
10          curr ← *x
11          if curr = old
12              *x ← new
13              return true
14          return false
```

but earlier reads and writes can happen after the acquire. A releasing operation is symmetrical: it prevents earlier operations from happening after the release, but later reads and writes may happen before the release. In short, operations outside an acquire-release pair may move inside it, but ones inside it may not move out. This is suitable for implementing critical sections.

Consistency models

The strongest *consistency model* is *strict consistency*, where every read, write and atomic operation occurs in the same order everywhere in the system.[7] Strict consistency implies that happens-before is a total order, with the order defined by some global clock. This is the easiest model to understand, and probably the way that most programmers think, but it is prohibitive to implement efficiently. In fact, given concurrently acting components, a total order may not even be well defined: some actions may happen at exactly the same clock cycle. A slightly weaker model is *sequential consistency*, in which the global happens-before order is any partial order consistent with every processor's program order. Small scale multiprocessors usually aim for sequential consistency or something close to it, because it is easier to program to than more relaxed models. *Weak consistency* is the model resulting from treating all atomic operations as total fences and otherwise allowing all reorderings.[8] The acquire-release model mentioned above is usually called *release consistency*. Intermediate in strength between sequential and weak consistency is *causal consistency*. This enforces happens-before between previous reads by a program and its subsequent writes, since the reads may causally influence the value written, and it enforces happens-before between a read and the write that stored the value obtained by the read. The term *relaxed consistency* is not a specific model but refers to any model weaker than sequential consistency.

While allowed reorderings depend to some extent on the interconnect and memory system, that is they may lie outside total control by the processor, difference processors enforce more strict or more relaxed consistency models. For example, Intel processors perform all store instructions in program order without any fences while ARM processors do not. All popular processors of which we are aware implement at least weak or release

---

[7]By 'occurs' we mean 'appears to occur' — a program cannot tell the difference.
[8]This is more or less what is called relaxed consistency in the C++11 memory model.

Algorithm 13.5: Trying to advance state atomically with compare-and-swap

```
1  compareThenCompareAndSwap(x):
2      if *x = interesting
3          z ← value for the desired next state
4          CompareAndSwap(x, interesting, z)
```

consistency. There are many subtleties that arise. For more background on memory consistency models, see Adve and Gharachorloo [1995, 1996].

Given the subtleties and variations that exist across hardware platforms, how might a programmer write portable but high performing code across them? From the programmer's perspective, the main question is how to prevent undesired reorderings that would harm program correctness. To assist with that, the C++ libraries provide a collection of accessing functions where the programmer can explicitly specify the desired ordering constraint. The compiler then takes care of emitting the right instructions for the target hardware that meet that constraint. For example, `atomic_store_explicit` allows choice among relaxed, release and sequentially consistent orders, and `atomic_load_explicit` allows the symmetrical choices of relaxed, acquire or sequentially consistent. The libraries also allow explicitly specifying orders on atomic update operations and on fences. These are based on what is known as the C++11 memory model. A number of other languages, such including C and Rust, now provide similar functions.

13.3 Hardware primitives

From some of the earliest computers onwards, processors have supported atomic read-modify-write primitives for locking and synchronisation. Section 13.1 introduced two primitives. `AtomicExchange` is perhaps the simplest in that it involves no computation or conditional action — it simply writes a new value to a memory location and returns the old value atomically, implying that no other write (atomic or otherwise) can interleave. `TestAndSet` is also quite simple in that it sets a single bit to 1 and returns the bit's previous value. However, it can be viewed as a conditional primitive that only sets the bit if its current value is zero. The other widely known and used atomic primitives include: compare-and-swap, also called compare-and-exchange; load-linked/store-conditionally, also called load-and-reserve/store-conditional or load-exclusive/store-exclusive (on ARM); and various atomic increment, decrement, add, and fetch-and-or primitives, notably fetch-and-add, also called exchange-and-add. We consider the most common of these below.

Compare-and-swap

The `CompareAndSwap` primitive and its close relation, `CompareAndSet`, are presented in Algorithm 13.4. `CompareAndSet` compares a memory location to an expected value `old`, and if the location's value equals `old`, it sets the value to `new`. In either case it indicates whether or not it updated the memory location. `CompareAndSwap` differs only in that it returns the value of the memory location observed by the primitive before any update, rather than returning a boolean truth value. The utility of the two primitives is essentially the same, although their semantics are not strictly equivalent.

`CompareAndSwap` is often used to advance a location from one state to another, such as 'locked by thread *t1*' to 'unlocked' to 'locked by thread *t2*'. It is common to examine the current state and then try to advance it atomically, following the pattern of Algorithm 13.5,

Algorithm 13.6: Semantics of load-linked/store-conditionally

```
 1   LoadLinked(address):
 2       atomic
 3           reservation ← address      /* reservation is a per-processor variable */
 4           reserved ← true            /* reserved is a per-processor variable */
 5           return *address
 6
 7   StoreConditionally(address, value):
 8       atomic
 9           if reserved
10               store(address, value)
11                   return true
12           return false
13
14   store(address, value):          /* at all processors, not necessarily simultaneously */
15       if address = reservation    /* granularity may be same cache line, and so on */
16           reserved ← false
17       *address ← value
```

sometimes called compare-then-compare-and-swap. There is a lurking trap in this approach, namely that it is possible that at the `CompareAndSwap` the state has changed multiple times, and is now again equal to the value sampled before. In some situations this may be all right, but in others it could be that the bit pattern, while equal, actually has a different meaning. This can happen in garbage collection if, for example, two semispace collections occur, and along the way a pointer was updated to refer to a different object that by coincidence lies where the original object was two collections ago. This inability of `CompareAndSwap` to detect whether a value has changed and then changed back to its original value is called the *ABA problem*.

Load-linked/store-conditionally

`LoadLinked` and `StoreConditionally` solve the ABA problem by having the processor remember the location read by the `LoadLinked` and use the processor's coherence mechanism to detect any update to that location. Assuming that the processor applies the semantics of the `store` function, Algorithm 13.6 describes `LoadLinked`/`StoreConditionally` more precisely. It still falls short, though, because the reservation is cleared not only by writes by the same processor, but also by writes coming from *other* processors. Because *any* write to the reserved location resets the `reserved` flag, the compare-then-compare-and-swap code can be rewritten to avoid the possible ABA problem, as shown in Algorithm 13.7.[9] `LoadLinked`/`StoreConditionally` is thus strictly more powerful than `CompareAndSwap`. In fact, it should be clear that the `LoadLinked`/`StoreConditionally` primitives allow a programmer to implement any atomic read-modify-write operation that acts on a *single* memory word. Algorithm 13.8 shows how to implement compare-and-swap with `LoadLinked`/`StoreConditionally`, and also an implementation of compare-and-set. One more behaviour of `LoadLinked`/`StoreConditionally` is worth mentioning: it is legal for a `StoreConditionally` to fail 'spuriously', that is, even if no processor wrote the location in question. There might be a variety of low-level

---

[9]A thread also loses its reservation on a context-switch.

Algorithm 13.7: Atomic state transition with load-linked/store-conditionally

---

1 observed ← LoadLinked(x)
2 compute desired new value z, using observed
3 **if not** StoreConditionally(x, z)
4   go back and recompute or otherwise handle interference

Algorithm 13.8: Implementing compare-and-swap with load-linked/store-conditionally

---

1 compareAndSwapByLLSC(x, old, new):
2   previous ← LoadLinked(x)
3   **if** previous = old
4   StoreConditionally(x, new)
5   **return** previous
6
7 compareAndSetByLLSC(x, old, new):
8   previous ← LoadLinked(x)
9   **if** previous = old
10   **return** StoreConditionally(x, new)
11   **return** false

---

hardware situations that can cause spurious failures, but notable is the occurrence of interrupts, including such things as page and overflow traps, and timer or I/O interrupts, all of which induce kernel activity. This is not usually a problem, but if some code between LoadLinked and StoreConditionally causes a trap every time, then the StoreConditionally will always fail.

Because LoadLinked/StoreConditionally solves ABA problems so neatly, code presented here will most generally prefer LoadLinked/StoreConditionally where CompareAndSwap would exhibit an ABA problem. It would typically be straightforward to convert such instances to use CompareAndSwap with an associated counter.

Strictly speaking, StoreConditionally's effect may be undefined if it writes to an address other than the one reserved. Some processor designs allow that, however, giving an occasionally useful atomic primitive that acts across two arbitrary memory locations.

Atomic arithmetic primitives

For completeness, Algorithm 13.9 defines several atomic arithmetic primitives. It is also easy to offer versions of AtomicIncrement and AtomicDecrement that return either the old or the new value using AtomicAdd or FetchAndAdd.[10] Furthermore, processors often set condition codes when executing these primitives, which can reveal whether the value is (or was) zero, and so on. In the realm of garbage collection, FetchAndAdd might be used to implement sequential allocation (that is, with a 'bump pointer') in a concurrent setting — though usually it is preferable to set up local allocation buffers as described in Section 7.7. FetchAndAdd could similarly be used to add or remove items from a queue, though wrap-around in a circular buffer requires care (see Section 13.8).

It has been shown that these atomic arithmetic primitives are strictly less powerful than CompareAndSwap, and thus also less powerful than LoadLinked/StoreCondition-

---

[10]Some processors offer atomic *and*, *or* and other arithmetic operators that may be of occasional use.

Algorithm 13.9: Atomic arithmetic primitives

```
1   AtomicIncrement(x):
2       atomic
3           *x ← *x + 1
4
5   AtomicDecrement(x):
6       atomic
7           *x ← *x − 1
8
9   AtomicAdd(x, v):
10      atomic
11          new ← *x + v
12          *x ← new
13          return new
14
15  FetchAndAdd(x, v):
16      atomic
17          old ← *x
18          *x ← old + v
19          return old
20
21  FetchAndOr(x, v):
22      atomic
23          old ← *x
24          *x ← old | v
25          return old
```

ally (see Herlihy and Shavit [2008]). In particular, each primitive has what is called a *consensus number*. If the consensus number of a primitive is k, then it can be used to solve the consensus problem among k threads, but not among more than k. The consensus problem is a multiprocessor algorithm where (i) each thread proposes a value, (ii) all threads agree on the result, (iii) the result is one of the values proposed and (iv) all threads always complete in a finite number of steps, that is, the algorithm is wait-free (see Section 13.4). Primitives that either set a value unconditionally, such as AtomicExchange, or that when commuted result in the same value for the variable being updated, such as AtomicIncrement and FetchAndAdd, have consensus number 2. On the other hand, CompareAndSwap and LoadLinked/StoreConditionally have consensus number ∞, that is, they can solve consensus in a wait-free manner for any number of threads, as will be illustrated presently in Algorithm 13.13.

One potential advantage to unconditional arithmetic primitives is that they will always succeed, whereas an emulation of these primitives with LoadLinked/StoreConditionally or CompareAndSwap can starve in the face of contention.[11]

---

[11]Of course if contention is that high, there may be the possibility of starvation at the hardware level, in trying to gain exclusive access to the relevant cache line.

Algorithm 13.10: Fallacious test and set patterns

```
1  testThenTestAndSetLock(x):                          /* fallacious! */
2      if *x = 0
3          TestAndSet(x)
4
5  testThenTestThenSetLock(x):                          /* fallacious! */
6      if *x = 0
7          other work
8          if *x = 0
9              *x ← 1
```

Algorithm 13.11: `CompareAndSwapWide`

```
1  CompareAndSwapWide(x, old0, old1, new0, new1):
2      atomic
3          curr0, curr1 ← x[0], x[1]
4          if curr0 = old0 && curr1 = old1
5              x[0], x[1] ← new0, new1
6          return curr0, curr1
7
8  CompareAndSetWide(x, old0, old1, new0, new1):
9      atomic
10         curr0, curr1 ← x[0], x[1]
11         if curr0 = old0 && curr1 = old1
12             x[0], x[1] ← new0, new1
13             return true
14         return false
```

Test then test-and-set

The 'test then test-and-set' pattern was illustrated in function `testAndTestAndSet` (see Algorithm 13.3). Because of the way that algorithm iterates, it is correct. Programmers should avoid two fallacious attempts at the same semantics, here called test-then-test-and-set and test-then-test-then-set, illustrated in Algorithm 13.10. Test-then-test-and-set is fallacious because it does not iterate, yet the `TestAndSet` could fail if x is updated between the `if` and the `TestAndSet`. Test-then-test-then-set is even worse: it fails to use any atomic primitive, and thus anything can happen in between the first and second read of x and the second read and the write. Notice that making x `volatile` does not solve the problem. There are similar patterns that might be called compare-then-compare-and-set or compare-then-compare-then-set that are equally fallacious. These traps illustrate the difficulty programmers have in thinking concurrently.

More powerful primitives

As mentioned above, `LoadLinked/StoreConditionally` is fully general, and hence the most powerful among single-word atomic update primitives. However, primitives that allow updating multiple independent words are even more powerful. In addition to

Algorithm 13.12: CompareAndSwap2

```
1   CompareAndSwap2(x0, x1, old0, old1, new0, new1):
2       atomic
3           curr0, curr1 ← *x0, *x1
4           if curr0 = old0 && curr1 = old1
5               *x0, *x1 ← new0, new1
6           return curr0, curr1
7
8   CompareAndSet2(x0, x1, old0, old1, new0, new1):
9       atomic
10          curr0, curr1 ← *x0, *x1
11          if curr0 = old0 && curr1 = old1
12              *x0, *x1 ← new0, new1
13              return true
14          return false
```

---

single-word primitives, some processors include double-word primitives such as double-word compare-and-swap, here called CompareAndSwapWide/CompareAndSetWide, in addition to single-word CompareAndSwap (see Algorithm 13.11). These are not of greater theoretical power. However, a wide double-word compare-and-swap can solve the ABA problem of single-word compare-and-swap by using the second word for a counter of the number of times the first word has been updated. It would take so long — 2^{32} updates for a 32-bit word — for the counter to wrap around that it may be safe to ignore the possibility. The same would hold even more strongly for updating two adjacent 64-bit words. Thus CompareAndSwapWide can be more convenient and efficient even if it has the same theoretical power as a regular compare-and-swap.

But while double-word atomic primitives are useful, it is even more useful to be able to update two *arbitrary* (not necessarily adjacent) words in memory atomically. The Motorola 88000 and Sun's Rock design offered a compare-and-swap-two instruction (also called double-compare-and-swap). Algorithm 13.12 illustrates this CompareAndSwap2 primitive. CompareAndSwap2 is complex to implement in hardware, so it is not surprising that no commercially produced machines presently support it. CompareAndSwap2 can be generalised to compare-and-swap-n, also called n-way compare-and-swap. This was the inspiration for transactional memory, which is to LoadLinked/StoreConditionally what n-way compare-and-swap is to compare-and-swap. We discuss transactional memory in Section 13.9.

Overheads of atomic primitives

One reason programmers fall into the traps just mentioned is that they know that atomic primitives are expensive, so they try to avoid them. Another reason may be that they improperly replicate the pattern of testAndTestAndSet. The primitives tend to be expensive for the two reasons previously mentioned, but it is helpful to distinguish them. One reason is the cost of cache coherence: an atomic read-modify-write primitive must acquire exclusive access to the relevant cache line. Also, it must do that, read the contents, compute the new value and write it, before the instruction is complete. While modern processors may overlap multiple instructions, often there are few instructions available in the pipeline since the next thing to do often depends strongly on the result of the atomic

Algorithm 13.13: Wait-free consensus using compare-and-swap

```
1  shared proposals[N]                             /* one entry per thread */
2  shared winner ← −1            /* indicates which thread got here first */
3  me ← myThreadId
4
5  decide(v):
6      proposals[me] ← v                            /* 0 ≤ thread id < N */
7      CompareAndSwap(&winner, −1, me)
8      return proposals[winner]
```

operation. Because of the need for coherence, an atomic update primitive often includes a bus or memory access, which consumes many cycles.

The other reason atomic primitives tend to be slow is that they either include memory fence semantics or else, by the way they are used, the programmer will need to insert fences manually, typically on both sides of the atomic operation. This undermines the performance advantage of overlapped and pipelined processing, and makes it difficult for the processor to hide the cost of any bus or memory access the primitive requires.

13.4 Progress guarantees

It is important to guarantee progress among threads that may be contending on the same data structure, such as a shared collected heap or collector data structures. This is especially true in real-time programming. It is also helpful to know the relative power of the various atomic hardware primitives in supporting progress guarantees. From strongest to weakest, useful progress guarantees include: wait-freedom, lock-freedom and obstruction-freedom. A concurrent algorithm is *wait-free* if every thread can always make progress, regardless of the actions of other threads. A concurrent algorithm is *lock-free* if, infinitely often, some thread finishes within a finite number of steps. A concurrent algorithm is *obstruction-free* if, given a long enough period of isolated execution, any thread will finish in a finite number of steps. Progress guarantees are almost always *conditional* in real systems. For example, an algorithm might be wait-free as long as it does not exhaust free storage. See Herlihy and Shavit [2008] for a thorough discussion of these concepts, how to implement them, and so on.

A wait-free algorithm typically involves the notion of threads helping each other along. That is, if thread $t2$ is about to undertake an action that would undermine thread $t1$ that is somehow judged to be ahead of $t2$, $t2$ will help advance the work of $t1$ and then do its own work. Assuming a fixed bound on the number of threads, there is a bound on helping to accomplish one work unit or operation on the data structure, and thus the total time for any work unit or operation can be bounded. However, not only is the bound large, but the typical time for an operation is rather higher than for weaker progress guarantees because of the additional data structures and work required. For the simple case of consensus, it is fairly easy to devise a wait-free algorithm with low time overhead, as illustrated in Algorithm 13.13. It is fairly easy to see that this meets all of the criteria to be a solution to the consensus problem for N threads, but it does have space overhead proportional to N.

Lock-freedom is easier to achieve. It only requires that at least one contender make progress on any occasion, though any particular individual can 'starve' indefinitely.

Obstruction-freedom is easier to achieve than lock-freedom, but may require scheduler cooperation. If threads can see that they are contending, they can use random increasing back-off so as to allow some thread to win. That is, each time they detect contention, they compute a longer possible back-off period T and randomly choose an amount of time between zero and T to wait before trying again. In a pool of contending threads, each will eventually succeed, probabilistically speaking.

Progress guarantees and concurrent collection

Parallel collectors use multiple threads simultaneously in the collector, but stop all mutator threads during collection. *Concurrent collectors* perform at least some parts of collection while mutators threads are still running, and generally use multiple collector threads too. Both parallel and concurrent collection algorithms typically have a number of phases, such as marking, scanning, copying, forwarding or sweeping, and concurrent collection also has mutator work trying to proceed at the same time. Multiple collector threads may aim to cooperate, yet sometimes interfere with one another and with mutator threads. In such a complex situation, how can collector correctness be described? Certainly the collector must do nothing blatantly wrong — at the least it must preserve the reachable parts of the object graph and support the mutations being performed by the mutators. Next, provided that an invocation of the collector eventually terminates, it should generally return some unreachable memory for reuse. However, the specific expectations vary by collector algorithm. A conservative (ambiguous roots) collector may over-estimate reachability and thus fail to reclaim some unreachable objects. Likewise, generational and other partial-heap collectors intentionally forgo reclaiming unreachable objects from some parts of the heap on any given invocation. A complete collection algorithm gives a stronger guarantee: eventually, if invoked enough times, it will reclaim any given piece of garbage.

Concurrent collectors bring additional interesting issues. One is what can happen to objects allocated during collection that then become unreachable, or objects previously allocated that become unreachable during collection. A given collector might or might not reclaim those during the current invocation.

But there is a more subtle issue and risk that arises with concurrent and parallel collection. Sequential algorithms have more obvious termination properties. For example, marking a reachable object graph maintains some representation of marked-and-scanned, marked-but-not-yet-scanned and unmarked object sets, and obeys rules where the first set grows, eventually to contain the entire graph of reachable objects. Correctness may sometimes be tricky to prove, but it is relatively easy to see that the algorithm terminates. It is less obvious with concurrent collection, because the object graph can grow because of allocation of new objects, and it can change during a collection cycle. If each mutator change forces more collector work, how can we know that the collector will ever catch up? Mutators may need to be throttled back or stopped completely for a time. Even if a proof deals with the issues of more collector work being created during collection, there remains a further difficulty: unless the algorithm uses wait-free techniques, interference can prevent progress indefinitely. For example, in a lock-free algorithm, one thread can continually fail in its attempts to accomplish a work step. In fact, two competing threads can even each prevent progress of the other indefinitely, an occurrence called *livelock*.

Different phases of collection may offer different progress guarantees — one phase might be lock-free, another wait-free. However, practical implementations, even of theoretically entirely wait-free algorithms, may have some (it is hoped small) portions that are stop-the-world. Given the code complexity and increased possibility of bugs when trying to implement stronger progress guarantees, it may not be worth the engineering effort to make every last corner wait-free. Further, notice that an overall collection algorithm can be judged wait-free from the standpoint of the mutators only if it can reclaim memory fast enough to ensure that a mutator will not block in allocation waiting for collection to complete. Put another way, the heap must not run out before the collector is done. This requires more than a wait-free guarantee for each phase — it requires overall balance between heap size, maximum live size, allocation rate and collection rate. Enough resources need to be devoted to collection — memory and processing time — for the collector to keep up. This may be required for critical real-time systems, and Chapter 19 discusses it in more detail. Most of the algorithms presented in succeeding chapters make weaker guarantees, such as lock-freedom, possibly only in certain phases. They are easier to implement and their guarantees are acceptable in many less stringent settings.

13.5 Notation used for concurrent algorithms

Given the considerations discussed previously, particularly atomicity, coherence and consistency, what a programmer writes is not always executed in the exact order presented — hardware and compilers can reorder and even eliminate some operations. Exactly what can occur depends strongly on the programming language, its compiler and run-time system, and the hardware. Yet here it is best to present algorithms in pseudocode independently of any particular hardware-software platform. In an algorithm, the relative order of some operations is typically important to correctness, but it is not generally necessary that all operations occur, and be perceived everywhere, in the order presented. Therefore, the code offered here for algorithms that may execute concurrently follows certain conventions. This makes it easier to translate the pseudocode into a working implementation in a given environment. Here are the conventions used.

Meaning of `atomic`: The actions within an `atomic` must be perceived by all processors as if they happened instantaneously — no other shared memory read or write can appear to happen in the middle. Moreover, `atomic` actions must be perceived as happening in the same order everywhere if they conflict (one writes and the other reads or writes the same shared variable), and in program execution order for the thread that executes them. Furthermore, `atomic` blocks act as fences for all other shared memory accesses. Since not all hardware includes fence semantics with atomic primitives, the programmer may need to add them. The code here may work with acquire-release fence semantics, but is designed assuming total fences.

Ordering effects of `LoadLinked` and `StoreConditionally`: Both the `LoadLinked` and `StoreConditionally` instructions act as total fences with respect to accesses to shared memory.

Marking variables: We explicitly mark shared variables; all other variables are private to each thread.

Arrays: Where we use arrays, we give the number of elements within brackets, such as `proposals[N]`. Declarations of arrays use `shared` or `private` explicitly, so as not to look like uses of the arrays, and may be initialised with a tuple, such as `shared pair[2]←[0,1]`, including tuples extended to the specified length, such as `shared level[N]←[−1,...]`.

References to shared variables: Each reference to a shared variable is assumed to result in an actual memory read or write, though not necessarily in the order presented.

Causality obeyed: Code assumes that if, subject to the sequential semantics of the pseudocode language, an action *x* causally precedes an action *y*, then *x* happens-before *y* in the actual system. An example is a dependent memory reference. If code accesses a shared pointer variable p then a field f of the structure that p references, namely (*p).f, then reading p causally preceded reading the field f. Similar remarks apply to accessing a shared index variable i then a shared array element a[i].

Obeying causality also implies obeying control dependence: the evaluation of an if, while, or similar expression that determines control flow causally precedes execution of the code it guards. The programmer must be careful not to allow speculative evaluation of conditional code so as to reorder accesses to shared variables. However, unconditional code following an if is not causally dependent on evaluation of the if expression. Similar remarks apply to moving code across loops.

Explicit fence points: Even with the conventions listed above, many operations may be freely reordered — but sometimes an algorithm requires a particular order for its correctness. Therefore, our conventions include the possibility of marking a line of code with a $, which indicates operations that must occur in the order presented. Furthermore, lines so marked also indicate total fences for shared memory accesses. It is convenient that pseudocode presented thus far in this chapter has not needed these markings. Notice that a line marked with $ may, for some processor architectures, need a fence of some kind before the line, after the line or both before and after. Usually it is a particular action of the line that is important not to reorder, that is, one store or one load. While the markers do not offer complete guidance on how to translate pseudocode into working code for a given platform, they do serve to indicate where caution is necessary.

13.6 Mutual exclusion

One of the most basic problems in concurrent computing is *mutual exclusion*, by which it is desired to guarantee that at most one thread at a time can be executing certain code, called a *critical section*. While atomic primitives can sometimes achieve a necessary state transition using one instruction, and techniques with stronger progress guarantees might be applied — though perhaps at greatest cost and almost certainly greater complexity — mutual exclusion remains convenient and appropriate in many cases. Atomic read-modify-write primitives make it fairly easy to construct lock/unlock functions, as shown in Algorithms 13.1 to 13.3. It is less obvious, but nevertheless true, that mutual exclusion can be achieved using only (suitably ordered) reads and writes of shared memory without stronger atomic update primitives. One of the classic techniques is Peterson's Algorithm for mutual exclusion between two threads, shown in Algorithm 13.14. Not only does this algorithm guarantee mutual exclusion, it also guarantees progress — if two threads are competing to enter the critical section, one will succeed — and that waits are bounded, that is, the number of turns taken by other processes before a requester gets its turn is bounded.[12] In this case the bound is one turn by the other thread.

It is not too hard to generalise Peterson's Algorithm to N threads, as shown in Algorithm 13.15, which highlights its similarity to the two-thread case. How the while loop works is a bit subtle. The basic idea is that a requesting thread can advance a level in the competition to enter the critical section if it sees no other thread at the same or higher level. However, if another thread enters its current level, that thread will change victim and the earlier arrival can advance. Put another way, the latest arrival at a given level waits for threads at all higher levels plus earlier arrivals at its own level. Meanwhile, later

---

[12]The time before this happens is not bounded unless a requesting thread whose turn it is enters and then leaves within bounded time.

Algorithm 13.14: Peterson's algorithm for mutual exclusion

```
1   shared interested[2] ← [false, false]
2   me ← myThreadId
3
4   petersonLock():
5       other ← 1 − me                              /* thread id must be 0 or 1 */
6       interested[me] ← true
7       victim ← me                                                          $
8       while victim = me && interested[other]                               $
9           /* do nothing: wait */
10
11  petersonUnlock():
12      interested[me] ← false
```

Algorithm 13.15: Peterson's algorithm for N threads

```
1   shared level[N] ← [−1,...]
2   shared victim[N]
3   me ← myThreadId
4
5   petersonLockN():
6       for lev ← 0 to N−1
7           level[me] ← lev                                  /* 0 ≤ thread id < N */
8           victim[lev] ← me                                                 $
9           while victim[lev] = me && (∃i ≠ me)(level[i] ≥ lev)              $
10              /* do nothing: wait */
11
12  petersonUnlockN():
13      level[me] ← −1
```

Algorithm 13.16: Consensus via mutual exclusion

```
1   shared winner ← −1
2   shared value                                  /* does not need to be initialised */
3   me ← myThreadId
4
5   decideWithLock(v):                       /* simple, but no strong progress guarantee */
6       lock()
7       if winner = −1
8           winner ← me
9           value ← v
10      unlock()
11      return value
```

arrivals at the same and lower levels will come strictly later. It does not matter that the `while` loop's condition is not evaluated atomically. Peterson's algorithm is illustrative of what is possible and of techniques for reasoning about concurrent programs, but atomic locking primitives are more convenient and practical.

The previous discussion of consensus in Section 13.3 described the wait-free version of the consensus problem. Mutual exclusion can solve consensus quite easily if stronger progress guarantees are not needed, as shown in Algorithm 13.16. Since Peterson's mutual exclusion algorithm implements mutual exclusion, it can also support this kind of consensus. However, if compare-and-swap is available it is usually a more appropriate solution (see Algorithm 13.13).

13.7 Work sharing and termination detection

It is common in parallel or concurrent collection algorithms to need a way to detect *termination* of a parallel algorithm. Note that this is quite distinct from demonstrating that a parallel algorithm will terminate; it concerns having the program detect that termination has actually been achieved in a specific instance. In particular, consider a generic situation in which threads consume work, and as they process work units, they may generate more work. If each thread is concerned only with its own work, detecting termination is simple — just have each thread set a `done` flag and when all the flags are set, the algorithm has terminated. However, parallel algorithms generally involve some sort of sharing of work items so as to try to balance the amount of work done by each thread and gain maximum speedup from the available processors. This balancing can take two forms: threads with a relatively large amount of work can *push* work to more lightly loaded threads, or lightly loaded threads can steal *work* from more heavily loaded threads.

Work movement must be atomic, or at least must guarantee that no work unit is lost.[13] Here, though, the concern is detecting termination of a work sharing algorithm. It is relatively easy to detect termination using a single shared counter of work units updated atomically by each thread, but such counters may become bottlenecks to performance if the threads update them frequently.[14] Therefore, a number of termination detection algorithms avoid atomic update primitives and rely on single word reads and writes. It is simplest to consider first algorithms in which detection is the responsibility of a separate thread whose only job is detection.

Algorithm 13.17 shows a simplified version of the shared-memory work sharing termination algorithm of Leung and Ting [1997].[15] It is designed for the push model. The basic idea is that workers indicate whether or not they are busy with their `busy` flags, which the detector scans. Notice that an idle worker will become busy again only if another worker pushes a job to it. However, the pusher can then finish processing and go idle. Since the detector's scan is not atomic, it might first see the job receiver as idle (because the job has not been sent yet) and then find the pusher idle (after it sends the job). In this situation the detector would falsely indicate termination. Hence, the algorithm includes

---

[13]Sometimes work is idempotent, so if it is done two or more times, the algorithm is still correct, though possibly wasteful of computing resources.

[14]Flood *et al.* [2001] use essentially this technique in their parallel collector, but with a single word that has one 'active' bit per thread. The termination condition is the same: the algorithm terminates when the status word becomes zero.

[15]The version shown eliminates the β flags of Leung and Ting [1997], which have to do with operating system sleeping and wakeup, which we elide here for simplicity. Here, we give their α and γ flags the more memorable names busy and jobsMoved. Leung and Ting also give a variant that detects termination a little faster by checking the jobsMoved flag every $\sqrt{N}$ iterations of the detector's scanning loop. Given the time needed to perform work in a collection algorithm, it is doubtful that such a refinement is worthwhile.

Algorithm 13.17: Simplified $\alpha\beta\gamma$ shared-memory termination [Leung and Ting, 1997]

```
 1  shared jobs[N] ← initial work assignments
 2  shared busy[N] ← [true,...]
 3  shared jobsMoved ← false
 4  shared allDone ← false
 5  me ← myThreadId
 6
 7  worker():
 8      loop
 9          while not isEmpty(jobs[me])
10              if the job set of some thread j appears relatively smaller than mine
11                  some ← chooseAndDequeueJobs()
12                  sendJobs(some, j)                                              $
13              else
14                  job ← dequeue(jobs[me])
15                  perform job
16          busy[me] ← false                                                      $
17          while isEmpty(jobs[me]) && not allDone                                $   $
18              /* do nothing: wait for work or termination */
19          if allDone return                                                     $
20          busy[me] ← true                                                       $
21
22  sendJobs(some, j):                   /* push jobs to more lightly loaded thread */
23      enqueue(jobs[j], some)                                                    $
24      while (not busy[j]) && (not isEmpty(jobs[j]))                             $
25          /* do nothing: wait for j to wake up */
26      /* indicate that some work moved */
27      jobsMoved ← true                                                          $
28
29  detect():
30      anyActive ← true
31      while anyActive
32          anyActive ← (∃i)(busy[i])
33          anyActive ← anyActive || jobsMoved                                    $
34          jobsMoved ← false                                                     $
35      allDone ← true                                                            $
```

the jobsMoved flag, which indicates whether any jobs have moved recently. The detector restarts detection in that case. It is also important that sendJobs waits until busy[j] is true to guarantee that before, during and immediately after the transfer at least one of the busy[i] is true: all busy[i] can be false only if there is no work in the system.

Algorithm 13.18 shows the similar algorithm for a work stealing (pull) model of sharing work. For example, Endo *et al.* [1997] uses essentially this algorithm to detect termination in their parallel collector. Also, while the lock-free collector of Herlihy and Moss [1992] is not based on work sharing, its termination algorithm at its heart uses the same logic as the busy and jobsMoved flags.

It is straightforward to refine these detection algorithms so that they wait on a single variable anyIdle until a scan might be useful, as shown in Algorithm 13.19. Likewise,

Algorithm 13.18: An $\alpha\beta\gamma$-style work stealing termination algorithm

```
1   me ← myThreadId
2
3   worker():
4       loop
5           while not isEmpty(jobs[me])
6               job ← dequeue(jobs[me])
7               perform job                                              $
8           if another thread j exists whose jobs set appears relatively large
9               some ← stealJobs(j)                                      $
10              enqueue(jobs[me], some)
11              continue
12          busy[me] ← false                                            $
13          while no thread has jobs to steal && not allDone            $
14              /* do nothing: wait for work or termination */
15          if allDone return                                          $
16          busy[me] ← true                                            $
17
18  stealJobs(j):
19      some ← atomicallyRemoveSomeJobs(jobs[j])
20      if not isEmpty(some)
21          jobsMoved ← true              /* indicate that some work moved */
22      return some
```

Algorithm 13.19: Delaying scans until useful

```
1   shared anyIdle ← false
2   me ← myThreadId
3
4   worker():
5       ...
6       busy[me] ← false                                               $
7       anyIdle ← true                                                 $
8       ...
9
10  detect():
11      anyActive ← true
12      while anyActive
13          anyActive ← false
14          while not anyIdle                                          $
15              /* do nothing: wait until a scan might be useful */
16          anyIdle ← false                                            $
17          anyActive ← (∃i)(busy[i])                                  $
18          anyActive ← anyActive || jobsMoved                         $
19          jobsMoved ← false                                          $
20      allDone ← true                                                 $
```

Algorithm 13.20: Delaying idle workers

```
 1   shared anyLarge ← false
 2   me ← myThreadId
 3
 4   worker():
 5       loop
 6           while not isEmpty(jobs[me])
 7               job ← dequeue(jobs[me])
 8               perform(job)                                              $
 9               if my job set is large
10                   anyLarge ← true                                      $
11           if anyLarge
12               anyLarge ← false              /* set false before looking */   $
13               if another thread j has a relatively large jobs set      $
14                   anyLarge ← true           /* could be more stealable work */   $
15                   some ← stealJobs(j)                                  $
16                   enqueue(jobs[me], some)
17                   continue
18           busy[me] ← false                                             $
19           while (not anyLarge) && (not allDone)                        $
20               /* do nothing: wait for work or termination */
21           if allDone return                                            $
22           busy[me] ← true                                              $
```

---

in the work stealing case there is a similar refinement so that workers wait on a single `anyLarge` flag (in addition to `allDone`), as shown in Algorithm 13.20.

The algorithms presented so far assume a separate detection thread. It is tempting to use idle threads to check termination, as shown in Algorithm 13.21. The problem is that this algorithm does not work. For example, suppose thread A finishes its work, sees no thread to steal from and starts detection. In its detection scan, it now sees that thread B has extra work, so A will give up on detection, and may be just about to set its `busy` flag. In the meantime, B finishes all of its work, enters detection, sees that all threads are done and declares termination. A simple approach to fix this is to apply mutual exclusion to detection as shown in Algorithm 13.22.

Hassanein [2016] found in a production system that symmetrically coded termination detection using mutual exclusion, with ever-increasing back-off on acquiring the lock, can lead to a long tail in the time to complete the termination detection. They found it to be better to have a distinguished detection thread, the one that first cannot find any work.

For completeness, Algorithm 13.23 shows termination detection using an atomically updated shared counter. For discussion of a lock-free data structure to support work sharing implemented as a concurrent *double-ended queue* (deque), see Section 13.8.

The discussion above has focused on coordination and termination of work stealing algorithms. What about how to implement `atomicallyRemoveSomeJobs`, the primitive that accomplishes the actual stealing? That will vary according to the data structures being used, a topic covered in Section 13.8. Historically, collectors that use work stealing have operated in terms of specific concrete items of work, say the address of one object to mark. In a design where the work items are more general tasks of some kind, perhaps represented

Algorithm 13.21: Symmetric termination detection

```
1  work():
2      ...
3      while I have no work && not allDone                                    $
4          /* this version is broken! */
5          detectSymmetric()
6      ...
7
8  detectSymmetric():
9      while not allDone                                                      $
10         while (not anyIdle) && (not anyLarge)                              $
11             /* do nothing: wait until a scan might be useful */
12         if anyLarge return                                                 $
13         anyIdle ← false
14         anyActive ← (∃i)(busy[i])                                          $
15         anyActive ← anyActive || jobsMoved                                 $
16         jobsMoved ← false                                                  $
17         allDone ← not anyActive                                            $
```

Algorithm 13.22: Symmetric termination detection repaired

```
1  shared detector ← −1
2  me ← myThreadId
3
4  work():
5      ...
6      while I have no work && not allDone                                    $
7          if detector ≥ 0
8              continue          /* wait for previous detector to finish before trying */
9          if CompareAndSet(&detector, −1, me)
10             detectSymmetric()                                              $
11             detector ← −1                                                  $
12         ...
```

Algorithm 13.23: Termination via a counter

```
1  shared numBusy ← N
2  worker():
3      loop
4          while work remaining
5              perform(work)
6          if AtomicAdd(&numBusy, −1) = 0
7              return
8          while nothing to steal && (numBusy > 0)                            $
9              /* do nothing: wait for work or termination */
10         if numBusy = 0
11             return
12         AtomicAdd(&numBusy, 1)
```

Algorithm 13.24: Rendezvous via a counter

```
1   shared numBusy ← N
2
3   barrier():
4       AtomicAdd(&numBusy, −1)
5       while numBusy > 0
6           /* do nothing: wait for others to catch up */
```

Algorithm 13.25: Rendezvous with reset

```
1   shared numBusy ← N
2   shared numPast ← 0
3
4   barrier():
5       AtomicAdd(&numBusy, −1)
6       while numBusy > 0
7           /* do nothing: wait for others to catch up */
8       if AtomicAdd(&numPast, 1) = N                    /* one winner does the reset */
9           numPast ← 0                                                              $
10          numBusy ← N                                                              $
11      else
12          while numBusy = 0                       /* the others wait (but not for long) */
13              /* do nothing: wait for reset to complete */
```

---

by *continuations* (in the programming language sense), more general techniques might be useful, such as those explored by Kumar *et al.* [2012, 2014].

Rendezvous barriers

Another common synchronisation mechanism in parallel and concurrent collectors is the need for all participants to reach the same point in the algorithm — essentially a point of termination of a phase of collection — and then to move on. In the general case one of the previously presented termination algorithms may be most appropriate. Another common case occurs when the phase does not involve work sharing or balancing, but it is required only to wait for all threads to reach a given point, called the *rendezvous barrier*. This can use a simplified version of termination detection with a counter (Algorithm 13.23), shown in Algorithm 13.24. Since a collector is usually invoked more than once as a program runs, these counters must be reset as the algorithm starts, or in any case before the phase is run again, and the resetting should be done with care to ensure that no thread can be depending on the value of the rendezvous counter at the time it is reset. Algorithm 13.25 shows such a resetting barrier.

13.8 Concurrent data structures

There are particular data structures commonly used in parallel and concurrent allocators and collectors, so it is helpful to review some of the relevant implementation techniques. It should be plain that data structure implementations for sequential programs are not

Algorithm 13.26: Counting lock

```
1   /* the lock packs into one word a thread id and a count */
2   shared lock ← ⟨thread: −1, count: 0⟩int
3   me ← myThreadId
4
5   countingLock():
6       old ← lock
7       if old.thread = me && old.count > 0
8           /* just increment the count; assume no overflow */
9           lock ← ⟨old.thread, old.count + 1⟩
10          return
11      loop
12          if old.count = 0
13              if CompareAndSet(&lock, old, ⟨thread: me, count: 1⟩)
14                  return
15          old ← lock
16
17  countingUnlock():
18      /* leaves thread id, but no harm even when count becomes 0 */
19      old ← lock
20      lock ← ⟨old.thread, old.count − 1⟩
```

---

suitable as is for parallel and concurrent systems — they will generally break. If a data structure is accessed rarely enough then it may suffice to apply mutual exclusion to an otherwise sequential implementation by adding a lock variable to each instance of the data structure, and have each operation acquire the lock before the operation and release it after. If operations can be nested or recursive, then a 'counting lock' is appropriate, as shown in Algorithm 13.26.

Some data structures have high enough traffic that applying simple mutual exclusion leads to bottlenecks. Therefore, a number of concurrent data structures have been devised that allow greater overlap between concurrent operations. If concurrent operations are overlapped, the result must still be safe and correct. An implementation of a concurrent data structure is said to be *linearisable* if any pair of overlapping operations produces state changes on the data structure and responses to the operations consistent with executing the two operations in a non-overlapped way in one order or the other [Herlihy and Wing, 1990]. Furthermore, if two operations do not overlap in time, they must appear to happen in the order in which they were invoked. For each operation there is a point in time at which the operation can be viewed as having taken place. This is called its *linearisation point*. Often an operation has many points in time that might be viewed as its linearisation point, but the relative order of the linearisation points of operations that affect each other will always be consistent with the logical order of the operations. If operations do not affect each other then they can linearise in either order. Many memory manager actions, such as allocation and changes to work lists, must be linearisable.

There is a range of generic strategies a programmer can employ in building a concurrent data structure. In order from lower to higher concurrency, and typically from simplest to most complex, they are as follows.[16]

---

[16]See Herlihy and Shavit [2008], Chapter 9, for details of each of these approaches applied to a set implemented as a linked list.

Coarse-grained locking: One 'large' lock is applied to the whole data structure (already mentioned).

Fine-grained locking: In this approach an operation locks individual elements of a larger data structure, such as the individual nodes of a linked list or tree. This can increase concurrency if the locales of access and update are spread around enough. A general concern to keep in mind is that if an operation locks multiple elements, it must ensure that no other invocation of the same operation, or of any other operation, will attempt to lock the same two elements in the opposite order — in that case, the operations can deadlock. A common technique on a data structure only accessed in a single direction, such as a singly linked list or a tree, is *lock coupling*. This locks a node A and then a node B pointed to by A. Then it releases the lock on A and acquires a lock on a node C pointed to by B, and so on. This 'hand-over-hand' walking of locks through a data structure guarantees that later-arriving threads cannot pass the current thread in the data structure, and supports safe execution of operations such as inserting or removing an item from a list or tree. A potential drawback of fine-grained locking is that the overhead of going to a shared bus or memory multiple times to lock individual elements may swamp the benefit of avoiding a coarser lock.

Optimistic locking: This refines fine-grained locking by doing any searching of the data structure without locks, then locking what appear to be the proper elements for the operation. However, in general, concurrent updates can have changed things, so after locking, the operation validates that it has locked the correct elements for its intended action. If the validation fails, it releases the locks and starts over. Avoiding locking until the latest time necessary reduces overhead and improves concurrency. Optimism is often a good strategy, but can result in poorer performance in the presence of frequent conflicting updates.

Lazy update: Even with optimistic locking, read-only operations may still need to lock a data structure. This can result in a concurrency bottleneck and also has the effect that a read-only operation performs writes (of locks). It is often possible to design a data structure so that read-only operations need no locking — but of course the updating operations are a bit more complex. Generally speaking, they make some change that *logically* accomplishes the operation, but may need further steps to complete it and get the data structure into a normalised form. An example may help in understanding this. For lazy update of a linked list representation of a set, the `remove` operation will first mark an element as being (logically) removed, by setting a boolean flag `deleted` in the element. After that it will unchain the deleted element by redirecting the predecessor's pointer. All this happens while holding locks in the appropriate elements, so as to prevent problems with concurrent updaters. The two steps are necessary so that readers can proceed without locking. Adding an element needs to modify only one `next` pointer in the data structure and therefore needs only one update (again, with appropriate locks held).

Non-blocking: There are strategies that avoid locking altogether and rely on atomic update primitives to accomplish changes to the state of data structures. Typically a state-changing operation has some particular atomic update event that is its linearisation point. This is in contrast to lock based methods, where some critical section marks the linearisation 'point'.[17] As previously mentioned, these can be characterised according to their progress guarantees, in order from easiest to implement

---

[17]Because of mutual exclusion, it is a point as far as any other operations are concerned. However, lazy update methods also tend to have a single linearisation point.

to hardest. Lock-free implementations may allow starvation of individual threads; obstruction-free implementations may require long enough periods in which a single thread can make progress without interference; and wait-free implementations guarantee progress of all threads. Some lock-free implementations are sketched below; for wait-free implementation, see Herlihy and Shavit [2008].

For data structures most relevant to implementing parallel and concurrent collection, implementation descriptions and code sketches are offered below. The implementation strategies generally follow those suggested by Herlihy and Shavit.

Concurrent stacks

First, we sketch ways to implement a concurrent stack using a singly linked list. Since there is only one locus of mutation for a stack, the performance of the various approaches to locking will be about the same. The code is obvious, so it is not illustrated. Algorithm 13.27 shows a lock-free implementation of a stack. It is easy to make push lock-free; pop is a little harder. The popABA routine is a simple compare-and-set implementation of pop that is lock-free — but that also has an ABA problem. Algorithm 13.27 also shows LoadLinked/StoreConditionally and CompareAndSetWide solutions that avoid the ABA problem, as concrete examples of how to do that. The problem occurs when some other thread(s) pop the node referred to by currTop, and that node is pushed later with its next different from the currTop.next read by this popping thread.

A concurrent stack based on an array is best implemented using a lock. However, concurrent stacks tend to be a bottleneck not just because of cache and memory issues, but because all the operations must serialise. It is possible to do better. Blelloch and Cheng [1999] provide a lock-free solution by requiring all threads accessing a shared stack either to be popping from it or all to be pushing onto it, thus allowing the stack pointer to be controlled by a FetchAndAdd instruction rather than a lock. We discuss this in detail in Chapter 14. Chapter 11 of Herlihy and Shavit discusses a concurrent lock-free stack implementation where threads that encounter high contention try to find matching operations in a side buffer. When a pop finds a waiting push, or a push finds a waiting pop, that push instantly satisfies that pop: the pair of operations eliminate each other. They linearise at that moment (push before pop, of course), regardless of what is happening at the 'main' stack.

Concurrent queue implemented with singly linked list

A concurrent queue is a more interesting example of concurrency than a concurrent stack, since it has two loci of modification: the head, where items are removed, and the tail, where they are added. It is convenient to include a 'dummy' node, before the next element to be removed from the queue. The head pointer refers to the dummy node, while the tail pointer refers to the node most recently added to the queue, or the dummy node if the queue is empty.

Algorithm 13.28 shows an implementation that does fine-grained locking. It has one lock for each locus. Notice that remove changes head to refer to the next node; thus, after the first successful remove, the original dummy node will be free, and the node with the value just removed becomes the new head. This version of a queue is unbounded. Algorithm 13.29 shows a similar implementation for a bounded queue. To avoid update contention on a single size field, it maintains counts of the number of items added and the number removed. It is fine if these counts wrap around — the fields storing them just

Algorithm 13.27: Lock-free implementation of a single-linked-list stack

```
1   shared topCnt[2] ← [null, any value]
2   shared topAddr ← &topCnt[0]                                    /* top */
3   shared cntAddr ← &topCnt[1]        /* count, only for popCount below */
4
5   push(val):
6       node ← new Node(value: val, next: null)
7       loop
8           currTop ← *topAddr
9           node.next ← currTop
10          if CompareAndSet(topAddr, currTop, node)
11              return
12
13  popABA():
14      loop
15          currTop ← *topAddr
16          if currTop = null
17              return null
18          /* code below can have an ABA problem if node is reused */
19          next ← currTop.next
20          if CompareAndSet(topAddr, currTop, next)
21              return currTop.value
22
23  pop():
24      loop
25          currTop ← LoadLinked(topAddr)
26          if currTop = null
27              return null
28          next ← currTop.next
29          if StoreConditionally(topAddr, next)
30              return currTop.value
31
32  popCount():
33      loop
34          currTop ← *topAddr
35          if currTop = null
36              return null
37          currCnt ← *cntAddr                                          $
38          nextTop ← currTop.next
39          if CompareAndSetWide(&topCnt, currTop, currCnt,
40                               nextTop, currCnt+1)
41              return currTop.value
```

Algorithm 13.28: Fine-grained locking for a single-linked-list queue

```
1   shared head ← new Node(value: dontCare, next: null)
2   shared tail ← head
3   shared addLock ← UNLOCKED
4   shared removeLock ← UNLOCKED
5
6   add(val):
7       node ← new Node(value: val, next: null)
8       lock(&addLock)
9       tail.next ← node
10      tail ← node
11      unlock(&addLock)
12
13  remove():
14      lock(&removeLock)
15      node ← head.next
16      if node = null
17          unlock(&removeLock)
18          return EMPTY                    /* or otherwise indicate emptiness */
19      val ← node.value
20      head ← node
21      unlock(&removeLock)
22      return val
```

Algorithm 13.29: Fine-grained locking for a single-linked-list bounded queue

```
1   shared head ← new Node(value: dontCare, next: null)
2   shared tail ← head
3   shared addLock ← UNLOCKED
4   shared removeLock ← UNLOCKED
5   shared numAdded ← 0
6   shared numRemoved ← 0
7
8   add(val):
9       node ← new Node(value: val, next: null)
10      lock(&addLock)
11      if numAdded − numRemoved = MAX
12          unlock(&addLock)
13          return false                        /* or otherwise indicate full */
14      tail.next ← node
15      tail ← node
16      numAdded ← numAdded + 1                  /* numeric wrap around is ok */
17      unlock(&addLock)
18      return true                             /* or otherwise indicate success */
19
20  remove():
21      lock(&removeLock)
22      node ← head.next
23      if numAdded − numRemoved = 0
24          unlock(&removeLock)
25          return EMPTY                        /* or otherwise indicate emptiness */
26      val ← node.value
27      head ← node
28      numRemoved ← numRemoved + 1              /* numeric wrap around is ok */
29      unlock(&removeLock)
30      return val
```

need to be able to store all $max + 1$ values from zero through max. Of course if these counts lie on the same cache line, this 'optimisation' may perform no better than using a single `size` field.

There is an important special case of this implementation: if either adding or removing or both is limited to one thread, then that end does not need a lock. In particular, if there is one adder and one remover, then this data structure needs no locks at all. A common case in collection is multiple adders and one remover, which is still an improvement over the general case.

Other locking approaches (such as optimistic or lazy update) offer no real advantage over fine-grained locking for this data structure.

Algorithm 13.30 shows a lock-free implementation. A tricky thing here is that adding a node happens in two steps. First, the current tail node is updated to point to the new node, and then `tail` is updated to refer to the new node. A lock-free implementation must provide for the possibility that other adders — and also removers — may see the intermediate state. This implementation addresses the issue by having any thread update `tail` if it notices that `tail` is 'out of sync'. This ensures that `tail` comes into sync without any thread waiting for another one to do it. This is a case of the *helping* typical of wait-free algorithms, even though this algorithm is not wait-free.

Concurrent queue implemented with array

A queue implemented with an array has higher storage density than one implemented with a linked list, and it does not require on the fly allocation of nodes from a pool. A bounded queue can be implemented with a circular buffer. Algorithm 13.31 shows a fine-grained locking version of that, which can be improved by folding together `head` and `numRemoved`, and also `tail` and `numAdded`, using modular arithmetic, shown in Algorithm 13.32. This is particularly attractive if `MAX` is a power of two, since then the modulus function can be performed with bit masking. The reason for `MODULUS` is that we need to distinguish the `MAX+1` possible values for the difference between `tail` and `head`, that is, the number of elements in the buffer. Thus our modulus for the modular arithmetic needs to be greater than `MAX`. At the same time, it must be a multiple of `MAX` so that we can reduce `head` and `tail` modulo `MAX` when indexing into the buffer. The value `MAX*2` is the smallest modulus that will work, and has the added virtue of being a power of two when `MAX` is. In the code we add `MODULUS` to `tail−head` to ensure we are taking the modulus of a positive number, which is not necessary if using masking or if the implementation language does a proper modulus (toward $-\infty$ as opposed to toward zero).

If there is a distinguished value that can mark empty slots in the buffer, then the code can be further simplified as shown in Algorithm 13.33.

It is often the case that the buffer has just a single reader and a single writer (for example, the channels used by Oancea *et al.* [2009]). In this case, the code for a circular buffer is much simpler; it appears in Algorithm 13.34. This algorithm is a good example for mentioning the adjustments a programmer needs to make to realise the algorithm on different platforms. The algorithm works as is on Intel x86 processors because they are strict about the order of stores to memory as perceived by other processors.

However, on the PowerPC the lines we mark with $ for ordering require attention. One approach is to insert fences, as indicated by Oancea *et al.*. In `add` we insert an `lwsync` instruction between the stores to `buffer[tail]` and `tail`, to serve as a store-store memory

Algorithm 13.30: Lock-free implementation of a single-linked-list queue

```
1   shared head ← new Node(value: dontCare, next: null)
2   shared tail ← head
3
4   add(val):
5       node ← new Node(value: val, next: null)
6       loop
7           currTail ← LoadLinked(&tail)
8           currNext ← currTail.next
9           if currNext ≠ null
10              /* tail appears to be out of sync: try to help */
11              StoreConditionally(&tail, currNext)
12              continue                          /* start over after attempt to sync */
13          if CompareAndSet(&currTail.next, null, node)
14              /* added to end of chain; try to update tail */
15              StoreConditionally(&tail, node)
16              /* ok if failed: someone else brought tail into sync, or will in the future */
17              return
18
19  remove():
20      loop
21          currHead ← LoadLinked(&head)
22          next ← currHead.next
23          if next = null
24              if StoreConditionally(&head, currHead)
25                  /* head has not changed, so truly empty */
26                  return EMPTY                   /* or otherwise indicate emptiness */
27              continue                           /* head may have changed so try again */
28
29          currTail ← tail
30          if currHead = currTail
31              /* not empty; appears to be out of sync; try to help */
32              currTail ← LoadLinked(&tail)
33              next ← currTail.next
34              if next ≠ null
35                  StoreConditionally(&tail, next)
36              continue
37
38          /* appears non–empty and in sync enough; try to remove first node */
39          val ← next.value
40          if StoreConditionally(&head, next)
41              return val
42          /* on failure, start over */
```

Algorithm 13.31: Fine-grained locking of a circular buffer

```
 1  shared buffer[MAX]
 2  shared head ← 0
 3  shared tail ← 0
 4  shared numAdded ← 0
 5  shared numRemoved ← 0
 6  shared addLock ← UNLOCKED
 7  shared removeLock ← UNLOCKED
 8
 9  add(val):
10      lock(&addLock)
11      if numAdded − numRemoved = MAX
12          unlock(&addLock)
13          return false                              /* indicate failure */
14      buffer[tail] ← val
15      tail ← (tail + 1) % MAX
16      numAdded ← numAdded + 1
17      unlock(&addLock)
18
19  remove():
20      lock(&removeLock)
21      if numAdded − numRemoved = 0
22          unlock(&removeLock)
23          return EMPTY                              /* indicate failure */
24      val ← buffer[head]
25      head ← (head + 1) % MAX
26      numRemoved ← numRemoved + 1
27      unlock(&removeLock)
28      return val
```

fence.[18] This will guarantee that if the remover orders its load instructions properly, it will not perceive the change to `tail` until after it can perceive the change to `buffer`. Likewise, we add an `isync` instruction, which serves as a load-store memory fence, before the store to `buffer`, to ensure that the processor does not speculatively begin the store before the load of `head` and thus possibly overwrite a value being read by the remover.[19]

Similarly, we insert an `lwsync` in `remove` between loading `buffer[head]` and updat-

---

[18]The `lwsync` instruction ensures that memory accesses by the issuing processor for instructions before the `lwsync` complete before any memory accesses for instructions after the `lwsync`, as viewed by all processors. It stands for 'light-weight sync' and is a version of the `sync`, where the 'heavy-weight' version, written just `sync`, deals with input/output device memory in addition to ordinary cached memory. Both `lwsync` and `sync` are somewhat expensive since their implementation typically involves waiting for the write buffer to drain before allowing future memory accessing instructions to issue. This implies waiting for inter-processor cache synchronisation to complete.

[19]The `isync` instruction ensures that all instructions previously issued by this processor complete before any future instruction of this processor. It is suitable for separating previous loads from future memory accesses. It does not guarantee that previous and future stores will be perceived by other processors in the locally issued order — that requires one of the `sync` instructions. One reason `isync` may be more efficient is that it involves only processor-local waiting, for the instruction pipeline to empty sufficiently; it does not itself require cache coherence activity.

Algorithm 13.32: Circular buffer with fewer variables

```
1   shared buffer[MAX]
2   MODULUS = MAX * 2                                         /* see text for explanation */
3   shared head ← 0                                           /* 0 ≤ head < MODULUS */
4   shared tail ← 0                                           /* 0 ≤ tail < MODULUS */
5   shared addLock ← UNLOCKED
6   shared removeLock ← UNLOCKED
7
8   add(val):
9       lock(&addLock)
10      if (tail − head + MODULUS) % MODULUS = MAX
11          unlock(&addLock)
12          return false                                      /* indicate failure */
13      buffer[tail % MAX] ← val
14      tail ← (tail + 1) % MODULUS
15      unlock(&addLock)
16      return true                                           /* indicate success */
17
18  remove():
19      lock(&removeLock)
20      if (tail − head + MODULUS) % MODULUS = 0
21          unlock(&removeLock)
22          return EMPTY                                      /* indicate failure */
23      local val ← buffer[head % MAX]
24      head ← (head + 1) % MODULUS
25      unlock(&removeLock)
26      return val
```

ing head, and an isync before loading from buffer, to serve as a load-load memory barrier between loading tail and loading from buffer.

Oancea *et al.* proposed a solution that includes writing null in remove as an explicit EMPTY value, and having both add (remove) watch its intended buffer slot until the slot appears suitably empty (non-empty), before writing its new value (EMPTY). Because there is only one reader and only one writer, only one thread writes EMPTY values, and only one writes non-EMPTY values, and each delays its write until it sees the other thread's previous write, accesses to the buffer cannot incorrectly pass each other. Likewise, only one thread writes each of head and tail, so at worst the other thread may have a stale view. This solution avoids fences, but the buffer writes by the remover may cause more cache ping-ponging than fences would. Oancea *et al.* actually combine both solutions, but as we just argued, each seems adequate on its own. This all shows the care needed to obtain a correctly working implementation of concurrent algorithms under relaxed memory orders.

If the queue is being used as a *buffer*, that is, if the order in which things are removed need not match *exactly* the order in which they were added, then it is not too hard to devise a lock-free buffer. First assume an array large enough that wrap-around will never occur. Algorithm 13.35 implements a lock-free buffer. It assumes that initially all entries are EMPTY. This algorithm does a lot of repeated scanning. Algorithm 13.36 adds an index lower from which to start scans. It requires distinguishing not just empty slots, but also

Algorithm 13.33: Circular buffer with distinguishable empty slots

```
 1  shared buffer[MAX] ← [EMPTY,...]
 2  shared head ← 0
 3  shared tail ← 0
 4  shared addLock ← UNLOCKED
 5  shared removeLock ← UNLOCKED
 6
 7  add(val):
 8      lock(&addLock)
 9      if buffer[tail] ≠ EMPTY
10          unlock(&addLock)
11          return false                          /* indicate failure */
12      buffer[tail] ← val
13      tail ← (tail + 1) % MAX
14      unlock(&addLock)
15      return true                               /* indicate success */
16
17  remove():
18      lock(&removeLock)
19      if buffer[head] = EMPTY
20          unlock(&removeLock)
21          return EMPTY                          /* indicate failure */
22      val ← buffer[head]
23      head ← (head + 1) % MAX
24      unlock(&removeLock)
25      return val
```

Algorithm 13.34: Single reader/single writer lock-free buffer [Oancea *et al.*, 2009]

```
 1  shared buffer[MAX]
 2  shared head ← 0            /* next slot from which to try removing */
 3  shared tail ← 0           /* next slot into which to add */
 4
 5  add(val):
 6      newTail ← (tail + 1) % MAX
 7      if newTail = head
 8          return false
 9      buffer[tail] ← val                                    $
10      tail ← newTail
11      return true
12
13  remove():
14      if head = tail
15          return EMPTY            /* or otherwise indicate emptiness */
16      value ← buffer[head]                                  $
17      head ← (head + 1) % MAX                               $
18      return value
```

Algorithm 13.35: Unbounded lock-free buffer implemented with an array

```
1   shared buffer[ ]← [EMPTY,...]              /* unrealisable unbounded buffer */
2   shared head ← 0                            /* next slot to fill */
3
4   add(val):
5       pos ← FetchAndAdd(&head, 1)
6       buffer[pos] ← val
7
8   remove():
9       limit ← head
10      pos ← −1
11      loop
12          pos ← pos + 1
13          if pos = limit
14              return null                     /* found nothing */
15          val ← LoadLinked(&buffer[pos])
16          if val ≠ EMPTY
17              if StoreConditionally(&buffer[pos], EMPTY)
18                  return val
```

ones that have been filled and then emptied, indicated by USED in the code. Further refinement is needed to produce a lock-free circular buffer implementation along these lines. In particular there needs to be code in the add routine that carefully converts USED slots to EMPTY ones before advancing the head index. It also helps to use index values that cycle through *twice* MAX as in Algorithm 13.32. The resulting code appears in Algorithm 13.37.

Concurrent deque for work stealing

To support work stealing, Arora *et al.* [1998] designed a lock-free implementation of a double-ended queue. The local worker thread can push *and* pop work items, while other threads can remove (steal) items. The design has the local worker push and pop at one end of the deque, while other threads remove from the opposite end (the deque is input-restricted). Algorithm 13.38 shows an implementation avoids an ABA problem by using load-linked/store-conditionally.[20] It is straightforward to pack a counter with the tail index to derive a safe implementation in terms of compare-and-swap.

Pushing a value is simple and involves no synchronisation. Popping checks to see if it is trying to get the last value remaining. If it is, it may be in a race with a non-local remover. Both threads will try to update tail; the winner 'gets' the value. In any case, the popper sets tail to zero. This will not confuse a contending remover. Either the remover lost the race, in which case it does not return a value, or it won and it already has the value and will leave tail alone. It is also important that pop sets top to zero first, before setting tail to zero — this keeps the top ≤ tail test working in remove. Notice that the conventions for top and tail ensure that top−tail is the number of items in the queue (except in the middle of resetting them both to zero, where the difference may be negative).

---

[20]The names of variables are different from Arora *et al.* [1998], and the algorithm here calls the local end's index *top* and the opposite end's index *tail*, so as to correspond better with the view that the local end of the deque is a stack and the other end is the tail (removal point) of a queue.

Algorithm 13.36: Unbounded lock-free array buffer with increasing scan start

```
1   shared buffer[ ]← [EMPTY,...]              /* unrealisable unbounded buffer */
2   shared head ← 0                                       /* next slot to fill */
3   shared lower ← 0                                /* position to look at first */
4
5   add(val):
6       pos ← FetchAndAdd(&head, 1)
7       buffer[pos] ← val
8
9   remove():
10      limit ← head
11      currLower ← lower
12      pos ← currLower − 1
13      loop
14          pos ← pos + 1
15          if pos = limit
16              return null                               /* found nothing */
17          val ← LoadLinked(&buffer[pos])
18          if val = EMPTY
19              continue
20          if val = USED
21              if pos = currLower
22                  /* try to advance lower */
23                  currLower ← LoadLinked(&lower)
24                  if pos = currLower
25                      StoreConditionally(&lower, pos+1)
26              continue
27          /* try to grab */
28          if StoreConditionally(&buffer[pos], USED)
29              return val
```

13.9   Transactional memory

A *transaction* consists of a collection of reads and writes that should appear to execute atomically. That is, the effect should be as if no other reads or writes interleave with those of a transaction. load-linked/store-conditionally achieves this semantics for transactions involving a single word, but the point is to allow transactions over multiple independent words. A suitable mechanism will generally include means to indicate:

- the *start* of a transaction;

- each *read* that is part of the current transaction;

- each *write* that is part of the current transaction; and

- the *end* of a transaction.

The end is usually called the (attempted) *commit* of the transaction. If it succeeds, then the transaction's effects appear; if it fails, then the writes are discarded and the software may respond by trying again, trying some other action, and so on. Thus, transactions

Algorithm 13.37: Bounded lock-free buffer implemented with an array

```
1   shared buffer[MAX] ← [EMPTY,...]
2   MODULUS = 2 * MAX
3   shared head ← 0                                          /* refers to next slot to fill */
4   shared lower ← 0                         /* slots from lower to head−1 may have data */
5
6   add(val):
7     loop
8       currHead ← head
9       /* could peek before using atomic operator */
10      oldVal ← LoadLinked(&buffer[currHead % MAX])
11      if oldVal = USED
12        currLower ← lower
13        if (currHead % MAX) = (currLower % MAX)
14             && (currHead ≠ currLower)
15          advanceLower()                              /* lower is a buffer behind */
16          continue
17        /* try to clean entry; ensure head has not changed */
18        if currHead = head
19          StoreConditionally(&buffer[currHead % MAX], EMPTY)
20        continue
21      if oldVal ≠ EMPTY
22        if currHead ≠ head
23          continue                                  /* things changed: try again */
24        return false                          /* indicate failure: buffer is full */
25      currHead ← LoadLinked(&head)                        /* try to claim slot */
26      /* recheck inside LL/SC */
27      if buffer[currHead % MAX] = EMPTY
28        if StoreConditionally(&head, (currHead + 1) % MODULUS)
29          buffer[currHead] ← val
30          return true                                      /* indicate success */
31
32  remove():
33    advanceLower()
34    limit ← head
35    scan ← lower − 1
36    loop
37      scan ← (scan + 1) % MODULUS
38      if scan = limit
39        return null                                         /* found nothing */
40      /* could peek at value first before using atomic operator */
41      val ← LoadLinked(&buffer[scan % MAX])
42      if val = EMPTY || val = USED
43        continue
44      /* try to grab */
45      if StoreConditionally(&buffer[scan % MAX], USED)
46        /* Note: always safe to grab entry that is not USED and not EMPTY */
47        return val
```

Algorithm 13.37 (continued): Bounded lock-free buffer implemented with an array

```
1   advanceLower():
2       if buffer[lower % MAX] ≠ USED
3           return                      /* quick return without using atomic operation */
4       loop
5           currLower ← LoadLinked(&lower)
6           if buffer[currLower % MAX] = USED
7               if StoreConditionally(&lower, (lower + 1) % MODULUS)
8                   continue
9           return
```

may be executed *speculatively*. It is necessary to mark their end so that speculation can be resolved and the transaction accepted, with its writes installed, and so on, or rejected and the software notified so that it can retry or take some other action.

Similar to the ACID properties of database transactions, transactional memory transactions ensure the following properties.

- *Atomicity:* All effects (writes) of a transaction appear or none do.

- *Consistency:* A transaction appears to execute at a single instant.

- *Isolation:* No other thread can perceive an intermediate state of a transaction, only a state before or a state after the transaction.

The *durability* property of database transactions, which ensures to very high probability that the results of a successful transaction will not be lost, is omitted from the requirements on transactional memory.[21]

The actual reads and writes of a transaction will be spread out over time. Thus, as transactions run, they may interfere with each other if they access the same locations. Specifically, transactions A and B conflict if one of them writes an item that the other reads or writes. Conflicting transactions must be ordered. In some cases, given the reads and writes a transaction has already performed, this is not possible. For example, if A and B have both read x, and then they both try to write to x, there is no way to complete both transactions so as to satisfy transactional semantics. In that case, one or both of A and B must be *aborted* (discarded), and the situation made to appear as if the aborted transaction had not run. Generally the software will try it again, which will likely force a suitable ordering.

Transactional memory provides a high-level programming abstraction that allows programmers to enclose code within transactional blocks. All shared memory accesses within a block (and their effects) are either committed all together or discarded as a group. Transactional memory can be implemented in hardware, software or a hybrid combination. Any implementation strategy must provide for: atomicity of writes, detection of conflicts and visibility control (for isolation). Visibility control may be part of conflict detection.

Atomicity of writes can be achieved either by *buffering* or by *undoing*. The buffering approach accumulates writes in some kind of scratch memory separate from the memory locations written, and updates those memory locations only if the transaction commits. Hardware buffering may be achieved by augmenting caches or using some other side buffer; software buffering might work at the level of words, fields or whole objects. With buffering, a transaction commit installs the buffered writes, while an abort discards

---

[21]We note, however, that Intel x86 hardware transactional memory transactions may be durable if executed over non-volatile memory on certain platforms.

Algorithm 13.38: Lock-free work stealing deque [Arora *et al.*, 1998]

```
1   shared deque[MAX]
2   shared top ← 0                              /* index one beyond the last used entry */
3   shared tail ← 0                                  /* index of the first used entry */
4
5   push(val):                        /* local worker function to push (enqueue) a value */
6      currTop ← top
7      if currTop ≥ MAX
8         return false                                       /* indicate overflow */
9      deque[currTop] ← val
10     top ← currTop + 1
11     return true                                            /* indicate success */
12
13  pop():                   /* local worker function to pop a value from the local end */
14     currTop ← top − 1
15     if currTop < 0
16        return null                                                  /* empty */
17     top ← currTop
18     val ← deque[currTop]
19     currTail ← LoadLinked(&tail)
20     if currTop > currTail
21        return val                     /* cannot be contending with other removers */
22     /* might be contending, and deque will be empty */
23     top ← 0
24     if StoreConditionally(&tail, 0)
25        return val                       /* I won on changing tail, so I get the value */
26     tail ← 0
27     return null
28
29  remove():                            /* steal a value from another thread's deque */
30     loop
31        currTail ← LoadLinked(&tail)
32        currTop ← top
33        if currTop ≤ currTail
34           return null                                        /* deque is empty */
35        val ← deque[currTail]
36        if StoreConditionally(&tail, currTail+1)
37           return val                  /* won on setting tail, so can return the value */
38        /* contended with another remover, or pop that emptied the deque */
39        /* if stealing is optional, could indicate failure instead of looping */
```

---

the buffer. This typically requires more work for commits, usually the more common case, and less work for aborts. Undoing works in a converse way: it updates modified data as a transaction runs, but saves in a side data structure called the *undo log* the previous value of each item it writes. If the transaction commits, it simply discards the undo log, but if the transaction aborts, it uses the undo log to restore the previous values. Undo logs can be implemented in hardware, software, or a combination, just as buffering can. Typical hardware transactional memory buffers writes in the cache marking the affected lines as tentative until the transaction commits and invalidating those lines if the transaction aborts.

Conflict detection may be implemented *eagerly* or *lazily*. Eager conflict checking checks each new access against the currently running transactions to see if it conflicts. If necessary it will cause one of the conflicting transactions to abort. Lazy conflict checking does the checks when a transaction attempts to commit. Some mechanisms also allow a transaction to request as it runs validation that there are no conflicts so far in the transaction. Software schemes may set flags in object headers or maintain a side table recording accesses. These are checked by transactional accesses to accomplish conflict detection. Hardware will typically associate flags with cache lines or words to the same end.

For purposes of presentation, let us discuss a simple hardware transactional memory interface consisting of these primitives, as introduced by Herlihy and Moss [1993]:[22]

TStart() indicates the beginning of a transaction.

TCommit() indicates that the transaction wants to commit. It returns a boolean that is true if and only if the commit succeeded.

TAbort() indicates that the transaction wants to abort, which is sometimes useful to request programmatically.

TLoad(addr) marks a transactional load from the indicated address. This adds that address to the transaction's read set and returns the current value in that memory location.

TStore(addr, value) marks a transactional store of the indicated value to the indicated address. This adds the address to the transaction's write set and performs the write transactionally, that is, in a way such that the effect of the write disappears if the transaction aborts, and so on.

These primitives can simplify the implementation of a variety of concurrent data structures. For example, Algorithm 13.30 simplifies to Algorithm 13.39. The add function is simpler because it can write two locations atomically, and remove is simpler because it can read two and even three values atomically. More importantly, it is easier to see that the transactional implementation is correct; verifying the other version requires more subtle arguments about orders of reads and writes.

Using transactional memory to help implement collection

There are two main relationships that transactional memory can have with garbage collection. Transactional memory can help implement the collector [McGachey *et al.*, 2008; Ritson *et al.*, 2014], or transactions may be part of the managed language semantics that the collector must play with nicely. This section considers transactional memory in support of garbage collection; the next section looks at garbage collection for a language that supports transactions.

---

[22]Intel's x86 Restricted Transactional Memory (RTM) works substantially like this.

Algorithm 13.39: Transactional memory version of a single-linked-list queue

```
1   shared head ← new Node(value: dontCare, next: null)
2   shared tail ← head
3
4   add(val):
5       node ← new Node(value: val, next: null)
6       loop
7           currTail ← TLoad(&tail)
8           TStore(&currTail.next, node)
9           TStore(&tail, node)
10          if TCommit()
11              return
12
13  remove():
14      loop
15          currHead ← TLoad(&head)
16          next ← TLoad(&currHead.next)
17          if next = null
18              if TCommit()                    /* the commit ensures we got a consistent view */
19                  return EMPTY                /* or otherwise indicate emptiness */
20              continue
21
22          /* appears non–empty; try to remove first node */
23          val ← TLoad(&next.value)
24          TStore(&head, next)
25          if TCommit()
26              return val
27          /* on failure, start over */
```

It should be clear that transactional memory, because of the way it can simplify the programming of concurrent data structures, can make it easier to implement parallel and concurrent allocation and collection. In particular it can simplify concurrent allocators, mutator and collector read and write barriers, and concurrent collector data structures. Given that there are no current hardware standards and an increasing variety of software packages available, it is not possible to be specific, but using transactional memory to support automatic memory management involves these caveats.

- *Software transactional memory* tends to involve significant overheads, even after optimisation. Given the desire for low overheads in most parts of automatic storage management, the scope for applying software transactional memory may be small. Still, coding of low traffic data structures might be simplified while continuing to avoid the difficulties with locks. However, software transactional memory can be used efficiently to support concurrent replication copying [Ritson *et al.*, 2014; Ugawa *et al.*, 2018]. Their insight is that fromspace and tospace replicas of an object need to be only *eventually* rather than *immediately* consistent, and therefore that a general-purpose transactional memory mechanism is not necessary.

- *Hardware transactional memory* will likely have idiosyncrasies. For example, it may handle conflict detection, access and updating all in terms of physical units such as cache lines. It will also likely have an upper limit on the number of data items involved in a transaction, because of hardware capacity limitations such as the number of lines per cache set in a set-associative cache, for some approaches to implementing hardware transactional memory. Because the mapping from what a programmer writes to the cache lines actually used may not be obvious, implementers must still be careful with low-level details.

• Transactional memory can, at most, guarantee lock-freedom, though it does that fairly easily. Even if the underlying commit mechanism of transactional memory is wait-free, *transactions* can conflict, leading to aborts and retries. Programming wait-free data structures will remain complex and subtle.

• Transactional memory can require careful performance tuning. One concern is inherent conflicts between transactions because they access the same data. An example is a concurrent stack: transactional memory will not solve the bottleneck caused by the need for every push and pop to update the stack pointer. Furthermore, exactly where in a transaction various reads and writes occur — nearer to the beginning or nearer to the end — can significantly affect conflicts and the overhead of retrying transactions.

All that said, a hardware transactional memory facility such as that offered on some Intel x86 processors can be useful. That hardware supports reading and writing at least a small number of completely independent cache lines in a transaction, which is enough to simplify the implementation of most of the concurrent data structures presented here. Whether the performance would be comparable, or even better, with hardware transactional memory remains an open question — hardware transactions tend to empty the processor pipeline. The simpler model of the world that transactional memory presents may result in fewer bugs and reduce development effort.

Supporting transactional memory in the presence of garbage collection

Consider now the quite different problem of implementing a language that offers both automatic memory management and transactions built using some form of transactional memory [Harris and Fraser, 2003; Welc *et al.*, 2004, 2005]. The key issue is the ways in which these two complex mechanisms — transactions and automatic memory management — may interfere, particularly in a highly concurrent implementation.

One kind of interference is that actions of the storage manager may cause transaction conflicts that result in higher overhead because of more retries, as well as making progress problematic for either a mutator, the collector or both. For example, if the mutator is attempting a long transaction, and collector actions conflict, the mutator transaction may be continually aborted by actions of the collector, or the collector may effectively block for a long time. The issue is particularly severe if the implementation exploits hardware transactional memory. For example, attempts by a concurrent collector to mark, forward or copy an object may cause mutator transactions to abort just because they touched the same memory word — even though the operations are carefully coded not to disturb each other's semantics. This would be harder to avoid with hardware transactional memory, since it is oblivious to the semantics of the data being managed, whereas a software transactional memory built for a particular language might give special treatment to object headers, as opposed to data fields.

Transactions can become involved in the semantics of memory reclamation. For example, if a transactional memory system uses a log of old values to support aborting transactions in an update-in-place implementation, then it is possible for the log to contain the only reference to an object. While the transaction remains in doubt, the referent object must be considered still to be reachable. Thus, transaction logs need to be included in the root set for collection. Furthermore, in the case of copying collection, pointers in the logs must not only be provided to the collector for tracing, they must also be updated to reflect the new locations of objects that have moved.

An interesting issue is how to handle allocation in a transactional language. In particular, it would seem logical that if a transaction allocates some objects and then aborts, it should somehow unallocate those objects. However, if the allocation data structures are shared, maintaining ability to roll back values exactly as they were would mean that transactions accessing free-lists or bump pointers effectively lock them until the transaction completes. This is probably undesirable. Therefore, allocation should be more a logical action than a physical one, when we consider how to undo it. A free-list system might go back through an aborting transaction's log and free the objects it allocated. This may put them in a different position on a free-list, and if a block had been split, it might not be recombined, and so forth. It is also possible that the semantics of the language may admit some non-transactional activity within a transaction. In that case an object allocated by the transaction might be revealed, so it can be unsafe to free the object. The implementation must further take care that if an object might be revealed in this way, the initialisation of its crucial contents, such as setting up the object header, is not undone. Concepts such as open nesting [Ni *et al.*, 2007] may help here. A generic strategy is to consider all automatic memory management actions of a transactional mutator to be open-nested actions. However, a simpler approach overall is to use local allocation buffers.

Finally, some transactional memory systems do significant allocation as part of how they function, and that has impact on allocators and collectors. In particular, many software transactional memory systems work by allocating a new version of an object for a writing transaction, which is only installed if the transaction commits. There may not be anything new here semantically for a collector to deal with, but the load may be a bit different. There is also a bit of a sibling relationship between transactional memory and collection in the sense that they may both need efficient concurrent data structures with adequate progress guarantees. For example, transaction commit is in part a consensus algorithm that ideally is wait-free.

13.10 Issues to consider

A first consideration cannot be overstated: getting concurrent algorithms correct is *hard!* Therefore, unless concurrency is absolutely necessary, it should be avoided. That said, concurrency has become more necessary than it was, and so we offer these additional considerations.

What is the range of platforms on which the system will run? What are the memory consistency properties and the fence and synchronisation primitives they offer? It is necessary to code to the weakest ordering to be supported, but it may be possible to elide some fences or other primitives on some platforms, as we discussed relative to Algorithm 13.34 in Section 13.8. What orderings will need fences?

What atomic update primitives are available? Although load-linked/store-conditionally is convenient and more powerful, many popular systems only offer compare-and-swap or equivalent. Without load-linked/store-conditionally, ABA problems can crop up, which can be addressed as we showed in Algorithm 13.27. Perhaps in the future transactional memory will be of use.

What progress guarantees are needed? Weaker guarantees are much easier to implement and to reason about. For low-traffic data structures, straightforward locking may be appropriate — it is much easier to code and to code *correctly* than lock-free or stronger guarantees. Further, even deployed systems that are wait-free for most cases may use simpler techniques for corner cases or for some short steps where the implementation effort to make them wait-free is not worth the benefit.

Does the system exhibit true concurrency (more than one thread running at once in hardware) or is it only multiprogrammed? Multiprogrammed concurrent algorithms are easier to deal with.

In the following chapters, we build on the ideas introduced here to construct parallel, incremental, concurrent and real-time collectors.

Chapter 14

Parallel garbage collection

Today's trend is for modern hardware architectures to offer increasing numbers of processors and cores. Sutter wrote as long ago as 2005 that "The free lunch is over," as many of the traditional approaches to improving performance ran out of steam. Energy costs, and the difficulty of dissipating that energy, have led hardware manufacturers away from increasing clock speeds (power consumption is a cubic function of clock frequency) towards placing multiple processor cores on a single chip (where the increase in energy consumption is linear in the number of cores); we discuss energy-aware garbage collection in Chapter 20. As there is no reason to expect this trend to change, designing and implementing applications to exploit the parallelism offered by hardware will become more and more important. On the contrary, heterogeneous and other non-uniform memory architectures will only increase the need for programmers to take the particular characteristics of the underlying platform into account.

Up to now we have assumed that, although there may be many mutator threads, there is only a single collector thread. Unless there are other demands for processors, this is a poor use of resources on modern multicore or multiprocessor hardware. In this chapter we consider how to parallelise garbage collection, although we continue to assume that no mutators run while garbage collection proceeds and that each collection cycle terminates before the mutators can continue. Terminology is important. Early papers used terms like 'concurrent', 'parallel', 'on-the-fly' and 'real-time' interchangeably or inconsistently. We shall be more consistent, in keeping with most usage today.

Figure 14.1a represents execution on a single processor as a horizontal bar, with time proceeding from left to right, and shows mutator execution in white while different collection cycles are represented by distinct non-white shades. Thus grey boxes represent actions of one collection cycle and black boxes those of the next. On a multiprocessor, suspension of the mutator means stopping *all* the mutator threads. Figure 14.1b shows the general scenario we have considered so far: multiple mutator threads are suspended while a single processor performs garbage collection work. An obvious way to reduce pause times is to have all processors cooperate to collect garbage (while still stopping all mutator threads), as illustrated in Figure 14.1c. This *parallel collection* is the topic of this chapter.

These scenarios, where collection cycles are completed while the mutators are halted, are called *stop-the-world collection*. We note in passing that pause times can be further diminished either by interleaving mutator and collector actions (*incremental collection*) or by allowing mutator and collector threads to execute in parallel (*concurrent collection*), but we defer discussion of these styles of collection to later chapters. In this chapter, we focus on parallelising tracing garbage collection algorithms. Reference counting is also a naturally parallel and concurrent technique which we discussed in Chapter 5; again, we defer

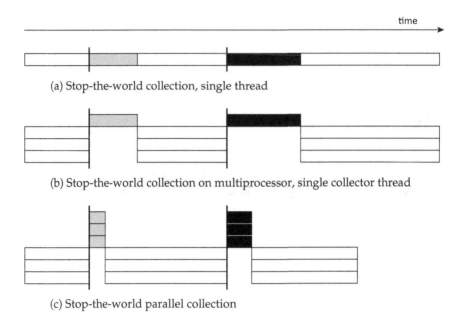

Figure 14.1: Stop-the-world collection: each bar represents an execution on a single processor. The coloured regions represent different collection cycles.

consideration of how this can be improved for a multiprocessor setting until Chapter 18. Here we consider how parallel techniques can be applied to each of the four major components of tracing garbage collection: marking, sweeping, copying and compaction.

14.1   Is there sufficient work to parallelise?

The goal of parallelising collection is to reduce the time overhead of garbage collection by making better use of available hardware resources. In the case of stop-the-world collection, parallel garbage collection will reduce pause times; in the case of incremental or concurrent collection, it will shorten garbage collection cycle times. As with parallelising any problem, the first requirement is to ensure that there is sufficient work to make a parallel solution worthwhile. Inevitably, parallel collection will require some synchronisation between cooperating garbage collection threads, and this will incur overhead. Different solutions may require the use of locks, or atomic primitive operations such as compare-and-swap, and careful design of auxiliary data structures. No matter how careful we are to optimise these mechanisms, they cannot be as efficient as uniprocessor solutions. The question therefore arises, is there sufficient garbage collection work available for the gains offered by a parallel solution to more than offset these costs?

Some garbage collection problems appear inimical to parallelising. For example, a mark-sweep collector may need to trace a list, but this is an inherently sequential activity: at each tracing step, the marking stack will contain only a single item, the next item in the list to be traced. In this case, only one collector thread will do work and all others will stall, waiting for work. Siebert [2008] shows that the number of times n that a processor stalls for lack of work during a parallel mark phase on a p-processor system is limited by the maximum depth of any reachable object o:

$$n \leq (p-1) \cdot \max_{o \in reachable} depth(o)$$

This formulation depends on the unrealistic assumption that all marking steps take the same amount of time. Of course, these steps are not uniform but depend on the kind of object being scanned. Although most objects in most programming languages are typically small — in particular they contain only a few pointers — arrays may be larger and often very much larger than the common case (unless they are implemented as a contiguous 'spine' which contains pointers to fixed-size *arraylets* that hold the array elements).

Fortunately, many typical applications comprise a richer set of data structures than a single list. For example, tracing a branching data structure such as a tree will generate more work at each step than it consumes until the trace reaches the leaves. Furthermore, there are typically multiple sources from which tracing can be initiated, including global variables, the stacks of mutator threads and, in the case of generational or concurrent collectors, remembered sets. In a study of small Java benchmarks, Siebert finds that not only do many programs have a fairly shallow maximum depth but, more significantly, that the ratio between the maximum depth and the number of reachable objects is very small: stalls would occur on fewer than 4% of the objects marked, indicating a high degree of potential parallelism, with all the benchmarks scaling well up to 32 processors (or even more in some cases).

Tracing is the garbage collection component that is most problematic for identifying potential parallelism. The opportunities for parallelising other components, such as sweeping or fixing up references to compacted objects, are more straightforward, at least in principle. An obvious way to proceed is to split those parts of the heap that need to be processed into a number of non-overlapping regions, each of which is managed in parallel by a separate processor. Of course, the devil is in the details.

14.2 Load balancing

The second requirement of a parallel solution is that work is distributed across available hardware resources in a way that minimises the coordination necessary yet keeps all processors as busy as possible. Without *load balancing*, naive parallelisation may lead to little speedup on multiprocessors [Endo *et al.*, 1997]. Unfortunately, the goals of load balancing and minimal coordination typically conflict. A *static balance* of work might be determined in advance of execution, at the startup of the memory manager or, at the latest, before a collection cycle. It may require no coordination of work between garbage collection threads other than to reach a consensus on when their tasks are complete. However, static partitioning may not always lead to an even distribution of work amongst threads. For example, a contiguous mark-compact space on an N-processor system might be divided into N regions, with each processor responsible for fixing up references in its own region. This is a comparatively simple task yet its cost is dependent on the number of objects in the region and the number of references they contain, and so on. Unless these characteristics are broadly similar across regions, some processors are likely to have more work to do than others. Notice also that as well as balancing the amount of *work* across processors, it is also important to balance *other resources* given to those processors. In a parallel implementation of Baker's copying collector [1978], Halstead [1984, 1985] gave each processor its own fixed fromspace and tospace. Unfortunately, this static organisation frequently led to one processor exhausting its tospace while there was room in other processors' spaces.

Many collection tasks require *dynamic* load balancing to distribute work approximately evenly. For jobs where it is possible to obtain a good estimate of the amount of work to be done in advance of performing it, even if this estimate will vary from collection to collection, the division of labour may be done quite simply, and in such a way that no further cooperation is required between parallel garbage collector threads. For example, in the compaction phase of a parallel mark-compact collector, after the marking phase has identified live objects, Flood *et al.* [2001] divide the heap into N regions, each containing approximately equal volumes of live data, and assign a processor to compact each region separately and in parallel.

More often it is not possible to estimate, and hence to divide, the work to be done in advance of carrying out that work. In this case, the usual solution is to *over-partition* the work into more subtasks than there are threads or processors, and then have each compete to claim one task at a time to execute. Over-partitioning has several advantages. It is more resilient to changes in the number of processors available to the collector due to load from other processes on the machine, since smaller subtasks can more easily be redistributed across the remaining processors. If one task takes longer than expected to complete, any further work can be carried out by threads that have completed their smaller tasks. For example, Flood *et al.* also over-partition the heap into M object-aligned areas of approximately equal size before installing forwarding pointers; M was typically chosen to be four times the number of collection threads. Each thread then competes to claim an area, counting the volume of live data in it and coalescing adjacent unmarked objects into a single garbage filler object that can be traversed in constant time. Notice how different load balancing strategies are used in different phases of this collector (which we discuss in more detail later).

We simplify the algorithms we present later in this chapter by concentrating on the three key subtasks of acquiring, performing and generating collection work. We abstract this by assuming in most cases that each collector thread t executes the following loop:

```
while not terminated()
    acquireWork()
    performWork()
    generateWork()
```

Here, `acquireWork` attempts to obtain one or possibly more units of work; `performWork` does the work; and `generateWork` may take one or more new work units discovered by `performWork` and place them in the general pool for collector threads to acquire.

14.3   Synchronisation

It might seem that the best possible load balancing would be to divide the work to be done into the smallest possible independent tasks, such as marking a single object. However, while such fine granularity might lead to a perfect balancing of tasks between processors since whenever a task was available any processor wanting work could claim it, the cost of coordinating processors makes this impractical. Synchronisation is needed both for correctness and to avoid, or at least minimise, repeating work. There are two aspects to correctness. It is essential to prevent parallel execution of garbage collector threads from corrupting either the heap or a collector's own data structures. Consider two examples. Any moving collector must ensure that only a single thread copies an object. If two threads were to copy it simultaneously, in the best case (where the object is immutable) space would be wasted, but the worst case risks the two replicas being updated later with conflicting values. Safeguarding the collector's own data structures is also essential. If all threads were to share a single marking stack, then all push and pop operations would have to be synchronised in order to avoid losing work when more than one thread manipulates the stack pointer or adds/removes entries.

Synchronisation between the collector threads has time and space overheads. Mechanisms to ensure exclusive access may use locks or wait-free data structures. Well-designed algorithms minimise the occasions on which synchronisation operations are needed, for example by using thread-local data structures. Where synchronisation is required, the fast case should be the common case: locks should be rarely contended and atomic operations like compare-and-swap should be expected to succeed. If they do not succeed, it is often preferable that they are allowed to compete for other work in a wait-free manner rather than having to retry. However, sometimes exclusive access is not essential for correctness and so some synchronisation actions can be omitted. For example, setting a mark bit in an object's header word is an idempotent operation. The only consequence of two threads setting the same bit is the risk of some unnecessary work, but this may be cheaper than the cost of making the action synchronised.

Implementations trade load balancing against coordination costs. Modern parallel collectors typically have worker threads compete to acquire larger tasks that they expect to complete without further synchronisation. These tasks may be organised in a variety of ways: as thread-local marking stacks, as heap regions to scan or as other pools of (usually fixed-size) buffers of work. Of course, employing such data structures also incurs a space cost on account of their metadata and fragmentation, but these costs tend to be small.

14.4 Taxonomy

In the rest of this chapter, we will consider particular solutions to the problems of parallelising marking, sweeping, copying and compaction. Throughout we assume that all mutator threads are halted at GC safe-points while the collector threads run to completion. As far as possible, we situate these case studies within a consistent framework. In all cases, we shall be interested in how the algorithms *acquire*, *perform* and *generate* collection work. The design and implementation of these three activities determines what synchronisation is necessary, the granularity of the workloads for individual collector threads and how these loads are balanced between processors.

Parallel garbage collection algorithms can be broadly categorised as either *processor-centric* or *memory-centric*. Processor-centric algorithms tend to have threads acquire work quanta that vary in size, typically by stealing work from other threads. Little regard is given to the location of the objects that are to be processed. However, as we have seen in earlier chapters, locality has significant effects on performance, even in the context of a uniprocessor. Its importance is even greater for non-uniform memory or heterogeneous architectures. Memory-centric algorithms, on the other hand, take locality into greater account. They typically operate on contiguous blocks of heap memory and acquire/release work from/to shared pools of buffers of work; these buffers are likely to be of a fixed size. These are most likely to be used by parallel copying collectors.

Finally, we are concerned with the termination of parallel collection. Threads not only acquire work to do but also generate further work dynamically. Thus, it is usually insufficient to detect termination of a collection cycle by, say, simply checking that a shared pool of work is empty, since an active thread may be about to add further tasks to that pool.

14.5 Parallel marking

Marking comprises three activities: acquisition of an object to process from a work list, testing and setting one or more marks and generating further marking work by adding the object's children to a work list. All known parallel marking algorithms are processor-centric. No synchronisation is necessary to acquire an object to trace if the work list is thread-local and non-empty. Otherwise, the thread must acquire work (one or more objects) atomically, either from some other thread's work list or from some global list. Atomicity is chiefly necessary to maintain the integrity of the list from which the work is acquired. Marking an object more than once or adding its children to more than one work list only affects performance rather than correctness in a non-moving collector. Although the worst case is that another thread might redundantly process an entire data structure in lockstep with the first collector thread, such scheduling is unlikely to occur in practice. Thus, if an object's mark is represented by a bit in its header or by a byte in a byte map, it can be tested and set with a non-atomic load and store. However, if marks are stored in a bitmap that is shared between marking threads, then the bit must be set with an atomic operation. The object's children can be added to the marking list without synchronisation if the list is private and unbounded. Synchronisation is necessary if the list is shared or if it is bounded. In the latter case, some marking work must be transferred to a global list whenever the local list is filled. If the object is a very large array of pointers, pushing all its children onto a work list as a single task may induce some load imbalance. Some collectors, especially those for real-time systems, process the slots of large objects incrementally, often by representing a large object as a linked data structure rather than a single contiguous array of elements or by breaking the work into separate portions.

Work stealing. Many parallel marking algorithms, including most of those we shall consider in this and the next few chapters, use *work stealing* to balance loads (early examples include Endo *et al.* [1997], Flood *et al.* [2001] and Siebert [2010]). Whenever a thread runs out of marking work, it steals work belonging to another thread. In a parallel implementation of the Boehm and Weiser [1988] conservative mark-sweep collector, Endo *et al.* provide each marker thread with its own local mark stack and a *stealable work queue* (Algorithm 14.1), an idea whose value was confirmed by Horie *et al.* [2018]. Periodically, each thread checks its own stealable mark queue and, if it is empty, transfers all its private mark stack (apart from local roots) to the queue. An idle thread acquires marking work by first examining its own stealable queue and then other threads' queues. When a thread finds a non-empty queue, it steals half of the queue's entries into its own mark stack. Multiple threads may seek work to steal at the same time, so the stealable queues are protected by locks. Endo *et al.* found that a claim-lock-then-steal approach led to processors spending considerable time trying to acquire locks so they replaced it by a try-lock-then-steal-else-skip strategy. If a thread observes that a queue is locked or if it fails to lock the queue, it gives up on that queue and skips to the next one. This sequence is 'lock-free'. Horie *et al.* [2018, 2019] explored refinements of this approach.

Any parallel collector needs to take care with how mark bitmaps are treated and how large arrays are processed. Bits in a mark bitmap word must be set atomically. Rather than locking the word then testing the bit, Endo *et al.* use a simple load to test the bit and only if it is not set attempt to set it atomically, retrying if the set fails (because bits are only set in this phase, only a limited number of retries are needed), illustrated in Algorithm 14.2. Collectors like that of Flood *et al.* [2001], which store the mark bit in the object header, can of course mark without atomic operations, though.

Processing large arrays of pointers has been observed to be a source of problems. Boehm and Weiser [1988] tried to avoid mark stack overflow by pushing large objects in smaller (128 word) portions. Similarly, Endo *et al.* split a large object into 512-byte sections before adding them to a stack or queue in order to improve load balancing; here, the stack or queue holds ⟨address, size⟩ pairs.

The Flood *et al.* [2001] parallel generational collector manages its young generation by copying and its old generation by mark-compact collection. In this section, we only consider parallel marking. Whereas Endo *et al.* used a stack *and* a stealable queue per processor, Flood *et al.* use just a single deque per collector thread. Their lock-free, work

Algorithm 14.1: The Endo *et al.* [1997] parallel mark-sweep algorithm

```
 1  shared stealableWorkQueue[N]                          /* one per thread */
 2  me ← myThreadId
 3
 4  acquireWork():
 5      if not isEmpty(myMarkStack)              /* my mark stack has work to do */
 6          return
 7      lock(stealableWorkQueue[me])
 8      /* grab half of my stealable work queue */
 9      n ← size(stealableWorkQueue[me]) / 2
10      transfer(stealableWorkQueue[me], n, myMarkStack)
11      unlock(stealableWorkQueue[me])
12
13      if isEmpty(myMarkStack)
14          for each j in Threads
15              if not locked(stealableWorkQueue[j])
16                  if lock(stealableWorkQueue[j])
17                      /* grab half of his stealable work queue */
18                      n ← size(stealableWorkQueue[j]) / 2
19                      transfer(stealableWorkQueue[j], n, myMarkStack)
20                      unlock(stealableWorkQueue[j])
21                      return
22
23  performWork():
24      while pop(myMarkStack, ref)
25          for each fld in Pointers(ref)
26              child ← *fld
27              if child ≠ null && not isMarked(child)
28                  setMarked(child)
29                  push(myMarkStack, child)
30
31
32  generateWork():              /* transfer all my stack to my stealable work queue */
33      if isEmpty(stealableWorkQueue[me])
34          n ← size(markStack)
35          lock(stealableWorkQueue[me])
36          transfer(myMarkStack, n, stealableWorkQueue[me])
37          unlock(stealableWorkQueue[me])
```

Algorithm 14.2: Parallel marking with a bitmap

```
 1  setMarked(ref):
 2      oldByte ← markByte(ref)
 3      bitPosition ← markBit(ref)
 4      loop
 5          if isMarked(oldByte, bitPosition)
 6              return
 7          newByte ← mark(oldByte, bitPosition)
 8          if CompareAndSet(&markByte(ref), oldByte, newByte)
 9              return
```

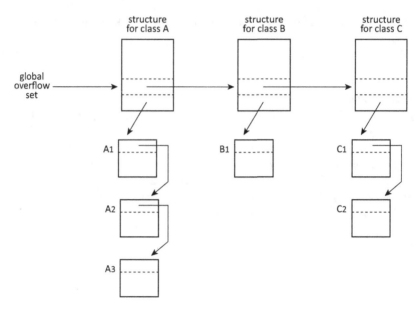

Figure 14.2: Global overflow set implemented as a list of lists [Flood *et al.*, 2001]. The class structure for each Java class holds the head of a list of overflow objects of that type, linked through the class pointer field in their header.

stealing algorithm is based on that of Arora *et al.* [1998]; its low overhead allows work to be balanced at the level of individual objects. The algorithm works as follows (see also the detailed presentation in Section 13.8). A thread treats the bottom of its deque as its mark stack; its push does not require synchronisation and its pop operation only requires synchronisation to claim the last element of the deque. Threads without work steal an object from the top of other threads' deques using the synchronised remove operation. One advantage of this work stealing design is that the synchronisation mechanism, with its concomitant overheads, is only activated when it is needed to balance loads. In contrast, other approaches (such as *grey packets*, which we discuss below) may have their load balancing mechanism permanently 'turned on'.

The Flood *et al.* thread deques are fixed size in order to avoid having to allocate during a collection. However, this risks overflow, so they provide a global overflow set with just a small, per class, overhead. The class structure for each Java class C is made to hold a list of all the overflow objects of this class, linked together through their type fields (illustrated in Figure 14.2). Although the overflow link overwrites the object's type — making this design inappropriate for a concurrent collector where mutators need quick access to the object's type — it can be recovered as the object is removed from the overflow list. Overflow is handled as follows. Whenever pushing an item onto the bottom of a thread's deque would cause it to overflow, items in the bottom half of the deque are moved into the overflow sets of their classes. Conversely, threads looking for work try to fill half of their deque from the overflow set before trying to steal from other threads' deques.

Siebert [2010] also uses work stealing for a parallel and concurrent implementation of the *Jamaica* real-time Java virtual machine. Jamaica breaks objects into linked blocks in order to bound the time of any mark step; thus, the collector works with blocks rather than objects. One consequence is that colours are associated with blocks. As we shall see in Chapter 15, concurrent mutators and collectors may both need to access lists of grey blocks. In order to avoid having to synchronise such accesses, the Jamaica virtual

Algorithm 14.3: The Flood *et al.* [2001] parallel mark-sweep algorithm

```
 1   shared overflowSet
 2   shared deque[N]                                          /* one per thread */
 3   me ← myThreadId
 4
 5   acquireWork():
 6       if not isEmpty(deque[me])
 7           return
 8       n ← size(overflowSet) / 2
 9       if transfer(overflowSet, n, deque[me])
10           return
11       for each j in Threads
12           ref ← remove(deque[j])                           /* try to steal from j */
13           if ref ≠ null
14               push(deque[me], ref)
15               return
16
17   performWork():
18       loop
19           ref ← pop(deque[me])
20           if ref = null
21               return
22           for each fld in Pointers(ref)
23               child ← *fld
24               if child ≠ null && not isMarked(child)
25                   setMarked(child)
26                   if not push(deque[me], child)
27                       n ← size(deque[me]) / 2
28                       transfer(deque[me], n, overflowSet)
29
30   generateWork():
31       /* nop */
```

machine uses processor-local grey lists. The cost of this design is that a block's colour is represented by a *word* rather than a few bits. A thread marks a block grey by using a compare-and-swap operation to link it through this colour word into a *local* grey list of the processor on which the thread is running. To balance loads, Siebert steals other threads' work lists wholesale: a thread without work attempts to steal *all* of another thread's grey list. To prevent two threads from working on the same grey block, a new colour *anthracite* is introduced for blocks while they are being scanned in a mark step. Thief threads also steal by attempting to change the colour of the head of the grey list of another processor to anthracite. This mechanism is very coarse, and best suited to the case that the victim thread is not performing any collection work but maybe only adding blocks to its grey list as it executes write barriers. This is a plausible scenario for a real-time, concurrent collector. However, if all threads are collecting garbage, it may degrade to a situation where all threads compete for a single remaining list of grey blocks. Siebert writes that this does not occur often in practice.

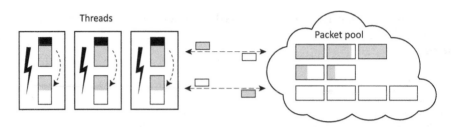

Figure 14.3: Grey packets. Each thread exchanges an empty packet for a packet of references to trace. Marking fills an empty packet with new references to trace; when it is full, the thread exchanges it with the global pool for another empty packet.

Termination with work stealing. Finally, the collector must be able to determine when a phase is complete, that is, when all the cooperating threads have completed their activities. Endo *et al.* [1997] originally tried to detect termination with a single global count of the number of mark stacks and stealable mark queues that were empty. However, contention to update this counter atomically serialised termination, with large systems (32 processors or more) spending a significant amount of time acquiring the lock. Their solution, presented in detail in Algorithm 13.18, was to provide each processor with two flags indicating whether their mark stack or queue was empty: no locks are necessary to set or clear these flags. To detect termination, a processor clears a global *detection-interrupted* flag and checks through all the other processors' flags. Finally, it checks the detection-interrupted flag again in case any other processor has reset it and started work. If not, termination is complete. This method required a strict protocol to be followed when a processor A steals all the tasks of processor B. First, A must clear its stack-empty flag, then set the detection-interrupted flag and finally B's queue-empty flag. Unfortunately, as Petrank and Kolodner [2004] point out, this protocol is flawed if more than one thread is allowed to detect termination, since a second detector thread may clear the detection-interrupted flag after the first detector thread has set it, thus fooling the first detector thread into believing that the flag remained clear throughout.

Petrank and Kolodner employ a solution common to many concurrency problems. They ensure that only one thread at a time can try to detect termination by introducing a lock: a synchronised, global, *detector-identity* word. Before attempting to detect termination, a thread must check that the detector-identity's is -1 (meaning that no thread is currently trying to detect termination) and, if so, try to set its own identity into the word atomically, or else wait. .

Flood *et al.* detect termination through a status word, with one bit for each participating thread, which must be updated atomically. Initially, all threads' statuses are active. When a thread has no work to do (and has not been able to steal any), it sets its status bit to be inactive and loops, checking whether all the status word's bits are off. If so, all threads have offered to terminate and the collection phase is complete. Otherwise, the thread peeks at other threads' queues, looking for work to steal. If it finds stealable work, it sets its status bit to active and tries to steal. If it fails to steal, it reverts the bit to inactive and loops again. This technique clearly does not scale to a number of threads beyond the number of bits in a word. Peter Kessler suggested using a count of active threads instead [Flood *et al.*, 2001].

Grey packets. Ossia *et al.* observe that mark stacks with work stealing is a technique best employed when the number of threads participating in a collection is known in advance

[Ossia *et al.*, 2002; Barabash *et al.*, 2005]. This will not be the case if each *mutator* thread also helps by performing a small increment of work, say at each allocation. They also note that it may be difficult both for a thread to choose the best queue from which to steal, and to detect termination. Instead, they balance work loads by having each thread compete for packets of marking work to perform. Their system had a fixed number (1,000) of packets available, and each packet was a fixed size (512 entries).

Each thread uses two packets; it processes entries in its input packet and adds work to be done to its output packet. Under the tricolour abstraction, the entries in both packets are grey, hence, we adopt the name *grey packets*, originally coined by Thomas *et al.* [1998] for Insignia's Jeode Java virtual machine.[1] A thread competes to acquire a new packet of work from the global pool. After processing all the entries in the packet, it returns that packet to the pool. When its output packet is full, it returns it to the pool and obtains a fresh packet. Ossia *et al.* maintain three linked lists of packets: a pool of empty packets, a pool of less than half full packets and a pool of nearly full packets, as illustrated in Figure 14.3. Threads prefer to obtain their input packet from the highest occupancy, non-empty list (procedure getInPacket in Algorithm 14.4), and their output packet from the lowest occupancy, non-empty list (procedure getOutPacket).

Grey packets offer a number of advantages. By separating input from output — Ossia *et al.* avoid swapping the roles of a thread's packets — work is distributed evenly between processors as a processor will tend not to consume its own output. Since a grey packet contains a queue of objects that will be processed in sequence, grey packets naturally support prefetching the next object to be marked. On the other hand, if threads do not consume their own output, threads miss out on the opportunity to process entries that are likely to be already in their cache.

Grey packets only require synchronisation when packets are acquired from or returned to the global lists. These operations are non-blocking if we use a compare-and-swap operation (with the thread's identifier added to the head of the list to avoid an ABA problem). They also reduce the number of fences that have to be inserted on architectures with weakly-ordered memory consistency. Rather than having to fence after marking and pushing each object, a fence is only required when a thread acquires or returns packets. Ossia *et al.* use a vector of *allocation bits* when they conservatively scan thread stacks in order to determine whether a putative reference really does point to an allocated object. Their allocation bits are also used for synchronisation between mutators and collectors. Their allocators use local allocation buffers. On local allocation buffer-overflow, the allocator performs a fence and then sets the allocation bits for all the objects in that local allocation buffer, thus ensuring that the stores to allocate and initialise new objects cannot precede the stores to set their allocation bits (Algorithm 14.5). Two further fences are needed. First, when a tracing thread acquires a new input packet, it tests the allocation bits of every object in the new packet, recording in a private data structure whether an object is safe to trace — its allocation bit has been set — or not. The thread then fences before continuing to trace all the safe objects in the input packet. Tracing unsafe objects is deferred; instead, they are added to a third, deferred, packet. At some point, this packet may be returned to a global pool of deferred packets. This protocol ensures that an object cannot be traced before its allocation bit has been loaded and found to be set. A tracing thread also fences when it returns its output packet to the global pool (in order to prevent the stores to the packet being reordered with respect to adding the packet back to the global pool). A fence is not needed for this purpose when getting an input packet since there is a data dependency between loading the pointer to the packet and accessing its contents, an ordering that most hardware respects.

---

[1]However, the first publication of this idea, other than through a patent application, was by Ossia *et al.* [2002].

Algorithm 14.4: Grey packet management

```
 1   shared fullPool                              /* global pool of full packets */
 2   shared halfFullPool                       /* global pool of half–full packets */
 3   shared emptyPool                           /* global pool of empty packets */
 4
 5   getInPacket():
 6       atomic
 7           inPacket ← remove(fullPool)
 8       if isEmpty(inPacket)
 9           atomic
10               inPacket ← remove(halfFullPool)
11       if isEmpty(inPacket)
12           inPacket, outPacket ← outPacket, inPacket
13       return not isEmpty(inPacket)
14
15   testAndMarkSafe(packet):
16       for each ref in packet
17           safe(ref) ← allocBit(ref) = true            /* private data structure */
18
19
20   getOutPacket():
21       if isFull(outPacket)
22           generateWork()
23       if outPacket = null
24           atomic
25               outPacket ← remove(emptyPool)
26       if outPacket = null
27           atomic
28               outPacket ← remove(halfFullPool)
29       if outPacket = null
30           if not isFull(inPacket)
31               inPacket, outPacket ← outPacket, inPacket
32               return
33
34   addOutPacket(ref):
35       getOutPacket()
36       if outPacket = null || isFull(outPacket)
37           dirtyCard(ref)
38       else
39           add(outPacket, ref)
```

Algorithm 14.5: Parallel allocation with grey packets

```
 1  sequentialAllocate(n):
 2      result ← free
 3      newFree ← result + n
 4      if newFree ≤ labLimit
 5          free ← newFree
 6          return result
 7
 8      /* LAB overflow */
 9      fence                                                        $
10      for each obj in lab
11          allocBit(obj) ← true
12      lab, labLimit ← newLAB()
13      if lab = null
14          return null                  /* signal 'Memory exhausted' */
15      sequentialAllocate(n)
```

Algorithm 14.6: Parallel tracing with grey packets

```
 1  shared fullPool                              /* global pool of full packets */
 2
 3  acquireWork():
 4      if isEmpty(inPacket)
 5          if getInPacket()
 6              testAndMarkSafe(inPacket)
 7              fence                                                $
 8
 9  performWork():
10      for each ref in inPacket
11          if safe(ref)
12              for each fld in Pointers(ref)
13                  child ← *fld
14                  if child ≠ null && not isMarked(child)
15                      setMarked(child)
16                      addOutPacket(child)
17          else
18              addDeferredPacket(ref)          /* defer tracing unsafe objects */
19
20  generateWork():
21      fence                                                        $
22      add(fullPool, outPacket)
23      outPacket ← null
```

Grey packets make it comparatively easy to track state. Each global pool has an associated count of the number of packets it contains, updated by an atomic operation after a packet is acquired or returned. Counting the number of packets is only approximate since the count may be read after a packet has been returned but before the counter has been incremented. However, the termination condition is simply that the size of the empty packet pool is the same as the total number of packets available. It is not necessary to make acquisition/return of a packet and the update of the counter a single, indivisible operation provided that threads observe the following discipline. In order to ensure that the empty count cannot drop to zero temporarily, each thread must obtain a new packet *before* it replaces the old one. Requiring a thread to obtain its input packet before its output packet at the start of a collection will ensure that attempts to acquire work packets when no tracing work remains will not prevent termination detection.

Grey packets limit the depth of the total mark queue, making it possible that marking may overflow. If a thread cannot obtain an output packet with vacant entries, it may swap the roles of its input and output packets. If both are full, some overflow mechanism is required. Ossia *et al.* continue to mark objects without adding them to an output packet, but when this happens they dirty the card table slots corresponding to these objects. Later, they scan the card table and continue marking from any marked object with unmarked children. An alternative would be to link overflow objects to the class structures corresponding to their type, as Flood *et al.* [2001] did.

Channels. Wu and Li [2007] suggest an architecture for load balancing on large-scale servers that does not require expensive atomic operations. Instead, threads exchange marking tasks through single writer, single reader channels (recall Algorithm 13.34), as shown in Algorithm 14.7. In a system with P marking threads, each thread has an array of $P - 1$ queues, implemented as circular buffers; null indicates that a slot in the buffer is empty. It is the restriction to one reader and one writer that allows this architecture to avoid the expense of atomic operations. It performed better than the Flood *et al.* [2001] work stealing algorithm on servers with a large number of processors.

Similar to the strategy used by Endo *et al.* [1997], threads proactively give up tasks to other threads. When a thread i generates a new task, it first checks whether any other thread j needs work and, if so, adds the task to the output channel $\langle i \to j \rangle$. Otherwise, it pushes the task onto its own marking stack. If its stack is empty, it takes a task from some input channel $\langle j \to i \rangle$. Unfortunately, a thread that is not generating any new marking tasks will not be able to keep other threads busy. In this case, the thread *drips* a task from the bottom (oldest end) of its local stack into the channel. Wu and Li report that this load balancing strategy can keep all threads busy. The choice of queue length will depend on how busily threads use their local mark stacks or whether they have to seek tasks. If threads do not often have to seek work, then shorter queues will be preferred. On a machine with 16 Intel Xeon processors, queues of length one or two were found to scale best. They use a termination detection solution similar to that of Petrank and Kolodner [2004], but select a *fixed* detector thread in order to avoid the conflicting detector problem.

14.6   Parallel copying

Parallelisation of copying algorithms faces many of the same issues faced by parallelisation of marking algorithms. However, as we noted earlier, it is essential that an object is copied only once whereas marking an object two or more times is often benign. We consider processor-centric and then memory-centric techniques.

Algorithm 14.7: Parallel tracing with channels

```
 1  shared channel[N,N]                    /* N×N single reader, single writer channels */
 2  me ← myThreadId
 3
 4  acquireWork():
 5      for each k in Threads
 6          if not isEmpty(channel[k,me])              /* k has work for me */
 7              ref ← remove(channel[k,me])
 8              push(myMarkStack, ref)                 /* onto my mark stack */
 9              return
10
11  performWork():
12      loop
13          if isEmpty(myMarkStack)
14              return
15          ref ← pop(myMarkStack)
16          for each fld in Pointers(ref)
17              child ← *fld
18              if child ≠ null && not isMarked(child)
19                  if not generateWork(child)  /* drip a task to another processor */
20                      push(myMarkStack, child)
21
22  generateWork(ref):
23      for each j in Threads
24          if needsWork(j) && not isFull(channel[me,j])
25              add(channel[me,j], ref)
26              return true
27      return false
```

Processor-centric techniques

Dividing work among processors. Blelloch and Cheng parallelise copying in the context of *replicating collection* [Blelloch and Cheng, 1999; Cheng and Blelloch, 2001; Cheng, 2001]. We discuss replicating collection in detail in Chapter 17 but, in brief, replicating collectors are incremental or concurrent collectors that copy live objects while the mutators are running, taking special care to fix up the values of any fields that a mutator might have changed during the course of a collection cycle. In this chapter, we only discuss the parallelism aspects of their design.

Each copying thread is given its own stack of work to do. Blelloch and Cheng claim that stacks offer easier synchronisation between copying threads and less fragmentation than Cheney queues (but we examine Cheney-style parallel copying collectors below). Load is balanced by having threads periodically transfer work between their local stacks and a shared stack (see Algorithm 14.8). As we noted earlier, a simple shared stack requires synchronisation between threads pushing and popping entries. Unfortunately, there is no way to increment or decrement a stack pointer and insert or remove a stack element atomically using primitive operations like fetch-and-add. A lock or use of load-linked/store-conditionally operations or transactional memory would sequentialise access to the shared stack, as shown in Section 13.8. However, we can use these instructions either to allow multiple threads to push elements or to allow multiple threads to pop elements, since

Algorithm 14.8: Parallel copying in Cheng and Blelloch [2001]

```
 1  shared sharedStack                              /* the shared stack of work */
 2  myCopyStack[k]                                  /* local stack has k slots max.*/
 3  sp ← 0                                          /* local stack pointer */
 4
 5  while not terminated()
 6      enterRoom()                                 /* enter pop room */
 7      for i ← 1 to k
 8          if isLocalStackEmpty()
 9              acquireWork()
10              if isLocalStackEmpty()
11                  break
12          performWork()
13      transitionRooms()
14      generateWork()
15      if exitRoom()                               /* leave push room */
16          terminate()
17
18  acquireWork():
19      sharedPop()                                 /* move work from shared stack */
20
21  performWork():
22      ref ← localPop()
23      scan(ref)                                   /* see Algorithm 4.2 */
24
25  generateWork():
26      sharedPush()                                /* move work to shared stack */
27
28  isLocalStackEmpty()
29      return sp = 0
30
31  localPush(ref):
32      myCopyStack[sp++] ← ref
33
34  localPop():
35      return myCopyStack[--sp]
36
37  sharedPop():                                    /* move work from shared stack */
38      cursor ← FetchAndAdd(&sharedStack, 1)       /* try to grab from shared stack */
39      if cursor ≥ stackLimit                      /* shared stack empty */
40          FetchAndAdd(&sharedStack, −1)           /* readjust stack */
41      else
42          myCopyStack[sp++] ← cursor[0]           /* move work to local stack */
43
44  sharedPush():                                   /* move work to shared stack */
45      cursor ← FetchAndAdd(&sharedStack, −sp) − sp
46      for i ← 0 to sp−1
47          cursor[i] ← myCopyStack[i]
48      sp ← 0
```

Algorithm 14.9: Push/pop synchronisation with rooms

```
 1   shared gate ← OPEN
 2   shared popClients                    /* number of clients currently in the pop room */
 3   shared pushClients                   /* number of clients currently in the push room */
 4
 5   enterRoom():
 6       while gate ≠ OPEN
 7           /* do nothing: wait */
 8       FetchAndAdd(&popClients, 1)                           /* try to start popping */
 9       while gate ≠ OPEN
10           FetchAndAdd(&popClients, −1)           /* back out since did not succeed */
11           while gate ≠ OPEN
12               /* do nothing: wait */
13           FetchAndAdd(&popClients, 1)                              /* try again */
14
15
16   transitionRooms():
17       gate ← CLOSED
18       FetchAndAdd(&pushClients, 1)              /* move from popping to pushing */
19       FetchAndAdd(&popClients, −1)
20       while popClients > 0
21           /* do nothing: cannot start pushing until none other popping */
22
23   exitRoom():
24       pushers ← FetchAndAdd(&pushClients, −1) − 1      /* stop pushing */
25       if pushers = 0                /* I was last in push room: check termination */
26           if isEmpty(sharedStack)                        /* no grey objects left */
27               gate ← OPEN
28               return true
29           else
30               gate ← OPEN
31               return false
```

these operations either all advance or all retreat the stack pointer. Once a thread has succeeded in moving the stack pointer (possibly by several slots), it can read from or write to those stack slots without risk of any races.

Blelloch and Cheng [1999] enforce such a discipline on access to the shared stack using what they later called 'rooms': at any time, at least one of the pushing room and the popping room must be empty. The algorithm is shown in Algorithm 14.9. At each iteration of the collection loop, a thread first enters the pop room and performs a fixed amount of work. It obtains slots to scan either from its own local stack or from the shared stack with a fetch-and-add. Any new work generated is added to its stack. The thread then leaves the pop room and waits until all other threads have also left the room before it tries to enter the push room. The first thread to enter the push room closes the gate to prevent any other thread entering the pop room. Once in the push room, the thread empties its local stack entirely onto the shared stack, again using fetch-and-add to reserve space on the stack. The last thread to leave the push room opens the gate.

The problem here is that any processor waiting to enter the push room must wait until all those in the pop room have finished greying their objects. The time to grey objects is considerable compared to fetching or depositing new work, and a processor trying to transition to the push phase must wait for all others already in the pop phase to finish greying their objects. Large variations in the time for different processors to grey their objects makes this idle time significant. A more relaxed abstraction would allow processors to leave the pop room without going into the push room. Since greying objects is not related to the shared stack, that work can be done outside the rooms. This greatly increases the chance that the pop room is empty and so a thread can move to the push room.

The original Blelloch and Cheng room abstraction allows straightforward termination detection. Each thread's local tracing stack will be empty when it leaves the push room, so the last thread to leave should detect whether the shared stack is also empty. However, the relaxed definition means that collection threads may be working outside the rooms. With this abstraction, the shared stack must maintain a global counter of how many threads have borrowed objects from it. The last thread to leave the push room must check whether this counter is zero as well as whether the shared stack is empty.

Copying objects in parallel. To ensure that only one thread copies an object, threads must race to copy an object and install a forwarding address in the old version's header. How threads copy an object depends on whether or not they share a single allocation region. By sharing a single region, threads avoid some wastage but at the cost of having to use an atomic operation to allocate. In this case, Blelloch and Cheng [1999] have threads race to write a 'busy' value in the object's forwarding pointer slot. The winning thread copies the object before overwriting the slot with the address of the replica; losing threads must spin until they observe a valid pointer value in the slot. An alternative, if each thread knows where it will copy an object (for example, because it will copy into its own local allocation buffer), is for threads to attempt to write the forwarding address atomically into the slot before they copy the object.

Marlow *et al.* [2008] compared two approaches in the context of the GHC Haskell system. In the first approach, a thread trying to copy an object first tests whether it has been forwarded. If it has, it simply returns the forwarding address. Otherwise, it attempts to compare-and-swap a busy value into the forwarding address word; this value should be distinguishable from either a 'normal' value to be expected in that slot (such as a lock or a hash code) or a valid forwarding address. If the operation succeeds, the thread copies the object, writes the address of its tospace replica into the slot and then returns this address. If the busy compare-and-swap fails, the thread spins until the winning thread has completed copying the object. In their second approach, they avoid spinning by having threads optimistically copy the object and then compare-and-swap the forwarding address. If the compare-and-swap fails, the copy must be retracted (for example, by returning the thread's free pointer to its original value). They found that this latter approach offered little benefit since collisions were rare. Marlow *et al.* [2009] found that copying immutable objects non-atomically, with the small but safe risk that some may be duplicated, significantly improved performance. Most Haskell objects are immutable but, although Haskell is a pure functional language, there are exceptions such as thunks and mutable arrays.

The collector built by Flood *et al.* [2001] that we discussed earlier in this chapter is generational. Its old generation was managed by mark-compact and its young generation by copying; both algorithms are parallel. Above, we discussed how they parallelise marking; here, we consider how they parallelise copying collection. The same work stealing queues are used once again to hold the list of objects to be scanned. However, parallel copying collection faces two challenges that parallel marking does not. First, it is desirable to minimise contention to allocate space for the copy and, second, it is essential that a live object

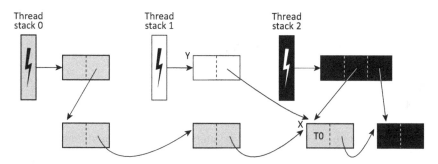

Figure 14.4: Dominant-thread tracing. Threads 0 to 2, coloured grey, white and black, respectively, have traced a graph of objects. Each object is coloured to indicate the processor to which it will be copied. The first field of each object is its header. Thread T0 was the last to lock object X.

is copied only once. Contention for space is minimised through the use of thread-local allocation buffers (see Section 7.7), both for copying to survivor spaces in the young generation and for promoting to the old generation. To copy an object, a thread makes a speculative allocation in its local allocation buffer and then attempts to compare-and-swap the forwarding pointer. If it succeeds, the thread copies the object. If the compare-and-swap fails, it will return the forwarding pointer that the winning thread installed.

As we have seen throughout this book, locality has a significant impact on performance. This is likely to become increasingly important for multiprocessors with non-uniform memory architectures. Here, the ideal is to place objects close to the processor that will use them most. Modern operating systems support standard *memory affinity policies*, used to determine the processor from which memory will be reserved. Typically, a policy may be *first-touch* or *local*, in which case memory is allocated from the processor running the thread that requested it, or *round-robin*, where memory allocation is striped across all processors. A processor-affinity thread scheduler will help preserve locality properties by attempting to schedule a thread to the last processor on which it ran. Ogasawara [2009] observes that, even with a local-processor policy, a memory manager that is unaware of a non-uniform memory architecture may not place objects appropriately. If local allocation buffers are smaller than a page and are handed out to threads linearly, then some threads will have to allocate in remote memory, particularly if the system is configured to use the operating system's large page (16 megabytes) feature to reduce the cost of local to physical address translation. Further, collectors that move objects will not respect their affinity.

In contrast, Ogasawara's memory manager is aware of non-uniform memory access and so splits the heap into segments of one or more pages. Each segment is mapped to a single processor. The allocator, used by both mutator and collector threads, preferentially obtains blocks of memory from the preferred processor. For the mutator, this will be the processor on which the thread is running. The collector threads always try to evacuate live objects to memory associated with their preferred processor. Since the thread that allocated an object may not be the one that accesses it most frequently, the collector also uses *dominant-thread* information to determine each object's preferred processor. First, for objects directly referred to from the stack of a mutator thread, this will be the processor on which that mutator thread was running; it may be necessary for mutator threads to update the identity of their preferred processor periodically. Second, the collector can use object locking information to identify the *dominant* thread. Locking schemes often leave the locking thread's identity in a word in the object's header. Although this only identifies the thread, and hence the preferred processor, that *last* locked the object, this is likely to be

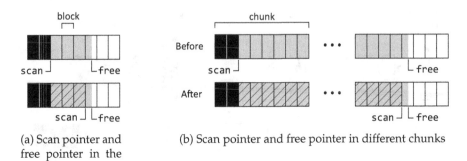

(a) Scan pointer and free pointer in the same chunk

(b) Scan pointer and free pointer in different chunks

Figure 14.5: Chunk management in the Imai and Tick [1993] parallel copying collector, showing selection of a scan block before (above) and after (below) overflow. Hatching denotes blocks that have been added to the global pool.

a sufficient approximation, especially as many objects never escape their allocating thread (although they may still be locked). Finally, the collector can propagate the preferred processor from parent objects to their children. In the example in Figure 14.4, three threads are marking. For simplicity, we assume they are all running on their preferred processor, identified in the figure by different colours. Thread T0 has at some time locked object X, indicated by writing its thread number in X's header. Each object has been coloured to indicate the processor to which a collector thread will copy it.

Memory-centric techniques

Per-thread fromspace and tospace. Copying collection lends itself naturally to a division of labour based on objects' locations. A simple solution to parallelising copying collection is to give each Cheney-style collector its own fromspace and tospace [Halstead, 1984]. In this way, each thread has its own contiguous chunk of memory to scan but still competes with other threads to copy objects and install forwarding pointers. However, this very simple design not only risks poor load balancing as one processor may run out of work while others are still busy, but also requires some mechanism to handle the case that one thread's tospace overflows although there is unused space in other tospaces.

Block-structured heaps. An obvious solution is to over-partition tospace and then allow threads to compete to claim both blocks to scan and blocks for copying allocation. Imai and Tick [1993] divided the heap into small, fixed-size chunks, giving each copying thread its own chunks to scan and into which to copy survivors. Copying used Cheney pointers rather than explicit work lists. When a thread's copy chunk was full, it was transferred to a global pool where idle threads competed to scan it, and a fresh, empty chunk was obtained from a free-chunk manager. Two mechanisms were used to ensure good load balancing. First, the *chunks* acquired for copying (which they called 'heap extension units') were comparatively small (only 256 words). The problem with using small chunks for linear allocation is that it may lead to excessive fragmentation since, on average, we can expect to waste half an object's worth of space at the end of each chunk. To solve this, Imai and Tick used big bag of pages allocation (see Chapter 7) for small objects; consequently each thread owned N chunks for copying. Larger objects and chunks were both allocated from the shared heap using a lock.

Second, they balanced load at a granularity finer than a chunk. Each chunk was divided into smaller *blocks* (which they called 'load distribution units'). These were maybe

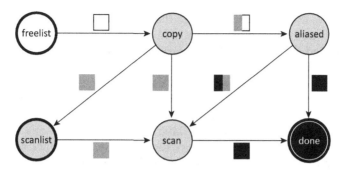

Figure 14.6: Block states and transitions in the Imai and Tick [1993] collector. Blocks in states with thick borders are part of the global pool, those with thin borders are owned by a thread.

copy	scan		
	aliased	▨ or ▆	▆
▨▮	(continue scanning)	(continue scanning)	scan → done copy → aliased
☐	aliased → copy scanlist → scan	(continue scanning)	scan → done scanlist → scan
▆▮	aliased → copy scanlist → scan	(cannot happen)	(cannot happen)
▨	aliased → scan freelist → copy	copy → scanlist freelist → copy	scan → done copy → scan freelist → copy
▆▯	aliased → scan freelist → copy	(cannot happen)	(cannot happen)
▆	aliased → done freelist → copy scanlist → scan	(cannot happen)	(cannot happen)

Table 14.1: State transition logic for the Imai and Tick collector

as small as 32 words — smaller blocks led to better speed ups. In this algorithm, each thread offered to give up some of its unscanned blocks whenever it needed a new scan block. After scanning a slot and incrementing its scan pointer, the thread checked whether it had reached the block boundary. If so, and the next object was smaller than a block, the thread advanced its scan pointer to the start of its current copy block. This helps reduce contention on the global pool since the thread does not have to compete to acquire a scan block. It also avoids a situation whereby the only blocks containing grey objects to scan are copy blocks. If there were any unscanned blocks between the old scan block and the copy block, these were given up to the global pool for other threads to claim. Figure 14.5 shows two example scenarios. In Figure 14.5a, a thread's scan and copy blocks are in the same chunk; in Figure 14.5b, they are in different chunks. Either way, all but one of the unscanned blocks in the thread's copy and scan blocks are given up to the global pool.

If the object was larger than a block but smaller than a chunk, the scan pointer was advanced to the start of the thread's current copy *chunk*. If the object was large, the thread continued to scan it. Any large objects copied were immediately added to the global pool.

Figure 14.6 shows the states of blocks and their transitions.[2] Blocks in the states *freelist*, *scanlist* and *done* are in the global pool; blocks in the other states are local to a thread. The transitions are labelled with the possible colourings of a block when it changes state. Under the Imai and Tick scheme, a block's state can only change when the scan pointer reaches the end of a scan block, the copy pointer reaches the end of a copy block or scan reaches free (the scan block is the same as the copy block — they are aliased). For example, a block must contain at least some empty space in order to be a copy block so all transitions into the state *copy* are at least partially empty. Table 14.1 shows the actions taken, depending on the state of the copy and scan blocks. For example, if the copy block contains both grey slots and empty space (▯) and the unaliased scan block is completely black (■), then we are finished with the scan block and continue scanning in the copy block — the copy and scan blocks are now aliases of one another.

Marlow *et al.* [2008] found this block-at-a-time load balancing over-sequentialised the collector when work was scarce in GHC Haskell. For example, if a thread evacuates its roots into a single block, it will export work to other threads only when its scan and free pointers are separated by more than a block. Their solution is to export partially full blocks to the global pool whenever (i) the size of the pool is below some threshold, (ii) the thread's copy block has sufficient work to be worth exporting and (iii) its scan block has enough unscanned slots to process before it has to claim a new block to scan. The optimum minimum quantum of work to export was 128 words (for most of their benchmarks, though some benefited from much smaller quanta). This design could be expected to suffer badly from fragmentation if threads were to acquire only empty blocks for copying while exporting partially filled ones. To avoid this, they have threads prefer to acquire blocks that are partly filled rather than empty. Despite the potential for exacerbating fragmentation through objects being too large to fit in the current block and also by dividing each generation of their collector into separate steps (see Chapter 9), Marlow *et al.* found the level of fragmentation was never more than 1% of total memory.

The algorithms above provide breadth-first copying. Breadth-first copying leads to poor mutator locality as it tends to separate parents from their children, tending to co-locate distant cousins instead (see Section 4.2). Depth-first copying, on the other hand, offers better locality but at the cost of an auxiliary stack to control tracing. Moon [1984] and Wilson *et al.* [1991] introduced *hierarchical* copying algorithms that led to mostly depth-first traversal but without the cost of a stack. However, their algorithms were sequential. Siegwart and Hirzel [2006] added hierarchical decomposition to the Imai and Tick parallel copying collector to manage the young generation of IBM's J9 Java virtual machine.[3]

In the sequential hierarchical decomposition collector [Wilson *et al.*, 1991] incompletely scanned blocks were associated with two pointers, a partial scan pointer and a free space pointer. Similarly, Imai and Tick used pairs of scan and free pointers for their blocks. The trick to obtaining a hierarchical traversal of the object graph with the parallel algorithm is therefore for threads to select the 'right' blocks to use next. Like both of these collectors, Siegwart and Hirzel prefer to alias copy and scan blocks,[4] in contrast to the approach that Ossia *et al.* [2002] used where they strove to have threads hold distinct input and output packets. Unlike Imai and Tick, who defer checking whether the copy and scan blocks can be aliased until the end of a block, Siegwart and Hirzel make the check immediately after scanning a grey slot. It is this immediacy that leads to the hierarchical decomposition order of traversal of the object graph.

---

[2]This particularly clear notation is due to Siegwart and Hirzel [2006].

[3]The old generation is managed by concurrent mark-sweep with occasional stop-the-world compaction.

[4]Each thread in their generational collector holds *two* copy blocks, one for young and one for old objects; only one at a time can be aliased with the scan block.

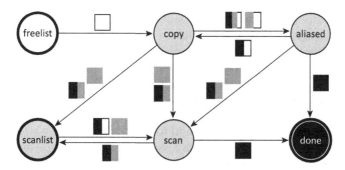

Figure 14.7: Block states and transitions in the Siegwart and Hirzel collector. Blocks in states with thick borders are part of the global pool, those with thin borders are local to a thread. A thread may retain one block of the *scanlist* in its local cache.

Siegwart and Hirzel [2006], doi: 10.1145/1133956.1133964
© 2006 Association for Computing Machinery, Inc. Reprinted by permission.

copy	scan		
	aliased	▨ or ▩	▪
▨ or ▨▯	(continue scanning)	scan → scanlist copy → aliased	scan → done copy → aliased
▯ or ▯▪	aliased → copy scanlist → scan	(continue scanning)	scan → done scanlist → scan
▨ or ▨▪	aliased → scan freelist → copy	copy → scanlist freelist → copy	scan → done copy → scan freelist → copy
▪	aliased → done freelist → copy scanlist → scan	(cannot happen)	(cannot happen)

Table 14.2: State transition logic for the Siegwart and Hirzel collector.

Siegwart and Hirzel [2006], doi: 10.1145/1133956.1133964
© 2006 Association for Computing Machinery, Inc. Reprinted by permission.

Figure 14.7 shows the states of blocks and their transitions under this scheme. As before, blocks in the states *freelist*, *scanlist* and *done* are in the global pool; blocks in the other states are local to a thread. The transitions are labelled with the possible colourings of a block when it changes state. Table 14.2 shows the actions taken, depending on the state of the copy and scan blocks. For example, if the copy block contains both grey slots and empty space (▨▯ or ▯▨) and the unaliased scan block also has grey slots, then we return the scan block to the scan list and continue scanning the copy block — the copy and scan blocks are now aliases of one another. Thus, the state transition system for Siegwart and Hirzel is a superset of that for Imai and Tick [1993].

Parallelising the algorithm places pressure on the global pool to acquire blocks to scan. For this reason, Siegwart and Hirzel have threads cache an extra scan block locally. Their blocks are also larger (128 kilobytes) than those of Imai and Tick. Thus, the transition *scanlist* → *scan* really obtains the cached block (if any), and *scan* → *scanlist* caches the block, possibly returning in its stead the previously cached block to the shared pool of blocks to be scanned. Parallel hierarchical copying is very effective in improving the spatial locality of connected objects. Most parents and children were within a page (4 kilobytes) of each other. In particular, it offers a promise of reduced translation lookaside buffer and cache miss rates. Thus, it can trade mutator speedup for collector slowdown. Whether or not this is effective depends on the application, implementation and platform.

Gidra *et al.* [2013] considered scalability of parallel copying on non-uniform memory access multicore processors. Many modern machines with more than one socket (chip) exhibit non-uniform memory access times to some degree. They examined the performance of OpenJDK's *Parallel Scavenging* collector and found two issues they addressed. One was a heavily contended lock. This they fixed by using a lock-free queue and by simplifying the initiation and termination protocol for the collector. The other issue is more to point for non-uniform memory access machines: dealing with load balancing and spatial locality. In building NAPS, the *NUMA-Aware Parallel Scavenging* collector, they first ensured that objects allocated by either a mutator or collector thread are allocated into physical memory located on that thread's processor. To do this efficiently, NAPS reserves contiguous virtual addresses on each processor large enough to hold an entire space. For example, since Parallel Scavenging uses an eden space, a fromspace, a tospace and an old space, each processor would reserve addresses for a complete eden space, a complete fromspace, and so on. However, the threads cooperate to ensure that the total amount of space actually used does not exceed the configured size of the space. They call this approach *fragmented spaces*.[5] They also looked at what they call *segregated spaces*, where collector threads only access pages local to their processor and send other pieces of work to their respective processors. They found that keeping allocation local did well, but that their segregated spaces rarely did better and was often worse.

NumaGiC [Gidra *et al.*, 2015] extends NAPS in several ways: (i) it uses the fragmented spaces idea of NAPS for the old space as well, improving parallel compaction; (ii) it partitions the card table so that each collector thread can find its own roots for a generational collection; and (iii) it has each collector thread process the stack of the mutator on the same processor. NumaGiC further implements work stealing, in a particular way. A collector thread will do only local work, called being in 'Local Mode,' until it runs out of that. Then it enters 'Stealing Mode'. When stealing, a collector thread looks for work in three places, in this order: (i) local buffers of work not yet sent to other processors; (ii) the receive side of the channels through which it sent work to other processors; and (iii) from other threads' pending work queues. When it finds work in a particular place, it keeps stealing from that place until it finds no more work to steal. A collector thread in Stealing Mode will periodically check (after every 1024 stolen objects) if it has any local work, and if so, it reverts to Local Mode. Gidra *et al.* [2015] found that NumaGiC performed better than NAPS, sometimes very much so.

Channels. Like Wu and Li [2007], Oancea *et al.* [2009] use channels to eliminate the need for atomic synchronisation operations. However, their architecture is memory-centric rather than processor-centric. It was designed to improve performance on non-uniform memory architectures although it also performs well on typical multicore platforms. The heap is divided into many more partitions than the number of processors. Each partition has its own work list, containing only references to tospace objects in that partition that need to be scanned. At any given time, at most one processor can own a given work list. The authors argue that binding work lists to memory-space semantics is likely to become increasingly hardware-friendly as the cost of inter-processor communication grows.

---

[5]*Distributed* or *striped* perhaps captures the notion better, since it is not related to 'fragmentation' as typically used in memory management.

As usual, a processor traces slots in its work lists. If it finds a reference to an object in its partition, it adds the reference to its work list. If the reference is to an object in another partition, the reference is sent to that partition. Processors exchange work through single-reader, single-writer channels. These are again implemented as fixed-size, circular buffers (see Algorithm 13.34). On Intel or AMD x86 architectures, no locks or expensive memory barriers are required to insert or remove a slot from a channel. However, architectures like the PowerPC that do not enforce strong access ordering require fences or a protocol where each slot alternates between null and non-null values. Atomic operations are only required to acquire a partition/work list. The partitions used here are larger at 32 kilobytes than those we have seen before. While a larger granularity reduces communication costs, it is less effective at load balancing than finer grained approaches.

While there is work left, each thread processes work in its incoming channels and its work list. The termination condition for a collector thread is that (i) it does not own any work list, (ii) all its input and output channels are empty, and (iii) all work lists (of all threads) are empty. On exit, each thread sets a globally visible flag. Oancea *et al.* take a pragmatic approach to the management of this collector. They use an initialisation phase that processes in parallel a number (30,000) of objects under a classical tracing algorithm and then places the resulting grey objects in their corresponding work lists, locking the partitions to do so, before distributing the work lists among the processors, and switching to the channel-based algorithm.

Card tables. Often a generational collector will use parallel copying to manage its young generation. This raises the additional question of how to deal with roots of that generation held in the remembered set. The set may be implemented with a linked list of buffers, with a hash table or with a card table. The first two cases can be handled by one of the techniques we discussed above. For example, if the set is a linked list of buffers, then loads can be balanced by having threads compete to claim the next buffer in the same way as block structured algorithms. It is more difficult to balance loads effectively with card tables. When a younger generation is collected, the parts of the heap corresponding to cards marked in the table must be scanned for possible inter-generational references. The obvious approach to parallelising card scanning would be to divide the heap into consecutive, equally sized blocks, either statically assigned to processors or which collector threads would compete to claim. However, the distribution of live objects among blocks tends to be uneven, with some blocks very densely populated and others very sparsely. Flood *et al.* [2001] found that this straightforward division of work led to uneven load balancing, as scanning the dense blocks dominated collection time. To address this, they over-partitioned the card table into N *stripes*,[6] each a set of cards separated by intervals of N cards. Thus, cards $\{0, N, 2N, \ldots\}$ comprise one stripe, cards $\{1, N + 1, 2N + 1, \ldots\}$ comprise the next, and so on. This causes dense areas to be spread across stripes. Instead of competing for blocks, threads compete to claim stripes. Iyengar *et al.* [2012a] later adopted a similar technique applied to mark bits stored in a bitmap.

14.7 Parallel sweeping

We consider next how to parallelise sweeping and compaction phases. Both share the property that the tracing work has been done, the live objects in the heap have been identified, and that this last phase is 'embarrassingly' parallel.

---

[6]They call these *strides*.

In principle, parallelising the sweep phase is straightforward: either statically partition the heap into contiguous blocks, or over-partition it and have threads compete for a block to sweep to a free-list. However, the effect of such a simple strategy is likely to be that the free-list becomes a bottleneck, sequentialising the collection. Fortunately, in any such parallel system, processors will have their own free-lists and most likely use segregated-fits allocation (see Chapter 7), so the issue of contention reduces to that of handling the return of completely free blocks to a global block allocator. Furthermore, lazy sweeping (see Chapter 2) is a naturally parallel solution to the problem of sweeping partially full blocks that balances loads according to the allocation rates of mutator threads.

The first and only step in the sweep phase of lazy sweeping is to identify completely empty blocks and return them to the block allocator. In order to reduce contention, Endo *et al.* [1997] gave each sweep thread several (for example, 64) consecutive blocks to process locally. His collector used bitmap marking, with the bitmaps held in block headers, stored separately from the blocks themselves. This makes it easy to determine whether a block is complete empty or not. Empty ones are sorted and coalesced, and added to a local free-block list. Partially full blocks are added to local reclaim lists (for example, one for each size class if segregated-fits allocation is being used) for subsequent lazy sweeping by mutator threads. Once a processor has finished with its sweep set, it merges its free-block list into the global free-block list. One remaining question is, what should a mutator thread do if it has run out of blocks on its local reclaim list and the global pool of blocks is empty? One solution is that it should steal a block from another thread. This requires synchronising the acquisition of the next block to sweep, but this is a reasonable cost to pay since acquiring a new block to sweep is less frequent than allocating a slot in a block, and we can expect contention for a block to sweep to be uncommon.

14.8   Parallel compaction

Parallelising mark-compact algorithms shares much of the issues discussed above. Live objects must be marked in parallel and then moved in parallel. However, parallel sliding compaction is simpler than parallel copying in some respects, at least in contiguous heaps. For example, once all the live objects have been marked, the destinations of objects to be moved are fixed: races only affect performance rather than correctness. After marking is complete, all compacting collectors require two or more further phases to determine the forwarding address of each object, to update references and to move objects. As we saw in Chapter 3, different algorithms may perform these tasks in different orders or even combine two tasks in a single pass over the heap.

Crammond [1988] implemented a locality-aware parallel collector for Parlog, a concurrent logic programming language. Logic programming languages benefit from preserving the order of objects in the heap. In particular, backtracking to 'choice points' is made more efficient by preserving the allocation order of objects in memory, since all memory allocated after the choice point can simply be discarded. Sliding compaction preserves the order. Crammond's collector parallelised the Morris [1978] threaded collector, which we discussed in Section 3.3; in this section, we only consider the parallelism aspects of the algorithm. Crammond reduced the cost by dividing the heap into regions associated with processors. A processor encountering an object in its own region marked and counted it without synchronisation. However, if the object was a 'remote' one, a reference to it was added to that processor's stack of indirect references and a global counter was incremented. The remote processor was responsible for processing the object and decrementing the global counter (which was used to detect termination). Thus, synchronisation (using locks) was only required for remote objects since the indirect stacks were single reader,

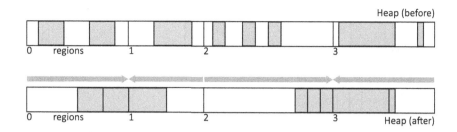

Figure 14.8: Flood *et al.* [2001] divide the heap into one region per thread and alternate the direction in which compacting threads slide live objects (shown in grey)

multiple writer structures. Crammond found that indirect references typically comprised less than 1% of the objects marked.

Flood *et al.* [2001] use parallel mark-compact to manage the old generation of their Java virtual machine. The collector uses three further phases after parallel marking (which we discussed above) to (i) calculate forwarding addresses, (ii) update references and (iii) move objects. An interesting aspect of their design is that they use different load balancing strategies for different phases of compaction. Uniprocessor compaction algorithms typically slide all live data to one end of the heap space. If multiple threads move data in parallel, then it is essential to prevent one thread from overwriting live data before another thread has moved it. For this reason, Flood *et al.* do not compact all objects into a single, dense end of the heap but instead divide the space into several regions, one for each compacting thread. Each thread slides objects in its region only. To reduce the (limited) fragmentation that this partitioning might incur, they also have threads alternate the direction in which they move objects in even- and odd-numbered regions (see Figure 14.8).

The first step is to install a forwarding pointer into the header of each live object. This will hold the address to which the object is to be moved. In this phase, they *over*-partition the space in order to improve load balancing. The space is split into M object-aligned *units*, each of roughly the same size; they found that a good choice on their eight-way UltraSPARC server was to use four times as many units as garbage collection threads, $M = 4N$. Threads compete to claim units and then count the volume of live data in each unit; to improve subsequent passes, they also coalesce adjacent garbage objects into single quasi-objects. Once they know the volume of live objects in each unit, they can partition the space into N unevenly sized *regions* that contain approximately the same amount of live data. These regions are aligned with the units of the previous pass. They also calculate the destination address of the first live object in each unit, being careful to take into account the direction in which objects in a region will slide. Collection threads then compete once again to claim units in order to install forwarding pointers in each live object of their units.

The next pass updates references to point to objects' new locations. As usual, this requires scanning mutator threads' stacks, references to objects in this heap space that are held in objects stored outside that space, as well as live objects in this space (for example, the old generation). Any suitable load balancing scheme can be used. Flood *et al.* reuse the unit partitions for scanning the space to be compacted (their old generation) although they scan the young generation as a single task. Their last phase moves the objects. Here they give each thread a region of objects to move. This balances effort between threads since these regions were chosen to contain roughly equal volumes of live data.

There are two disadvantages to the way this algorithm compacts objects. First, it makes three passes over the heap. As we saw in Chapter 3, other algorithms make fewer passes.

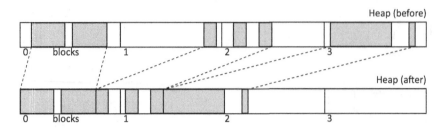

Figure 14.9: Inter-block compaction. Rather than sliding object by object, Abuaiadh *et al.* [2004] slide only complete blocks: free space within each block is not squeezed out.

Second, rather than compacting all live objects to one end of the heap, Flood *et al.* compact into N dense piles, leaving $\lceil (N+1)/2 \rceil$ gaps for allocation. Each pile is compacted densely, in the sense that space need only be wasted in a pile due to object alignment requirements. However, it is possible that if a very large number of threads/regions were to be used, it may be difficult for mutators to allocate very large objects.

Abuaiadh *et al.* [2004] address the first problem by calculating rather than storing forwarding addresses, using the mark bitmap and an offset vector that holds the new address of the first live object in each small block of the heap, as we described in Section 3.4. Their solution to the second problem is to over-partition the heap into a number of fairly large areas. For example, they suggest that a typical choice may be to have 16 times as many areas as processors, while ensuring that each area is at least 4 megabytes. The heap areas are compacted in order. Threads race to claim an area, using an atomic operation to increment a global area index (or pointer). If the operation is successful, the thread has obtained this area to compact. If it was not successful, then another thread must have claimed it and the first thread tries again for the next area. Thus, acquisition of areas is wait-free. A table holds pointers to the beginning of the free space for each area. After winning an area to compact, the thread competes to acquire an area into which it can move objects. A thread claims an area by trying to write null atomically into its corresponding table slot. Threads never try to compact from a source area nor into a target area whose table entry is null, and objects are never moved from a lower to a higher numbered area. Progress is guaranteed since a thread can always compact an area into itself. Once a thread has finished with an area, it updates the area's free space pointer in the table. If an area is full, its free space pointer will remain null.

Abuaiadh *et al.* explored two ways in which objects could be moved. The best compaction, with the least fragmentation, is obtained by moving individual live objects to their destinations, as we described above. Note that because every object in a block is moved to a location partly determined by the offset vector for that block, a block's objects are never split between two destination areas. They also tried trading quality of compaction for reduced compaction time by moving whole blocks at a time (256 bytes in their implementation), illustrated in Figure 14.9. Because objects in a linearly allocated space tend to live and die in clumps, they found that this technique could reduce compaction time by a fifth at the cost of increasing the size of the compaction area by only a few percent. On the other hand, it is not hard to invent a worst case that would lead to no compaction at all.

The calculate-rather-than-store the forwarding address mechanism was later adopted by the Compressor [Kermany and Petrank, 2006]. However, the Compressor introduced some changes. First, as the second phase of the collector passes over the mark bitmap, it calculates a *first-object* vector as well as the offset vector.[7] The first-object table is a vector indexed by the pages that will hold the relocated objects. Each slot in the table holds the address in fromspace of the first object that will be moved into that page. Compaction itself starts by updating the roots (using the information held in the mark and offset vectors).

The second difference is that each thread then competes to claim a tospace page from the first-object table. A successful thread maps a new physical page for its virtual page, and copies objects starting from the location specified in this slot of the first-object table, using the offset and mark vectors. Acquisition of a fresh page to which to evacuate objects allows Compressor to use parallel collector threads, whereas the description we gave in Chapter 3 sequentialised sliding of objects. At first sight, this may look as if it is a copying algorithm rather than a mark-compact one. However, Compressor truly is a sliding mark-compact collector. It manages fromspace and tospace pages at a cost in physical memory of typically only one page per collector thread, in stark contrast to a traditional semispace collector which requires twice as much heap space. The trick is that, although Compressor needs to map fresh tospace pages, it can also unmap each fromspace page as soon as it has evacuated all the live objects from it.

This design minimises overheads for synchronisation between compacting threads. A thread only needs to synchronise to claim a slot in the first-object table corresponding to a tospace page into which it can evacuate objects. This process is wait-free since a thread never needs to retry a page: if it fails to claim it, then another thread is evacuating to it so this thread can try the next slot in the table. Termination is equally simple: a thread exits when it reaches the end of the table. One subtlety is how to handle objects that span pages. In a stop-the-world implementation, one can arbitrarily decide that such an object is associated with the first tospace page on which it will be placed. However, this solution will not work for a concurrent implementation (which we discuss in Section 17.5), so we copy precisely the data that belongs to a single tospace page, including the end of the object that starts on the previous page and the beginning of one that ends on the next page.

14.9 Garbage collection on the GPU?

We have seen in this chapter how it is possible to improve the performance of the garbage collector by using multiple threads. So far, we have assumed that these threads run on one or more standard multicore processors, each of which typically provides a small number of hardware cores (at the time of writing, in the tens but not hundreds) compared with the number provided by a modern *graphics processing unit* (GPU). However, modern general-purpose GPUs may offer many more execution units, either *integrated* on the same wafer as the host CPU or on a separate, *discrete graphics card*. For example, Intel's Iris X^e-LP low power, integrated graphics processor provides up to 96 execution units whereas a high-end graphics card, such as nVidia's GeForce RTX 3090 has 10,496. It is natural to ask, therefore, whether it is possible to take advantage of modern, highly parallel, graphics processors to accelerate garbage collection. In this section, we look at some approaches that have been tried, but we note that technology in this area, and hence the design trade-offs that are possible, is evolving very fast.

GPU background

We start by briefly outlining the architecture and programming model of the GPU. These devices provide a *Single Instruction, Multiple Thread* (SIMT) programming model, accessed through programming frameworks such as nVidia's CUDA or OpenCL from the Khronos

---

[7] At 512 bytes, their blocks are also larger than those of Abuaiadh *et al.* [2004].

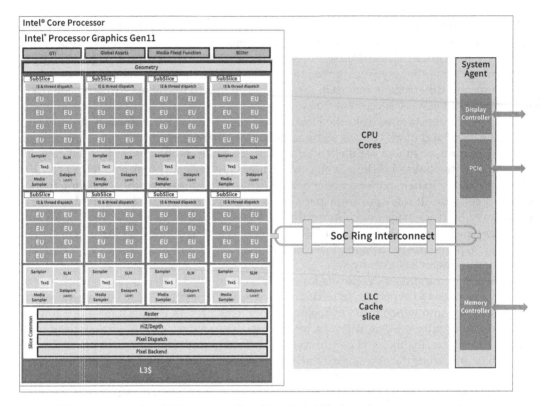

Figure 14.10: Intel Processor Graphics Gen11, showing a core processor, System-on-a-Chip and its ring interconnect achitecture

Graphic courtesy of Intel Corporation

Group. We will use OpenCL (respectively, CUDA) terminology. GPUs comprise a large number of *processing elements* or *stream processors* (SPs), each of which has a private register file and a number of integer and floating point units. Groups of typically 4 to 64 processing elements (stream processors) are organised into *compute units* (*streaming multiprocessors*; or *subslices* in Intel's Iris graphics architecture), along with an instruction decoder, an instruction cache, and a data cache or memory shared by its processing elements. A GPU is then composed of multiple compute units (streaming multiprocessors, subslices) along with global assets which might include a shared L3 cache. Global memory may either be dedicated hardware on a discrete GPU device or, on an integrated GPU, an area of the main system memory, and hence providing a unified view of memory, accessible to both CPU and GPU. If memory is not shared, then it will be necessary to copy data between CPU and GPU buffers using Direct Memory Access (DMA). In contrast, shared physical memory enables *zero-copy transfers* between CPU and GPU. Integrated GPUs may or may not also share a last-level cache with the host CPU. Dashti and Fedorova [2017] provide an overview of memory management on integrated systems.

Code is run by having the CPU launch a program *kernel* on the GPU. The latency of a kernel launch is high, maybe about 1 ms for an initial launch, lower for subsequent ones. Each kernel is composed of a number of *workgroups* (CUDA *blocks*). A workgroup is further broken down into *wavefronts* (*warps*), each consisting of a number of *work-items* (*threads*), each assigned a unique ID. GPUs schedule wavefronts rather than individual work-items, under a SIMT model. All the work-items of a wavefront execute the same instructions in lockstep, with hardware *execution masking* (also called *predicated execution*) handling divergent control paths (that is, when one work-item takes a branch but another does not): both sides of a branch will be executed but only some of the work-items will be enabled in each case.

Memory sizes (whether private to a processing element, shared by all processing elements in a compute unit or shared by all compute units) on the GPU are likely to be more restricted than those available to conventional processors; one consequence is a lack of support for deep recursion. If zero-copy transfers are not available, then the amount of data copied between CPU and GPU should be minimised. It is desirable to design algorithms and data structures that cause work-items (threads) in a workgroup (warp) to access sequences of addresses that fall within a single cache line, as this allows the GPU to coalesce accesses into a single load or store. Operations like indirection are also more expensive on the GPU than on a CPU. Atomic instructions provided by GPUs tend to be much more expensive than those provided by CPUs. For example, Dashti and Fedorova [2020] found that atomically marking objects on the GPU was $6.5\times$ slower on average than non-atomic marking, whereas atomic marking on the CPU was only around $4.1\times$ slower. This makes conventional approaches to load balancing, like work stealing where hundreds of threads may diverge while trying to access a concurrent queue, less suitable.

The predominant activities of garbage collectors include tracing recursive data structures, compacting live objects and sweeping regions of the heap. In Section 14.1, we asked if there is sufficient work to deploy in parallel to multiple processors or are there structural limits to parallelism. For instance, tracing a linked list is an inherently sequential activity, whereas tracing a broader structure offers more opportunity for parallel execution. This question becomes even more germane in the context of garbage collection on the GPU where performance gains will only be made if sufficiently many processing elements are kept busy. Barabash and Petrank [2010] examined the shape of data structures in the SPECjvm98, SPECjbb2005 and DaCapo 2006 benchmark suites for Java, measuring the number of objects found at each depth from the roots. They found that although many benchmarks had a large number of objects at smaller depths, several had very long tails of very narrow width. Maas *et al.* [2012] reached similar conclusions and observed that any effective GPU solution to tracing must include a mechanism for dealing with long tails in the heap graph. Although some garbage collection activities might appear ripe for parallelisation, it is clear that algorithms and data structures designed to run on multiprocessors cannot be naively transferred to run on GPUs [Dashti and Fedorova, 2020]. Here, we look at some approaches that have been tried.

Heap reference graphs

Processing heap data structures on the GPU is problematic. The heap may be too large for the GPU, especially if a unified view of memory is not available. In this case, it is essential to minimise the volume of data that has to be transferred between CPU and GPU, especially if zero-copy transfers are not available. Object representations are commonly GPU-unfriendly. Typically, object headers hold a pointer to a table that indicates where pointer fields lie in objects of the given type, implemented as either a bitmap or a vector of offsets of pointer fields (see Section 11.2). Following pointers in either implementation requires one or more levels of indirection and possibly branching to discover fields from the table, both of which are best avoided in kernel code. Several GPU-based garbage collection algorithms have therefore used *heap reference graphs*: more compact, more GPU-friendly representations of the heap that better support vector loads and stores. In these representations, each object in the heap is mapped to an entry in a *vertex array*. A vertex array entry may include the number of pointer fields in the object plus:

- a consecutive sequence of edges (indices of child vertices in the vertex array) [Maas *et al.*, 2012]; or

- the index of the first outgoing edge held in a separate *edge vector*, that holds the indices of child vertices [Abhinav and Nasre, 2016];

as well as other metadata such as the address of the object in the heap, whether the object has been marked, whether its fields have been scanned or whether it is an array, depending on the implementation. Such implementations require that vertices are created in the heap reference graph whenever a new object is allocated, and that the edge lists are up-to-date at collection time (all the algorithms discussed here assume stop-the-world collection). Maas *et al.* scan the objects in the heap reference graph immediately before collection in order to update the edge lists. In contrast, Abhinav and Nasre update the heap reference graph while mutators are executing. Their *FastCollect* algorithm is implemented with Intel's OpenCL 1.2 which supports zero-copy transfers, allowing the host Hotspot Java virtual machine to maintain the heap reference graph on-the-fly. However, this turns every mutator pointer update into a double write, one to the object graph and one to the heap reference graph. FastCollect assumes that pointer updates are race-free — as they do not synchronise their write barrier which is already fairly expensive as it has to interrogate the object's header and type descriptor in order to update the correct slot in the edge vector. Clearly, heap reference graphs incur a substantial overhead, in both space and time. Bidirectional layouts, where pointer fields are placed on one side of the object reference point and non-pointer fields on the other side, would also provide a GPU-friendly layout, without need for a separate heap reference graph.

Marking on the GPU

Researchers have explored a number of different approaches to marking on the GPU. Most of these are prototypes.

Veldema and Philippsen [2011] describe a parallel, stop-the-world, mark-sweep collector for programs running on discrete GPUs. Their heap is managed in chunks of 128 bytes, with smaller objects rounded up to that size. After initial bump pointer allocation, kernels allocate from $N = 1024$ free-lists of small objects (≤ 128 bytes) and $M = 32$ segregated free-lists of larger objects (with request sizes in powers of two from $2^8 \ldots 2^{28}$) in order to reduce contention. Thus, kernel K allocates small objects from free-list K modulo N and from bucket K modulo M for larger ones. The state of each chunk is summarised in a statically allocated array of 32-byte `ObjectInfo` structures that hold whether the chunk has been allocated, whether it has been seen in the marking phase, whether the fields it contains have been scanned, whether it is an array of references, the number of pointers it contains and a pointer to a table of integers indicating the offsets into an object at which there are references to other objects. The key idea in their collector is to partition the memory into fixed-size segments spanning several chunks. Initially, the CPU makes a parallel-call to the GPU to mark all roots in parallel. At each subsequent iteration of the marking loop, the CPU makes a parallel-call to the GPU to scan those segments where objects were marked in the previous iteration. The result of an iteration on the GPU is a boolean `device_marked_array` indicating those segments containing an object marked in that iteration, that is, those to be scanned later. At the start of each iteration, this array is copied to a `host_marked_array` before being cleared. Work-items then scan those segments for which a bit is set in the `host_marked_array`. If the `ObjectInfo` for a chunk in the segment indicates that an object has been allocated in the chunk, and marked but not yet scanned, then the object is scanned, its children are marked with the current mark-phase value (an object is garbage if it holds an old mark-phase value after marking), and a bit is set in a `device_marked_array`. Sweeping is performed in a similar manner.

Veldema and Philippsen suggest a number of optimisations to improve marking. To avoid having a kernel scan the elements of a large array sequentially, the marker can push a pair (reference, number of elements) to a queue. Once the segment is fully marked and control has returned to the CPU, the CPU copies the queue from the GPU before, for each array in the queue, parallel-calling a GPU kernel to mark all the array's elements in parallel. As we have seen, marking of deeply nested structures is also likely to be problematic. Their solution is that, after returning to the host a given number (say, ten) times, the collector marks recursively from inside the scan method using a small, fixed-size to-do queue, thus trading a reduced number of context switches for a possible reduction in parallelism.

This algorithm makes a GPU kernel call, and transfers data between CPU and GPU, at each iteration of the marking loop. In contrast, the following heap reference graph based algorithms invoke the marking kernel on the GPU only once per collection cycle.

Maas *et al.* [2012] initiate a collection cycle by constructing a heap reference graph and copying it to the GPU (the device drivers of the version of Linux they used did not support zero-copy transfers). They mark from a breadth-first queue of objects. At each iteration of the marking loop, the kernel in parallel removes, say, 256 items from the queue, marks them and appends the addresses of any children to the queue. Once marking is complete, marks from the heap reference graph are transferred back to the host. To avoid synchronising accesses to the queue, their algorithm calculates the offsets where any child references will be stored in the queue. Although they originally used a prefix-sum algorithm to calculate offsets in the queue (thus storing all references of an object in consecutive slots), they found that a histogram-based approach (where the first references from all objects/work-items with at least one reference appear first, followed by the second references, the third references and so on) performed better. To avoid stalling other work-items when one member of the workgroup encounters an object with high out-degree, their algorithm limits the number of references processed for each object (currently, 16). Objects with more children than this are stored on a non-blocking stack and processed in the same iteration by having each work-item in parallel deal with one reference. As we mentioned above, workloads with long, narrow tails are problematic to trace in parallel. Maas *et al.* deal with these by returning marking to the CPU once the length of the work queue drops below a threshold, on the assumption that caching on a CPU is more effective than on a GPU.

FastCollect [Abhinav and Nasre, 2016] is a lock-free, parallel, generational garbage collection algorithm targeted at integrated GPUs. It uses the compressed sparse-row representation described above for the heap reference graph for each generation. Marking runs multiple depth-first traces (adopted for better locality), one from each root. Each work-item uses a *hybrid stack*, stored in both local and global memory, which it accesses without synchronisation (although objects are marked with a compare-and-swap instruction). Each marking thread pushes entries (vertex indices) onto its hybrid stack in its local memory until it runs out of space. It then threads further stack entries through a shared array of vertex indices. When a young generation object is marked, FastCollect records its vertex index in a to-be-promoted array which is passed after marking is complete to the HotSpot host for copying. FastCollect implements a form of load balancing, at the risk of some duplication in marking. Each work-item is assigned an area of the shared mark stack to search. When a work-item has completed marking from its own stack, it searches this area, pushing any vertex found onto its own stack.

A problem not yet solved

While researchers have made interesting progress toward developing efficient garbage collection algorithms running on the GPU, it is clear that these solutions are prototypes. Although some algorithms have shown remarkable speed-ups, for example in the marking loop, compared with parallel collectors running on CPUs, they have incurred significant overheads elsewhere. Maas *et al.* [2012] report that their collector was 40% to 80% slower than a CPU-based collector. Much of this overhead was incurred in the construction and copying of their heap reference graph. Object allocation added 7% to 25% to execution time with the DaCapo benchmarks, and filling the heap reference graph before each collection took several times as long as the mark phase; marks also had to be copied back. An integrated GPU with zero-copy transfers, which their device drivers did not support, may reduce these overheads. Abhinav and Nasre [2016] claim excellent performance for FastCollect on an integrated GPU that *did* provide zero-copy transfer. For a subset of the DaCapo Java benchmarks, its marking phase outperformed HotSpot's Parallel collector by around 4×, leading to an overall reduction in execution time of around 10%, when using 128 work-items, each with a local stack of 128 elements. However, this was achieved by omitting any mechanism to guarantee the consistency of the heap and the heap reference graph; in order to support programs with races, the write barrier would have to include some form of synchronisation which is likely to be expensive. Finally, some obstacles appear impossible to overcome. There is no parallel solution to the inherently sequential problem of tracing very long lists. The difference in hardware models provided by different GPU vendors leads to fundamentally different optimisations and trade-offs. Thus, porting algorithms between different platforms is likely to remain difficult.

14.10   Issues to consider

Terminology

Earlier work was often inconsistent in the terminology it used to describe parallel garbage collection. Papers in the twentieth century often used 'parallel', 'concurrent' and even 'real-time' interchangeably. Fortunately, since around 2000, authors have adopted a consistent usage. Thus, a parallel collector is now one that uses multiple garbage collector threads, running in parallel. The world may or may not be stopped while parallel collection threads run. It seems clear that it is sensible to allow parallel collection if the underlying platform has the capability to support this, in the same way that it is desirable to allow mutator threads to use all available parallel resources.

Is parallel collection worthwhile?

The first question to ask is, recalling Amdahl's law,[8] is there sufficient work available to parallelise? It is easy to imagine scenarios that offer no opportunity for parallel execution: a common example might be tracing a list. Fortunately, there is evidence that real applications use a richer set of data structures and that these do indeed offer a high degree of potential parallelism [Siebert, 2008]. Garbage collection activities other than tracing offer much more obvious opportunities to exploit parallel hardware. For example, sweeping and compaction are eminently parallelisable (even if a little care needs to be taken with the

---

[8]Amdahl's law states that the speedup obtained from parallelising a program depends on the proportion of the program that can be parallelised. Thus, if s is the amount of time spent (by a serial processor) on serial parts of a program, and p is the amount of time spent (by a serial processor) on parts that can be done in parallel by n processors, then the speedup is $1/(s + p/n)$.

latter). Even in the tracing phase, thread stacks and remembered sets can be scanned in parallel and with little synchronisation overhead; completing the trace in parallel requires more careful handling of work lists in order to limit the synchronisation costs while at the same time using parallel hardware resources as efficiently as possible.

Strategies for balancing loads

It should be clear that parallelising collection effectively requires carefully trading off the need to balance loads between processors and limiting the amount of synchronisation necessary to do so safely. We want to balance loads to ensure that no processors are inactive while others do all the work. It is also important to balance other resources, such as memory. Synchronisation is essential to protect the integrity of the collector's work lists and the application's heap allocated structures. For example, allowing two threads to manipulate a mark stack pointer simultaneously risks losing entries. Furthermore, allowing two threads to copy an object simultaneously risks changing the topology of the heap. However, the finest grain balancing is likely to involve very high synchronisation costs.

The general solution is to assign to each collector thread a quantum of work that it can perform without further synchronisation with other threads. This begs the question of how the work can be divided between threads. The cheapest division, in the sense of the least synchronisation overhead, is to partition the work statically, at either build time, on program startup or before each collection cycle. In this case, the coordination between threads will be limited to consensus on termination. However, static partitioning may not lead to good load balancing. On the other hand, loads can be balanced by over-partitioning the work available and having threads compete to acquire tasks and having them return new tasks to a global pool. This offers the finest grain load balancing but at the cost of the most synchronisation. In between these two extremes, it is often possible to apply different load balancing strategies in different phases of the execution of a collection cycle. For example, information gathered by one phase (typically, the mark phase) can be used to estimate a fair division between threads of the work to done by subsequent phases. The Flood *et al.* [2001] collector is a good example of this approach.

Managing tracing

Tracing the heap involves consuming work (objects to mark or copy) and generating further work (their untraced children). Some structure, such as a stack or a queue, is needed to keep track of work to do. A single, shared structure would lead to high synchronisation costs, so collection threads should be given their own private data structures. However, in order to balance loads, some mechanism is required that can transfer work between threads. The first decision is what mechanism to use. We have discussed several in this chapter. Work stealing data structures can be used to allow work to be transferred safely from one thread to another. The idea is to make the common operation (pushing and popping entries while tracing) as cheap (that is, unsynchronised) as possible while still allowing infrequent operations (transferring work safely between threads). Endo *et al.* [1997] give each thread its own stack and a stealable work queue, whereas Flood *et al.* [2001] have each thread use just one double-ended queue both for tracing and stealing. Grey packets provide a global pool of buffers of work to do (hence their name) [Thomas *et al.*, 1998; Ossia *et al.*, 2002]. Here, each thread competes for a packet of work to do and returns new work to the pool in a fresh packet. Cheng and Blelloch [2001] resolve the problem of synchronising stack pushes and pops by splitting tracing into steps, which they call 'rooms'. At its simplest, all threads are in the push room or all are in the pop room. In each case, every thread wants to move the stack pointer in the same direction, so an atomic operation like fetch-and-add can be used. Other authors eliminate the need for atomic operations by having tracing threads communicate through single-writer, single-reader channels [Wu and Li, 2007; Oancea *et al.*, 2009].

The second decision is how much work to transfer and when to transfer it. Different researchers have proposed different solutions. The smallest unit of transfer is a single entry from the stack. However, if data structures are small, this may lead to a higher volume of traffic between threads. In the context of a parallel, concurrent and real-time collector, Siebert [2010] has a processor with no work steal all of another's work list. This is only a sensible decision if it is unlikely that processors will run out of work to do at around the same time (in this case, because they are executing mutator code concurrently). A common solution is to transfer an intermediate amount of work between threads. Fixed-size grey packets do this naturally; other choices include transferring half of a thread's mark stack. If mark stacks are a fixed size, then some mechanism must be employed to handle overflow. Again, grey packets handle this naturally: when an output packet is filled, it is returned to the global pool and an empty one is acquired from the pool. Flood *et al.* [2001] thread overflow sets through Java class objects, at the cost of a small, fixed space overhead per class. Large arrays are problematic for load balancing. One solution, commonly adopted in real-time systems, is to divide large, logically contiguous objects into linked data structures. Another is to record in the mark stack a sequence of sections of the array to scan for pointers to trace, rather than requiring all of the array to be scanned in a single step.

The techniques above are processor-centric: the algorithms concern the management of thread- (processor-) local work lists. The alternative is to use memory-centric strategies that take into account the location of objects. This may be increasingly important in the context of non-uniform memory architectures where access to a remote memory location is more expensive than access to a local one. Memory-centric approaches are common in parallel copying collectors, particularly where work lists are Cheney queues [Imai and Tick, 1993; Siegwart and Hirzel, 2006]. Here the issues are (i) the size of the blocks (the quanta of work), (ii) which block to process next and which to return to the global pool of work and (iii) which thread 'owns' an object. There are two aspects to choosing sizes of blocks. First, any moving collector should be given its own, private region of the heap into which it can allocate. These chunks should probably be large in order to reduce contention on the chunk manager. However, large chunks do not offer an appropriate granularity for balancing the load of copying threads. Instead, chunks should be broken into smaller blocks which can act as the work quanta in a Cheney-style collector. Second, the choice of which object to process next affects the locality of both the collector and the mutator (as we saw in Section 4.2). In both cases, it seems preferable to select the next unscanned object in the block that is being used for allocation, returning intermediate, unscanned or incompletely scanned blocks to the global pool. Making this decision at the end of scanning a block may improve the collector's locality; making this decision after scanning each object may improve the mutator's locality as well because it causes the live object graph to be traversed in a more depth-first-like (hierarchical) order. Finally, the decision might be made on which processor is most likely to use an object next. Oancea *et al.* [2009] use the notion of a 'dominant thread' to guide the choice of which processor should copy an object (and hence the location to which it should be copied). In a generational collector for Parallel Haskell, Marlow *et al.* [2009] maintain exactly one *Haskell Execution Context* (HEC) per physical CPU. They emphasise locality: each HEC allocates into its own private region of the heap, has its own remembered set and traces its own root set. They found that *not* load balancing improved performance by not moving data between caches (although their benchmarks were only small to medium-sized).

Low-level synchronisation

As well as synchronising operations on collector data structures, it may also be necessary to synchronise operations on individual objects. In principle, marking is an idempotent operation: it does not matter if an object is marked more than once. However, if a collector uses a vector of mark bits, it is essential that the marker sets these bits atomically, perhaps using an operation such as fetch-and-or. However, it can be more efficient to simply set a byte non-atomically. On the other hand, if the mark bit is held in the object's header, or the mark vector is a vector of bytes (one per object), then no synchronisation is necessary since double writing the mark is safe.

A copying collector must not 'mark' (that is, copy) an object more than once, as this would change the topology of the graph, with possibly disastrous consequences for mutable objects. It is essential that copying an object and setting the forwarding address is seen by other collector threads to be a single, indivisible operation. The details come down to how the forwarding address is handled. A number of solutions have been adopted. A collector may attempt to write a 'busy' value into the forwarding address slot atomically, then copy the object and write the forwarding address with a simple store operation. If another thread sees a 'busy' value, it must spin until it sees the forwarding address. The synchronisation cost can be reduced by testing the forwarding address slot before attempting the atomic 'busy' write. Another tactic might be to copy the object if there is no forwarding address and then attempt to store the forwarding address atomically, retracting the copy if the store is unsuccessful. The effectiveness of such a tactic will depend on the frequency of collisions when installing forwarding addresses.

It is important that certain actions be made visible in the proper order to other processors on platforms with weakly consistent memory models. This requires the compiler to emit memory fences in the appropriate places. Atomic operations such as compare-and-swap often act as fences, but in many cases weaker instructions suffice. One factor in the choice of algorithm will be the complexity of deciding where to place fences, the number that need to be executed and the cost of doing so. It may well be worth trading simplicity of programming (and hence confidence that the code is correct) for some reduction in performance.

Sweeping and compaction

Sweeping and compaction phases essentially sweep linearly through the heap (in more than one pass in the case of compaction). Thus, these operations are well suited to parallelisation. The simplest load balancing strategy might be to divide the heap into as many partitions as there are processors. However, this can lead to uneven load balancing if the amount of work is uneven between partitions. To first approximation, the amount of work to be done is proportional to the number of objects in a partition. This information is available from the mark phase and can be used to divide the heap into unequally sized (but object aligned) partitions, each of which contains roughly the same amount of work.

However, this strategy assumes that each partition can be processed independently of the others. This will not be true if processing one partition may destroy information on which another partition depends. For example, a sliding compaction collector cannot move objects in an arbitrary order to their destinations, as this would risk overwriting live but not yet moved data. In this case, it may be necessary to process partitions in address order. Here, the solution is to over-partition the heap and have threads compete for the next partitions to use (one for the object to be moved and one into which to move them).

Termination

Finally, termination of any collection phase must be determined correctly. The use of parallel threads clearly makes termination detection more complex. The problem is fundamentally that one thread may be attempting to detect whether the phase has terminated while another is generating more work. Unfortunately, flawed termination detection algorithms are quite easy to write! One (correct) solution to the problem is to nominate a single thread to detect termination and have threads indicate atomically whether they are busy or not; care is needed with the protocol for raising and lowering flags and processing work, and in placement of fences in the presence of relaxed memory orders. Systems with a global pool of work can offer simpler protocols that allow any number of threads to detect termination. For example, grey packet systems may allow the number of packets in the global pool to be counted: if they are all present (and empty), then the phase is complete.

Chapter 15

Concurrent garbage collection

The basic principles of *concurrent collection* were initially devised as a means to reduce pause times for garbage collection on uniprocessors. Early papers used terms such as 'concurrent', 'parallel', 'on-the-fly' and 'real-time' interchangeably or inconsistently. In Chapter 14 we defined the modern usage of 'parallel'. Here, we define the remaining terms. So far, we have assumed that the mutator is suspended while garbage collection proceeds, and that each collection cycle terminates before the mutator can continue. Figure 14.1 illustrated different stop-the-world collection styles by one or more horizontal bars, with time proceeding from left to right, and showed mutator execution in white while each collection cycle is represented as a distinct non-white shade. Thus, grey boxes represent actions of one garbage collection cycle, and black boxes those of the next. In Chapter 14 we saw that one way to reduce pause times on a multiprocessor is to run a full collection cycle with multiple collector threads acting in parallel while all the mutators are stopped, as illustrated in Figure 14.1c.

Another way to reduce pause times on a uniprocessor is to interleave mutator execution with collector execution, as illustrated in Figure 15.1a. Interleaving mutator and collector execution in this way is called *incremental collection*, since the collection cycle is broken down into multiple finer-grained increments. However, incremental collection is not as straightforward as it might first seem, since the collection cycle is no longer atomic with respect to mutation of the object graph, so the reachability of objects can change from one increment to the next. Thus, incremental collectors must have some way of keeping track of changes to the graph of reachable objects, perhaps re-scanning objects or fields in the face of those changes. There are many different ways to cope with this problem.

Although interleaving provides the illusion of concurrency between mutator and collector, incremental collection assumes that the mutator and collector do not execute in parallel — that is, that the mutator is stopped for each increment of the collector cycle. It is possible to maintain this property on a multiprocessor by making sure that all parallel mutators are stopped for each increment, as illustrated in Figure 15.1b. The increments can also be parallelised, as in Figure 15.1c.

It is a conceptually simple step to go from interleaving of the mutator with the collector on a uniprocessor to concurrent execution of (multiple) mutators in parallel with the collector on a multiprocessor. The main added difficulty is ensuring that the collector and mutators synchronise properly to maintain a consistent view of the heap, and not just for reachability. For example, inconsistency can occur when a mutator attempts to manipulate partially scanned or copied objects, or to access metadata, concurrently with the collector.

The degree and granularity of this synchronisation necessarily impacts application throughput (that is, end-to-end execution time including both mutator and collector work),

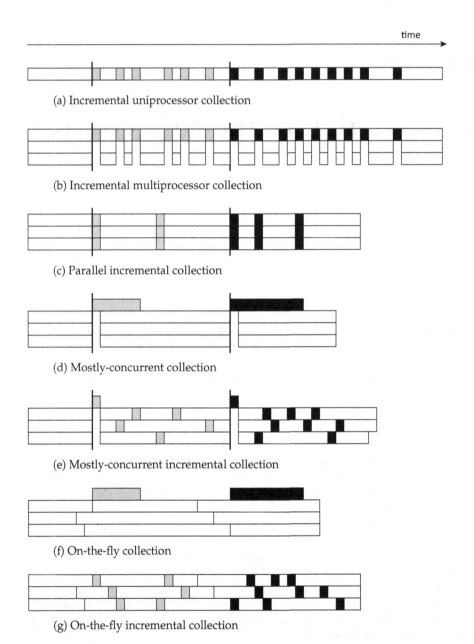

Figure 15.1: Incremental and concurrent garbage collection. Each bar represents an execution on a single processor. The coloured regions represent different garbage collection cycles.

and synchronisation is more easily maintained in some phases of collection than others. Thus, *mostly-concurrent collection* avoids some synchronisation overhead by assuming that all the mutators are stopped at the same time for brief periods during each collector cycle, often at the beginning of the cycle, which may include obtaining stack roots from the stopped mutators, and at the end of the marking phase to ensure that all live objects have been marked. This is true whether the collection cycle is monolithic (Figure 15.1d) or incremental (Figure 15.1e). The (hopefully brief) global stop-the-world phase ensures that all the mutators are simultaneously aware that some phase of a collection cycle has begun (or completed).

Relaxing the need for a global stop-the-world phase yields purely concurrent *on-the-fly collection*, which executes in parallel with the mutators (Figure 15.1f), possibly incrementally (Figure 15.1g). The vertical lines indicate that each mutator may need to synchronise with the garbage collector prior to each collection cycle, even though there is no global stop-the-world phase.[1]

15.1 Correctness of concurrent collection

A *correct* concurrent collector must satisfy two properties:

- *safety* requires the collector to retain *at least* all reachable objects;

- *liveness* requires the collector eventually to complete its collection cycle.

Concurrent collectors are only correct insofar as they are able to control mutator and collector interleavings. As we shall soon see, concurrent mutator and collector operations will be specified as operating atomically, allowing us to interpret a sequence of interleaved operations as being generated by a single mutator (and single collector), without loss of generality. Any concurrent schedule for executing these atomic operations that preserves their appearance of atomicity will be permitted, leaving the actual implementation of the concurrency control for these operations to the discretion of the implementer. Perhaps the easiest way to preserve atomicity of these operations is to alternate collector and mutator work by running the collector incrementally, stopping all the mutator threads while each collector increment runs. Other approaches permit finer-grained synchronisation. We reviewed techniques for doing so in Chapter 13.

The tricolour abstraction, revisited

Correctness of concurrent collectors is often reasoned about most easily by considering invariants based on the *tricolour abstraction* that the collector and mutator must preserve. All concurrent collectors preserve some realisation of these invariants, but they must retain at least all the reachable objects (safety) even as the mutator modifies objects. Recall that:

White objects have not yet been reached by the collector; this includes all objects at the beginning of the collection cycle. Those left white at the end of the cycle will be treated as unreachable garbage.

Grey objects have been reached by the collector, but one or more of their fields still need to be scanned (they may still point to white objects).

---

[1]Historically, concurrent collection in general was referred to as 'on-the-fly' [Dijkstra *et al.*, 1976, 1978; Ben-Ari, 1984]. However, on-the-fly has since come to mean more specifically never stopping all the mutator threads simultaneously.

Black objects have been reached by the collector and all their fields have been scanned; thus, immediately after they were scanned none of the outgoing pointers were to white objects. Black objects will not be rescanned unless their colour changes.

The garbage collector can be thought of as advancing a grey wavefront, the boundary between black (was reachable at some time and scanned) and white (not yet visited) objects. When the collector cycle can complete without mutators concurrently modifying the heap, there is no problem. The key problem with concurrent mutation is that the collector's and the mutator's views of the world may become inconsistent, and that the grey wavefront no longer represents a proper boundary between black and white.

Let us reconsider the earlier definition of the mutator `Write` operation, which we can recast as follows by introducing a redundant load from the field right before the store:

```
atomic Write(src, i, new):
    old ← src[i]
    src[i] ← new
```

The `Write` operation *inserts* the pointer src→new into the field src[i] of object src. As a side effect it *deletes* the pointer src→old from src[i]. We characterise the operation as `atomic` to emphasise that the old and new pointers are exchanged instantaneously without any other interleaving of mutator/collector operations. Of course, on most hardware the store is naturally atomic, so no explicit synchronisation is required.

When the mutator runs concurrently with the collector and modifies objects ahead of the wavefront — grey objects (whose fields still need to be scanned) or white objects (as yet unreached) — correctness ensues since the collector will still visit those objects at some point (if they are still reachable). There is also no problem if the mutator modifies objects behind the wavefront — black objects (whose fields have already been scanned) — so long as it only inserts or deletes a pointer to a black or grey object (which the collector has already decided is reachable). However, other pointer updates may lead to the mutator's and the collector's view of the set of live objects becoming incoherent [Wilson, 1994], and thus live objects being freed incorrectly. Let us consider an example.

The lost object problem

We show the two scenarios under which a white pointer can be inserted behind the wavefront in Figure 15.2. The first scenario in Figure 15.2a illustrates how the mutator can hide a white object initially *directly* reachable from a grey object by inserting its pointer behind the wavefront and then deleting its link from the grey object. The initial state of the heap shows a black object X and grey object Y, having been marked reachable from the roots. White object Z is directly reachable from Y. In Step D1 the mutator inserts pointer b from X to Z by copying pointer a from grey object Y. In Step D2 the mutator deletes unscanned pointer a from the only unscanned object (Y) that refers to Z. In Step D3 the collector scans object Y to make it black, and then terminates its marking phase. In the sweep phase, white object Z will be erroneously reclaimed, even though it is reachable via pointer b.

The second scenario in Figure 15.2b shows how the mutator can hide a white object *transitively* reachable via a chain of pointers from a grey object by inserting its pointer behind the wavefront, and then deleting some *other* link in the chain. In this scenario no pointer to the lost object itself is deleted, unlike the *direct* case which does delete a pointer to the lost object. The initial state of the heap shows a black object P and grey object Q, having been marked reachable from the roots. White object R is directly reachable from Q, while white object S is transitively reachable from Q via R. In Step T1 the mutator inserts

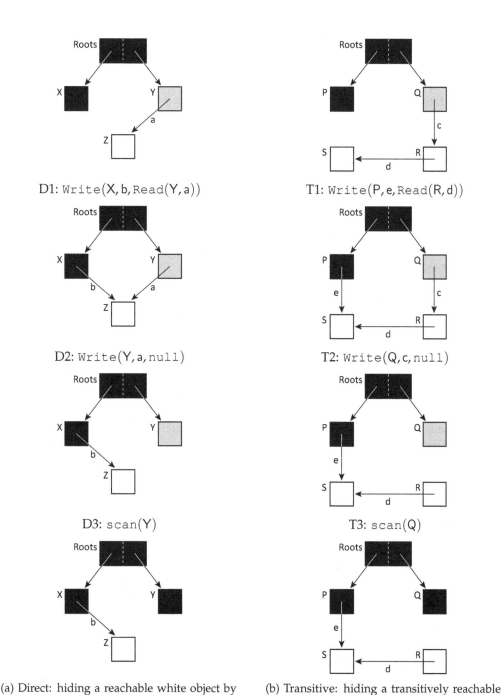

D1: Write(X, b, Read(Y, a))

T1: Write(P, e, Read(R, d))

D2: Write(Y, a, null)

T2: Write(Q, c, null)

D3: scan(Y)

T3: scan(Q)

(a) Direct: hiding a reachable white object by dropping a direct link from grey

(b) Transitive: hiding a transitively reachable white object by breaking an indirect chain from grey

Figure 15.2: The lost object problem: a reachable white object is hidden from the collector by making it unreachable from any grey object.

With kind permission from Springer Science+Business Media: Vechev *et al.* [2005], figures 3–4, pages 584–5 pointer e from P to S by copying pointer d from white object R. In Step T2 the mutator deletes pointer c to R, destroying the path from the only unscanned object Q that leads to S. In Step T3 the collector scans the object Q to make it black, and terminates its marking phase. In the sweep phase, white object S will be erroneously reclaimed, even though it is reachable via pointer e.

Wilson [1994] observes that objects can only become lost if two conditions hold at some point during tracing:

Condition 1: the mutator stores a pointer to a white object into a black object, and

Condition 2: all paths from any grey objects to that white object are destroyed.

Inserting a white pointer (that is, a pointer to a white object) into a black object will cause problems if the collector never encounters another pointer to the white object. It would mean that the white object is reachable (from the black object, Condition 1), but the collector will never notice since it does not revisit black objects. The collector could only discover the white object by following a path of unvisited (that is, white) objects starting from an object that the collector has noticed but not finished with (that is, a grey object). But Condition 2 states that there is no such path.

The strong and weak tricolour invariants

To prevent live objects from being reclaimed incorrectly, we must ensure that both conditions cannot hold simultaneously. To guarantee that the collector will not miss any reachable objects, it must be sure to find every white object that is pointed to by black objects. So long as any white object pointed to by black objects is also protected from deletion, it will not be missed. It is sufficient for such an object to be directly reachable from some grey object, or transitively reachable from some grey object through a chain of white objects. In this case Condition 2 never holds. We say that such an object is *grey protected*. Thus, we must preserve:

- **The *weak tricolour invariant*:** All white objects pointed to by a black object are grey protected (that is, reachable from some grey object, either directly or through a chain of white objects).

Non-copying collectors have the advantage that all white pointers automatically turn into grey/black pointers when their target object is shaded grey or black. Thus, white pointers in black objects are not a problem because their grey protected white targets are eventually shaded by the collector — all white pointers in black objects eventually become black before the collection cycle can terminate.

In contrast, concurrent copying collectors are more restricted because they explicitly have two copies of every live object at the end of the collection cycle (the fromspace white copy, and the tospace black copy), at which point the white copies are discarded along with the garbage. By definition, black objects are never revisited by the collector. Thus, a correct concurrent copying collector must never allow a white fromspace pointer (to a white fromspace object) to be stored in a black tospace object. Otherwise, the collector will complete its cycle while leaving dangling white pointers from black tospace into the discarded white fromspace. That is, they must preserve:

- **The *strong tricolour invariant*:** There are no pointers from black objects to white objects.

Clearly, the strong invariant implies the weak invariant, but not the other way round. Because problems can only occur when the mutator inserts a white pointer into a black object, it is sufficient simply to prohibit that. Preserving the strong tricolour invariant is a strategy equally suited to both copying and non-copying collectors.

In both the scenarios in the example, the mutator first wrote a pointer to a white object into a black object (D1/T1), breaking the strong invariant. It then destroyed all paths to that white object from grey objects (D2/T2), breaking the weak invariant. The result was that a (reachable) black object ended up pointing to a (presumed garbage) white object, violating correctness. Solutions to the lost object problem operate at either the step that writes the pointer to the white object (D1/T1) or the step that deletes a remaining path to that object (D2/T2).

Precision

Different collector algorithms, which achieve safety and liveness (of collector) in different ways, will have varying degrees of *precision* (as determined by the set of objects they retain at the end of the collection cycle), *efficiency* (throughput) and *atomicity* (degree of concurrency). Varying precision means that they may retain some varying superset of the reachable objects, and hence affects the promptness of reclamation of dead objects. A stop-the-world collector obtains maximal precision (all unreachable objects are collected) at the expense of any concurrency with the mutator. Finer-grained atomicity permits increased concurrency with the mutator at the expense of possibly retaining more unreachable objects and the overhead to ensure atomicity of key operations. It is difficult to identify the minimal yet sufficient set of critical sections to place in tracing. Vechev *et al.* [2007] shows how this search can be semi-automated. Unreachable objects that are nevertheless retained at the end of the collection cycle are called *floating garbage*. It is usually desirable, though not strictly necessary for correctness, that a concurrent collector also ensure *completeness* in collecting floating garbage in some later collection cycle.

Mutator colour

In classifying algorithms, it is also useful to talk about the colour of the mutator roots as if the mutator itself were an object. A grey mutator either has not yet been scanned by the collector so its roots are still to be traced, or its roots have been scanned but need to be rescanned. Thus, grey mutator roots may refer to objects that are white, grey or black. A black mutator has been scanned by the collector so its roots have been traced, and will not be scanned again. Under the strong invariant this means that a black mutator's roots can refer only to objects that are grey or black but not white. Under the weak invariant, a black mutator can hold white references so long as their targets are protected from deletion.

The colour of the mutator has implications for termination of a collection cycle. By definition, concurrent collection algorithms that permit a grey mutator need to rescan its roots. This will lead to more tracing work if a reference to a non-black object is found. When this trace is complete, the roots must be scanned again, in case the mutator has added to the roots yet another non-black reference, and so on. It is generally necessary for grey mutator algorithms to halt all mutator threads for a final scan of their roots.

As mentioned earlier, our simplifying assumption for now is that there is only a single mutator. However, on-the-fly collectors distinguish among multiple mutator threads because they do not suspend them all at once to sample their roots. These collectors must operate with mutator threads of different colours, both grey (unscanned) and black (scanned). Moreover, some collectors may separate a single mutator thread's roots into scanned (black) and unscanned (grey) portions. For example, the top frame of a thread's stack may be scanned to make it black, while the remaining stack frames are left unscanned (grey). Returning or unwinding into the grey portion of the stack forces the new top stack frame to be scanned.

Allocation colour

Mutator colour also influences the colour objects receive when they are allocated, since allocation results in the mutator holding the pointer to the newly allocated object, which must satisfy whichever invariant applies given the colour of the mutator. But the allocation colour also affects how quickly a new object can be freed once it becomes unreachable. If an object is allocated black or grey, then it will not be freed during the current collection cycle (since black and grey objects are considered to be live), even if the mutator drops its reference without storing it into the heap. A grey mutator can allocate objects white and so avoid unnecessarily retaining new objects. A black mutator cannot allocate white (whether the strong or weak invariant applies), unless (under the weak invariant) there is a guarantee that the white reference will be stored to a live object ahead of the wavefront so the collector will retain it. Otherwise, there is nothing to prevent the collector from reclaiming the object even though the black mutator retains a pointer to it. Note also that, initially, a new object contains no outgoing references, so allocating black is always safe.

Pointer tagging

While colour — white, grey or black — applies to *objects*, it is also possible to associate information with *pointers*. For example, a bit within each pointer might indicate whether that pointer is marked through or not. This bit stealing introduces tags on pointers.[2] Such tags allow finer-grained recording of progress in scanning (marking through) the pointers of an object. It leads to invariants that are further refined. Using the strong tricolour invariant, the target of a marked-through pointer must not be white. A black object may only contain marked-through pointers; a white object may only contain unmarked-through pointers; and a grey object may contain either. Pointer tags can help in maintaining a black mutator invariant, since a marked-through pointer is good for a black mutator to hold but an unmarked-through one may not be. Some systems use double mapping (Section 11.10) to support using one or more higher-order bits for the pointer tags while sometimes avoiding explicit tests of those bits.

Incremental update solutions

Wilson [1994] calls solutions that address D1/T1 mutations *incremental update* techniques because they inform the collector of incremental changes made by the mutator to the set of objects known to be live, and hence of additional objects that need to be (re)scanned. Incremental update solutions conservatively treat an object as live (non-white) if a pointer to it is ever inserted behind the wavefront (into a black object), speculating that the mutator may yet delete all other paths to the object ahead of the wavefront. Thus, incremental update techniques preserve the strong invariant. They use a *write barrier* to protect against the insertion of a pointer to a white object into a black object. In the example above, the write barrier would re-colour the source or destination of pointer b so that the pointer is no longer black to white.

---

[2]Tagged pointers have also been called *coloured pointers*. We prefer the term *tagged pointer* in order to avoid confusion with a pointer to a coloured object.

When a black mutator loads a reference from the heap it is effectively inserting a pointer in a black object (itself). Incremental update techniques can use a mutator *read barrier* to protect from insertion of white pointers in a black mutator.

Snapshot-at-the-beginning solutions

Wilson calls solutions that address D2/T2 mutations *snapshot-at-the-beginning* techniques since they preserve the set of objects that were live at the start of the collection. They inform the collector when the mutator deletes a white pointer from a grey or white object (ahead of the wavefront). Snapshot-at-the-beginning solutions conservatively treat an object as live (non-white) if a pointer to it ever existed ahead of the wavefront, speculating that the mutator may have also inserted that pointer behind the wavefront. This maintains the weak invariant, because there is no way to delete every path from some grey object to any object that was live at the beginning of the collection cycle. Snapshot-at-the-beginning techniques use a write barrier to protect against deletion of grey or white pointers from grey or white objects.

Snapshotting the mutator means scanning its roots, making it black. We must snapshot the mutator at the beginning of the collection cycle to ensure it holds no white pointers. Otherwise, if the mutator held a white pointer that was the only pointer to its referent, it could write that pointer into a black object and then drop the pointer, breaking the weak invariant. A write barrier on black could catch such insertions, but degenerates to maintaining the strong invariant. Thus, snapshot collectors only operate with a black mutator.

15.2 Barrier techniques for concurrent collection

Following Pirinen [1998], barrier techniques that maintain one of the two tricolour invariants rely on a number of actions to cope with insertion or deletion of pointers. They can:

- add to the wavefront by *shading* an object grey, if it was white; Shading an already grey or black object has no effect.

- advance the wavefront by *scanning* an object to make it black; or

- retreat the wavefront by *reverting* an object from black back to grey.

The only other actions — reverting an object to white or shading an object black without scanning — would break the invariants. Algorithms 15.1 to 15.2 enumerate the range of classical barrier techniques for concurrent collection. Following Hellyer *et al.* [2010], we have marked barriers as `atomic`, but this can be relaxed with care. For each processor type (memory model) the implementer will need to determine where to use individual atomic operations or to place fences to prevent incorrect orderings of memory accesses.

Grey mutator techniques

We first consider approaches that operate with a grey mutator. All these techniques preserve the strong invariant by using an *insertion barrier*[3] when writing references into the heap to protect from storing white pointers into black objects. Because the mutator is grey, they do not need a read barrier. They are incremental update techniques.

---

[3]We believe that *insertion barrier* is a clearer term for the mechanism than *incremental update barrier*. Likewise, we prefer the term *deletion barrier* to *snapshot barrier*.

Algorithm 15.1: Grey mutator barriers

(a) Steele [1975, 1976] barrier

```
1  atomic Write(src, i, ref):
2      src[i] ← ref
3      if isBlack(src)
4          if isWhite(ref)
5              revert(src)
```

(b) Boehm *et al.* [1991] barrier

```
1  atomic Write(src, i, ref):
2      src[i] ← ref
3      if isBlack(src)
4          revert(src)
```

(c) Dijkstra *et al.* [1976, 1978] barrier

```
1  atomic Write(src, i, ref):
2      src[i] ← ref
3      if isBlack(src)
4          shade(ref)
```

Algorithm 15.2: Black mutator barriers

(a) Baker [1978] barrier

```
1  atomic Read(src, i):
2      ref ← src[i]
3      if isGrey(src)
4          ref ← shade(ref)
5      return ref
```

(b) Appel *et al.* [1988] barrier

```
1  atomic Read(src, i):
2      if isGrey(src)
3          scan(src)
4      return src[i]
```

(c) Abraham and Patel [1987] / Yuasa barrier

```
1  atomic Write(src, i, ref):
2      if isGrey(src) || isWhite(src)
3          shade(src[i])
4      src[i] ← ref
```

Hellyer *et al.* [2010], doi: 10.1145/1806651.1806666
© 2010 Association for Computing Machinery, Inc. Reprinted by permission.

Algorithm 15.3: Pirinen [1998] black mutator hybrid barrier

```
1   atomic Read(src, i):
2       ref ← src[i]
3       if isWhite(src)
4           shade(ref)
5       return ref
6
7   atomic Write(src, i, ref):
8       if isGrey(src)
9           shade(src[i])
10      src[i] ← ref
```

- Steele [1975, 1976] devised the barrier illustrated in Algorithm 15.1a. It yields the most precision of all the techniques because it simply notes the source object being modified. It does not change any decision about reachability of any object, but re-treats the wavefront by changing the modified source object from black back to grey. It defers deciding reachability of the target white object until the source object can be rescanned (the inserted pointer might be deleted before rescanning). This precision comes at the cost of progress, since the wavefront is retreated.

- Boehm *et al.* [1991] implemented a variant of the Steele barrier which ignores the colour of the inserted pointer, as shown in Algorithm 15.1b. They originally im-plemented this barrier using virtual memory dirty bits to record pages modified by the mutator without having to mediate the heap writes in software, which meant a less precise barrier that did not originally have the conditional test that the reverted source object is actually black. Boehm *et al.* use a stop-the-world phase to terminate collection at which time the dirty pages are rescanned.

- Dijkstra *et al.* [1976, 1978] designed a barrier (Algorithm 15.1c) that yields less pre-cision than Steele's since it commits to shading the target of the inserted pointer as reachable (non-white), even if the inserted pointer is subsequently deleted. This loss of precision aids progress by advancing the wavefront. The original formulation of this barrier shaded the target without regard for the colour of the source, with a fur-ther loss of precision. Omitting this extra check allows atomicity to be relaxed, so long as the store and the shade operations are separately atomic. The store must still be performed ahead of the shade operation so as to avoid a subtle race when the col-lector transitions from one collector cycle to the next in the middle. If the operations are inverted, then a collector cycle transition right after shading the stored `ref` grey can revert it to white and scan the `src` to black before the store, which then creates a black to white pointer violating the strong invariant [Stenning, 1976].

Black mutator techniques

The first two black mutator approaches apply incremental updates to maintain the strong invariant using a read barrier to prevent the mutator from acquiring white pointers (that is, to protect from inserting a white pointer in a black mutator). The third, a snapshot tech-nique, uses a *deletion barrier* on pointer writes into the heap to preserve the weak invariant (that is, to protect from deleting the last pointer keeping an object live that was reachable at the time of the snapshot). Under the weak invariant, a black mutator can still hold white references; it is black because its roots do not need to be rescanned, even if it has since loaded pointers to white objects, because those white objects are protected from deletion by the write barrier.

- Baker [1978] used the read (mutator insertion) barrier shown in Algorithm 15.2a. This approach has less precision than that of Dijkstra *et al.*, since it retains otherwise white objects whose references are loaded by the mutator at some time during the collection cycle, as opposed to those actually inserted behind the wavefront. Note that Baker's read barrier was designed originally for a copying collector, where the act of shading copies the object from fromspace to tospace, so the `shade` routine returns the tospace pointer.

- Appel *et al.* [1988] implemented a coarse-grained (less precise) variant of Baker's read barrier (Algorithm 15.2b), using virtual memory page protection primitives of the operating system to trap accesses by the mutator to grey pages of the heap without having to mediate those reads in software. Having scanned (and unprotected) the page, the trapped access is allowed to proceed. This barrier can also be used with a copying collector since scanning will forward any fromspace pointers held in the source object, including that in the field being loaded.

- Abraham and Patel [1987] and Yuasa [1990] independently devised the deletion barrier of Algorithm 15.2c. At D2 it directly shades Z grey. At T2 it shades R grey so that S can eventually be shaded. This barrier offers the least precision of all the techniques, since it retains any unreachable object to which the last pointer was deleted during the collection cycle. With an insertion barrier at least we know that the mutator has had some interest in objects retained by the barrier (whether to acquire or store its reference), whereas the deletion barrier retains objects regardless of whether the mutator manipulated them. This is evident in that shading R retains it as floating garbage — it is not otherwise reachable — solely to preserve S. In its original form, this snapshot barrier was unconditional: it simply shaded the target of the overwritten pointer, regardless of the colour of the source. Abraham and Patel exploited this to drive their snapshot barrier using virtual memory copy-on-write mechanisms.

Completeness of barrier techniques

Pirinen [1998] argues that these barrier techniques cover the complete range of all possible approaches, if augmented with the read and write barrier combination illustrated in Algorithm 15.3. This combines an insertion read barrier on a black mutator with a deletion barrier on the heap. The combination preserves a weak invariant: all black-to-white pointers have a copy in some grey object (this is slightly stronger than the basic weak invariant that requires only a chain of white references from grey to white). The black mutator can safely acquire a white pointer from some grey source object since the target object will eventually be shaded grey when the grey source is scanned, or the write barrier will shade the target grey if the source field is modified. The read barrier makes sure that the mutator never acquires a white pointer from a white object. Thus, every reachable white object has a grey object directly keeping it alive throughout the collection cycle.

Variations on the techniques listed above can be obtained in various ways by short-circuiting, coarsening or refining some steps, including the following.

- Shading an object grey can be short-circuited by immediately scanning the object to make it black.

- A deletion barrier that shades the target of the deleted pointer grey can instead (and more coarsely) scan the source object that contained the pointer to black before the store.

- A read barrier that shades the target of the loaded pointer grey can instead (and more coarsely) scan the source object to black so that it contains no pointers to white objects, ensuring that the loaded pointer cannot be white. Thus, the read barrier of Appel *et al.* coarsens that of Baker. Conversely, the Baker read barrier can be refined to consider only properties of the loaded target reference (ignoring the colour of the source). For example, if the target is white, then the barrier can shade it to grey to prevent the black mutator from acquiring a pointer to a white object. We discuss variants of this refinement in more detail on the facing page.

- An insertion barrier that shades the target of the inserted pointer grey can instead revert the source to grey. This is how the barriers of Steele and Boehm *et al.* gain precision over that of Dijkstra *et al.*

Algorithm 15.4: Baker [1978]-style load barrier. This barrier becomes self-healing with the addition of line 5.

```
1  atomic Read(src, i):
2     ref ← src[i]
3     if isWhite(ref)
4        ref ← shade(ref)
5        src[i] ← ref                    /* optional self–healing */
6     return ref
```

Clearly, all strong invariant (incremental update) techniques must at least protect a grey mutator from inserting white pointers into black, or protect a black mutator from acquiring or using white pointers. The strong techniques all do one of these two things and need not do any more.

We have already argued that weak invariant (snapshot) techniques must operate with a black mutator. Under the weak invariant, a grey object does not merely capture a single path to reachable white objects. It may also be a placeholder for a pointer from a black object to some white object on that path. Thus, the snapshot barrier must preserve any white object directly pointed to from a grey one. The least it can do is to shade the white object when its pointer is deleted from a grey one.

To deal with white objects transitively reachable via a white path from a grey object (which may also be pointed to from a black one) we can either prevent the mutator from obtaining pointers to white objects on such paths so it can never modify the path [Pirinen, 1998], or make sure that deleting a pointer from a white object (which may be on such a path) makes the target of the pointer at least grey [Abraham and Patel, 1987; Yuasa, 1990].

Load barriers

We use the term *load barrier*[4] for a read barrier that only focuses on properties of the target being loaded, ignoring properties of the source object. A load barrier aims to maintain an invariant on the pointers held by a mutator as it loads them, as opposed to when the pointers are used.

For example, Baker's read barrier ensures that a black mutator never holds a pointer to a white object. Rather than testing if the source object is grey (and making sure to shade the loaded target in case it is white), a load barrier version of the Baker read barrier can instead test if the target of the loaded reference is white before shading it, as shown in Algorithm 15.4.

Load barriers can also be self-healing. For example, Baker's read barrier used with a copying collector might not only copy a white target object from fromspace to tospace, but it might also update the source slot with the tospace pointer by adding line 5 to Algorithm 15.4. Self-healing avoids repeatedly triggering the load barrier's work on the same loaded reference.

In the presence of pointer tags, we obtain additional variations. Rather than considering the colour of the source object whose field is being read, or the colour of the target referent of a field, pointer tags allow focus on a property of the *pointer* being loaded, which may be connected with, but not the same as, the colour of its referent. Furthermore, since the focus is on the pointer, not the source object, the barrier may take action before the

---

[4]The Pauseless/C4 collectors [Click *et al.*, 2005; Tene *et al.*, 2011] use the term *loaded value barrier*; Shenandoah calls these *loaded reference barriers* [Kennke, 2019].

reference is used. This is of particular advantage on speculative hardware, since properties of the loaded pointer are not dependent on properties of its target referent object. For example, the tag might reveal that its pointer refers to a fromspace white object instead of a tospace (grey or black) copy. The barrier can check for that and forward the reference accordingly, preserving a tospace invariant for the black mutator. The Pauseless/C4 collector uses such a barrier (see Section 17.5 [Click *et al.*, 2005; Tene *et al.*, 2011]).

In summary, all of the barrier techniques enumerated here cover the minimal requirements to maintain their invariants, but variations on these techniques can be obtained by short-circuiting, refining or coarsening.

Concurrent write barrier mechanisms

In order to preserve either the strong or the weak invariant, write barriers must detect all writes to object fields of interesting pointers and record either their source, their target or the target originally stored in the field. References to these grey objects must be recorded in some data structure. However, concurrently with mutators adding references to the structure, the collector will remove and trace them. It is essential that insertions and removals be efficient and correct in the face of mutator-mutator and mutator-collector races.

One way to record grey objects is to add them to a log. We considered a variety of concurrent data structures and efficient ways to manage them in Chapter 13. In this section, we consider a popular and alternative mechanism: card tables. The basic operation of card tables for stop-the-world collectors was described in Chapter 11. Here we extend that discussion to examine how mutator-collector concurrency complicates their operation and how this can be resolved.

Recall that remembered sets can be implemented by associating a byte in a card table with each small (say, 512 bytes) contiguous area of the heap. Card tables can be used by both generational and concurrent collectors. A write barrier records the location of a grey object by dirtying the byte in the card table that corresponds to the card containing the object. Concurrently, the collector scans the card table for dirty cards. The collector must then search any dirty cards, trace grey objects and clean the cards. Clearly, this presents a race between mutators and collector that raises questions of correctness.

What constitutes a grey entity depends on the style of collector and its write barrier. In a generational collector, object fields are grey if the object is in an older generation and the field holds a reference to an object in a younger generation. In a concurrent collector that uses a Steele-style retreating barrier, an object is grey if it has already been marked (that is, was once black) but now holds a reference to an unmarked child. With a Dijkstra-style advancing barrier or a Yuasa-style deletion barrier, all objects in a dirty card must be considered grey. While this barrier may seem very imprecise since it will preserve garbage neighbours of live objects, note that Abuaiadh *et al.* [2004] found that compacting small blocks rather than individual objects led to an increase in memory footprint of only a few percent.

The card table is the concurrent collector's work list. The collector must scan it looking for dirty cards and cleaning them until all cards are clean. Since mutators may dirty cards after the collector has cleaned them, the collector must repeatedly scan the card table. An alternative might be to delay processing the card table until a final stop-the-world phase, but this is likely to cause the concurrent part of the tracing phase to terminate too soon [Barabash *et al.*, 2003, 2005].

One-level card tables

The simplest organisation is a one-level card table, as described above. Here, a card may be in one of three states: dirty, refining or clean. Mutator write barriers will set the state to be dirty using a simple store instruction rather than an atomic primitive such as compare-and-swap [Detlefs *et al.*, 2002a]. The collector thread sets the status to refining before searching the card for interesting pointers and determining a new status for the card. The simplest would be dirty but Detlefs *et al.* can also 'summarise' cards (see Chapter 11). The collector now attempts to write the new status back to the card. First, it checks that the card's status is still refining and that no mutator has dirtied the card while the collector was searching it. If the status is still refining, the collector must try to change the value atomically to the new status, for example with a compare-and-swap. If this fails, then a mutator must have dirtied the card concurrently, meaning that it may contain an unprocessed grey object. Detlefs *et al.* simply leave this card dirty and proceed to the next dirty card, but one might also try to clean the card again.

Two-level card tables

Because the overwhelming majority of cards are likely to be clean, two-level card tables reduce the cost of searching the card table for dirty cards. Each entry in a second, coarse-grain card table records the state of 2^n fine grained cards. Cleaning a two-level card table proceeds similarly to cleaning a one-level table. When a dirty coarse-grain card is found, its status is set to refining and the corresponding fine-grained cards are searched. Once all the fine-grain cards are clean, the collector attempts atomically to set the state of the coarse-grain card to clean. However, there is a subtle concurrency issue here. Because write barrier actions are not atomic with respect to the card-cleaning thread, the write barrier must dirty the fine-grained card before dirtying the corresponding coarse-grained card, while the collector reads them in the opposite order. We note that obtaining the proper order may have extra cost on machines that require a memory fence to force it.

Reducing work

One solution that reduces the amount of redundant work done by the collector is to try to avoid scanning any object more than once [Barabash *et al.*, 2003, 2005]. Here, the authors defer cleaning cards for as long as there is other tracing work for the collector to do. Their mostly-concurrent collector uses a Steele-style retreating insertion barrier. Such collectors must scan marked objects on dirty cards and trace all their unmarked children. The first technique for reducing the amount of redundant scanning is not to trace through an object on a dirty card: it suffices to mark the object as it will be traced through when the card is cleaned. Although objects that are traced through before their card is dirtied will still be scanned twice, this eliminates rescanning objects that are marked after their card is dirtied. Barabash *et al.* observe that this can improve the collector's performance and reduce the number of cache misses it incurs. Note that although changes in the order of memory accesses on a weakly consistent platform may cause this optimisation to be missed, the technique is still safe.

Their second approach is to reduce the number of dirty cards. Recall that it is necessary for a Steele-style barrier to dirty a card only if the modified object has already been traced by the collector. If it has not, then the collector will notice it eventually so there is no need to dirty the card. In other words, there is no need to shade a white object grey. Card marking is used by collectors because it is a fast, unconditional operation. The question, therefore, is how this check can be made efficient.

One solution is to mark the cards dirty unconditionally but maintain a second table indicating whether a card contains an object that has been traced. Periodically, the dirty card table can be undirtied as follows, without need for atomic operations assuming the tables hold bytes rather than bits:

```
for each dirty card C
    if not isTraced(C)                                                          $
        setClean(C)
        if isTraced(C)
            setDirty(C)
```

Their second solution rests on the observation that for many programs most pointer writes are made to young objects and that these typically reside in local allocation buffers. Instead of keeping a second card table, a bit is used for each object to indicate whether it is part of an active local allocation buffer. If this bit is set, the collector defers tracing the object to a later time, instead adding the object to a deferred list. When the buffer overflows — the allocation slow path — the mutator sets all the cards in the buffer to be clean and clears all the `defer` bits for all objects in the buffer. One reason that this is effective is that Barabash *et al.* found that the collector rarely reaches objects in an active local allocation buffer.

Some care is needed with this solution on weakly consistent platforms. The simplest approach is to have the collector execute a fence after marking a card traced and before tracing an object, and have the undirtying procedure execute a fence between checking whether each card is dirty and checking whether it is traced (as above). Note that in both cases only the collector threads execute the fence. An alternative method is to have the undirtying procedure start by scanning the card table, and cleaning and recording (in a list or an additional card table) all cards that are dirty but have not yet been traced. Next, the undirtying procedure handshakes with the collector, requesting the concurrent collector to run a synchronisation barrier. When both have run the handshake, the undirtying procedure rescans all the cards whose dirty bit was cleared and marks them dirty again if the card has been traced.

Eliminating read barriers

For systems with much concurrency, a technique of Sivaramakrishnan *et al.* [2012] allows eliminating read barriers. They do this by preventing the creation of pointers that cross generations or regions, that is, pointers that would force the referent object to be copied and necessitate the installation of a forwarding address. Instead, the write barrier simply blocks the thread until after the next local collection has occurred. In systems without much mutator concurrency, this would probably not work well, but they obtained favorable results (20% to 30% performance improvement) across multiple hardware platforms with large numbers of processors executing large numbers of mutator threads.

15.3 Ragged phase changes

Tracing garbage collectors comprise several phases, for example with the collector idle, marking roots, tracing the object graph, and so on. It is essential that phase changes are coordinated between mutator and collector threads. This is straightforward for stop-the-world or mostly-concurrent collectors as all mutator threads are halted when the collector changes from one phase to another (Figure 15.3a). This ensures the following.

- Once the collector has entered a new phase B, no mutator observes a collector state S_A corresponding to the previous phase A; and

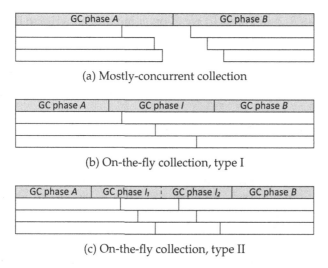

(a) Mostly-concurrent collection

(b) On-the-fly collection, type I

(c) On-the-fly collection, type II

Figure 15.3: Ragged phase changes

- At any time, all mutators observe a coherent collector state, that is, all observe S_A or all observe S_B.

In contrast, on-the-fly collectors typically stop each mutator independently, for example to scan its stack. A mutator will not recognise that a phase has been changed until it reaches a GC safe-point. This causes two problems.

1. The collector cannot start collection work until it has determined that all mutators have recognised that the phase has been changed.

2. There is a time window in which different mutators observe different collection states.

Ugawa *et al.* [2018] identify a general design pattern that subsumes previous approaches. They assert that it is sufficient to capture all types of ragged phase change.   Problem 1 requires an intermediate phase (Figure 15.3b) between the main phases, where the collector simply handshakes with each mutator to ensure that the mutator has recognised the change of main phases and changed its local state. Each mutator should respond to this handshake request at its next GC safe-point. Once the collector has completed a handshake with every mutator, it is guaranteed that all mutators have recognised that the collector is going to move to the new phase. They call this type of ragged phase change *Type I*.

Problem 2 recognises the possibility of a mutator-mutator conflict. Any mutator that has not recognised the new phase will be running with assumptions based on an invariant for the previous phase. This may conflict with the invariant assumed by mutators that have recognised the change. Two intermediate phases, I_1 and I_2 (Figure 15.3c), solve this problem as follows. Before the ragged phase change, mutators respect the invariants of the current Phase A. The purpose of Phase I_1 is for mutators to change their local collection state to an intermediate state, S_I. Typically, a mutator in this intermediate state will run with a more complex barrier that respects the invariants of both main Phases A and B, that is, each mutator is prepared for another mutator acting according to the invariants of Phase B, but none is doing so yet. In Phase I_2, mutators know that no other mutator is still in Phase A but some may be in Phase B. At the end of Phase I_2, all mutators will be respecting the invariants of Phase B. Ugawa *et al.* call this type of ragged phase change *Type II*. As an example, consider how an on-the-fly collector might change from no collection (Phase

A) to marking (Phase B). In Phase I_1, we allow a mutator to write to black objects safely but to allocate only white objects. At the transition from Phase I_1 to I_2, the collector knows that all mutators are ready for black objects. In Phase I_2, mutators can allocate new objects black. At the end of this phase, the collector knows that all mutators are allocating black and so can transition to state S_B.

15.4 Issues to consider

Garbage collectors that are incremental (mutator interleaved with collector) or concurrent (mutator and collector in parallel) have one primary purpose: minimising the collector pauses observed by the mutator. Whether the pause is due to an increment of collection work needing to be performed by the mutator, or is caused by the mutator having to synchronise with (and possibly wait for) the collector to finish some work, incremental/concurrent techniques usually trade increased elapsed time (mutator throughput) for reduced disruption by the collector. In an ideal world, concurrent collectors may be able to reduce elapsed time by running collector work completely in parallel with the mutator. Unfortunately, there is no free lunch. As we have already seen, concurrent collectors require some level of communication and synchronisation between the mutator and the collector, in the form of mutator barriers. Moreover, contention between the mutator and collector for processor time or for memory (including disturbance of the caches by the collector) can also slow the mutator down.

Conversely, incremental or concurrent collection can improve throughput for some applications. The collectors impose overhead on individual mutator actions (loads or stores) in order to reduce the pauses observed by the application's users. However, an application's user may be another program, and this client may be very sensitive to delays. Ossia et al. [2004] offer three-tier transaction processing systems as an example. They point out that delays for stop-the-world collections may cause transactions to time out and to be retried. By doing a little extra work (executing write barriers), much more extra work (reprocessing transactions that timed out) can be avoided.

The concurrent collection techniques that we consider in subsequent chapters each have their own particular impact on these costs. Concurrent reference counting collectors may impose a particularly high overhead on pointer loads and stores. Concurrent mark-sweep collectors, which do not move objects, have relatively low overhead for pointer accesses (varying with the barrier), but they may suffer from fragmentation. Concurrent collectors that relocate objects require additional synchronisation to protect the mutator from, or inform the mutator about, objects that the collector moves. Copying collectors also impose additional space overhead that adds to memory pressure. In all concurrent collectors, whether a read barrier or write barrier is used will affect throughput differently, based on the relative frequency of reads and writes, and the amount of work the barrier performs.

Concurrent mark-sweep collectors typically use a write barrier to notify the marker of an object to mark from. Many concurrent copying and compacting collectors use a read barrier to protect the mutator from accessing stale objects that have been copied elsewhere. However, concurrent replicating collectors typically only use write barriers except for pointer comparisons. There is a trade-off between the frequency of barrier execution and the amount of work it must do. A barrier that triggers copying and scanning will be more expensive than one that simply copies, which will be more expensive than one that simply redirects the source pointer. Similarly, performing more work early may result in fewer later barriers needing to do much work. All of these factors depend on the granularity of work performed, across a scale from references through objects to pages.

The amount of floating garbage is another factor in the costs of concurrent collection. Not having to collect floating garbage will allow faster termination of the current collection cycle, at the expense of additional memory pressure.

Whether the mutator (threads) must be stopped at the beginning of the collection cycle (to make sure the collector has seen all the roots), at the end (to check for termination) or between intermediate phases, also has an impact on throughput. Termination criteria also affect the amount of floating garbage.

A further consideration is that most concurrent collectors offer only loose assurances on pauses and space overhead. Providing the hard bounds on space and time needed for real-time applications means making well-defined progress guarantees for mutator operations that interact with the heap, and space guarantees that derive solely from knowledge of the memory allocation footprint of the application.

Incremental or concurrent collection can be particularly desirable when the volume of live data is expected to be very large. In this case, even stop-the-world parallel collection using every processor available would lead to unacceptable pause times. However, one drawback of incremental and concurrent collectors is that they cannot recycle any memory until the marking phase of a collection cycle is complete; we must provide sufficient headroom in the heap or give the collector a sufficiently generous share of processor resources (at the expense of the mutator) to ensure that the mutator does not run out of memory before the collection cycle completes. We consider garbage collector scheduling when we address the problem of real-time collection in Chapter 19; there, the problem is particularly acute.

An alternative approach is to use hybrid generational/concurrent collection. The young generation is managed in the usual generational way, stopping the world for each minor collection. The old generation is managed by a concurrent collector. A variation on this approach is used by the LXR collector [Zhao *et al.*, 2022a] which combines coalesced reference counting to reclaim many, especially short-lived, objects in both generations promptly with background concurrent mark-sweep collection only of garbage cycles; we discuss LXR in Section 18.1. These generational strategies have several advantages. Nursery collections are usually short enough not to be disruptive. Since most objects tend to die young — the weak generational hypothesis — we can expect memory to be recycled promptly for further allocation, thus reducing the space overhead required to avoid running out of memory. There is no need to apply the concurrent write barrier to objects in the young generation as it is collected stop-the-world: the generational write barrier in the slow path suffices. Concurrent collectors typically allocate new objects black, guaranteeing that they will survive a collection even though most objects will not live that long. However, by allocating new objects generationally, this problem disappears. Finally, old objects have much lower mutation rates than young ones [Blackburn and McKinley, 2003]. This is the ideal scenario for an incremental or concurrent collector since their write barrier is less frequently invoked.

!

Chapter 16

Concurrent mark-sweep

In the previous chapter we looked at the need for incremental or concurrent garbage collection, and identified the problems faced by all such collectors. In this chapter, we consider one family of these collectors: concurrent mark-sweep collectors. As we noted before, the most important issue facing concurrent collection is correctness. The mutator and collector must communicate with each other in order to ensure that they share a coherent view of the heap. This is necessary on the mutator's part to prevent live objects from being hidden from the collector. It is necessary for collectors that move objects to ensure that the mutator uses the correct addresses of moved objects.

The mark-sweep family includes the simplest of the concurrent collectors. Because they do not change pointer fields, the mutator can freely read pointers from the heap without needing to be protected from the collector. Thus, there is no inherent need for a read barrier for non-moving collectors. Read barriers are otherwise generally considered too expensive for use in maintaining the strong invariant for a non-moving collector, since heap reads by the mutator are typically much more frequent than writes. For example, Zorn [1990] found that the static frequencies of pointer loads and stores in SPUR Lisp were 13% to 15% and 4%, respectively. He measured the running-time overhead of inlined write barriers as ranging from 2% to 6%, and up to 20% for read barriers. The exception to this general rule is when compiler optimisation techniques can be brought to bear on eliminating redundant barriers [Hosking *et al.*, 1999; Zee and Rinard, 2002], and to folding some of the barrier work into existing overheads for null pointer checks [Bacon *et al.*, 2003a]. For this reason, mark-sweep collectors usually adopt the Dijkstra *et al.* [1976, 1978] incremental update or Steele [1976] insertion write barriers, or their coarser Boehm *et al.* [1991] variant, or the snapshot-at-the-beginning Yuasa [1990] deletion write barrier.

16.1 Initialisation

Instead of allowing the mutator to run until memory is exhausted, concurrent collectors run while the mutator is still allocating. However, when to trigger the beginning of a new marking phase is a critical decision. If a collection is triggered too late, it can happen that there will be insufficient memory to satisfy some allocation request, at which point the mutator will stall until the collection cycle can complete. Once the collection cycle begins, the collector's steady-state work-rate must be sufficient to complete the cycle before the mutator exhausts memory, while minimising its impact on mutator throughput. How and when to trigger a garbage collection cycle, ensuring that sufficient memory is available

Algorithm 16.1: Mostly-concurrent mark-sweep allocation

```
 1   New():
 2       handshake1()
 3       ref ← allocate()                        /* must initialise black if mutator is black */
 4       if ref = null
 5           gcStart()
 6           while gcRunning
 7               /* wait for collection to finish */
 8           ref ← allocate()
 9           if ref = null
10               error "Out of memory"
11       return ref
12
13   handshake1():
14       if not gcRunning && behind()                        /* GC checkpoint */
15           gcStart()
16       if markingTerminating()                        /* only for grey mutators */
17           ackHandshake()
18           while markingTerminating()
19               /* wait for marking/sweeping to finish (with lazy or eager sweep) */
```

for allocation to keep the mutator satisfied even as concurrent collection proceeds, and reaching termination of the collection cycle so that garbage can be reclaimed and recycled, all depend on scheduling collection work alongside the mutator.

Algorithm 16.1 illustrates the mutator allocation sequence for a concurrent mark-sweep garbage collector that triggers the collector to start work based on a policy decision as to whether collection is 'behind' and needs to begin in order to avoid running out of memory before the collection cycle completes. Collection is synchronised with concurrent mutator threads executing mutator barriers or allocations, as indicated by the atomic modifier. There may also be multiple collector threads if the code is adjusted to use a suitable termination algorithm to end marking and likewise sweeping may be parallelised. The decision as to when to start the collector is captured by the utility routine behind, which makes sure that the mutator does not get so far ahead of the collector that the allocate routine will not block waiting for the collector to finish.

Algorithm 16.2 shows what happens when collection work is triggered. The gcStart routine forces initialisation of the collector by scanning the roots to prime the work list. Assuming that scanning the roots also means stopping and scanning all the mutator threads, then at this point no mutator thread holds a white reference. Thus, this example operates in mostly-concurrent mode, with a stop-the-world phase to initiate collection. The now-grey root objects represent the initial scanning wavefront from which tracing proceeds. Having scanned the roots, mutator threads can now continue either as black (since they hold no white references) or grey, depending on the mutator barriers being used.

Stopping the world may result in unacceptable pauses. With grey mutator barriers in place, it is possible simply to enable the barriers and defer scanning all the roots until later, concurrently with the mutator. Section 16.6 describes techniques that relax the need to stop the mutator threads in order to sample their roots. Still, at least one root must be scanned to prime the work list and initiate tracing.

Algorithm 16.2: Mostly-concurrent marking

```
 1   shared worklist ← empty
 2
 3   atomic gcStart():
 4       if not gcRunning
 5           scan(Roots)                              /* invariant: mutator holds no white references */
 6           gcRunning ← true
 7       return
 8
 9   gcThread():
10       while true                                  /* one iteration per collection cycle */
11           while not gcRunning
12               /* wait for cycle start */
13           while not isEmpty(worklist)
14               ref ← remove(worklist)
15               scan(ref)
16           rescan()                                /* only for grey mutators */
17           sweep()                                 /* eager or lazy sweep */
18           gcRunning ← false
19
20   rescan():                                       /* only needed for grey mutators */
21       setMarkingTerminating(true)
22       handshake2()
23       scan(Roots)
24       while not isEmpty(worklist)
25           ref ← remove(worklist)
26           scan(ref)
27       setMarkingTerminating(false)
28
29   handshake2():                                   /* wait for all mutators to stop */
30       waitForAllMutatorsToAckHandshake()
```

16.2 Termination

Termination of the collector cycle for a black mutator is a relatively straightforward procedure. When there are no grey objects in the work list remaining to be scanned, the collector terminates. At this point, even with the weak tricolour invariant the mutator can contain only black references, since there are no white objects reachable from grey objects still held by the mutator (since there are no grey objects). Because the mutator is black, there is no need to rescan its roots.

Termination for a grey mutator is a little more complicated, since the mutator may acquire white pointers after its roots were scanned to initiate the collection. Thus, the grey mutator roots must be rescanned before the collector cycle can terminate. Provided that rescanning the mutator roots does not expose any fresh grey objects, the collection cycle is done. Algorithm 16.2 simply follows a single marking pass by stopping all the mutator threads in order to rescan their stacks and mark to completion before entering the sweep phase. An alternative would be to repeat the process of stopping mutators, scanning their stacks, and marking while the mutators are restarted a number of times, before a final stop-the-world rescan and mark to completion. This approach is likely to lead to a shorter pause to complete marking. Note that there is also a choice in `handshake1` (Algorithm 16.1) of whether to halt mutators just until marking is complete (and then lazily sweep the heap) or to halt them until after the (eager) sweep is also complete.

Pizlo [2017] describes a technique for ensuring that rescanning eventually terminates. In this scheme, time is broken down into quanta of, say, two milliseconds. The collector (if running) always gets at least 30% of a quantum. The remaining 70% is split according to what fraction of the reserve space is left, the reserve being the amount of space into which the mutator may allocate while the collector is running. If fraction H of the reserve is left, the mutator gets that fraction of the 70% of the quantum. Note that in the extreme (when the reserve is exhausted) the collector will run to completion without interruption. This resource allocation approach helps prevent the collector from getting too far behind and, assuming that mutators continue to allocate, guarantees eventual completion.

16.3   Allocation

Notice that the allocator must initialise the mark state (colour) of the new object according to the colour of the mutator. If the mutator is black, then new objects must be allocated black (marked) under the strong invariant, unless (under the weak invariant) the new object is also made reachable from some grey object. This last guarantee is generally difficult to make, so black mutators usually allocate black even under the weak invariant [Abraham and Patel, 1987; Yuasa, 1990]. However, a grey mutator admits a number of alternatives that several implementations exploit.

Kung and Song [1977] simply allocate black during the marking phase and white otherwise. Their choice is guided by the observation that new objects are usually immediately linked to existing reachable objects, at which point their write barrier (unconditional Dijkstra-style incremental update) would simply shade the object anyway. Moreover, because the new object contains no references, it is safe to allocate straight to black and avoid unnecessary work scanning it for non-existent children.

Steele [1976] chooses to vary the colour of allocation during marking, depending on the pointer values that are used to initialise the new object. Assuming that the initial values of a new object's reference fields are known at the time of allocation permits a bulk test of the colour of the targets of those references. If none of them are white, then the new object can safely be allocated black. Furthermore, if none of them are white, then it is a possible sign that the marker is close to terminating and that the new object will not be discarded. Conversely, if any of the initialising pointers is white, then the new object is allocated white. The Steele collector marks mutator stacks last, and scans them from bottom (least volatile) to top (most volatile), so most cells will be allocated white to reduce floating garbage.

During sweeping, Steele allocates white or black according to where the sweeper is in its pass through the heap. Allocation is white if the free cell being allocated is from space that has already been swept, and black otherwise (to prevent the sweeper from misinterpreting the newly allocated object as free).

One problem with allocating new objects white instead of black is that the new object may over time accumulate a long chain of white objects which, if it remains reachable, must eventually be traversed before the collection cycle can terminate (consider what happens when a grey mutator allocates a large new data structure white). Allocating black avoids dragging out termination in this way, but at the cost of wasted space since it defers freeing any newly allocated but now unreachable data until the next cycle [Boehm *et al.*, 1991; Printezis and Detlefs, 2000]. Vechev *et al.* [2006] propose a compromise solution in which they colour newly allocated objects with a fourth colour: *yellow* objects are treated as if they are white for purposes of retention (they may yet die before the cycle completes), but black with respect to the tricolour invariant. That is, a yellow object will be shaded straight to black (reachable) without being scanned. Thus, terminating tracing with a grey mutator that holds yellow references means not needing to trace beyond the yellow object.

16.4 Concurrent marking and sweeping

So far we have considered running marking concurrently only with the mutator, with marking and sweeping proceeding in series. Lazy sweeping means that allocation requests by the mutator may also trigger concurrent sweeping from the previous marking phase, even as a new collection cycle is running the next marking phase. This can potentially lead to a confusion about the colours of objects. The trick is to distinguish true garbage white objects from the previous marking phase (needing to be swept) from (as-yet unmarked) white objects in the next marking phase (which may yet be marked). Lamport [1976] pipelines the execution of marking and sweeping phases by introducing a new colour, *purple*, to distinguish the former from the latter. At the completion of the marking phase, all (garbage) white objects are recoloured purple. Sweeping will collect purple objects, adding them to the free-list (recoloured black or white, depending on allocation colour). Lamport envisions several concurrent marking and sweeping threads, with a collection cycle proceeding as follows.

1. Wait until all markers and sweepers have finished.

2. Change all white nodes to purple and all black nodes to white (preferably white to avoid floating garbage) or grey (in the case the node has been shaded concurrently by the mutator write barrier).

3. Shade all roots.

4. Start the markers and sweepers.

Marking ignores all purple objects: the mutator can never acquire a reference to a purple object, so grey objects never point to purple and purple objects are never shaded. Of course, the difficulty with this approach is that the conversion of white to purple might require touching colour state associated with all of the garbage objects, which must be completed before sweeping can begin. Similarly, when starting the marking phase, all black objects (from the previous cycle) must be recoloured white.

Lamport describes an elegant solution to this problem in which the colours are reinterpreted at Step 2 by rotating through a range of colour values. Each object is tagged with a two-bit basic hue (white, black, purple) plus a one-bit `shaded` flag. If the hue is white, then setting the `shaded` flag shades the object grey (that is, a `shaded` white hue is grey). If the hue is black, then setting the `shaded` flag has no effect (that is, black hue means black whether the `shaded` flag is set or not). If the hue is purple, then the `shaded` flag will never be set since garbage objects will not be traced. The sense of the hue bits is determined by a global variable `base` encoding the value of white (=`base`), black (=`base`+1) and purple (=`base`+2). At Step 2 there are no grey or purple nodes because marking and sweeping have finished, so flipping from black to white and white to purple is achieved simply by incrementing `base` modulo 3. Table 16.1 shows the three possible values of `base` encoded in binary (00, 01, 10) and the two possible values of the `shaded` flag (0, 1), which together make up the possible colours, along with examples for the three possible values of `base`. The entries in the 'value' columns are determined using arithmetic modulo 3. Note that

| tag | | GC 1: base=00 | | GC 2: base=01 | | GC 3: base=10 | |
hue	shaded	value	colour	value	colour	value	colour
00	0	base	white	base+2	purple	base+1	black
00	1	base	grey	base+2	impossible	base+1	black
01	0	base+1	black	base	white	base+2	purple
01	1	base+1	black	base	grey	base+2	impossible
10	0	base+2	purple	base+1	black	base	white
10	1	base+2	impossible	base+1	black	base	grey

Table 16.1: Lamport [1976] mark colours: 'hue and shaded' encoding of colours for concurrent marking and sweeping. The colour encoding is: white as hue=base/shaded=0, grey as hue=base/shaded=1, black as hue=base+1 and purple as hue=base+2. Note that a garbage (purple) object can never be shaded. When all markers and sweepers have finished, there are no grey or purple nodes, so flipping from black to white/grey and white to purple is achieved simply by incrementing base modulo 3.

the combination hue=base+2/shaded=1 is impossible because purple (garbage) objects are never shaded grey. Subsequent increments cycle the hue interpretation accordingly.

To make sure that Step 2 does not leave a node grey from one cycle to the next unless it was recently shaded by a mutator, whenever a marker thread makes a grey node black it must also clear the shaded flag. Otherwise, the grey node will be retained as floating garbage. Also, to speed up the identification of garbage, markers and sweepers can take the opportunity to clear the shaded flag whenever they encounter a black object.

Queinnec *et al.* [1989] propose an alternative solution to this problem, using separate colour information for odd and even collection cycles. Thus, marking in one cycle can proceed independently of sweeping from the previous cycle because they operate on independent colour state.

16.5   Garbage-First: collecting young and old regions

Most of the concurrency issues faced in the marking phase of a mostly-concurrent collector are addressed by the use of write barriers, which we considered at length in the previous chapter. As an example, we now discuss the OpenJDK *Garbage-First* (G1) collector which employs collector threads, running concurrently with mutator threads, to mark live objects, although it stops the world to copy survivors from condemned regions.

In Section 10.4 we focused on G1's organisation of the heap and on 'young only' collection of young generation regions. To recap, G1 organises the heap into equal-sized regions. To enable these to be collected independently, G1 requires for each collected region a remembered set that records where other regions might contain a reference to this region; G1 implements remembered sets as sets of cards. Management of these remembered sets is crucial to G1's performance and space utilisation.

As configured in OpenJDK, G1 is a generational collector. Most collections are 'young only', stopping the world to evacuate young generation regions and reclaim in-place any dead humongous objects. In this section, we consider how a *mixed collection* of young and old regions operates, describing its phases in some detail. Here, G1 marks the whole heap concurrently but still evacuates any regions selected with mutators paused. Thus, it is a 'mostly mark-sweep collector.' G1 has evolved considerably from the implementation described by Detlefs [2004a]; here we discuss the techniques used in OpenJDK 20. One of the most significant changes lies in the handling of remembered sets, which can grow very large unless stale and duplicate entries are removed, which was time-consuming and did not eliminate all remembered set fragmentation. G1 therefore no longer builds remembered sets on the fly for all old regions but on demand only for those being evacuated; remembered sets for young regions are always maintained.

G1 starts in 'young only' mode, evacuating in stop-the-world pauses only live objects in young generation regions (see Section 10.4). Eventually, it will become necessary to reclaim space in old generation regions as well. This necessitates a 'mixed collection' that starts by initiating concurrent marking adaptively, based on the size of the old generation, promotion rate, prediction of the length of time to mark and other metrics. 'Mixed collections' comprise a number of stop-the-world and concurrent phases.

Start: This stop-the-world phase is piggy-backed on a 'young only' collection that seeds the roots for concurrent marking. To avoid explicitly marking recently allocated objects, G1 sets a *Top At Mark Start* (TAMS) variable for each region; any objects allocated at addresses above the TAMS for a region will be considered implicitly live/marked. This simplifies allocation, as there is no need to mark the bitmap[1] for new objects. This phase also records those memory ranges to which the young collection copied objects (in the survivor space or old generation). These ranges will be searched subsequently for roots into the condemned set; simply recording these ranges avoids expensive iteration and marking during this pause.

Concurrent Clear Claimed Marks: Initialise collection of classes and class loaders.

Concurrent Scan Root Regions: The 'young only' collection did not follow references to old generation objects. In this phase, multiple threads scan the previously recorded ranges of addresses occupied by survivors of the 'young only' collection for references to the old generation, and mark the referenced objects. This phase runs concurrently with the mutators and must complete before the next stop-the-world 'young only' collection can start.

Concurrent Mark From Roots: Now that all roots have been marked, live objects below each region's TAMS are traced and marked concurrently by parallel threads, using a snapshot-at-the-beginning algorithm, with mutators using a deletion barrier (as in Algorithm 15.2c). G1 marking threads use the approach described by Printezis and Detlefs [2000]. Each thread first claims a region to mark by atomically advancing a *global* 'finger' to the right. To scan a region, the thread advances a *local* finger through the region's bitmap. When it encounters a mark, the thread tries to mark atomically the corresponding object's unmarked children. If an unmarked child is to the left of the global finger, the thread pushes it onto its local mark stack. Otherwise, it takes no further action as the object will be encountered later by some marking thread.

The threads use work stealing to balance loads, where necessary pushing or stealing work between their local mark stacks and a global mark stack or other threads' local mark stacks. Several stop-the-world 'young only' collections may take place while concurrent marking is in progress. Marking threads synchronise with pending GC safe-points by regularly polling, based on a dynamic number of objects and words scanned metric.

Concurrent Pre-clean: Optionally, process weak reference objects discovered by concurrent marking. Any such object that holds null or a reference to a live object needs no further processing and is dropped from the list of discovered references.

---

[1] Recall that in JDK 20 G1 uses only a single bitmap for marking (it originally used two [Detlefs, 2004a]).

Remark: In this stop-the-world phase, G1 completes marking. Should this cause the global mark stack to overflow, G1 will start another Concurrent Mark round. Otherwise, it processes weak references according to the Java specification (see the discussion of weak references in Section 12.2) and unloads unused classes. It then reclaims any completely empty regions and identifies candidate regions for evacuation according to the volume of live data in each region, ignoring any whose occupancy exceeds a threshold (default, 85%) and therefore whose reclamation would yield little free space. In the next phase, G1 will need to scan live objects for inter-region references. To assist this, the Remark phase sets a *Top At Rebuild Start* (TARS) variable for each old generation region. It will be sufficient to scan live objects in a region only up to its TARS, since any objects above this threshold whose reference fields are updated will be handled by the write barrier. The barrier will also handle *all* objects mutated after they have been scanned.

Concurrent Rebuild Remembered Sets: In this phase, mutators are restarted. G1 now starts to gather information needed for reclaiming space in the old generation, rebuilding the remembered sets for those old regions selected for evacuation. In versions prior to JDK 20, G1 obtained liveness information from its 'current' and 'previous' bitmaps (and 'current' and 'previous' TAMSes), which it used alternately. JDK 20 drops the second bitmap and TAMSes in favour of reformatting the heap in order to facilitate later parsing and scanning it. Here, G1 replaces sequences of dead objects and gaps with filler objects (using liveness information from the mark bitmap) in order to improve heap parsability. It then scans live objects for inter-region references, adding any cross-region references to the appropriate remembered set. The pre-JDK 20 method had the disadvantages not only of the space needed for the second bitmap but also that iterating over the live objects (below the TAMS) required the use of the bitmap rather than simply walking over holes now occupied by single dead objects. All these actions — reformatting the heap, scanning and rebuilding remembered sets — are 'embarrassingly' parallel. Again, there is regular synchronisation at safe-points where 'young only' collections may occur.

Cleanup: In this stop-the-world phase, G1 calculates the efficiency of evacuating each region in the condemned set, based on each region's occupancy and connectedness. It drops any regions from the condemned set, along with their remembered sets, whose efficiency would be too low. At this point, G1 is ready to start the Space Reclamation phase but first runs a further stop-the-world Prepare Mixed 'young only' collection. This is needed because the Cleanup pause interrupted a mutator execution that had been sized to maintain minimum mutator utilisation requirements using predictions for a non-mixed collection pause; changing the type of garbage collection invalidates these predictions.

Concurrent Cleanup for Next Mark: Clears the bitmap, ready for the next marking cycle.

Space Reclamation: Over the next few stop-the-world pauses for 'young only' collections, parallel threads also scan the card table looking for live objects in old generation regions to evacuate. The only difference here between 'young only' and 'mixed' collections is the contents of the condemned set. In each pause, G1 continues to evacuate regions in the condemned set until it estimates that it would exceed its pause time goal.

In summary, G1 is intended to support applications running on multiprocessor machines using heap sizes of tens of gigabytes or larger, with over half the heap occupied by live data. It is capable of defragmenting the heap while at the same time balancing throughput and latency. Management of remembered sets has proved critical to its performance. Earlier implementations could lead to remembered sets as large as 20%[2] of the heap in some circumstances. Building remembered sets on demand and only for those old regions selected for evacuation and removing the second bitmap can reduce the space needed to around 3% of the heap size in typical cases. Nevertheless, G1 may require careful tuning to meet throughput and latency goals for some applications.

16.6 On-the-fly marking

So far, we have assumed that the mutator threads are all stopped at once so that their roots can be scanned, whether to initiate or terminate marking. Thus, after the initial root scan, the mutator holds no white references. At this point, the mutator threads can be left to run as black (so long as a black mutator barrier is employed), or grey (with a grey mutator barrier) with the proviso that to terminate marking the collector must eventually stop and rescan grey mutators until no more work can be found. These stop-the-world actions reduce concurrency. An alternative is to sample the roots of each mutator thread separately, and concurrently with other mutator threads. This approach introduces complexity because of the need to cope with some threads operating grey and some operating black, all at the same time, and how it affects termination.

On-the-fly collection never stops the mutator threads all at once. Rather, the collector engages each of the mutators in a series of soft *handshakes*: these do not require a single global hard synchronisation at the command of the collector. Instead, the collector merely prompts each mutator thread asynchronously, one-by-one, to halt gracefully at some convenient point. The collector can then sample (and perhaps modify) each thread's state (stacks and registers) before releasing it on its way. While one mutator thread is stopped, others can continue to run. Furthermore, if stack barriers are used, as described in Section 11.5, the collector can restrict its examination of the stopped thread to just the top active stack frame (all other frames can be captured synchronously with a stack barrier) so the handshake can be very quick, minimising mutator interruption.

Write barriers for on-the-fly collection

Synchronisation operations for on-the-fly collectors need some care. A common approach for mostly-concurrent collectors, which stop all threads together to scan their stacks, is to use a deletion barrier with a black mutator. Furthermore, new objects are allocated black. This approach simplifies the termination of marking: black stacks do not need to be rescanned and allocation does not lead to more work for the collector. However, this approach is not sufficient for an on-the-fly collector, as Figure 16.1 illustrates. Because stacks are scanned on the fly, some may be white. The heap is allowed to contain black objects before all threads have been scanned and before tracing has started because we allocate new objects black. The deletion barrier is not triggered on stack operations and there is no insertion barrier, so neither X nor Y is shaded grey. Typically, on-the-fly algorithms employ an incremental update insertion barrier to avoid propagating pointers unnoticed before the deletion barrier can be enabled. In summary, correct mutator-collector synchronisation for on-the-fly marking is a subtle issue that requires substantial care on the part of the algorithm designer.

---

[2]Thomas Schatzl, Free and Open Source Software Developers' European Meeting (FOSDEM), 2018, `https://archive.fosdem.org/2018/schedule/event/g1/`.

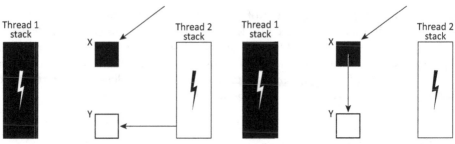

(a) The deletion barrier is 'on'. Thread 1 has been scanned, but thread 2 has not. X has been newly allocated black.

(b) X is updated to point to Y; thread 2's reference to Y is removed. Neither action triggers a deletion barrier.

Figure 16.1: On-the-fly collectors that allocate black need more than a deletion barrier to prevent the scenario of a white object reachable only from a black object.

Doligez-Leroy-Gonthier

Using soft handshakes to initiate marking was first used in a mark-sweep garbage collector tailored for the ML programming language. Dubbed *Doligez-Leroy-Gonthier*, after the names of its authors [Doligez and Leroy, 1993; Doligez and Gonthier, 1994], this collector uses private thread-local heaps to allow separate garbage collection of data allocated solely on behalf of a single thread, and not shared with other threads. A global heap allows sharing of objects among threads, with the proviso that the global shared objects never contain pointers into private heaps. A dynamic escape detection mechanism copies private objects into the shared heap whenever a reference to them is stored outside the private heap. Only immutable objects (the vast majority in ML) can be allocated privately, so making a copy of one in the shared heap does not require updating all the sources of its pointers (though it does require copying its transitive closure of reachable immutable objects). But mutation is rare in ML, so this happens infrequently. These rules permit a private heap to be collected independently, stopping only the mutator that owns that heap.

Doligez-Leroy-Gonthier uses concurrent mark-sweep collection in the shared heap, to avoid having to update references from each of the threads. The steady-state concurrent mark-sweep collector operates in the usual black mutator snapshot mode, employing a Yuasa-style snapshot deletion barrier. Initiating steady-state collection proceeds using a series of soft handshakes to transition mutator threads from grey to black, as follows. In terms of Ugawa *et al.* [2018] (Section 15.3), this is a Type II transition.

The collector and mutator threads each track their own view of the state of the collection with a private status variable. To initiate the collection cycle, the collector sets its status to $Sync_1$. The mutator threads are then made to acknowledge, and update their own status, via soft handshakes. Once all have acknowledged the $Sync_1$ handshake, the collector is said to be in Phase $Sync_1$. Mutator threads ignore handshakes while storing to a pointer field or allocating, to ensure that these operations first complete, making them atomic with respect to phase changes. Having acknowledged this handshake, each mutator thread now runs with the write barrier in Algorithm 16.3a, which shades both the old and new values of modified pointer fields, combining both the black mutator Yuasa-style snapshot deletion barrier and the grey mutator Dijkstra-style incremental update insertion barrier. Shading by the mutator does not place the shaded object directly into the collector's work list for scanning (like Kung and Song [1977]), but simply colours a white object explicitly grey and resets a global `dirty` variable to force the collector to scan for the

Algorithm 16.3: Doligez-Leroy-Gonthier write barriers. Both ignore the handshake.

<table>
<tr><td colspan="2">(a) The Sync barrier</td><td colspan="2">(b) The Async barrier</td></tr>
</table>

```
1  Write_Sync(src, i, new):        1  Write_Async(src, i, new):
2      old ← src[i]                2      old ← src[i]
3      shade(old)                  3      if not isBlack(old)
4      shade(new)                  4          shade(old)
5      src[i] ← new                5          if old ≤ scanned
                                   6              dirty ← true
                                   7      src[i] ← new
```

newly grey object (in the style of Dijkstra *et al.* [1978]). This avoids the need to synchronise explicitly between the mutator and the collector (other than for soft handshakes, where atomicity is accomplished simply by delaying acknowledging the handshake), but does mean that worst-case termination requires rescanning the heap for grey objects. Because mutation is rare in ML, this is not a significant impediment. At this point, the grey mutator threads are still allocating white, as they were before the collection cycle was initiated.

Once all of the mutators have acknowledged the $Sync_1$ handshake the collector moves to Phase $Sync_2$ with another round of handshakes. Because the write barrier is atomic only with respect to handshakes, it does not impose mutator-mutator synchronisation. This leaves the possibility that a mutator from before the $Sync_1$ handshake, which is not running the write barrier, could insert some other pointer X into the src[i] field right after the load old←src[i]. Thus, shade(old) will not shade the pointer X that actually gets overwritten by the store src[i]←new. The transition to Phase $Sync_2$ avoids such problems by ensuring that all mutator threads have completed any unmonitored atomic allocation or write in *Async* before transitioning to $Sync_1$. At that point, all mutators will be running the write barrier (with insertion protection), so even if the mutators interleave their write barrier operations, there will not be a problem. The collector can then safely move into the steady-state snapshot marking phase, *Async*. Each mutator thread acknowledges the *Async* handshake by scanning (shading from) its roots for the collector (making itself black), starting to allocate black, and reverting to the standard snapshot barrier augmented with resetting the global dirty flag (similarly to Dijkstra *et al.* [1978]) to force the collector to rescan if the shaded object is behind the scanning wavefront, shown in Algorithm 16.3b. Table 16.2 shows the phases as observed by collector and mutators.

Once marking finishes, sweeping commences. Like Steele [1975], the collector's sweep pointer determines the mutator allocation colour to minimise floating garbage: white if allocating from memory already swept (so already noted free in this cycle), black if not yet swept (to avoid sweeping it to the free-list), and grey if at the point where the collector is currently sweeping (to avoid the race with the sweeper at the boundary).

Doligez-Leroy-Gonthier for Java

Domani *et al.* [2000] consider Doligez-Leroy-Gonthier-style collection in the context of Java, where they offer several improvements to cope with much higher mutation rates, and language features such as weak references and finalisation. Because Java lacks general support for immutable objects they do not consider independently collected thread-local heaps, but simply a global shared heap, collected on the fly. They also support correct execution on multiprocessors that have a more relaxed memory model than sequential consistency, which was assumed for the original Doligez-Leroy-Gonthier implementation.

Phase	Collector	Mutators	Meaning
Async	*Async*	*Async*	No mutators are executing barriers
	$Sync_1$	*Async*, $Sync_1$	Some mutators may be running the *Sync* barrier
$Sync_1$	$Sync_2$	$Sync_1$, $Sync_2$	Some mutators may be black and running the *Async* barrier; others are running the *Sync* barrier
$Sync_2$	$Sync_2$	$Sync_2$	All mutators are running the *Async* barrier
	Async	$Sync_2$, *Async*	Some mutators are black; all are running the *Async* barrier
Async	*Async*	*Async*	All mutators are black; the collector can complete marking, scanning and sweeping

Table 16.2: Phases in the Doligez and Gonthier collector

To avoid rescanning for fresh mutator-shaded grey objects (which are more common in a mutation-oriented language like Java), Domani *et al.* dedicate an output-restricted double-ended queue to each mutator thread, to which it can enqueue grey objects at one end, while the collector is able to poll for work from the other end. This minimises synchronisation between the mutator and collector in the write barriers.

Sliding views

Azatchi *et al.* [2003] offer further improvements to on-the-fly marking by exploiting the *sliding views* approach to sampling mutator roots without stopping the world [Levanoni and Petrank, 1999]. In place of the deque used by Domani *et al.*, the sliding views approach implements the snapshot deletion barrier by logging to a thread-local buffer the state of *all* the fields of an object before it is modified (dirtied) for the first time while the collector is marking. The buffers are drained via soft handshakes, with marking terminated once all the buffers are empty. Like Doligez-Leroy-Gonthier, after the initial handshake, and before the deletion barrier can be enabled for each mutator, the mutators also execute a Dijkstra-style incremental update insertion barrier to avoid propagating pointers unnoticed before the mutator snapshot can be gathered. These *snooped* stores also become mutator roots. The snooped stores are disabled once all threads are known to be logging the snapshot. We discuss further details of this approach in Section 18.7.

16.7   Abstract concurrent collection

Concurrent collectors have many common design features and mechanisms, while differing in small but important details. To highlight these similarities and differences, we can adopt a common abstract framework for concurrent garbage collection [Vechev *et al.*, 2005, 2006; Vechev, 2007]. As discussed previously, the correctness of a concurrent collector depends on cooperation between the collector and the mutator in the presence of concurrency. Thus, the abstract concurrent collector logs events of mutual interest to the collector and mutator by appending to the shared list log. These events are tagged as follows:

- **T**⟨src, fld, old, new⟩ records that the collector has Traced pointer field fld of source object src, and that the field initially contained reference old which the collector has replaced by reference new. That is, the collector has traced an edge in the object graph src→old and replaced it with an edge src→new.

- **N**⟨ref⟩ records that the mutator has allocated a **New** object ref.

- **R**⟨src, fld, old⟩ records that the mutator has performed a **Read** from the heap by loading the value old from field fld of source object src.

- **W**⟨src, fld, old, new⟩ records that the mutator has performed a **Write** to the heap by storing the value new into field fld of source object src which previously contained value old. If fld is a pointer field, then the mutator has replaced an edge src→old with an edge src→new.

Each of src, fld, old, new are the addresses of the source object and source field, and old and new target object addresses, respectively. Collector event **T** captures the fields that have already been scanned by the mutator. For a non-moving collector tracing does not modify the references in the heap, so old=new for **T** events. Mutator event **N** captures allocations by the mutator. Mutator events **R** and **W** capture the fields that the mutator has accessed or modified.

An abstract concurrent mark-sweep collector is illustrated by Algorithm 16.4, which takes the abstract tracing collector of Algorithm 6.1 and augments it to handle the fact that the collector executes concurrently with the mutator. The algorithm proceeds in the usual way, scanning reachable objects by tracing from the roots, before sweeping to reclaim unreachable objects. Units of scanning work performed by scanTracingInc occur atomically; except to note that sweeping must also be properly synchronised, we omit details of sweepTracing.

Initialisation of the collector atomically samples the mutator roots using the routine rootsTracing and clears the log. This is performed atomically (stop-the-world) to avoid the complication of concurrent mutation of the roots by the mutator threads. On-the-fly collectors can sample the roots without stopping the world.

The collector then proceeds concurrently with the mutator, repeatedly both scanning objects and adding origins to be considered by the collector due to concurrent writes performed by the mutator.

At some point, the loop terminates as a result of some non-deterministic choice (denoted by ⑦), when the collector moves to a termination phase in which the remaining origins and objects to be scanned are processed atomically (that is, preventing the mutator from writing). This is performed atomically to prevent concurrent writes during termination, which may be needed to guarantee that the collector will complete its cycle. For some practical algorithms, this atomic termination phase can be eliminated.

The scanTracingInc procedure implements the usual collector traversal of the heap, but incrementally, interleaved with the mutator. It differs from the original procedure scanTracing of Algorithm 6.1 only in that it atomically records to the log each traced field and the reference it contains.

The addOrigins procedure reveals that the abstract concurrent collector is parametrised by an as-yet-undefined function *expose* which takes a log prefix and returns a set of objects that should be considered as additional origins for live references. Different implementations for this function yield different abstract concurrent collector algorithms corresponding to concrete algorithms in the literature, as discussed further below when we describe how to instantiate specific collectors. It is the log that permits dealing with concurrent mutations that cause reachable objects to be hidden from the scan routine, which otherwise would remain unmarked.

The collector wavefront

Cooperation between the collector and the mutator guarantees correctness in the presence of concurrency. The log records the tracing progress of the collector through the heap — the *wavefront* — in the form of **T** events. Key to cooperation is how interleaved mutator

Algorithm 16.4: Mostly-concurrent incremental tracing garbage collection

---

```
 1   shared log ← ()
 2
 3   collectTracingInc():
 4       atomic
 5           rootsTracing(W)
 6           log ← ()
 7       repeat
 8           scanTracingInc(W)
 9           addOrigins(W)
10       until ⓘ
11       atomic
12           addOrigins(W)
13           scanTracingInc(W)
14       sweepTracing()
15
16   scanTracingInc(W):
17       while not isEmpty(W)
18           src ← remove(W)
19           if ρ(src) = 0                                    /* reference count is zero */
20               for each fld in Pointers(src)
21                   atomic
22                       ref ← *fld
23                       log ← log · T⟨src, fld, ref, ref⟩
24                   if ref ≠ null
25                       W ← W + [ref]
26           ρ(src) ← ρ(src)+1                                /* increment reference count */
27
28   addOrigins(W):
29       atomic
30           origins ← expose(log)
31       for each src in origins
32           W ← W + [src]
33
34   New():
35       ref ← allocate()
36       atomic
37           ρ(ref) ← 0
38           log ← log · N⟨ref⟩
39       return ref
40
41   atomic Write(src, i, new):
42       if src ≠ roots
43           old ← src[i]
44           log ← log · W⟨src, &src[i], old, new⟩
45           src[i] ← new
```

events (**N**, **R**, and **W**) are treated, depending on whether they occur to the portion of the heap already scanned by the collector (behind the wavefront) or not yet scanned (ahead of the wavefront). The wavefront itself comprises the set of pending fields still to be scanned (specifically not the values of the pointers in those fields). Practical collectors may approximate the wavefront more or less precisely, from field granularity up through granularity at the level of objects to pages or other physical or logical units.

Adding origins

The addOrigins procedure uses the log to select a set of additional objects to be considered live, even if the collector has not yet encountered those objects in its trace, since it is possible that some number of reachable pointers were hidden by the mutator behind the wavefront. The precise choice of the set of origins is returned by the *expose* function.

Mutator barriers

The procedures New and Write represent the usual barriers performed by the mutator (here they are suitably atomic), which in the abstract algorithm coordinate with the collector by appending their actions to the log. Logging **N**ew objects allows subsequent mutator events to distinguish loading/storing fields of new objects, and loading/storing references to new objects. A freshly allocated object always has a unique reference until that reference has been stored to more than one field in the heap. Moreover, it does not contain any outgoing references (so long as its fields have not been modified, since they are initialised to null). This event allows concrete collectors to vary in how they decide liveness of objects that are allocated during the collection cycle (some collectors treat all such objects as live regardless of their reachability, leaving those that are unreachable to be reclaimed at the next collection cycle). Others will retain only those new objects whose references are stored to live objects.

As usual, the mutator Write operation assigns src[i]←new (with new≠null) so the pointer to destination object new is *inserted* in field src[i] of source object src. Similarly, the old pointer old previously in field src[i] of source object src is *deleted*. When the source field is behind the collector wavefront, then the pointers new/old are inserted/deleted behind the wavefront. Otherwise, the pointers are inserted/deleted ahead of the wavefront. Logging **W**rite events captures both the inserted and deleted pointers.

Recall also that the wavefront can be expressed using the tricolour abstraction, where those objects/fields ahead of the wavefront are white, those at the wavefront are grey, and those behind the wavefront are black.

Precision

The abstract concurrent collector of Algorithm 16.4 preserves a fixed level of atomicity (as specified by the atomic blocks) while instantiating the function *expose* in different ways to vary precision. Varying this parameter of the abstract concurrent collector is sufficient to capture a representative subset of concrete concurrent collectors that occur in the literature, but there are other real collectors that cannot be instantiated directly from Algorithm 16.4 since they vary also in what they treat atomically. For example, Algorithm 16.4 assumes that roots can be obtained atomically from the mutator threads, which implies that they must be sampled simultaneously perhaps by stopping them all briefly (that is, Algorithm 16.4 is mostly-concurrent, not fully on-the-fly).

Instantiating collectors

Instantiating specific concurrent collectors within this framework requires defining a corresponding *expose* function. For example, consider a Steele-style concurrent collector that
rescans all objects modified up to and including the wavefront. The wavefront at an object
and field granularity is captured by (last) Trace operations in the log for each object/field.
The objects modified are captured by the src component of all the Write records in the
log, and the modified fields by the fld component. The Steele-style *expose* function atomically rescans modified fields that have already been traced. The traditional implementation tracks the wavefront at the object granularity (src component of Trace records) using per-object mark bits, but the abstract framework highlights that the wavefront might
also operate at the field (fld) granularity given a mechanism for marking distinct fields.
Thus, one need only rescan modified fields that have already been traced as opposed to
whole modified objects that have already been traced. Moreover, Steele [1976] assumes
that mutator thread stacks are highly volatile, so *expose* must rescan them right to the end.
Termination requires that every Trace record have no matching (at the field or object level)
Write record occurring after it in the log.

A classical Dijkstra-style collector that unconditionally shades the target of any reference stored to the heap will expose the new component of all the Write records up to and
including matching Trace records at the wavefront. Note that these new references are
extracted directly from the log without rescanning. Termination is similar to Steele.

Conversely, a Yuasa-style snapshot collector exposes the old component of all Write
records that have no matching Trace record after them in log. Tracing that stays ahead
of the mutator will successfully append Trace records to the log before the mutator can
modify the fields they record, offering speedier termination than for incremental update.

16.8   Issues to consider

Many of the issues facing concurrent mark-sweep garbage collection are common to all
concurrent collectors. Concurrent collectors are without doubt more complex to design,
implement and debug than stop-the-world collectors. Do the demands made of the collector warrant this additional complexity? Or would a simpler solution such as a generational
collector suffice?

Generational collectors can offer expected pause times for most applications of a few
milliseconds or even less. However, their worst case — a full heap collection — may pause
an application for very much longer, depending on the size of the heap, the volume of
live objects and so on. Such delays may not be acceptable. Concurrent collectors, on the
other hand, offer shorter and more predictable pause times. As we shall see in Chapter 19,
properly specified real-time collectors can guarantee submillisecond pause times, but this
typically comes at the cost of significant overhead on both the mutator and the collector.
To bound pause times, the collector must not only be concurrent but also on-the-fly: it
must stop mutators only one at a time in order to process their roots (unless the mutators
can be processed concurrently).

Other questions for concurrent mark-sweep collection are the same as those for its
stop-the-world counterpart. Non-moving memory managers are vulnerable to fragmentation. As well as defragmenting the heap, copying and compacting collectors permit bump
pointer allocation which may be faster than free-list allocation and may also provide better
locality for the mutator(s). On the other hand, mark-sweep collectors make better utilisation of space than copying collectors since they do not require a copy reserve. However,
non-moving concurrent collectors have a further advantage over other concurrent collec-

tors: a simpler heap coherency model. All concurrent collectors require mutators to inform the collector of changes to the topology of the heap in order to prevent a mutator from hiding objects from a collector. In addition, collectors that move objects must ensure both that only one collector thread moves an evacuated object and that it appears to mutators that *all* references to a moved object are updated atomically.

Concurrent mark-sweep collection also presents a number of tactical choices to the implementer. As with other concurrent collectors, objects may be allocated black, grey or white. Black mutators require that all objects be allocated black. Grey mutators allow further possibilities. New objects may be allocated black, grey or white, or the decision may be varied depending on the phase of the collector, the initial values of the new object's fields or the progress of the sweeper.

In the remaining chapters, we examine concurrent copying and compacting collectors and conclude with collectors that can provide pause time guarantees sufficient for hard real-time systems, that is, those that must meet every deadline.

Chapter 17

Concurrent copying and compaction

In this chapter we discuss approaches to defragmenting the heap concurrently with the mutator, relocating live objects either by concurrent copying or by concurrent compaction. Here we consider how the mark-compact approaches of Chapter 3 and the copying approaches of Chapter 4 extend to operate concurrently with the mutator.

We focus initially on collection techniques based on copying (evacuating or scavenging) reachable objects out of a fromspace into a tospace, after which the fromspace can be reclaimed. These collectors face the problem that mutators may encounter references to either fromspace or tospace objects, although note that replicating collectors relax this complication by having mutators continue to operate on fromspace originals whilst the collector constructs a replica of the live heap in tospace. We then consider concurrent collection techniques based on compaction. Typically, such collectors divide the heap into a number of regions and then identify only some of these for evacuation.

Recall that when scanning object fields the collector must convert all fromspace pointers to tospace pointers, replacing each fromspace pointer with the forwarding address of its fromspace target, copying the fromspace target the first time it is encountered. Concurrent copying collectors must not only protect the collector against mutation but also protect the mutator against concurrent copying. Moreover, concurrent updates by the mutator must be propagated to the copies being constructed in tospace by the collector.

For copying collectors, a black mutator must by definition only hold tospace pointers. If it held fromspace pointers, then the collector would never revisit and forward them, violating correctness. This is called the black mutator *tospace invariant*: the mutator operates at all times ahead of the wavefront in tospace. Similarly, a grey mutator must by definition only hold fromspace pointers at the beginning of the collector cycle. In the absence of a read barrier to forward a fromspace pointer to the tospace copy, the grey mutator cannot directly acquire tospace pointers from fromspace objects (since the copying collector does not forward pointers stored in fromspace objects). This is called the grey *mutator fromspace invariant*. Of course, for termination of a copying algorithm, all mutator threads must end the collection cycle holding only tospace pointers, so any copying collector that allows grey mutator threads to continue operating in fromspace must eventually switch them all over to tospace by forwarding their roots. Moreover, updates by the mutator in fromspace must also be reflected in tospace or else they will be lost.

17.1 Mostly-concurrent copying

Maintaining a tospace invariant for all mutator threads is perhaps the simplest approach to concurrent copying because it guarantees that the mutator threads never see objects that the collector is yet to copy, or is in the middle of copying. Establishing the tospace invariant in a mostly-concurrent world requires stopping all the mutator threads (atomically) to sample and forward their roots (copying their targets) at the beginning of the collection cycle. At this point, the now-black mutators contain only (grey) tospace pointers, but the (unscanned) grey targets will still contain fromspace pointers.

Baker's algorithm

Baker's [1978] black mutator read barrier was first formulated for incremental collection to protect against a mutator acquiring one of these fromspace pointers, and was subsequently extended by Halstead [1985] for concurrent copying. The read barrier presents the illusion to the mutator threads that the collection cycle has completed, by preventing them from crossing the collector wavefront boundary between tospace and fromspace.

Baker-style concurrent collection is illustrated in Algorithm 17.1, as a revision of the non-concurrent copying of Algorithm 4.2. Notice that the read barrier only needs to trigger when loading from a grey tospace object (ahead of the collector wavefront). Only then is the forward operation needed to ensure that the loaded reference is to a tospace object, copying any uncopied fromspace object as necessary. As specified here, synchronisation between mutator and collector is relatively coarse-grained (at the level of objects): the collector atomic block scans the next grey object, while the mutator atomic read barrier forwards any reference loaded from a grey object. The atomic blocks ensure that a mutator thread can never load a reference from an object that is in the middle of being scanned (to turn it from grey to black).

As presented in Algorithm 17.1, atomicity of the Read operation ensures that the mutator sees the correct state of the src object (grey or not) and the target object (forwarded or not), as well as allowing the mutator to copy the target object if it is in fromspace, without interfering with ongoing copying by the collector in process. Thus, the mutator's atomic Read operation may incur overhead proportional to the size of the object being copied. It is possible to obtain finer-grained atomicity by synchronising each of these operations more carefully with the collector.

One approach is to allow finer-grained synchronisation using a work list holding field addresses rather than object references. A difficulty then is how to distinguish grey fields from black fields. The problem is ensuring that the wavefront is easily determined by the mutator. At the granularity of objects, it is simple enough to set a grey bit in the header of each grey object, but for fields there is not usually a cheap place to store this information although side metadata can be used for this purpose [Zhao *et al.*, 2022a,b]. However, with Cheney scanning the scan pointer can be advanced (atomically) as each field is scanned, so black fields lie behind the scan pointer and grey fields in front. In this case, the read barrier might look something like:

```
atomic Read(src, i):
    ref ← src[i]
    if ref ≠ null && scan ≤ &src[i]              /* src[i] is grey */
        ref ← forward(ref)
    return ref
```

Of course, this description leaves out all the machinery needed to advance the wavefront atomically through each of the fields. We will see techniques for achieving this finer-grained processing in Chapter 19, where minimising interruptions by the collector becomes important for real-time systems.

Algorithm 17.1: Mostly-concurrent copying

```
 1   shared worklist ← empty
 2
 3   collect():
 4       atomic
 5           flip()
 6           for each fld in Roots
 7               process(fld)
 8       loop
 9           atomic
10               if isEmpty(worklist)
11                   break                           /* exit loop */
12               ref ← remove(worklist)
13               scan(ref)
14
15   flip():
16       fromspace, tospace ← tospace, fromspace
17       free, top ← tospace, tospace + extent
18
19   scan(toRef):
20       for each fld in Pointers(toRef)
21           process(fld)
22
23   process(fld):
24       fromRef ← *fld
25       if fromRef ≠ null
26           *fld ← forward(fromRef)       /* update with tospace reference */
27
28   forward(fromRef):
29       toRef ← forwardingAddress(fromRef)
30       if toRef = null                        /* not copied (not marked) */
31           toRef ← copy(fromRef)
32       return toRef
33
34   copy(fromRef):
35       toRef ← free
36       free ← free + size(fromRef)
37       if free > top
38           error "Out of memory"
39       move(fromRef, toRef)
40       forwardingAddress(fromRef) ← toRef              /* mark */
41       add(worklist, toRef)
42       return toRef
43
44   atomic Read(src, i):
45       ref ← src[i]
46       if isGrey(src)
47           ref ← forward(ref)
48       return ref
```

Mostly-concurrent, mostly-copying collection

Mostly-concurrent collection also naturally applies to *mostly-copying collection*. Recall that a mostly-copying collector must treat ambiguous roots conservatively, pinning all objects that they reference. The collector is free to move the remaining objects not directly referenced by ambiguous roots. It is straightforward to use the brief stop-the-world phase of a mostly-concurrent collector to mark (and pin) all the objects referenced by the ambiguous roots in the mutator thread stacks and registers. At this point all the mutator threads are black, and a Baker-style read barrier will ensure that the mutator threads never subsequently acquire references to uncopied objects.

DeTreville [1990] used this approach for concurrently collecting Modula-2+ and subsequently for Modula-3 [Cardelli *et al.*, 1992], both systems-oriented programming languages whose compilers were not sophisticated enough to generate accurate stack maps. Also, because their compilers did not emit an explicit barrier for heap accesses, DeTreville applied an Appel *et al.* read barrier to synchronise the mutator with the collector using virtual memory page protection. Detlefs [1990] used the same technique for C++, modifying the AT&T C++ compiler to derive automatically the accurate pointer maps for heap objects needed to allow copying of objects not referenced directly from ambiguous roots.

Subsequently, Hosking [2006] replaced use of coarse-grained virtual memory page protection as the read barrier mechanism with compiler-generated object-grained read barrier support. The motivation for this was the difficulty of managing page protections atomically in the presence of mutator threads that are preemptively scheduled by the operating system. Because the read barrier is only needed during the copying phase of collection, after all the mutator threads have been stopped to scan their ambiguous roots and make them black, it is possible to avoid expensive atomic instructions in the fast path of the barrier that checks if the source object is grey. Atomic operations are thus only needed to ensure atomicity of the forwarding operation.

17.2   Brooks's indirection barrier

An alternative approach to requiring a tospace invariant is to allow the mutator to make progress without concern for the wavefront. Brooks [1984] observes that if every object (whether in fromspace or tospace) has a non-null forwarding pointer (either to its fromspace original or to its copy in tospace), then the test on the `src` object in the read barrier can be eliminated. A fromspace object that has not yet been copied will have an indirection field that points to itself. When copying an object, the fromspace indirection field is atomically updated to refer to the tospace copy. The tospace copy has an indirection field that points to itself. All heap accesses, both reads and writes, of pointers, non-pointers and mutable values in header words, now always require an unconditional dereference operation in order to follow any indirection pointer to the tospace copy if one exists. Thus, the `Read` barrier for the mutator is rewritten by Brooks as in Algorithm 17.2.

Now the only problem, other than the need for an additional dependent load, is that the read barrier can still read a field ahead of the wavefront that might refer to an uncopied fromspace object. Fortunately, the ubiquitous indirection field relaxes the need for the tospace invariant imposed by Baker so the mutator is allowed to operate grey and hold fromspace references. To ensure termination Brooks imposes a Dijkstra-style write barrier to prevent the insertion of fromspace pointers behind the wavefront, as in Algorithm 17.2.

Because mutator threads now operate grey, once copying is finished they need a final scan of their stacks to replace any remaining unforwarded references. The alternative, as

Algorithm 17.2: Brooks's indirection barriers

```
1  atomic Read(src, i):
2      src ← forwardingAddress(src)
3      return src[i]
4
5  atomic Write(src, i, ref):
6      src ← forwardingAddress(src)
7      if isBlack(src)                    /* src is behind wavefront in tospace */
8          ref ← forward(ref)
9      src[i] ← ref
```

performed in the original incremental Brooks collector, is simply to scan the thread stacks and registers of each mutator thread after each collector increment, in order to redirect any references they may hold to copied objects before they can resume.

17.3 Self-erasing read barriers

Baker-style collectors require a read barrier to preserve their black mutator invariant. Read barriers are often considered to be more expensive than write barriers since reads are more prevalent than writes. Furthermore, read barriers are conditional: given a Read(src,i), they must test whether src[i] is in tospace and evacuate it if not. Cheadle *et al.* [2004] eliminated this test and all overheads in accessing a black tospace object for a Baker-style incremental copying collector in the Glasgow Haskell Compiler (GHC). The first word of every object (*closure*) in GHC points to its *entry code*: the code to execute (*enter*) when the closure is evaluated. They provided two versions of this code. In addition to the standard version, a second version scavenged the closure before entering the standard code. Let us see how this scheme operated. When the collector was off, the entry-code word pointed to the standard, non-scavenging code. However, when an object was copied to tospace, this word was hijacked and set to point to the self-scavenging code. If the object, now in tospace, was entered, the self-scavenging code was executed first to copy the object's children to tospace. Then the original value of the entry-code word was reinstated. Finally, the standard version of the code was entered. The beauty of this scheme was that if the closure was evaluated in the future, then its standard code would have been entered unconditionally: the read barrier had been erased. The cost of this scheme was some duplication of code: Cheadle *et al.* found the overhead to be 25% over that of a stop-the-world copying collector. However, GHC's later introduction of pointer tagging is incompatible with this technique as it eliminates many mutator calls to entry code in order to reduce the number of branch prediction misses [Marlow *et al.*, 2007]. Cheadle *et al.* [2008] applied the same technique to flip method-table pointers in the Jikes RVM Java virtual machine. To do so, they had to virtualise most accesses to an object (all method calls and accesses to fields unless they are static or private). However, they were able to recoup some of this cost by using the run-time compiler to inline aggressively. Note that a self-healing *load barrier* is similar in intent, though different in implementation: it also seeks to repair the condition that the barrier detects, and updates the slot to prevent the barrier action in the future. However, it does so using explicit code, not an indirect call.

17.4   Replication copying

The Brooks indirection barrier imposes a time and space penalty. Following an indirection pointer adds (bounded) overhead to every mutator heap access (both reads and writes, pointers and non-pointers), and the indirection pointer adds an additional pointer word to the header of every object. It has the advantage of avoiding the need for Baker's tospace invariant which forces the mutator to perform copying work when loading a fromspace reference from the heap, while preserving the essential property that accesses (both reads and writes) go to the tospace copy whenever one is present. This has the important result that heap updates are never lost because they occur either to the fromspace original before it is copied or to the tospace copy afterwards.[1]

Replication copying collectors [Nettles *et al.*, 1992; Nettles and O'Toole, 1993] relax this requirement by allowing the mutator to continue operating against fromspace originals even while the collector is copying them to tospace. That is, the mutator threads obey a fromspace invariant, updating the fromspace objects directly, while a write barrier logs all updates to fromspace objects to record the differences that must still be applied to their tospace copies. In other words, replication copying collectors allow the state of the tospace copy to lag behind that of its fromspace original, so long as by the time the collector is finished copying, but before it can discard fromspace, all mutator updates have been applied from the log to the tospace copy and all mutator roots have been forwarded. Thus, the termination condition for collection is that the mutation log is empty, the mutator's roots have all been scanned, and all of the objects in tospace have been scanned.

Concurrent replication copying requires synchronisation between the mutator and collector via the mutation log, and when updating the roots from the mutators. Thread-local buffers and work stealing techniques can minimise the synchronisation overhead when manipulating the mutation log [Azagury *et al.*, 1999]. The collector must use the mutation log to ensure that all replicas reach a consistent state before the collection terminates. When the collector modifies a replica that has already been scanned, it must rescan the replica to make sure that any object referenced as a result of the mutation is also replicated in tospace. Termination of the collector requires that each mutator thread be stopped to scan its roots. When there are no more objects to scan, the mutator log is empty, and no mutator has any remaining references to uncopied objects, then the collection cycle is finished. At this point, all the mutator threads are stopped together briefly to switch them over to tospace by redirecting their roots.

The resulting algorithm imposes only short pauses to sample (and at the end redirect) the mutator roots: each mutator thread is stopped separately to scan its roots, with a brief stop-the-world phase at the end of the cycle to switch all the threads over to tospace.

The downside to replication copying is that *every* mutation of the heap, not just pointers, needs to be logged by the mutator threads. This imposes a much higher write barrier overhead than for traditional pointer-only write barriers, and the mutation log can become a bottleneck. For languages that discourage mutation, such as the functional language ML used by Nettles and O'Toole, this is less of an issue so performance does not suffer.

Multi-version copying

Nettles and O'Toole [1993] still require global stop-the-world synchronisation of the mutator threads to transition them to tospace. Their algorithm is not lock-free because no mutator can make progress while this transition occurs. Herlihy and Moss [1992] dispense with

---

[1] Atomic copying of an object and installation of the forwarding address from the old copy to the new one is not always simple.

the need for a global transition. They adapt Halstead's [1985] multiprocessor refinement of Baker's [1978] algorithm, which divides the heap into multiple per-processor regions. Each processor has its own fromspace and tospace, and is responsible for evacuating into its own tospace any fromspace object it discovers while scanning. Halstead uses locking to handle races between processors that compete to copy the same object, and for updates to avoid writing to an object while it is being evacuated. He also retains global synchronisation to have all the processors perform the flip into their tospace before discarding their fromspace. To eliminate this global synchronisation, Herlihy and Moss decouple fromspace reclamation from the flip. They divide each processor region into a single tospace plus *multiple* (zero or more) fromspaces. As copying proceeds, multiple fromspace versions of an object can accumulate in different spaces. Only one of these versions is current, while the rest are obsolete.

Each processor[2] alternates between its mutator task and a scanning task that checks local variables and its tospace for pointers to fromspace versions. When such a pointer is found, the scanner locates the object's current version. If that version is in a fromspace, then it copies it to a new current version in its tospace (the old version is now obsolete).

In this way, the processors cooperate to move objects from fromspaces to tospaces, and to redirect reachable pointers to the tospaces. Each processor is responsible for scanning its own tospace for fromspace pointers, and for copying any fromspace object it finds (including objects in fromspaces of other processors) that does not have a current tospace copy in some processor. A processor can flip at any time during its mutator task (when its tospace is full and so long as it has sufficient free space to allocate a new tospace), but not in the middle of a scan. It cannot free its fromspaces until it can be sure no other processor holds references to any of its fromspace objects.

To manage versions, Herlihy and Moss maintain a forwarding pointer field `next` at all times in each object, so that each obsolete fromspace version refers to its next version, terminating at the current version which has a `null` forwarding pointer. When copying a fromspace object into its own tospace, a scanning processor atomically installs the tospace copy at the end of the version chain using compare-and-swap, making it current. Thus, every mutator heap access must traverse to the end of the chain of versions before performing the access. Moreover, to preserve lock-freedom while ensuring that heap updates are not lost, every store into an object creates a new version of the object in the mutating processor's tospace, using compare-and-swap to make it current. Thus, scanning and copying require no global synchronisation, while preserving all mutator updates.

A processor owning fromspaces (the *owner*) can discard them only if no other scanning processor (scanners) holds any of its fromspace pointers. A scan is *clean* with respect to a given owner if the scan completes without finding any pointers to versions in any of the owner's fromspaces, otherwise it is dirty. A *round* is an interval during which every processor starts and completes a scan. A *clean* round is one in which every scan is clean and no processor executes a flip. After a processor executes a flip, the resulting fromspace can be reclaimed after completion of a subsequent clean round.

An owner detects that another scanner has started and completed a scan using two atomic *handshake* bits, each written by one processor and read by the other. Initially, both bits agree. To start a flip, the owner creates a new tospace, marks the old tospace as a fromspace, and inverts its handshake bit. At the start of a scan, the scanner reads the owner's handshake bit, performs the scan, and sets its handshake bit to the value read from the owner's. Thus, the handshake bits will agree once the scanner has started and completed a scan in the interval since the owner's bit was inverted.

---

[2]Herlihy and Moss use the term *process* for what might now be called a thread, but we continue to use *processor* here to match Halstead [1985] and to emphasise that the heap regions should be thought of as per-processor.

However, an owner must detect that *all* processes have started and completed a scan, and every processor is symmetrically both an owner and a scanner, so the handshake bits are arranged into two arrays. An *owner* array contains the owner handshake bits, indexed by owner processor. A 2-dimensional scanner array contains the scanner handshake bits, with an element for each owner-scanner pair. Because a scan can complete with respect to multiple owners, the scanner must copy the entire *owner* array into a local array on each scan. At the end of the scan, the scanner must set its corresponding scanner bits to these previously saved values. An owner detects that the round is complete as soon as its owner bit agrees with the bits from all scanners. An owner cannot begin a new round until the current round is complete.

To detect whether a completed round was clean, the processors share an array of *dirty* bits, indexed by processor. When an owner executes a flip, it sets the *dirty* bit for all other processors. Also, when a scanner finds a pointer into another processor's fromspace it sets that processor's *dirty* bit. If an owner's *dirty* bit is clear at the end of a round, then the round was clean, and it can reclaim its fromspaces. If not, then it simply clears its *dirty* bit and starts a new scan. By associating *dirty* bits with fromspaces rather than processor regions, and having scanners set the *dirty* bit for the target fromspace when they find a pointer, it is also possible to reclaim fromspaces individually rather than all at once.

Herlihy and Moss prove safety and liveness (of collector) for their algorithm, but they do not explore performance of an actual implementation. The liveness (of collector) argument relies on the observation that if each processor always eventually scans, then some processor always eventually reclaims its fromspaces. At worst, because each processor will eventually exhaust its free spaces, further flips will cease, and all processors will eventually focus on scanning until a clean round ensues. Of course, this resource exhaustion has the effect of causing blocking in the system as a whole.

Extensions to avoid copy-on-write

The novelty of this multi-versioning algorithm is that it is entirely lock-free. Its downside is the need to create a new version on every heap update, though this may be useful on a non-uniform memory architecture multiprocessor to improve locality. Herlihy and Moss consider several alternatives to avoiding versioning on every update:

Update in place with `CompareAndSwap2`. The first extension assumes the availability of the `CompareAndSwap2` operator which allows both performing the update and ensuring that the forwarding pointer `next` remains `null` as a single atomic operation. Unfortunately, `CompareAndSwap2` is not widely implemented on modern multiprocessors. Transactional memory might be a viable alternative; in fact, this algorithm inspired the work leading to Herlihy and Moss [1993].

Owner update in place. Another approach simply uses compare-and-swap, but it requires additional fields in the header of object a: seq(a) is a modulo two *sequence number*, index(a) is the index of the slot being updated and value(a) is the new value for that slot. Also, the forwarding pointer field next(a) is permitted to hold a sequence number, in addition to a pointer or `null` (this is easy enough to achieve by tagging the forwarding pointer field with a low bit to distinguish pointers to suitably aligned objects from a sequence number). There only need be two values for sequence numbers: if seq(a)=next(a), then the current update is installed, and otherwise it is ignored.

To perform a store using the full write barrier, a processor chains down the list of versions until it finds the current version (one with `null` or a sequence number stored in its

Algorithm 17.3: Herlihy and Moss [1992] Owner update in place

```
1   Write_Local(a, next, i, v):
2       seq ← (next + 1) % 2
3       seq(a) ← seq                                              $
4       index(a) ← i
5       value(a) ← v
6       if CompareAndSet(&next(a), next, seq)
7           scan(a[i])
8           a[i] ← v
9       else
10          Write(a, i, v)
```

next field). If the current version is local, then the processor performs the Write$_{Local}$ operation illustrated in Algorithm 17.3. This takes the current version a, the observed next field (either null or a sequence number), the index i of the slot to be modified, and the new value of the slot v. It then uses compare-and-set to install the new sequence number in the next field. If successful, then the processor performs a deletion barrier to scan any pointer overwritten by the store (this preserves the invariant that scanning has inspected every pointer written into tospace), before performing the store. Otherwise, the processor locates the newer version and retries the update by invoking the full write barrier. Having the owning process update in place is well suited to a non-uniform memory architecture where it is more efficient to update local objects.

If the object is remote, then the new owner makes a local tospace copy as before, except that after making the copy, but before performing the store, it must check whether next(a)=seq(a). If they are equal, then it must first complete the pending update, performing the deletion barrier to scan the slot indicated by the index field and storing the value from the value field into that slot. The same action must be performed when the scanner evacuates an object into tospace. This ensures that any writes performed on the original object while it is being copied are linearised before writes performed to the copy.

Locking update in place. Finally, there is the alternative of giving up on lock-freedom and using compare-and-swap to lock the object while it is updated. As before, only the owner of the current version may update in place. The owner locks an object by:

1. using compare-and-swap to lock the object by installing a distinguished *locked* value in its next field;

2. scanning the pointer (if any) being overwritten by the store;

3. performing the update;

4. scanning the pointer (if any) being stored; and

5. unlocking the object by setting next back to null.

Since the owner is the only processor that updates the object in place, there is no need to synchronise with the scanner. The deletion barrier in Step 2 ensures that pointers possibly seen by other processors will be scanned. The insertion barrier in Step 4 ensures that if the object has already been scanned, then the new pointer will not be mistakenly omitted.

Sapphire

A problem with symmetric division of the heap into independently collected regions per processor as done by Halstead [1985] and Herlihy and Moss [1992] is that it ties the heap structure to the topology of the multiprocessor. Unfortunately, application heap structures and thread-level parallelism may not map so easily to this configuration. Moreover, one processor can become a bottleneck because it happens to own a particularly large or knotty portion of the heap, causing other processors to wait for it to complete its scanning before they can discard their fromspaces, so they may end up stalling if they have no free space in which to allocate. It may be possible to steal free space from another processor, but this requires the ability to reconfigure the per-processor heap regions dynamically. These issues were discussed earlier in Chapter 14. Instead, concurrent collectors place collector work asymmetrically on one or more dedicated collector threads, whose priority can easily be adjusted to achieve a balance of throughput between mutator and collector threads.

Sapphire [Hudson and Moss, 2001, 2003] is a concurrent copying algorithm designed to work well in the presence of a large number of mutator threads on small- to medium-scale shared memory multiprocessors. It extends previous concurrent replication copying algorithms to allow one thread at a time to flip from operating in fromspace to operating in tospace, as opposed to having to stop them to transition them all at once over to tospace. This minimises the amount of time that any given application thread may need to block to support the collector. To cope with mutators operating in both fromspace and tospace at the same time, Sapphire requires that they update both the fromspace and tospace copies of an object, when both exist.

Transactional Sapphire

Transactional Sapphire [Ugawa *et al.*, 2018] extends Sapphire with parallel collector threads, and introduces transactions, in either hardware or software, for object copying, and a simpler mechanism to handle volatile fields in order to support lock-free programs that employ fine-grain synchronisation using atomic operations. Like Sapphire, Transactional Sapphire assumes that Java programs are well-synchronised, that is that accesses by different threads to a field should either be protected by a lock or the field should be declared `volatile`. Otherwise, surprising results[3] may occur.

The Transactional Sapphire collector starts as an incremental update collector supported by insertion barriers, before transitioning to a snapshot collector supported by deletion barriers (see the discussion in Section 16.6 on page 357). It allocates most objects in replicated from- and tospaces. Whereas Hudson and Moss had to adopt a complex protocol to manage objects with volatile fields safely, Transactional Sapphire avoids the costs and complexities of synchronising accesses to such objects with replicating them by allocating these objects (and large objects) in a space managed by mark-sweep collection; the volume of these objects is expected to be small. Transactional Sapphire has four major groups of phases (Algorithm 17.4). Throughout the Mark and Copy phases, it maintains the invariant that mutators read from and write to the originals in fromspace in the replicated heap; the Flip phase transitions mutators in several steps to accessing tospace objects. Most of these phase changes are Type I (see Section 15.3), but changing from 'collector idle' to the StackMark phase and from the Copy phase to the HeapFlip phase requires Type II phase changes (the names of intermediate phases are prefixed with 'Pre').

Mark: The first group of phases marks all reachable objects. For objects in replicated spaces, the collector creates an empty shell in tospace and installs forwarding pointers; for objects in mark-sweep spaces, the collector sets a mark in the object header.

---

[3]Of course, in Java 'surprises' can also result from unsynchronised accesses to `double` and `long` values.

Algorithm 17.4: Transactional Sapphire phases

```
 1  Mark:
 2      PreMark1                          /* install Mark phase write barrier */
 3      PreMark2                             /* toggle allocation colour */
 4      StackMark                            /* process mutators' stacks */
 5      RootMark                             /* blacken global variables */
 6      HeapMark                          /* process collector mark queue */
 7      ReferenceProcess         /* mark reference types and terminate marking */
 8
 9  Copy:
10      PreCopy                          /* install Copy phase write barrier */
11      Copy                      /* copy fromspace objects to their tospace shells */
12
13  Flip:
14      PreFlip1              /* install the limited self–flip and equality barriers */
15      PreFlip2                         /* install the full self–flip barrier */
16      HeapFlip              /* flip non–replicated spaces to point to tospace */
17      RootFlip                     /* flip global roots to point to tospace */
18      StackFlip                    /* flip mutator stacks to point to tospace */
19
20  Reclaim                       /* turn off barriers; reclaim fromspace */
```

Copy: The second group of phases copies fields of reachable objects in fromspace to their replica shells in tospace. During these phases, the mutators read from the originals in fromspace, but must mirror their writes to the tospace copies. The fromspace and tospace copies are kept loosely coherent by relying on the programming language memory model (in this case for Java [Manson *et al.*, 2005; Gosling *et al.*, 2015]). This means that the updates to each copy need not be atomic or simultaneous. Rather, a well-synchronised Java application need only perceive that the values in the copies cohere at application-level synchronisation points. Any changes made by a mutator thread to fromspace copies between two synchronisation points will be propagated to the tospace copies before passing the second synchronisation point. If all threads are at synchronisation points, then the fromspace and tospace copies will be consistent with one another. This is important during the third, Flip, group of phases, when mutators can observe both fromspace and tospace copies.

Flip: In this group, the collector forwards pointers in global variables and thread stacks and registers, flipping them one at a time into tospace. Unflipped mutator threads may hold references to both fromspace and tospace copies (even of the same object). Previous concurrent copying collectors either imposed a tospace invariant using a read barrier to redirect mutators out of fromspace [Baker, 1978], or imposed a fromspace invariant while replicating and then flipped all at once [Nettles and O'Toole, 1993]. Incremental flipping without a read barrier (except for pointer equality tests) means that mutators may access both fromspace and tospace at the same time, which requires slightly tighter synchronisation of updates to both copies.

Reclaim: As mutators and global roots no longer hold fromspace references, the collector can now release the old fromspace.

Algorithm 17.5: Transactional Sapphire write barriers

(a) The `Mark` phase write barrier

```
1   checkAndEnqueue(ref):                              /* shade ref */
2       if inFromspace(ref)
3           if not forwarded(ref)                      /* white */
4               tobeCopiedQueue.enqueue(ref)
5       else
6           if not testAndMark(ref)                    /* white */
7               add(worklist, ref)
8
9   Write_Mark(src, i, ref):
10      src[i] ← ref
11      checkAndEnqueue(ref)
```

(b) The `ReferenceProcess` phase write barrier

```
1   Write_ReferenceProcess(src, i, ref):
2       checkAndEnqueue(src[i])
3       src[i] ← ref
4       if isFirstStackScan()
5           checkAndEnqueue(ref)      /* active only while switching barriers */
```

(c) The `Copy` phase write barrier

```
1   Write_Copy(src, i, ref):
2       src[i] ← ref
3       if inFromspace(src)
4           repl ← src.forwardingPointer
5           if inFromspace(ref)
6               repl[i] ← ref.forwardingPointer
7           else
8               repl[i] ← ref
```

Marking. The Mark group of phases comprises six steps. Termination relies on use of deletion barriers and allocating new objects black, that is, with replicas in both fromspace and tospace.

To allocate a new object, the fromspace replica is allocated first,[4] after checking that there is enough space for both objects; this ensures that although a mutator may be blocked until the end of the collection cycle if there is insufficient memory, the subsequent allocation of the tospace replica can never fail. Maintaining the invariant that there are no black-white pointers requires care. Because there is no stop-the-world rendezvous, different mutators may be in different phases. The transition from 'collector idle' to the start of the main marking phase, StackMark, must therefore be Type II[5] (see Section 15.3). The

---

[4]The original Sapphire allocated new objects black in a separate *newspace*.

[5]An alternative design decision might be to allocate grey in this phase, which would allow the phase change to be Type I, thus removing a handshaking step. However, delaying turning on the deletion barrier would require scanning objects newly allocated during the Mark phase.

role of the first intermediate phase, PreMark1, is to install the insertion barrier shown in Algorithm 17.5a. Mutators do not perform any marking directly, but rather enqueue objects for the collector to process. If the referent `ref` of a pointer update `src.i = ref` is in fromspace, and if it has not been forwarded (the collector has not created a shell for it), the barrier shades the object by adding it to a `tobeCopiedQueue`. The barrier does not create the shell immediately, since that allocation path might include a GC safe-point and hence a potential phase change. An unmarked object in a non-replicating space is marked and added to a separate work list so that its children can be traced. Each mutator has its own queue, so enqueuing does not normally need synchronisation.

In the StackMark phase, each collector thread competes to claim and halt a mutator, scan its stack and then resume it. The number of mutators blocked at any time is at most the number of collector threads, typically significantly fewer than the number of CPU cores. As with the mutator barrier, as it scans a mutator's stack, the collector simply adds references found to its work queue rather than immediately creating tospace shells. In the RootMark phase, the collector scans global roots — for Jikes RVM, vectors of references for static variables and Java Native Interface references. All writes to these vectors are protected by an insertion barrier so mutators do not need to be halted for scanning. To support load balancing between collector threads, the RootMark phase comprises two stages. The first is a global stage in which the master collector measures each vector to balance loads in the following stage where all collectors scan the vectors in parallel. It is essential that this is global, since the size of a vector's live area may change as mutators run. If the range of a vector were to be computed asynchronously, some slots may be scanned by multiple collectors and others not at all. Protecting the vectors with a write barrier allows the live area to be enlarged or contracted safely (although contraction may mean that the collector traverses dead objects).

In the HeapMark phase, collectors traverse reachable objects, creating shells in tospace and writing a forwarding pointer to each shell in a distinct word in the fromspace object's header. Care is taken to handle any races between collector and collector, or collector and mutator. Roots for the traversals are the queues filled by the collectors in the StackMark and RootMark Phases and by the mutator write barrier. Each tospace shell's header (a status word and a back pointer to its fromspace replica) is created immediately. The back pointer is used in the Flip Phases to propagate mutator updates to both copies of an object.

Until the ReferenceProcess phase, Transactional Sapphire uses the insertion barrier shown in Algorithm 17.5a, both for safe initialisation and because insertion barriers preserve less floating garbage than deletion barriers. In this phase, the algorithm switches on both an insertion and a deletion barrier (Algorithm 17.5b), as per Doligez and Gonthier [1994], to give both quicker termination and a guarantee of progress. For termination, insertion barrier techniques require mutator stacks to be scanned repeatedly until no new references are found. In contrast, collectors using a deletion barrier do not have to rescan stacks. Transactional Sapphire faces two problems here. First, deletion barriers are a black mutator technique (see Section 15.2), but the insertion barrier used so far does not prevent a mutator from holding a reference to an otherwise unreachable white object. Thus, the stacks must be rescanned to blacken them. After each mutator's stack has been scanned again, it suffices that the mutator only use the deletion barrier. Second, Java's semantics allow a mutator to call `get` at any time on a weak reference whose referent is only weakly-reachable, causing the referent to become strongly-reachable if the reference has not yet been cleared. Once the referent becomes strongly-reachable, the collector must not clear the weak reference, and must retain any objects that just became strongly-reachable. If multiple weak reference objects refer to the same target, they must behave consistently: at any time, all calls to `get` on these weak reference objects must either all return `null` or all return a reference to the target. For example, if a and c are weak references to an object b, at all times the invariant `a.get() = c.get()` must hold.

Algorithm 17.6: The collector's word-copying algorithm using compare-and-swap

```
 1  copyWord(p, q):
 2      loop
 3          currentValue ← *q;
 4          toValue ← *p                                                    $
 5          if isPointer(toValue)
 6              toValue ← forwardObject(toValue)
 7          if toValue = currentValue
 8              return
 9          if not CompareAndSwap(q, currentValue, toValue)                 $
10              return
```

Without a stop-the-world phase, this race between the mutator calling get and the collector attempting to finish marking strongly-reachable objects before proceeding to clearing reference objects with unmarked referents necessitates the collector to iterate until no new calls to get have been made. Transactional Sapphire uses a global state, with values normal, tracing, repeat and clearing, to manage this. The collector starts by changing the state from normal to tracing. When it believes its tracing work is complete, it attempts to change the state atomically to clearing. Meanwhile, any get will attempt to set the state atomically to repeat, which will prevent the collector from proceeding to clearing references but cause it to continue tracing from the newly greyed referents. Note that a further benefit of using a deletion barrier is that the number of weak references at the start of the ReferenceProcessing stage is known, and any new weak reference objects will be allocated black, hence termination of marking is guaranteed without a stop-the-world pause. In contrast, with an insertion barrier, the collector may have to chase references escaping back and forth between a Reference object and the stack repeatedly.

Copying. By the end of the Mark group of phases, all live fromspace objects have been marked with forwarding pointers to tospace shells. In the Copy phase, the collector copies the contents of each fromspace object into its shell; mutators continue to access fromspace objects and to allocate new objects black. The collector first installs the Copy phase write barrier (Algorithm 17.5c) in the PreCopy phase. Whenever a mutator writes to a fromspace object, this barrier writes the semantically equivalent value to the corresponding field of its tospace copy.

It is important that mutator updates are never lost, even when the collector copies the same object at the same time, and are wait-free. Any concurrent copying collector must deal with races between mutators updating and collectors copying an object. The target platform for Transactional Sapphire is x86 systems, for which most memory operations are guaranteed to be executed in order: only loads may be reordered with preceding store instructions. It is assumed that all reference fields are word-aligned: copying word by word rather than field by field improves performance, while still handling reference types and double-word types in accordance with the Java specification. Transactional Sapphire offers three solutions: it can copy an arbitrary number of words atomically and efficiently using a compare-and-swap in a loop, it can use hardware transactional memory (such as Intel's Restricted Transactional Memory extensions) or it can use a minimal form of software transactional memory.

The compare-and-swap method shown in Algorithm 17.6 copies word by word. This is efficient because multiple non-reference fields within the same word can be processed in a single iteration of the loop, and it also deals correctly with reference fields, which are

Algorithm 17.7: Transactional Sapphire: copying with software transactional memory

```
 1  copyObjectTransactional(p, q):
 2      for i ← 0 to words(q)                              /* copying step */
 3          toValue ← p[i]
 4          if isPointerField(p, i)
 5              buf[i] ← toValue
 6              toValue ← forward(toValue)
 7          q[i] ← toValue
 8
 9      memoryBarrier
10
11      for i ← 0 to words(q)                              /* verification step */
12          if isPointerField(p, i)
13              if p[i] ≠ buf[i]
14                  goto FAIL
15          else if p[i] ≠ q[i]
16              goto FAIL
17
18      return
19
20  FAIL:
21      copyObject(p, q)              /* fall back to copying word at a time with CAS */
```

word-aligned and sized. If the contents of the old and new words differ, then the collector atomically updates the tospace word using a compare-and-swap. Failure means that a mutator has updated this word with a newer value so the collector does not need to copy this word. Unfortunately, success does not mean that the collector has written the newest value, as there is a risk of an ABA problem. If the mutator were to change the values held in p and q between line 3 and line 4, then the test in line 7 would fail, so the collector would prepare to compare-and-swap toValue into q. In the absence of any further mutator action, this compare-and-swap would fail, which is safe as noted above. But if the mutator were to update p and q again with their original value, then the compare-and-swap would succeed, updating q with a stale toValue! To resolve this, the algorithm double checks in the next iteration of the loop. The risk to progress is very small: the mutator would have to continually update the words to prevent progress.

The simplest hardware transactional memory approach is to copy a single object in each transaction, word by word, dereferencing for forwarding where necessary, using normal load/store instructions within an XBEGIN...XEND block. If the transaction fails, then the algorithm falls back to copying using compare-and-swap. Since objects are typically smaller than a cache line, it is possible to copy several objects in a single transaction, but note that the expected read set of a transaction for a single object may be larger as semantic copying requires dereferencing each reference field of a source object. However, the size of a transaction can be reduced by visiting objects as part of the heap scan and adding them to a 'to be copied' list (until it reaches a limit) before initiating the transaction; this planning removes scanning traffic from the transaction's read set and hence also reduces the risk of aborts.

Previous concurrent copying collectors have also attempted to leverage transactional memory, but at some cost. For example, McGachey *et al.* [2008] describe a lock-free, on-the-fly, copying collector in a strongly atomic software transactional memory system that uses versioning for reads, and strict two-phase locking and eager versioning for writes. In order to guarantee consistency, mutators and collectors must wrap reads and writes of both reference and scalar fields in transactions (although note that the transactional mutator needs such barriers anyway).

However, copying does not require such a general purpose transactional memory mechanism, as it is only necessary for fromspace and tospace replicas to be *eventually* rather than immediately consistent, since tospace fields are not read until after the Copy group of phases is complete. The Transactional Sapphire garbage collector can therefore use either hardware transactions, or a custom software transactional method comprising a copying and a verification step for each object; both transactional methods were found to offer similar copying speeds and to significantly improve over the original Sapphire technique which used compare-and-swap instructions [Ritson *et al.*, 2014]. The copying step implemented with software transactions semantically copies the object using normal load/store instructions. In the verification step, the contents of the tospace replica are compared to the fromspace object. If the two are semantically consistent, then the object has been successfully replicated. If any word is found to be inconsistent with its replica, then the object is copied again using the fallback compare-and-swap method. A memory fence (MFENCE on x86) separating the copying and verification steps is essential, but is the only fence needed. Without it, a store to the tospace replica could be reordered after the loads performed in the verification step, risking the loss of a mutator store. Anderson *et al.* [2015] use a broadly similar software verification step in *Chihuahua*, a concurrent, semispace collector, which uses Brooks forwarding pointers rather than replication to redirect mutator accesses to the most up-to-date location of an object. However, Chihuahua requires the mutator to use not only a read barrier — an extra, unconditional dereference to follow the forwarding pointer — but also atomic instructions in the write barrier.

Flip. In this phase, the collector flips fromspace references in non-replicated spaces, global roots and mutators' stacks to point to tospace. Before this phase, mutators never access tospace objects, but after this phase mutators never access fromspace objects. In order to avoid conflicting mutator invariants, another Type II phase transition is needed. During this transition, mutators must be ready to deal with references to any space.

The PreFlip1 phase installs two barriers: Algorithm 17.8a shows a pointer-equality read barrier that tests the equivalence of references to the fromspace and tospace replicas of the same object (in preparation for subsequent phases that store tospace references), and Algorithm 17.8b a double-update write barrier that propagates a write to a fromspace/tospace object to its tospace/fromspace replica, respectively. Note that mutators in the PreFlip1 phase do not yet have access to tospace objects. In the PreFlip2 phase, the full self-flip barrier (Algorithm 17.8c) is installed: from now on, this mutator never writes a reference to a fromspace object. Note that it was not possible to install this barrier in PreFlip1 as other mutators might still have been in a Copy phase, expecting to see only fromspace references. In the HeapFlip and RootFlip phases, the collector flips the non-replicated spaces and global roots, respectively. From the StackFlip phase onwards, the allocator must return a tospace reference while also allocating a fromspace replica.

In summary, Transactional Sapphire extends previous concurrent copying algorithms and has much in common with replication schemes. It permits one thread at a time to flip from fromspace to tospace rather than all at once, and minimises thread blocking (pauses) while avoiding a read barrier for all but pointer-equality tests in the Flip phase. Mutators simply update both the fromspace and tospace copies of an object (when both exist) to keep them coherent. We have omitted the subtleties of dealing with locks, status words and hash codes, and the swapping of the roles of fromspace and tospace; we refer readers to Ugawa *et al.* [2018] for details.

Algorithm 17.8: Transactional Sapphire `Flip` phase barriers

(a) Pointer equivalence read barrier

```
1  pointerEQ(p, q)                                    /* p == q */
2     if p = q
3        return true
4     if inFromspace(p)
5        return p.forwardingPointer = q
6     if inFromspace(q)
7        return q.forwardingPointer = p
8     return false
```

(b) `PreFlip` phase write barrier with limited self-flipping

```
1  Write_preFlip(src, i, ref):
2     if inFromspace(ref) && inTospace(src)
3        ref ← ref.forwardingPointer
4     src[i] ← ref
5     if inFromspace(src) || inTospace(src)
6        repl ← src.forwardingPointer
7        if inFromspace(ref) ||
8              (inTospace(ref) && inFromspace(repl))
9           repl[i] ← ref.forwardingPointer
10       else
11          repl[i] ← ref
```

(c) Full self-flip write barrier

```
1  Write_Flip(src, i, ref):
2     if inFromspace(ref)
3        ref = ref.forwardingPointer
4     src[i] ← ref
5     if inFromspace(src) || inTospace(src)
6        repl ← src.forwardingPointer
7        repl[i] ← ref
```

Platinum

The *Platinum* collector [Wu *et al.*, 2020b] aims to deal with long application latency tails (caused by garbage collection pauses) and to improve the utilisation of the CPU in a mostly-concurrent, generational, replicating collector. They take two measures to address CPU utilisation. First, they use fewer collector threads than cores, ensuring that resources will be available for mutators to keep running during collection. Second, each collector thread is bound to a particular core. When the collector is not running, mutators may use any core, but when the collector is running they are restricted to the cores where collector threads are *not* running. This strategy helps guarantee high CPU utilisation for the collector threads.

Wu *et al.* also exploit two hardware features found on some modern Intel processors, transactional memory and memory protection keys, to keep mutator write barrier overheads low. Memory protection keys allow the programmer to use a system call to associate a particular protection key with a range of pages. The programmer can set any access restrictions, such as to make the pages read-only, by setting a register that can be accessed cheaply without a system call. These additional restrictions can be changed at will, though they cannot allow more access rights than the underlying page table entry does. The critical point is that protection keys allow different threads to have different access rights to the same virtual memory pages.

Platinum sets up two protection keys. During collection, one is associated with pages to which only the collector threads should have write access, and Platinum arranges that the mutators set their protection keys to disallow writes to these pages. The other protection key is associated with pages to which mutators *do* have write access.

Platinum uses the heap layout from HotSpot's Parallel collector: an old generation and a young generation split into an eden and two survivor spaces. During collection, mutators access only fromspace replicas of objects. Collector threads have write access to most of the heap — the *Collection* region. In contrast, mutators have write access only to the blocks that saw recent allocation — the *Pinned* region — and blocks reserved for allocation — the *Allocation* region. These regions are not scavenged. When the collector copies an object, it places forwarding- and back-pointers in the fromspace and tospace replicas. When a mutator attempts to modify an object in a page in the Collection region, to which it does not have write access, it takes a trap. If the object being mutated has been copied, the trap handler adjusts the mutator's protection key temporarily in order to update the field in both copies of the object in a hardware transaction. In contrast, Transactional Sapphire protects the collector's copying in a transaction (hardware or software).

As with other mostly-concurrent collectors, Platinum needs an initial and a final stop-the-world phase. As usual, in the first pause, the collectors scan thread stacks. However, Platinum needs to do more work in the final stop-the-world phase. Because collector threads do not scavenge the Pinned and Allocation regions in the concurrent phase, Platinum must not only update references in thread stacks to objects in the Collection region that have been moved but must also sweep these two regions to update any references.

17.5   Concurrent compaction

Chapter 3 discussed approaches to garbage collection that split into two phases, marking and compacting. Recall that compaction is decoupled from the tracing phase that determines reachable objects. This allows greater freedom than a copying collector over the order in which objects are relocated (by address, say, rather than in order of tracing for reachability). It can further give freedom as to which regions are compacted and which are left alone. In principle, these compacting collectors could defragment the entire heap one region at a time — thus, at the memory overhead of a single region — unlike a copying collector which must reserve sufficient space to accommodate all the objects that it copies, in the worst case, the size of fromspace.

Compressor

Compressor [Kermany and Petrank, 2006], presented earlier in Section 3.4 and Section 14.8, exploits the freedom allowed by separating marking from copying to perform compaction concurrently with the mutator threads.

Recall that Compressor first computes an auxiliary 'first-object' table that maps a to-space page to the first fromspace object that will be moved into the page. Parallel compactor threads then race to claim an unmapped tospace virtual page, map it to a physical page, populate it with its live copies from fromspace pages, and redirect each pointer field in the copies to refer to tospace. Once all the live objects in a fromspace page have been copied, it is immediately unmapped.

To enable concurrent compaction, Compressor exploits virtual memory page protection primitives similarly to Appel *et al.* [1988] (where protection served as the read barrier for concurrent copying collection in order to prevent the mutator from accessing tospace pages whose objects have not yet been copied or which contain unforwarded pointers). Ossia *et al.* [2004] also used protection simply to allow concurrent forwarding of pointers in pages containing compacted objects, but Compressor drives both compaction and forwarding using page protection. Compressor protects the tospace pages from read and write access (without yet mapping them to physical pages). Computing the first-object table and protecting tospace occurs concurrently with mutator threads operating in fromspace. Compressor then briefly stops all the mutator threads to switch their roots to refer to tospace addresses before releasing the threads. Of course, the contents of those pages have not yet been copied. At this point, if a mutator accesses a protected tospace page, it will trap. Handling the trap requires doing the work of compaction to map and populate the page with its copies (the mutator performs incremental compaction work as if it was a compactor thread), and forward the references in those copies, before the mutator can resume and access the page. Note that only the data for this page is copied, thus the handler will not evacuate the beginning of an object that starts on the previous page or the end of one that continues onto the next page. Concurrent compaction requires that a compactor thread be able to access the page while other mutator threads are still protected from access. To support this, Compressor double-maps each physical page when its contents are to be copied, once in its 'natural' (still-protected) tospace virtual page, and again in an unprotected virtual page private to the compactor thread (see also double mapping in Section 11.10). Once the compaction work has been done for that page, the tospace virtual page can be unprotected so mutators can proceed, and the private mapping is discarded.

In essence, Compressor applies the standard tricolour invariant. Fromspace pages are white, protected tospace pages are grey, and unprotected tospace pages are black. Initially, the mutator threads operate grey in fromspace while the first-object table is computed along with the tospace addresses. When the mutator threads are flipped over to tospace, they are black. The protection-driven double mapping read barrier prevents the black mutator threads from acquiring stale fromspace references from grey pages that are still in the process of being populated with their fromspace copies.

Compressor must also handle other aspects of the tricolour invariant. In particular, after marking and before the task of determining the first-object table begins, mutators must allocate all new objects in tospace to prevent those allocations from interfering with the relocation map (otherwise, allocating to a hole in fromspace would interfere). Moreover, these newly allocated objects must eventually have their pointer fields scanned after the mutators flip to tospace, to redirect any stale fromspace references in those fields over to tospace, and similarly for global roots. Thus, both newly allocated tospace objects and the global roots must be protected from access by mutators, with traps on their pages forcing scanning to redirect their pointers.

Because the performance of Compressor depends heavily on the cost of virtual memory page mapping and protection primitives, which can be onerous [Hosking and Moss, 1993b], it is important to batch these operations as much as possible. For example, Compressor actually protects and double-maps the entire tospace at the beginning of collection (to avoid the cost of double mapping each page as it is processed). Similarly, it moves eight virtual pages per trap (to better amortise the trap overhead on mutator threads).

One downside of Compressor is that when a mutator traps on access to a protected tospace page, then it must not only copy *all* of that page's objects, it must also forward *all* the pointers in those objects to refer to their relocated (or soon to be relocated) targets. This can impose significant pauses on the mutator. In a moment, we will discuss the Pauseless collector, which reduces the amount of incremental work needed to be performed by a mutator to copying at most one object (without needing to forward any of the stale fromspace references it contains). Before doing so, let us briefly review the way in which Compressor drives compaction using page protection, as illustrated in Figure 17.1. The figures show the *logical* grouping of virtual pages into distinct categories (the *linear* address-ordered layout of the heap is intentionally not represented).

Live: pages containing (mostly) live objects (initially dark grey in the figures)

Condemned: pages containing some live objects, but mostly dead ones, which are good candidates for compaction (light grey in the figures, with dark grey live objects)

Free: pages currently free but available for allocation (dashed borders)

New Live: pages in which copied live objects have been allocated but not yet copied (dashed borders, with dashed space allocated for copies)

Dead: unmapped pages that can be recycled (freed for allocation) once there are no pointers to them (shown hatched in the figures)

Figure 17.1a illustrates the initial state in which live objects have been identified along with those to be relocated. For ease of later comparison with Pauseless and its generational successor C4, we take the liberty here to restrict compaction only to pages sparsely occupied by live objects. In Compressor, live tospace pages containing stale references that need forwarding, and tospace pages into which objects are yet to be relocated, must first be protected to prevent the mutators from accessing them. Concurrently with the mutators, the forwarding information for the live objects is prepared on the side in auxiliary data structures. At this point, the heap pages are configured as in Figure 17.1b, and the mutator roots are all flipped over to refer to only the protected tospace pages. Compaction can now proceed concurrently with the mutators, which will trap if they try to access an unprocessed tospace page. Trapping on a live tospace page causes all of the references in that page to be forwarded to refer to tospace, as in Figure 17.1c. Trapping on a reserved tospace page evacuates objects from condemned fromspace pages to fill the page, and the references contained in these copied objects are forwarded to refer to tospace (Figure 17.1d). When all the live objects in a condemned fromspace page have been evacuated, it is completely dead and its physical page can be unmapped and returned to the operating system, though its virtual page cannot be recycled until all references to it have been forwarded. Compaction ceases when all tospace pages have been processed and unprotected (Figure 17.1e). We now contrast this approach with that of the Pauseless and C4 collectors.

Pauseless and C4

Azul Systems found that stop-the-world collection of the young generation led to long pauses in enterprise-scale systems and applications (such as portals, replicated in-memory data and messaging systems) that hold a large amount of data for each session. Their *Pauseless* collector [Click *et al.*, 2005; Azul, 2008] and its generational extension, the *Continuously Concurrent Compacting Collector* (C4) [Tene *et al.*, 2011], address this problem. Pauseless protects fromspace pages that contain objects being moved, instead of protecting tospace pages containing moved objects and/or stale pointers. Rather than needing to protect all of the tospace pages like Compressor, Pauseless and C4 protect the much smaller set of fromspace pages whose objects are actually being moved (focusing on sparsely populated pages that will yield most space), and these pages can be protected incrementally

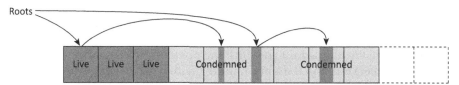

(a) Initial Compressor configuration. All pages are in fromspace.

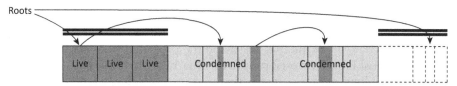

(b) Compute forwarding information, protect all tospace pages (illustrated by the double horizontal bars). These include those reserved to hold evacuated objects and those Live pages not condemned for evacuation. Then flip mutator roots to tospace. Mutators accessing a protected tospace page will now trap.

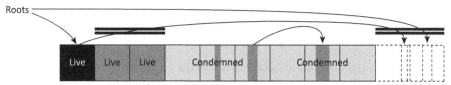

(c) Trapping on a Live page forwards pointers contained in that page to refer to their tospace targets. Unprotect the Live page once all its stale fromspace references have been replaced with tospace references.

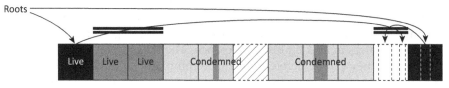

(d) Trapping on a reserved tospace page evacuates objects from fromspace pages to fill the page. The fields of these objects are updated to point to tospace. Unprotect the tospace page and unmap fully evacuated fromspace pages (releasing their physical pages, shown as hatched).

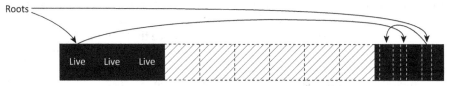

(e) Compaction is complete when all Live pages have been scanned to forward references they contain, and all live objects in condemned pages have been copied into tospace and the references they contain have been forwarded.

Figure 17.1: Compressor

Figure 17.2: C4's tagged pointer layout. The a bits are the address. The two SS bits identify the space (generation) in which the object resides and N is the NMT bit. The virtual address to which the pointer refers is indicated by the p (page number) bits and the a bits (address within the page).

when they become a source for evacuation.   Pauseless uses a self-healing *loaded value barrier* (LVB) to intercept and repair (heal) stale fromspace references *before* the mutator traps trying to use them, copying their target object as necessary. This avoids blocking the mutator to evacuate all of the live objects on the protected fromspace page. The initial implementation of Pauseless used proprietary hardware to implement the read barrier directly as a special load-reference instruction, but on stock hardware Pauseless and C4 compile the necessary logic inline with every load-reference operation by the mutator.

Pauseless steals one address bit from the 64-bit address space to use as a pointer tag. This *Not-Marked-Through* (NMT) bit is used by the LVB during the concurrent marking phase of the collector to decide whether the reference has previously been scanned by the collector. The collector maintains a desired value for the NMT bit and the LVB ensures that every loaded reference has been safely scanned by the collector *and* points to the current location of its safely accessible (unprotected) target object (that is, the evacuated object in tospace if it has been copied).

The C4 generational collector extends this scheme to support simultaneous and independently active concurrent collections of different generations. While Pauseless maintains a single, global, currently expected value of the NMT state, C4 instead maintains a different expected value for each generation. C4 steals an additional pointer tag bit per generation to encode the generation in which the referent resides. This allows the LVB to quickly check the NMT value for the proper generation, which can differ because collections of young and old generations proceed independently. Moreover, a reference's generation never changes without relocating its target object. Figure 17.2 shows the layout of C4's tagged pointers in a 64-bit object reference. The tagged pointers must be stripped of their tag before they can be dereferenced. The compiler can modify all dereferences to strip the tag before use, and reuse the stripped reference where the reuse does not cross a GC safe-point. Alternatively, an implementation can multi-map memory or alias address ranges so that the tag is effectively ignored.

During an active mark phase, if the LVB encounters a loaded reference with a NMT state that does not match the expected state for its target generation, the LVB will remedy that by logging the reference on the collector's work list to be scanned. Self-healing repairs the slot from which the reference was loaded. Null references are ignored.

Likewise, if the LVB also encounters a loaded reference that points to a protected fromspace page whose live objects are being evacuated, the LVB will obtain the new location of the reference's target (copying the object if it has not yet been evacuated), and repair the slot from which the mutator loaded the fromspace reference.

The initial implementation of Pauseless and C4 used proprietary hardware which implemented the LVB as a special single-cycle instruction that implicitly interprets the pointer tag bits, but on stock hardware this can be emulated at some cost as instructions inlined to interpret the pointer tag explicitly at every load-reference operation by the mutator. Algorithm 17.9 shows the interpretation of the tags and and pseudocode for a representative LVB implementation in C4. Note that the specifics differ with the context in which the LVB is generated: interpreter, compiler optimisation level or in the run-time system itself.

Algorithm 17.9: Pauseless/C4 *loaded value barrier* (LVB)

```
1   Expected[4] = {0, 0, 0, 0}
2
3   // Space ID Values:
4   // 00 NULL and non-heap pointers
5   // 01 Old generation references
6   // 10 New generation references
7   // 11 Unused
8
9   Read(src, i):
10      src_ptr ← src & 0x1FFFFFFFFF        /* strip tags from reference */
11      addr ← &src_ptr[i]                    /* address of source slot */
12      value ← *addr                /* load target reference from source slot */
13
14      // target referent may need to be marked or may be in protected fromspace page
15      trigger_mark ← value.NMT ≠ Expected[value.space]
16      trigger_copy ← protected(value.page)
17      if trigger_mark || trigger_copy /* may need to mark and/or copy referent */
18          value ← shade(addr, value, trigger_mark, trigger_copy)
19      return value
20
21  shade(addr, value, trigger_mark, trigger_copy):
22      oldValue ← value
23      if trigger_mark                         /* fix the trigger conditions */
24          value.NMT ← not value.NMT
25          add(worklist, value)               /* enqueue to marker's work list */
26      if trigger_copy
27          value ← forward(value)          /* copy referent if not yet copied */
28      loop                        /* will only repeat if CAS fails spuriously */
29          if oldValue = CompareAndSwap(addr, oldValue, value)
30              return value                   /* CAS succeeded, so we are done */
31          if oldValue ≠ *addr
32              return value      /* Another thread updated slot but value is ok */
```

Here, the LVB executes first the load, followed by the LVB logic. If the loaded reference does not have the expected NMT value for the generation to which it refers then the reference needs to be queued for the collector to mark as necessary, also correcting its NMT value. If it refers to a protected page (which is currently being evacuated by the collector), then the reference needs to be corrected to point to its relocated referent. Both of these situations trigger execution of slow path code to correct the situation. When the triggering reference points to an object that has not yet been relocated, then the LVB will first cooperatively relocate the object before forwarding the reference to point to its new location. Unlike a Brooks-style indirection barrier there is no null check, no memory access, no load-use penalty, no need for a forwarding word in the object header and no cache footprint imposed on the fast path, making it efficient and predictable.

The Pauseless and C4 garbage collection phases. Both collectors divide their work into three main phases, each of which is fully parallel and concurrent.

Mark is responsible for periodically refreshing the mark bits. In the process of doing that, it will set the NMT bit for all references to the desired value (in C4's case, the desired value for the generation being collected) and gather liveness statistics for each page. The marker starts from the roots (static global variables and mutator stacks) and begins marking reachable objects. The NMT bit assists in making the Mark phase fully concurrent, as described further below.

Relocate uses the most recently available mark bits to find sparse pages with little live data, to compact those pages (relocating their objects), and to free their physical backing memory. The Relocate phase starts by protecting sparsely occupied fromspace pages against mutator access and then copies live objects out of those pages. Forwarding information maintained on the side tracks the locations of relocated objects. If a mutator loads a reference to a protected page, the LVB will trigger and replace the stale protected-page reference with the correctly forwarded reference. After the page contents have been relocated, the Relocate phase frees the physical memory, which can be immediately recycled by the operating system. Virtual memory cannot be freed until no more stale references to that page remain in the heap. A Relocate phase runs continuously, freeing memory to keep pace with mutator allocation. It runs standalone or concurrently with the next mark phase.

Remap updates every remaining pointer in the heap whose target has been relocated. Collector threads traverse the object graph executing the LVB against every reference in the heap, forwarding stale references as if triggered by a mutator. At the end of this phase, no live heap reference can refer to a page protected by the previous Relocate phase, so virtual memory for those pages is freed. Since both the Remap and Mark phases traverse all live objects, Pauseless and C4 are able to fold them together. The Remap phase for the previous collection cycle runs concurrently with the Mark phase for the current cycle.

Pauseless and C4 have several qualitative advantages. Firstly, there is no 'rush' to finish any given phase. No phase imposes a substantial burden on the mutators that needs to be relieved by ending the phase quickly. There is no 'race' to finish some phase before collection can begin again — the Relocate phase runs continuously and can immediately free memory at any point. Since all phases are parallel, the collector can keep up with any number of mutator threads simply by adding more collector threads. Unlike some other concurrent marking collectors, marking is guaranteed to complete in a single traversal regardless of the mutation rate (there is no need to re-mark — revert to grey — previously marked objects, nor to stop the mutators in a final mark step to ensure termination). Collector threads will compete with mutator threads for CPU time, though any spare CPU can be employed by the collector.

Secondly, the phases incorporate a self-healing effect, where mutators use the LVB immediately to correct any mis-tagged reference by replacing it with the corrected reference in the slot from which it was loaded (marking and relocating its target as necessary). On Azul's proprietary Vega hardware, this was reported to result in a drop in mutator utilisation for a short period (a 'trap storm') following a phase shift, with an minimum mutator utilisation penalty of approximately 20 milliseconds spread over a few hundred milliseconds. But Pauseless has no stop-the-world pauses where all threads must be simultaneously stopped. We now discuss the phases in more detail.

Mark. The Mark phase manipulates mark bits managed on the side. It begins by clearing the current cycle's mark bits. Each object has two mark bits, one for the current cycle and one for the previous cycle.

The Mark phase then marks all global references, scans each mutator thread's root set, and flips the per-thread expected NMT value. For C4, the root set also includes the remembered set of references from old to young objects. The remembered set is maintained by a precise card marking barrier that leverages the same reference metadata as the LVB to filter out unnecessary card marks without need for address range comparisons. Running mutators cooperate by marking their own root set at a ragged handshake. Blocked (or stalled) mutators are marked in parallel by mark phase collector threads. Each mutator thread can immediately proceed once its root set has been marked (and expected NMT flipped), but the Mark phase cannot proceed until all threads have executed the handshake.

After the root sets have been marked, marking proceeds in parallel and concurrently with the mutators in the style of Flood *et al.* [2001]. The markers ignore the NMT bit in references loaded from their work lists. The NMT bit is only used for loads from heap objects. This continues until all live objects have been marked. New objects are allocated in live pages. Because mutators can only hold (and thus store) marked-through references, the initial state of the mark bit for new objects does not matter for marking.

The NMT bit is crucial to completion of the Mark phase in a single pass over the live objects, regardless of stores by the mutator, because the load barrier prevents mutators from acquiring unmarked references. A mutator that loads a reference with the wrong value in the NMT bit will trigger the LVB to communicate the reference to the marker threads. Because it can never acquire an unmarked reference, a mutator can never store and propagate an unmarked reference. The self-healing nature of the LVB also stores the corrected (marked) reference back to memory, so that particular reference can never trigger again in the current cycle. This self-healing effect means that a phase-change will not make the mutators wait until the marker threads can flip the NMT bits in the objects on which the mutator is working. Instead, each mutator flips each reference it encounters as it runs. Steady state NMT triggers are rare.

The mutator must take care that updating the triggering reference does not clobber a store to the same location by another thread since the NMT-trigger occurred. Thus, the LVB uses a compare-and-swap operation so that the memory is only updated if it has not changed since the triggering thread read from that location. Because a ragged handshake is used to initiate the Mark phase, different mutators may briefly have a different view of the desired NMT value. It is possible for mutators on different sides of the handshake to compete, possibly more than once, over a single reference's NMT value triggering in the LVB and updating in memory. This can only last until the unflipped thread passes its next GC safe-point where it will mark through its stack, and cross the handshake. Note that it is not possible for a single thread to hold the same reference twice in its root set with different NMT settings, so pointer equality can always be implemented as a direct comparison of (loaded) pointer values.

The scalability of marking can be improved by reducing cache contention. Pauseless held mark bits on the side in a bitmap, which avoids compare-and-swap on object headers, but Iyengar *et al.* [2012a] improve on this for C4 by *striping*[6] cache lines of the bitmap across processors, based on the addresses of those lines. A marking thread works only on its own stripe. When it finds a pointer whose mark bit lies in a different stripe, it enqueues that pointer for another thread to work on, without examining the mark bit. While it is possible to have one worker per stripe, they found that four workers per stripe reduced contention well enough and usefully reduced the number of queues needed. The queues accumulate a fixed number of entries, and when one fills, the thread publishes the group of entries to a global pool, where other threads can claim the group and work on it. When a worker's own queue becomes empty, it publishes any partial queues it has for other threads. Iyengar

---

[6]Flood *et al.* [2001] did the same thing; they used the term *stride* as opposed to *stripe*.

et al. showed that this striping approach improved scalability, scaling linearly up to the number of cores on a socket. They further observed that when a mutator enqueues a reference for marking, the referent of the reference is usually in the mutator's own cache so it can be advantageous to process the reference using a marking thread that is topologically near the queueing mutator. They found using a topology aware preference when marking threads claim queued pointers to mark gave approximately 10% improvement when the number of marking threads exceeds the number of cores per socket.

C4 permits multiple young generation collections to occur while it is simultaneously collecting the old generation. Mostly, these collections are independent, but some cross-generational coordination is necessary. Old generation marking starts with a set of young-to-old roots gathered by a special young generation collection triggered at the start of every old generation collection cycle; further young generation collections running during this old generation collection cycle will ignore any new-to-old pointers they find. The collectors need to synchronise whenever the young generation collector needs to access objects that the old generation collector is relocating or otherwise modifying. Examples include metadata objects that the collector needs to access to discover an object's layout, and re-membered set cards that the young generation collector reads to discover the source of old-to-young pointers. In order to access such objects safely, the young generation collector waits briefly until the old generation collector has completed relocating objects on a page, at which point the old generation collector waits for the young generation collector. After the young generation collector has scanned the card(s), it signals the old generation collector to resume relocation.

Termination of the Mark phase only needs to worry about the race between a mutator having loaded an unmarked reference but not having yet completed the LVB. The LVB never spans a GC safe-point, so it is sufficient that all the mutators cross a GC safe-point without triggering an LVB. Thus, the Mark phase requests an empty handshake. Any references discovered before the handshake will be marked as normal. When all mutators have executed the handshake without reporting a new reference for marking, then the Mark phase is complete. Otherwise, the marker threads will consume the new references for marking and the handshake can be repeated. Because no new references can be created with the wrong NMT bit, this process must eventually terminate.

Relocate. The Relocate phase starts by finding sparsely occupied pages. Figure 17.3a shows a logical grouping of virtual pages into distinct categories (again, the linear address-ordered layout of the heap is intentionally not illustrated). There are references from both the mutator roots and live pages into sparse pages whose live objects are to be compacted by evacuation. The Relocate phase first builds side arrays to hold forwarding pointers for the objects to be relocated. These cannot be held in the fromspace originals because the physical storage for the fromspace pages will be reclaimed immediately after copying and long before all the fromspace references have been forwarded. The side array of forwarding data is not large because only sparse pages are relocated, so it can be implemented easily as a hash table. The Relocate phase then protects the mostly dead condemned pages from access by the mutators as in Figure 17.3b. Objects in these pages are now considered stale and can no longer be modified. Also, if a mutator loads a reference that points into a protected page, then it will trigger the LVB to repair the reference.

At the time the fromspace pages are protected, running mutators may have stale references in their root set. These are already past their load barrier and will not get caught directly. Instead, the mutators are asked to forward any existing stale references from their root set with a ragged handshake, relocating the fromspace targets as necessary (Figure 17.3c). Once all the mutators have executed this handshake, copying of the remaining

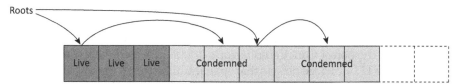

(a) Initial Pauseless configuration. All pages are in fromspace.

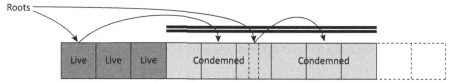

(b) Compute forwarding information, protect all condemned fromspace pages (illustrated by the double horizontal bars), but leave tospace pages unprotected. These include those reserved to hold evacuated objects and those live pages not condemned for evacuation.

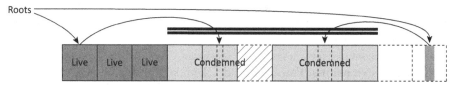

(c) Flip mutator roots to tospace, copying their targets, but leaving the references they contain pointing to fromspace. Mutators accessing an object on a protected fromspace page will trap and wait until the object is copied.

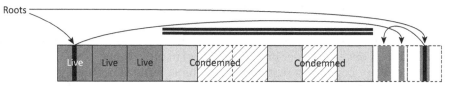

(d) Mutators loading a reference to a protected page will now trigger the LVB, copying their targets.

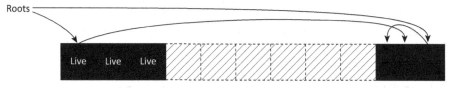

(e) Compaction is finished when all live objects in condemned pages have been copied to tospace, and all tospace pages have been scanned to forward references they contain.

Figure 17.3: Pauseless

live objects into tospace can proceed concurrently with the mutators. The load barrier prevents the mutators from seeing a stale object before it has finished moving.

As in the Mark phase, the load barrier in the Relocate phase prevents the mutator from loading a stale reference. The self-healing LVB forwards the reference and updates the memory location using compare-and-swap. If the fromspace object has not yet been copied, then the mutator will copy the object on behalf of the collector rather than waiting. The mutator copies the object from the collector's double mapped view of the page. This is illustrated in Figure 17.3d. Large objects that span multiple pages are not relocated, nor are objects in mostly live pages. An object that consumes about half of a page can be copied in about a millisecond.[7]

To amortise the cost of modifying page protections and forwarding the mutator roots, Pauseless batches up groups of sparse pages for compaction, typically protecting (and relocating and freeing) a few gigabytes at a time. The rate at which relocation must proceed is dictated only by the need to keep up with the allocation rate of the mutators.

Remap. Virtual memory is not freed immediately. The final step of forwarding the remaining stale references in the live pages and reclaiming virtual memory falls to the Remap phase. At the end of the Remap phase, there are no more stale references to the fromspace pages so their virtual memory can now be recycled (Figure 17.3e), the side array of forwarding pointers can be reclaimed, and the collection cycle is complete. Recall that *real* memory for evacuated pages was reclaimed long before, during the Relocate phase. Further recall that the Remap phase for the current collection cycle runs concurrently with the Mark phase for the next cycle.

Operating system extensions. Pauseless and C4 make aggressive and sustained use of virtual memory mapping and physical memory manipulation. This functionality can be implemented using standard operating system primitives, but the performance and rates at which that functionality can be deployed using the standard primitives is prohibitive. Pauseless-specific extensions to the operating system's memory manager result in significant performance improvements [Azul, 2010]. Enterprise Java applications commonly see allocation rates of from 200 to 500 megabytes/second per core, which must be matched by a sustained garbage collection rate to avoid pauses. In Pauseless/C4, each page will eventually be remapped once (and later unmapped once) in order to reclaim dead object space. No physical memory copying is required, so the remap rate is not significantly sensitive to memory bandwidth. Instead, the cost of the remapping operations dominate. Typical operating systems support remapping with three limitations.

1. Each page remap includes an implicit translation lookaside buffer invalidation operation. Since translation lookaside buffer invalidations require multiple cross-CPU interrupts (over all cores) the cost of remapping grows with the number of active threads in the program. This happens even when the active threads do not participate in the remapping, or have no interaction with the remapped memory.

2. Only small (typically 4-kilobyte) page mappings can be remapped.

3. Remap operations are single-threaded within a process (grabbing a common write lock).

To address these shortcomings, Pauseless/C4 benefits from operating system extensions that support bulk remapping with a single system-wide translation lookaside buffer invalidation for a batch of remaps, remapping of large (typically 2-megabyte) page mappings,

---

[7]Recall that Pauseless's pages are quite large.

and multiple concurrent remaps within the same process. These operating system improvements result in approximately three orders of magnitude speedup compared to a stock operating system, scaling almost linearly as the number of active threads doubles.

Summing up, Pauseless/C4 is designed as a fully parallel, generational and concurrent collector for large multiprocessor systems. It requires no stop-the-world pauses and reclaiming of dead objects happens throughout a collector cycle rather than, say, only at the end. There are no phases where the collector must race to finish before the mutators run out of free memory. Mutators can perceive a period of reduced utilisation during trap storms at some phase shifts, but the self-healing property of the LVB serves to recover utilisation quickly.

Collie

Can mutator utilisation be further improved during collection? *Collie* is another full-heap parallel compacting collector that uses transactional memory to ensure consistency [Iyengar *et al.*, 2012b] and wait-freedom. It was developed on Azul Systems' Vega system which provided hardware assisted transactional memory as well as the self-healing LVB instruction used by Pauseless/C4 described above [Click *et al.*, 2005; Tene *et al.*, 2011]. Collie extends Pauseless but attempts to compact most objects inside transactions. If a transaction fails to relocate an object, the object is pinned to its location, without compaction, but at a mirrored virtual address on a tospace page mapped to the same physical page (the fromspace and mirrored tospace addresses differ by only the value of a high-order bit not interpreted as an address). An evacuating transaction will fail if there is a potentially inconsistent concurrent write or an inconsistent concurrent read of a memory location that is written to.

Collie relies on the notion of stable referrer sets. A *referrer set* is the set of locations that point to an object. An object's referrer set is said to be *stable* after marking completes if (i) it does not contain any thread stack or register references before the collector starts to relocate the object, and (ii) once relocation begins, no new references are added to the object's referrer set. In other words, an object is guaranteed to be inaccessible to mutators as long as its referrer set is stable, and thus can be safely relocated to a fresh location. Objects whose referrer sets are either not stable before an attempt to evacuate them or which do not remain stable during the evacuation are pinned at their mirrored tospace virtual addresses.

The stability of an object's referrer set is identified through a combination of the Collie mutator's load and write barriers, and transactions used by the collector in its compacting phase. The write barrier intercepts heap reference stores and pins their target by setting a bit in its header. Note that Collie identifies referrer sets conservatively: a write may cause some object's precise referrer set to shrink. Once the compaction phase starts, Collie's LVB ensures that any load of a fromspace reference will cause the barrier to attempt to replace it atomically with a mirrored-tospace reference and then reload the reference from the heap location (Algorithm 17.10). If the barrier succeeds in replacing the old reference value, it has effectively pinned the object. If the replacement fails, then the value at address must have been changed, either by a racing mutator or by the collector's having evacuated the target object; either way, the newly loaded reference will be a valid tospace reference.

Wait-free concurrent marking is similar to that of Pauseless/C4 but also constructs the per-object, heap-stable (containing all heap references to the object) referrer sets. Evaluation suggests that capping referrer set sizes at four words is sufficient to capture most objects. Popular objects with more references than can fit in a referrer set (or objects that fail to have a referrer set allocated for them) are pinned. The concurrent compaction phase copies live objects to tospace, replacing fromspace references with objects' tospace addresses. Just

Algorithm 17.10: Collie's load barrier trap

```
1  GCtrap(address, oldRef):
2      mirror = mirror(oldRef)
3      CompareAndSwap(address, oldRef, mirror)
4      return *address
```

like Pauseless/C4, Collie compacts at page granularity and releases fromspace physical pages early, allowing them to be reused. By the end of the marking phase, Collie has established heap-stable referrer sets but these also include references in thread stacks and registers. Thread stacks are next scanned individually in a pre-compaction ragged handshake, pinning the target of any reference encountered — note that this does not require a global rendezvous. This handshake also arms the LVB to trap on the load of any reference to an object on a page that was relocatable at the start of the handshake. By the end of the handshake, all objects either have stable referrer sets (and so are potentially movable) or are pinned.

Individually movable objects are moved to tospace by first copying their contents and then updating the references in their referrer sets to point at their new locations. The copy can be performed outside a transaction since any concurrent mutator access would pin the object, but transactional memory is used to update the referrer set atomically with respect to other threads. After the transaction is started, each reference in the object's stable referrer set is checked to ensure that it does not point to the object's tospace mirror's virtual address (which would indicate that the reference in the referrer set has been updated); the transaction aborts if any reference to a mirror address is found. Then, each reference in the referrer set is replaced with a reference to the object's new tospace location. Finally, the transaction is committed. If a transaction fails or aborts for any reason, the object is rendered pinned. The last step of a collection is to fix up references to pinned objects to ensure that they point to the objects' virtual addresses in the mirrored tospace. Because the LVB is self-healing, this fixup traversal can be delayed and rolled into the next mark phase, just as Pauseless/C4 do.

Compared with Pauseless, Collie has been shown to offer significantly better minimum mutator utilisation (MMU) and improved throughput in the compaction phase on Azul's Vega platform. The aborting load barrier may cause fragmentation as objects are pinned on mirrored tospace pages, as with Staccato [McCloskey *et al.*, 2008] or Chicken [Pizlo *et al.*, 2008], but this is limited to the working set of the mutators during collection. Finally, although Collie was developed on Azul's Vega specialised hardware which was withdrawn in 2013 in favour of software-only solutions, Iyengar *et al.* expect Collie to be implementable on other hardware transactional memory systems such as Intel's Restricted Transactional Memory. We are unaware of any attempts to do so and Azul has not deployed Collie, believing that C4 offers sufficient performance.

ZGC

ZGC [Lidén, 2018] is a non-generational, mostly-concurrent, parallel, mark-compact, region-based collector.[8] ZGC's original goals were to provide pause times of no more than 10 milliseconds (today these are typically less than a millisecond) at a throughput no more than 15% worse than the OpenJDK G1 collector, and to handle a wide range of heap sizes including very large ones.

---

[8]We are indebted to Yang and Wrigstad [2022] from whose primer on ZGC we have drawn heavily.

(a) Non-generational tagged pointer layout. The F bit is used for concurrent marking through with finalisers, the R bit is the relocated bit, and the two MM bits are mark bits.

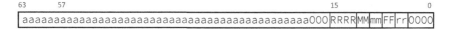

(b) Generational tagged pointer layout. The four R bits indicate the good colour (only one of which is set at any time), the M and m bits are mark bits for the old and young generations, respectively, the F bits are used for concurrent marking through with finalisers and the two r bits indicate whether the field is tracked in a remembered set.

Figure 17.4: ZGC tagged pointer layouts. The a bits are the address the pointer holds (with 64-bit alignment, the three lower-order bits are 000).

Like Pauseless , ZGC uses tagged pointers and self-healing load barriers. Figure 17.4a shows its tagged pointer layout. A group of four higher-order bits determine a *colour*. The four bits are named F (finalisable), R (relocated), M1 and M0 (marked). A given pointer will have only one of R, M0 and M1 set, so these can be thought of as the colour of the pointer. We explain on page 403 how F is used in dealing with Java finalisation. At any given time, only one of R, M0 or M1 is the *good* colour; loading pointers of other colours forces a load barrier slow path (see Algorithm 17.11). To allow direct access to objects using a pointer of any colour, the heap is triple mapped.

ZGC is a mostly-concurrent algorithm, with main phases similar to those of Pauseless. In particular, the Mark and Remap steps are run side-by-side. The main phases are:

STW1: The initial stop-the-world phase comprises three steps. (i) Flip the good colour to either M0 or M1 (they alternate from cycle to cycle). As will be seen, the previous good colour will have been R, so this colour change immediately invalidates all pointers (causes them to have a bad colour). (ii) Arrange for threads to allocate from fresh regions. All objects in the new regions will be considered live throughout this collection cycle. (iii) Scan the roots, replacing non-null pointers with a version of good colour, obtained by applying the self-healing *mark barrier*, and push them onto the mark stack. The mark barrier is the same as the load barrier in Algorithm 17.11 but does not return a result and therefore is streamlined in the obvious ways.

Mark/Remap: Marking takes the typical steps: pop an item from the marking thread's mark stack; try to mark the object; and if that succeeds, proceed to process the pointer slots of the object, using the self-healing mark barrier. Marking also records the volume of live data in the marked object's region. Just as with Pauseless, ZGC may discover a stale reference to a region condemned in the previous collection cycle. The mark barrier remaps these references to point to the new location of their target and tints them with the good colour.

STW2: The second handshake's purpose is to check if marking is complete, and it may be entered more than once. To reduce the number of times it is needed, ZGC does individual handshakes with each thread first to ascertain if the thread has any remaining marking work.

Reference Processing/Condemned Regions: This phase combines the identification of condemned regions (called evacuation candidates in ZGC), namely regions containing objects that should be evacuated, with the processing of weak reference objects. Both the ZGC and Shenandoah collectors handle reference processing in a similar intricate fashion, so we cover it separately on page 403. This phase uses the volume of live data associated with each region to determine which regions to evacuate. Since ZGC only allocates into fresh regions, lightly occupied regions waste space. Like other compacting collectors, ZGC prioritises evacuating the most sparsely occupied regions in order to reclaim the most space with the least effort.

STW3: The third stop-the-world handshake establishes an invariant that mutators never see a pointer to an object in a condemned region. It does this by relocating objects in condemned regions referenced by roots and updating the roots to point to the relocated copies of their targets. To maintain this invariant, this handshake also changes the good colour to R (for relocated), which immediately invalidates all pointers (they now have a bad colour).

Relocate: In this phase, collector threads relocate objects in condemned regions. If mutators encounter a pointer to such an object, they attempt to relocate it, and will self-heal the pointer. As more than one thread may attempt to relocate an object at the same time, ZGC uses a compare-and-swap to set the forwarding address in the relocation table; the winner's copy will be used and other competing threads will back out of their bump pointer allocations. As usual, a region's relocation table is kept outside the region so that its physical pages can be reclaimed as soon as all the live objects it contains have been evacuated. Relocation completes when all live objects in condemned regions have been relocated. However, some objects may retain R-coloured pointers. These pointers will be healed, either when a mutator next loads them or, at the latest, by the end of the Map/Remap step of the next collection cycle.

Choosing condemned regions. The policy used by ZGC to choose condemned regions is to rank regions according to their occupancy, in order to maximise storage reclaimed per byte copied. It selects regions with occupancy of no more than 75%.

Yang *et al.* [2020] suggest using the evacuation mechanism to segregate objects according to their hotness. Their *Hot-Cold Segregated Garbage Collector* (HCSGC) considers an object to be *hot* if it has been accessed since the last collection cycle. The goal of this new policy is not only to reclaim space but also to improve locality. It follows the principle that the future order of mutator accesses is likely to follow their past order. Therefore, whereas the previous policy aimed to have collector threads do as much evacuation as possible, this policy aims to have *mutators* do it. That way, evacuated objects will be laid out in the order they were accessed by mutators, leading to better cache locality and hardware prefetching.

HCSGC uses an additional bitmap to indicate whether an object is considered hot. It clears this bitmap at the start of each collection cycle. An object's hot bit will be set by a mutator if it encounters the object on the slow path of the load barrier. The object's hot bit will also be set by a collector thread if it encounters an R-coloured pointer to the object, which indicates that a mutator accessed the object since the STW3 phase of the last collection cycle. Collector threads maintain two allocation regions, one for hot objects and one for cold, placing the new copies into one or other region according to their hot bit. In contrast, mutators continue to use a single region since all objects they evacuate are hot, by definition.

To shift evacuation work more to mutators, HCSGC defers the Relocation step of ZGC until the start of the *next* collection cycle (but still before STW1). Relocation will then

Algorithm 17.11: ZGC's self-healing load barrier

```
 1  Read(src, i):
 2      addr ← &src[i]
 3      value ← *addr
 4      if isNull(value) || isGoodColour(value)
 5          return value
 6      if pointsIntoCondemned(value)
 7          good ← remap(value)                 /* looks up forwarding address */
 8      else
 9          good ← goodColour(value)       /* tints value with current good colour */
10      push(markStack, good)
11      selfHeal(addr, value, good)
12      return good
13
14  selfHeal(addr, value, good):
15      if isNull(good)
16          return
17      loop
18          old ← CompareAndSwap(addr, value, good)
19          if old = value || isNull(old) || isGoodColour(old)
20              return
21          value ← old
```

evacuate objects in condemned regions that mutators have not yet encountered, with most of them being placed into collector threads' regions for cold objects.

Yang and Wrigstad [2022] evaluated ZGC using SPECjbb2015, a benchmark suitable for testing response time (as opposed to throughput). They found that both typical and more extremal pause times are shorter for ZGC— on the order of 1 millisecond versus about 3 milliseconds for Shenandoah, and 100 milliseconds or more for OpenJDK's G1 and Parallel collectors.

Generational ZGC. Originally, ZGC was not generational but *Generational ZGC* Karlsson [2022] uses two logical generations, each of which can be collected independently and concurrently. It uses a different representation of pointer colours from the non-generational version, with many more tag bits. This means that it cannot use multiple mappings, and instead has its load and store barriers deal with the tag bits explicitly. The load barrier strips pointers of their colour as they are loaded, so references in registers and on the stack are *colourless*. This means that it must use a store barrier to restore a proper colour when a reference is written to the heap. These store barriers are now responsible for helping marking; the load barrier is now only responsible for updating stale pointers after Generational ZGC has relocated objects. In these ways, it differs from both non-generational ZGC and Pauseless/C4.

Figure 17.4b shows the layout of Generational ZGC's tagged pointers. It uses the *low*-order 16 bits of pointers for colours rather than the four higher-order bits that non-generational ZGC uses. Note that this layout also offers the possibility to increase the maximum heap size from 16 to 128 terabytes. Of the 16 bits reserved for colours, 12 are used. Schematically, the colour bits are RRRRMMmmFFrr0000. The RRRR bits are used by the load barrier: exactly one is set in the good colour at any given time, thus encoding which generation (or neither or both) is being relocated (hence the name, R) as follows. These bits encode a relocation parity per generation, which is flipped at the start of the corresponding generation's relocation pause. This parity can be encoded as two bits, let's call them o (for old) and y (for young), and write them as oy. So if for example the number is 10 and relocation of an old generation starts, the parity will flip to 00, and if then a young relocation starts, it will flip to 01, and so on. The binary number oy denotes the index of the corresponding RRRR bit that is expected to be set. This encoding avoids ABA problems when phasing out stale pointers. The other bits are explained below.

At any given time a current *shift factor* indicates the number of positions that the good colour can be shifted until its low-order set bit just shifts out of low end of the word. On an x86 processor such shifting places that bit in the carry flag, and simultaneously checks whether the resulting value is zero. A ja (jump above) instruction will branch if both the carry and zero flags are 0. Thus, if it branches, the value is a non-null pointer of bad colour. A similar technique works for the ARM instruction set. This design avoids any further shifting in the fast path case by having the shifted good pointer value be the address of the referent. Note that an implication of this is that a pointer's address bits need to be shifted left different numbers of bit positions depending on the current good colour. The shift factor is embedded in the shifting instructions for speed, so when the colour changes, instructions have to be updated. This is accomplished by faking a flush of the cache of generated code to cause the system to take a slow path that patches the shift factors.

The MM bits alternate between 01 and 10 according to the marking cycle of the old generation; mm acts likewise for the young generation. The FF bits indicate which cycle of finaliser reachability bits the collector is currently using for the old generation (young generation collections do not check finaliser reachability). Lastly, the rr bits deal with re-membered sets, indicating whether the pointer is currently remembered. Values 01 or 10 (depending on the young generation collection cycle) indicate that the field containing the pointer is remembered. The normal ('cleared') value for the rr bits is 11, explained below. Note that all pointer values need to be coloured, including null values, so that all remembered set entries get inserted correctly.

The store barrier first checks whether any of the old pointer's colour bits are bad, using a testw instruction on the x86 and a mask of bad colour bits (similar methods will work on other platforms). This is why this system uses the somewhat space-inefficient coding of the alternating cycles as 01 or 10: to make it time-efficient to test whether all the colours match the current cycle (have 0 in all the right places). If this test fails, the code branches to a slow path that can take action, such as inserting the field into a remembered set, or otherwise doing self-healing barrier work for atomic operations appropriate to the phase, as in non-generational ZGC. The test mask is updated similarly to the shift factor in the load barriers. The store barrier fast path shifts the pointer left by the shift factor and inserts the current good colour before doing the actual store. The slow path of the store barrier occurs at the first store of a pointer, exactly what is needed for efficient remembered set maintenance (as well as snapshot-at-the-beginning marking). We can now explain why the normal value of the rr bits is 11: it causes the testw always to conclude the colour is bad, forcing a slow path check as to whether the new pointer should be remembered. Notice that Generational ZGC uses double-buffered remembered sets and records the locations of updated fields precisely in a bitmap. Each old generation region has two remembered set bitmaps, one actively used by the store buffers and one used by the collector as a read-only record of all old generation fields that potentially point to the young generation. Swapping the two bitmaps atomically at the start of each young generation collection means that mutator threads do not have to wait for the bitmaps to be cleared, and that store barriers do not have to use a memory fence when recording old-young generation pointers.

A young generation collection works as usual from statics, thread stacks and the remembered set to find all references to young objects, which can be evacuated after marking as in non-generational ZGC. One detail here is that if a pointer previously in the remembered set is found no longer to point into the young generation, then its rr bits are set to the 'clear' value, `11`. Young generation collections allow regions to be aged without relocating their contents. This cheap promotion allows large objects to be allocated in the young generation rather than the old one, as many generational collectors do. On the other hand, only full heap collections process weak references or unload classes.

Shenandoah

Shenandoah [Flood *et al.*, 2016] is a parallel, compacting collection algorithm aimed at providing short pause times for applications using large heaps. Like many other modern compacting collectors, it is a region-based collector that prioritises sparsely occupied regions (identified in the marking phase) for evacuation. At the time of writing, Shenandoah is non-generational. In 2016 Flood *et al.* argued that programs such as web caches hold onto objects just long enough to defeat generational collectors so, instead, Shenandoah focuses its effort on regions with fewer live objects, regardless of whether those objects are young or old. They also argued that generational collection requires some kind of remembered set, typically a card table, accesses to which lead to cache contention. However, it is not clear that these concerns still hold and implementation of a generational version of Shenandoah is in progress.

Shenandoah's equally sized regions may contain newly allocated objects, older objects or a mixture. Its default policy is to choose regions for evacuation with at least 60% garbage and to start a collection cycle when 75% of the regions have been allocated. Humongous objects larger than a region are only copied during a full, stop-the-world collection.

Shenandoah uses a deletion write barrier for marking. Originally, it also used a combination of this barrier and a Brooks-style read barrier in its evacuation phase, with the forwarding pointer placed immediately before the object (thus separate from the Java class pointer and the header word used for marking and locking, allowing the indirection barrier to be simple and thus faster). Shenandoah made some effort to optimise these barriers away. First, its compiler employed global value numbering, which can identify and remove redundant barriers. Both load and write barriers can be avoided if the value is newly allocated (since it will be in tospace), the value is a null pointer, the value is a constant or the value itself came from a write barrier. Further, load barriers can be eliminated if the value must be the same in both fromspace and tospace (Java `final` fields) or the value came from a load barrier and there can be no interfering write barrier.

However, these barriers have now been replaced in the evacuation phase with a single[9] load barrier applied immediately after loading a reference (Algorithm 17.12). Like the Pauseless and ZGC load barriers, this barrier is self-healing — where necessary, the load barrier cooperates with the collector to copy not yet evacuated objects — but unlike those barriers, it does not use pointer tags. Replacing the read and write barriers with a load barrier simplified the implementation and improved its performance in a number of ways. (i) The strong tospace invariant that threads only ever see a canonical reference to an object makes it easier to reason about the state of collection and objects. (ii) The number of places where barriers are inserted is reduced. (iii) Equality tests are simpler because there is only one copy of an object. (iv) Barriers are placed where references are loaded rather than the typically hotter locations where the references are used. (v) As the fromspace copy is

---

[9]Different flavours of this load barrier are used for normal objects and weak references.

Algorithm 17.12: Shenandoah's self-healing load barrier

```
1   Read(src, i):
2       addr ← &src[i]
3       obj ← *addr
4       if not isGCactive()                    /* fast path: accesses thread–local flag */
5           return obj
6       if not isInCollectionSet(obj)
7           return obj
8
9       fwd = resolveForwardee(obj)             /* access forwarding pointer, if one */
10      if obj ≠ fwd
11        CAS(addr, fwd, obj)                               /* self–heal */
12       return fwd
13
14      fwd = loadSlowpath(obj)        /* once per location with non–forwarded object */
15      CAS(addr, fwd, obj)
16      return fwd
```

---

no longer used, Shenandoah can write the forwarding pointer into it rather than having to dedicate an extra word to the forwarding pointer; this reduces both heap and cache pressure. (vi) Finally, rather than being always on, the load barrier can be made conditional on whether a collection is in progress and the referent is in a condemned region.

The Shenandoah collection cycle consists of the following phases. Note that recent improvements have reduced the time spent in stop-the-world phases (on the next page).

STW1: Initial stop-the-world marking phase to prepare the heap and application threads.

Mark: Concurrently scan thread stacks using stack barriers (see Section 11.5) to ensure consistency. Trace the heap marking objects. Mutators use a deletion write barrier to ensure consistency. The collector threads use work stealing for load balancing. Note that pointers to objects evacuated in the previous collection cycle are no longer updated in this phase but in a subsequent one.

STW2: Final stop-the-world marking phase drains marking queues. There is no need to rescan roots as Shenandoah uses a deletion write barrier. This phase also selects condemned regions.

Concurrent roots and reference processing: Evacuate and update all references in threads and all weak references, and clear and enqueue any unreachable weak references. Evacuate and update all weak roots (such as JNI weak references and some internal structures like the interned string table), and clear unreachable weak roots. Free any regions with no live objects. Unload unused classes and process any remaining strong roots such as references in compiled code regions.

Relocate: Concurrently evacuate live objects from condemned regions. Shenandoah requires that objects in condemned regions not be updated by mutators. Rather, the object must first be copied and may then be updated. Mutators cooperate with collector threads in this regard. There may be a race between copying an object and installing the indirection to the new copy, but the algorithm uses a compare-and-swap for the update, so one thread will win the race and the others can simply rewind their allocation pointers.

Update references: Concurrently sweep the heap to update any remaining pointers to evacuated objects.

Concurrent cleanup: Free the condemned regions.

Reducing stop-the-world time in Shenandoah and ZGC

The original version of Shenandoah [Flood *et al.*, 2016] completed marking in a stop-the-world phase. As well as ensuring that all live objects are marked, this phase dealt with a number of issues that are tricky to handle concurrently. These include processing weak references and finalisers, and class unloading. Handling these matters took up more than half the time of the final mark phase. More recently, Shenandoah and ZGC have adopted similar approaches to reduce the time spent in stop-the-world phases. These include using stack barriers to allow the collector to process thread stacks concurrently, and concurrent reference processing and class unloading. All of these improvements reduced pause times substantially.

Concurrent reference processing. As we noted earlier in this chapter, Java's semantics make concurrent reference processing delicate. First, there may be a race between the collector processing a weak reference by nulling its referent field and a mutator resurrecting the referent by making it strongly-reachable. Second, if multiple weak reference objects refer to the same target, they must behave consistently. ZGC and Shenandoah use five steps to process weak references concurrently.

1. During the Map/Remap phase of a cycle, marking builds a *discovered list* of addresses of weak reference objects found whose referent was not strongly marked at the time the weak reference object was discovered. The discovered list is a superset of the weak references that should be cleared. Note that a `SoftReference` also requires that the system's policy hold for it (for example, an 'always clear' policy or an 'LRU max heap' policy, which clears the `SoftReference` if it has not been used recently enough).

2. In stop-the-world phase STW2, resurrection is disabled. Fetching the target of a weak reference (other than a `PhantomReference`) will return null if the target is not marked or a pointer to its target if it is marked.

3. In the concurrent Reference Processing phase, the discovered list is pruned to remove any weak references that should not be cleared and to clear those that should be.

4. After this, resurrection is re-enabled.

5. Finally, the discovered list is made available to components that use it to post weak reference objects to their registered queues.

Objects with finalisers need to be marked specially, as finalisably reachable. This is because these objects need to be retained until they are finalised, but not treated as if they are strongly-reachable. Three mark states are needed: (strongly) marked, finalisably marked and unmarked. Marking propagates the strongly marked and finalisably marked wave-fronts together, in one pass. In the case of ZGC, any tagged pointers that are followed in this finalisable trace are updated with both F and the good colour. Strong marking is preferred: if an object previously marked as finalisable is discovered, its transitive closure is strongly marked (in ZGC's case, clearing the F bit).

Class unloading is important for applications that make heavy use of class loaders, such as application servers and integrated development environments (IDEs), and is also relevant to Java's anonymous classes and lambdas. Class unloading requires determining whether a class loader is reachable, and unlinking and cleaning any unreachable loader, class or other data structure including compiled code. This is usually performed in a stop-the-world phase, but ZGC and Shenandoah manage class unloading concurrently by using *compiled method entry barriers*, which indicate that the compiled code may have been invalidated. The aim is to evacuate and update references in a method before it executes and to handle other methods concurrently. A compiled method entry barrier is invoked before a method is first executed in a cycle in order to scan the method's code for embedded constants, evacuating the referent and updating the reference. These barriers are enabled in the final stop-the-world pause of a collection cycle and disabled when a collector thread processes the method or when a Java thread is first about to execute the method.

17.6   Issues to consider

This chapter has laid out the basic principles of concurrent copying collection and concurrent compaction to reduce fragmentation, while also avoiding long pauses. As in any concurrent collector algorithm, the collector must be protected against mutations that can otherwise cause lost objects. But because the collector is moving objects, the mutator must also be protected against accessing stale copies. Some algorithms protect the mutator by making sure it operates with a tospace invariant so that it can never hold references to stale fromspace objects [Baker, 1978]. Others protect the mutator by making it forward to tospace copies as they are created but otherwise allow it to continue operating in fromspace [Brooks, 1984]. Still others permit continued operation in fromspace, so long as updates eventually propagate to tospace [Nettles *et al.*, 1992; Nettles and O'Toole, 1993]. Once copying has finished, all the mutators flip to tospace in a single step. Dispensing with this global transition can mean accumulating chains of multiple versions, which mutators must traverse to find the most up-to-date copy [Herlihy and Moss, 1992]. Alternatively, by performing updates on both copies, mutators can be transitioned one at a time [Hudson and Moss, 2001, 2003; Ugawa *et al.*, 2018]. Compaction can be performed in similar ways but without the need to copy all objects at every collection [Kermany and Petrank, 2006; Click *et al.*, 2005; Azul, 2008; Flood *et al.*, 2016; Lidén, 2018].

These approaches may result in longer pauses than non-moving concurrent collection: on any given heap access, the mutator may need to wait for an object (or objects) to move or indirect to the current version. Indeed, Baker [1992a] devised his Treadmill algorithm as an antidote to the churn present in his original copying collector [Baker, 1978]. While copying or compaction are needed to avoid fragmentation, they can present particular difficulties for applications that are sensitive to prolonged or frequent pauses. Often, such applications also operate in environments where memory is unusually constrained, such as embedded systems, where defragmentation can be even more important.

Many of the concurrent collectors discussed in this chapter rely on parallel threads, trading much increased CPU cycles for lower latencies. This increased use of resources does not come for free in a multi-tenancy system. In the next chapter, we discuss alternative ways to reduce expected latency times with lower total resource use. The following Chapter 19 then considers how to manage concurrent copying or concurrent compaction while tightly bounding pause times for more demanding applications.

Chapter 18

Concurrent reference counting

We discussed reference counting in Chapter 5. The two chief issues facing naive reference counting were its inability to collect garbage cycles and the high cost of manipulating reference counts, particularly in the face of races between different mutator threads. The solution to cyclic garbage was trial deletion (partial tracing). We used deferred reference counting to avoid having mutators manipulate reference counts on local variables and coalescing to avoid having to make 'redundant' changes to reference counts that would be cancelled out by later mutations; a useful side effect of coalescing is that it tolerates mutator races. All three solutions required stopping the world while the collector reconciled reference counts and reclaimed any garbage. In this chapter, we will relax this requirement and consider the changes that need to be made in order to allow a reference counting collector thread to run concurrently with mutator threads but, before we do, we look at LXR, a high-performance, mostly non-concurrent (mostly)-reference counting algorithm.

18.1 LXR: Latency-critical ImmiX with Reference counting

Latency-critical ImmiX with Reference counting (LXR) [Zhao *et al.*, 2022a,b] is primarily a high-performance, coalescing, generational, deferred, sticky reference counter but uses a concurrent, snapshot-at-the-beginning tracing collector to reclaim both garbage cycles and objects whose reference counts are stuck. LXR applies reference count increments in stop-the-world pauses during which it can also defragment the heap by opportunistically evacuating either young objects or mature objects in sparsely occupied blocks; its decrements are applied lazily and concurrently with mutators' execution. One of the most interesting aspects of LXR is that it raises the question of whether the complexity of concurrent copying/compacting garbage collectors is worthwhile. Implemented in OpenJDK with the MMTk memory management toolkit,[1] LXR has demonstrated performance that is competitive with other modern collectors such as G1 in large heaps but offers better throughput and especially better latency in heaps as tight as $1.3\times$ minimum heap size. It also uses fewer total resources such as CPU cycles [Zhao *et al.*, 2022b, Section 5.5].

Heap structure. LXR builds on the *RC Immix* heap structure [Shahriyar *et al.*, 2013] where heap organisation was identified as the principal cause of the performance gap between existing high-performance reference counters and modern tracing collectors such as immix [Blackburn and McKinley, 2008]. As we noted earlier, heap management based on free-lists

---

[1]MMTk: a high-performance language-independent memory management framework, https://mmtk.io.

suffers from a number of problems including internal and external fragmentation. Free-list layout also leads to poor cache locality as objects allocated contemporaneously may be dispersed, for instance among several segregated free-lists, in contrast to bump pointer allocation which would allocate these objects together. RC Immix modified the authors' previous reference counter [Shahriyar *et al.*, 2012] by replacing its free-list allocation with immix's heap structure of 32-kilobyte blocks of 256-byte lines. Bump pointer allocation also allows whole blocks or contiguous free lines within a block to be zeroed more efficiently, *en masse*, rather than an object at a time, as a free-list allocator must do. Both immix and RC Immix bump allocate small and medium-sized objects into gaps of contiguous whole lines in partially filled blocks (see Section 10.6). The allocator places new objects contiguously into empty lines, skipping occupied lines; objects may span lines, but not blocks. Lines and blocks are not reclaimed until all the objects they contain are dead.

Reference counting. Whereas RC Immix tracks the number of live objects on a line and in a block, LXR stores a two-bit, sticky reference count for each object in a side reference count table; objects whose reference count reaches three become 'stuck' and can only be reclaimed by a concurrent tracing collector thread. Importantly, objects in LXR are born dead, with a reference count of zero. As with other coalesced reference counters (see Section 5.4), reference count increments and decrements are applied in frequent epochs. Increments and decrements are generated either by the LXR write barrier (Algorithm 18.1), or when root scanning at each reference counting epoch boundary (when LXR applies an increment to each object reachable from the roots — recursively for young objects — and buffers a corresponding decrement for the next epoch). The barrier is field rather than object remembering and uses one `unlogged` bit per field (also held in side metadata). The log lock (again, in side metadata) can be per-field or of coarser granularity, though for efficiency `markAsLoggedAndUnlock` should be able to clear the `unlogged` bit and release the log lock in one step. As noted in Algorithm 18.1, looping is not needed if the log locks are per-field (not coarse).

As usual for a coalesced reference counter, at each epoch boundary LXR first applies increments to the referents of all the fields in the `modifiedFieldsBuffer` and then applies decrements to objects recorded in the `decrementsBuffer`. Whenever an object's reference count is reduced to zero, LXR enqueues the dead object for recursive decrements of the referents of its fields. An epoch is complete when both the `decrementsBuffer` and the recursive decrement queue are empty. To avoid long pauses, LXR restarts mutators and processes decrements lazily in a separate thread which runs immediately after each stop-the-world pause and completes before the next pause starts.

Coalesced reference counting allows LXR (and RC Immix to handle short-lived objects very efficiently by treating them as *implicitly dead*, with a reference count of zero. Young objects (allocated in the current epoch) cannot generate decrements since (i) their pointer fields are originally null, and (ii) there were no pointers to them from the stack or the heap at the start of the epoch. Furthermore, LXR generates increments from a young object only if and when the object receives its first reference count increment (from zero to one) at the end of the epoch in which it was created (thus transitively applying increments to surviving young objects). If the weak generational hypothesis holds, most objects will die within an epoch and therefore can be reclaimed without *any* reference counting increments or decrements. Instead, LXR sweeps all young blocks at the end of the reference counting pause, adding each one to its two global lists of either free or partially free blocks. After lazy decrement processing is complete, LXR sweeps mature blocks, but only those that contain an object that has received a decrement.

Algorithm 18.1: LXR field-logging write barrier

```
 1  Write(src, i, ref):
 2      field ← &src[i]
 3      if unLogged(field)            /* unsynchronised test of per–field unlogged bit */
 4          log(field)
 5      src[i] ← value
 6
 7  log(field):
 8      do                            /* looping only needed if lock is coarse */
 9          if tryLogLock(field)      /* returns false if another thread is logging */
10              old ← *field          /* remember old referent */
11              markAsLoggedAndUnlock(field)
12              push(decrementsBuffer, old)       /* log old referent*/
13              push(modifiedFieldsBuffer, field)    /* log field address */
14          else:                     /* must wait for old referent to be logged */
15              waitUntilLogUnlocked(field)
16      while unLogged(field)
```

Concurrent tracing. LXR (and RC Immix use a tracing collector in the background, as needed, to reclaim garbage cycles. In LXR, this collector also handles objects whose reference counts are stuck. The write barrier needed by coalesced reference counting to capture the referents of overwritten fields is also just what is needed for LXR's Yuasa-style concurrent snapshot-at-the-beginning tracing collector. A run of the tracing collector is seeded from the roots set of a reference counting collection but may span several epochs. An optimisation is to have the trace visit only mature objects, ignoring objects with a zero reference count — normally a snapshot-at-the-beginning algorithm would preserve young objects. In order to avoid interference with a running trace, the reference counter immediately marks and scans (for reference count decrementing) any mature object that it determines to be dead unless the trace has already marked it. Note that, since marking and reference count work are mutually exclusive, the former being done only outside of pauses and the latter only during pauses, there is no race condition. This allows the reference counter to reclaim objects promptly but prevents the trace from following a pointer to a deleted object. Unmarked objects are reclaimed in the first epoch after the trace has completed. To limit their cost, LXR triggers traces only if a reference counting epoch finds too few empty blocks or if the predicted volume of uncollected dead mature objects exceeds a threshold.

Evacuation. The LXR design is based on the belief that concurrent copying is intrinsically expensive. It reclaims most objects without copying. However, some copying is necessary to defragment the heap: LXR can do this opportunistically but only during mutator pauses. Shahriyar *et al.* [2013] noted that any young object that survives its first epoch will receive an increment from every referent. This pause is an opportunity to move surviving young objects (which are identified by their reference counts incrementing from zero to one). LXR targets all blocks that contain only young objects, evacuating their contents into partially free (preferentially) or completely empty blocks, if any are available. Most notably, LXR respects pause time targets, stopping copying when a time threshold is reached, at which point further objects are left in place. Mature objects can also be compacted opportunistically as the LXR write barrier supports the maintenance of remembered sets. This 'double duty' of the LXR write barrier is one of its key insights and innovations. Each remembered set tracks all pointers into a condemned set of blocks within a contiguous 4-megabyte region of the heap. Before each concurrent trace, LXR identifies blocks that are estimated from the reference count table to be most sparsely occupied; these form the condemned sets. LXR does not maintain remembered sets continuously but initialises them by piggybacking on a concurrent trace, which must traverse every pointer into the condemned sets, and discards the remembered sets in the pause when the condemned sets are evacuated. The write barrier remembers any new reference into the sets created subsequently. Remembered sets that are maintained for more than one epoch risk having entries that are stale because the object has been reclaimed by the reference counter. LXR avoids this by tagging each line and each remembered set pointer source entry with a *reuse counter*. Line reuse counts are incremented whenever the line is reused (and all reuse counts are reset to zero at the start of each trace). If evacuation finds that a remembered set entry's reuse count is older than that of the line to which the entry refers, it discards the entry. LXR may evacuate one or more condemned sets at each stop-the-world pause, depending on time budget. It evacuates each set by tracing from roots and the remembered set, copying objects and leaving forwarding pointers. Any reference to something outside the condemned set is ignored, thus bounding the number of objects traced.

While LXR does not represent generations explicitly, it is essentially generational in character, using frequent pauses to copy young survivors opportunistically (with a non-zero tenuring threshold). Thus it exploits the weak generational hypothesis. Both LXR and explicitly generational collectors use remembered sets for evacuation. The LXR increment buffer also resembles a remembered set but remembers unconditionally all old object fields that have been modified, whereas a filtering generational remembered set might remember only where an old-young pointer has been stored. However, LXR runs collections of young objects (typically by stop-the-world copying) and mature objects (concurrent tracing) simultaneously and somewhat independently. Reference counting is key here to the prompt reclamation of dead objects.

Triggers. LXR uses a number of heuristics to control collection. As well as triggering a pause if the heap is full, it also triggers a pause if the number of increments or the predicted number of survivors exceed thresholds. These heuristics guard against long pauses due to increment processing and copying of young objects. The survivor predictor is an exponential decay predictor, conservatively biased to higher survival rates. To manage fragmentation, LXR triggers concurrent tracing based on the number of free blocks or the predicted heap wastage, defined as uncollected dead mature objects plus fragmentation.

Scalability and performance. LXR was designed with scalability and immediacy in mind. It supplies fresh blocks in a lock-free manner to thread-local allocators, with minimal contention. Reference counts are inherently local so increments and decrements can be applied in parallel. Work stealing is used for load balancing and very large arrays are partitioned. Most decrements are performed concurrently. The field remembering write barrier is reported to have a geometric mean overhead of only 1.6% compared with no barrier. Only the tertiary mechanism, concurrent tracing, has significant potential for scalability issues.

Measuring the overheads of garbage collectors is difficult, as is ascribing the causes of these overheads; see, for example, the methodology of Cai *et al.* [2022] for measuring overheads — they also provide a detailed analysis of a number of modern collectors, serial, parallel and concurrent, implemented in OpenJDK 17. Zhao *et al.* show that LXR offers excellent latency and throughput, compared with other collectors implemented in Open-JDK 11, when running the DaCapo benchmarks,[2] which require minimum heap sizes in

---

[2] DaCapo Chopin evaluation release, 2021.

Thread 1 Write(o,i,x)	**Thread 2** Write(o,i,y)
addReference(x)	addReference(y)
old ←o[i]	old ←o[i]
deleteReference(old)	deleteReference(old)
o[i]←x	o[i]←y

Figure 18.1: Reference counting must synchronise the manipulation of counts with pointer updates. Here, two threads race to update an object field. Note that old is a local variable of each thread's Write method.

the range of 7 to 3,689 megabytes. LXR delivered throughput competitive with G1 and better than the concurrent compacting collectors Shenandoah and ZGC , but with significantly lower 99.99% latency and overall resource consumption compared with all of those collectors. We can ask why LXR demonstrates better performance than some modern concurrent copying collectors. Garbage collection is a time-space trade-off, and concurrent copying collectors often need large heaps, especially for applications with very high allocation rates, if they are not to revert to stop-the-world collection. In particular, concurrent compacting collectors cannot reclaim any space until marking is complete, and can then release early only those regions that are completely empty. Consequently, they require more headroom in the heap than deferred reference counting which reclaims space occupied by dead objects much more promptly (in LXR's case, for all objects that are not reachable only from garbage cycles). Throughput is affected by the cost of barriers, and concurrent copying is inherently expensive. Even with self-healing load barriers, the frequency and CPU cycle cost of using read barriers is higher than that of write barriers, which LXR uses. Furthermore, LXR avoids applying barriers to most objects since they are allocated dead and most die young. The opportunity cost of running multiple threads is also a consideration in many environments. Cai *et al.* [2022] found that the total cost (CPU cycles across all threads) of Shenandoah and ZGC was much higher than that of G1. However, LXR's behaviour is more comparable to G1 in this respect while anecdotal results suggest it consistently uses fewer CPU cycles.

18.2 Simple reference counting revisited

We now return to think about concurrent reference counting. To be correct, reference counting algorithms must preserve the invariant that an object's reference count is equal to the number of references to that object. Maintaining this invariant becomes more complicated with multiple mutator threads. At first sight, it may seem that it is more difficult to Write safely than to Read safely. Updating a pointer slot requires three actions: the reference count of the new target must be incremented, that of the old target be decremented and the pointer written. It is important that these three actions be coordinated, even though multiple mutator threads may manipulate pointers to the objects in question.[3] Objects must not be reclaimed prematurely (for example, because their reference count has temporarily dropped to zero) nor is it desirable for garbage to float indefinitely in the heap. Figure 18.1 illustrates the problem. Here, even if all the reference count increments and decrements are performed atomically, some thread interleavings may lead to an incorrect result because the reference count of old may be decremented twice and the reference count of one of the new targets may be too high.

---

[3]Note that we are not concerned about the correctness of the user program in the face of races, but we must ensure the consistency of the heap.

Algorithm 18.2: Eager reference counting with locks

```
 1  Read(src, i):
 2      lock(src)
 3          tgt ← src[i]
 4          addReference(tgt)
 5      unlock(src)
 6      return tgt
 7
 8  Write(src, i, ref):
 9      addReference(ref)
10      lock(src)
11          old ← src[i]
12          src[i] ← ref
13          deleteReference(old)
14      unlock(src)
```

The difficulty of concurrent reference counting does not lie solely with incrementing or decrementing reference count fields. This can be done easily enough with an atomic primitive operation such as AtomicIncrement, discussed in Chapter 13. The harder problem is to synchronise reference count modifications with pointer loads or stores; in Algorithm 5.1 we simply required the mutator Read and Write actions to be atomic. The simplest way to do this is to lock the object containing the field that is being read or written, src, as illustrated in Algorithm 18.2. This is safe. After Read has locked src, the value of field i cannot change. If it is null, Read is trivially correct. Otherwise, src holds a reference to some object tgt. The reference counting invariant ensures that tgt's reference count cannot drop to zero before src is unlocked since there is a reference to tgt from src. Thus, we can guarantee that tgt cannot be freed during the Read and that addReference will be able to update the count rather than potentially corrupting memory. A similar argument establishes the safety of Write.

It is appealing to hope that we can find a lock-free solution, using commonly available primitive operations. Unfortunately, single memory location primitives are insufficient to guarantee safety. The problem does not lie in Write. Imagine that, instead of the coarser grain lock, we use atomic increments and decrements to update reference counts and compare-and-swap for the pointer write, as in Algorithm 18.3. If ref is non-null, then the writing thread holds a reference to it so ref cannot be reclaimed until Write returns (whether or not we use eager or deferred reference counting). Write spins, attempting to set the pointer field until we are successful: at that point, we know that next we will decrement the count of the correct old object and that only the winning thread will do this. Note that the reference count of this old target remains an overestimate until deleteReference(old) is called, and so old cannot be prematurely deleted.

We cannot apply the same tactic in Read, though. Even if Read uses a primitive atomic operation to update the reference count, unless we lock src it is possible that some other thread will delete the pointer src[i] and reclaim its target between the point that we load the reference (line 19) and the increment of the reference count. The attempt to increment the reference count may corrupt memory that has been freed and maybe reallocated.

Although single memory location primitive operations are insufficiently powerful to provide a solution, Detlefs *et al.* [2001, 2002b] show that the CompareAndSet2 primitive discussed in Section 13.3 *is* sufficient. CompareAndSet2 can atomically update two inde-

Algorithm 18.3: Eager reference counting with compare-and-swap is broken

```
 1  Write(src, i, ref):
 2     if ref ≠ null
 3        AtomicIncrement(&rc(ref))              /* ref guaranteed to be non–free */
 4     loop
 5        old ← src[i]
 6        if CompareAndSet(&src[i], old, ref)
 7           deleteReference(old)
 8           return
 9
10  deleteReference(ref):                        /* ref guaranteed to be null or non–free */
11     if ref ≠ null
12        AtomicDecrement(&rc(ref))
13        if rc(ref) = 0
14           for each fld in Pointers(ref)
15              deleteReference(*fld)
16           free(ref)
17
18  Read(src, i):
19     tgt = src[i]
20     AtomicIncrement(&rc(tgt))                 /* oops! */
21     return tgt
```

Algorithm 18.4: Eager reference counting with `CompareAndSet2`

```
 1  Read(src, i, root):
 2     loop
 3        tgt ← src[i]
 4        if tgt = null
 5           return null
 6        rc ← rc(tgt)
 7        if CompareAndSet2(&src[i], &rc(tgt), tgt, rc, tgt, rc+1)
 8           return tgt
```

pendent memory locations. Although this is not sufficient to maintain accurate reference counts at all times, it is sufficient to guarantee the weaker invariant that (i) while there remains a pointer to an object, its reference count cannot be zero, and (ii) if there are no pointers to an object, its reference count will eventually become zero. In Algorithm 18.4, `CompareAndSet2` is used to increment the reference count and simultaneously to check that the pointer to the object still exists, thus avoiding the possibility of modifying an object's header after it has been freed. An alternative if it is available is transactional memory, though using a transaction for each write may have high cost.

18.3   Biased reference counting

Choi *et al.* [2018] found that, in a selection of Swift programs, 99% of client and 93% of server objects were private, and that the overwhelming majority of reference counting operations were to private objects (93% for client and 87% for server programs). Their *biased reference counting* technique takes advantage of this by using two reference count fields. The owner thread updates the first, *biased*, counter using non-atomic operations, while non-owner threads use atomic operations to update the second, *shared*, counter. Both 14-bit counters, two flag bits (Merged and queued) and a thread ID are stored in the 64-bit word that Swift uses for a reference count. The algorithm can be understood by considering the five invariants that it maintains.

I1: An object can only be deallocated if the sum of the biased and shared reference counts is zero.

I2: The biased reference count must be non-negative. When the biased reference count reaches zero, the owner sets the Merged flag, making the biased reference count inaccessible.

I3: The shared reference count may be negative. For instance, a thread may create an object and point a global reference to it, only for this reference to be removed by a non-owner. To prevent a leak, when a non-owner removes a reference that would cause the shared count to become negative for the first time, it adds a reference to the object to the owner's QueuedObjects list and sets the Queued flag.

I4: The owner gives up ownership when it merges counters either implicitly when the biased reference count becomes zero or explicitly if it finds the object in its Queued-Objects list. Periodically, the owning thread examines this list.

I5: An object can only be placed in QueuedObjects list once and is removed from the list when the counters are explicitly merged.

Choi *et al.* found that biased reference counting reduced the average execution time of client programs by 22.5% and boosted the average throughput of server programs by 7.3%.

18.4   Buffered reference counting

Eager reference counting schemes require either locks or multi-word atomic primitives, which are (currently) not widely available. Deferred reference counting partially finesses the problem we saw in the previous section by not applying reference count operations to local variables and deferring reclamation of objects with zero reference counts (see Section 5.3). This leaves the question of how to reduce the overhead of pointer writes to object fields. We now turn to look at *buffered reference counting* techniques that only use simple loads and stores in the mutator write barrier, yet support multithreaded applications.

In order to avoid the cost of synchronising reference count manipulations by different mutator threads, DeTreville [1990] had mutators log the old and new referents of each pointer update to a buffer (in a hybrid collector for Modula-2+ that used mark-sweep as an occasional backup collector to handle cycles). A single, separate reference counting thread processed the log and adjusted objects' reference counts, thereby ensuring that the modifications were trivially atomic. In order to prevent inadvertently applying a reference count decrement before an increment that causally preceded it (and hence prematurely reclaiming an object), increments were applied before decrements. Unfortunately, buffering updates does not resolve the problem of coordinating the reference count manipulations with the pointer write. DeTreville offered two solutions, neither of which is entirely satisfactory. His first approach was, as above, to protect the entire Write operation with a lock.

This ensures that records are correctly appended to the shared buffer as well as synchronising the updates. To avoid the cost of making every write atomic, his second solution provided each mutator thread with its own buffer, which was periodically passed to the reference counting thread, but this required the programmer to take care to ensure that pointer writes were performed atomically, if necessary performing the locking manually, to avoid the problems illustrated by Figure 18.1.

Bacon and Rajan [2001] also provided each thread with a local buffer but required the update of the pointer field to be atomic, as for example in Algorithm 18.5; a compare-and-swap with retry could be used to do this. The mutator write barrier on a processor adds the old and new values of slot i to its local `myUpdates` buffer (line 9). Once again, reference counting of local variables is deferred, and time is divided into *ragged epochs* to ensure that objects are not prematurely deleted, by using a single shared epoch number plus per-thread local epoch numbers. Periodically, just as with deferred reference counting, a processor will interrupt a processor and scan all the stacks of each local thread that has been active in that epoch, logging references found to a local `myStackBuffer`. The processor then transfers its `myStackBuffer` and `myUpdates` to the collector, and updates its local epoch number, e. Finally, it schedules the collector thread of the next processor before resuming the interrupted thread.

The collector thread runs on the last processor. In each collection cycle k, the collector applies the increments of epoch k and the decrements of epoch $k - 1$. Finally, it increments the global epoch counter (for simplicity, we assume an unbounded number of global `updatesBuffers` in Algorithm 18.5). The advantage of this technique is that it is never necessary to halt all mutators simultaneously: the collector is on-the-fly and the state transitions are simply Type I (see Section 15.3). Note how the collector uses a variant of deferred reference counting. At the start of the collection, the counts of objects directly referenced from thread stacks (in this epoch) are incremented; at the end of the cycle, those of objects directly reachable from the stacks in the previous epoch are decremented.

18.5 Concurrent, cyclic reference counting

This leaves the question of collecting garbage cycles by reference counting without introducing stop-the-world pauses. The *Recycler* [Bacon *et al.*, 2001; Bacon and Rajan, 2001] reclaims cyclic garbage by tracing candidate subgraphs, applying trial deletion to reference counts. Although buffering successfully devolves reference counting to a spare processor, the Recycler faces three problems in collecting cycles in a concurrent world.

- It cannot guarantee that it will retrace the same subgraph since the graph may be modified by mutators while the Recycler is detecting garbage cycles.

- Pointer deletions may disconnect portions of the subgraph.

- Reference counts may be out of date.

To resolve these problems, the asynchronous Recycler operates in two phases. The first phase is much the same as the synchronous collector described in Chapter 5. However, the asynchronous collector defers the freeing of objects discovered by `collectWhite` (Algorithm 5.5) to the next phase which checks that these objects are indeed still garbage. There are several disadvantages to this approach. In theory, but probably not in practice, it is possible for some garbage cycles not to be collected — the collector is not guaranteed to be complete. Further, trial deletion cannot use the original reference count but must add a second, cyclic reference count field to object headers. Third, the algorithm must trace candidate cycles again, in the second phase, in order to avoid incorrectly reclaiming live

Algorithm 18.5: Concurrent buffered reference counting

```
 1   shared epoch
 2   shared updatesBuffer[]                              /* one buffer per epoch */
 3
 4   Write(src, i, ref):
 5       if src = Roots
 6           src[i] ← ref
 7       else
 8           old ← AtomicExchange(&src[i], ref)
 9           log(old, ref)
10
11   log(old, new):
12       myUpdates ← myUpdates + [⟨old, new⟩]
13
14   collect():
15       /* each processor passes its buffers on to a global updatesBuffer */
16       myStackBuffer ← []
17       for each local ref in myStacks            /* deferred reference counting */
18           myStackBuffer ← myStackBuffer + [⟨ref, ref⟩]
19       atomic
20           updatesBuffer[e] ← updatesBuffer[e] + myStackBuffer
21       atomic
22           updatesBuffer[e] ← updatesBuffer[e] + myUpdates
23       myUpdates ← []
24       e ← e + 1
25
26       me ← myProcessorId
27       if me < MAX_PROCESSORS            /* schedule collect() on the next processor */
28           schedule(collect, me+1)
29       else                           /* the last processor updates the reference counts*/
30           for each ⟨old, new⟩ in updatesBuffer[epoch]
31               addReference(new)
32           for each ⟨old, new⟩ in updatesBuffer[epoch−1]
33               deleteReference(old)
34           release(updatesBuffer[epoch−1])              /* free the old buffer */
35           epoch ← epoch + 1
```

objects. It also adds overhead to the reference counting write barrier, as it must fix the colours of objects left white or grey by improper traversals.

The fundamental problem is that the Recycler is trying to apply an algorithm designed for synchronous collection in a world where the topology of the object graph is continually changing. Next, we see below how this circle can be squared by providing the Recycler with a fixed snapshot of the heap.

18.6   Taking a snapshot of the heap

We saw in Chapter 5 how coalesced reference counting provided the collector with a snapshot of the heap. Thread-local buffers, passed synchronously to the collector, held replicas

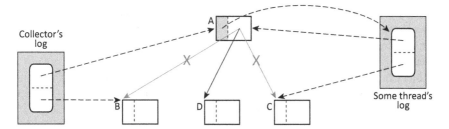

Figure 18.2: Concurrent coalesced reference counting: in the previous epoch A was modified to point to C and the values of its reference fields logged. However, A has been modified again in this epoch (to point to D), and so marked dirty and logged again. The original referent B can be found in the collector's global log, just as in Figure 5.2. The reference to C that was added in the previous epoch will be in some thread's current log: this log can be found from A's `getLogPointer` field.

Algorithm 18.6: Sliding views: update reference counts

```
 1  incrementNew(entry):              /* use the entry in the collector's log */
 2      obj ← objFromLog(entry)                        /* the current object */
 3      if not dirty(obj)
 4          replica ← copy(obj)            /* copy the object's reference slots */
 5          if dirty(obj)
 6              replica ← getLogPointer(obj)    /* entry in some thread's log */
 7      else
 8          replica ← getLogPointer(obj)
 9
10      for each fld in Pointers(replica)
11          child ← *fld
12          if child ≠ null
13              rc(child) ← rc(child) + 1
14              mark(child)                     /* if tracing young generation */
```

of objects into which pointers had been written. Every thread was halted at the start of a collection cycle, its buffers were transferred to the collector, and fresh buffers allocated. The collector simply used the replica to find and decrement the reference counts of the old targets, and the current version of the object to find and increment reference counts of the new targets. All dirty objects were cleaned.

Let us see first how we can allow the reference counting thread to run concurrently with the mutators (after a brief pause to transfer buffers), and then consider how to make that concurrent algorithm on-the-fly. In the first case, all the mutator threads can be stopped temporarily while their buffers are transferred to the collector. However, once all the mutator threads have transferred their buffers, they can be restarted. The collector's task is to modify the reference counts of the old and new children of every modified object. Reference decrements can be handled as before, using the replicas in the logs, but handling increments is more involved (Algorithm 18.6). The task is to increment the reference counts of the children of each object in the collector's log, using the state of the object *at the time that the log was transferred*. There are two cases to consider, since the logged object may have been modified since the logs were transferred to the collector.

If the object remains clean, its state has not changed, so the reference counts of its current children are incremented. Note that incrementNew in Algorithm 18.6 must check again after making a replica of a clean object in case it was dirtied while the copy was being taken.

If the object has been modified since the logs were transferred, then it will have been re-marked dirty and its state at the time of the transfer can be found in a fresh log buffer of some mutator. The object's dirty pointer will now refer to this log, which can be read without synchronising with that thread. Consider the example in Figure 18.2. A has been modified again in this epoch, which complicates finding C, the target of the last update to A in the previous epoch. As A is dirty, its previous contents will be held in some thread's current local log (shown on the right of the figure): the log refers to C. Thus, we can decrement the reference count of B and increment the reference count of C. In the next epoch, C's reference count will be decremented to reflect the action Write(A, 0, D).

18.7   Sliding views reference counting

For the snapshot of the heap, we stopped the world while threads' modification buffers were transferred to the collector. We relax that restriction now, instead stopping threads one at a time, on-the-fly. This gives a distorted view of the heap. In this *sliding view*, the values of different objects are recorded (and transferred to the collector thread) at different times. Sliding views require neither locks nor atomic instructions (at least, assuming sequential consistency), but coordinate mutators and collector threads with four handshakes between each mutator thread and the collector thread. We consider what modifications need to be made to the algorithm to support weaker consistency models later. Sliding views can be used in several contexts: for plain reference counting [Levanoni and Petrank, 1999, 2001, 2006], for managing the old generation of generational [Azatchi and Petrank, 2003] and age-oriented [Paz et al., 2003, 2005b] collectors, and for integration with cyclic reference counting collectors [Paz et al., 2005a, 2007]. Here, we consider how sliding views can be used in an age-oriented collector and then extend it to reclaim cyclic structures.

Age-oriented collection

Age-oriented collectors partition the heap into young and old generations. Unlike traditional generational collectors, both generations are collected at the same time: there are no nursery collections and inter-generational pointers do not need to be trapped. Appropriate policies and techniques are chosen for the management of each generation. Since the weak generational hypothesis expects most objects to die young, and young objects are likely to have high mutation rates (for example, as they are initialised), a young generation benefits from a collector tuned to low survival rates. In contrast, the old generation can be managed by a collector tuned to lower death and mutation rates. Paz et al. [2003] adopt a mark-sweep collector for the young generation (since it need not trace large volumes of dead objects) and a sliding views reference counting collector for the old generation (as it can handle huge live heaps). Their age-oriented collector does not move objects: instead, each object has a bit in its header denoting its generation.

On-the-fly collection starts by gathering a sliding view (Algorithm 18.7). Incremental collection of a sliding view requires careful treatment of modifications made while the view is being gathered. Pointer writes are protected by adding an incremental update write barrier called *snooping* (Algorithm 18.8) to the Write operation of Algorithm 5.3. This prevents missing a referent o whose only reference is removed from a slot s_1 before the sliding view reads s_1, and then is written to another slot s_2 after s_2 is added to the view.

Algorithm 18.7: Sliding views: the collector

```
 1   shared updates
 2   shared snoopFlag[MAX_PROCESSORS]                    /* one per processor */
 3
 4   collect():
 5       collectSlidingView()
 6       on-the-fly handshake 4:
 7           for each thread t
 8               suspend(t)
 9               scanStack(t)
10               snoopFlag[t] ← false
11               resume(t)
12       processReferenceCounts()
13       markNursery()
14       sweepNursery()
15       sweepZCT()
16       collectCycles()
17
18   collectSlidingView():
19       on-the-fly handshake 1:
20           for each thread t
21               suspend(t)
22               snoopFlag[t] ← true
23               transfer t's buffers to updates
24               resume(t)
25       clean modified and young objects
26       on-the-fly handshake 2:
27           for each thread t
28               suspend(t)
29               find modify-clean conflicts
30               resume(t)
31       reinforce dirty objects
32       on-the-fly handshake 3:
33           for each thread t
34               suspend(t)
35               resume(t)
36
37   processReferenceCounts():
38       for each obj in updates
39           decrementOld(obj)
40           incrementNew(obj)
41
42   collectCycles():
43       markCandidates()
44       markLiveBlack()
45       scan()
46       collectWhite()
47       processBuffers()
```

Algorithm 18.8: Sliding views: `Write`

```
1   shared logs[MAX_PROCESSORS]                          /* one per processor */
2   shared snoopFlag[MAX_PROCESSORS]                      /* one per processor */
3   me ← myProcessorId
4
5   Write(src, i, ref):
6       if src = Roots
7           src[i] ← ref
8       else
9           if not dirty(src)
10              log(src)                                                      $
11          src[i] ← ref                                                      $
12          snoop(ref)                                   /* for sliding view */
13
14  log(ref):
15      for each fld in Pointers(ref)
16          if *fld ≠ null
17              add(logs[me], *fld)
18      if not dirty(ref)                 /* commit the entry if ref is still clean */
19          entry ← add(logs[me], ref)
20          logPointer(ref) ← entry
21
22  snoop(ref):
23      if snoopFlag[me] && ref ≠ null
24          mySnoopedBuffer ← mySnoopedBuffer + [ref]            /* mark grey */
```

Algorithm 18.9: Sliding views: `New`

```
1   New():
2       ref ← allocate()
3       add(myYoungSet, ref)
4       setDirty(ref)                                          /* allocate dirty */
5       return ref
```

At the start of a cycle, each thread's `snoopFlag` is raised (without synchronisation). While the sliding view is being collected (and the `snoopFlag` is up for this thread), the new referent of any modified object is recorded in the thread's local `mySnoopedBuffer` (line 24 of Algorithm 18.8). In terms of the tricolour abstraction, this Dijkstra-style barrier marks `ref` grey. Objects are allocated dirty in the young generation (Algorithm 18.9) in order to avoid activating the write barrier when their slots are initialised.

In the first handshake, each thread is stopped, one at a time, its `snoopFlag` raised and its local log and young set transferred to the collector's `updates` buffer.

Next, all modified and young objects are cleaned. This risks a race. As cleaning is performed while mutator threads are running, it may erase the dirty state of objects modified concurrently with cleaning. A second handshake therefore pauses each thread, again on the fly, and scans its local log to identify objects modified during cleaning. The dirty state of these objects is restored ('reinforced').

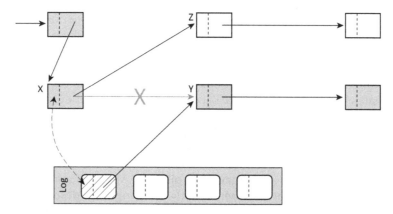

Figure 18.3: Sliding views allow a fixed *snapshot* of the graph to be traced by using values stored in the log. Here, the shaded objects indicate the state of the graph at the time that the pointer from X to Y was overwritten to refer to Z. The old version of the graph can be traced by using the value of X's field stored in the log.

A third, empty handshake ensures that no thread has fallen behind. The collector is now ready to begin to mark the young generation and update the reference counts of the old generation.

Concurrent marking starts with a fourth handshake, again suspending threads one at a time to scan their stacks in the usual way for mark-sweep and deferred reference counting collectors. Each thread's snoop flag can then be dropped.

The items in each thread's `mySnoopedBuffer` are transferred to the work list asynchronously. The collector is then ready to process reference counts in the old generation. Notice that the nursery cannot be marked until the old generation has been processed since an update may have added a pointer from an old to a young object.

Processing the old generation also requires the counts of old and new objects in the `updates` buffer to be processed: if the reference count of a young object is updated (it is reachable from the old generation and will be promoted), and that object has not been marked, it is added to the marker's work list.

Once the old generation has been processed and all inter-generational references have been discovered, the young generation is traced (`markNursery`), marking objects with the `incrementNew` procedure, and swept (`sweepNursery`), freeing any unmarked object.

Objects in the old generation can be reclaimed in the same way as with deferred reference counting. Any object that is unmarked, has a zero reference count and is not directly referenced by a root, is reclaimed (`sweepZCT`). If an object with a zero reference count is dirty, recursive freeing decrements the reference counts of its descendants, found from its log entry (see Figure 18.3); otherwise, its current fields are used.

Sliding views cycle reclamation

As presented so far, the age-oriented collector can reclaim cycles in the nursery but not in the old generation. Paz *et al.* [2007] combine the Recycler's cycle collection algorithm with an age-oriented collector. The difficulty that faced the asynchronous Recycler was that the topology of the heap could vary under its feet. In contrast, sliding views presents the collector with a fixed view of the heap, using the original version of unmodified objects or the logged copy of modified objects (see Figure 18.3). It is therefore possible for each pass of the trial deletion algorithm to retrace the steps of the first pass. Thus, by working on the sliding view of the heap, we can apply the simpler synchronous algorithm rather than the more complicated, multi-coloured asynchronous algorithm of Bacon and Rajan [2001].

Paz *et al.* introduce a number of optimisations that can further reduce the number of objects that trial deletion must trace. Like Bacon and Rajan [2001], they ignore scalar objects that cannot be members of cycles. Mature objects are considered for cycle reclamation only if they have survived several collections. This requires a queue of candidate buffers rather than a single one (they found a delay of two collection cycles to be effective). Paz *et al.* also try to avoid considering objects that might be live, including root referents, snooped objects and objects modified after the sliding view was collected. An additional markBlack phase pre-processes these objects, marking them and their sliding view descendants black. This raises a dilemma. The set of objects known to be live (actually, a subset of the dirty objects) is not fixed during the collection, so it is not possible to identify how many reference count modifications the collector might have made to an object before it became dirty. Hence, it is not possible to restore its original count. Instead, cycle detection operates on a second, cyclic, reference count. The alternative, to consider these objects regardless, would lead to more objects being processed by the reference counter.

Memory consistency

The sliding views algorithms presented above assume sequential consistency, which processors do not always guarantee. On the mutator side, it is important that the order of operations in Write are preserved to ensure that (i) the values seen in the log are the correct ones (that is, they represent a snapshot of the modified object as it was before the collection cycle started); (ii) the collector only reads completed log entries; and (iii) object fields cannot be updated after a collection starts without being snooped. The handshakes used by the algorithm solve some dependency issues on weakly consistent platforms (ensuring that the collector only sees complete log entries, or that new references are snooped during the collection cycle). Two further modifications are necessary. First, on the mutator side, synchronisation must be added in the write barrier around the logging to ensure that it is seen before the modification of the pointer. Levanoni and Petrank [2006] do this by placing a memory fence before and after log(src) (line 10 in Algorithm 18.8). Second, something similar is needed on the collector side. However, the approach above would be inefficient since most objects are unlikely to be dirty since their log pointers have been reset. Instead, on a weakly consistent platform, the collector can reduce the cost of synchronisation by reading batches of values from the buffers into a local array before processing them.

18.8   Issues to consider

The immediate problem facing reference counting is how to ensure that objects' reference counts are correct in the face of concurrent modifications to the object graph. The simplest solution is to require mutators to lock an object before it is modified. If the cost of locking is considered to be too high, then an alternative solution must be found. Current solutions rest on avoiding races between mutators that compromise the consistency of reference counts. Note that the memory manager is only concerned to preserve the consistency of the heap; whether or not mutator races violate the correctness of the user program is of no interest to it.

To preserve coherence, we must ask how we can serialise pointer writes and reference count operations. A partial solution is to use deferred reference counting, since this defers reclamation of garbage objects and, in particular, devolves the task to a single collector thread. However, this only accounts for pointer loads and stores, and not for writes into object fields. Thus, the question becomes, how can we devolve reference count modifications necessitated by writes to pointer fields from the mutator threads to a collector thread? One solution is for each mutator to buffer its reference counting operations and periodically pass them to the collector. A further step, coalesced reference counting, extends this by taking a snapshot of objects before they are modified: this allows the collector thread to avoid applying any redundant reference count modifications. In both cases reference count manipulation and object reclamation is separated from the action of writing pointers and is performed by a single collector thread (although it would be relatively straightforward to use parallel collector threads). Taking a snapshot of the state of the heap also simplifies concurrent cyclic reference counting. Trial deletion algorithms need to traverse a subgraph of the heap multiple times. By traversing the snapshot, the collector can ensure that it traces the *same* subgraph each time, even in the face of concurrent mutator activity.

Safe memory reclamation

Finally we note that there is a large and growing literature on safe reclamation of memory when using dynamic memory structures, from the *ABA-prevention tags* used in IBM's System 370 onwards. We pick out only a selection here. Broadly, these schemes require a thread to reserve the set of objects that it is using in order to prevent premature reclamation of an object by another thread. Proposed schemes have been manual or automatic, supported by atomic reference counting. Mechanisms may be *epoch-based* or *pointer-based*. Differences between safe memory reclamation algorithms include the costs of *protecting* a pointer and *retiring* an object (making it available for deallocation unless it is still in use by other threads), the bounds on the number of objects retired but not yet deallocated and restrictions on programming style.

Epoch-based memory management (see, for example, Fraser [2004] or Hart *et al.* [2007]), which is often the fastest approach, relies on a global epoch counter to reserve objects. Before a thread starts to use a data structure, it logs the current epoch in a global record. This implicitly reserves *all* objects that were not retired before the start of this epoch. To retire an object, depending on the algorithm, a thread might append the object to a list of retired objects, record the current epoch in the object's header and update the epoch (either immediately or after every so many retirements). An object can only be reclaimed if it was retired before the earliest epoch reserved by any active thread. These techniques are scheduler-dependent and tend to be vulnerable to the delay or failure of a single thread. If some thread stalls while it is using a reserved data structure, all other threads may be prevented from reclaiming reserved objects.

In contrast, pointer-based schemes avoid the stalling problem by reserving only those individual objects that a thread is using, but they tend to have higher overheads. The *Pass The Buck* (PTB) scheme [Herlihy *et al.*, 2002] provides lock-free progress to protect pointers and wait-free progress to retire objects but requires a double-word compare-and-swap atomic instruction. Each thread creates a list of retired objects which may be proportional to the number of threads. *Hazard pointers* [Michael, 2004] require only a single-word atomic primitive. Before accessing an object, a thread must publish a pointer in a globally shared data structure. Typically, a thread must load the pointer, write it to a hazard pointer, issue a store-load (write-read) fence and then re-read the pointer to check that it has not changed. Periodically, the hazard pointers of all threads are scanned to reclaim any object on the retired list for which there is no hazard pointer. *Drop The Anchor* [Braginsky *et al.*, 2013] is an extension of hazard pointers with improved performance to protect pointers. However, it may require non-trivial changes to algorithms that use it. *Automatic Optimistic Access*

[Cohen and Petrank, 2015] and *Free Access* [Cohen, 2018] are other lock-free reclamation schemes that require programs to be written in a particular style.

Ramalhete and Correia [2017] combine the lower overhead of epoch-based reclamation with the non-blocking properties of hazard pointer by recording *hazard eras* rather than hazard pointers. Publishing an era e guarantees that no object with a lifetime that overlaps e will be reclaimed. All currently live objects are protected but objects created after this era may be reclaimed, which is not possible in epoch-based reclamation.

Anderson *et al.* [2021] combine ideas from reference counting and hazard pointers to provide concurrent reference counting with wait-free, constant-time overhead, deferring reference count decrements until no other thread can be incrementing them, and eliding or deferring increments for short-lived objects.

In contrast with epoch-based reclamation, in which threads reserve *all* objects created after a certain time, or pointer-based reclamation schemes that reserve only *individual* objects, *interval-based reclamation* [Wen *et al.*, 2018] allows a thread to reserve all blocks known to have existed in a *bounded interval* of time. Like hazard pointers, interval-based reclamation avoids the risk of a stalled thread retaining an unbounded number of objects but, unlike hazard pointers, does not need a memory fence on pointer loads.

The *Hyaline* algorithm [Nikolaev and Ravindran, 2021] in its 'robust' versions bounds memory usage by adopting the birth eras approach of hazard eras and interval-based reclamation, marking each object with a global counter in order to ensure that stalled threads can only retain older objects. Unlike those two approaches, Hyaline relies on reference counting but only during reclamation and not while accessing objects.

OrcGC [Correia *et al.*, 2021] is an automatic lock-free memory reclamation scheme that combines counts of references from other objects (but not from thread stacks) with a pointer-based mechanism, *Pass The Pointer*. It requires C++ type annotations to indicate which references should be tracked. Pointers are protected in the same way as with hazard pointers or Pass The Buck and, similarly, to retire an object all hazardous pointers are scanned. However, if a pointer to an object is found, the responsibility for freeing that object is passed to the protecting thread. *Beware And Cleanup* [Gidenstam *et al.*, 2009] is another manual scheme that combines hazard pointers with atomic reference counting.

Chapter 19

Real-time garbage collection

The concurrent and incremental garbage collection algorithms of the preceding chapters strive to reduce the pause times perceived by the mutator by interleaving small increments of collector work on the same processor as the mutator or by running collector work at the same time on another processor. Many of these algorithms were developed with the goal of supporting applications where long pauses result in the application providing degraded service quality (such as jumpy movement of a mouse cursor in a graphical user interface). Thus, early incremental and concurrent collectors were often called 'real-time' collectors, but they were only real-time under certain strict conditions (such as restricting the size of objects). However, as real-time systems are now understood, none of the previous algorithms live up to the promise of supporting true real-time behaviour because they cannot provide strong progress guarantees to the mutator. When the mutator must take a lock (within a read or write barrier or during allocation), its progress can no longer be guaranteed. Worse, preemptive thread scheduling may result in the mutator being descheduled arbitrarily in favour of concurrent collector threads. True *real-time collection* must account precisely for all interruptions to mutator progress, while ensuring that space bounds are not exceeded. Fortunately, there has been much progress in real-time garbage collection that extends the advantages of automatic memory management to real-time systems.

19.1 Real-time systems

Real-time systems impose operational deadlines on particular tasks within an application. These real-time tasks must be able to respond to application inputs (events) within a fixed time window. A task that fails to meet its real-time constraint may degrade service (for example, dropping a frame while displaying digital video), or much worse, cause catastrophic failure of the system (such as mis-timing the spark-plug ignition signal resulting in damage to an internal combustion engine). Thus, a real-time system must not only be correct logically, it must also be correct with respect to responsiveness to real-time events.

A *soft real-time system* (like video display) can tolerate missed deadlines at the expense of service quality. Too many missed deadlines will result in unacceptable quality of service, but the occasional missed deadline will not matter much. Printezis [2006] suggests for systems a soft real-time goal that specifies a maximum garbage collection time, a time slice duration and an acceptable failure rate. In any interval in this time slice duration, the collector should avoid using more than the allowed maximum collection time, and any violations of this goal should be within the acceptable failure rate.

Such a soft goal is inadequate for *hard real-time systems* (like engine control) which consider missed deadlines to mean failure of the system. A correct hard real-time system

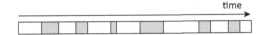

Figure 19.1: Unpredictable frequency and duration of conventional collectors. Collector pauses in grey.

must guarantee that all real-time constraints will be satisfied. In the face of such timing constraints, it is important to be able to characterise the responsiveness of garbage collection in real-time systems in ways that reflect both needs of the application (hard or soft real-time) and the behaviour of the garbage collector [Printezis, 2006].

Overall performance or throughput in real-time systems is less important than *predictability* of performance. The timing behaviour of a real-time task should be able to be determined analytically by design, or empirically during testing, so that its response-time when deployed in the field can be known ahead of time (to some acceptable degree of confidence). The *worst-case execution time* (WCET) of a task is the maximum length of time the task could take to execute in isolation (that is, ignoring re-scheduling) on a particular hardware platform. Multitasking real-time systems must schedule tasks so that their real-time constraints are met. Knowing that these constraints will be met at run time involves performing *schedulability analysis* ahead-of-time, assuming a particular (usually priority-based) run-time scheduling algorithm.

Real-time applications are often deployed to run as embedded systems dedicated to a specific purpose, such as the example above of a control system for engine timing. Single-chip processors predominate in embedded systems, so incremental garbage collection techniques translate naturally to embedded settings, but with multicore embedded processors becoming increasingly common, techniques for concurrent and parallel collection also apply. Moreover, embedded systems often impose tighter space constraints than general-purpose platforms.

For all of these reasons, stop-the-world, parallel or even concurrent garbage collectors that impose unpredictable pause times are not suited to real-time applications. Consider the collector schedule illustrated in Figure 19.1 which results when the effort required to reclaim memory depends on the total amount and size of objects that the application uses, the interconnections among those objects and the level of effort required to free enough memory to satisfy future allocations. Given this schedule, the mutator cannot rely on predictable and sustained utilisation of the processor.

19.2   Scheduling real-time collection

When and how to trigger collector work is the main factor affecting the impact of the collector on the mutator. Stop-the-world collectors defer all collector work until some allocation attempt detects that space is exhausted and triggers the collector. An incremental collector will piggyback some amount of collector work on each heap access (using read/write barriers) or allocation, or both. A concurrent collector will trigger some amount of collector work to be performed concurrently (possibly in parallel) with the mutator, but imposes mutator barriers to keep the collector synchronised with the mutator. To maintain steady-state space consumption, the collector must free and recycle dead objects at the same rate (measured by space allocated) as the mutator allocates new objects. Fragmentation can lead to space being wasted so that in the worst case an allocation request cannot be satisfied unless the collector itself or a separate compaction phase is able to relocate objects. But object relocation imposes an additional burden that can adversely affect real-time bounds. While in general we are cautious about using minimum mutator utilisation where response time is a more appropriate measure, given the usually known bounds on mutator work needed to meet deadlines in real-time systems, minimum mutator utilisation is a reasonable metric in this setting.

There are a number of alternative techniques for scheduling the work of real-time garbage collectors and for characterising how that work can affect the mutator [Henriksson, 1998; Detlefs, 2004b; Cheng and Blelloch, 2001; Pizlo and Vitek, 2008]. *Work-based scheduling* imposes collector work as a tax on units of mutator work. *Slack-based scheduling* runs collector work in the slack portions of the real-time task schedule (that is, when no real-time task is running). The slack can be a significant fraction of overall time when real-time tasks are infrequent or *periodic* (executing briefly at some known frequency). This can be achieved easily in a priority-scheduled system by giving the collector a lower priority than any of the real-time tasks. *Time-based scheduling* reserves a pre-defined portion of execution time solely for collector work during which the mutator is stopped. This allows meeting some pre-defined minimum mutator utilisation guarantee.

19.3 Work-based real-time collection

The classic Baker [1978] incremental semispace copying collector was one of the earliest attempts at real-time collection. It uses a precise model for analysing for real-time behaviour founded on the limiting assumption that objects (in this case Lisp `cons` cells) have a fixed size. Recall that Baker's read barrier prevents the mutator from accessing fromspace objects by making the mutator copy any fromspace object it encounters into tospace. This work is bounded because the objects have a single fixed size. Also, each mutator allocation performs some bounded amount of collector work (scanning some fixed number of grey tospace fields, copying their fixed-size fromspace targets as necessary). The more fields scanned per allocation, the faster the collection will finish, but the slower the mutator will run. Baker derived bounds on both time and space for his collector. His space bound was $2R(1 + 1/k)$, where R is the reachable space, and k is the adjustable time bound defined to be the number of fields scanned at each allocation. Baker did offer some solutions for incremental copying of variable-sized arrays, but these do not feature in his analysis.

Parallel, concurrent replication

Blelloch and Cheng [1999] extended the analysis of Baker for multiprocessor collection by devising a concurrent and parallel replicating copying collector for which they derive bounds on space and time. In evaluating their subsequent practical implementation of this collector, Cheng and Blelloch [2001] were the first to characterise intrusiveness of collection in terms of minimum mutator utilisation. Because their collector is still work-based, regardless of the efforts to which it goes towards minimising pause times, it can still suffer from unpredictable variation in the distribution of pauses that make it difficult to obtain real-time guarantees for the mutator. In Section 19.5 we will see that minimum mutator utilisation can also be used to drive time-based scheduling of real-time garbage collection by making minimum mutator utilisation an input constraint to the collector. Still, Blelloch and Cheng offer useful insights into the way in which pause times can be tightly bounded, while also bounding space, so we consider its detailed design here.

Machine model. Blelloch and Cheng assume an idealised machine model. A real implementation must grapple with differences between this idealised model and the actual target machine. The machine assumed is a typical shared-memory symmetric multiprocessor, having atomic test-and-set and fetch-and-add instructions for synchronisation. These are supported directly in hardware or can be implemented easily on modern symmetric multiprocessors using load-linked/store-conditionally or compare-and-swap, though it is important that fetch-and-add be implemented fairly (with strict time bounds) so that all processors make progress. They also assume a simple interrupt that is used to start and stop incremental collection on each of the processors. This can be implemented using GC safepoints, as described in Section 11.6. More importantly, they assume memory accesses to be sequentially consistent, which makes practical implementation of the collector more difficult, since some memory accesses must be ordered appropriately to ensure correctness.

The memory is organised as a contiguous set of locations addressable from $[2..M+1]$ (so pointers with value 0 and 1 have special meaning) where M is the maximum memory size. Each location can hold at least a pointer.

For timing analysis, the longest time taken by any one instruction is used as the cost of all instructions (interrupts occur between instructions and do not count towards this time).

Application model. The application model assumes the usual mutator operations Read and Write, and New(n) which allocates a new object with n fields and returns a pointer to the first field; it also includes a header word for use by the memory manager. In addition, Blelloch and Cheng require that on each processor every New(n) is followed by n invocations of InitSlot(v) to initialise each of the n fields of the last allocated object of the processor with v, starting at slot 0. A processor must complete all n invocations of InitSlot before it uses the new object or executes another New, though any number of other operations including Read and Write can be interleaved with the InitSlots. Furthermore, the idealised application model assumes that Write operations are atomic (no two processors can overlap execution of a Write). The memory manager further uses a function isPointer(p,i) to determine whether the ith field of the object referenced by p is a pointer, a fact often determined statically by the type of the object, or its class in an object-oriented language.

The algorithm. The collector is structured as a replicating collector in the style of Nettles and O'Toole [1993] except that, instead of a fromspace invariant and logging updates, the mutators obey a replication invariant: whenever the collector is active and a mutator wishes to update an object, it must update both the primary and its replica (if one exists). When the collector is active, all allocations make both a primary and a replica in tospace for the mutators to manipulate. Blelloch and Cheng also use a snapshot-at-the-beginning Yuasa-style deletion write barrier to ensure correctness.

Blelloch and Cheng assume a header field forwardingAddress(p) on each primary object p and copyCount(r) on each replica r (these can be stored in the same slot because they only apply to a primary or replica, respectively). The header is used for several purposes: for synchronisation on the primary to control which thread generates the replica, as a forwarding pointer from the primary to the replica, as a count in the replica of how much remains to be copied to it from the primary and to synchronise on the replica among mutators and the thread copying the object. When a primary object p is white, there is only a primary copy and its header is zero (forwardingAddress(p)=null). When the object turns grey and space has been allocated for the replica r, the header of the primary points to the replica (forwardingAddress(p)=r), and the header of the replica contains how many fields remain to be copied (copyCount(r)=n). When the object turns black (is fully copied), then the header of the replica will be zero (copyCount(r)=0).

The heap is configured into two semispaces as shown in Figure 19.2. Fromspace is bounded by the variables fromBot and fromTop which are private to each thread. The

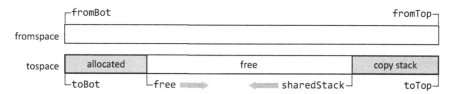

Figure 19.2: Heap structure in the Blelloch and Cheng work-based collector

collector maintains an explicit copy stack in the top part of tospace holding pointers to the grey objects. As noted in Section 14.6, Blelloch and Cheng offer several arguments that this explicit copy stack allows better control over locality and synchronisation than Cheney queues in sharing the work of copying among concurrent collector threads. The area between `toBot` and `free` holds all replicas and newly allocated objects. The area between `sharedStack` and `toTop` holds the copy stack (growing down from `toTop` to `sharedStack`). When `free=sharedStack`, the collector has run out of memory. If the collector is off when this happens, then it is turned on. Otherwise, an out of memory error is reported. The variables `toBot` and `toTop` are also private to each thread, whereas `free` and `sharedStack` are shared.

The code for copying a slot from a primary object to its replica is shown in Algorithm 19.1, where `copyOneSlot` takes the address of the grey primary object p as its argument, copies the slot specified by the current count stored in the replica, shades the object pointed to by that slot (by calling `makeGrey`), and stores the decremented count. Finally, the primary object p is still grey if it has fields that still need to be copied, in which case it is pushed back onto the local copy stack (the operations on the local stack are defined earlier in Algorithm 14.8).

The `makeGrey` function turns an object grey if it is white (has no replica allocated for it) and returns the pointer to the replica. The atomic test-and-set[1] is used to check if the object is white, since many processors could try to shade an object simultaneously, and it is undesirable to allocate more than one replica in tospace. The processor that manages to win this *copy-copy* race is the *designated copier*. The `makeGrey` function distinguishes three cases for the header `forwardingAddress(p)`.

1. The `testandset` returns zero so this processor becomes the designated copier and allocates the tospace replica r, sets its header `copyCount(r)` to the length of the object, sets the header `forwardingAddress(p)` of the primary to point to the replica, pushes a reference to the primary on a private stack and returns the pointer to r.

2. The `TestAndSet` returns non-zero, and the value of the header is a valid forwarding pointer so this pointer to the replica can be returned.

3. The `TestAndSet` returns non-zero, but the value in the header is 1, so another processor is the designated copier but has not yet set the forwarding pointer. The current processor must wait until it can return the proper forwarding pointer.

Algorithm 19.2 shows the code for the mutator operations when the collector is on. The `New` operation allocates space for the primary and replica copies using `allocate`, and sets some private variables that parametrise the behaviour of `InitSlot`, saying where it should write initial values. The variable `lastA` tracks the address of the last allocated object, `lastL` notes its length, and `lastC` holds the count of how many of its slots have

---

[1]Recall that this primitive, as we defined it, sets the word to 1 only if the whole word's value is 0 — it does not operate on just the low bit of the word. It is equivalent to a compare-and-swap of new value 1 for old value 0.

Algorithm 19.1: Copying in the Blelloch and Cheng work-based collector

```
 1   shared gcOn ← false
 2   shared free                                         /* allocation pointer */
 3   shared sharedStack                                  /* copy stack pointer */
 4
 5   copyOneSlot(p):                      /* p is the primary copy of a grey object */
 6       r ← forwardingAddress(p)                  /* pointer to the replica copy */
 7       i ← copyCount(r) − 1                       /* index of slot to be copied */
 8       copyCount(r) ← −(i+1)          /* lock slot to prevent write while copying */
 9       v ← p[i]
10       if isPointer(p, i)
11           v ← makeGrey(v)                          /* grey if it is a pointer */
12       r[i] ← v                                             /* copy the slot */
13       copyCount(r) ← i               /* unlock object with decremented index */
14       if i > 0
15           localPush(p)                           /* push back on local stack */
16
17   makeGrey(p):                               /* p must be a primary copy */
18       if TestAndSet(&forwardingAddress(p)) ≠ 0  /* race to replicate primary */
19           /* we lost the race */
20           while forwardingAddress(p) = 1
21               /* do nothing: wait for a valid forwarding address */
22       else
23           /* we won the race */
24           count ← length(p)                          /* length of primary */
25           r ← allocate(count)                          /* allocate replica */
26           copyCount(r) ← count              /* set copy counter for replica */
27           forwardingAddress(p) ← r       /* set forwarding address for primary */
28           localPush(p)              /* push primary on stack for copying */
29       return forwardingAddress(p)
30
31   allocate(n):
32       ref ← FetchAndAdd(&free, n)
33       if ref + n > sharedStack                      /* is tospace exhausted? */
34           if gcOn
35               error "Out of memory"
36           interrupt(collectorOn)    /* interrupt mutators to start next collection */
37           allocate(n)                                      /* try again */
38       return ref
```

already been initialised. The `InitSlot` function stores the value of the next slot to be initialised in both the primary and replica copies and increments `lastC`. These initialising stores shade any pointers that are stored to preserve the strong tricolour invariant that black objects cannot point to white objects. The statement `collect(k)` incrementally copies k words for every word allocated. By design, the algorithm allows a collection cycle to start while an object is only partially initialised (that is, when a processor has `lastC≠lastL`).

Algorithm 19.2: Mutator operations in the Blelloch and Cheng collector (gcOn=true)

```
 1  lastA                                            /* per–processor pointer to last allocated object */
 2  lastL                                            /* per–processor length of last allocated object */
 3  lastC                                            /* per–processor count of number of slots last filled */
 4
 5  Read(p, i):
 6      return p[i]
 7
 8  New(n):
 9      p ← allocate(n)                                            /* allocate primary */
10      r ← allocate(n)                                            /* allocate replica */
11      forwardingAddress(p) ← r                         /* primary forwards to replica */
12      copyCount(r) ← 0                                 /* replica has no slots to copy */
13      lastA ← p                                               /* set last allocated */
14      lastC ← 0                                                        /* set count */
15      lastL ← n                                                       /* set length */
16      return p
17
18  atomic Write(p, i, v):
19      if isPointer(p, i)
20          makeGrey(p[i])                                           /* grey old value */
21      p[i] ← v                                       /* write new value into primary */
22      if forwardingAddress(p) ≠ 0                    /* check if object is forwarded */
23          while forwardingAddress(p) = 1
24              /* do nothing: wait for forwarding address */
25          r ← forwardingAddress(p)                         /* get pointer to replica */
26          while copyCount(r) = −(i+1)
27              /* do nothing: wait while slot concurrently being copied */
28          if isPointer(p, i)
29              v ← makeGrey(v)                     /* update replica with grey new value */
30          r[i] ← v                                                 /* update replica */
31      collect(k)                                             /* execute k copy steps */
32
33  InitSlot(v):                                   /* initialise next slot of last allocated */
34      lastA[lastC] ← v                                           /* initialise primary */
35      if isPointer(lastA, lastC)
36          v ← makeGrey(v)                           /* replica gets grey initial value */
37      forwardingAddress(lastA)[lastC++] ← v                     /* initialise replica */
38      collect(k)                                             /* execute k copy steps */
```

The Write operation first shades any overwritten (deleted) pointer grey (to preserve snapshot reachability), and then writes the new value into the corresponding slot of both the primary and the replica (if it exists). When writing to a grey object, it is possible that the designated copier is also copying the same slot. This *copy-write* race can lead to a lost update if the mutator writes to the replica after the copier has read the slot from the primary but before it has finished copying the slot to the replica. Thus, the Write operation waits for the copier, both to allocate the replica and to finish copying the slot. It is not a

Algorithm 19.3: Collector code in the Blelloch and Cheng work-based collector

```
 1  collect(k):
 2     enterRoom()
 3     for i ← 0 to k−1
 4        if isLocalStackEmpty()                         /* local stack empty */
 5           sharedPop()                      /* move work from shared stack to local */
 6           if isLocalStackEmpty()                  /* local stack still empty */
 7              break                               /* no more work to do */
 8        p ← localPop()
 9        copyOneSlot(p)
10     transitionRooms()
11     sharedPush()                            /* move work to shared stack */
12     if exitRoom()
13        interrupt(collectorOff)                    /* turn collector off */
```

problem for the mutator to write to the primary before the copier locks the slot, since the copier will then copy that value to the replica. The `while` statements that force the mutator to wait are both time-bounded, the first by the time it takes for the copier to allocate the replica and the second by the time it takes for the copier to copy the slot.

`InitSlot` is used for initialising stores instead of `Write` because it is much cheaper. The uninitialised slots are implicitly `null` so do not need a deletion barrier to preserve the snapshot. Also, the new object always has a replica so there is no need to check for the replica's presence. Finally, the collector is designed so that if a collection cycle starts while an object is only partially initialised, only the initialised slots will be copied (see `collectorOn` in Algorithm 19.4).

Algorithm 19.3 shows the collector function `collect(k)`, which copies k slots. The shared copy stack allows the copy work to be shared among the processors. To reduce the number of invocations of the potentially expensive `sharedPop` operation (which uses fetch-and-add), to improve the chances for local optimisation, and to enhance locality, each processor takes most of its work from a private local stack (the shared and private stack operations are defined earlier in Algorithm 14.8). Only when there is no work available in this local stack will the processor fetch additional work from the shared copy stack. After copying k slots, `collect` places any remaining work back into the shared stack. Note that no two processors can simultaneously execute the code to copy slots (obtaining additional work from the shared copy stack) in lines 2–10 *and* move copy work back to the copy stack after copying k slots in lines lines 10–12. This is enforced using the 'rooms' of Algorithm 14.9, which we discussed in Section 14.6.

Algorithm 19.4 shows the code to start (`collectorOn`) and stop (`collectorOff`) the collector. Here, the only roots are assumed to reside in the fixed number of registers `REG` private to each processor. The `synch` routine implements barrier synchronisation to block a processor until all processors have reached that barrier. These are used to ensure a consistent view of the shared variables `gcOn`, `free`, and `sharedStack`. When a new collection cycle begins, each processor sets the replica header of its partially initialised last allocated object to the last initialised slot `lastC` so that only the initialised slots need to be copied. When the collection cycle ends, the registers and the last allocated object are forwarded to refer to their replicas.

Algorithm 19.4: Stopping and starting the Blelloch and Cheng work-based collector

```
 1   shared gcOn
 2   shared toTop
 3   shared free
 4   shared count ← 0                           /* number of processors that have synched */
 5   shared round ← 0                           /* the current synchronisation round */
 6
 7   synch():
 8       curRound ← round
 9       self ← FetchAndAdd(&cnt, 1) + 1
10       if self = numProc                      /* round is done, reset for next one */
11           cnt ← 0
12           round++
13       while round = curRound
14           /* do nothing: wait until last processor changes round */
15
16   collectorOn():
17       synch()
18       gcOn ← true
19       toBot, fromBot ← fromBot, toBot                                    /* flip */
20       toTop, fromTop ← fromTop, toTop
21       free, sharedStack ← toBot, toTop
22       stackLimit ← sharedStack
23       synch()
24       r ← allocate(lastL)                    /* allocate replica of last allocated */
25       forwardingAddress(lastA) ← r           /* forward last allocated */
26       copyCount(r) ← lastC                   /* set number of slots to copy */
27       if lastC > 0
28           localPush(lastA)                   /* push work onto local stack */
29       for i ← 0 to length(REG)               /* make roots grey */
30           if isPointer(REG, i)
31               makeGrey(REG[i])
32       sharedPush()                           /* move work to shared stack */
33       synch()
34
35   collectorOff():
36       synch()
37       for i ← 0 to length(REG)               /* make roots grey */
38           if isPointer(REG, i)
39               REG[i] ← forwardingAddress(REG[i])    /* forward roots */
40       lastA ← forwardingAddress(lastA)
41       gcOn ← false
42       synch()
```

Other practical improvements. The original formulation of the real-time replication algorithm [Blelloch and Cheng, 1999] and its subsequent practical implementation [Cheng and Blelloch, 2001; Cheng, 2001] describe a number of other practical improvements to this algorithm. Instead of using fetch-and-add in every invocation of `allocate`, each processor can allocate from a private allocation area as described in Section 7.7. Instead of spin-waiting for the forwarding pointer in `makeGrey`, because the processor can know the location at which it is going to place an object in its private space, it can then use a compare-and-swap instead of test-and-set. Other improvements include deferring the collector work performed in `New` and `InitLoc` until each local allocation area fills up with (small) objects, avoiding the cost of double allocations (primary and replica) in `New` and how to make `Write` atomic using rooms synchronisation (only one writer can enter the 'writing room' at any particular time).

Time and space bounds. The considerable effort taken by this algorithm to place a well-defined bound on each increment of collector work allows for precise bounds to be placed on space and the time spent in garbage collection. Blelloch and Cheng [1999] prove that the algorithm requires at most $2(R(1 + 2/k) + N + 5PD)$ memory words, where P is the number of processors, R is the maximum reachable space during a computation (number of words accessible from the root set), N is the maximum number of reachable objects, D is the maximum depth of any object and k controls the tradeoff between space and time, bounding how many words are copied each time a word is allocated. They also show that mutator threads are never stopped for more than time proportional to k non-blocking machine instructions. These bounds are guaranteed even for large objects and arrays, because `makeGrey` progresses the grey wavefront a field at a time rather than a whole object at a time.

Performance. Cheng and Blelloch [2001] implemented their collector for ML, a statically typed functional language. ML programs typically have very high allocation rates, posing a challenge to most collectors. Results reported are for a 64-processor Sun Enterprise 10000, with processor clock speeds on the order of a few hundred megahertz. On a single processor, the collector imposes an average (across a range of benchmarks) overhead of 51% compared to an equivalent stop-the-world collector. These are the costs to support both parallel (39%) and concurrent (12%) collection. Nevertheless, the collector scales well for 32 processors (17.2× speedup), while the mutator does not scale quite so well (9.2× speedup), and near perfectly for 8 processors (7.8× and 7.2×, respectively). Minimum mutator utilisation for the stop-the-world collector is zero or near zero for all benchmarks at a granularity of 10 milliseconds, whereas the concurrent collector supports a minimum mutator utilisation of around 10% for $k = 2$ and 15% for $k = 1.2$. Maximum pause times for the concurrent collector range from 3 to 4 milliseconds.

Uneven work and its impact on work-based scheduling

The argument against work-based scheduling for real-time garbage collection is that it results in uneven minimum mutator utilisation, with the operations of the mutator so tightly coupled to those of the collector. A worst-case execution time analysis for work-based copying collection must assume the worst-case time for all mutator operations on the heap. For the Baker [1978] collector, reading a pointer slot may require copying its target. For Lisp `cons` cells this is a bounded cost, but variable-sized objects like arrays cause problems. Allocation can cause some fixed amount of collector work, and at the beginning of the collection cycle will also involve the flip, scanning the roots and copying their targets. This includes the global variables (bounded in each particular program) and

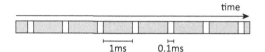

Figure 19.3: Low mutator utilisation even with short collector pauses. The mutator (white) runs infrequently, while the collector (grey) dominates.

local (thread stack) variables (potentially unbounded up to stack overflow). In summary, the worst case is so far from the usual case that the resulting worst-case execution time analysis is virtually useless for schedulability analysis.

There have been several attempts at containing these worst-case overheads for work-based scheduling. To bound the cost of stack scanning, Cheng and Blelloch [2001] propose dividing the stack into fixed-size *stacklets*. The flip only needs to scan the top-most stacklet in which the mutator is currently active, leaving the other stacklets for later scanning in due course. To prevent a mutator from returning to an unscanned stacklet, this approach adds a *stack barrier* (recall Section 11.5) to the operations that pop the stacklets as the mutator executes, requiring the mutator to scan the stacklet being returned to. Detlefs [2004b] notes two approaches for handling the case in which the mutator attempts to return into a stacklet that is already in the process of being scanned by the collector: either the mutator must wait for the collector or the collector must abort the scanning of that stacklet, deferring that work to the mutator.

Similarly, variable-sized objects can be broken into fixed-size *oblets*, and arrays into *arraylets*, to place bounds on the granularity of scanning/copying to advance the collector wavefront. Of course, these non-standard representations require corresponding changes to the operations for accessing object fields and indexing array elements, increasing space and time overheads for the additional indirections [Siebert, 1998, 2000, 2010].

Nevertheless, Detlefs considers the asymmetric overheads of pure work-based scheduling to be the final nail in its coffin. For example, in the Baker concurrent copying collector mutator operations have costs that vary greatly depending on where in the collector cycle they occur. Before a flip operation, the mutator is only taxed for the occasional allocation operation in order to progress the wavefront, while reads are most likely to load references to already copied objects. For some time after the flip, when only mutator roots have been scanned, the average cost of reads may come close to the theoretical worst case as they are forced to copy their targets. Similarly, for the Blelloch and Cheng [1999] collector, even though writes are much less common than reads, there is still wide variability in the need to replicate an object at any given write.

This variability can yield collector schedules that preserve predictably short pause times, but do not result in satisfactory utilisation because of the frequency and duration of collector work. Consider the schedule in Figure 19.3 in which pauses are bounded at a millisecond, but the mutator is only permitted a tenth of a millisecond between them in which to run. Even though collector work is split into predictably short bounded pauses, there is insufficient time remaining for a real-time mutator to meet its deadlines.

While work-based scheduling may result in collector overhead being spread evenly over mutator operations, on average, the big difference between average cost and worst-case cost leaves worst-case execution time analysis for work-based scheduling ineffective. The result is unnecessary over-provisioning of processor resources resulting in reduced utilisation of the processor by the mutator.

In a non-copying concurrent collector, where the mutator write barrier simply shades the source or old/new target object, mutator overheads for accessing the heap are rela-

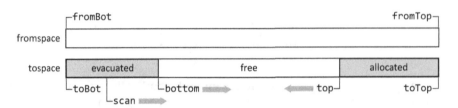

Figure 19.4: Heap structure in the Henriksson slack-based collector

tively tightly bounded. However, because allocations come in bursts, work-based scheduling still results in wide variation in the garbage collection overheads imposed on mutators.

For this reason, more advanced scheduling approaches treat collector work as something that must be budgeted for in a way that does not make it a pure tax on mutator work, essentially by treating garbage collection as another real-time task that must be scheduled. This results in mutator worst-case execution time analysis that is much closer to actual average mutator performance, allowing for better processor utilisation. Rare but potentially costly operations, such as flipping the mutator, need only be short enough to complete during the portion of execution made available to the collector.

19.4 Slack-based real-time collection

Henriksson attacks the real-time collector scheduling problem by adopting the rule that garbage collection should be completely avoided while high priority (real-time) tasks are executing [Magnusson and Henriksson, 1995; Henriksson, 1998]. Garbage collection work is instead delayed until no high-priority tasks are eligible for execution. Allocation by high-priority tasks is not taxed, while low-priority tasks perform some collector work when allocating. A special task, the *high-priority garbage collection* task, is responsible for performing collector work that was omitted while the high-priority tasks were executing, as implied by the allocations performed by the high-priority tasks. The high-priority garbage collection task has a priority lower than other high-priority tasks, but higher than the low-priority tasks. It must always ensure that enough free memory is initialised and available for allocation to meet the requirements of the high-priority tasks. Thus, collector work operates entirely in the slack in the real-time task schedule.

The heap is configured into two semispaces as shown in Figure 19.4. New objects are allocated at the top of tospace, at the position of the pointer `top`. Evacuated objects are placed at the bottom of tospace, at the position designated by `bottom`. The collector scans the evacuated objects in the usual Cheney style, evacuating all fromspace objects they refer to. Low-priority threads perform some evacuation work incrementally as new objects are allocated at the top of tospace. The position of `scan` indicates the progress of the collector in scanning the evacuated objects.

Henriksson describes his approach in the context of a Brooks-style concurrent copying collector that uses an indirection barrier on all accesses, including a Dijkstra insertion write barrier to ensure that the new target object is in tospace, copying it if not. This maintains a strong invariant for concurrent collection: no tospace object contains references to fromspace objects. However, Henriksson does not impose the full copying cost of the write barrier on high-priority tasks. Instead, objects are evacuated lazily. The write barrier simply allocates space for the tospace copy, but without actually transferring the contents of the fromspace original. Eventually, the garbage collector will run (whether as the high-priority garbage collection task or as a tax on allocation by low-priority tasks)

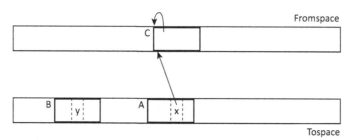

(a) Before a high-priority task performs B.y←A.x. The write barrier catches the assignment since the fromspace C object is not previously evacuated or scheduled for evacuation.

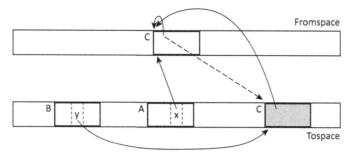

(b) After having reserved a tospace location for C. A temporary `toAddress` pointer (dashed) to the reserved area prevents multiple tospace reservations for C. Forwarding pointers prevent access to the uninitialised reserved space.

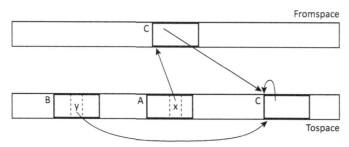

(c) When the high-priority task pauses, the collector finishes evacuating C to its reserved tospace location and sets the forwarding pointers to refer to the tospace copy. A.x will be forwarded later when the A object is scanned by the collector.

Figure 19.5: Lazy evacuation in the Henriksson slack-based collector

Henriksson [1998]. Reprinted by permission.

and perform the deferred copying work when it comes to scan the contents of the tospace copy. Before scanning the tospace version, the collector must copy the contents over from the fromspace original. To prevent any mutator from accessing the empty tospace copy before its contents have been copied over, Henriksson exploits the Brooks indirection barrier by giving every empty tospace shell a back-pointer to the fromspace original. This lazy evacuation is illustrated in Figure 19.5.

As sketched in Algorithms 19.5 and 19.6, the collector is similar to that of concurrent copying (Algorithm 17.1), but uses the Brooks indirection barrier to avoid the need for a tospace invariant on the mutators and (like Sapphire) defers any copying from the mutator write barrier to the collector. Note that the temporary toAddress pointer allows the collector to forward references held in tospace copies, even while the mutator continues to operate in fromspace, since this toAddress pointer is distinct from the forwardingAddress header word used by the mutator.

The collector itself is specified as a coroutine, so that collector execution interleaves with the low-priority mutator tasks at well-defined yield points, though high-priority tasks can preempt the collector at any time to regain control. If the collector is in the middle of copying an object, the copy is simply aborted and restarted when the collector resumes. Also, Henriksson assumes that the execution platform is a uniprocessor, so that disabling scheduler interrupts is sufficient to implement atomic operations.

Scheduling the collector work

The amount of work to perform in each collector increment (controlled by the call to behind) must ensure that fromspace is completely evacuated before tospace fills up, thus finishing a collector cycle. Let us assume that the amount of work (in terms of bytes processed) needed in the worst case to evacuate all live objects out of fromspace and to initialise enough memory to satisfy allocation requests of the high-priority threads during a collection cycle is W_{max}, and that after the flip at least F_{min} bytes of memory must be free and available for allocation. That is, W_{max} indicates the maximum work needed to complete a collection cycle and F_{min} the minimum space that must be free when the cycle completes. Then, the *minimum* garbage collection ratio GCR_{min} is defined as:

$$GCR_{min} = \frac{W_{max}}{F_{min}}$$

The *current* garbage collection ratio GCR is the ratio between performed garbage collection work W and the amount A of new allocated objects in tospace:

$$GCR = \frac{W}{A}$$

Allocation by the mutator causes A to increase, while garbage collection work increases W. The collector must perform enough work W to make sure that the current garbage collection ratio is no less than the minimum garbage collection ratio ($GCR \geq GCR_{min}$). This will guarantee that fromspace is empty (all live objects have been evacuated) before tospace is filled, even in the worst case.

Allocation of memory by low-priority tasks is throttled so that the current garbage collection ratio GCR does not drop too low (below GCR_{min}), by giving the collector task priority. The upper bound on the collector work performed during allocation will be proportional to the size of the allocated object.

If a high-priority task is activated shortly before a semispace flip is due then the remaining memory in tospace may not be sufficient to hold both the last objects to be allocated by

Algorithm 19.5: The Henriksson slack-based collector

```
 1  coroutine collector:
 2      loop
 3          while bottom < top                          /* tospace is not full */
 4              yield /* revert to mutator */
 5          flip()
 6          for each fld in Roots
 7              process(fld)
 8              if not behind()
 9                  yield /* revert to mutator */
10          while scan < bottom
11              scan ← scanObject(scan)
12              if not behind()
13                  yield /* revert to mutator */
14
15  flip():
16      toBot, fromBot ← fromBot, toBot
17      toTop, fromTop ← fromTop, toTop
18      bottom, top ← toBot, toTop
19      scan ← bottom
20
21  scanObject(toRef):
22      fromRef ← forwardingAddress(toRef)
23      move(fromRef, toRef)
24      for each fld in Pointers(toRef)
25          process(fld)
26      forwardingAddress(fromRef) ← toRef
27      return toRef + size(toRef)
28
29  process(fld):
30      fromRef ← *fld
31      if fromRef ≠ null
32          *fld ← forward(fromRef)                      /* update with tospace reference */
33
34  forward(fromRef):
35      toRef ← forwardingAddress(fromRef)
36      if toRef = fromRef                               /* not evacuated */
37          toRef ← toAddress(fromRef)
38          if toRef = null              /* not scheduled for evacuation (not marked) */
39              toRef ← schedule(fromRef)
40      return toRef
41
42  schedule(fromRef):
43      toRef ← bottom
44      bottom ← bottom + size(fromRef)
45      if bottom > top
46          error "Out of memory"
47      toAddress(fromRef) ← toRef                       /* schedule for evacuation (mark) */
48      return toRef
```

Algorithm 19.6: Mutator operations in the Henriksson slack-based collector

```
1   atomic Read(src, i):
2       src ← forwardingAddress(src)                    /* Brooks indirection */
3       return src[i]
4
5   atomic Write(src, i, ref):
6       src ← forwardingAddress(src)                    /* Brooks indirection */
7       if ref in fromspace
8           ref ← forward(ref)
9       src[i] ← ref
10
11  atomic New_HighPriority(size):
12      top ← top − size
13      toRef ← top
14      forwardingAddress(toRef) ← toRef
15      return toRef
16
17  atomic New_LowPriority(size):
18      while behind()
19          yield /* wake up the collector */
20      top ← top − size
21      toRef ← top
22      if bottom > top
23          error "Out of memory"
24      forwardingAddress(toRef) ← toRef
25      return toRef
```

the high-priority task and the last objects to be evacuated from fromspace. The collector must ensure a buffer between bottom and top for these objects large enough to hold all new objects allocated by the high-priority tasks while the collector finishes the current cycle. To do this, the application developer must estimate the worst-case allocation needed by the high-priority tasks in order to run, as well as their periods and worst-case execution times for each period. Henriksson suggests that this job is easy enough for the developer because high-priority tasks in a control system are written to be fast and small, with little need to allocate memory. He provides an analytical framework for deciding schedulability and the memory headroom needed by high-priority tasks, given a large set of program parameters such as task deadlines, task periods, and so on.

Execution overheads

The overhead to high-priority tasks for collector activity consists of tight bounds on the instructions required for memory allocation, pointer dereferencing and pointer stores. Of course, instruction counts alone are not always a reliable measure of time, in the face of loads that may miss in the cache. Worst-case execution time analysis must either assume caches are disabled (slowing down all loads), or the system must be tested empirically to ensure that real-time deadlines are met under the expected system load.

Heap accesses require single instruction indirection through the forwarding pointer, plus the overhead of disabling interrupts. Pointer stores have worst-case overhead on the order of twenty instructions to mark the target object for later evacuation. Allocation requires simply bumping a pointer and initialising the header (to include the forwarding pointer and other header information), having overhead on the order of 10 instructions.

Low-priority tasks have the same overheads for heap accesses and pointer stores. On allocation, the worst-case requirement is to perform collector work proportional to the size of the new object. The exact worst case for allocation depends on the maximum object size, total heap size, maximum live object set, and the maximum collector work performed within any given cycle.

Worst-case latency for high-priority tasks depends on the time for the collector to complete (or abort) an ongoing item of `atomic` work, which is short and bounded. Henriksson states that latency is dominated more by the cost of the context switch than the cost of completing an item of `atomic` work.

Programmer input

The programmer must provide sufficient information about the application program, and the high-priority tasks, to compute the minimum garbage collection ratio and to track the garbage collection ratio as the program executes so that the collector does not disrupt the high-priority tasks. The period and worst-case execution times for each high-priority task is required, along with its worst-case allocation need for any one of its periodic invocations, so as to calculate the minimum buffer requirements to satisfy high-priority allocations. The programmer must also provide an estimate of the maximum live memory footprint of the application. These parameters are sufficient to perform worst-case execution time analysis, and schedulability analysis, for the high-priority real-time tasks. Henriksson [1998] provides further details.

19.5 Time-based real-time collection: Metronome

Slack-based scheduling of the collector requires sufficient slack available in the schedule of high-priority real-time tasks in which to run the collector. Time-based scheduling treats minimum mutator utilisation as an input to the scheduling problem, with the scheduler designed to maintain minimum mutator utilisation while providing real-time bounds. This approach was first used in the *Metronome* real-time garbage collector for Java [Bacon et al., 2003a]. Metronome is an incremental mark-sweep collector with partial on-demand compaction to avoid fragmentation. It uses a deletion write barrier to enforce the weak tricolour invariant, marking live any object whose reference is overwritten during a write. Objects allocated during marking are black. The overhead of simply marking on writes is much lower (and more predictable) than replicating as in Blelloch and Cheng [1999].

After sweeping to reclaim garbage, Metronome compacts if necessary, to ensure that enough contiguous free space is available to satisfy allocation requests until the next collection. Like Henriksson [1998], Metronome uses Brooks-style forwarding pointers, imposing an indirection on every mutator access.

Mutator utilisation

Metronome guarantees the mutator a predetermined percentage of execution time, with use of the remaining time at the collector's discretion: any time not used by the collector will be given to the mutator. By maintaining uniformly short collector pause times, Metronome is able to give finer-grained utilisation guarantees than traditional collectors. Using

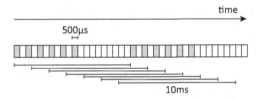

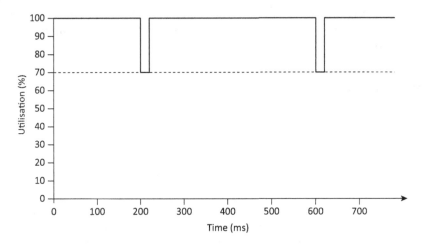

Figure 19.6: Metronome utilisation. Collector quanta are shown in grey and mutator quanta in white.

Figure 19.7: Overall mutator utilisation in Metronome

collector quanta of 500 microseconds over a 10-millisecond window, Metronome sets a default mutator utilisation target of 70%. This target utilisation can also be tuned further for the application to meet its space constraints. Figure 19.6 shows a 20-millisecond Metronome collector cycle split into 500-microsecond time slices. The collector preserves 70% utilisation over a 10-millisecond sliding window: there are at most 6 collector quanta and correspondingly at least 14 mutator quanta in any window. Here, each collector quantum is followed by at least one mutator quantum so that pauses are limited to the length of one quantum, even if utilisation would still be preserved by back-to-back quanta so as to minimise pauses. Given a minimum mutator utilisation target below 50%, a window may schedule more collector quanta than mutator quanta, so some instances of back-to-back collector quanta will be needed to ensure that the collector gets its share of the window.

Of course, when the collector is not active all quanta can be used by the mutator, giving 100% utilisation. Overall, the mutator will see utilisation drop during periods that the collector is running, but never lower than the target utilisation. This is illustrated in Figure 19.7, which shows overall mutator utilisation dropping for each collector cycle.

Figure 19.8 shows mutator utilisation over the same collector cycle that was illustrated in Figure 19.6 (grey bars indicate each collector quantum while white is the mutator). At time t on the x-axis this shows utilisation for the 10-millisecond window leading up to time t. Note that while the schedule in Figure 19.6 is perfect in that utilisation is exactly 70% over the collector cycle, real schedules will not be quite so exact. A real scheduler will typically allow collector quanta to run until minimum mutator utilisation is close to the target MMU and then back off to prevent overshooting the target.

Section A of the figure is a staircase graph where the descending portions correspond to collector quanta and the flat portions correspond to mutator quanta. The staircase shows

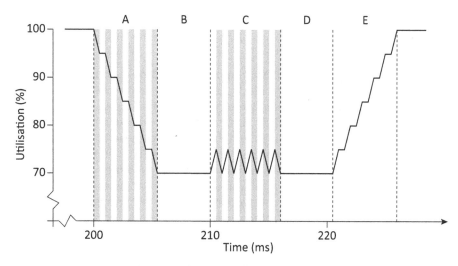

Figure 19.8: Mutator utilisation in Metronome during a collection cycle

First published on IBM developerWorks: http://www.ibm.com/developerworks

the collector maintaining low pause times by interleaving with the mutator, as utilisation steps down to the target. Section B comprises only mutator activity so as to preserve mutator utilisation across all sliding windows that cover that section. It is common to see this pattern showing collector activity only at the beginning of a window because the collector runs whenever it is allowed to (while preserving pause times and utilisation). This means the collector will exhaust its allotted time at the beginning and then allow the mutator to recover for the remainder of the window. Section C shows collector activity when mutator utilisation is near the target. Ascending portions represent mutator quanta, where the scheduler detects utilisation rising above the target, and descending portions are collector quanta where the scheduler permits the collector to run to bring utilisation back close to the target. The sawtooth results from the interleaving of the mutator with the collector to preserve low pause times while also preserving the target utilisation. Section D shows that once the collector finishes its cycle, the mutator must run for a while before utilisation begins to rebound. In Section E the mutator regains 100% utilisation stepping up the staircase from the target.

Supporting predictability

Metronome uses a number of techniques to achieve deterministic pause times while guaranteeing collector safety. The first of these addresses the unpredictability of allocating large objects when the heap becomes fragmented. The remainder advance predictability by keeping collector pause times deterministically short.

Arraylets. Metronome was implemented to support *arraylets* to allow allocation of arrays in multiple chunks. This allows a degree of tolerance to fragmentation without the need to perform compaction (which can adversely affect predictability). Large arrays can be allocated as a single contiguous spine object, which then contains pointers to separately allocated fixed-size arraylets that contain the array elements. The size is a power of two so that the division operation needed for indexing can be implemented using a shift. This allows simple computation of the element position, using an extra indirection through the spine. Metronome uses an arraylet size of two kilobytes and a maximum block size of 16 kilobytes for the spine, allowing arrays of up to 8 megabytes in size.

Read barrier. Like Henriksson [1998], Metronome uses a Brooks-style read barrier to ensure that the overhead for accessing objects has uniform cost even if the collector has moved them. Historically, read barriers were considered too expensive to implement in software — Zorn [1990] measured their running-time overhead at around 20% — but Metronome applies several optimisations to reduce their overhead to 4% on average (and we saw in earlier chapters that several modern collectors have adopted load barriers). First, it uses an eager read barrier, forwarding all references as they are loaded from the heap, to make sure that they always refer to tospace. Thus, accesses from the stacks and registers via these references incur no indirection overhead. In contrast, a lazy read barrier would incur indirection every time a reference held in the stacks or registers is used. The cost for this is that whenever a collector quantum moves objects, it must also forward all references held in the registers and stacks. Second, Metronome applies several common compiler optimisations to reduce the cost of read barriers, such as common subexpression elimination and specialised optimisations such as barrier sinking to move the barrier to the point of use, allowing the barrier and use null-checks to be combined [Bacon et al., 2003a].

Scheduling the collector. Metronome uses two different threads to control for both consistent scheduling and short, uninterrupted pause times. The *alarm thread* is a very high priority thread (higher than any mutator thread) that wakes up every 500 microseconds. It acts as the 'heartbeat' for deciding whether to schedule a collector quantum. If so, it initiates suspension of the mutator threads and wakes the *collector thread*. The alarm thread is active only long enough to carry out these duties (typically under 10 microseconds) so that it goes unnoticed by the application.

The *collector thread* performs the actual collector work for each collector quantum. It must first complete the suspension of the mutator threads that was initiated by the alarm thread. Then it will perform collector work for the remainder of the quantum, before restarting the mutator threads and going back to sleep. The collector thread can also preemptively sleep if it is unable to complete its work before the quantum ends.

Metronome produces consistent CPU utilisation because the collector and mutator are interleaved using fixed time quanta. However, time-based scheduling is susceptible to variations in memory requirements if the mutator allocation rate varies over time.

Suspending the mutator threads. Metronome uses a series of short incremental pauses to complete each collector cycle. However, it must still stop all the mutator threads for each collector quantum, using a handshake mechanism to make all the mutator threads stop at a GC safe-point. At these points, each mutator thread will release any internally held run-time metadata, store any object references from its current context into well-described locations, signal that it has reached the safe-point and then sleep while waiting for a resume signal. Upon resumption, each thread will reload object pointers for the current context, reacquire any necessary run-time metadata that it previously held and then continue. Storing and reloading object pointers allows the collector to update the pointers if their targets move during the quantum. GC safe-points are placed at regularly spaced intervals by the compiler so as to bound the time needed to suspend any mutator thread.

The suspend mechanism is only used for threads actively executing mutator code. Threads that do not access the heap, threads executing non-mutator 'native' code and already suspended mutator threads (such as those waiting for synchronisation purposes) are ignored. If these threads need to begin (or return to) mutating the heap (for example, when returning from 'native' code, invoking operations of the Java Native Interface, or accessing other Java run-time structures), they will suspend themselves and wait for the collector quantum to complete.

Ragged root scanning. Metronome scans each complete thread stack within a single collector quantum so as to avoid losing pointers to objects. Developers must make sure not to use deep stacks in their real-time applications so as to permit each stack to be scanned in a single quantum. Though each whole stack must be scanned atomically in a single quantum, Metronome does allow scanning of distinct thread stacks to occur in different quanta. That is, the collector and mutator threads are allowed to interleave their execution while the collector is scanning the thread stacks. To support this, Metronome imposes an insertion write barrier on all unscanned threads, to make sure they do not hide a root reference behind the wave front before the collector can scan it.

Analysis

One of the biggest contributions of Metronome is a formal model of the scheduling of collection work and its characterisation in terms of mutator utilisation and memory usage [Bacon et al., 2003a]. The model is parametrised by the instantaneous *allocation rate* $A^*(\tau)$ of the mutator over time, the instantaneous *garbage generation rate* $G^*(\tau)$ of the mutator over time and the *garbage collector processing rate* P (measured over the live data). All are defined in units of data volume per unit time. Here, time τ ranges over *mutator time*, idealised for a collector that runs infinitely fast (or in practice assuming there is sufficient memory to run without collecting).

These parameters allow simple definitions of the amount of memory allocated during an interval of time (τ_1, τ_2) as:

$$\alpha^*(\tau_1, \tau_2) = \int_{\tau_1}^{\tau_2} A^*(\tau)\, d\tau \tag{19.1}$$

and similarly for garbage generated as:

$$\gamma^*(\tau_1, \tau_2) = \int_{\tau_1}^{\tau_2} G^*(\tau)\, d\tau. \tag{19.2}$$

The maximum memory allocated for an interval of size $\Delta\tau$ is:

$$\alpha^*(\Delta\tau) = \max_\tau \alpha^*(\tau, \tau + \Delta\tau) \tag{19.3}$$

which gives the maximum allocation rate:[2]

$$a^*(\Delta\tau) = \frac{\alpha^*(\Delta\tau)}{\Delta\tau}. \tag{19.4}$$

The instantaneous memory requirement of the program (excluding garbage, overhead, and fragmentation) at a given time τ is:

$$m^*(\tau) = \alpha^*(0, \tau) - \gamma^*(0, \tau). \tag{19.5}$$

Of course, real time must also include the time for the collector to execute, so it is helpful to introduce a function $\Phi : t \to \tau$ that maps from real time t to mutator time τ,

---

[2]Note carefully here the distinction between a^* (the maximum allocation *rate* over an interval) and α^* (the maximum allocated memory over an interval).

where $\tau \leq t$. A function that operates in mutator time is written f^*, whereas a function that operates in real time is written f. Thus, the live memory of the program at time t is:

$$m(t) = m^*(\Phi(t)) \tag{19.6}$$

and the maximum memory requirement over the entire program execution is:

$$m = \max_t m(t) = \max_\tau m^*(\tau). \tag{19.7}$$

Time utilisation. Time-based scheduling has two additional parameters: the *mutator quantum* Q_T and the *collector quantum* C_T, being the amount of time that the mutator and collector, respectively, are allowed to run before yielding. These allow derivation of minimum mutator utilisation as:

$$u_T(\Delta t) = \frac{Q_T \cdot \lfloor \frac{\Delta t}{Q_T + C_T} \rfloor + x}{\Delta t} \tag{19.8}$$

where $Q_T \cdot \lfloor \frac{\Delta t}{Q_T + C_T} \rfloor$ is the length of whole mutator quanta in the interval and x is the size of the remaining partial mutator quantum, defined as:

$$x = \max \left(0, \Delta t - (Q_T + C_T) \cdot \lfloor \frac{\Delta t}{Q_T + C_T} \rfloor - C_T \right). \tag{19.9}$$

Asymptotically, minimum mutator utilisation approaches the expected ratio of total time given to the mutator versus the collector:

$$\lim_{\Delta t \to \infty} u_T(\Delta t) = \frac{Q_T}{Q_T + C_T}. \tag{19.10}$$

For example, consider a perfectly scheduled system that has a collector quantum $C_T = 10$, which is the maximum pause that will be experienced by the mutator. Figure 19.9 plots minimum mutator utilisation for mutator quanta of $Q_T = 2.5$, $Q_T = 10$ and $Q_T = 40$. Notice that $u_T(\Delta t)$ converges to $\frac{Q_T}{Q_T + C_T}$ in the limit for large Δt, and that more frequent collection (reducing the mutator quantum Q_T) leads to faster convergence. Also, note that the x term has more impact at the small time scales of interest in real-time systems. Of course, in practice the collector will usually only run intermittently, so $u_T(\Delta t)$ is only a lower bound on mutator utilisation.

Space utilisation. As already noted, space utilisation will vary depending on the mutator allocation rate. Assuming constant collector rate P, at time t the collector will run for time $m(t)/P$ to process the $m(t)$ live data (work is proportional to the tracing needed to mark the live data). In that time, the mutator will run for quantum Q_T per quantum C_T of the collector. Thus, to run a collection at time t requires an excess space overhead of:

$$e_T(t) = \alpha^* \left(\Phi(t), \Phi(t) + \frac{m(t)}{P} \cdot \frac{Q_T}{C_T} \right) \tag{19.11}$$

allowing definition of the maximum excess space required as:

$$e_T = \max_t e_T(t). \tag{19.12}$$

Freeing an object in Metronome can take as long as three collection cycles: one to collect the object, two if the object became garbage only after the current snapshot cycle began so

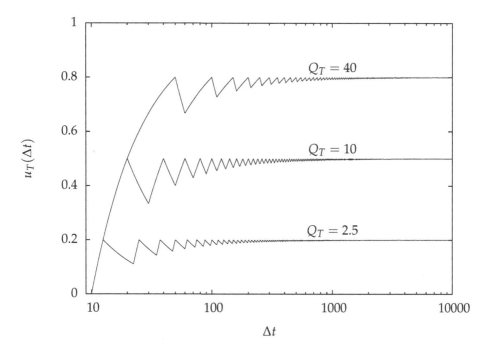

Figure 19.9: Minimum mutator utilisation $u_T(\Delta t)$ for a perfectly scheduled time-based collector. $C_T = 10$. Utilisation converges to $\frac{Q_T}{Q_T + C_T}$. Increasing the frequency of the collector (reducing the mutator quantum) produces faster convergence.

it cannot be collected until the next cycle, and three if the object needs also to be relocated before its space can be reused.

Thus, the space required (ignoring internal fragmentation) at time t is:

$$s_T(t) \leq m(t) + 3e_T \qquad (19.13)$$

while the overall space needed is:

$$s_T \leq m + 3e_T. \qquad (19.14)$$

These are in the worst case that all garbage objects are dragged into the next collector cycle and that they all need to be moved. The expected space needed is simply $m + e_T$.

Mutation. Mutation also has a space cost because the write barrier must record every deleted and inserted reference. It must filter `null` references and marked objects so as to place a bound on collector work (at most, all the objects in the heap will be marked live), while keeping the cost of the write barrier constant. Thus, in the worst case, the write log can have as many entries as there are objects. This space must be accounted for by treating allocation of the log entries as an indirect form of allocation.

Sensitivity. Metronome will behave as predicted only when given accurate estimates of the parameters used to describe the application and the collector: the application allocation rate $A^*(t)$ and garbage generation rate $G^*(t)$, and the collector processing rate P and the quantisation parameters Q_T and C_T. Utilisation u_T depends solely on Q_T and C_T, so utilisation will remain steady (subject only to any jitter in the operating system delivering a timely quantum signal and the minimum quantum it can support).

The excess space required for collection $e_T(t)$, which determines the total space s_T needed, depends on both maximum application memory usage m and the amount of memory allocated over an interval. If the application developer underestimates either the total space required m or the maximum allocation rate a^*, then the total space requirement s_T may grow arbitrarily. Time-based collectors suffer from such behaviour particularly when there are intervals of time in which the allocation rate is very high. Similarly, the estimate of the collector processing rate P must be a conservative underestimate of the actual rate.

Fortunately, a collection cycle runs for a relatively long interval of mutator execution time:

$$\Delta \tau = \frac{m(t)}{P} \cdot \frac{Q_T}{C_T}$$

so the allocation rate in that time will be close to the average allocation rate, resulting in little variation in space consumed so long as the estimate of maximum memory required m is accurate.

Comparison with work-based scheduling. A similar analysis of work-based scheduling yields the opportunity to compare time-based and work-based scheduling. However, this analysis is compromised because operations of the mutator can affect the time allocated to it. More formally, for time-based scheduling the time dilation Φ from t to τ is linear and fixed, whereas for work-based scheduling the dilation is variable and non-linear, and dependent on the application.

The parameters for work-based scheduling reflect that the mutator and collector interleave by triggering the collector after some amount of allocation to perform some amount of collector work: the work-based mutator quantum Q_W and collector quantum C_W being the amount of memory that the mutator and collector, respectively, are allowed to allocate/process before yielding.

Because work-based time dilation is variable and non-linear, there is no way to obtain a closed-form solution for minimum mutator utilisation. Each collector increment processes C_W memory at rate P, so each pause for collection takes time $d = C_W/P$. Each mutator quantum involves allocation of Q_W memory, so the minimum total mutator time $\Delta \tau_i$ for i quanta is the minimum $\Delta \tau_i$ that solves the equation:

$$\alpha^*(\Delta \tau_i) = iQ_W. \tag{19.15}$$

Increasing the time interval does not decrease the maximum amount of allocation in that time, so $\alpha^*(\Delta \tau)$ increases monotonically. Thus, $\Delta \tau_i > \Delta \tau_{i-1}$, so Equation 19.15 can be solved using an iterative method. Let k be the largest integer such that:

$$kd + \Delta \tau_k \leq \Delta t \tag{19.16}$$

so that the minimum mutator utilisation over an interval Δt is:

$$u_W(\Delta t) = \frac{\Delta \tau_k + y}{\Delta t} \tag{19.17}$$

where $\Delta \tau_k$ is the time taken by k whole mutator quanta in Δt and y is the size of the remaining partial mutator quantum, defined as:

$$y = \max(0, \Delta t - \Delta \tau_k - (k+1) \cdot d). \tag{19.18}$$

Note that minimum mutator utilisation $u_W(\Delta t)$ will be zero for $\Delta t < d$. Moreover, any large allocation of nQ_W bytes will force the collector to perform n units of work leading to a pause lasting time nd in which the mutator will experience zero utilisation. This reveals analytically that the application developer must take care with a work-based collector to achieve real-time bounds by avoiding large allocations and making sure that allocation is spaced evenly.

Now, minimum mutator utilisation depends on the allocation rate $a^*(\Delta\tau)$, where $\Delta\tau \leq \Delta t$, and on the collector processing rate P. Suppose that the interval Δt over which we require real-time performance is small (say, 20 milliseconds), so the peak allocation rate for this interval is likely to be quite high. Thus, at real-time scales work-based minimum mutator utilisation $u_W(\Delta t)$ will vary considerably with the allocation rate. In contrast, note that the $\Delta\tau$ in which the time-based collector is dependent on allocation rate is at a much larger scale: the time needed for a complete garbage collection cycle.

Analysing for space, the excess space required to perform a collection at time t is:

$$e_W(t) = m(t) \cdot \frac{Q_W}{C_W} \tag{19.19}$$

and the excess space required for a collection cycle over its whole execution is:

$$e_W = m \cdot \frac{Q_W}{C_W}. \tag{19.20}$$

These will be accurate as long as the application developer's estimate of total live memory m is accurate. Also, note that the excess e_W for a whole collection cycle will exceed the maximum memory m needed for execution of the program unless $Q_W < C_W$. The space requirement of the program at time t is:

$$s_W(t) \leq m(t) + 3e_W \tag{19.21}$$

and the space required overall is:

$$s_W = m + 3e_W. \tag{19.22}$$

To sum up, while a work-scheduled collector will meet its space bound so long as m is correctly estimated, its minimum mutator utilisation will be heavily dependent on the allocation rate over a real-time interval, while a time-based collector will guarantee minimum mutator utilisation easily but may fluctuate in its space requirements.

Robustness

Time-based scheduling yields the robustness needed for real-time collection, but when the input parameters to the collector are not accurately specified, it may fail to reclaim sufficient memory. The only way for it to degrade gracefully is to slow down the allocation rate.

One approach to reducing the total allocation rate is to impose a generational scheme. This treats the nursery as a filter to reduce the allocation rate into the primary heap. Focusing collector effort on the portion of the heap most likely to yield free memory results in higher mutator utilisation and also reduces the amount of floating garbage. However, traditional nursery collection is unpredictable both in terms of the time to collect and the quantity of data that is promoted. *Syncopation* is an approach for performing nursery collection synchronously with the mature-space collector, where the nursery is evacuated at the beginning of the mature-space collection cycle and at the start of sweeping, as well as outside the mature-space collection cycle [Bacon *et al.*, 2005]. It relies on an analytic solution for utilisation in generational collection taking the nursery survival rate as a parameter and sizing the nursery such that evacuation is only needed once per real-time window.

The analysis informs whether generational collection should be used in any given application. Syncopation handles the situation where temporary spikes in allocation rate make it impossible to evacuate the nursery quickly enough to meet real-time bounds by moving the work triggered by the temporary spike to a later time. Frampton *et al.* [2007] adopt a different approach, allowing nursery collection to be performed incrementally so as to avoid having pause times degenerate to the time needed to evacuate the nursery.

Another strategy for slowing the allocation rate is simply to add an element of work-based collection to slow the mutator down, but of course this can lead to missed deadlines. Alternatively, slack-based scheduling achieves this by preempting the low-priority threads as necessary for the collector to keep up with allocation. So long as sufficient low-priority slack is available, real-time deadlines will be preserved. These observations lead to the following Tax-and-Spend methodology that combines slack-based and time-based scheduling.

19.6 Combining scheduling approaches: Tax-and-Spend

Metronome works best on dedicated uniprocessor or small multiprocessor systems, because of its need to suspend the mutator while an increment of collector work is performed. Typical work-based collectors can suffer latencies that are orders of magnitude worse than time-based schemes. Henriksson's slack-based scheduling is best suited to periodic applications and is fragile under overload conditions when there is no available slack. To address these limitations, Auerbach *et al.* [2008] devised a general scheduling methodology called *Tax-and-Spend* that subsumes the work-based, slack-based and time-based approaches. When applied to Metronome, the Tax-and-Spend methodology results in latencies almost three times shorter, comparable utilisation at a time window two and a half times shorter, and mean throughput improvements of 10% to 20%.

The basic principle of Tax-and-Spend is that each mutator thread is required to engage in some amount of collection work (taxation) at a rate and intervals appropriate to its desired minimum mutator utilisation. Collection work also proceeds in any available slack left over by the mutators, building up credits that mutators can later spend to preserve or improve their utilisation by avoiding some amount of collector work.

Taxation can occur at any GC safe-point as a result of some global decision, but a thread-specific check for pending collector work is imposed on every slow path allocation (when the thread's local allocation buffer is exhausted) that also enables a decision based on mutator work (measured by units of allocation, thread execution time, safe-points executed, absolute physical time, or whatever virtualised time makes sense).

Tax-and-Spend scheduling

As we have already seen, minimum mutator utilisation is simple for developers to reason about because they can consider the system as just running somewhat slower than the native processor speed until the responsiveness requirements approach the quantisation limits of the garbage collector. As a measure of garbage collector intrusiveness, minimum mutator utilisation is superior to maximum pause time since it accounts for clustering of the individual pauses that cause missed deadlines and pathological slowdowns. Tax-and-Spend scheduling allows different threads to run at different utilisations, providing flexibility when threads have widely varying allocation rates, or for threads having particularly stringent deadlines that must be interrupted as little as possible. Also, background threads on spare processors can be used to offload collector work to obtain high utilisation for mutator threads. The time metric can be physical or virtual as best suits the application.

Of course, this does mean that any analysis of the application must compose the real-time constraints of the individual threads to obtain a global picture of application behaviour.

Per-thread scheduling. To manage per-mutator utilisation, Tax-and-Spend must measure and schedule collector work based on per-thread metrics and allow a collector increment to be charged to a single mutator thread. All collector-related activity can be accounted for in each thread (including the overheads of extending the mutation log, initialising an allocation page, and other bookkeeping activities). The collector can track all of these so as to avoid scheduling too much work on any given mutator thread.

Also, by piggybacking collector increments on mutator threads before a thread voluntarily yields to the operating system (say, to take an allocation slow path or to perform I/O or execute native code that does not access the heap) Tax-and-Spend avoids having the operating system scheduler assume that the thread has finished with its operating system time quantum and schedule some unrelated thread in its place. This is particularly important in a loaded system. By interleaving mutation and collection on the same operating system thread the operating system scheduler is less likely to interfere in the scheduling of the collection work.

Allowing different threads to run with different utilisations is important when allocation rates vary significantly across threads or when high-priority threads like event handlers desire minimal interruption. This also permits threads that can tolerate less stringent timing requirements to lower their quantisation overheads by running with larger quanta, and so increase throughput.

Tax-based versus slack-based scheduling. Slack-based scheduling works well in classical periodic real-time systems, but it degrades badly when the system is overloaded and has insufficient slack. This makes it poorly suited to queuing, adaptive (where the system saturates the processor to compute as accurate a result as possible but tolerates less accuracy to avoid total overload) or interactive real-time systems. Work-based scheduling taxes mutator allocation work, choosing some amount of collector work proportional to allocation work that will permit the collector to finish its cycle before memory is exhausted. It often suffers from poor minimum mutator utilisation and wide variations in pause time. Time-based scheduling taxes mutator utilisation to interleave the collector with the mutator for given amounts of processor time. It is robust to overload because the tax continues to be assessed, but when there is sufficient slack in the system it can result in unnecessary jitter since collection can occur at any time so long as minimum mutator utilisation requirements are preserved.

Combining tax-based and slack-based scheduling. Tax-and-Spend combines these different scheduling approaches by adopting an economic model. Each mutator thread is subject to a tax rate that determines how much collector work it must perform for a given amount of execution time, specified as a per-thread minimum mutator utilisation. Dedicated collector threads run at low or idle priority during slack periods and accumulate tax credits for their work. Credits are typically deposited in a single global account, though it is possible to consider policies that use multiple accounts.

The aggregate tax over all threads, combining the tax on the mutator threads with the credits contributed by the collector threads, must be sufficient for the collector to finish its cycle before memory is exhausted. The number of background collector threads is typically the same as the number of processors, configured so that they naturally run during slack periods in overall system execution. They execute a series of quanta each adding the corresponding amount of credit. On real-time operating systems, it is desirable to run these threads at some low real-time priority rather than the standard idle priority so that they are scheduled similarly to other threads that perform real work rather than as a true idle thread. These low-priority real-time threads will still sleep for some small amount of time, making it possible for non-real-time processes to make progress even when collection might saturate the machine. This enables administrators to log in and kill run-away real-time processes as necessary.

Each mutator thread is scheduled according to its desired minimum mutator utilisation, guaranteeing that it can meet its real-time requirements while also allowing the collector to make sufficient progress. When a mutator thread is running and its tax is due, it first attempts to withdraw credit from the bank equal to its tax quantum. If this is successful, then the mutator thread can skip its collector quantum because the collector is keeping up, so the mutator only pays tax when there is insufficient slack-scheduled background collection. Even if only a partial quantum's credit is available, then the mutator can perform a smaller quantum of collector work than usual. Thus, if there is any slack available, the mutator can still run with both higher throughput and lower latencies without having the collector falling behind. This treats slack in a uniprocessor and excess capacity in a multiprocessor in the same way.

Tax-and-Spend prerequisites

Tax-and-Spend requires an underlying garbage collector that is both incremental (so collector work can be levied as a work-scheduled tax on the mutator threads) and concurrent (so slack-scheduled collector work can run on a spare processor concurrently with the mutators). To exploit multiprocessors effectively it should also be parallel (so slack-scheduled collector work can run concurrently with work-scheduled collector work). While Metronome is incremental, it was not originally devised to be concurrent, because time-based scheduling requires that the mutator interleave with the collector at precise intervals, with the mutator suspended while the collector executes. Thus, Tax-and-Spend makes two key changes. First, collector work occurs in collector threads concurrently with mutator threads. This makes it easy for the collector threads to exploit any available slack on some processors while the other processors continue to run mutator threads. Second, mutator threads can be *taxed* by piggybacking an increment of collector work on them when the load on the system makes it necessary to steal some time from the mutator.

Concurrent collection by itself is insufficient, since it devolves scheduling of the collector threads to the operating system which does not provide the precision needed to meet real-time guarantees and prevent heap exhaustion. Even a real-time operating system cannot account for the allocation patterns and space needs of the application in making its scheduling decisions.

We describe below how Tax-and-Spend extends Metronome to achieve on-the-fly, concurrent, parallel and incremental collection. These extensions are similar to those of other on-the-fly and parallel collectors, but we reiterate them this context for completeness.

Ragged epochs for global consensus. Rather than stopping all the mutator threads to impose global consensus about the current activities of the collector, Tax-and-Spend substitutes a ragged epoch protocol. This is used for several purposes. For example, during certain phases of the collector all the mutators must install a particular write barrier. Alternatively, for termination of the collector, all mutator threads must have drained their private store buffer. The thread installing the barrier, or checking for termination, uses the epoch mechanism to assert that the new state is in effect for all threads.

The epoch mechanism uses a single shared epoch number that can be atomically incremented by any thread to initiate a new epoch, plus a per-thread local epoch number.

Each thread updates its local epoch number by copying the shared epoch, but it does so only at GC safe-points. Thus, each thread's local epoch is always less than or equal to the shared epoch. Any thread can examine the local epochs of all threads to find the least local epoch, which is called the *confirmed epoch*. Only when the confirmed epoch reaches or passes the value a thread sets for the global epoch can it be sure that all other threads have noticed the change. On weakly ordered hardware, a thread must use a memory fence before updating its local epoch. To cope with threads waiting on I/O or executing native code, Tax-and-Spend requires that they execute a GC safe-point on return to update their local epoch before they resume epoch-sensitive activities. Thus, such threads can always be assumed to be at the current epoch, so there is no need to wait for them.

Phase agreement using 'last one out'. Metronome easily achieved agreement on the collector phase (such as marking, sweeping, finalising and so on) because all collector work occurred on dedicated threads that could block briefly to effect a phase change, so long as there was enough remaining time in their shared collector quantum. With concurrent collection piggy-backed on the mutator threads, each mutator might be at a different place in its taxation quantum, so it is essential that phase detection be non-blocking or else a taxed mutator might fail to meet its deadlines. Using ragged epochs for this is not efficient because it does not distinguish taxed mutator threads from others. Instead, the *'last one out'* protocol operates by storing a phase identifier and worker count in a single shared and atomically updatable location.

Every taxed mutator thread atomically increments the worker count, leaving the phase identifier unchanged. When a mutator thread exhausts its taxation quantum without completing the phase, it atomically decrements the worker count, also leaving the phase identifier unchanged. When any thread believes that the phase might be complete because there is (apparently) no further work to do in that phase, and it is the only remaining worker thread (the count is one), then it will change the phase and decrement the worker count in one atomic operation to establish the new phase.

This protocol only works so long as each worker thread returns any incomplete work to a global work queue when it exits. Eventually there will be no work left, some thread will end up being the last one and it will be able to declare the next phase.

Unfortunately, termination of the mark phase in Metronome is not easily achieved using this mechanism, because the deletion barrier employed by Metronome deposits the overwritten pointer into a per-thread mutation log. Mark phase termination requires that all threads have an empty mutation log (not just those performing collector work). Thus, Tax-and-Spend introduces a final marking phase in which the remaining marking work is handled by one thread which uses the ragged epoch mechanism to ensure that there is global agreement that all the mutation logs are empty. If this check fails, then the deciding thread can declare a false alarm and switch back to parallel marking. Eventually all the termination conditions will be met and the deciding thread can move to the next post-marking phase.

Per-thread callbacks. Most phases of a collection cycle need just enough worker threads to make progress, but others require that something be done by (or to) every mutator thread. For example, the first phase of collection must scan every mutator stack. Other phases require that the mutator threads flush their thread-local state to make information available to the collector. To support this, some phases impose a *callback* protocol instead of 'last one out'.

In a callback phase, some collector master thread periodically examines all the mutator threads to see if they have performed the desired task. Every active thread that has not is asked to call back at their next GC safe-point to perform the required action (stack scanning, cache flushing, and so on). Threads waiting on I/O or executing native code are prevented from returning while the action is performed on their behalf. Thus, the maximum delay to any thread during a callback phase is the time taken to perform the action.

Priority boosting to ensure progress. A real-time collector must make progress so that it finishes collection before the heap is exhausted. All three of the prior protocols (ragged epochs, last one out and callback) can be prevented from making progress if some lower priority thread is unable to respond because higher priority threads are saturating the processors. The solution is to boost the priority of the lower priority thread temporarily until it has been heard from.

19.7   Controlling fragmentation

A real-time collector must bound both its time and its space consumption. Unfortunately, over time, fragmentation can eat away at the space bound. Accounting for fragmentation is impossible without precise characterisation of application-specific behaviours such as pointer density, average object size and locality of object size. Thus, a real-time collector must be designed to manage and limit fragmentation in some way. One way to achieve this is through compaction. Another approach is to allocate objects in fragments (oblets and arraylets) so as to preclude external fragmentation at the expense of some (bounded) internal fragmentation and overhead on the mutator to access the appropriate fragment during reads and writes to the heap. In this section we discuss both of these approaches.

The challenge in concurrent compaction is for the collector to relocate objects concurrently with the mutator while guaranteeing that mutator accesses retain tight time bounds. The replicating collectors discussed in Chapter 17 and that of Blelloch and Cheng [1999] were originally devised expressly to allow concurrent copying but they maintain two copies of each object. Keeping these copies consistent on modern multiprocessors that lack strict coherence usually requires some form of locking, particularly for `volatile` fields. Moreover, replicating collectors may rely on a synchronous termination phase to ensure that the mutator roots have been forwarded. Per-object locking does not scale. Compressor and Pauseless rely on page-level synchronisation using page protection, but suffer from poor minimum mutator utilisation both because of the cost of the traps and because they are work-based, with a trap storm following a phase shift.

The absence of lock-freedom means we cannot guarantee progress of the mutator, let alone preserve time bounds. There are a number of approaches to making mutator accesses wait-free or lock-free in the presence of concurrent compaction, which we now discuss.

Incremental compaction in Metronome

Metronome was designed as a mostly non-copying collector under the assumption that external fragmentation is rare. It uses arraylets to break large objects (arrays) into chunks which form the largest contiguous units allocated by the system. This combination greatly reduces the number of objects that must be copied in order to minimise fragmentation. Bacon *et al.* [2003b] derive an analytical framework to decide how many pages to defragment during each collection so as to ensure that the mutator never needs to wait for any allocation request. Because Metronome is an incremental collector, it can perform defragmentation while all the mutator threads are stopped. When the mutator threads resume, they are forwarded to any copies as necessary via the Brooks indirection barrier. There is no need to be concerned with mutators seeing objects in the middle of being copied. The only cost to the mutator is the cost of the extra indirection, which has tight time bounds.

Algorithm 19.7: Replication copying for a uniprocessor

```
1   atomic Read(p, i):
2       return p[i]
3
4   atomic Write(p, i, value):                    /* p may be primary or replica */
5       /* deletion barrier code also needed here for snapshot collection */
6       p[i] ← value
7       r ← forwardingAddress(p)
8       r[i] ← value
9       /* insertion barrier code also needed here for incremental update collection */
```

The Tax-and-Spend extension of Metronome is a concurrent collector but it does not perform any compaction.

The Bacon *et al.* framework divides the defragmentation work (as determined by the derived defragmentation target) as evenly as possible across the size classes of their segregated-fits allocator. Each size class consists of a linked list of pages (as opposed to individual objects). The algorithm for defragmenting a size class consists of the following steps.

1. Sort the pages by the number of unused (free) objects per page from dense to sparse.

2. Set the allocation page to the first (densest) non-full page in the resulting list.

3. Set the page to evacuate to the last (sparsest) page in the list.

4. While the target number of pages to evacuate in this size class has not been met, and the page to evacuate is not the page in which to allocate, move each live object from the sparsest page to the next available free cell on the allocation page (moving to the next page in the list whenever the current allocation page fills up).

This moves objects from the sparsest pages to the densest pages. It moves the minimal number of objects and produces the maximal number of completely full pages. The choice of the first allocation page in Step 2 as the densest non-full page may result in poor cache locality because previously co-located objects will be spread among the available dense pages. To address this, one can set a threshold for the density of the page in which to allocate at the head of the list, so that there are enough free cells in the page to satisfy the locality goal.

References to relocated objects are redirected as they are scanned by the subsequent tracing mark phase. Thus, at the end of the next mark phase, the relocated objects of the previous collection can be freed. In the meantime, the Brooks forwarding barrier ensures proper mutator access to the relocated objects. Deferring update of references to the next mark phase has three benefits: there is no extra 'fixup' phase, fewer references need to be fixed (since any object that dies will never be scanned) and there is the locality benefit of piggybacking fixup on tracing.

Incremental replication on uniprocessors

Before considering more complicated schemes for concurrent compaction, it is worth noting that many real-time applications run in embedded systems, where uniprocessors have been the predominant platform. Preserving atomicity of mutator operations (with respect to the collector and other mutators) is simple on a uniprocessor, either by disabling scheduler interrupts or by preventing thread switching except at GC safe-points (making sure that mutator barriers never contain a GC safe-point). In this setting, the collector can freely copy objects so long as mutators subsequently access only the copy (using a Brooks indirection barrier to force a tospace invariant), or they make sure to update *both* copies (in case other mutators are still reading from the old version in a replicating collector).

Kalibera [2009] compares replication copying to copying with a Brooks barrier in the context of a real-time system for Java running on uniprocessors. His replication scheme maintains the usual forwarding pointer in all objects, except that when the object is replicated the forwarding pointer in the replica refers back to the original instead of to itself (in contrast to Brooks [1984]). This arrangement allows for very simple and predictable mutator barriers. On `Read` the mutator need not be concerned whether it is accessing a fromspace or tospace object, and can simply load the value from whichever version the mutator references. All that `Write` needs to do is to make sure that the update is performed on both versions of the object to keep them coherent. Pseudo-code for these barriers (omitting the support necessary for concurrent tracing) is shown in Algorithm 19.7. Not surprisingly, avoiding the need to forward every read is a significant benefit, and the cost of the double-write is negligible given that most of the time both writes will be to the same address because the forwarding address is a self-reference.

Concurrent compaction on a multiprocessor prevents us from assuming that `Read` and `Write` can be made straightforwardly atomic. For that we must consider more fine-grained synchronisation among mutators, and between mutator and collector, as follows.

Stopless: lock-free garbage collection

Pizlo *et al.* [2007] describe an approach to concurrent compaction for their lock-free *Stopless* collector that ensures lock-freedom for mutator operations (allocation and heap accesses) even while compaction proceeds concurrently. Unlike Blelloch and Cheng [1999], Stopless does not require that the mutator update both copies of an object to keep them coherent. Instead, it enforces a protocol that always updates just one definitive copy of the object. The innovation in Stopless is to create an intermediate 'wide' version of the object being copied, where each field has an associated status word, and to use a double-word `CompareAnd-SwapWide` to synchronise copying of those fields with mutation. The field's status word changes atomically with its data and indicates the up-to-date location of the data (in the fromspace original, the wide copy, or the final tospace copy). As in Blelloch and Cheng [1999] a header word on each object stores a Brooks forwarding pointer, either to the wide copy or to the tospace copy. During the compaction phase, mutator and collector threads race to create the wide copy using compare-and-swap to install the forwarding pointer.

Once the wide copy has been created, and its pointer installed in the original's forwarding pointer header field, the mutator can only update the wide copy. The status word on each field lets the mutator know (via read and write barriers) where to read/write the up-to-date field, encoding the three possibilities: `inOriginal`, `inWide` and `inCopy`. All status words on the fields in the wide object are initialised to `inOriginal`. So long as the status field is `inOriginal`, then mutator reads occur on the fromspace original. All updates (both by the collector as it copies each field and the mutator as it performs updates) operate on the wide copy, atomically updating both the field and its adjacent status to `inWide` using `CompareAndSwapWide`. The collector must assert that the field is `inOriginal` as it copies the field. If this fails, then the field has already been updated by the mutator and the copy operation can be abandoned.

Once all fields of an object have been converted to `inWide` (whether by copying or mutation), the collector allocates its final 'narrow' version in tospace, whose pointer is then installed as a forwarding pointer into the wide copy. At this point there are three versions of the object: the out-of-date fromspace original which forwards to the wide copy, the up-to-date wide copy which forwards to the tospace copy, and the uninitialised tospace copy. The collector concurrently copies each field of the wide copy into the narrow tospace copy, using `CompareAndSwapWide` to assert that the field is unmodified and to set its status to `inCopy`. If this fails, then the field was updated by the mutator and the collector tries again to copy the field. If the mutator encounters an `inCopy` field when trying to access the wide copy, then it will forward the access to the tospace copy.

Because Stopless forces all updates to the most up-to-date location of a field, it also supports Java `volatile` fields without the need for locking. It is also able to simulate application-level atomic operations like compare-and-swap on fields by the mutator. For details see Pizlo *et al.* [2007]. The only remaining issue is coping with atomic operations on double-word fields (such as Java `long`) where the `CompareAndSwapWide` is not able to cover both the double-word field and its adjacent status word.[3] The authors of Stopless propose a technique based on emulating *n*-way compare-and-swap using the standard compare-and-swap [Harris *et al.*, 2002].

Some might object to the space overhead of Stopless (three copies including one double-width), but Pizlo[4] points out that so long as sparse pages are being evacuated, with at most one-third occupancy, one can make use of the dead space for the wide copies. Of course, the reason for evacuating the page is that it is fragmented, so there may not be sufficient contiguous free space available for all the copies. But if segregated-fits allocation is used, then the free portions are uniformly sized, and it is possible to allocate the wide objects in multiple wide fragments so as to allocate each data field and its status word side-by-side. In Stopless, the space for the wide objects is retained until the next mark phase has completed, having forwarded all pointers to their tospace copies.

Staccato: best-effort compaction with mutator wait-freedom

Whereas Metronome performs compaction while the mutator is stopped during a collector quantum, *Staccato* [McCloskey *et al.*, 2008] permits concurrent compaction without requiring the mutators to use locks or atomic operations like compare-and-swap in the common case, even on multiprocessors with weak memory ordering. Storms of atomic operations are avoided by moving few objects (only as necessary to reclaim sparsely occupied pages) and by randomising their selection.

Staccato inherits the Brooks-style indirection barrier of Metronome, placing a forwarding pointer in every object header. It also relies on *ragged synchronisation*: the mutators are instrumented to perform a memory fence (on weakly ordered machines like the PowerPC) at regular intervals (such as GC safe-points) to bring them up to date with any change to global state. The collector reserves a bit in the forwarding pointer to denote that the object is being copied (Java objects are always word-aligned, so a low bit in the pointer can be used). This `COPYING` bit and the forwarding pointer can be changed atomically using compare-and-swap/set. To move an object, the collector performs the following steps.

1. Set the `COPYING` bit using compare-and-swap/set. Mutators access the forwarding pointer without atomic operations, so this change takes some time to propagate to the mutators.

2. Wait for a ragged synchronisation where every mutator performs a read fence to ensure that all mutators have seen the update to the `COPYING` bit.

3. Perform a read fence (on weakly ordered machines) to ensure that the collector sees all updates by mutators from before they saw the change to the `COPYING` bit.

---

[3] We observe that some processors offer a 16-byte compare-and-swap that can be used to solve this problem.
[4] Filip Pizlo, personal communication.

Algorithm 19.8: Copying and mutator barriers (while copying) in Staccato

```
 1  copyObjects(candidates):
 2      for each p in candidates
 3          /* set COPYING bit */
 4          CompareAndSet(&forwardingAddress(p), p, p | COPYING)
 5          waitForRaggedSynch(writeFence; readFence)
 6                          /* ensure mutators flush pending writes & see COPYING bits */
 7      readFence()              /* ensure collector sees mutator updates from before CAS */
 8      for each p in candidates
 9          r ← allocate(length(p))                        /* allocate the copy */
10          move(p, r)                                     /* copy the contents */
11          forwardingAddress(r)                    /* the copy forwards to itself */
12          add(replicas, r)                              /* remember the copies */
13      writeFence()                    /* flush the copies so the mutators can see them */
14      waitForRaggedSynch(readFence)             /* ensure mutators see the copies */
15      for each (p in candidates, r in replicas)
16          /* try to commit the copy */
17          if not CompareAndSet(&forwardingAddress(p), p | COPYING, r)
18              /* the commit failed so deal with it */
19              free(r)                                 /* free the aborted copy */
20              add(aborted, p)                           /* remember the aborts */
21      return aborted
22
23  Access(p):
24      r ← forwardingAddress(p)                    /* load the forwarding pointer */
25      if r & COPYING = 0
26          return r                   /* only use the forwarding pointer if not copying */
27      /* try to abort the copy */
28      if CompareAndSet(&forwardingAddress(p), r, p)
29          return p                                     /* the abort succeeded */
30      /* collector committed or another aborted */
31      atomic                       /* force reload of current forwardingAddress(p) */
32          r ← forwardingAddress(p)
33      return r
34
35  Read(p, i):
36      p ← Access(p)
37      return p[i]
38
39  Write(p, i, value):
40      p ← Access(p)
41      p[i] ← value
```

4. Allocate the copy, and copy over the fields from the original.

5. Perform a write fence (on weakly ordered machines) to push the newly written state of the copy to make it globally visible.

6. Wait for a ragged synchronisation where every mutator performs a read fence to ensure that it has seen the values written into the copy.

7. Set the forwarding address to point to the copy and simultaneously clear the COPY-ING bit using compare-and-swap/set. This commits the move of the object. If this fails, then the mutator must have modified the object at some point and the move is aborted.

The collector will usually want to move a number of objects, so the cost of the ragged synchronisation can be amortised by batching the copying, as illustrated by the copyObjects routine in Algorithm 19.8. This takes a list of candidates to be moved and returns a list of aborted objects that could not be moved.

Meanwhile, when the mutator accesses an object (to examine or modify its state for any reason), it performs the following steps:

1. Load the forwarding pointer.

2. Use the forwarding pointer as the object pointer only if the COPYING bit is clear.

3. Otherwise, try to abort the copy by using a compare-and-set to clear the COPYING bit (which is the same as storing the original pointer).

4. Use the forwarding pointer (with the COPYING bit cleared) as the object pointer only if the compare-and-set succeeds.

5. Otherwise, the failure of the compare-and-set means either that the collector committed the copy or else another mutator aborted it. So, reload the forwarding pointer using an *atomic* read (needed on weakly ordered machines), guaranteed to see the current value of the forwarding pointer (that is, the value placed there by the collector or other mutator).

These steps are shown in the Access barrier helper function, used by both Read and Write in Algorithm 19.8.

We note that when using compare-and-swap (instead of compare-and-set) Access can avoid the atomic read of the forwarding pointer and simply use the value that Compare-AndSwap returns, as shown in Algorithm 19.9, clearing its COPYING bit just in case the compare-and-swap succeeded.

McCloskey *et al.* note that frequently accessed objects might prove difficult to relocate because their move is more likely to be aborted. To cope with this, they suggest that when such a popular[5] object is detected, then its page can be made the target of compaction. That is, instead of moving the popular object off of a sparsely populated page, it suffices simply to increase the population density of the page.

Also, abort storms can occur when the collector chooses to move objects that have temporal locality of access by the mutator, so degrading its minimum mutator utilisation because of the need to run an increased number of compare-and-swap operations in a short time. This is unlikely because only objects on sparsely populated pages are moved, so objects allocated close together in time are unlikely all to move together. The probability of correlated aborts can be reduced by breaking the defragmentation into several phases

---

[5]Not to be confused with an object that is the target of many heap references.

Algorithm 19.9: Heap access (while copying) in Staccato using compare-and-swap

```
1  Access(p):
2      r ← forwardingAddress(p)              /* load the forwarding pointer */
3      if r & COPYING = 0
4          return r              /* only use the forwarding pointer if not copying */
5      /* otherwise try to abort the copy */
6      r ← CompareAndSwap(&forwardingAddress(p), r, p)
7      /* failure means collector committed or another aborted so r is good */
8      return r & ~COPYING         /* success means we aborted so clear COPYING bit */
```

to shorten the time window for aborts. Also, the set of pages chosen for defragmentation in each phase can be randomised. Finally, by choosing to run several defragmentation threads at much the same time (though not synchronously, and respecting minimum mutator utilisation requirements), there will be fewer mutator threads running so reducing the likelihood of aborts.

Chicken: best-effort compaction with mutator wait-freedom for x86

Pizlo *et al.* [2008] offer a solution similar to Staccato. *Chicken* (Algorithm 19.10), developed independently, is essentially the same as Staccato, though they assume the stronger memory model of x86/x86-64. This means that only writes need abort a copy (because atomic operations order reads) and that the ragged synchronisations need not perform the read fence. Both Staccato and Chicken support wait-free mutator reads and writes, and wait-free copying at the cost that some copy operations might be aborted by the mutator.

Clover: guaranteed compaction with probabilistic mutator lock-freedom

Pizlo *et al.* describe an alternative approach called *Clover* that relies on probabilistic detection of writes by the mutator to deliver guaranteed copying with lock-free mutator accesses (except in very rare cases) and lock-free copying by the collector. Rather than preventing data races between the collector and the mutator, Clover detects when they occur, and in that rare situation may need to block the mutator until the copying phase has finished. Clover picks a random value α to mark fields that have been copied and assumes that the mutator can never write that value to the heap. To ensure this, the write barrier includes a check on the value being stored and will block the mutator if it attempts to do so.

As the collector copies the contents of the original object to the copy it marks the original fields as copied by overwriting them with the value α using compare-and-swap. Whenever the mutator reads a field and loads the value α it knows that it must reload the up-to-date value of the field via the forwarding pointer (which points to the original if its copy has not been made yet, or the copy if it has). This works even if the true value of the field is α from before the copy phase began.

Whenever the mutator tries to overwrite a field containing the value α, it knows that it must store to the up-to-date location of the field via the forwarding pointer. If the mutator actually tries to store the value α, then it must block until copying ends (so that α no longer means a copied field that must be reloaded via the forwarding pointer). We sketch Clover's collector copying routine and mutator barriers in Algorithm 19.11.

For some types α can be guaranteed not to clash with a proper value: pointers usually have some illegal values that can never be used and floating point numbers can use any

Algorithm 19.10: Copying and mutator barriers (while copying) in Chicken

```
 1  copyObjects(candidates):
 2      for each p in candidates
 3          /* set COPYING bit */
 4          forwardingAddress(p) ← p | COPYING
 5      waitForRaggedSynch()                    /* ensure mutators see COPYING bits */
 6      for each p in candidates
 7          r ← allocate(length(p))                        /* allocate the copy */
 8          move(p, r)                                     /* copy the contents */
 9          forwardingAddress(r)                    /* the copy forwards to itself */
10          /* try to commit the copy */
11          if not CompareAndSet(&forwardingAddress(p), p | COPYING, r)
12              /* the commit failed so deal with it */
13              free(r)                                   /* free the aborted copy */
14              add(aborted, p)                        /* remember the aborts */
15      return aborted
16
17  Read(p, i):
18      r ← forwardingAddress(p)                    /* load the forwarding pointer */
19      return r[i]
20
21  Write(p, i, value):
22      r ← forwardingAddress(p)                    /* load the forwarding pointer */
23      if r & COPYING ≠ 0          /* only use the forwarding pointer if not copying */
24          /* otherwise try to abort the copy */
25          CompareAndSet(&forwardingAddress(p), r, r & ~COPYING)
26          /* failure means collector committed or another aborted */
27          r ← forwardingAddress(p)         /* reload forwardingAddress(p) */
28      r[i] ← value
```

one of the NaN (Not a Number) forms so long as the program never generates them. For other types, α needs to be chosen with care to minimise overlap with values used in the program. To make the chance of overlap virtually impossible, Pizlo *et al.* [2008] offer an innovative solution using a random choice for α. They use the largest width Compare-AndSwapWide available on the processor to assert copying of multiple fields at once. For example, modern x86-64 processors support a 128-bit compare-and-swap, resulting in the infinitesimal chance of overlap of 2^{-128}. Of course, this implies that when testing for α every Read/Write must look at the full aligned 128-bit memory location and extract/insert the value to load/store.

Stopless versus Chicken versus Clover

Pizlo *et al.* compare Chicken and Clover to their earlier Stopless collector as well as to a non-compacting concurrent mark-sweep collector. Qualitatively, Stopless cannot guarantee progress to the collector, because there is a chance that repeated writes to a field in a 'wide' copy may cause copying to be postponed indefinitely. Chicken guarantees progress for the collector, at the expense of aborting some copies. Pizlo *et al.* claim that Clover can

Algorithm 19.11: Copying and mutator barriers (while copying) in Clover

```
 1  copySlot(p, i):
 2      repeat
 3          value ← p[i]
 4          r ← forwardingAddress(p)
 5          r[i] ← value
 6      until CompareAndSet(&p[i], value, α)
 7
 8  Read(p, i):
 9      value ← p[i]
10      if value = α
11          r ← forwardingAddress(p)
12          value ← r[i]
13      return value
14
15  Write(p, i, newValue):
16      if newValue = α
17          sleep until copying ends
18      repeat
19          oldValue ← p[i]
20          if oldValue = α
21              r ← forwardingAddress(p)
22              r[i] ← newValue
23              break
24      until CompareAndSet(&src[i], oldValue, newValue)
```

guarantee collector progress, though in the simple formulation presented here it may stall waiting to install α into a field it is copying while the mutator repeatedly updates the field, causing its compare-and-swap to fail repeatedly.

All three algorithms aim for lock-free heap access, but with subtle differences. Chicken guarantees wait-free access for both reads and writes. Clover and Stopless provide only lock-free writes, and reads require branching. Clover's lock-free writes are only probabilistic, since it is possible that a heap write must be stalled until copying is complete as noted above.

Clover never aborts an object copy. Stopless can abort copying an object in the unlikely situation that two or more mutator threads write to the same field at much the same time during entry into the compaction phase (see Pizlo *et al.* [2007] for details). Chicken is much less careful: any write to an object while it is being copied will force the copy to abort.

Benchmarks comparing these collectors and non-compacting concurrent mark-sweep collection show that throughput is highest for the non-compacting collector (because it has much simpler barriers). The copying collectors install their copying-tailored barriers only during the compaction phase by hot-swapping compiled code at phase changes using the techniques of Arnold and Ryder [2001]. Chicken is fastest (three times slow-down while copying according to Pizlo[6]), though it results in many more copy aborts, followed by Clover (five times slower while copying) and Stopless (ten times slower while copying). All the collectors scale well on a multiprocessor up to six processors. Because of the throughput slow-downs, copying degrades responsiveness to real-time events for both

---

[6]Filip Pizlo, personal communication.

Clover and Stopless. Responsiveness for Chicken is much better because it stays out of the mutator's way by aborting copies quickly when necessary.

Fragmented allocation

The preceding discussion of compaction for real-time systems reveals that any real-time collector relying on defragmentation to ensure space bounds must trade off throughput and responsiveness to real-time events against the level of fragmentation it is willing to tolerate. Wait-freedom of mutator heap accesses was guaranteed only by Chicken/Staccato at the price of aborting some copies. Stopless and Clover offer stronger space guarantees but only with the weaker progress guarantee of lock-freedom for heap accesses. A real-time collector needing hard space bounds may find this tradeoff unacceptable.

For this reason, Siebert has long advocated bounding external fragmentation by allocating all objects in (logically if not physically) discontiguous fixed-size chunks [Siebert, 1998, 2000, 2010], as implemented in his Jamaica virtual machine for real-time Java. Jamaica splits objects into a list of fixed-size *oblets*, with each successive oblet requiring an extra level of indirection to access, starting at the head of the list. This results in linear-time access for object fields, depending on the field index. Similarly, arrays are represented as a binary tree of arraylets arranged into a *trie* data structure [Fredkin, 1960]. Thus, accessing an array element requires a number of indirections logarithmic in the size of the array. The main problem with this scheme is this variable cost of accessing arrays. Worst-case execution time analysis requires knowing (or bounding) statically the size of the array being accessed. However, array size in Java is a dynamic property, so there is no way to prove general bounds for programs in which array size is not known statically. Thus, in the absence of other knowledge, the worst-case access time for trie-based arrays can in general be bounded only by the size of the largest allocated array in the application, or (worse) the size of the heap itself if that bound is unknown.

To solve this problem, Pizlo *et al.* [2010b] marry the spine-based arraylet allocation techniques of Metronome to the fragmented allocation techniques of Jamaica in a system they call *Schism*. By allowing objects and arrays to be allocated as fixed-size fragments, there is no need to worry about external fragmentation. Moreover, both object and array accesses have strong time bounds: indirecting a statically known number (depending on the field offset) of oblets for object accesses, and indirecting through the spine to access the appropriate arraylet for array accesses. To a first order approximation (ignoring cache effects) both operations require constant time. Schism's scheme for allocating fragmented objects and arrays is illustrated in Figure 19.10. An object or array is represented by a 'sentinel' fragment in the heap. Every object or array has a header word for garbage collection and another to encode its type. The sentinel fragment, representing the object or array, contains these and additional header words to encode the remaining structure. All references to an object or array point to its sentinel fragment.

Objects are encoded as a linked list of oblets (Figure 19.10a). An array that fits in a single fragment is encoded as in Figure 19.10b. Arrays requiring multiple arraylet fragments are encoded with a sentinel that refers to a spine that contains pointers to each of the arraylet fragments. The spine can be 'inlined' into the sentinel fragment if it is small enough, as in Figure 19.10c. Otherwise, the spine must be allocated separately. Stilkerich *et al.* [2014] proposed a modification of this scheme that incorporates bidirectional object layouts.

The novelty of Schism is that separately allocated array spines need not be allocated in the object/array space. That space is managed entirely as a set of fixed-size fragments using the allocation techniques of the immix mark-region collector. The 128-byte lines of immix are the oblet and arraylet fragments of Schism. Schism adds fragmented allocation and on-the-fly concurrent marking to immix, using an incremental update Dijkstra-style

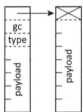
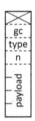

(a) A two-fragment object with a payload of six to twelve words. The sentinel fragment has three header words: a fragmentation pointer to the next object fragment, a garbage collection header and a type header. Each fragment has a header pointing to the next.

(b) A single-fragment array with a payload of up to four words. The sentinel fragment has four header words: a `null` fragmentation pointer, a garbage collection header, a type header and an actual length $n \leq 4$ words, followed by the inlined array fields.

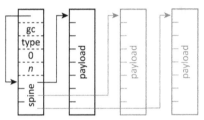

(c) A multi-fragment array with a payload of up to three fragments (up to 24 words). The sentinel fragment has five header words: a non-`null` fragmentation pointer to the inlined array spine, a garbage collection header, a type header, a pseudo-length 0 indicating fragmentation and an actual length $4 < n \leq 24$ words, at negative offsets from the inlined spine. Payload fragments have no headers.

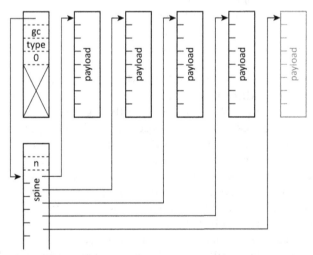

(d) An array with a payload of four or more fragments (more than 24 words). The sentinel fragment has four header words: a non-`null` fragmentation pointer to the separately allocated array spine, a garbage collection header, a type header and a pseudo-length 0 indicating fragmentation, followed by the rest of the sentinel which is unused. The spine has a two-word header: the actual length and a forwarding pointer (at the same negative offsets from the spine as in (c)). Payload fragments have no headers.

Figure 19.10: Fragmented allocation in Schism

Pizlo *et al.* [2010b], doi: 10.1145/1806596.1806615

insertion barrier. The fragments never move, but so long as there are sufficient free fragments available, any array or object can be allocated. Thus, fragmentation is a non-issue, except for the variable-sized array spines.

To bound the fragmentation due to array spines, Schism allocates them in a separately managed space that uses replication copying collection to perform compaction. Because the array spines are immutable (they contain only pointers to arraylet fragments, which never move), there is no problem of dealing with updates to the spines. Indeed, a mutator can use either a fromspace primary spine or tospace replica spine without fear. Moreover, each spine has a reference from at most one array sentinel. When replicating, the reference to the primary from the sentinel can be lazily replaced with a reference to the replica at the collector's leisure, without needing to synchronise with the mutator. Mutators can freely continue to use the spine primary or switch over to using the spine replica when next they load the spine pointer from the sentinel. Once replication of the spines has finished, the fromspace spines can be discarded without needing to fix any other pointers because the tospace spines have only the single reference from their sentinel. A ragged synchronisation of the mutators ensures that they all agree and are no longer in the middle of any heap access that is still using a fromspace spine.

Schism has a number of desirable properties. First, mutator accesses to the heap are wait-free and tightly bounded (costing constant time). Second, fragmentation is strictly controlled. Indeed, Pizlo *et al.* prove that given the number and type of objects and arrays (including their size) in the maximum live set of the program, then total memory needed for the program can be strictly bounded at $1.3104\,b$ where b is the size of the maximum live set. Third, as proposed for Jamaica virtual machine by Siebert [2000], Schism can run with contiguous allocation of arrays (objects are always fragmented) when there is sufficient contiguous space. Contiguous arrays are laid out as in Figure 19.10d, except with the payload extending into successive contiguous fragments. This allows for much faster array access without indirection through the spine. These properties mean that Schism has superior throughput compared to other production real-time collectors, while also being tolerant of fragmentation by switching to fragmented allocation of arrays when contiguous allocation fails. This comes at the cost of some slow-down to access the fragmented arrays. The cost of the read and write barrier machinery to access fragmented arrays is a reduced throughput that is 77% of that for pure concurrent mark-region garbage collection (without the fragmented array access support).

For application developers requiring predictability of the cost for array accesses, Schism can be configured always to use fragmented allocation for arrays at the cost of having to perform spine indirections on all array accesses. The benefit for this is much improved maximum pause times. Since all allocations are performed in terms of fragments, pauses due to allocation are essentially the cost of zero-initialising a 4-kilobyte page in the slow path of allocation — 0.4 milliseconds on a 40-megahertz embedded processor. When allocating arrays contiguously, the allocator must first attempt to locate a contiguous range of fragments, which slows things down enough to cause maximum pauses around a millisecond on that processor.

19.8   Issues to consider

Real-time systems demand precise control over garbage collection to ensure short pauses and predictable minimum mutator utilisation. This chapter has brought together techniques from all the previous chapters in order to achieve these goals. In the absence of parallelism and concurrency, real-time collection is conceptually straightforward so long as collection can be scheduled to preserve adequate responsiveness and performance. Our focus here has been on the real-time collection algorithms themselves, and not so much on how to integrate their schedulability with that of the application. Real-time application developers still need accurate analysis of worst-case execution time to feed into schedulability analyses that will ensure that real-time constraints will be met [Wilhelm *et al.*, 2008].

The literature on real-time systems offers an abundance of guidance on analysis of garbage collected applications for worst-case execution time and schedulability [Kim *et al.*, 2001; Robertz and Henriksson, 2003; Chang and Wellings, 2005, 2006a,b; Chang, 2007; Chang and Wellings, 2010; Cho *et al.*, 2007, 2009; van Assche *et al.*, 2006; Kalibera *et al.*, 2009; Feizabadi and Back, 2005, 2007; Goh *et al.*, 2006; Kim *et al.*, 1999, 2000, 2001; Kim and Shin, 2004; Schoeberl, 2010; Zhao *et al.*, 1987]. Kalibera *et al.* [2011] examined different techniques for scheduling the work of collectors in the context of the Minuteman real-time collection framework, built on top of a real-time Java virtual machine that is compiled to C ahead of time. Choosing the scheduling strategy is a key part of the design of a real-time system. Kalibera *et al.* found that neither slack-based nor time-based scheduling was superior to the other. Although hybrid scheduling such as that of Auerbach *et al.* [2008] is strictly more powerful than time-based scheduling, neither does it subsume slack-based scheduling nor does slack-based scheduling subsume hybrid scheduling. Some workloads were only schedulable with a time-based collector, while others were only schedulable with a slack-based one. However, hybrid scheduling performed best in their experiments.

While we have focused on minimum mutator utilisation as the primary metric for measuring garbage collector responsiveness over time, we note that other metrics may be just as important. Printezis [2006] argues that application-specific metrics are often more appropriate. Consider a periodic real-time task that must deliver a response within a fixed window. From the perspective of this task, minimum mutator utilisation is immaterial, so long as the real-time expectations of that task are met. Moreover, minimum mutator utilisation and maximum pause time may be difficult to account for when the only pauses related to garbage collection that the mutator experiences are those due to executing the non-inlined slow path of a read or write barrier, or the slow path during allocation when the thread's local allocation buffer is exhausted. For some collectors, such as Schism, these are the only collector-related pauses that the mutator will see (assuming collector work can be offloaded to another processor). Should these pauses be charged to the garbage collector? If so, then how can a system account for them? Pizlo *et al.* [2010a] even go so far as to account for these slow paths using specialised hardware for on-device profiling of an embedded processor. To aid developers lacking such specialised hardware, Pizlo *et al.* [2010b] provide a worst-case execution mode for their Schism collector that forces slow path execution so that developers can get some reasonable estimate of worst-case execution times during testing.

Chapter 20

Energy-aware garbage collection

While the vast majority of work on garbage collection has been about improving performance in execution time or possibly in space requirements, the energy consumed by computer systems has become a primary concern. While this may be obvious for systems that run from limited power such as smart phones and unplugged laptops, it is also of concern more broadly as computing consumes an increasingly large share of energy worldwide. Therefore, some researchers have considered the energy consumption of managed systems and in particular the impact of garbage collection.

To first approximation, one would expect that if one collector configuration results in shorter execution time or higher throughput than another, then it consumes less power (energy per unit time). This may often be the case, but given the complexities of modern computer systems, it is far from universally true, because different components consume energy at different rates and also because their energy consumption can be controlled to some extent via such features as dynamic voltage and frequency scaling (DVFS) of processors, lower power modes for selected memory banks and scheduling on processors with different micro-architectures (such as simple in-order versus aggressively superscalar out-of-order). We now turn our attention to analyses of garbage collection energy consumption and approaches to controlling and mitigating it.

First, here is a simplified overview of the causes of energy consumption in processors and memories. Typical processors consist mostly of CMOS (complementary metal-oxide silicon) logic gates. These gates consume power in two basic ways, dynamic and leakage, leading to the power equation $P_{cpu} = P_{dyn} + P_{leak}$. Without going into the physics and electronics in detail, a useful model for dynamic power is $P_{dyn} = a\,CVf^2$, where C is the overall capacitance of the processor (a given, as far as we are concerned), V is the power supply voltage and f is the clock frequency. The constant a has to do with how many bits change value, on average, at each clock cycle, either from 0 to 1 or 1 to 0, which is a function both of processor design and the code being executed, but again essentially a constant for our purposes. For internal devices to have time to acquire enough electric charge during a clock cycle, at higher frequencies f the voltage V must be higher as well. This leads to P_{dyn} scaling more like f^α for some α where $2 < \alpha < 3$. P_{leak}, on the other hand, acts more like a power loss across a resistor and is thus proportional to V but not affected by f. Now we can see why DVFS can be used to control energy consumption: lower voltages and frequencies reduce both P_{dyn} and P_{leak}. Note, though, that *energy* is power over time. Running an algorithm more slowly consumes less power (energy *per unit time*) but may consume more energy overall because the algorithm takes more time.

Moving from processors to memories, memory can be *static* or *dynamic*. Static memory consumes power continuously to maintain the state of each bit. Dynamic memory keeps

465

the state in small capacitors that slowly (compared to computer clock speeds) leak charge. Their bits need to be read periodically and rewritten, called *refreshing*. Static memory bits require more area on an integrated circuit, but they operate much faster. They are typically used for registers and on-chip caches, where speed is critical. Dynamic random access memory (*DRAM*) is typically used for the larger main memory. Dynamic memory draws more power than static memory when idling, because of its refreshing, but both draw substantially more power when accessed. Dynamic memory reads are destructive and require writing back, similar to a refresh cycle. Also a dynamic memory typically reads out many more bits than a single word — though they can be held in a buffer and used to provide results for accesses to nearby locations or larger transfers, often a cache line at a time. Static CMOS memories consume power similarly to the processor, and can be modeled with it. Dynamic memory power can also be modeled with $aCVf^2$ where a will have to do with the number of accesses, and V and f are not as adjustable as the processor is with DVFS. It also has a time-dependent component because of refresh, which plays a role similar to P_{leak} in processors. Detailed DRAM power consumption is affected by many factors concerning the spatial and temporal distribution of accesses, bits flipped in each direction, and so on, but for general understanding we can think of the energy consumption as varying with the number of accesses a and the overall time.

While our discussion here is definitely over-simplified, it helps explain why the total energy consumed by a workload might be higher at very low clock frequencies (leakage and DRAM refresh might dominate) and at very high clock frequencies (because of the dependence of energy consumption on f^α).

Changing collector algorithm. Several researchers have considered how the choice of collection algorithm impacts energy consumption. Velasco *et al.* [2005] characterised energy consumption of five tracing stop-the-world collectors from the JMTk suite of collectors available at the time with Jikes RVM. Their evaluation was conducted by running simulations with *Dynamic Simple Scalar*, an extension of *SimpleScalar* [Austin *et al.*, 2002] that handles dynamic code generation, and using the *CACTI* tool [Shivakumar and Jouppi, 2001] to estimate power consumption. They compared five SPECjvm98 benchmarks under these collectors: *MarkSweep* (non-generational mark-sweep), *SemiSpace* (non-generational semispace copying), *GenCopy* (generational with copying in the old generation), *GenMS* (generational with a semispace nursery and mark-sweep in the old generation) and *CopyMS* (generational where survivors are immediately copied to the old generation and managed by mark-sweep thereafter).

Their findings included: (i) allocation has a significant impact on energy consumption, and sequential allocation via a bump pointer does better than free-list allocation; (ii) L2 cache miss rates also have a significant impact, with CopyMS and GenMS providing the best results in that regard; and (iii) heap size affects which algorithm consumes the least energy, with SemiSpace doing better in larger heaps and worse in smaller ones. With no single technique dominating, these results suggest that managed language implementations might do well to offer choice from several collection algorithms if the goal is to minimise energy consumption.

Griffin *et al.* [2005] considered how to improve energy efficiency in a Java virtual machine designed for embedded devices (such as smart phones). They developed a modified version of Sun's *Kilobyte Virtual Machine* (KVM). KVM employed a simple non-generational mark-compact algorithm, which induces a lot of copying of objects and significant pauses. Their modified collector employed deferred reference counting and used the original mark-compact algorithm as a backup to reclaim cyclic garbage. They further developed two techniques that helped reduce the cost of stack scanning. The first was *frame tagging*, used to help avoid generating stack maps over and over. A stack frame has a tag that can have one of three values: (i) *dirty*, which indicates that the frame's stack map has not been generated; new frames start dirty; (ii) *clean*, which indicates that the frame's stack map has been generated and is available via a pointer in the frame; and (iii) *saved*, which indicates that the frame's referents have had their reference counts incremented in the heap, as if the frame were heap resident. Working from the top (most recently pushed) frame, the tags must obey the order: all dirty before all clean before all saved. Re-entering a clean or saved frame requires reverting it to dirty, and in the case of a saved frame, decrementing reference counts. This can be accomplished with a stack barrier. Frame tagging offered considerable savings and might be applied in other collectors. However, this may have had to do with the more frequent collections required on a device with limited memory.

The second optimisation technique they applied was pointer tagging. In this optimisation, pointers in clean frames that had already been seen in a scan from the oldest clean frame to the newest were tagged by setting a stolen bit. The referents had their reference counts incremented only once, rather than multiple times, helping reduce the number of reference count overflows. This technique could also be applied in other systems.

When objects are reclaimed because of reference count decrements, their space is put onto lists that are searched first when allocating, thus aiming to reuse space before trying to allocate from or near the wilderness. If, after processing deferred reference counts, an allocation request still cannot be satisfied, then adjacent free blocks are coalesced and placed on wilderness lists. If the allocation still cannot be satisfied, the system falls back to the original mark-compact algorithm.

Griffin *et al.* evaluated their collector on six benchmarks and found that it reduced the number of mark-compact collections by 93% to 100%. It also reduced energy consumption, with up to 85% reduction in memory access energy and smaller reductions in execution energy. A three-bit reference count field captured over 99% of the reference counts. It seems that the deferred reference counting approach acted similarly to generational collection in reducing the number of full tracing collections of the heap, similar to experience with the LXR collector.

Hussein *et al.* [2015b] examined concurrent collectors in the Android Dalvik Java virtual machine. They measured energy consumption in an actual system at a high (48,000 per second) sampling rate. The schemes they compared were: Dalvik's usual concurrent mark-sweep (*CMS*); CMS extended to scan thread stacks on-the-fly; generational CMS (*GenCMS*), where mutators may perform young generation collection themselves; GenCMS with all work performed by mutators in the foreground (*GenCMSfg*); and GenCMS with all work performed by a separate collector thread (*GenCMSbg*). Their findings included: (i) increased throughput from using a larger heap does not necessarily result in lower energy consumption, which is related to DVFS decisions; (ii) the GenCMSbg scheme causes increased energy consumption because it induces more context switches and also heap size reductions; and (iii) multithreaded applications benefited in their responsiveness (minimum mutator utilisation) from GenCMSfg collection, but GenMSbg and GenCMS concurrent collectors were better for larger heaps. They suggested that energy consumption could be better managed by controlling when the background collector thread is enabled and by having the heap size adjustment policy integrated with DVFS decision making.

DVFS. Hussein *et al.* [2015a] considered the effect on execution time and energy consumption of applying DVFS to collector threads. Their setting was again the Android Dalvik Java virtual machine platform and its concurrent mark-sweep collector. They measured a live system running DaCapo and specJVM benchmarks. By pinning the collector threads and varying their processors' voltage and frequency, they found they could achieve 30% energy savings at a speed reduction of 10%, about a 20% reduction in energy-delay product (our calculation).

Global coordination. An approach complementary to adjusting the collection algorithm is to use a coordinated central *collection service*. This requires an environment of trust. Hussein *et al.* [2017] examine this approach in the context of the Android Run-Time (ART), which differs from the original Dalvik virtual machine in that it compiles applications to native code when they are installed. It also features a much improved allocator and its collector supports non-moving generational collection. The collection service runs as a separate thread and handles all collection requests when it is running. (The system falls back to having each application collect separately if the service is not running.) When the service receives a request, generally because some thread is running low on memory, it typically chooses to collect the heap of the thread that it judges to have the most garbage. Some of the memory reclaimed can then be given to the original requestor, which may be running in a different heap than the one that was collected. The service applies techniques including trimming the heap with the highest fragmentation first, delaying collection when memory is available, and adjusting individual heap allocation thresholds based on allocation rates rather than static thresholds. To enable this centralised decision making, the service gathers statistics globally (such as available memory), from each process, and from each heap. Additionally, when performing collection the clock frequency of the processor running the collector is capped, to reduce energy consumption. The results they obtained from running selected benchmarks were: 50% fewer collections, 10% reduction in memory required, reduced execution time and energy consumption (each by a few percent) and shorter pause times (order of 10%).

Sartor and Eeckhout [2012] also explored global policies which related to running multithreaded Java programs on multicore processors. Their findings included: (i) isolating the collector threads to particular cores can *increase* execution time by up to 20%; (ii) lowering the clock frequency of cores running collector threads affects performance less than does lowering the frequency of cores running application threads; (iii) on a single socket system, it is best to have the number of application and collector threads be the same, and both be the number of cores on the socket; (iv) on a two socket system, it is best to co-locate application threads and their collector threads, and to have the number of collector threads be half the number of application threads; and (v) pinning threads to specific cores does not always improve performance and sometimes makes things worse.

Asymmetric multicore processors. Given that collector threads often make demands different from those of mutators, asymmetric multicore processors present opportunity to save energy as with DVFS: running the collector on a less capable, slower processor can save substantial energy without slowing down the overall application much. Cao *et al.* [2012] showed that collection is often memory-bound, that is, collector threads' processors are often waiting on memory and do not exhibit as much instruction-level parallelism as do mutators. Hence, the collector does not benefit as much as mutators do from being run on, say, a superscalar out-of-order processor versus a simpler in-order one. Akram *et al.* [2016] considered in more detail when to run collector threads on 'big' (faster, more energy hungry) cores versus 'small' ones. They found that stop-the-world phases benefited from being run on 'big' cores, and that otherwise the critical factor was whether or not the application would end up waiting for the collector to finish. When finishing the collection is on the critical path, it should be run on 'big' cores; otherwise, small cores are fine. They also found that giving the collector threads longer scheduling quanta (a larger share of processor time) compared to mutators helped when collection was on the critical path.

Cache management. There are several impacts of typical collection algorithms on caches and the processor memory subsystem. Consider this common sequence of interaction.

1. Some memory has been used, but becomes unreachable.

2. Because the cache lines for that memory are dirty and have not been used in a long time, the cache writes them back to memory.

3. Some time later, the allocator zeroes the memory when preparing it for a mutator to use.

This pattern of memory use involves two unnecessary interactions with the memory. First, writing the dirty line back is useless to the application since the value in the line will never be looked at again. Second, zeroing the line causes those old contents to be fetched from memory, whereupon they are immediately overwritten with zeroes. While the write back may happen in the background, and thus will not always slow execution down, it does waste energy. The fetch from memory is more likely to slow execution down, and also wastes energy. Sartor *et al.* [2014] considered the possible benefits of providing special cache operations to avoid these costs. They considered these operations.

clinvalidate: directly invalidate a given line at all levels of the cache;

clundirty: clear a given line's dirty bit, making it appear clean, at all levels of the cache;

clclean: clear a given line's dirty bit, making it appear clean, at all levels of the cache, and record it as least recently used (more likely to be dropped from the cache if other data are accessed); and

clzero$k$: zero a given line at level k of the cache.

Note that what some processor descriptions call 'clean' is actually a request to write back a dirty line, not what is desired here. They found that *clinvalidate, clundirty* and *clclean* all reduced write backs to memory. When any of those operations are used along with *clzero2*, then the memory reads for zeroing were also reduced. These reductions improved both execution time and energy consumption. The reason that *clzero2* stood out in their experiments, versus *clzero1* or *clzero3*, is that they zeroed 32 kilobytes at a time, which better matched their L2 cache size. They further found that the best reductions happened when the nursery size matched the cache size. While not all popular processors support these operations, some do offer *clinvalidate* and *clzero*.

Ismail and Suh [2018] considered a different hardware approach, where the application can inform the hardware of ranges of virtual addresses whose data are not needed ('invalid'). Accesses to those addresses supply zero values and remove the addresses from the range of 'invalid' ones. The expected benefits would be similar to those of Sartor *et al.*.

20.1   Issues to consider

Garbage collection has a clear impact on energy consumption. To first approximation, a collector that takes less time (at a given clock speed) does less work and thus tends to consume less energy. Likewise, better locality tends to imply reduced energy consumption. Garbage collection is often more memory bound and often has less available instruction-level parallelism than mutator code. Thus its total energy, or its energy-delay product, may be less at a lower clock speed. Likewise, it is less impacted by being run on a simpler 'small' processor core than on a more complex 'big' one, compared to mutator code. In concurrent collection, if the collector becomes the bottleneck, then reducing its resources may be counter-productive to energy consumption or energy-delay product. Cache management techniques, and careful choice of allocator and of heap sizing should also be considered when tuning for better energy use.

Chapter 21

Persistence and garbage collection

Persistence is the ability of a heap and the objects it contains to outlive the execution of a program.[1] Persistence has a significant literature in programming languages, dating back at least to the 1980s but was largely pushed aside by developments in databases such as object-relational mapping that enabled continued reliance on trusted commercial relational database technologies for persistent storage of application data.[2] The more recent introduction of byte-addressable *non-volatile memory* has renewed interest in persistent programming languages, and thus in collection of persistent heaps. Baldassin *et al.* [2021] offer a useful survey of persistence, to which we are indebted in developing our discussion of the topic. Our purpose here is to focus on issues of garbage collection, not on persistence generally nor on persistent programming languages.

21.1 Persistence: concepts, issues and implementation

As with database management systems, a key challenge with persistence is maintaining the *integrity* of the persistent heap in the face of various kinds of failures. We generally want resistance to corruption of the heap caused by system failures ('crashes'), which we call *resilience*. As we discuss below, this requires careful updating of persistent memory.

It is possible to implement resilience at the granularity of individual updates to the persistent heap, though the overhead may be high. Therefore, many systems support persistence either via occasional *checkpoints* (also called snapshots), likely at times chosen by the application or user of the system, or else by grouping updates into larger batches that achieve useful and logical changes to the heap, that is, transactions.[3]

In addition to resilience to failures, it is helpful for a persistent heap to resist corruption by software defects ('bugs'). Transactions help with that as well, since a software failure in the middle of a transaction can be arranged to cause a transaction abort. Our earlier discussion of transactions concerned their atomicity in the face of concurrency, which we call *concurrency atomicity*. Persistence demands *durability*: heap updates should outlive program execution and survive system failures. Durability leads to the need for *failure atomicity*, the requirement that a transaction's set of changes to the persistent heap either all occur, or none do. This concept applies equally to both checkpointing and transactional

---

[1]This is distinguished from another use of the term 'persistent' in computer science to refer to a data structure that incorporates the history of operations performed on the data structure.

[2]Hence the previous edition of this book made the choice not to explore garbage collection in these languages since they were no longer under much active use or development.

[3]See Section 13.9. While that discussion focuses on transactional memory, the transaction concepts here are the same, with the addition of *durability*.

approaches. It is also important that changes to the persistent heap occur in an order consistent with the order of commits of transactions that conflict with one another, that is, they need to be ordered with respect to each other.

Resilience is always with respect to a *failure model* and *probability of unrecoverable failure*. Consideration of this topic in depth is beyond our scope here. However, a common failure model is *fail-stop*. In this model, a failure cannot cause arbitrary behaviour. Rather, failure causes the system simply to stop, with its volatile state lost and its non-volatile state surviving as is. Persistent systems are often built under this or similar assumptions. We observe that guaranteeing that non-volatile memory state will not be lost is often addressed in hardware, using schemes such as error checking and correcting codes (ECC), spare units of memory within the devices or, for block-oriented devices, redundancy such as mirrored disks or redundant arrays (RAID). Software can apply similar techniques to decrease the likelihood of unrecoverable failure even further. We assume the fail-stop model here and consider the persistent memory to be perfectly reliable, that is, as reliable as the application needs. We will mostly not get into the details, but after a failure a *recovery* procedure may be needed to move the persistent heap to a good state, one in which there are no partial effects of failed transactions or incomplete checkpoints.

Providing durability

The general principle involved in achieving durability is that, when trying to move forward toward the next persistent state, at any moment we must be able either to go back to the previous persistent state, forward to the next persistent state or both. This generally requires maintaining some encoding of both the old and the new state at least until the new state is installed.

Checkpointing. A simple technique for *checkpointing* is to write an entire new copy of the persistent heap. This is typical of some single-user programming environments such as Smalltalk. A more incremental approach is to consider the heap as a collection of disjoint blocks or pages. As the system runs and modifies blocks, it preserves the original blocks, replacing them by updated copies of blocks that are changed. This approach is called *copy-on-write*, and the new mapping is sometimes called a *shadow copy*. This mechanism can be built fairly transparently using page protections in virtual memory. A checkpoint then just records the current mapping of addresses to page (block) contents. Once the updated blocks and map have been recorded in persistent memory, the system writes a separate record indicating that the new checkpoint is complete and thus captures the most recent state of the system.

A possible objection to copy-on-write is that new checkpoints have their pages scattered around the actual persistent memory and addresses require mapping or translation to the actual locations of the data. An alternative approach that avoids this is a *redo log*. In this design, new block versions are written into alternate locations while the system runs, and the updated map is saved, but then the new versions of blocks are copied to where the old versions reside. This can be done in background. It avoids permanent scattering of blocks in persistent memory, but still requires mapping.

A third approach, *undo logging*, overcomes that objection. When a block is about to be modified, the system saves a copy of its contents on the side, in the undo log, and then allow changes to the original copy. This keeps data in their original locations, but requires processing the undo log if there is a failure: the old copies of blocks need to be copied back to the original location. This implies that undo log information must be recorded reliably before the application can modify the original block.

Transactions. While checkpointing typically operates at page or block granularity, *transactions* more often deal with smaller units, such as objects, memory words or granules more the size of cache lines. Durability for transactions can be provided using any of the three methods we enumerated for checkpointing: shadow copies, redo logs or undo logs. A difference is that each running transaction will have its own shadow copy or log, whereas checkpointing is a system-wide notion. In a single-threaded system, the two are very similar in their mechanics, although the API offered to programmers is a little different.

Durable commits. An important detail we have glossed over so far is that part of a transaction commit (checkpoint) is ensuring that all necessary data have been recorded in persistent memory *before* the transaction (checkpoint) is recorded as complete. When dealing with block-oriented devices this involves not only writing the blocks, but waiting for confirmation from the device that it has accepted responsibility for the durability of the writes, and only then writing the record of the commit. If the device can be told to order the writes, then the system may avoid having to wait before sending the commit record.

With byte-addressable non-volatile memory the situation is slightly trickier. Data become durable once written back from the cache to the persistent main memory. Since cache write backs can happen at any time, the system must be careful about the ordering of its memory writes. Also, to guarantee that the contents of given memory words have been made durable, the system may need to write back cache lines explicitly, using instructions such as `clflush`, `clflushopt`, or `clwb` on Intel processors,[4] and employing memory fences to make sure those write backs have happened before performing any further writes that depend on their durability.

For readers interested in delving more deeply into methods of implementing transactions with durability, Gray and Reuter [1993] remains a good resource.

Issues raised by persistence

Persistence adds a new dimension to programming languages, memory management and heaps. Thus it brings a number of new issues. We now describe some of the more significant issues, focusing on those most relevant to garbage collection.

What is persistent? Various systems might persist different parts of the overall system state. Assuming the heap persists, then so do objects and sufficient metadata for using those objects and performing memory management. A system might go further and include types, classes or even code, which may lead to a need to collect those as well. Going even further, threads and stacks might persist. While some of these entities may require special decoding to find references they hold, and perhaps need collection policies suited to their life-times and behaviours, they do not otherwise present difficulty in collection.

Some systems only allow objects of particular types, or specifically designated objects to persist. Another approach is *persistence by reachability*. Usually in that approach certain variables are designated as *persistent roots*, and objects reachable from them become persistent. In either case, collection only demands the ability to enumerate roots and to find and follow edges in the object graph.

Can a program connect to multiple persistent heaps? If a program can connect to more than one persistent heap, then it may wish to create references that point from one heap to another. These probably require special treatment, and imply that garbage collection either

---

[4]If the caches are part of the persistence domain, then write backs are not needed though a fence still is. Such systems are becoming available as of this time of writing.

processes a whole set of interconnected heaps at once, or else applies methods similar to distributed garbage collection, which lie beyond the scope of this handbook.

Is there also a non-persistent heap or region? If a system includes non-persistent regions as well as persistent ones, then issues arise concerning references from one to the other. What does it mean if there is a pointer from the persistent heap to a non-persistent object, and a system failure then occurs? Under persistence by reachability, this should not be allowed, except possibly during the middle of a transaction. Then such objects and the transitive closure of non-persistent objects reachable from them should be moved to the persistent heap, rather like generational copying collection or copying globally reachable objects out of a thread-local heap. Thus a non-persistent region may function similarly to a young generation. This may be helpful in avoiding moving short-lived objects to durable storage. This approach leads to the possibility of barriers for tracking references from persistent to non-persistents objects.

Addressing objects. In non-persistent heaps, objects are usually located either via a direct pointer or by using an object table indexed by some form of object identifier. For a variety of reasons, these simple methods for addressing objects may not meet the needs of a persistent system. However, for purposes of supporting collection, all we need is *some* means of tracing the object graph.

Persistence technology and means of access. There are two fundamentally different ways in which systems provide access to durable (persistent) storage: transferring whole blocks of data and direct access at the byte level. Block-oriented access was the only method available until byte-addressable non-volatile memory came on the market. Block-oriented systems may work directly with files in a file system. In that case, the system itself must deal with the proper ordering of writes to durable storage and forcing writes from buffers to the actual device(s). It must also support means of recovery, such as a write-ahead log. An alternative is to store blocks of bytes in a database management system, or at least to use its transaction processing and storage layer, which makes it easier to build the desired functionality.

Block-oriented persistence incurs some inherent slowdowns. One cause is that data are necessarily copied between memory and durable storage. Depending on the operating system interface, data may be copied *twice*, once between the device and operating system buffers, and again between those buffers and user space. An interface that supports page mapping avoids copying between user space and operating system buffers, but cannot avoid the transfers to and from the device. There is also the overhead of operating system calls. Further, devices that provide durable storage are often themselves slow to access compared with typical computer memories.

Byte-addressable non-volatile memory offers the advantage of fast access without intermediate copying or software layers. In fact, its speed approaches that of volatile memories such as dynamic RAM and tends to offer comparable bandwidth. Its strength of direct access is also a weakness, however. Block-oriented access supports atomic updating of whole blocks and also allows control over when data are written to durable storage. Non-volatile memories and systems currently available guarantee atomic update of word-sized units, but not necessarily anything larger. Also, since a cache between the processor and the non-volatile memory can choose to write back modified data at any time, the only control a system has over such ordering is that it can use cache write-back instructions to force particular data to be written back. Additionally, it can use memory fences to constrain the relative order of writes to the cache, write-backs from the cache to the non-volatile memory, and so on. Another challenge is that data still in the processor and its caches is lost when power is removed.[5]

21.2 Impacts of persistence on garbage collection

There are several significant ways in which persistence impacts the design of a garbage collector: the format of the heap and of the objects it contains, barriers, and interactions with any transaction and crash recovery mechanisms. Additional factors that affect the design include: persistent heaps may be large (possibly larger than a processor's available memory), system failures may occur *during* garbage collection, and various of the issues mentioned above.

Heap design. Ways in which persistence affects the overall design of the heap include:

- There is increased need for the heap to be *self-describing*. For example, a typical design would place a heap in a single file. When a mutator opens the file to connect to the heap, the mutator needs to be able to decode the overall structure of the heap, discover how to allocate new objects (structures describing free memory), how to interpret existing objects, and so on.

- The heap must include one or more persistent roots, where a mutator can start in traversing the object graph. This might include a flat or hierarchical name space, similar to those of file systems.

- The heap must also be interpretable after a crash, perhaps requiring an intervening recovery process by a special recovery tool, or else employing integrated crash recovery. The details depend on the transaction or checkpoint mechanisms, of course. Not only must mutator activity be cleanly recovered, but so must any collector activity. It is desirable that collection be able to complete eventually if crashes are far enough apart to allow some progress.

- Supporting cross-heap references requires going beyond usual heap designs to allow means to describe which heap contains the target object of a cross-heap reference, and the specific target object. These might have semantics more like symbolic links (a name lookup) or more like 'hard' links (a specific address or object identifier).

Barriers and remembered sets. In addition to any read and write barriers required by the collection algorithm, persistence may require load and store barriers to facilitate access to objects in the persistent heap. A load barrier provides additional actions required to be able to locate and access the target object of a reference. It may be combined with read barrier actions where read barriers are necessary. Generally speaking, if load barriers are needed, they are needed in more situations than read barriers are. A store barrier likewise provides actions that help maintain addressability of persistent objects, such as converting a reference from internal to external form before storing it into an object. Further, in order to support transaction semantics, a persistent system may need to track updates to objects, including to non-pointer fields. These are also store barriers, though of a slightly different kind. These barriers do not tend to affect collection algorithms directly. Rather, they need to be incorporated appropriately in collector code that manipulates objects and references.

---

[5]This particular problem can be overcome by providing enough reserve power for these data to be saved, building that functionality into the processor or the operating system, triggered by a power-fail interrupt or similar means. As previously noted, systems are becoming available that support this.

We do note that the possibility of references from persistent to non-persistent objects and vice versa may require additional write barriers, to maintain tables of such references needed to implement persistence by reachability or to fix up references when persistent objects are removed from the address space. Transaction semantics may require remembering or logging objects read and written by a transaction, another case of what can be considered barriers and remembered sets.

21.3   Barriers in support of persistence

We now delve deeper into how barriers support persistence, as useful background when we discuss specific collectors of persistent heaps. As mentioned above, persistent heaps may require load and store barriers to support persistence, apart from or combined with read and write barriers that support collection. Even though these barriers are not intrinsic to collection, we briefly survey them here because they may require integration with the memory manager. The two main approaches to implementing barriers are to exploit hardware support or to use software only.

Software barriers

We begin by describing LOOM, the *Large Object-Oriented Memory*, a design for a Smalltalk system whose heap size could exceed the memory available on its machine [Kaehler and Krasner, 1983; Kaehler, 1986]. Although old, we find it useful to present LOOM because it exemplifies in a clear way mechanisms and techniques for managing a heap of objects larger than a machine's address space (or at least larger than one chooses to load at once). It is thus relevant to the implementation of persistent heaps that are not mapped or loaded in their entirety.

In LOOM, an object is always *accessed* via its object table entry, and is *identified* by its address within the disk file containing the Smalltalk snapshot. When an object is resident, references from other resident objects point to its object table entry. For resident objects that point to non-resident ones, LOOM used two different techniques. One was to provide a proxy for the non-resident object, called a *leaf*. The leaf is marked as such and contains the object identifier to support fetching the object. Once the object is fetched, it replaces the leaf in the object table. The other technique is a specially marked pointer which LOOM calls a *lambda* (in the sense of a null pointer, not in the sense of a lambda expression). In that case the object identifier resides in the disk version of the referring object and that object must be fetched in order to locate the target object. Notice that LOOM supports both specially marked nodes and specially marked edges in the object graph to support object faulting. The conversion between the external form (object identifiers) and internal form (pointers to object table entries) has come to be called *pointer swizzling*.

It is fairly easy to see how the object graph can be faulted into memory incrementally. However, LOOM can also shrink it incrementally. First, the system can write an object back to disk and replace its object table pointer with a pointer to a leaf. Then it can replace pointers to object table entries that refer to the leaf by lambdas, eventually reaching a state where the object table entry can be reused for some other object. The latter step is facilitated by maintaining a reference count on the object table entry. (Note that this is not the same as a reference count on the *object* which would include references from non-resident objects.)

LOOM also maintains 'clean' and 'untouched' bits in object table entries. These allow the system to avoid writing back objects that have not been updated, and to detect which objects have been accessed recently when selecting candidates for eviction. Maintaining these bits is load and store barrier work.

It identifies leaf objects via a designated bit in their object table entry, and lambdas by their specific value (they are object number 0). These properties must be checked in appropriate places, and LOOM uses a number of techniques to reduce the frequency of these checks. Again, this is load and store barrier work.

Another Smalltalk system that extended its heap beyond the computer memory was *Alltalk* [Straw *et al.*, 1989]. Alltalk avoided swizzling, always using the object identifier to access each object, doing so through a hashed object table. In this case the load barrier is the hashed lookup in the object table.

Persistent Smalltalk [Hosking and Moss, 1993a] did not use an object table. It used an analogue of LOOM's leaf objects, called *fault blocks*. The difference is that an object table based system *always* has a level of indirection to access an object. In Persistent Smalltalk, such indirection occurred only in the case of fault blocks, and once the target object was resident, the fault block (called an indirect block in this case) could be bypassed, a step that can be pushed onto the collector. The converse — converting a regular object into a fault block — was easily done since a fault block fits within the space needed by a regular object. Persistent Smalltalk accomplished many of its object residency checks via Smalltalk's message dispatch (method call) mechanism. First, a marked edge, that is, a pointer tagged to indicate that it points to a non-resident object, was detected during the check of low-order tag bits. This check is already necessary since the target object could be a `SmallInteger`, character, boolean or other type, which each have their own low-bit tags. Thus, marked edges simply used a previously unused tag value. Second, a marked node, that is, a fault block, has a 'fake' class arranged to cause an object fault and then forward the original message (call) to the faulted-in target. The same can happen with indirect blocks, skipping the faulting step. Persistent Smalltalk also employed additional techniques to try to bypass indirect blocks more aggressively.

These Smalltalk systems cover a substantial range of the main approaches to supporting persistence in a managed object-oriented language. Similar approaches have been developed for adding persistence to Modula-3 [Hosking and Chen, 1999] and Java [Daynès and Atkinson, 1997; Printezis *et al.*, 1997], among others. Our aim here is a brief introduction to the techniques, so further consideration of persistent programming languages, as opposed to garbage collection for such languages, lies beyond our scope. Likewise we omit details of systems built on top of database managers. For an introduction to that literature see, for example, White and Dewitt [1992] or Amsaleg *et al.* [1994, 1995].

To sum up, barriers in support of *persistence*, as opposed to just for collection, have mainly to do with expanding, shrinking and accessing a resident object graph. Software barriers for persistence may exploit specially marked edges (pointers), nodes (objects) or both in the object graph.

Hardware barriers

The *Texas persistent object store* [Singhal *et al.*, 1992] exemplifies approaches that use standard page trap hardware for persistence barriers. Where LOOM uses software checks for leaves or lambdas, Texas uses a fault handler invoked when protected pages are accessed. Thus, a LOOM leaf object corresponds to a page of objects in Texas. The objects in a leaf page contain references to other objects in an external form. When a leaf page is accessed, the references it contains are swizzled, and updated to point to their resident targets (if the targets are indeed resident) or to leaf pages for non-resident objects. Thus, Texas maintains a mapping table between internal and external forms of object references. It employs techniques analogous to LOOM's to grow and shrink the resident object graph. The virtue of Texas's hardware approach is that C/C++ code could work unmodified except for connecting to the store and accessing the first object.

While Texas does not perform collection, Persistent Smalltalk [Hosking and Moss, 1993a] and *Persistent Modula-3* [Hosking and Chen, 1999], which support page faulting as an alternative to software-only barriers, do, using barrier techniques similar to those of Texas. Hardware approaches that use non-stock hardware are out of scope here.

Software versus hardware barriers

Do software or hardware barriers offer better performance? Hosking and Moss [1993a,b] answered that question for the hardware and software of the time. They concluded, perhaps contrary to intuition, that software barriers could outperform hardware ones. Much has changed in both hardware and software since that time. The time required for an operating system kernel to field a page trap and direct it to a process's signal handler was comparatively long; modern kernels may be faster. At the same time, modern out-of-order processors may be able to perform software barrier work overlapped with other operations, particularly for store and write barriers, which are not on the critical path. Load barrier latency may be harder to hide. This is an area that is technology-dependent, so the best approach is to make careful measurements. It is clear, though, that software barriers have the strong advantage of flexibility. Further, they are amenable to clever compiler optimisations to eliminate them or simplify their code.

21.4   Overview of implemented collectors for persistent heaps

A reasonable question is whether persistent heaps lend themselves more to some collection algorithms than others or, put another way, whether any collection algorithms become practically impossible in the presence of persistence. The answer is that there are implementations of persistent heaps across the full spectrum of collection algorithms. Rather than discuss a large number of systems in detail — a survey that would rapidly become dated — we enumerate various kinds of collectors and offer citations of representative systems. We discuss the collectors of some of these systems in more detail as an introduction to some of the techniques developed to date. We only mention systems targeting non-volatile memory, the focus of current, and likely most future, efforts. Again, the interested reader may find the Baldassin *et al.* [2021] survey helpful in relation to the current state of the art in persistence.

In terms of the basic collection algorithms, reference counting [Coburn *et al.*, 2011; Denny *et al.*, 2016; Memaripour and Swanson, 2018; Hoseinzadeh and Swanson, 2021], mark-sweep [George *et al.*, 2020; Krauter *et al.*, 2021; Lee *et al.*, 2020; Perez *et al.*, 2020], mark-compact [Perez *et al.*, 2020] and copying collection [Krauter *et al.*, 2021; Shull *et al.*, 2019a; Wu *et al.*, 2018] are all represented. The full spectrum of concurrency is also represented, including stop-the-world, parallel and concurrent collection. Furthermore, there are implementations of persistent heaps for a considerable range of programming languages, including C/C++ [Coburn *et al.*, 2011; Denny *et al.*, 2016; Krishnan *et al.*, 2020; Lee *et al.*, 2020], with at least one system supporting persistence by reachability [Guerra *et al.*, 2012], Go [George *et al.*, 2020], Haskell [Krauter *et al.*, 2021], Java [Perez *et al.*, 2020; Shull *et al.*, 2019a; Wu *et al.*, 2018] and Rust [Hoseinzadeh and Swanson, 2021].

Persistent reference counting

Coburn *et al.* [2011] describe the reference counting implementation of their *NV-heaps* system. NV-heaps offers transactions with durability using redo logs for low-level allocation and reference count update operations, and undo logs for other changes to objects during transactions. Each object has two reference counts, one for references from non-volatile objects and one for references from volatile ones. To facilitate and simplify crash recovery, each NV-heap maintains a *generation number*, the number of times the NV-heap has been loaded into memory. The count of references from volatile objects also includes the generation number, and if it does not match the current generation number of the NV-heap, then that count is treated as having value zero. In this way the volatile reference counts are effectively cleared upon crash recovery without any additional work. The reference counts have an associated lock to use when updating the counts. We observe that there are deep similarities between this two-count approach and that of deferred reference counting and biased reference counting, even though their purposes are somewhat different.

Decrementing one reference count can cause a cascade of further decrements and reclaiming of unreachable objects. To make this process more easily recoverable, NV-heaps employs a novel technique whereby, during processing one logged decrement that results in a reference count becoming zero, the system tracks the root object deletion and the current non-root object being deleted. Since successful deletion clears the reference to the deleted object, recovery can simply restart from the root and non-root objects. Coburn *et al.* note that it is possible that some object destructors may be invoked more than once, but say it is generally easy to program around that.

NV-heaps supports weak references using proxy objects, similar to Java's `WeakReference` class. The authors note that some technique for reclaiming cyclic garbage is necessary, and offer weak references as their solution.

NV-heaps was implemented before byte-addressable non-volatile memory was available, so their results relied on simulation. It is also worth noting that they assumed a hardware mechanism called epoch barriers, devised by Condit *et al.* [2009], which has not been implemented to our knowledge. However, alternative means for forcing durability could certainly work with the NV-heaps design. *NVL-C* [Denny *et al.*, 2016] took an approach very similar to that of Coburn *et al.* [2011], so we omit details.

Memaripour and Swanson [2018] describe the *Breeze* system, which also offers reference counting persistence over non-volatile memory. However, they handle persistent reference count updates in an entirely deferred way. As a transaction commits, it records what they call an *activation record*, which details the pointer updates performed by the transaction. Breeze updates the actual reference counts in two phases. Phase 1 examines activation records and determines what the new reference count values should be. It records these changes in a redo log. Phase 2 processes that redo log, making the actual changes. In this way reference count updating is off the main path and performed in the background. It is also recoverable/restartable. Breeze supports weak references.

Hoseinzadeh and Swanson [2021] present *Corundum*, which is integrated with the Rust programming language. Rust already supports reference counting, so extending that to persistent objects is natural for Rust. There is no need to track references from volatile to persistent objects because Rust can prevent their outliving the transaction that created them. Corundum does, however, provide a version of weak references that *can* outlive their creating transaction, but that become null if their referent is reclaimed. The authors do not offer details on the durability mechanisms beyond mentioning journaling, probably using an undo log. To facilitate reclamation of cyclic structures, they provide non-volatile weak references as well as the volatile ones. The overall design seems well integrated with Rust, following its design philosophy well.

Persistent mark-sweep and mark-compact

George *et al.* [2020] presented *go-pmem*, adding persistence to the Go programming language. They employed a breadth-first mark-sweep collector. The system logs allocation metadata, including information about where pointer fields lie within objects. In crash recovery, that log is used to restore the metadata, which resides in volatile memory. Transaction processing uses an undo log. The collector extends the usual Go collector. When tracing the persistent heap, it takes care to trace not only the current target of each pointer in a persistent object, but also pointers in any pending undo log record of a pending transaction. Thus if a transaction replaces the last pointer to an object, that object will be retained, which is necessary if the transaction aborts or the system crashes. Such objects will generally be reclaimed at the following collection.

JaphaVM [Perez *et al.*, 2020] is a modification of *JamVM* [Lougher, 2014]. JaphaVM provides persistence by doing all allocations and updates using the libpmemobj library [libpmemobj], which supports durability with an undo log. JaphaVM considers execution of Java `synchronized` methods to be transactions, and also executes certain Java bytecodes as transactions if they are executed outside of `synchronized` method. Garbage collection is also handled as a transaction, which can be subsumed inside an already running transaction, or can be run asynchronously outside of mutator transactions. The JamVM collector is stop-the-world and can be run in either mark-sweep or mark-compact modes.

Krauter *et al.* [2021] present *Persistent Software Transactional Memory* (PSTM) for the Haskell programming language, building on Haskell's existing software transactional memory support. Access to the persistent heap works somewhat as in LOOM (Section 21.3), except that rather than fetching one object at a time into volatile memory, PSTM fetches the transitive closure of objects reachable from a `PSTVar` (persistent software transaction variable) all at once. This simplifies object 'faulting.' Likewise, transitive closures are written out at transaction commit. Unlike the usual Haskell collector, PSTM uses a modified version of the *Alligator* collector [Gamari and Dietz, 2020] for the old generation, including the persistent heap — a mark-sweep collector. Updates to the persistent heap are made durable using a redo log.

Persistent copying

AutoPersist adds persistence by reachability to Java over byte-addressable non-volatile memory [Shull *et al.*, 2019a]. Its persistence by reachability mechanism works by leaving behind a *forwarding object* for each object moved from volatile to non-volatile memory. This technique requires dynamic forwarding checks. The system applies various techniques to reduce the frequency of checks [Shull *et al.*, 2019b], the details of which lie beyond our scope. However, the collector fixes pointers to bypass such forwarding objects. Moving objects to non-volatile memory occurs within transactions and is not part of the collector itself, though the process of moving does trace a transitive closure of objects, similar to a tracing collection.

AutoPersist's collector does stop-the-world copying collection. It first marks from the persistent roots, to identify those objects that must remain in the persistent heap. It then performs a copying collection, which generally moves reachable volatile objects to volatile tospace and non-volatile objects to non-volatile tospace. However, if it encounters a volatile pointer to a non-volatile object that was *not* marked in the first, marking, pass, it will copy that object to volatile tospace. This can be prevented by setting a special 'requested non-volatile' flag on the object.

AutoPersist implements durability using an undo log and the cache line write-back (`clwb`) and `sfence` instructions available on certain Intel processors.

Wu *et al.* [2018] describe the *Espresso* system that also implements persistent Java using byte-addressable non-volatile memory. They segregate persistent types and objects from volatile ones, not offering persistence by reachability. On the theory that memory management policies for persistent objects should be analogous to those for old generations of volatile heaps, Espresso only offers non-generational collection for the persistent space.

Collection in Espresso proceeds in three phases: (i) mark from persistent roots, saving the mark information in a bitmap; (ii) determine the new location for reachable objects; and (iii) copy the reachable objects to their new locations, carefully. Here is what 'carefully' means. First, before starting to copy objects, save a snapshot of the mark bitmap and the new location information. Second, after each object is copied, the current collection number is written to the header of the old copy of the object. The combination of the snapshot and the collection number timestamp makes copying restartable after a crash. For performance, the persistent space is split into a number of separate regions, which can be copied independently in parallel.

Wu *et al.* [2020a] present a follow-on to Espresso called *GCPersist*. The aim of GCPersist is to reduce the cost of saving objects persistently by doing the copying to durable storage more in bulk, during a collection of the old generation. GCPersist can do this in a way that maintains a single copy of each object, similar to Espresso, or it can maintain a copy also in volatile memory, called snapshot mode. The goal of snapshot mode is to improve speed even further when running using non-volatile memory whose read access time in their system is noticeably slower than that of main memory DRAM. GCPersist does not introduce a new collector implementation so much as put collection and persistence together in a different way. An example application of GCPersist is the building of a read-only or read-mostly collection of data that may take some time to build but will be more static after initial construction.

21.5 Issues to consider

Collection of persistent heaps implemented on byte-addressable non-volatile memory is a relatively new phenomenon. Undoubtedly, new and different ways of integrating durability with automatic memory management will emerge. We offer the following somewhat speculative thoughts.

Overall durability is probably harder to provide and has a larger impact on performance than does garbage collection, so careful design of durability mechanisms may outweigh efficiency of collection. This will likely remain true even if future hardware lowers the cost of durability. Of course garbage collection must 'play well' with the persistence mechanisms, suggesting that strong designs may have each rely on the strengths of the other. Lastly, persistent heaps are likely to be large, suggesting more incrementality, both to spread out collector work and to facilitate recovery after crashes *during* collection. Likewise, large heaps suggest investigating designs that can be parallelised.

Glossary

A comprehensive glossary can also be found at http://www.memorymanagement.org.

ABA problem the inability of certain **atomic** operations to distinguish reading the same value twice from a memory **location** as 'nothing changed' versus some other **thread(s)** changing the value after the first read and then changing it back before the second read

accurate see **type-accurate**

activation record a record that saves the state of computation and the return address of a method, also called a (stack) **frame**

address conventionally, a fixed-length unsigned integer representing the **location** of a datum in **virtual** or **physical memory**

address space a set of **addresses**, physical or virtual, available to the program

age-based collection a **collection** technique that partitions the **heap** into **spaces** by age

aging space a **subspace** of a **generation**, typically the **youngest generation**, into which **objects** are **copied** for a few **collections** before **promoting** them

alignment hardware or **virtual machine** constraints may require that **objects** and **fields** be stored only on certain **address** boundaries

allocation the action of finding a suitable **free cell** and making it available for use

allocation site a location in code that **allocates** a **cell** or **object**

allocator the **memory manager** component responsible for creating (allocating) **objects** (but not initialising them)

ambiguous pointer a value that may or may not be a true **pointer** to an **object**; see **conservative collection**

ambiguous root a **root** that is an **ambiguous pointer**

arbitrary compaction a **compaction** technique that moves **objects** without regard for their original order in memory or any **reference** relationship; see **compaction order**

arraylet a fixed-size **chunk** representing some subset of the **cells** of an array

asymmetric multicore processor a **multicore processor** where the **cores** are heterogeneous, typically in terms of processing power (and energy consumption), though possibly also in their instruction set

atomic the property of a **primitive** operation that it appears to execute indivisibly and instantaneously with respect to other **primitive** operations

atomic add, decrement, exchange and increment primitives that **atomically** modify a memory **location** using the indicated operation; see also **compare-and-swap**, **compare-and-set**, **fetch-and-add**, **fetch-and-or**, **load-linked/store-conditionally** and **test-and-set**

barrier (read, write, etc.) an action (typically a sequence of code emitted by the compiler) mediating access to an **object**; see also **read barrier, write barrier, stack barrier, load barrier** and **store barrier**

belt a set of **increments** used by the Belt-way **collector**

best-fit allocation a **free-list allocation** strategy that places an **object** in a **cell** in the **heap** that most closely matches the **object's** size

big bag of pages allocation (BiBoP) a **segregated-fits allocation** strategy that places **objects** with the same attribute (such as type) in the same **block**, thus allowing the type to be associated with the **block** rather than with individual **objects**

bit stealing using one or more low- or high-order bits of a word to indicate the type or some other attribute of the word's value, such as distinguishing **pointers** from other values or indicating the **space** to which a **tagged pointer** refers

bitmap an array of bits (or often, bytes), each associated with an **object** or **granule**

bitmapped-fits allocation a **sequential fits allocation** strategy that uses a **bitmap** to record the **free granules** in the **heap**

black an **object** is black if the **collector** has finished processing it and considers it to be **live** (and by extension, a **mutator** if it cannot access **white objects**); see also **tri-colour abstraction**

blacklisting an **address** range that has been found to be a target of a **false pointer** may be blacklisted in **conservative collection** to prevent space **leaks**

block an **aligned chunk** of a particular size, usually a power of two

block-based allocation see **big bag of pages allocation**

block-structured heap a **heap** comprised of a set of typically contiguous **blocks** of memory, rather than a single contiguous range of **addresses**

boundary tag structures on the boundaries of **blocks** that assist **coalescing**

bounded mutator utilisation (BMU) the **minimum mutator utilisation** observed for a given time window or any larger one; **BMU** is monotonically increasing, whereas **MMU** is not

branch predictor a unit in the CPU that tries to predict the target of each branch in order to avoid stalls in the instruction pipeline

breadth-first traversal a **traversal** of the **object** graph in which an **object's** siblings are visited before its descendants (**referents**)

break table a table of **forwarding addresses** placed by a **mark-compact collector** in the break between already moved and yet to be moved **objects**

bucket a **subspace** used to segregate **objects** by age *within* a **step**

bucket brigade an approach to **generational collection** using **buckets**

buddy system a **segregated-fits allocation** strategy that **allocates blocks**, typically in power of two sizes to allow easy **splitting** and **coalescing**; see also **Fibonacci buddy system**

buffered reference counting a form of **reference counting** in which **mutators** buffer **reference counting** operations and subsequently send them for execution to the **collector**

bump pointer allocation see **sequential allocation**

byte map see **bitmap**

cache a fast memory which stores copies of data from frequently accessed memory **locations**

cache block see **cache line**

cache coherence the degree to which two or more **caches** agree on the contents of memory

cache hit a memory access that finds its containing **cache line** in the **cache**

cache line the unit of memory that can be transferred between the **cache** and memory

cache miss a memory access that does not find its containing **cache line** in the **cache**

call stack a **stack** holding the **stack frames** (also called **activation records**) of the methods being executed by a **thread**

car (1) the unit of **collection** in the Mature Object Space ('Train') **collector**; (2) the word in a **cons cell** that holds or points to the list element, from 'Content of the Address part of the Register' referring to an early Lisp implementation

card a small, power of two sized and **aligned** area of the **heap**

card marking a technique used by the **mutator** to record the source of **pointers** of interest to the **collector**; the **write barrier** updates a **card** table

causal consistency a store A is said to *causally precede* another store B if the **process** performing store B observed store A before performing store B; a system is *causally consistent* if whenever some store A causally precedes another store B, all **processes** must observe A and B in that order

cdr the word in a **cons cell** that holds or points to the next **cons cell** in the list, from 'Content of the Decrement part of the Register' referring to an early Lisp implementation

cell a contiguous group of **granules**, which may be **allocated** or **free**, or even wasted or unusable

channel a single-reader, single-writer communication mechanism, for example, between two **threads**

checkpoint a **persistent** record of the state of a **heap** at a moment in time

Cheney scanning a technique used with **copying collection** for **tracing** live **objects** without using a **stack**

chip multiprocessor (CMP) a **multiprocessor** that has more than one **processor** on a single integrated circuit chip; see also **multicore processor** and **many-core processor**

chunk a large contiguous group of **granules**

circular first-fit allocation see **next-fit allocation**

class loader An **object** responsible for locating and loading classes, usually on demand

closure a record consisting of a function and bindings (values) for one or more of the variables it uses; see also **thunk**

coalesced reference counting a form of **buffered reference counting** that avoids applying redundant **reference count** operations

coalescing recombining adjacent free **cells** into a single **cell**; see also **segregated-fits allocation**

coherence protocol a **cache** management protocol for maintaining some memory **consistency model**

collection a single instance of executing a **collector**; typically this instance will **reclaim** at least all **objects** in the **space** being collected that were **dead** at the time that the **collector** was called

collection cycle a complete execution of the **collector**

collector a system component responsible for **garbage collection**

compacting relocating **marked (live) objects** and updating the **pointer** values of all **live references** to **objects** that have moved; its purpose is to eliminate **external fragmentation**

compaction order the order in which a **compacting collector** rearranges **objects**; this may be **arbitrary**, **linearising** or **sliding**

compare-and-set an **atomic** instruction that compares a memory **location** to an expected value old, and if the **location's** value equals old, sets the value to new. In either case it indicates whether or not it updated the memory **location**; see also **atomic**

compare-and-swap (also called compare-and-exchange) like **compare-and-set** but returns the value of the memory **location** observed before any update rather than returning a boolean truth value; see also **atomic**

completeness the property of a **collector** that guarantees to **reclaim** all **garbage**

eventually; for example, **reference counting** is not complete because it cannot **reclaim cycles** of **dead objects**

compute unit OpenCL term for a set of **processing elements** in a GPU along with other elements such as an instruction decoder, instruction **cache** and data **caches** or memory shared by its **processing elements**; called a *streaming multiprocessor* on CUDA or a *subslice* on Intel

concurrent collection execution of the **garbage collector** concurrently with execution of **mutator threads**

condemned space the **space** or **subspace** chosen to be **collected**, typically by **evacuating** its **live** contents to another **space**

connectivity-based (garbage) collection a **collection** technique that partitions the **heap** into **spaces** based on connectivity

cons cell a double-word **cell** used by Lisp for storing the spine of a list

conservative collection a technique for **collection** that receives no assistance from a language's compiler or **run-time system** and so must make over-estimates of the set of **live objects**

consistency model a specification of how the memory system will appear to the programmer, placing restrictions on the values that can be returned by a read in a shared-memory program execution

copy reserve a **space** reserved as a target for **copying** in **copying collection**

copying see **evacuating**

copying collection collection that **evacuates live objects** from one **semispace** to another (after which, the space occupied by the former can be **reclaimed**)

core (1) a **processor** of a **multicore** or **many-core processor**; (2) the main memory of a system, even though magnetic cores are no longer used

creation space see **nursery**

critical section a section of code in which a thread manipulates a shared resource; see also **mutual exclusion**

crossing map a map that decodes how **objects** span areas (typically **cards**)

cyclic data structure a self-referential data structure

dangling pointer a **pointer** to an **object** that has been **reclaimed** by the **memory manager**

dead an **object** is dead if it cannot be accessed at any time in the future execution of the **mutator**, usually approximated by the **object's** being **unreachable**

deallocation the action of freeing an **allocated cell**

deferred reference counting a **reference counting** scheme in which some **reference count** operations (typically those on local variables) are deferred to a later time

deletion barrier a **write barrier** that detects the removal of a **reference**; see also **snapshot-at-the-beginning**

dependent load a load from a memory **location** whose **address** depends on the result of a prior load

depth-first traversal a **traversal** of the **object** graph in which an **object's** descendants (**referents**) are visited before its siblings

derived pointer a **pointer** obtained by adding an offset to an **object** reference

direct collection a **collection** algorithm that determines whether an **object** is **live** simply from that **object** itself, in contrast to **indirect collection**; an example is **reference counting**, particularly **eager reference counting**

discrete GPU a card dedicated to the **GPU**, in contrast to an **integrated GPU**

disentangled a property of a hierarchy of **heaplets** in which an **object** may only **reference** another **object** if it is in the same **heaplet** or in an ancestor **heaplet**; thus, **heaplets** cannot contain down-**pointers** or cross-**pointers**

double mapping a technique that maps the same **physical page** at two different **virtual addresses** with different protections

double-ended queue (deque) a data structure allowing adding to and removing from both the front (head) and back (tail)

durability the ability of changes to a **persistent heap** to survive failures and outlive the execution of a program

dynamic voltage and frequency scaling (DVFS) adjusting the voltage and clock frequency of a **processor** while it runs, typically to control the tradeoff between speed and energy consumed

eager reference counting an eager **reference counting memory manager** applies **reference count** increments and decrements immediately, rather than deferring them; see also **buffered reference counting, coalesced reference counting, deferred reference counting, lazy reference counting**

eager sweeping sweeping immediately as opposed to **lazy sweeping**

eden see **nursery**

en masse promotion generational collection scheme in which all **survivors** of a **minor collection** are **promoted**

epoch a period of execution of a **reference counting collector** during which synchronised operations can be eliminated or replaced by unsynchronised operations

escape analysis an analysis (usually static) that determines whether an **object** may become **reachable** from outside the method or **thread** that created it

evacuating moving an **object** from a **condemned space** to its new **location** (in **to-space**); see **copying collection** and **mark-compact collection**

explicit deallocation the action of **deallocation** under the control of the programmer, rather than automatically

external fragmentation space wasted outside any **cell**; see also **internal fragmentation**

false pointer a value that was falsely assumed to be a **pointer** to an **object**; see **conservative collection**

false sharing the coincidence of different **processors** accessing different memory **locations** that happen to lie in the same **cache line**, resulting in increased **cache coherence** traffic

fast (slow) path most **memory managers** take care to optimise the common case (fast path) for **allocation** or **barriers**; the fast path is typically inlined code with the less common case (slow path) handled with a procedure call

fast-fits allocation a **sequential fits allocation** strategy that uses an index to search for the first or next **cell** that satisfies the **allocation** request

fat pointer a **pointer** that also holds additional **metadata**, for example, a version number

fence see **memory fence**

fetch-and-add and fetch-and-or (also called exchange-and-add) an **atomic** instruction that **atomically** increments the value of a **location** by a specified value (fetch-and-add), or performs a logical or of the value of the **location** with a specified value (fetch-and-or), and returns the **location's** original value; see also **atomic**

Fibonacci buddy system a **buddy system** in which the **size classes** form a Fibonacci sequence

field a component of an **object** holding a **reference** or **scalar** value

filler object a pseudo-**object** allocated in the gaps between real **objects** to support **heap parsability**

finalisation an action performed on an **object** when it is determined to be no longer **reachable**

finaliser a method that runs when the **collector** determines that the **object** is no longer **reachable**

first-fit allocation a **free-list allocation** strategy that places an **object** in the first **cell** in the **heap** that can contain the **object**

first-in, first-out (FIFO) see **queue**

flip the swapping of **fromspace** and **tospace** in **copying collection** at the start of a **collection cycle**

floating garbage garbage that was not reclaimed in a previous **collection cycle**

footprint (memory) the volume of memory that a program uses while running

forward (1) cause **mutators** to refer to the **tospace** copy of an **object**; (2) insert a **forwarding address**

forwarding address the **address** to which an **object** has been **evacuated** (stored in the **fromspace** object's **header** or in side metadata)

fragmentation the inability to use **free** memory because of the arrangement of **objects**; see also **internal fragmentation** and **external fragmentation**

frame (1) a power of two sized and **aligned chunk** (typically a discontiguous **space** comprises a number of frames); (2) see **activation record**

free the state of a **cell** that is available for reallocation; see also **reclaim**

free pointer a **pointer** to the **free granules** of a **chunk**; see **sequential allocation**

free-list allocation a **sequential fits allocation** strategy that uses a data structure to record the **location** and size of **free cells**

fromspace the **semispace** from which **copying collection** copies objects

fromspace invariant the invariant that the **mutator** holds only **fromspace references**

garbage an **object** that is not **live** but whose space has not been **reclaimed**

garbage collection (GC) an automatic approach to **memory management** that reclaims memory occupied by **objects** that are no longer in use by the program (**mutator**)

garbage collector see **collector**

GC check-point a point in **mutator** code that may trigger **garbage collection**, but where **collection** would not otherwise be triggered, such as a branch that closes a

loop; every **GC check-point** must be a **GC safe-point**, but not necessarily vice versa

GC-point see **GC safe-point**

GC safe-point a point in the **mutator** code at which it is safe for **garbage collection** to occur, although a **collection** might or might not actually be triggered here on a given occasion; certain points in code, such as **allocations** or where a **thread** might suspend, *must* be **GC safe-points**

generation a **space** characterised by the age of the **objects** it contains

generational collection **collection** that segregates **objects** by age into **generations** and preferentially collects the **youngest generation**

generational hypothesis a hypothesis that **object** lifetime is correlated with age; see also **weak generational hypothesis** and **strong generational hypothesis**

gibibyte (GiB) standard usage unit meaning 2^{30} bytes; see also **gigabyte**

gigabyte (GB) common usage unit meaning 2^{30} bytes; see also **gibibyte**

globalise in a **thread**-local **collector**, the action of making a local **object** accessible to other **threads**, typically by copying it from a **thread**-local **heaplet** to the shared, global **heap**

granule the smallest unit of **allocation**, say a word or a double-word

graphics processing unit (GPU) a specialised **processor** with a large number of **cores**, originally designed to accelerate 3D graphics but now also widely used to accelerate workloads in high performance computing, deep learning and other applications

grey an **object** is grey if the **collector** has determined that it is **reachable** but has not yet finished processing it (and by extension, a **mutator** if it may access **white** objects); see also **tricolour abstraction**

grey packet a unit of **collector** work used for **load balancing** that contains a fixed number of **grey objects** for a **collector** to process; see also **tricolour abstraction**

guard page a **page** mapped with no-access protection so as to cause a trap when accessing beyond an allowed limit, thus avoiding the need for an explicit range limit check

handle a structure holding a **reference** to an **object**, and optionally additional status information; typically, a handle is not moved by the **collector** whereas its target **object** might be

handshake a protocol for **mutator** and **collector threads** to **rendezvous** at **garbage collection phase** boundaries

happens-before a requirement on the order in which operations occur on memory

hard real-time system a **real-time system** in which all deadlines must be met within a strict bound; missing a deadline is a critical system failure

header a part of an **object** used to store **metadata** used by the **run-time system**

headroom additional space for **allocation** required to avoid **thrashing tracing collectors** and those **reference counting collectors** that do not **reclaim garbage** immediately

heap a data structure in which **objects** may be **allocated** or **deallocated** in any order, independent of the lifetime of the method invocation that created them

heap allocation **allocation** of an **object** in the **heap**

heap parsability the capability to advance through the **heap** from one **object** to the next

heap reference graph a compact representation of the **heap**, typically intended to be better suited to processing by a **GPU**

heaplet a subset of the **heap** containing **objects** accessible to only a single **thread**

hyperthreading see **simultaneous multithreading**

immediacy the degree to which a **collector** reclaims garbage shortly after it dies; related to **promptness**

immutable data that does not change, in constrast to **mutable** data

increment (1) a unit of **collection** in the Beltway **collector**; (2) see **incremental collection**

incremental collection **collection** in which the **mutator** performs small quanta of **collection** work interlaced with its own work; see also **concurrent collection**

incremental update a technique for solving the **lost object problem** that informs the **collector** of incremental changes made by the **mutator** to the set of **objects** known to be **live**

incremental update barrier see **insertion barrier**

indirect collection a **collection** algorithm that does not detect **garbage** per se, but rather identifies all **live objects** and then concludes that anything else must be garbage

insertion barrier a **write barrier** that detects the insertion of a **reference**; see also **incremental update**

integrated GPU a system where the **GPU** is built onto the same die as the CPU, in contrast to a **discrete GPU**

interior pointer a **derived pointer** to a **field** of an **object**

internal fragmentation space wasted inside a **cell**, for example due to rounding up requested sizes; see also **external fragmentation**

JVM a **virtual machine** for the Java language

kernel (1) a procedure executed on the **GPU**; (2) the privileged controlling code of the operating system

kibibyte (KiB) standard usage unit meaning 2^{10} bytes; see also **kilobyte**

kilobyte (KB) common usage unit meaning 2^{10} bytes; see also **kibibyte**

large object space (LOS) a **space** reserved for **objects** larger than a given threshold, and typically managed by a non-moving **collector**

last-in, first-out (LIFO) see **stack**

latency the delay from the start of some action to its completion, typically from a request delivered to an application until the application's response

lazy reference counting deferring **freeing** of **objects** with **reference counts** of zero until they are subsequently acquired by the **allocator**, at which point their children can be processed

lazy sweeping **sweeping** only on demand (when fresh space is required)

leak see **memory leak**

limit pointer a pointer to the end of a **chunk**; see **sequential allocation**

line an **aligned chunk** used by the immix **collector** and its relatives, roughly sized to match the architecture's **cache line**

linear allocation see **sequential allocation**

linearisable an execution history of concurrent operations that appear to execute serially in some non-overlapped way, where if two operations do not overlap in the history then they must appear to happen in the order they were invoked

linearisation point the point in time at which an operation in a **linearisable** history appears instantaneously to occur

linearising compaction a **compaction** technique that attempts to place **objects** next to those that they **reference**; see **compaction order**

live an **object** is live if it could be accessed at some time in the future execution of the **mutator**; usually this is approximated by the **object's** being **reachable**

livelock a situation in which two (or more) competing **threads** prevent progress of the other(s) indefinitely

liveness (1) the property of an **object** that it will be accessed at some time in the future execution of the **mutator**; (2) the property

of a (**concurrent** or **incremental**) **collector** that it eventually completes its **collection cycle**

load balancing distributing work across available hardware resources in a way that minimises the coordination necessary yet keeps all **processors** as busy as possible

load barrier (also called a loaded value barrier) a **barrier** on loads by the **mutator** and possibly the **collector**, distinguished by the fact action may be taken with respect to the value or **reference** being loaded rather than the **reference** being used; a load barrier may be concerned with low-level **reference** encoding, with properties such as the space in which the **referent** lies, or with both

load-linked/store-conditionally (also called load-and-reserve/store-conditional or load-exclusive/store-exclusive) **atomic** instruction pair that first reserves a **location** and then updates it only if the **processor's coherence protocol** confirms that its value has not been changed since the reservation was made; see also **atomic**

loaded value barrier (LVB) see **load barrier**

local allocation buffer (LAB) a **chunk** of memory used for **allocation** by a single **thread**

locality the degree to which items (**fields**, **objects**) are accessed together in space or time; see also **spatial locality** and **temporal locality**

location an addressable unit of memory, having a unique **address**

lock a synchronisation mechanism for controlling access to a resource by multiple concurrent **threads**; usually only one **thread** at a time can hold the lock, while all other **threads** must wait

lock-free a guarantee of system-wide progress, although individual **threads** may fail to make progress; implies **obstruction-free**; see also **non-blocking**

log (1) a record, often sequential, related to changes made to a data structure, such as a **persistent heap**; see also **redo log** and **undo log**; (2) a record related to **remembered sets**, **buffered reference counting** and so on

lost object problem a situation that can arise when interleaved execution results in the **mutator's** hiding **references** from the **collector** so that the **collector** erroneously **reclaims live objects**

major collection collection of both the **old generation** and **young generation**; see also **generational collection**

malloc a function in the C standard library that **allocates** memory in the **heap**

managed code application code running on a **managed run-time**

managed language a programming language that has a **managed run-time** that supports **managed code**

managed run-time a **run-time system** that provides services such as automatic **memory management**

many-core processor a kind of **multiprocessor** that has a large number of **processors** on a single integrated circuit chip; sometimes distinguished from a **multicore processor** in that the **cores** of a **many-core processor** are smaller and simpler

mark bit a bit (stored in the **object's header** or on the side in a mark **bitmap**) recording whether an **object** is **live**

mark stack (or queue) a stack (or queue) used as the work list for the **marking** process

mark-compact collection a **tracing collection** that typically operates in three or more **phases**, first **marking** all **live objects** and then **compacting** these **objects** and updating **references** to them to eliminate **fragmentation**

mark-region collection **marking** both **objects** and **lines**, used by the immix **collector**

mark-sweep collection a **tracing collection** that typically operates in two **phases**, first

marking all live **objects** and then **sweeping** through the **heap**, **reclaiming** the storage of all **unmarked**, and hence **dead**, **objects**

mark/cons ratio a common **garbage collection** metric that compares the amount of work done by the **collector** ('marking') with the amount of **allocation** ('consing') done; see **cons cell**

marking recording that an **object** is **live**, often by setting a **mark bit**

mature object space (MOS) a **space** reserved for older (mature) **objects** managed without respect to their age in the Mature Object Space **collector**

mebibyte (MiB) standard usage unit meaning 2^{20} bytes; see also **megabyte**

megabyte (MB) common usage unit meaning 2^{20} bytes; see also **mebibyte**

memory fence an operation on a **processor** that prevents certain reorderings of memory accesses

memory leak a failure to **reclaim** memory that is no longer in use by the program

memory manager component responsible for **allocating** and **reclaiming** memory

memory order the order of writes (and reads) to multiple memory **locations** at **caches** or memories, and thus as perceived by other **processors**; see also **program order**

memory protection keys a hardware feature that associates additional memory protection restrictions with chosen **pages** of memory under programmer control

meta-object an **object** that describes another **object**, typically providing information on the layout of **fields**

metadata data used by the **virtual machine** or **memory manager** but not part of the running application

minimum mutator utilisation (MMU) the minimum **mutator utilisation** for a given time window

minor collection collection of only the **young generation** or **nursery**; see also **generational collection**

mmap a Unix system call that creates a mapping for a range of **virtual addresses**

mostly-concurrent collection a technique for **concurrent collection** that may pause *all* **mutator threads** briefly

mostly-copying collection a technique for **copying collection** that **copies** most **objects** but does not move others (because of **pinning**)

moving collection any **collection** technique that moves **objects**

multi-tasking virtual machine a **virtual machine** that runs several applications (**tasks**) within a single invocation of the **virtual machine**

multicore processor see **chip multiprocessor** and **many-core processor**

multiprocessor a computer that provides more than one **processor**

multiprogramming the execution of multiple **processes** or **threads** on a single **processor**

multitasking the execution of multiple **tasks** on a single **processor**

multithreading the execution of multiple **threads** on one or more **processors**

mutable data that may be changed, in constrast to **immutable**

mutator the user program, so called because from the **collector's** point of view it simply mutates the graph of **objects**

mutator utilisation the fraction of **CPU** time used by the **mutator**, as opposed to the **collector**

mutual exclusion an approach to avoiding concurrent use of a shared resource; see also **critical section**

nepotism the situation where a **dead object** in an **uncollected space** preserves an otherwise **dead object** in the **condemned space**

newspace the **space** in which **objects** are allocated

next-fit allocation a **free-list allocation** strategy that places an **object** in the next

cell in the **heap** that can contain the **object**

node see **object**

non-blocking a guarantee that **threads** competing for a shared resource do not have their execution delayed indefinitely; see also **obstruction-free**, **lock-free**, **wait-free**

non-uniform memory access (NUMA) a **multiprocessor** in which a shared memory unit is associated with each **processor**, giving that **processor** faster access to that memory unit

non-volatile memory (1) memory whose state is not **volatile**, that is, which is retained without application of external power; (2) more specifically, non-volatile byte-addressable main memory, as opposed to external memory accessed via block transfer

Not-Marked-Through (NMT) a state of a **reference** indicating that it has not been **traced** through by the Pauseless/C4 **collector** to assure that its target **object** has been **marked**

null a distinguished reference value that does not refer to any **object**

nursery a **space** in which **objects** are created, typically by a **generational collector**

object a **cell allocated** for use by the application

object inlining an optimisation technique that replaces a **reference** to a unique **object** with that **object's fields**; see also **scalar replacement**

object table a table of **handles**, which refer to **objects**

oblet a fixed-size **chunk** representing some subset of the **cells** of an **object**

obstruction-free a guarantee that at any point, a single **thread** executed in isolation (that is, with all obstructing **threads** suspended) will complete its operation within a bounded number of steps; see also **non-blocking**

old generation a **space** into which **objects** are **promoted** or **tenured**

on-stack replacement a technique for re-placing a method's code with new code while it still has active invocations

on-the-fly collection a technique for **concurrent collection** that stops **mutator threads** at most one at a time

padding extra space inserted by the **allocator** to meet **alignment** constraints

page a **block** of **virtual memory**

paging the transfer of memory in a **virtual memory** system between main memory and secondary storage (also called swapping); if overly active, called **thrashing**

parallel collection use of multiple **processors** or **threads** to perform **collection**; not to be confused with **concurrent collection**

partial tracing **tracing** only a subset of the graph of **objects**; typically used to refer to a **trial deletion** algorithm that **traces** a subgraph that is suspected of being **garbage**

pause time the time during which **mutators** are halted while **stop-the-world collection** runs

persistence the ability of a **heap** and of **objects** within it to outlive the execution of a program

persistence by reachability **persistence** of **objects** by **reachability** from **persistent roots**

persistent root a **root** whose **transitive closure** is made to **persist**

phantom reference in Java, the weakest kind of **reference**; phantom references are typically used for scheduling cleanup actions more flexibly than is possible with **finalisation**

phase a part of a **collection cycle** that does particular work or expects or establishes particular invariants

physical memory the memory that is actually available on a given machine; see also **virtual memory**

pinning (1) preventing a **collector** from moving a particular **object** (typically because it is accessible to code that is not

collector-aware); (2) forcing a particular **thread** to run on a particular **core**

pointer a value that is an **address** in memory, typically of an **object**

pointer field a **field** that contains a **pointer** to another **object**

pointer swizzling The conversion of an **object reference** between its internal and external form

prefetching fetching a value into the **cache** earlier than it would naturally be fetched

prefetching on grey fetching the first **cache line** of an **object** when that **object** is marked **grey**

pretenuring allocating an **object** directly into an **old generation**

primitive (instruction) an instruction directly executable by a hardware **processor**

process an instance of a computer program that is executing within its own **address space**; a process may comprise multiple **threads** executing concurrently

processing element OpenCL term for an Arithmetic-Logic Unit (ALU) on which **work-items** execute; the CUDA term is *streaming processor*

processor (CPU) a unit of hardware that executes (**primitive**) machine instructions

program order the order of writes (and reads) to multiple memory **locations** as they appear to be executed in the program's machine code; see also **memory order**

prolific type an **object** type having many instantiations

promote move an **object** into an **old generation** in a **generational collector** or to an ancestor **heaplet** in a **thread**-local **collector**

promptness the degree to which a **collector** **reclaims** all **garbage** at each **collection cycle**; related to **immediacy**

queue a **first-in, first-out** data structure, allowing adding to the back (tail) and removing from the front (head)

ragged handshake a **handshake** that is performed with each **mutator** independently as opposed to stopping all **mutators** for a **handshake** at the same time

raw pointer a plain **pointer** (in contrast to a **smart pointer**)

reachable the property of an **object** that it can be accessed by following a chain of **references** from a set of **mutator roots**; typically used as a safe approximation to **live**

read barrier a **barrier** on **reference** loads by the **mutator**

real-time (garbage) collection a technique for **concurrent** or **incremental collection** supporting a **real-time system**

real-time system a hardware or software system that is subject to deadlines from event to system response

reclaim return storage occupied by an **object** to the **memory manager** for reuse

recursion if this is not clear, see **recursion**

redo log a record of changes made to a data structure allowing a system to push the data structure forward to a new state; see also **log** and **undo log**

reference the canonical **pointer** used to identify an **object**

reference count a count of the number of **references** that point to an **object**, typically stored in the **object's header**

reference counting a direct collection scheme that manages **objects** by maintaining a count of the number of **references** to each **object**

reference listing a direct collection scheme that manages **objects** by maintaining a list rather than a count of **references** to each **object**

referent the target of a **reference**

referentially transparent an expression is called referentially transparent if it can be replaced with its corresponding value (and vice versa) without changing the program's behaviour; this requires that the expression be pure: its value must depend only on its inputs and its evaluation must have no side effects

referrer set the set of **locations** that point to a particular **object**, notably used in the Collie **collector**

region (1) a **space** visible to and managed by the programmer or (typically inferred automatically by the) compiler in a region-based system; a region can typically be made **free** in constant time; (2) a set of usually contiguous **addresses**, often power-of-two **aligned**, that are treated in the same way by a **collector**, at least during a given **collection**

region inferencing a static analysis that determines the **region** into which to place an **object** in a **region**-based **memory management** scheme

register a quickly accessible location provided by a **processor**, usually not addressable with a memory **address**

relaxed consistency a **consistency model** that is weaker than **sequential consistency**

release consistency a **consistency model** in which acquire operations prevent later accesses from occurring before the acquire, but earlier accesses can happen after the acquire, and release operations prevent earlier accesses from happening after the release but later accesses can happen before the release

remembered set (remset) a set of **objects** or **fields** that the **collector** must process; typically, **mutators** supported by **generational**, **concurrent** or **incremental collection** add entries to the remembered set as they create **pointers** of interest to the **collector**

remset see **remembered set**

rendezvous barrier a code point at which each **thread** waits until all other **threads** have reached that point

replica (in a **copying collector**) the **copy** in **tospace** of a **fromspace object**, or vice versa

replicating collection a technique for **concurrent copying collection** that maintains two (or more) **copies** of **live objects**

resilience the ability of a system to survive failures ('crashes')

restricted deque a **double-ended queue** where one of the actions of adding or removing is allowed at only one end of the queue

resurrection an action performed by a **finaliser** that causes the previously **unreachable object** to become **reachable**

root a **reference** that is *directly* accessible to the **mutator** without going through other **objects**

root object an **object** in the **heap** referred to directly by a **root**

run-time system the code that supports the execution of a program, providing services such as **memory management** and **thread** scheduling

safety the property of a **collector** that it never **reclaims** a **live object**

scalar a non-**reference** value

scalar field a **field** that contains a **scalar** value

scalar replacement an optimisation technique that replaces a **reference** to a unique **object** with local variables representing its **fields**; see also **object inlining**

scan pointer a **pointer** to the next **location** to be **scanned**; typically used in **Cheney scanning**

scanning processing each **pointer field** of an **object** or other contiguous set of **addresses**

scavenging picking out **live objects** from the **fromspace**, typically leaving **forwarding addresses** behind; see **copying collection**

schedulability analysis the analysis of a set of **real-time tasks** to decide whether they can be **scheduled** so that none of them misses a deadline

scheduler an operating system component that chooses which **threads** to execute on which **processors** at any given time

scheduling choosing when to execute a unit of **collection**

segregated-fits allocation an allocation strategy that partitions the **heap** by **size class** in order to minimise **fragmentation**

self-healing barrier a **barrier** that repairs the condition that the **barrier** is detecting, often by writing an updated value back into the **slot** from which a **reference** was loaded

semispace one of two **spaces** into which a **copying collection** divides the **heap**

semispace copying see **copying collection**

sequential allocation an **allocation** strategy that **allocates objects** consecutively from one end of a **free chunk**; often called **bump pointer allocation** or **linear allocation**

sequential consistency consistency model in which all memory operations appear to execute one at a time, and the operations of each **processor** appear to execute in its **program order**

sequential fits allocation a **free-list allocation** strategy that searches the free-list sequentially for a **cell** that satisfies the **allocation** request

sequential store buffer (SSB) an efficient implementation of a **remembered set**, such as a chain of **blocks** of slots, which allows new entries to be stored quickly but does not prevent duplicate entries

shade to colour a **white object grey**; see **tri-colour abstraction**

shared pointer a form of **smart pointer** defined for C++ (`shared_ptr`), and Rust (`Rc` and `Arc`) based on **reference counting**

shell an empty **object** structure, typically **allocated** in **tospace** by a **replicating collector** with the expectation that its **fields** will be filled in later

simultaneous multithreading (SMT)   the capability of a **processor** to execute multiple independent **threads** at the same time

Single Instruction, Multiple Thread (SIMT) an execution model used by **GPUs** whereby instructions of all **threads** execute in lock-step

size class a logical set of **objects** that are managed by the same **allocation** and **collection** policies and whose size falls within a specific range; the amount **allocated** is generally rounded up to the largest size in the class

slack-based scheduling a technique for **scheduling real-time collection** that performs **collector** work when no **real-time task** is running

sliding compaction a **compaction** technique that preserves the order in memory of **live objects**; see **compaction order**

slot see **field**

slow path see **fast (slow) path**

smart pointer a form of **pointer** upon which operations such as copying or dereferencing are overloaded in order to perform **memory management** operations

snapshot barrier see **deletion barrier**

snapshot-at-the-beginning a technique for solving the **lost object problem** that preserves the set of **objects live** at the start of the **collection cycle**

socket (1) a place on a hardware circuit board where an integrated circuit computer chip may be inserted; (2) that chip

soft real-time system a **real-time system** (controversially) in which most deadlines must be met within strict bounds to preserve quality of service; completion of an operation after its deadline results in degraded service

soft reference in Java, a **reference** that is stronger than a **weak reference** but not as strong as a **strong reference**; soft references are typically used to build caches that the **garbage collector** can **reclaim** when it comes under memory pressure

space a subset of the **heap** managed by a particular **collection** policy

space utilisation the fraction of **heap** space usable for **mutators'** data; that is, excluding **garbage collector metadata**, other **semispaces**, and so on

spatial locality the degree to which two items (**fields**, **objects**) are likely to be **allocated** close to each other (for example, on the same **page** or **cache line**)

spin lock a **lock** where the waiting **threads** simply 'spin' in a loop until they can acquire the **lock**

splitting dividing a **cell** into two adjacent free **cells**; see also **segregated-fits allocation**

stack (1) a **last-in, first-out** data structure, allowing adding and removing only from the front (top); (2) see **call stack**

stack allocation **allocation** of an **object** in the **stack frame** of its allocating method

stack barrier a **barrier** on returning (or throwing an exception) beyond a given **stack frame** in a **thread's call stack**

stack frame an **activation record** allocated in the **call stack**

stack map a data structure indicating which **addresses** in a **call stack** the **collector** should consider to be **references** to **objects**

static allocation **allocation** of an **object** at an **address** known at program build time

step a **subspace** used to segregate **objects** by age *within* a **generation**

sticky reference count a **reference count** that has been incremented to the maximum permissible value, not changed by subsequent **pointer** updates

stop-the-world collection a technique for **collection** during which all **mutator threads** are halted

store barrier a **barrier** on **reference** (and possibly value) stores by the **mutator** and possibly the **collector**, distinguished by the fact that it relates to the low-level encoding of the datum while a **write barrier**

is concerned more with properties such as the space in which a **referent** lies

store buffer see **write buffer**; not to be confused with a **sequential store buffer**

strict consistency a **consistency model** in which every memory access and **atomic** operation appears to occur in the same order everywhere

strong generational hypothesis assumption that the older an **object** is, the less likely it is to die

strong reference a **reference** to an **object** that contributes to its **reachability**; normal **references** are usually strong

strong tricolour invariant a **tricolour** abstraction invariant that no **black object** ever refers to a **white object**

survival rate the fraction of **objects** that **survive** a **collection**

survivor an **object** that is **live** at the time of a **collection** and thus not **reclaimed**

swapping see **paging**

sweeping reclaiming unmarked (**dead**) **objects** in a linear pass through (a subset) of the **heap**

symmetric multiprocessor (SMP) a **multiprocessor** with identical separate **processors** and shared, possibly **non-uniform memory access**, memory

synthetic benchmark an artificially constructed benchmark intended only to evaluate a system; although the behaviour of synthetic benchmarks may be stochastic, such benchmarks may not reproduce the interactions exhibited by real programs, or may have working sets too small to exhibit their **locality** effects

tagged pointer a **pointer** some of whose bits are a tag indicating some attribute of the **pointer** or its **referent** such as which **space** it refers to; sometimes called a *coloured pointer*

task a unit of work performed by a **process** or **thread**, usually in a **real-time system**

tebibyte (TiB) standard usage unit meaning 2^{40} bytes; see also **terabyte**

temporal locality the degree to which two items (**fields**, **objects**) are likely to be accessed close to each other in time

tenuring see **promote**

terabyte (TB) common usage unit meaning 2^{40} bytes; see also **tebibyte**

test-and-set an **atomic** instruction that sets that value of a **location** to "1" only if it is currently "0"; in any case, it indicates whether it succeeded; see also **atomic**

test-and-set lock see **spin lock**

test-and-test-and-set lock lower-cost variant of a **test-and-set lock** that uses (expensive) **atomic** hardware primitives only when the **lock** appears to be free

thrash overly frequent **collections** (or **paging**), at the expense of **mutator** activity

thread the smallest unit of processing that can be **scheduled** for execution by an operating system; multiple **threads** may execute in the same **address space**; see also **process**

thread-local collection garbage collection of only those **objects** accessible to a single **thread**

threaded compaction a technique for **compacting** that links **objects** so that all those originally pointing to a given **object** can be discovered from that **object**

throughput the rate at which data is processed by the **mutator(s)** (alternatively, by the **collector(s)**)

thunk an unevaluated application of a function to its arguments; see also **closure**

tidy pointer the canonical **pointer** used as an **object's reference**

time-based scheduling a technique for **scheduling real-time collection** that reserves a pre-defined portion of execution time solely for **collector** work during which the **mutator** is stopped

tospace the **semispace** to which **copying collection** evacuates **live objects**

tospace invariant the invariant that the **mutator** holds only **tospace references**

tracing visiting the **reachable objects** by **traversing** all or part of an **object** graph

tracing collection a technique for **indirect collection** that operates by **tracing** the graph of **live objects**

train a component of the Mature Object Space ('Train') **collector**

transaction a collection of reads and writes that must appear to execute **atomically**

transaction abort the unsuccessful termination of a **transaction** which discards its effects

transaction commit the successful completion of a **transaction** which ensures that its effects are made visible, and possibly **durable**

transactional memory a mechanism analogous to database **transactions** for controlling concurrent access to shared memory; it may be implemented in hardware or software

transitive (referential) closure given a set of **objects**, **fields** or other **locations** (**roots**), the transitive referential closure of the set of **roots** is the set of **objects** that can be reached from those **roots** by following **references**

translation lookaside buffer (TLB) a small associative memory that **caches** some translations between **virtual** and **physical addresses**

traversal visiting each **node** in a graph exactly once

trial deletion the temporary deletion of a **reference** in order to discover whether this causes an **object's reference count** to drop to zero

tricolour abstraction a characterisation of the work of the **garbage collector** as partitioning **objects** into **white** (not yet visited) and **black** (need not be revisited), using **grey** to represent the remaining work (to be revisited)

type-accurate a property of a **garbage collector** that it can precisely identify every **slot** or **root** that contains a **pointer**

type-safe in the context of this book, a programming language is type-safe if it cannot manufacture a **reference** value from a non-**reference** type

ulterior reference counting a **reference counting** scheme that manages **young objects** by **copying** and **older** ones by **reference counting**, used in the **collector** of the same name

undo log a record of changes made to a data structure allowing a system to roll the data structure back to its previous state; see also **log** and **redo log**

uniprocessor a computer that provides a single **processor**; contrasted with **multiprocessor**

unique pointer a **smart pointer** that retains sole ownership of an **object** through a **pointer** and destroys the **object** when the **unique pointer** goes out of scope (called unique because two different unique pointers cannot manage the same **object**); defined for C++ (`unique_ptr`) and Rust (`Box`)

vector load load several words in a single operation; see also **vector store**

vector store store several words in a single operation; see also **vector load**

virtual address an address in the **virtual memory**

virtual machine a **run-time system** that abstracts away details of the underlying hardware and operating system

virtual memory an idealised abstraction of the **physical memory** that is actually available on a given machine; **pages** in virtual memory are mapped to actual **pages** in **physical memory**, not necessarily in a contiguous manner, and at any point some virtual **pages'** contents may reside in file storage rather than **physical memory**

volatile (1) subject to change by other **threads**; (2) in the context of **persistence**, not able to survive failures or outlive the execution of a program, the opposite of **durable**

wait-free a guarantee of both system-wide (**lock-free**) and per-**thread** progress so that a **thread** will complete its operation in a bounded number of steps; see also **non-blocking**

wavefront (1) the boundary, comprising **grey objects** (still to be processed), separating **black objects** (already processed) from **white objects** (not yet processed); (2) the OpenCL term for a group of **work-items** assigned to a **compute unit**, executing in lock-step — the CUDA term is *warp*

weak consistency any **consistency model** which treats each **atomic** operation as a total **memory fence**

weak generational hypothesis assumption that most **objects** die young

weak head normal formal an expression is in weak head normal form when its outermost part has been evaluated to a data constructor or a lambda abstraction

weak reference a **reference** to an **object** that does not contribute to its **reachability**; Java for example provides several kinds of weak reference (see **soft reference** and **phantom reference**)

weak tricolour invariant a **tricolour abstraction** invariant that any **white object** pointed to by a **black object** must also be **reachable** from some **grey object** either directly or through a chain of **white objects**

white an **object** is white if the **collector** has not processed it so that, at the end of a **collection cycle**, white **objects** are considered **dead**; see also **tricolour abstraction**

wilderness the last free **chunk** in the **heap**

wilderness preservation a policy of **allocating** from the **wilderness** only as a last resort

work stealing a technique for **balancing** work among **threads** where lightly loaded **threads** pull work from more heavily loaded **threads**

work-based scheduling a technique for **scheduling real-time collection** that imposes **collector** work as a tax on units of **mutator** work

work-item OpenCL term for one of a collection of parallel executions of a **kernel** invoked on a device; the CUDA term is *thread*

workgroup OpenCL term for a collection of related **work-items** executing the same **kernel** on a single **compute unit** and sharing local memory; the CUDA term is *block*

worst-case execution time (WCET) the maximum time an operation can take on a specific hardware platform; knowing worst-case execution times is necessary for **schedulability analysis** of a **hard real-time system**

write barrier a **barrier** on **reference** stores by the **mutator**; see also **store barrier**

write buffer a hardware buffer in a **processor** that holds pending writes to memory, also called a **store buffer** (not to be confused with a **sequential store buffer**)

young generation see **nursery**

zero count table (ZCT) a table of **objects** whose **reference counts** are zero

zero-copy transfer an operation which transfers data from one memory area to another without having to physically copy it, typically requiring the CPU and **GPU** to share a unified address space; also relevant to access in **persistent heaps**

Bibliography

This bibliography contains about 600 references. However, our comprehensive database at http://www.cs.kent.ac.uk/~rej/gcbib/ contains over 2500 garbage collection related publications. This database can be searched online or downloaded as BIBT_EX, PostScript or PDF. As well as details of the article, papers, books, theses and so on, the bibliography also contains abstracts for some entries and URLs or DOIs for most of the electronically available ones. We continually strive to keep this bibliography up to date as a service to the community. Here you can help: Richard (R.E.Jones@kent.ac.uk) would be very grateful to receive further entries (or corrections).

Abhinav and Rupesh Nasre. FastCollect: Offloading generational garbage collection to integrated GPUs. In *Proceedings of the International Conference on Compilers, Architectures and Synthesis for Embedded Systems (CASES'16)*, Pittsburgh, PA, 2016. ACM Press. doi: 10.1145/2968455.2968520. (pages 322, 323 and 324)

Santosh G. Abraham and Janak H. Patel. Parallel garbage collection on a virtual memory system. In *International Conference on Parallel Processing (ICPP'87)*, University Park, Pennsylvania, August 1987, pages 243–246. Pennsylvania State University Press. Also technical report CSRD 620, University of Illinois at Urbana-Champaign, Center for Supercomputing Research and Development. (pages 338, 340, 341 and 352)

Diab Abuaiadh, Yoav Ossia, Erez Petrank and Uri Silbershtein. An efficient parallel heap compaction algorithm. In OOPSLA 2004, pages 224–236. doi: 10.1145/1028976.1028995. (pages 36, 42, 50, 318, 319 and 342)

Sarita V. Adve and Kourosh Gharachorloo. Shared memory consistency models: A tutorial. WRL Research Report 95/7, Digital Western Research Laboratory, September 1995. https://www.hpl.hp.com/techreports/Compaq-DEC/WRL-95-7.pdf. (page 253)

Sarita V. Adve and Kourosh Gharachorloo. Shared memory consistency models: A tutorial. *IEEE Computer*, 29(12):66–76, December 1996. doi: 10.1109/2.546611. (page 253)

Ole Agesen. GC points in a threaded environment. Technical Report SMLI TR-98-70, Sun Microsystems Laboratories, Palo Alto, CA, 1998. http://dl.acm.org/citation.cfm?id=974974. (pages 199 and 200)

Shoaib Akram, Jennifer B. Sartor, Kenzo Van Craeynest, Wim Heirman and Lieven Eeckhout. Boosting the priority of garbage: Scheduling collection on heterogeneous multicore processors. *ACM Transactions on Architecture and Code Optimization*, 13(1): 4:1–4:25, March 2016. doi: 10.1145/2875424. (page 468)

Rafael Alonso and Andrew W. Appel. An advisor for flexible working sets. In *ACM SIGMETRICS International Conference on Measurement and Modeling of Computer Systems*, Boulder, CO, May 1990, pages 153–162. ACM Press. doi: `10.1145/98457.98753`. (pages 220 and 221)

Laurent Amsaleg, Michael Franklin and Olivier Gruber. Efficient incremental garbage collection for workstation/server database systems. Technical report, Inria Paris-Rocquencourt, November 1994. `https://hal.inria.fr/inria-00074266`. Also University of Maryland Institute for Advanced Computer Studies report UMIACS-TR-94-121. (page 477)

Laurent Amsaleg, Michael Franklin and Olivier Gruber. Efficient incremental garbage collection for client-server object database systems. In *Twenty-first International Conference on Very Large Databases (VLDB95)*, Zurich, Switzerland, September 1995. `http://www.vldb.org/conf/1995/P042.PDF`. (page 477)

Daniel Anderson, Guy E. Blelloch and Yuanhao Wei. Concurrent deferred reference counting with constant-time overhead. In PLDI 2021. doi: `10.1145/3453483.3454060`. (page 422)

Todd A. Anderson. Optimizations in a private nursery-based garbage collector. In ISMM 2010, pages 21–30. doi: `10.1145/1806651.1806655`. (page 153)

Todd A. Anderson, Melissa O'Neill and John Sarracino. Chihuahua: A concurrent, moving, garbage collector using transactional memory. In *10th ACM SIGPLAN Workshop on Transactional Computing*, Portland, OR, June 2015. (page 382)

Andrew W. Appel. Garbage collection can be faster than stack allocation. *Information Processing Letters*, 25(4):275–279, 1987. doi: `10.1016/0020-0190(87)90175-X`. (pages 131 and 182)

Andrew W. Appel. Simple generational garbage collection and fast allocation. *Software: Practice and Experience*, 19(2):171–183, 1989a. doi: `10.1002/spe.4380190206`. (pages 127, 128, 129, 131, 132, 136, 137, 150, 207, 208, 220 and 221)

Andrew W. Appel. Runtime tags aren't necessary. *Lisp and Symbolic Computation*, 2: 153–162, 1989b. doi: `10.1007/BF01811537`. (pages 181 and 183)

Andrew W. Appel. Tutorial: Compilers and runtime systems for languages with garbage collection. In PLDI 1992. doi: `10.1145/143095`. (page 119)

Andrew W. Appel. Emulating write-allocate on a no-write-allocate cache. Technical Report TR-459-94, Department of Computer Science, Princeton University, June 1994. `http://www.cs.princeton.edu/research/techreps/TR-459-94`. (pages 105, 175 and 176)

Andrew W. Appel and Zhong Shao. An empirical and analytic study of stack vs. heap cost for languages with closures. Technical Report CS–TR–450–94, Department of Computer Science, Princeton University, March 1994. `http://www.cs.princeton.edu/research/techreps/TR-450-94`. (page 182)

Andrew W. Appel and Zhong Shao. Empirical and analytic study of stack versus heap cost for languages with closures. *Journal of Functional Programming*, 6(1):47–74, January 1996. doi: `10.1017/S095679680000157X`. (page 182)

Andrew W. Appel, John R. Ellis and Kai Li. Real-time concurrent collection on stock multiprocessors. In PLDI 1988, pages 11–20. doi: `10.1145/53990.53992`. (pages 338, 339, 340, 370 and 385)

Apple. *The Swift Programming Language (Swift 5.5)*. Swift Programming Series. Apple Inc, September 2021. (page 241)

J. Armstrong, R. Virding, C. Wikström and M. Williams. *Concurrent Programming in Erlang*. Prentice-Hall, second edition, 1996. (page 152)

Matthew Arnold and Barbara G. Ryder. A framework for reducing the cost of instrumented code. In PLDI 2001, pages 168–179. doi: `10.1145/378795.378832`. (page 460)

Jatin Arora, Sam Westrick and Umut A. Acar. Provably space-efficient parallel functional programming. In *48th Annual ACM SIGPLAN Symposium on Principles of Programming Languages*, January 2021. ACM Press. doi: `10.1145/3434299`. (pages 113 and 155)

Nimar S. Arora, Robert D. Blumofe and C. Greg Plaxton. Thread scheduling for multiprogrammed multiprocessors. In *10th ACM Symposium on Parallel Algorithms and Architectures*, Puerto Vallarta, Mexico, June 1998, pages 119–129. ACM Press. doi: `10.1145/277651.277678`. (pages 281, 285 and 298)

Joshua Auerbach, David F. Bacon, Perry Cheng, David Grove, Ben Biron, Charlie Gracie, Bill McCloskey, Aleksandar Micic and Ryan Sciampacone. Tax-and-spend: Democratic scheduling for real-time garbage collection. In *8th ACM International Conference on Embedded Software*, Atlanta, GA, 2008, pages 245–254. ACM Press. doi: `10.1145/1450058.1450092`. (pages 448 and 464)

Todd M. Austin, Eric Larson and Dan Ernst. SimpleScalar: An infrastructure for computer system modeling. *Computer*, 35(2):59–67, 2002. doi: `10.1109/2.982917`. (page 466)

Thomas H. Axford. Reference counting of cyclic graphs for functional programs. *Computer Journal*, 33(5):466–470, 1990. doi: `10.1093/comjnl/33.5.466`. (page 71)

Alain Azagury, Elliot K. Kolodner and Erez Petrank. A note on the implementation of replication-based garbage collection for multithreaded applications and multiprocessor environments. *Parallel Processing Letters*, 9(3):391–399, 1999. doi: `10.1142/S0129626499000360`. (page 372)

Hezi Azatchi and Erez Petrank. Integrating generations with advanced reference counting garbage collectors. In *12th International Conference on Compiler Construction*, Warsaw, Poland, May 2003, pages 185–199. Volume 2622 of *Lecture Notes in Computer Science*, Springer-Verlag. doi: `10.1007/3-540-36579-6_14`. (page 416)

Hezi Azatchi, Yossi Levanoni, Harel Paz and Erez Petrank. An on-the-fly mark and sweep garbage collector based on sliding views. In OOPSLA 2003, pages 269–281. doi: `10.1145/949305.949329`. (page 360)

Azul. Pauseless garbage collection. White paper AWP–005–020, Azul Systems Inc., July 2008. (pages 386 and 404)

Azul. Comparison of virtual memory manipulation metrics. White paper, Azul Systems Inc., 2010. (page 394)

David F. Bacon and V.T. Rajan. Concurrent cycle collection in reference counted systems. In Jørgen Lindskov Knudsen, editor, *15th European Conference on Object-Oriented Programming*, Budapest, Hungary, June 2001, pages 207–235. Volume 2072 of *Lecture Notes in Computer Science*, Springer-Verlag. doi: 10.1007/3-540-45337-7_12. (pages 64, 72, 76, 77, 79, 114, 167, 413 and 420)

David F. Bacon, Clement R. Attanasio, Han Bok Lee, V.T. Rajan and Stephen E. Smith. Java without the coffee breaks: A nonintrusive multiprocessor garbage collector. In PLDI 2001, pages 92–103. doi: 10.1145/378795.378819. (pages 72 and 413)

David F. Bacon, Perry Cheng and V.T. Rajan. A real-time garbage collector with low overhead and consistent utilization. In POPL 2003, pages 285–298. doi: 10.1145/604131.604155. (pages 349, 439, 442 and 443)

David F. Bacon, Perry Cheng and V.T. Rajan. Controlling fragmentation and space consumption in the Metronome, a real-time garbage collector for Java. In LCTES 2003, pages 81–92. doi: 10.1145/780732.780744. (pages 452 and 453)

David F. Bacon, Perry Cheng and V.T. Rajan. A unified theory of garbage collection. In OOPSLA 2004, pages 50–68. doi: 10.1145/1035292.1028982. (pages 81, 85 and 141)

David F. Bacon, Perry Cheng, David Grove and Martin T. Vechev. Syncopation: Generational real-time garbage collection in the Metronome. In LCTES 2005, pages 183–192. doi: 10.1145/1065910.1065937a. (page 447)

Scott B. Baden. Low-overhead storage reclamation in the Smalltalk-80 virtual machine. In Krasner [1983], pages 331–342. (pages 67 and 68)

Brenda Baker, E.G. Coffman and D.E. Willard. Algorithms for resolving conflicts in dynamic storage allocation. *Journal of the ACM*, 32(2):327–343, April 1985. doi: 10.1145/3149.335126. (page 145)

Henry G. Baker. List processing in real-time on a serial computer. *Communications of the ACM*, 21(4):280–294, 1978. doi: 10.1145/359460.359470. Also AI Laboratory Working Paper 139, 1977. (pages 144, 293, 338, 339, 340, 341, 368, 370, 371, 372, 373, 377, 404, 425, 432 and 433)

Henry G. Baker. The Treadmill, real-time garbage collection without motion sickness. *ACM SIGPLAN Notices*, 27(3):66–70, March 1992a. doi: 10.1145/130854.130862. (pages 110, 145 and 404)

Henry G. Baker. CONS should not CONS its arguments, or a lazy alloc is a smart alloc. *ACM SIGPLAN Notices*, 27(3), March 1992b. doi: 10.1145/130854.130858. (page 155)

Henry G. Baker. 'Infant mortality' and generational garbage collection. *ACM SIGPLAN Notices*, 28(4):55–57, April 1993. doi: 10.1145/152739.152747. (page 112)

Jason Baker, Antonio Cunei, Filip Pizlo and Jan Vitek. Accurate garbage collection in uncooperative environments with lazy pointer stacks. In *International Conference on Compiler Construction*, Braga, Portugal, March 2007. Volume 4420 of *Lecture Notes in Computer Science*, Springer-Verlag. doi: 10.1007/978-3-540-71229-9_5. (page 505)

Jason Baker, Antonio Cunei, Tomas Kalibera, Filip Pizlo and Jan Vitek. Accurate garbage collection in uncooperative environments revisited. *Concurrency and Computation: Practice and Experience*, 21(12):1572–1606, 2009. doi: `10.1002/cpe.1391`. Supersedes Baker *et al.* [2007]. (page 182)

Alexandro Baldassin, João Barreto, Daniel Castro and Paolo Romano. Persistent memory: A survey of programming support and implementations. *ACM Computing Surveys*, 54 (7), 2021. doi: `10.1145/3465402`. (pages 471 and 478)

Subarno Banerjee, David Devecsery, Peter M. Chen and Satish Narayanasamy. Sound garbage collection for C using pointer provenance. In *ACM SIGPLAN Conference on Object-Oriented Programming, Systems, Languages, and Applications*, November 2020. ACM Press. (page 178)

Katherine Barabash and Erez Petrank. Tracing garbage collection on highly parallel platforms. In ISMM 2010, pages 1–10. doi: `10.1145/1806651.1806653`. (page 321)

Katherine Barabash, Yoav Ossia and Erez Petrank. Mostly concurrent garbage collection revisited. In OOPSLA 2003, pages 255–268. doi: `10.1145/949305.949328`. (pages 342 and 343)

Katherine Barabash, Ori Ben-Yitzhak, Irit Goft, Elliot K. Kolodner, Victor Leikehman, Yoav Ossia, Avi Owshanko and Erez Petrank. A parallel, incremental, mostly concurrent garbage collector for servers. *ACM Transactions on Programming Languages and Systems*, 27(6):1097–1146, November 2005. doi: `10.1145/1108970.1108972`. (pages 301, 342, 343 and 344)

David A. Barrett and Benjamin Zorn. Garbage collection using a dynamic threatening boundary. In *ACM SIGPLAN Conference on Programming Language Design and Implementation*, La Jolla, CA, June 1995, pages 301–314. ACM SIGPLAN Notices 30(6), ACM Press. doi: `10.1145/207110.207164`. (page 129)

David A. Barrett and Benjamin G. Zorn. Using lifetime predictors to improve memory allocation performance. In PLDI 1993, pages 187–196. doi: `10.1145/155090.155108`. (page 120)

Joel F. Bartlett. Compacting garbage collection with ambiguous roots. WRL Research Report 88/2, DEC Western Research Laboratory, Palo Alto, CA, February 1988a. `https://www.hpl.hp.com/techreports/Compaq-DEC/WRL-88-2.pdf`. Also appears as Bartlett [1988b]. (pages 32 and 110)

Joel F. Bartlett. Compacting garbage collection with ambiguous roots. *Lisp Pointers*, 1(6): 3–12, April 1988b. doi: `10.1145/1317224.1317225`. (page 505)

Joel F. Bartlett. Mostly-Copying garbage collection picks up generations and C++. Technical Note TN–12, DEC Western Research Laboratory, Palo Alto, CA, October 1989a. `https://www.hpl.hp.com/techreports/Compaq-DEC/WRL-TN-12.pdf`. (pages 181 and 203)

Joel F. Bartlett. SCHEME->C: a portable Scheme-to-C compiler. WRL Research Report 89/1, DEC Western Research Laboratory, Palo Alto, CA, January 1989b. `https://www.hpl.hp.com/techreports/Compaq-DEC/WRL-89-1.pdf`. (page 180)

George Belotsky. C++ memory management: From fear to triumph. O'Reilly linuxdevcenter.com, July 2003. `http://www.linuxdevcenter.com/pub/a/linux/2003/08/07/cpp_mm-3.html`. (page 3)

Mordechai Ben-Ari. Algorithms for on-the-fly garbage collection. *ACM Transactions on Programming Languages and Systems*, 6(3):333–344, July 1984. doi: `10.1145/579.587`. (page 331)

Emery Berger, Kathryn McKinley, Robert Blumofe and Paul Wilson. Hoard: A scalable memory allocator for multithreaded applications. In *9th International Conference on Architectural Support for Programming Languages and Operating Systems*, Cambridge, MA, November 2000, pages 117–128. ACM SIGPLAN Notices 35(11), ACM Press. doi: `10.1145/356989.357000`. (page 106)

Peter B. Bishop. *Computer Systems with a Very Large Address Space and Garbage Collection*. PhD thesis, MIT Laboratory for Computer Science, May 1977. doi: `1721.1/16428`. Technical report MIT/LCS/TR–178. (pages 109 and 146)

Stephen Blackburn and Kathryn S. McKinley. Immix: a mark-region garbage collector with space efficiency, fast collection, and mutator performance. In PLDI 2008, pages 22–32. doi: `10.1145/1375581.1375586`. (pages 33, 92, 105, 162, 163, 169, 197 and 405)

Stephen M. Blackburn. Design and analysis of field-logging write barriers. In ISMM 2019, pages 103–114. doi: `10.1145/3315573.3329981`. (page 204)

Stephen M. Blackburn. We live in interesting times. Keynote talk, June 2022. (pages xxvii and xxviii)

Stephen M. Blackburn and Antony L. Hosking. Barriers: Friend or foe? In ISMM 2004, pages 143–151. doi: `10.1145/1029873.1029891`. (page 214)

Stephen M. Blackburn and Kathryn S. McKinley. In or out? putting write barriers in their place. In ISMM 2002, pages 175–184. doi: `10.1145/512429.512452`. (page 84)

Stephen M. Blackburn and Kathryn S. McKinley. Ulterior reference counting: Fast garbage collection without a long wait. In OOPSLA 2003, pages 344–458. doi: `10.1145/949305.949336`. (pages 53, 59, 65, 67, 79, 114, 167, 168, 169 and 347)

Stephen M. Blackburn, Sharad Singhai, Matthew Hertz, Kathryn S. McKinley and J. Eliot B. Moss. Pretenuring for Java. In OOPSLA 2001, pages 342–352. doi: `10.1145/504282.504307`. (pages 116 and 138)

Stephen M. Blackburn, Richard E. Jones, Kathryn S. McKinley and J. Eliot B. Moss. Beltway: Getting around garbage collection gridlock. In PLDI 2002, pages 153–164. doi: `10.1145/512529.512548`. (pages 136, 137, 146 and 214)

Stephen M. Blackburn, Perry Cheng and Kathryn S. McKinley. Myths and realities: The performance impact of garbage collection. In *ACM SIGMETRICS International Conference on Measurement and Modeling of Computer Systems*, June 2004a, pages 25–36. ACM SIGMETRICS Performance Evaluation Review 32(1), ACM Press. doi: `10.1145/1005686.1005693`. (pages 50, 53, 58, 59, 83, 92, 111, 132, 136 and 214)

Stephen M. Blackburn, Perry Cheng and Kathryn S. McKinley. Oil and water? High performance garbage collection in Java with MMTk. In *26th International Conference on Software Engineering*, Edinburgh, May 2004b, pages 137–146. IEEE Computer Society Press. doi: `10.1109/ICSE.2004.1317436`. (pages 28, 113, 122, 206 and 208)

Stephen M. Blackburn, Robin Garner, Chris Hoffman, Asjad M. Khan, Kathryn S. McKinley, Rotem Bentzur, Amer Diwan, Daniel Feinberg, Daniel Frampton, Samuel Z. Guyer, Martin Hirzel, Antony Hosking, Maria Jump, Han Lee, J. Eliot B. Moss, Aashish Phansalkar, Darko Stefanović, Thomas VanDrunen, Daniel von Dincklage and Ben Wiedermann. The DaCapo benchmarks: Java benchmarking development and analysis. In *ACM SIGPLAN Conference on Object-Oriented Programming, Systems, Languages, and Applications*, Portland, OR, October 2006a, pages 169–190. ACM SIGPLAN Notices 41(10), ACM Press. doi: `10.1145/1167473.1167488`. (page 11)

Stephen M. Blackburn, Robin Garner, Chris Hoffmann, Asjad M. Khan, Kathryn S. McKinley, Rotem Bentzur, Amer Diwan, Daniel Feinberg, Daniel Frampton, Samuel Z. Guyer, Martin Hirzel, Antony Hosking, Maria Jump, Han Lee, J. Eliot B. Moss, Aashish Phansalkar amd Darko Stefanović, Thomas VanDrunen, Daniel von Dincklage and Ben Wiedermann. The DaCapo benchmarks: Java benchmarking development and analysis (extended version). Technical report, The DaCapo Group, 2006b. `http://dacapobench.sourceforge.net/dacapo-TR-CS-06-01.pdf`. (pages 64, 120 and 131)

Stephen M. Blackburn, Matthew Hertz, Kathryn S. Mckinley, J. Eliot B. Moss and Ting Yang. Profile-based pretenuring. *ACM Transactions on Programming Languages and Systems*, 29(1):1–57, 2007. doi: `10.1145/1180475.1180477`. (pages 116 and 138)

Bruno Blanchet. Escape analysis for object oriented languages: Application to Java. In OOPSLA 1999, pages 20–34. doi: `10.1145/320384.320387`. (page 155)

Ricki Blau. Paging on an object-oriented personal computer for Smalltalk. In *ACM SIGMETRICS International Conference on Measurement and Modeling of Computer Systems*, Minneapolis, MN, August 1983, pages 44–54. ACM Press. doi: `10.1145/800040.801394`. Also appears as Technical Report UCB/CSD 83/125, University of California, Berkeley, Computer Science Division (EECS). (page 54)

Guy E. Blelloch and Perry Cheng. On bounding time and space for multiprocessor garbage collection. In PLDI 1999, pages 104–117. doi: `10.1145/301618.301648`. (pages 272, 305, 307, 308, 425, 426, 427, 428, 429, 430, 431, 432, 433, 439, 452 and 454)

Daniel G. Bobrow. Managing re-entrant structures using reference counts. *ACM Transactions on Programming Languages and Systems*, 2(3):269–273, July 1980. doi: `10.1145/357103.357104`. (page 71)

Hans-Juergen Boehm. Mark-sweep vs. copying collection and asymptotic complexity, September 1995. `http://www.hboehm.info/gc/complexity.html`. (page 29)

Hans-Juergen Boehm. Reducing garbage collector cache misses. In ISMM 2000, pages 59–64. doi: `10.1145/362422.362438`. (pages 25 and 29)

Hans-Juergen Boehm. Destructors, finalizers, and synchronization. In POPL 2003, pages 262–272. doi: `10.1145/604131.604153`. (pages 229, 230, 231 and 233)

Hans-Juergen Boehm. The space cost of lazy reference counting. In *31st Annual ACM SIGPLAN Symposium on Principles of Programming Languages*, Venice, Italy, January 2004, pages 210–219. ACM SIGPLAN Notices 39(1), ACM Press. doi: 10.1145/604131.604153. (page 64)

Hans-Juergen Boehm. Space efficient conservative garbage collection. In PLDI 1993, pages 197–206. doi: 10.1145/155090.155109. (pages 111 and 178)

Hans-Juergen Boehm and Mike Spertus. Garbage collection in the next C++ standard. In ISMM 2009, pages 30–38. doi: 10.1145/1542431.1542437. (page 3)

Hans-Juergen Boehm and Mark Weiser. Garbage collection in an uncooperative environment. *Software: Practice and Experience*, 18(9):807–820, 1988. doi: 10.1002/spe.4380180902. (pages 25, 35, 84, 99, 100, 110, 143, 173, 178, 220 and 296)

Hans-Juergen Boehm, Alan J. Demers and Scott Shenker. Mostly parallel garbage collection. In PLDI 1991, pages 157–164. doi: 10.1145/113445.113459. (pages 213, 338, 339, 340, 349 and 352)

Michael Bond and Kathryn McKinley. Tolerating memory leaks. In *ACM SIGPLAN Conference on Object-Oriented Programming, Systems, Languages, and Applications*, Nashville, TN, October 2008, pages 109–126. ACM SIGPLAN Notices 43(10), ACM Press. doi: 10.1145/1449764.1449774. (page 220)

Anastasia Braginsky, Alex Kogan and Erez Petrank. Drop the anchor: Lightweight memory management for non-blocking data structures. In *25th ACM Symposium on Parallelism in Algorithms and Architectures*, Montréal, Canada, 2013, pages 33–42. ACM Press. doi: 10.1145/2486159.2486184. (page 421)

Tim Brecht, Eshrat Arjomandi, Chang Li and Hang Pham. Controlling garbage collection and heap growth to reduce the execution time of Java applications. In OOPSLA 2001, pages 353–366. doi: 10.1145/504282.504308. (page 220)

Tim Brecht, Eshrat Arjomandi, Chang Li and Hang Pham. Controlling garbage collection and heap growth to reduce the execution time of Java applications. *ACM Transactions on Programming Languages and Systems*, 28(5):908–941, September 2006. doi: 10.1145/1152649.1152652. (page 220)

R.P. Brent. Efficient implementation of the first-fit strategy for dynamic storage allocation. *ACM Transactions on Programming Languages and Systems*, 11(3):388–403, July 1989. doi: 10.1145/65979.65981. (page 145)

Rodney A. Brooks. Trading data space for reduced time and code space in real-time garbage collection on stock hardware. In LFP 1984, pages 256–262. doi: 10.1145/800055.802042. (pages 370, 371, 372, 382, 389, 401, 404, 434, 436, 439, 442, 452, 453, 454 and 455)

David R. Brownbridge. Cyclic reference counting for combinator machines. In Jean-Pierre Jouannaud, editor, *Conference on Functional Programming and Computer Architecture*, Nancy, France, September 1985, pages 273–288. Volume 201 of *Lecture Notes in Computer Science*, Springer-Verlag. doi: 10.1007/3-540-15975-4_42. (page 71)

Rodrigo Bruno, Luís Picciochi Oliveira and Paulo Ferreira. NG2C: Pretenuring garbage collection with dynamic generations for HotSpot big data applications. In ISMM 2017, pages 2–13. doi: 10.1145/3092255.3092272. (page 116)

F. Warren Burton. A buddy system variation for disk storage allocation. *Communications of the ACM*, 19(7):416–417, July 1976. doi: `10.1145/360248.360259`. (page 101)

Albin M. Butters. Total cost of ownership: A comparison of C/C++ and Java. Technical report, Evans Data Corporation, June 2007. `http://docplayer.net/24861428-Total-cost-of-ownership-a-comparison-of-c-c-and-java.html`. (pages 1 and 4)

Zixian Cai, Stephen M. Blackburn, Michael D. Bond and Martin Maas. Distilling the real cost of production garbage collectors. In *IEEE International Symposium on Performance Analysis of Systems and Software*, Singapore, May 2022. IEEE Press. (pages 7, 8, 10, 408 and 409)

Brad Calder, Chandra Krintz, S. John and T. Austin. Cache-conscious data placement. In *8th International Conference on Architectural Support for Programming Languages and Operating Systems*, San Jose, CA, October 1998, pages 139–149. ACM SIGPLAN Notices 33(11), ACM Press. doi: `10.1145/291069.291036`. (page 54)

D.C. Cann and Rod R. Oldehoeft. Reference count and copy elimination for parallel applicative computing. Technical Report CS–88–129, Department of Computer Science, Colorado State University, Fort Collins, CO, 1988. (page 64)

Dante Cannarozzi, Michael P. Plezbert and Ron Cytron. Contaminated garbage collection. In PLDI 2000, pages 264–273. doi: `10.1145/349299.349334`. (page 155)

Ting Cao, Stephen M. Blackburn, Tiejun Gao and Kathryn S. McKinley. The yin and yang of power and performance for asymmetric hardware and managed software. In *39th Annual ACM/IEEE International Symposium on Computer Architecture*, Portland, OR, June 2012. ACM Press. `https://dl.acm.org/doi/10.5555/2337159.2337185`. (page 468)

Luca Cardelli, James Donahue, Lucille Glassman, Mick Jordan, Bill Kalsow and Greg Nelson. Modula-3 language definition. *ACM SIGPLAN Notices*, 27(8):15–42, August 1992. doi: `10.1145/142137.142141`. (page 370)

Patrick J. Caudill and Allen Wirfs-Brock. A third-generation Smalltalk-80 implementation. In OOPSLA 1986, pages 119–130. doi: `10.1145/28697.28709`. (pages 120 and 144)

CC 2005. *14th International Conference on Compiler Construction*, Edinburgh, April 2005. Volume 3443 of *Lecture Notes in Computer Science*, Springer-Verlag. doi: `10.1007/b107108`. (page 533)

Pedro Celis, Per-Åke Larson and J. Ian Munro. Robin Hood hashing. In *26th Annual Symposium on Foundations of Computer Science*, Portland, OR, October 1985, pages 261–288. IEEE Computer Society Press. doi: `10.1109/SFCS.1985.48`. (page 206)

Yang Chang. *Garbage Collection for Flexible Hard Real-time Systems*. PhD thesis, University of York, 2007. (page 464)

Yang Chang and Andy J. Wellings. Integrating hybrid garbage collection with dual priority scheduling. In *11th International Conference on Embedded and Real-Time Computing Systems and Applications (RTCSA)*, August 2005, pages 185–188. IEEE Press, IEEE Computer Society Press. doi: `10.1109/RTCSA.2005.56`. (page 464)

Yang Chang and Andy J. Wellings. Low memory overhead real-time garbage collection for Java. In *4th International Workshop on Java Technologies for Real-time and Embedded Systems*, Paris, France, October 2006a. doi: 10.1145/1167999.1168014. (page 464)

Yang Chang and Andy J. Wellings. Hard real-time hybrid garbage collection with low memory requirements. In *27th IEEE Real-Time Systems Symposium*, December 2006b, pages 77–86. doi: 10.1109/RTSS.2006.25. (page 464)

Yang Chang and Andy J. Wellings. Garbage collection for flexible hard real-time systems. *IEEE Transactions on Computers*, 59(8):1063–1075, August 2010. doi: 10.1109/TC.2010.13. (page 464)

David R. Chase. *Garbage Collection and Other Optimizations*. PhD thesis, Rice University, August 1987. doi: 10.5555/914500. (page 110)

David R. Chase. Safety considerations for storage allocation optimizations. In PLDI 1988, pages 1–10. doi: 10.1145/53990.53991. (page 110)

A.M. Cheadle, A.J. Field and J. Nyström-Persson. A method specialisation and virtualised execution environment for Java. In David Gregg, Vikram Adve and Brian Bershad, editors, *4th ACM SIGPLAN/SIGOPS International Conference on Virtual Execution Environments*, Seattle, WA, March 2008, pages 51–60. ACM Press. doi: 10.1145/1346256.1346264. (pages 181 and 371)

Andrew M. Cheadle, Anthony J. Field, Simon Marlow, Simon L. Peyton Jones and R.L While. Non-stop Haskell. In *5th ACM SIGPLAN International Conference on Functional Programming*, Montreal, September 2000, pages 257–267. ACM Press. doi: 10.1145/351240.351265. (pages 180, 181 and 182)

Andrew M. Cheadle, Anthony J. Field, Simon Marlow, Simon L. Peyton Jones and Lyndon While. Exploring the barrier to entry — incremental generational garbage collection for Haskell. In ISMM 2004, pages 163–174. doi: 10.1145/1029873.1029893. (pages 103, 181, 182 and 371)

Wen-Ke Chen, Sanjay Bhansali, Trishul M. Chilimbi, Xiaofeng Gao and Weihaw Chuang. Profile-guided proactive garbage collection for locality optimization. In PLDI 2006, pages 332–340. doi: 10.1145/1133981.1134021. (page 57)

C.J. Cheney. A non-recursive list compacting algorithm. *Communications of the ACM*, 13 (11):677–8, November 1970. doi: 10.1145/362790.362798. (pages 47, 48, 50, 51, 52, 53, 54, 55, 59, 145, 151, 152, 158, 166, 305, 310, 326, 368, 427 and 434)

Perry Cheng and Guy Blelloch. A parallel, real-time garbage collector. In PLDI 2001, pages 125–136. doi: 10.1145/378795.378823. (pages 8, 198, 305, 306, 325, 425, 432 and 433)

Perry Cheng, Robert Harper and Peter Lee. Generational stack collection and profile-driven pretenuring. In *ACM SIGPLAN Conference on Programming Language Design and Implementation*, Montreal, Canada, June 1998, pages 162–173. ACM SIGPLAN Notices 33(5), ACM Press. doi: 10.1145/277650.277718. (pages 116, 138 and 152)

Perry Sze-Din Cheng. *Scalable Real-Time Parallel Garbage Collection for Symmetric Multiprocessors*. PhD thesis, Carnegie Mellon University, September 2001. http://reports-archive.adm.cs.cmu.edu/anon/2001/CMU-CS-01-174.pdf. SCS Technical Report CMU-CS-01-174. (pages 305 and 432)

Chen-Yong Cher, Antony L. Hosking and T.N. Vijaykumar. Software prefetching for mark-sweep garbage collection: Hardware analysis and software redesign. In Shubu Mukherjee and Kathryn S. McKinley, editors, *11th International Conference on Architectural Support for Programming Languages and Operating Systems*, Boston, MA, October 2004, pages 199–210. ACM SIGPLAN Notices 39(11), ACM Press. doi: 10.1145/1024393.1024417. (pages 30 and 55)

Trishul M. Chilimbi and James R. Larus. Using generational garbage collection to implement cache-conscious data placement. In ISMM 1998, pages 37–48. doi: 10.1145/301589.286865. (page 57)

Trishul M. Chilimbi, Mark D. Hill and James R. Larus. Cache-conscious structure layout. In PLDI 1999, pages 1–12. doi: 10.1145/301618.301633. (page 54)

Hyeonjoong Cho, Chewoo Na, Binoy Ravindran and E. Douglas Jensen. On scheduling garbage collector in dynamic real-time systems with statistical timing assurances. *Real-Time Systems*, 36(1–2):23–46, 2007. doi: 10.1007/s11241-006-9011-0. (page 464)

Hyeonjoong Cho, Binoy Ravindran and Chewoo Na. Garbage collector scheduling in dynamic, multiprocessor real-time systems. *IEEE Transactions on Parallel and Distributed Systems*, 20(6):845–856, June 2009. doi: 10.1109/TPDS.2009.20. (page 464)

Jiho Choi, Thomas Shull and Josep Torrellas. Biased reference counting: Minimizing atomic operations in garbage collection. In *27th International Conference on Parallel Architectures and Compilation Techniques*, Limassol, Cyprus, November 2018, page 12. ACM Press. doi: 10.1145/3243176.3243195. (pages 64, 411 and 412)

Douglas W. Clark and C. Cordell Green. An empirical study of list structure in Lisp. *Communications of the ACM*, 20(2):78–86, February 1977. doi: 10.1145/359423.359427. (page 77)

Cliff Click, Gil Tene and Michael Wolf. The Pauseless GC algorithm. In VEE 2005, pages 46–56. doi: 10.1145/1064979.1064988. (pages 341, 342, 386, 395 and 404)

Daniel Clifford, Hannes Payer, Michael Starzinger and Ben L. Titzer. Allocation folding based on dominance. In ISMM 2014, pages 15–24. doi: 10.1145/2602988.2602994. (page 175)

Daniel Clifford, Hannes Payer, Michael Stanton and Ben L. Titzer. Memento Mori: Dynamic allocation-site-based optimizations. In ISMM 2015, pages 105–117. doi: 10.1145/2754169.2754181. (page 242)

Marshall P. Cline and Greg A. Lomow. *C++ FAQs: Frequently Asked Questions*. Addison-Wesley, 1995. (page 3)

William D. Clinger and Lars T. Hansen. Generational garbage collection and the radioactive decay model. In PLDI 1997, pages 97–108. doi: 10.1145/258915.258925. (page 134)

Michael Coblenz, Michelle L. Mazurek and Michael Hicks. Garbage collection makes Rust easier to use: A randomized controlled trial of the Bronze garbage collector. In *44th International Conference on Software Engineering*, Pittsburg, PA, May 2022, pages 1021–1032. IEEE Computer Society Press. doi: 10.1145/3510003.3510107. (pages 3, 4 and 156)

Joel Coburn, Adrian M. Caulfield, Ameen Akel, Laura M. Grupp, Rajesh K. Gupta, Ranjit Jhala and Steven Swanson. NV-Heaps: Making persistent objects fast and safe with next-generation, non-volatile memories. In Todd Mowry, editor, *16th International Conference on Architectural Support for Programming Languages and Operating Systems*, Newport Beach, CA, March 2011, pages 105–118. ACM Press. doi: 10.1145/1950365.1950380. (pages 478 and 479)

Jacques Cohen and Alexandru Nicolau. Comparison of compacting algorithms for garbage collection. *ACM Transactions on Programming Languages and Systems*, 5(4): 532–553, October 1983. doi: 10.1145/69575.357226. (page 38)

Nachshon Cohen. Every data structure deserves lock-free memory reclamation. In *ACM SIGPLAN Conference on Object-Oriented Programming, Systems, Languages, and Applications*, October 2018. ACM Press. doi: 10.1145/3276513. (page 422)

Nachshon Cohen and Erez Petrank. Automatic memory reclamation for lock-free data structures. In *ACM SIGPLAN Conference on Object-Oriented Programming, Systems, Languages, and Applications*, Pittsburgh, PA, October 2015. ACM Press. doi: 10.1145/2814270.2814298. (page 422)

George E. Collins. A method for overlapping and erasure of lists. *Communications of the ACM*, 3(12):655–657, December 1960. doi: 10.1145/367487.367501. (pages 2 and 61)

W.T. Comfort. Multiword list items. *Communications of the ACM*, 7(6):357–362, June 1964. doi: 10.1145/512274.512288. (page 98)

Jeremy Condit, Edmund B. Nightingale, Christopher Frost, Engin Ipek, Benjamin C. Lee, Doug Burger and Derrick Coetzee. Better I/O through byte-addressable, persistent memory. In Jeanna Neefe Matthews and Thomas E. Anderson, editors, *Proceedings of the 22nd ACM Symposium on Operating Systems Principles SOSP*, Big Sky, MT, October 2009, pages 133–146. ACM Press. doi: 10.1145/1629575.1629589. (page 479)

Eric Cooper, Scott Nettles and Indira Subramanian. Improving the performance of SML garbage collection using application-specific virtual memory management. In LFP 1992, pages 43–52. doi: 10.1145/141471.141501. (pages 220 and 221)

Andreia Correia, Pedro Ramalhete and Pascal Felber. OrcGC: Automatic lock-free memory reclamation. In *26th ACM SIGPLAN Symposium on Principles and Practice of Parallel Programming*, February 2021, page 205–218. ACM Press. doi: 10.1145/3437801.3441596. (page 422)

Erik Corry. Optimistic stack allocation for Java-like languages. In ISMM 2006, pages 162–173. doi: 10.1145/1133956.1133978. (page 155)

Jim Crammond. A garbage collection algorithm for shared memory parallel processors. *International Journal Of Parallel Programming*, 17(6):497–522, 1988. doi: 10.1007/BF01407816. (pages 316 and 317)

Mohammad Dashti and Alexandra Fedorova. Analyzing memory management methods on integrated CPU-GPU systems. In ISMM 2017, pages 59–69. doi: 10.1145/3092255.3092256. (page 320)

Mohammad Dashti and Alexandra Fedorova. Trash talk: Accelerating garbage collection on integrated GPUs is worthless. https://arxiv.org/pdf/2012.06281.pdf, December 2020. (page 321)

Laurent Daynès and Malcolm P. Atkinson. Main-memory management to support orthogonal persistence for Java. In *2nd International Workshop on Persistence and Java (PJW2)*, Half Moon Bay, CA, August 1997. `https://www.semanticscholar.org/paper/Main-Memory-Management-to-support-Orthogonal-for-Dayn%C3%A8s-Atkinson/0bdabcd014ebb89b9e360280eb163e295fc713f2`. (page 477)

Ulan Degenbaev, Michael Lippautz and Hannes Payer. Concurrent marking of shape-changing objects. In ISMM 2019, pages 89–102. doi: `10.1145/3315573.3329978`. (pages 242 and 243)

Alan Demers, Mark Weiser, Barry Hayes, Hans Boehm, Daniel G. Bobrow and Scott Shenker. Combining generational and conservative garbage collection: Framework and implementations. In *17th Annual ACM SIGPLAN Symposium on Principles of Programming Languages*, San Francisco, CA, January 1990, pages 261–269. ACM Press. doi: `10.1145/96709.96735`. (page 122)

Joel E. Denny, Seyong Lee and Jeffrey S. Vetter. NVL-C: Static analysis techniques for efficient, correct programming of non-volatile main memory systems. In *Proceedings of the 25th ACM International Symposium on High-Performance Parallel and Distributed Computing*, Kyoto, Japan, May 2016, pages 125–136. ACM Press. doi: `10.1145/2907294.2907303`. (pages 478 and 479)

David Detlefs. Automatic inference of reference-count invariants. In *2nd Workshop on Semantics, Program Analysis, and Computing Environments for Memory Management (SPACE)*, Venice, Italy, January 2004a. `http://forskning.diku.dk/topps/space2004/space_final/detlefs.pdf`. (pages 162, 354 and 355)

David Detlefs. A hard look at hard real-time garbage collection. In *7th International Symposium on Object-Oriented Real-Time Distributed Computing*, Vienna, May 2004b, pages 23–32. IEEE Press. doi: `10.1109/ISORC.2004.1300325`. Invited paper. (pages 425 and 433)

David Detlefs, William D. Clinger, Matthias Jacob and Ross Knippel. Concurrent remembered set refinement in generational garbage collection. In *2nd Java Virtual Machine Research and Technology Symposium*, San Francisco, CA, August 2002a. USENIX Association. `https://www.usenix.org/conference/java-vm-02/concurrent-remembered-set-refinement-generational-garbage-collection`. (pages 97, 207, 209, 210, 213 and 343)

David Detlefs, Christine Flood, Steven Heller and Tony Printezis. Garbage-First garbage collection. In ISMM 2004, pages 37–48. doi: `10.1145/1029873.1029879`. (pages 158 and 169)

David L. Detlefs. Concurrent garbage collection for C++. Technical Report CMU-CS-90-119, Carnegie Mellon University, Pittsburgh, PA, May 1990. `http://repository.cmu.edu/compsci/1956`. (page 370)

David L. Detlefs, Paul A. Martin, Mark Moir and Guy L. Steele. Lock-free reference counting. In *20th ACM Symposium on Distributed Computing*, Newport, Rhode Island, August 2001, pages 190–199. ACM Press. doi: `10.1145/383962.384016`. (page 410)

David L. Detlefs, Paul A. Martin, Mark Moir and Guy L. Steele. Lock-free reference counting. *Distributed Computing*, 15:255–271, 2002b. doi: 10.1007/s00446-002-0079-z. (page 410)

John DeTreville. Experience with concurrent garbage collectors for Modula-2+. Technical Report 64, DEC Systems Research Center, Palo Alto, CA, August 1990. https://www.hpl.hp.com/techreports/Compaq-DEC/SRC-RR-64.pdf. (pages 370 and 412)

L. Peter Deutsch and Daniel G. Bobrow. An efficient incremental automatic garbage collector. *Communications of the ACM*, 19(9):522–526, September 1976. doi: 10.1145/360336.360345. (pages 65, 67 and 111)

Sylvia Dieckmann and Urs Hölzle. The allocation behaviour of the SPECjvm98 Java benchmarks. In Rudolf Eigenman, editor, *Performance Evaluation and Benchmarking with Realistic Applications*, chapter 3, pages 77–108. MIT Press, 2001. (page 64)

Sylvia Dieckmann and Urs Hölzle. A study of the allocation behavior of the SPECjvm98 Java benchmarks. In Rachid Guerraoui, editor, *13th European Conference on Object-Oriented Programming*, Lisbon, Portugal, July 1999, pages 92–115. Volume 1628 of *Lecture Notes in Computer Science*, Springer-Verlag. doi: 10.1007/3-540-48743-3_5. (pages 64, 119, 120 and 131)

Edsger W. Dijkstra, Leslie Lamport, A.J. Martin, C.S. Scholten and E.F.M. Steffens. On-the-fly garbage collection: An exercise in cooperation. In *Language Hierarchies and Interfaces: International Summer School*, volume 46 of *Lecture Notes in Computer Science*, pages 43–56. Springer-Verlag, Marktoberdorf, Germany, 1976. doi: 10.1007/3-540-07994-7_48. (pages 13, 23, 331, 338, 339 and 349)

Edsger W. Dijkstra, Leslie Lamport, A.J. Martin, C.S. Scholten and E.F.M. Steffens. On-the-fly garbage collection: An exercise in cooperation. *Communications of the ACM*, 21(11):965–975, November 1978. doi: 10.1145/359642.359655. (pages 13, 23, 331, 338, 339, 340, 349 and 359)

Robert Dimpsey, Rajiv Arora and Kean Kuiper. Java server performance: A case study of building efficient, scalable JVMs. *IBM Systems Journal*, 39(1):151–174, 2000. doi: 10.1147/sj.391.0151. (pages 33, 105, 158, 161, 162 and 197)

Amer Diwan, J. Eliot B. Moss and Richard L. Hudson. Compiler support for garbage collection in a statically typed language. In PLDI 1992, pages 273–282. doi: 10.1145/143095.143140. (pages 190, 191, 194 and 195)

Amer Diwan, David Tarditi and J. Eliot B. Moss. Memory subsystem performance of programs using copying garbage collection. In POPL 1994, pages 1–14. doi: 10.1145/174675.174710. (pages 105 and 175)

Julian Dolby. Automatic inline allocation of objects. In PLDI 1997, pages 7–17. doi: 10.1145/258915.258918. (page 156)

Julian Dolby and Andrew A. Chien. An automatic object inlining optimization and its evaluation. In PLDI 2000, pages 345–357. doi: 10.1145/349299.349344. (page 156)

Julian Dolby and Andrew A. Chien. An evaluation of automatic object inline allocation techniques. In *ACM SIGPLAN Conference on Object-Oriented Programming, Systems, Languages, and Applications*, Vancouver, Canada, October 1998, pages 1–20. ACM SIGPLAN Notices 33(10), ACM Press. doi: 10.1145/286936.286943. (page 156)

Damien Doligez and Georges Gonthier. Portable, unobtrusive garbage collection for multiprocessor systems. In POPL 1994, pages 70–83. doi: 10.1145/174675.174673. (pages 113, 114, 153, 358, 360 and 379)

Damien Doligez and Xavier Leroy. A concurrent generational garbage collector for a multi-threaded implementation of ML. In *20th Annual ACM SIGPLAN Symposium on Principles of Programming Languages*, Charleston, SC, January 1993, pages 113–123. ACM Press. doi: 10.1145/158511.158611. (pages 113, 114, 153 and 358)

Tamar Domani, Elliot K. Kolodner and Erez Petrank. A generational on-the-fly garbage collector for Java. In PLDI 2000, pages 274–284. doi: 10.1145/349299.349336. (pages 359 and 360)

Tamar Domani, Elliot K. Kolodner, Ethan Lewis, Erez Petrank and Dafna Sheinwald. Thread-local heaps for Java. In ISMM 2002, pages 76–87. doi: 10.1145/512429.512439. (pages 115, 116, 152 and 154)

Kevin Donnelly, Joe Hallett and Assaf Kfoury. Formal semantics of weak references. In ISMM 2006, pages 126–137. doi: 10.1145/1133956.1133974. (page 241)

R. Kent Dybvig, Carl Bruggeman and David Eby. Guardians in a generation-based garbage collector. In PLDI 1993, pages 207–216. doi: 10.1145/155090.155110. (page 232)

ECOOP 2007, Erik Ernst, editor. *21st European Conference on Object-Oriented Programming*, Berlin, Germany, July 2007. Volume 4609 of *Lecture Notes in Computer Science*, Springer-Verlag. doi: 10.1007/978-3-540-73589-2. (pages 516 and 546)

Daniel R. Edelson. Smart pointers: They're smart, but they're not pointers. In *USENIX C++ Conference*, Portland, OR, August 1992. USENIX Association. (pages 62 and 78)

Toshio Endo, Kenjiro Taura and Akinori Yonezawa. A scalable mark-sweep garbage collector on large-scale shared-memory machines. In *ACM/IEEE Conference on Supercomputing*, San Jose, CA, November 1997. doi: 10.1109/SC.1997.10059. (pages 265, 293, 296, 297, 300, 304, 316 and 325)

A.P. Ershov. On programming of arithmetic operations. *Communications of the ACM*, 1(8): 3–6, August 1958. doi: 10.1145/368892.368907. (page 180)

Shahrooz Feizabadi and Godmar Back. Java garbage collection scheduling in utility accrual scheduling environments. In *3rd International Workshop on Java Technologies for Real-time and Embedded Systems (JTRES)*, San Diego, CA, 2005. http://people.cs.vt.edu/~gback/papers/jtres2005-cadus.pdf. (page 464)

Shahrooz Feizabadi and Godmar Back. Garbage collection-aware utility accrual scheduling. *Real-Time Systems*, 36(1–2), July 2007. doi: 10.1007/s11241-007-9020-7. (page 464)

Robert R. Fenichel and Jerome C. Yochelson. A Lisp garbage collector for virtual memory computer systems. *Communications of the ACM*, 12(11):611–612, November 1969. doi: 10.1145/363269.363280. (pages 47, 48, 54 and 113)

Stephen J. Fink and Feng Qian. Design, implementation and evaluation of adaptive recompilation with on-stack replacement. In *1st International Symposium on Code Generation and Optimization (CGO)*, San Francisco, CA, March 2003, pages 241–252. IEEE Computer Society Press. doi: 10.1109/CGO.2003.1191549. (page 201)

David A. Fisher. Bounded workspace garbage collection in an address order preserving list processing environment. *Information Processing Letters*, 3(1):29–32, July 1974. doi: 10.1016/0020-0190(74)90044-1. (page 40)

John P. Fitch and Arthur C. Norman. A note on compacting garbage collection. *Computer Journal*, 21(1):31–34, February 1978. (page 46)

Robert Fitzgerald and David Tarditi. The case for profile-directed selection of garbage collectors. In ISMM 2000, pages 111–120. doi: 10.1145/362422.362472. (pages 6, 81 and 214)

Christine Flood, Dave Detlefs, Nir Shavit and Catherine Zhang. Parallel garbage collection for shared memory multiprocessors. In JVM 2001. http://www.usenix.org/events/jvm01/flood.html. (pages 38, 40, 264, 294, 296, 298, 299, 300, 304, 308, 315, 317, 318, 325, 326 and 391)

Christine H. Flood, Roman Kennke, Andrew Dinn, Andrew Haley and Roland Westrelin. Shenandoah: An open-source concurrent compacting garbage collector for OpenJDK. In *ACM International Symposium on Principles and Practice of Programming in Java*, Lugano, Switzerland, August 2016, pages 13:1–13:9. ACM. doi: 10.1145/2972206.2972210. (pages 401, 403 and 404)

John K. Foderaro and Richard J. Fateman. Characterization of VAX Macsyma. In *1981 ACM Symposium on Symbolic and Algebraic Computation*, Berkeley, CA, 1981, pages 14–19. ACM Press. doi: 10.1145/800206.806364. (page 119)

John K. Foderaro, Keith Sklower, Kevin Layer *et al.*. *Franz Lisp Reference Manual*. Franz Inc., 1985. (page 29)

Daniel Frampton, David F. Bacon, Perry Cheng and David Grove. Generational real-time garbage collection: A three-part invention for young objects. In ECOOP 2007, pages 101–125. doi: 10.1007/978-3-540-73589-2_6. (page 448)

Keir Fraser. *Practical Lock-Freedom*. PhD thesis, University of Cambridge, 2004. https://www.cl.cam.ac.uk/techreports/UCAM-CL-TR-579.pdf. (page 421)

Edward Fredkin. Trie memory. *Communications of the ACM*, 3(9):490–499, September 1960. doi: 10.1145/367390.367400. (page 461)

Daniel P. Friedman and David S. Wise. Reference counting can manage the circular environments of mutual recursion. *Information Processing Letters*, 8(1):41–45, January 1979. doi: 10.1016/0020-0190(79)90091-7. (page 71)

Ben Gamari and Laura Dietz. Alligator collector: A latency-optimized garbage collector for functional programming languages. In ISMM 2020, pages 87–99. doi: 10.1145/3381898.3397214. (page 480)

Robin Garner, Stephen M. Blackburn and Daniel Frampton. Effective prefetch for mark-sweep garbage collection. In ISMM 2007, pages 43–54. doi: 10.1145/1296907.1296915. (pages 26, 28 and 31)

Robin J. Garner, Stephen M. Blackburn and Daniel Frampton. A comprehensive evaluation of object scanning techniques. In ISMM 2011, pages 33–42. doi: 10.1145/1993478.1993484. (page 181)

Alex Garthwaite. *Making the Trains Run On Time*. PhD thesis, University of Pennsylvania, 2005. (page 206)

Alex Garthwaite, Dave Dice and Derek White. Supporting per-processor local-allocation buffers using lightweight user-level preemption notification. In VEE 2005, pages 24–34. doi: `10.1145/1064979.1064985`. (pages 106 and 206)

Alexander T. Garthwaite, David L. Detlefs, Antonios Printezis and Y. Srinivas Ramakrishna. Method and mechanism for finding references in a card in time linear in the size of the card in a garbage-collected heap. United States Patent 7,136,887 B2, Sun Microsystems, November 2006. (page 212)

David Gay and Bjarne Steensgaard. Fast escape analysis and stack allocation for object-based programs. In *9th International Conference on Compiler Construction*, Berlin, April 2000, pages 82–93. Volume 2027 of *Lecture Notes in Computer Science*, Springer-Verlag. doi: `10.1007/3-540-46423-9_6`. (pages 155 and 156)

GC 1990, Eric Jul and Niels-Christian Juul, editors. *OOPSLA/ECOOP Workshop on Garbage Collection in Object-Oriented Systems*, Ottawa, Canada, October 1990. doi: `10.1145/319016.319042`. (pages 522 and 545)

GC 1991, Paul R. Wilson and Barry Hayes, editors. *OOPSLA Workshop on Garbage Collection in Object-Oriented Systems*, October 1991. doi: `10.1145/143776.143792`. (pages 522 and 546)

GC 1993, J. Eliot B. Moss, Paul R. Wilson and Benjamin Zorn, editors. *OOPSLA Workshop on Garbage Collection in Object-Oriented Systems*, October 1993. (pages 521 and 545)

Jerrin Shaji George, Mohit Verma, Rajesh Venkatasubramanian and Pratap Subrahmanyam. go-pmem: Native support for programming persistent memory in Go. In Ada Gavrilovska and Erez Zadok, editors, *2020 USENIX Annual Technical Conference*, July 2020, pages 859–872. USENIX Association. `https://www.usenix.org/conference/atc20/presentation/george`. (pages 478 and 479)

Andy Georges, Dries Buytaert and Lieven Eeckhout. Statistically rigorous Java performance evaluation. In *ACM SIGPLAN Conference on Object-Oriented Programming, Systems, Languages, and Applications*, Montréal, Canada, October 2007, pages 57–76. ACM SIGPLAN Notices 42(10), ACM Press. doi: `10.1145/1297027.1297033`. (pages 11 and 12)

Anders Gidenstam, Marina Papatriantafilou, Høakan Sundell and Philippas Tsigas. Efficient and reliable lock-free memory reclamation based on reference counting. *IEEE Transactions on Parallel and Distributed Systems*, 20(8), 2009. doi: `10.1109/TPDS.2008.167`. (page 422)

Lokesh Gidra, Gaël Thomas, Julien Sopena and Marc Shapiro. A study of the scalability of stop-the-world garbage collectors on multicores. In *Proceedings of the Eighteenth International Conference on Architectural Support for Programming Languages and Operating Systems (ASPLOS)*, Houston, Texas, 2013, pages 229–240. ACM Press. doi: `10.1145/2451116.2451142`. (page 314)

Lokesh Gidra, Gaël Thomas, Julien Sopena, Marc Shapiro and Nhan Bguyen. NumaGiC: a garbage collector for big data on big NUMA machines. In *Proceedings of the Seventeenth International Conference on Architectural Support for Programming Languages*

and Operating Systems (ASPLOS), Istanbul, Turkey, March 2015.
doi: `10.1145/2694344.2694361`. (page 314)

Joseph (Yossi) Gil and Itay Maman. Micro patterns in Java code. In OOPSLA 2005, pages
97–116. doi: `10.1145/1094811.1094819`. (page 138)

O. Goh, Yann-Hang Lee, Z. Kaakani and E. Rachlin. Integrated scheduling with garbage
collection for real-time embedded applications in CLI. In *9th International Symposium on
Object-Oriented Real-Time Distributed Computing*, Gyeongju, Korea, April 2006. IEEE
Press. doi: `10.1109/ISORC.2006.41`. (page 464)

Benjamin Goldberg. Tag-free garbage collection for strongly typed programming
languages. In PLDI 1991 [PLDI 1991], pages 165–176. doi: `10.1145/113445.113460`.
(pages 181 and 183)

Benjamin Goldberg. Incremental garbage collection without tags. In *European Symposium
on Programming*, Rennes, France, February 1992, pages 200–218. Volume 582 of *Lecture
Notes in Computer Science*, Springer-Verlag. doi: `10.1007/3-540-55253-7_12`. (page
181)

Benjamin Goldberg and Michael Gloger. Polymorphic type reconstruction for garbage
collection without tags. In LFP 1992, pages 53–65. doi: `10.1145/141471.141504`.
(pages 181 and 183)

Marcelo J.R. Gonçalves and Andrew W. Appel. Cache performance of fast-allocating
programs. In *Conference on Functional Programming and Computer Architecture*, La Jolla,
CA, June 1995, pages 293–305. ACM Press. doi: `10.1145/224164.224219`. (page 175)

David Goodell, Pavan Balaji, Darius Buntinas, Gábor Dózsa, William Gropp, Sameer
Kumar, Bronis R. de Supinski and Rajeev Thakur. Minimizing MPI resource contention
in multithreaded multicore environments. In *2010 IEEE International Conference on
Cluster Computing*, 2010, pages 1–8. doi: `10.1109/CLUSTER.2010.11`. (page 167)

James Gosling, Bill Joy, Guy Steele, Gilad Bracha and Alex Buckley. *The Java Language
Specification*. Addison-Wesley, Java SE 8 edition, February 2015.
`https://docs.oracle.com/javase/specs/jls/se8/jls8.pdf`. (page 377)

Eiichi Goto. Monocopy and associative algorithms in an extended LISP. Technical Report
74-03, Information Science Laboratories, Faculty of Science, University of Tokyo, 1974.
(page 180)

Michael Gottesman. Ownership SSA. LLVM Developers' Meeting, 2019.
`https://www.youtube.com/watch?v=qy3iZPHZ88o`. (page 64)

Jim Gray and Andreas Reuter. *Transaction Processing: Concepts and Techniques*. Morgan
Kaufmann, 1993. (page 473)

David Gries. An exercise in proving parallel programs correct. *Communications of the
ACM*, 20(12):921–930, December 1977. doi: `10.1145/359897.359903`. (page 541)

Paul Griffin, Witawas Srisa-An and J. Morris Chang. An energy efficient garbage collector
for Java embedded devices. In LCTES 2005, pages 230–238.
doi: `10.1145/1070891.1065943`. (pages 77, 183, 466 and 467)

Dan Grossman, Greg Morrisett, Trevor Jim, Michael Hicks, Yanling Wang and James
Cheney. Region-based memory management in Cyclone. In PLDI 2002, pages 282–293.
doi: `10.1145/512529.512563`. (page 112)

Chris Grzegorczyk, Sunil Soman, Chandra Krintz and Rich Wolski. Isla Vista heap sizing: Using feedback to avoid paging. In *5th International Symposium on Code Generation and Optimization (CGO)*, San Jose, CA, March 2007, pages 325–340. IEEE Computer Society Press. doi: 10.1109/CGO.2007.20. (page 221)

Adrien Guatto, Sam Westrick, Ram Raghunathan, Umut Acar and Matthew Fluet. Hierarchical memory management for mutable state. In PPOPP 2018, pages 81–93. doi: 10.1145/3178487.3178494. (pages 113, 153 and 154)

Jorge Guerra, Leonardo Mármol, Daniel Campello, Carlos Crespo, Raju Rangaswami and Jinpeng Wei. Software persistent memory. In *2012 USENIX Annual Technical Conference*, Boston, MA, June 2012, pages 319–331. USENIX Association. https://www.usenix.org/conference/atc12/technical-sessions/presentation/guerra. (page 478)

Samuel Guyer and Kathryn McKinley. Finding your cronies: Static analysis for dynamic object colocation. In OOPSLA 2004, pages 237–250. doi: 10.1145/1028976.1028996. (pages 116, 139 and 149)

B.K. Haddon and W.M. Waite. A compaction procedure for variable length storage elements. *Computer Journal*, 10:162–165, August 1967. (page 46)

Robert H. Halstead. Implementation of Multilisp: Lisp on a multiprocessor. In LFP 1984, pages 9–17. doi: 10.1145/800055.802017. (pages 293 and 310)

Robert H. Halstead. Multilisp: A language for concurrent symbolic computation. *ACM Transactions on Programming Languages and Systems*, 7(4):501–538, October 1985. doi: 10.1145/4472.4478. (pages 293, 368, 373 and 376)

Lars Thomas Hansen. *Older-first Garbage Collection in Practice*. PhD thesis, Northeastern University, November 2000. (pages 134 and 135)

Lars Thomas Hansen and William D. Clinger. An experimental study of renewal-older-first garbage collection. In *7th ACM SIGPLAN International Conference on Functional Programming*, Pittsburgh, PA, September 2002, pages 247–258. ACM SIGPLAN Notices 37(9), ACM Press. doi: 10.1145/581478.581502. (page 134)

David R. Hanson. Storage management for an implementation of SNOBOL4. *Software: Practice and Experience*, 7(2):179–192, 1977. doi: 10.1002/spe.4380070206. (page 45)

Tim Harris and Keir Fraser. Language support for lightweight transactions. In OOPSLA 2003, pages 388–402. doi: 10.1145/949305.949340. (page 288)

Timothy Harris. Dynamic adaptive pre-tenuring. In ISMM 2000, pages 127–136. doi: 10.1145/362422.362476. (page 138)

Timothy L. Harris, Keir Fraser and Ian A. Pratt. A practical multi-word compare-and-swap operation. In Dahlia Malkhi, editor, *International Conference on Distributed Computing*, Toulouse, France, October 2002, pages 265–279. Volume 2508 of *Lecture Notes in Computer Science*. doi: 10.1007/3-540-36108-1_18. (page 455)

Thomas E. Hart, Paul E. McKenney, Angela Demke Brown and Jonathan Walpole. Performance of memory reclamation for lockless synchronization. *Journal of Parallel Distributed Computing*, 67(12):1270–1285, 2007. doi: 10.1016/j.jpdc.2007.04.010. (page 421)

Pieter H. Hartel. *Performance Analysis of Storage Management in Combinator Graph Reduction*. PhD thesis, Department of Computer Systems, University of Amsterdam, Amsterdam, 1988. (page 77)

Wessam Hassanein. Understanding and improving JVM GC work stealing at the data center scale. In ISMM 2016, pages 46–54. doi: 10.1145/2926697.2926706. (page 267)

Barry Hayes. Using key object opportunism to collect old objects. In *ACM SIGPLAN Conference on Object-Oriented Programming, Systems, Languages, and Applications*, Phoenix, AZ, November 1991, pages 33–46. ACM SIGPLAN Notices 26(11), ACM Press. doi: 10.1145/117954.117957. (pages 25, 105 and 120)

Barry Hayes. Finalization in the collector interface. In IWMM 1992, pages 277–298. doi: 10.1007/BFb0017196. (page 233)

Barry Hayes. Ephemerons: A new finalization mechanism. In *ACM SIGPLAN Conference on Object-Oriented Programming, Systems, Languages, and Applications*, Atlanta, GA, October 1997, pages 176–183. ACM SIGPLAN Notices 32(10), ACM Press. doi: 10.1145/263698.263733. (page 240)

Laurence Hellyer, Richard Jones and Antony L. Hosking. The locality of concurrent write barriers. In ISMM 2010, pages 83–92. doi: 10.1145/1806651.1806666. (pages 337 and 338)

Fergus Henderson. Accurate garbage collection in an uncooperative environment. In ISMM 2002, pages 150–156. doi: 10.1145/512429.512449. (page 182)

Roger Henriksson. *Scheduling Garbage Collection in Embedded Systems*. PhD thesis, Lund Institute of Technology, July 1998. https://lucris.lub.lu.se/ws/portalfiles/portal/5860617/630830.pdf. (pages 425, 434, 435, 436, 437, 438, 439, 442 and 448)

Maurice Herlihy and J. Eliot B Moss. Lock-free garbage collection for multiprocessors. *IEEE Transactions on Parallel and Distributed Systems*, 3(3):304–311, May 1992. doi: 10.1109/71.139204. (pages 265, 372, 373, 374, 375, 376 and 404)

Maurice Herlihy and Nir Shavit. *The Art of Multiprocessor Programming*. Morgan Kaufman, April 2008. (pages xxviii, 2, 245, 256, 259, 270 and 272)

Maurice Herlihy and Jeannette M. Wing. Linearizability: A correctness condition for concurrent objects. *ACM Transactions on Programming Languages and Systems*, 12(3): 463–492, 1990. doi: 10.1145/78969.78972. (page 270)

Maurice P. Herlihy and J. Eliot B. Moss. Transactional memory: Architectural support for lock-free data structures. In *20th Annual ACM/IEEE International Symposium on Computer Architecture*, San Diego, CA, May 1993, pages 289–300. IEEE Press. doi: 10.1145/165123.165164. (pages 286 and 374)

Maurice P. Herlihy, Victor Luchangco and Mark Moir. The repeat offender problem: A mechanism for supporting dynamic-sized lock-free data structures. In *16th International Symposium on Distributed Computing*, Toulouse, France, October 2002, pages 339–353. Volume 2508 of *Lecture Notes in Computer Science*, Springer-Verlag. doi: 10.1007/3-540-36108-1_23. (page 421)

Matthew Hertz. *Quantifying and Improving the Performance of Garbage Collection*. PhD thesis, University of Massachusetts, September 2006. `https://cse.buffalo.edu/~mhertz/thesis.pdf`. (page 220)

Matthew Hertz and Emery Berger. Quantifying the performance of garbage collection vs. explicit memory management. In OOPSLA 2005, pages 313–326. doi: `10.1145/1094811.1094836`. (pages 32 and 59)

Matthew Hertz, Yi Feng and Emery D. Berger. Garbage collection without paging. In Vivek Sarkar and Mary W. Hall, editors, *ACM SIGPLAN Conference on Programming Language Design and Implementation*, Chicago, IL, June 2005, pages 143–153. ACM SIGPLAN Notices 40(6), ACM Press. doi: `10.1145/1064978.1065028`. (pages 10, 83, 114, 116, 166 and 220)

Matthew Hertz, Jonathan Bard, Stephen Kane, Elizabeth Keudel, Tongxin Bai, Kirk Kelsey and Chen Ding. Waste not, want not — resource-based garbage collection in a shared environment. Technical Report TR–951, The University of Rochester, December 2009. doi: `1802/8838`. (pages 221 and 222)

D.S. Hirschberg. A class of dynamic memory allocation algorithms. *Communications of the ACM*, 16(10):615–618, October 1973. doi: `10.1145/362375.362392`. (page 101)

Martin Hirzel, Amer Diwan and Matthew Hertz. Connectivity-based garbage collection. In OOPSLA 2003, pages 359–373. doi: `10.1145/949305.949337`. (pages 149, 150 and 169)

Urs Hölzle. A fast write barrier for generational garbage collectors. In GC 1993. `https://www.cs.utexas.edu/ftp/garbage/GC93/hoelzle.ps`. (page 209)

Michihiro Horie, Hiroshi Horii, Kazunori Ogata and Tamiya Onodera. Balanced double queues for GC work-stealing on weak memory models. In ISMM 2018, pages 109–119. doi: `10.1145/3210563.3210570`. (page 296)

Michihiro Horie, Kazunori Ogata, Mikio Takeuchi and Hiroshi Horii. Scaling up parallel GC work-stealing in many-core environments. In ISMM 2019, pages 27–40. doi: `10.1145/3315573.3329985`. (page 296)

Morteza Hoseinzadeh and Steven Swanson. Corundum: statically-enforced persistent memory safety. In Tim Sherwood, Emery D. Berger and Christos Kozyrakis, editors, *26th International Conference on Architectural Support for Programming Languages and Operating Systems*, April 2021, pages 429–442. ACM Press. doi: `10.1145/3445814`. ASPLOS 2021 was a virtual event. (pages 478 and 479)

Antony L Hosking. Portable, mostly-concurrent, mostly-copying garbage collection for multi-processors. In ISMM 2006, pages 40–51. doi: `10.1145/1133956.1133963`. (pages 32 and 370)

Antony L. Hosking and Jiawan Chen. PM3: An orthogonally persistent systems programming language. In *International Conference on Very Large Data Bases*, Edinburgh, Scotland, September 1999, pages 587–598. `http://www.vldb.org/conf/1999/P55.pdf`. (pages 477 and 478)

Antony L. Hosking and Richard L. Hudson. Remembered sets can also play cards. In GC 1993. `https://www.cs.utexas.edu/ftp/garbage/GC93/hosking.ps`. (page 213)

Antony L. Hosking and J. Eliot B. Moss. Object fault handling for persistent
   programming languages: A performance evaluation. In *ACM SIGPLAN Conference on
   Object-Oriented Programming, Systems, Languages, and Applications*, Washington, DC,
   October 1993a. ACM SIGPLAN Notices 28(10), ACM Press.
   doi: `10.1145/165854.165907`. (pages 477 and 478)

Antony L. Hosking and J. Eliot B. Moss. Protection traps and alternatives for memory
   management of an object-oriented language. In *14th ACM SIGOPS Symposium on
   Operating Systems Principles*, Asheville, NC, December 1993b, pages 106–119. ACM
   SIGOPS Operating Systems Review 27(5), ACM Press.
   doi: `10.1145/168619.168628`. (pages 385 and 478)

Antony L. Hosking, J. Eliot B. Moss and Darko Stefanović. A comparative performance
   evaluation of write barrier implementations. In *ACM SIGPLAN Conference on
   Object-Oriented Programming, Systems, Languages, and Applications*, Vancouver, Canada,
   October 1992, pages 92–109. ACM SIGPLAN Notices 27(10), ACM Press.
   doi: `10.1145/141936.141946`. (pages 143, 144, 204, 205, 207, 208, 210, 213, 214 and
   217)

Antony L. Hosking, Nathaniel Nystrom, Quintin Cutts and Kumar Brahnmath.
   Optimizing the read and write barrier for orthogonal persistence. In Ronald Morrison,
   Mick J. Jordan and Malcolm P. Atkinson, editors, *8th International Workshop on Persistent
   Object Systems (August, 1998)*, Tiburon, CA, 1999, pages 149–159. Advances in Persistent
   Object Systems, Morgan Kaufmann.
   `http://hosking.github.io/links/Hosking+1998POS.pdf`. (page 349)

Xianlong Huang, Stephen M. Blackburn, Kathryn S. McKinley, J. Eliot B. Moss, Z. Wang
   and Perry Cheng. The garbage collection advantage: Improving program locality. In
   OOPSLA 2004, pages 69–80. doi: `10.1145/1028976.1028983`. (pages 56, 57 and 180)

Richard L. Hudson. Finalization in a garbage collected world. In GC 1991.
   doi: `10.1145/143776.143792`. (page 233)

Richard L. Hudson and Amer Diwan. Adaptive garbage collection for Modula-3 and
   Smalltalk. In GC 1990. doi: `10.1145/319016.319042`. (page 207)

Richard L. Hudson and J. Eliot B. Moss. Sapphire: Copying GC without stopping the
   world. In *Joint ACM-ISCOPE Conference on Java Grande*, Palo Alto, CA, June 2001, pages
   48–57. ACM Press. doi: `10.1145/376656.376810`. (pages 376 and 404)

Richard L. Hudson and J. Eliot B. Moss. Sapphire: Copying garbage collection without
   stopping the world. *Concurrency and Computation: Practice and Experience*, 15(3–5):
   223–261, 2003. doi: `10.1002/cpe.712`. (pages 376 and 404)

Richard L. Hudson and J. Eliot B. Moss. Incremental collection of mature objects. In
   IWMM 1992, pages 388–403. doi: `10.1007/BFb0017203`. (pages 115, 136, 143, 146,
   149, 168, 214 and 220)

Richard L. Hudson, J. Eliot B. Moss, Amer Diwan and Christopher F. Weight. A
   language-independent garbage collector toolkit. Technical Report COINS 91-47,
   University of Massachusetts, September 1991. `https:`
   `//web.cs.umass.edu/publication/docs/1991/UM-CS-1991-047.pdf`.
   (pages 125 and 144)

R. John M. Hughes. A semi-incremental garbage collection algorithm. *Software: Practice and Experience*, 12(11):1081–1082, November 1982. doi: `10.1002/spe.4380121108`. (page 28)

A.H. Hunter, Chris Kennelly, Paul Turner, Darryl Gove, Tipp Moseley and Parthasarathy Ranganathan. Beyond malloc efficiency to fleet efficiency: a hugepage-aware memory allocator. In *15th USENIX Symposium on Operating Systems Design and Implementation (OSDI 21)*, July 2021, pages 257–273. USENIX Association. `https://www.usenix.org/conference/osdi21/presentation/hunter`. (page xxviii)

Ahmed Hussein, Antony L. Hosking, Mathias Payer and Christopher A. Vick. Don't race the memory bus: Taming the GC leadfoot. In ISMM 2015. doi: `10.1145/2754169.2754182`. (page 467)

Ahmed Hussein, Mathias Payer, Antony L. Hosking and Christopher A. Vick. Impact of GC design on power and performance for Android. In *ACM International Systems and Storage Conference*, Haifa, Israel, May 2015b. SYSTOR. doi: `10.1145/2757667.2757674`. (page 467)

Ahmed Hussein, Mathias Payer, Antony L. Hosking and Chris Vick. One process to reap them all: Garbage collection as-a-Service. In Erez Petrank, Dan Tsafrir and Martin Hirzel, editors, *Proceedings of the 13th ACM SIGPLAN/SIGOPS International Conference on Virtual Execution Environments*, Xi'an, China, March 2017, pages 171–186. ACM Press. doi: `10.1145/3050748.3050754`. (page 468)

Akira Imai and Evan Tick. Evaluation of parallel copying garbage collection on a shared-memory multiprocessor. *IEEE Transactions on Parallel and Distributed Systems*, 4 (9):1030–1040, 1993. doi: `10.1109/71.243529`. (pages 310, 311, 312, 313 and 326)

Mohamed Ismail and G. Edward Suh. Hardware-software co-optimization of memory management in dynamic languages. In ISMM 2018, pages 45–58. doi: `10.1145/3210563.3210566`. (page 469)

ISMM 1998, Simon L. Peyton Jones and Richard Jones, editors. *1st ACM SIGPLAN International Symposium on Memory Management*, Vancouver, Canada, October 1998. ACM SIGPLAN Notices 34(3), ACM Press. doi: `10.1145/286860`. (pages 511, 533 and 539)

ISMM 2000, Craig Chambers and Antony L. Hosking, editors. *2nd ACM SIGPLAN International Symposium on Memory Management*, Minneapolis, MN, October 2000. ACM SIGPLAN Notices 36(1), ACM Press. doi: `10.1145/362422`. (pages 507, 516, 519, 535, 540 and 541)

ISMM 2002, Hans-J. Boehm and David Detlefs, editors. *3rd ACM SIGPLAN International Symposium on Memory Management*, Berlin, Germany, June 2002. ACM SIGPLAN Notices 38(2 supplement), ACM Press. doi: `10.1145/773146`. (pages 506, 515, 520, 525, 535 and 536)

ISMM 2004, David F. Bacon and Amer Diwan, editors. *4th ACM SIGPLAN International Symposium on Memory Management*, Vancouver, Canada, October 2004. ACM Press. doi: `10.1145/1029873`. (pages 506, 510, 513, 526, 532, 537, 539 and 547)

ISMM 2006, Erez Petrank and J. Eliot B. Moss, editors. *5th ACM SIGPLAN International Symposium on Memory Management*, Ottawa, Canada, June 2006. ACM Press. doi: `10.1145/1133956`. (pages 512, 515, 521, 530, 539, 540 and 547)

ISMM 2007, Greg Morrisett and Mooly Sagiv, editors. *6th ACM SIGPLAN International Symposium on Memory Management*, Montréal, Canada, October 2007. ACM Press. doi: 10.1145/1296907. (pages 516, 529, 534 and 539)

ISMM 2008, Richard Jones and Steve Blackburn, editors. *7th ACM SIGPLAN International Symposium on Memory Management*, Tucson, AZ, June 2008. ACM Press. doi: 10.1145/1375634. (pages 525, 530 and 539)

ISMM 2009, Hillel Kolodner and Guy Steele, editors. *8th ACM SIGPLAN International Symposium on Memory Management*, Dublin, Ireland, June 2009. ACM Press. doi: 10.1145/1542431. (pages 508, 532 and 544)

ISMM 2010, Jan Vitek and Doug Lea, editors. *9th ACM SIGPLAN International Symposium on Memory Management*, Toronto, Canada, June 2010. ACM Press. doi: 10.1145/1806651. (pages 502, 505, 520 and 539)

ISMM 2011, Hans Boehm and David Bacon, editors. *10th ACM SIGPLAN International Symposium on Memory Management*, San Jose, CA, June 2011. ACM Press. doi: 10.1145/1993478. (pages 516, 526, 529, 542 and 544)

ISMM 2012, Kathryn McKinley and Martin Vechev, editors. *11th ACM SIGPLAN International Symposium on Memory Management*, Beijing, China, June 2012. ACM Press. doi: 10.1145/2258996. (pages 525, 529, 538, 539 and 547)

ISMM 2013, Erez Petrank and Perry Cheng, editors. *12th ACM SIGPLAN International Symposium on Memory Management*, Seattle, WA, June 2013. ACM Press. doi: 10.1145/2491894.

ISMM 2014, Samuel Z. Guyer and David Grove, editors. *13th ACM SIGPLAN International Symposium on Memory Management*, Edinburgh, June 2014. ACM Press. doi: 10.1145/2602988. (pages 511, 536 and 542)

ISMM 2015, Mike Bond and Tony Hosking, editors. *14th ACM SIGPLAN International Symposium on Memory Management*, Portland, OR, June 2015. ACM Press. doi: 10.1145/2754169. (pages 511 and 523)

ISMM 2016, Zheng Zhang and Christine Flood, editors. *15th ACM SIGPLAN International Symposium on Memory Management*, Santa Barbara, CA, June 2016. ACM Press. doi: 10.1145/2926697. (page 520)

ISMM 2017, Christoph Kirsch and Ben Titzer, editors. *16th ACM SIGPLAN International Symposium on Memory Management*, Barcelona, June 2017. ACM Press. doi: 10.1145/3092255. (pages 508 and 512)

ISMM 2018, Hannes Payer and Jennifer Sartor, editors. *17th ACM SIGPLAN International Symposium on Memory Management*, Philadelphia, June 2018. ACM Press. doi: 10.1145/3210563. (pages 521 and 523)

ISMM 2019, Harry Xu and Jeremy Singer, editors. *18th ACM SIGPLAN International Symposium on Memory Management*, Phoenix, AZ, June 2019. ACM Press. doi: 10.1145/3315573. (pages 506, 513 and 521)

ISMM 2020, Martin Maas and Chen Ding, editors. *19th ACM SIGPLAN International Symposium on Memory Management*, June 2020. ACM Press. doi: 10.1145/3381898. (page 516)

ISMM 2021, Tobias Wrigstad and Zhenlin Wang, editors. *20th ACM SIGPLAN International Symposium on Memory Management*, June 2021. ACM Press. doi: `10.1145/3459898`. (page 532)

ISMM 2022, David Chisnall and Michael Lippautz, editors. *21st ACM SIGPLAN International Symposium on Memory Management*, June 2022. ACM Press. doi: `10.1145/3520263`.

IWMM 1992, Yves Bekkers and Jacques Cohen, editors. *International Workshop on Memory Management*, St Malo, France, 17–19 September 1992. Volume 637 of *Lecture Notes in Computer Science*, Springer. doi: `10.1007/BFb0017181`. (pages 520, 522, 528 and 531)

IWMM 1995, Henry G. Baker, editor. *International Workshop on Memory Management*, Kinross, Scotland, 27–29 September 1995. Volume 986 of *Lecture Notes in Computer Science*, Springer. doi: `10.1007/3-540-60368-9`. (pages 529 and 545)

Balaji Iyengar, Edward Gehringer, Michael Wolf and Karthikeyan Manivannan. Scalable concurrent and parallel mark. In ISMM 2012, pages 61–72. doi: `10.1145/2258996.2259006`. (pages 315 and 391)

Balaji Iyengar, Gil Tene, Michael Wolf and Edward Gehringer. The Collie: a wait-free compacting collector. In ISMM 2012, pages 85–96. doi: `10.1145/2258996.2259009`. (pages 395 and 396)

Ivan Jibaja, Stephen M. Blackburn, Mohammad R. Haghighat and Kathryn S. McKinley. Deferred gratification: Engineering for high performance garbage collection from the get go. In Jeffrey Vetter, Madanlal Musuvathi and Xipeng Shen, editors, *Workshop on Memory System Performance and Correctness*, San Jose, CA, June 2011. doi: `10.1145/1988915.1988930`. (page 62)

Erik Johansson, Konstantinos Sagonas and Jesper Wilhelmsson. Heap architectures for concurrent languages using message passing. In ISMM 2002, pages 88–99. doi: `10.1145/512429.512440`. (page 152)

Mark S. Johnstone. *Non-Compacting Memory Allocation and Real-Time Garbage Collection*. PhD thesis, University of Texas at Austin, December 1997. `https://www.cs.utexas.edu/ftp/garbage/johnstone-dissertation.ps.gz`. (page 161)

Richard Jones and Chris Ryder. A study of Java object demographics. In ISMM 2008, pages 121–130. doi: `10.1145/1375634.1375652`. (pages 25, 112, 119 and 120)

Richard E. Jones. *Garbage Collection: Algorithms for Automatic Dynamic Memory Management*. Wiley, Chichester, July 1996. `http://www.cs.kent.ac.uk/people/staff/rej/gcbook/gcbook.html`. With a chapter on Distributed Garbage Collection by R. Lins. (pages xxix, 6, 19, 32, 46, 58, 71, 84, 123, 125, 130, 144, 148, 158 and 177)

Richard E. Jones and Andy C. King. Collecting the garbage without blocking the traffic. Technical Report 18–04, Computing Laboratory, University of Kent, September 2004. `http://www.cs.kent.ac.uk/pubs/2004/1970/`. This report summarises King [2004]. (page 526)

Richard E. Jones and Andy C. King. A fast analysis for thread-local garbage collection with dynamic class loading. In *5th IEEE International Workshop on Source Code Analysis and Manipulation (SCAM)*, Budapest, September 2005, pages 129–138. IEEE Computer Society Press. doi: `10.1109/SCAM.2005.1`. This is a shorter version of Jones and King [2004]. (pages 113, 115, 151, 152 and 169)

H.B.M. Jonkers. A fast garbage compaction algorithm. *Information Processing Letters*, 9(1): 26–30, July 1979. doi: `10.1016/0020-0190(79)90103-0`. (pages 36, 41 and 42)

Maria Jump, Stephen M. Blackburn and Kathryn S. McKinley. Dynamic object sampling for pretenuring. In ISMM 2004, pages 152–162. doi: `10.1145/1029873.1029892`. (page 138)

JVM 2001. *1st Java Virtual Machine Research and Technology Symposium*, Monterey, CA, April 2001. USENIX Association.
`https://www.usenix.org/legacy/event/jvm01/`. (pages 516 and 535)

Ted Kaehler. Virtual memory on a narrow machine for an object-oriented language. In OOPSLA 1986, pages 87–106. doi: `10.1145/28697`. (page 476)

Ted Kaehler and Glenn Krasner. LOOM — large object-oriented memory for Smalltalk-80 systems. In Krasner [1983], pages 251–271. (page 476)

Tomas Kalibera. Replicating real-time garbage collector for Java. In *7th International Workshop on Java Technologies for Real-time and Embedded Systems (JTRES)*, Madrid, Spain, September 2009, pages 100–109. ACM Press. doi: `10.1145/1620405.1620420`. (page 454)

Tomas Kalibera and Richard Jones. Handles revisited: Optimising performance and memory costs in a real-time collector. In ISMM 2011, pages 89–98.
doi: `10.1145/1993478.1993492`. (page 195)

Tomas Kalibera, Filip Pizlo, Antony L. Hosking and Jan Vitek. Scheduling hard real-time garbage collection. In *30th IEEE Real-Time Systems Symposium*, Washington, DC, December 2009, pages 81–92. IEEE Computer Society Press.
doi: `10.1109/RTSS.2009.40`. (page 464)

Tomas Kalibera, Filip Pizlo, Antony L. Hosking and Jan Vitek. Scheduling real-time garbage collection on uniprocessors. *ACM Transactions on Computer Systems*, 3(1):8:1–29, August 2011. doi: `10.1145/2003690.2003692`. (page 464)

Stefan Karlsson. JDK 8272979: Generational ZGC. Technical report, OpenJDK, October 2022. `https://bugs.openjdk.org/browse/JDK-8272979`. (page 399)

Roman Kennke. Shenandoah GC in JDK 13, part 1: Load reference barriers. *Red Hat Developer*, June 2019.
`https://developers.redhat.com/blog/2019/06/27/shenandoah-gc-in-jdk-13-part-1-load-reference-barriers`. (page 341)

Haim Kermany and Erez Petrank. The Compressor: Concurrent, incremental and parallel compaction. In PLDI 2006, pages 354–363. doi: `10.1145/1133981.1134023`. (pages 42, 43, 213, 318, 384 and 404)

Hongjune Kim, Seonmyeong Bak and Jaejin Lee. Lightweight and block-level concurrent sweeping for Javascript garbage collection. In *ACM SIGPLAN/SIGBED Conference on Languages, Compilers, and Tools for Embedded Systems*, Edinburgh, UK, 2014, pages 155–164. ACM Press. doi: `10.1145/2597809.2597824`. (page 233)

Taehyoun Kim and Heonshik Shin. Scheduling-aware real-time garbage collection using dual aperiodic servers. In *Real-Time and Embedded Computing Systems and Applications*, 2004, pages 1–17. Volume 2968 of *Lecture Notes in Computer Science*, Springer-Verlag. doi: `10.1007/978-3-540-24686-2_1`. (page 464)

Taehyoun Kim, Naehyuck Chang, Namyun Kim and Heonshik Shin. Scheduling garbage collector for embedded real-time systems. In *ACM SIGPLAN Workshop on Languages, Compilers, and Tools for Embedded Systems (LCTES)*, Atlanta, GA, May 1999, pages 55–64. ACM SIGPLAN Notices 34(7), ACM Press. doi: `10.1145/314403.314444`. (page 464)

Taehyoun Kim, Naehyuck Chang and Heonshik Shin. Bounding worst case garbage collection time for embedded real-time systems. In *6th IEEE Real-Time Technology and Applications Symposium (RTAS)*, Washington, DC, May/June 2000, pages 46–55. doi: `10.1109/RTTAS.2000.852450`. (page 464)

Taehyoun Kim, Naehyuck Chang and Heonshik Shin. Joint scheduling of garbage collector and hard real-time tasks for embedded applications. *Journal of Systems and Software*, 58(3):247–260, September 2001. doi: `10.1016/S0164-1212(01)00042-5`. (page 464)

Andy C. King. *Removing Garbage Collector Synchronisation*. PhD thesis, Computing Laboratory, The University of Kent at Canterbury, 2004. `http://www.cs.kent.ac.uk/pubs/2004/1981/`. (pages 151 and 525)

Kenneth C. Knowlton. A fast storage allocator. *Communications of the ACM*, 8(10):623–625, October 1965. doi: `10.1145/365628.365655`. (page 101)

Donald E. Knuth. *The Art of Computer Programming*, volume I: Fundamental Algorithms. Addison-Wesley, second edition, 1973. (pages 93 and 102)

David G. Korn and Kiem-Phong Vo. In search of a better malloc. In *USENIX Summer Conference*, Portland, Oregon, 1985, pages 489–506. USENIX Association. (pages 105 and 162)

Glenn Krasner, editor. *Smalltalk-80: Bits of History, Words of Advice*. Addison-Wesley, 1983. (pages 504 and 526)

Nicolas Krauter, Patrick Raaf, Peter Braam, Reza Salkhordeh, Sebastian Erdweg and André Brinkmann. Persistent software transactional memory in Haskell. *Proceedings of the ACM on Programming Languages*, 5(ICFP):63:1–63:29, August 2021. doi: `10.1145/3473568`. (pages 478 and 480)

R. Madhava Krishnan, Jaeho Kim, Ajit Mathew, Xinwei Fu, Anthony Demeri, Changwoo Min and Sudarsun Kannan. Durable transactional memory can scale with TimeStone. In James R. Larus, Luis Ceze and Karin Strauss, editors, *25th International Conference on Architectural Support for Programming Languages and Operating Systems*, Lausanne, Switzerland, March 2020, pages 335–349. ACM Press. doi: `10.1145/3373376.3378483`. ASPLOS 2020 was canceled because of COVID-19. (page 478)

Tomohiro Kudoh, Hideharu Amano, Takashi Matsumoto, Kei Hiraki, Yulu Yang, Katsunobu Nishimura, Koichi Yoshimura and Yasuhito Fukushima. Hierarchical bit-map directory schemes on the RDT interconnection network for a massively parallel processor JUMP-1. In Prithviraj Banerjee, editor, *Proceedings of the 1995 International*

Conference on Parallel Processing, Urbana-Champain, Illinois, USA, August 14-18, 1995. Volume I: Architecture, 1995, pages 186–193. CRC Press. (page 97)

Vivek Kumar, Daniel Frampton, Stephen M. Blackburn, David Grove and Olivier Tardieu. Work-stealing without the baggage. In OOPSLA 2012, page 297–314. doi: 10.1145/2398857.2384639. (page 269)

Vivek Kumar, Stephen M. Blackburn and David Grove. Friendly barriers: Efficient work-stealing with return barriers. In Erez Petrank, Dan Tsafrir and Martin Hirzel, editors, *10th ACM SIGPLAN/SIGOPS International Conference on Virtual Execution Environments*, Salt Lake City, UT, March 2014. ACM Press. doi: 10.1145/2576195.2576207. (pages 198 and 269)

H.T. Kung and S.W. Song. An efficient parallel garbage collection system and its correctness proof. In *IEEE Symposium on Foundations of Computer Science*, Providence, Rhode Island, October 1977, pages 120–131. IEEE Press. doi: 10.1109/SFCS.1977.5. (pages 352 and 358)

Michael S. Lam, Paul R. Wilson and Thomas G. Moher. Object type directed garbage collection to improve locality. In IWMM 1992, pages 404–425. doi: 10.1007/BFb0017204. (pages 56 and 57)

Leslie Lamport. Garbage collection with multiple processes: an exercise in parallelism. In *International Conference on Parallel Processing (ICPP'76)*, 1976, pages 50–54. IEEE Press. (pages 353 and 354)

Bernard Lang and Francis Dupont. Incremental incrementally compacting garbage collection. In *Symposium on Interpreters and Interpretive Techniques*, St Paul, MN, June 1987, pages 253–263. ACM SIGPLAN Notices 22(7), ACM Press. doi: 10.1145/29650.29677. (pages 143, 157, 158, 159 and 169)

LCTES 2003. *ACM SIGPLAN/SIGBED Conference on Languages, Compilers, and Tools for Embedded Systems*, San Diego, CA, June 2003. ACM SIGPLAN Notices 38(7), ACM Press. doi: 10.1145/780732. (pages 504 and 536)

LCTES 2005. *ACM SIGPLAN/SIGBED Conference on Languages, Compilers, and Tools for Embedded Systems*, Chicago, IL, June 2005. ACM SIGPLAN Notices 40(7), ACM Press. doi: 10.1145/1065910. (pages 504 and 518)

Dokeun Lee, Youjip Won, Yongjun Park and Seongjin Lee. Two-tier garbage collection for persistent object. In *Proceedings of the 35th Annual ACM Symposium on Applied Computing*, New York, NY, USA, March 2020, pages 1246–1255. ACM Press. doi: 10.1145/3341105.3373986. (page 478)

Ho-Fung Leung and Hing-Fung Ting. An optimal algorithm for global termination detection in shared-memory asynchronous multiprocessor systems. *IEEE Transactions on Parallel and Distributed Systems*, 8(5):538–543, May 1997. doi: 10.1109/71.598280. (pages 264 and 265)

Yossi Levanoni and Erez Petrank. An on-the-fly reference counting garbage collector for Java. In OOPSLA 2001, pages 367–380. doi: 10.1145/504282.504309. (pages 167 and 416)

Yossi Levanoni and Erez Petrank. An on-the-fly reference counting garbage collector for Java. *ACM Transactions on Programming Languages and Systems*, 28(1):1–69, January 2006. doi: 10.1145/1111596.1111597. (pages 114, 416 and 420)

Yossi Levanoni and Erez Petrank. A scalable reference counting garbage collector. Technical Report CS–0967, Technion — Israel Institute of Technology, Haifa, Israel, November 1999. (pages 68, 360 and 416)

LFP 1984, Guy L. Steele, editor. *ACM Conference on LISP and Functional Programming*, Austin, TX, August 1984. ACM Press. doi: 10.1145/800055. (pages 508, 519, 531 and 541)

LFP 1992. *ACM Conference on LISP and Functional Programming*, San Francisco, CA, June 1992. ACM Press. doi: 10.1145/141471. (pages 512 and 518)

libpmemobj, 2022. https://pmem.io/pmdk/libpmemobj. (page 480)

Per Lidén. JEP 377: ZGC: A scalable low-latency garbage collector (production). Technical report, OpenJDK, 2018. http://openjdk.java.net/jeps/377. (pages 396 and 404)

Henry Lieberman and Carl E. Hewitt. A real-time garbage collector based on the lifetimes of objects. *Communications of the ACM*, 26(6):419–429, June 1983. doi: 10.1145/358141.358147. Also report TM–184, Laboratory for Computer Science, MIT, Cambridge, MA, July 1980 and AI Lab Memo 569, 1981. (pages 109 and 124)

Rafael D. Lins. Cyclic reference counting with lazy mark-scan. *Information Processing Letters*, 44(4):215–220, 1992. doi: 10.1016/0020-0190(92)90088-D. Also Computing Laboratory Technical Report 75, University of Kent, July 1990. (pages 75 and 76)

Anton Lorenzen and Daan Leijen. Reference counting with frame limited reuse. In *27th ACM SIGPLAN International Conference on Functional Programming*, Nara, Japan, September 2022. ACM Press. (page 62)

Robert Lougher. JamVM, 2014. http://jamvm.sourceforge.net. (page 480)

Martin Maas, Philip Reames, Jeffrey Morlan, Krste Asanović, Anthony D. Joseph and John Kubiatowicz. GPUs as an opportunity for offloading garbage collection. In ISMM 2012, pages 25–36. doi: 10.1145/2258996.2259002. (pages 321, 322, 323 and 324)

Boris Magnusson and Roger Henriksson. Garbage collection for control systems. In IWMM 1995, pages 323–342. doi: 10.1007/3-540-60368-9_32. (page 434)

Jeremy Manson, William Pugh and Sarita V. Adve. The Java memory model. In *32nd Annual ACM SIGPLAN Symposium on Principles of Programming Languages*, Long Beach, CA, January 2005, pages 378–391. ACM SIGPLAN Notices 40(1), ACM Press. doi: 10.1145/1040305.1040336. (page 377)

Sebastien Marion, Richard Jones and Chris Ryder. Decrypting the Java gene pool: Predicting objects' lifetimes with micro-patterns. In ISMM 2007, pages 67–78. doi: 10.1145/1296907.1296918. (pages 116 and 138)

Simon Marlow and Simon L. Peyton Jones. Multicore garbage collection with local heaps. In ISMM 2011, pages 21–32. doi: 10.1145/1993478. (pages 113 and 154)

Simon Marlow, Alexey Rodriguez Yakushev and Simon Peyton Jones. Faster laziness using dynamic pointer tagging. In *12th ACM SIGPLAN International Conference on Functional Programming*, Freiburg, Germany, September 2007, pages 277–288. ACM Press. doi: 10.1145/1291151.1291194. (page 371)

Simon Marlow, Tim Harris, Roshan James and Simon L. Peyton Jones. Parallel generational-copying garbage collection with a block-structured heap. In ISMM 2008, pages 11–20. doi: `10.1145/1375634.1375637`. (pages 122, 139, 308 and 312)

Simon Marlow, Simon L. Peyton Jones and Satnam Singh. Runtime support for multicore Haskell. In *14th ACM SIGPLAN International Conference on Functional Programming*, Edinburgh, Scotland, September 2009, pages 65–78. ACM Press. doi: `10.1145/1596550.1596563`. (pages 308 and 326)

Johannes J. Martin. An efficient garbage compaction algorithm. *Communications of the ACM*, 25(8):571–581, August 1982. doi: `10.1145/358589.358625`. (page 42)

A.D. Martinez, R. Wachenchauzer and Rafael D. Lins. Cyclic reference counting with local mark-scan. *Information Processing Letters*, 34:31–35, 1990. doi: `10.1016/0020-0190(90)90226-N`. (page 75)

John McCarthy. Recursive functions of symbolic expressions and their computation by machine, Part I. *Communications of the ACM*, 3(4):184–195, April 1960. doi: `10.1145/367177.367199`. (pages 2, 20 and 31)

John McCarthy. History of LISP. In Richard L. Wexelblat, editor, *History of Programming Languages I*, pages 173–185. ACM Press, 1978. doi: `10.1145/800025.1198360`. (page xxvii)

Bill McCloskey, David F. Bacon, Perry Cheng and David Grove. Staccato: A parallel and concurrent real-time compacting garbage collector for multiprocessors. IBM Research Report RC24505, IBM Research, 2008. `https://dominoweb.draco.res.ibm.com/98391b79c5acd00b852574440055084e.html`. (pages 396, 455 and 457)

Phil McGachey and Antony L Hosking. Reducing generational copy reserve overhead with fallback compaction. In ISMM 2006, pages 17–28. doi: `10.1145/1133956.1133960`. (page 133)

Phil McGachey, Ali-Reza Adl-Tabatabi, Richard L. Hudson, Vijay Menon, Bratin Saha and Tatiana Shpeisman. Concurrent GC leveraging transactional memory. In *ACM SIGPLAN Symposium on Principles and Practice of Parallel Programming*, Salt Lake City, UT, February 2008, pages 217–226. ACM Press. doi: `10.1145/1345206.1345238`. (pages 286 and 381)

Amirsaman Memaripour and Steven Swanson. Breeze: User-level access to non-volatile main memories for legacy software. In *36th IEEE International Conference on Computer Design (ICCD)*, Orlando, FL, October 2018, pages 413–422. IEEE Computer Society Press. doi: `10.1109/ICCD.2018.00069`. ISSN: 2576-6996. (pages 478 and 479)

Maged M. Michael. Hazard pointers: Safe memory reclamation for lock-free objects. *IEEE Transactions on Parallel and Distributed Systems*, 15(6):491–504, June 2004. doi: `10.1109/TPDS.2004.8`. (page 421)

James S. Miller and Guillermo J. Rozas. Garbage collection is fast, but a stack is faster. Technical Report AIM-1462, MIT AI Laboratory, March 1994. doi: `1721.1/6622`. (page 182)

Man Yue Mo. Chrome in-the-wild bug analysis: CVE-2021-37975, October 2021. `https://securitylab.github.com/research/in_the_wild_chrome_cve_2021_37975`. (page 241)

David A. Moon. Garbage collection in a large LISP system. In LFP 1984, pages 235–245. doi: `10.1145/800055.802040`. (pages 54, 55, 213 and 312)

F. Lockwood Morris. A time- and space-efficient garbage compaction algorithm. *Communications of the ACM*, 21(8):662–5, 1978. doi: `10.1145/359576.359583`. (pages 41, 46 and 316)

F. Lockwood Morris. On a comparison of garbage collection techniques. *Communications of the ACM*, 22(10):571, October 1979. (pages 41 and 46)

F. Lockwood Morris. Another compacting garbage collector. *Information Processing Letters*, 15(4):139–142, October 1982. doi: `10.1016/0020-0190(82)90094-1`. (pages 41, 42 and 46)

J. Eliot B. Moss. Working with persistent objects: To swizzle or not to swizzle? *IEEE Transactions on Software Engineering*, 18(8):657–673, August 1992. doi: `10.1109/32.153378`. (page 219)

MPLR 2022, Tobias Wrigstad and Elisa Gonzalez Boix, editors. *ACM SIGPLAN International Conference on Managed Programming Languages and Runtimes*, Brussels, Belgium, September 2022. ACM Press. (pages 537 and 546)

Todd Mytkowicz, Amer Diwan, Matthias Hauswirth and Peter F. Sweeney. Producing wrong data without doing anything obviously wrong! In Mary Lou Soffa, editor, *14th International Conference on Architectural Support for Programming Languages and Operating Systems*, Seattle, WA, March 2008, pages 265–276. ACM SIGPLAN Notices 43(3), ACM Press. doi: `10.1145/1508244.1508275`. (page 11)

John Nagle. Re: Real-time GC (was Re: Widespread C++ competency gap). USENET comp.lang.c++, January 1995. (page 4)

Scott Nettles and James O'Toole. Real-time replication-based garbage collection. In PLDI 1993, pages 217–226. doi: `10.1145/155090.155111`. (pages 372, 377, 404 and 426)

Scott M. Nettles, James W. O'Toole, David Pierce and Nicholas Haines. Replication-based incremental copying collection. In IWMM 1992, pages 357–364. doi: `10.1007/BFb0017201`. (pages 372 and 404)

Yang Ni, Vijay Menon, Ali-Reza Adl-Tabatabai, Antony L. Hosking, Richard L. Hudson, J. Eliot B. Moss, Bratin Saha and Tatiana Shpeisman. Open nesting in software transactional memory. In *ACM SIGPLAN Symposium on Principles and Practice of Parallel Programming*, San Jose, CA, March 2007, pages 68–78. ACM Press. doi: `10.1145/1229428.1229442`. (page 289)

Ruslan Nikolaev and Binoy Ravindran. Snapshot-free, transparent, and robust memory reclamation for lock-free data structures. In PLDI 2021. doi: `10.1145/3453483.3454090`. (page 422)

Gene Novark, Trevor Strohman and Emery D. Berger. Custom object layout for garbage-collected languages. Technical report, University of Massachusetts, 2006. `https://web.cs.umass.edu/publication/docs/2006/UM-CS-2006-007.pdf`. New England Programming Languages and Systems Symposium, March, 2006. (page 57)

Cosmin E. Oancea, Alan Mycroft and Stephen M. Watt. A new approach to parallelising tracing algorithms. In ISMM 2009, pages 10–19. doi: 10.1145/1542431.1542434. (pages 276, 279, 280, 314, 315 and 326)

Takeshi Ogasawara. NUMA-aware memory manager with dominant-thread-based copying GC. In *ACM SIGPLAN Conference on Object-Oriented Programming, Systems, Languages, and Applications*, Orlando, FL, October 2009, pages 377–390. ACM SIGPLAN Notices 44(10), ACM Press. doi: 10.1145/1640089.1640117. (page 309)

Hiro Onozawa, Tomoharu Ugawa and Hideya Iwasaki. Fusuma: Double-ended threaded compaction. In ISMM 2021. doi: 0.1145/3459898.3463903. (page 42)

OOPSLA 1986. *ACM SIGPLAN Conference on Object-Oriented Programming, Systems, Languages, and Applications*, Portland, OR, November 1986. ACM SIGPLAN Notices 21(11), ACM Press. doi: 10.1145/28697. (pages 509 and 526)

OOPSLA 1999. *ACM SIGPLAN Conference on Object-Oriented Programming, Systems, Languages, and Applications*, Denver, CO, October 1999. ACM SIGPLAN Notices 34(10), ACM Press. doi: 10.1145/320384. (pages 507 and 541)

OOPSLA 2001. *ACM SIGPLAN Conference on Object-Oriented Programming, Systems, Languages, and Applications*, Tampa, FL, November 2001. ACM SIGPLAN Notices 36(11), ACM Press. doi: 10.1145/504282. (pages 506, 508 and 528)

OOPSLA 2002. *ACM SIGPLAN Conference on Object-Oriented Programming, Systems, Languages, and Applications*, Seattle, WA, November 2002. ACM SIGPLAN Notices 37(11), ACM Press. doi: 10.1145/582419. (pages 538 and 547)

OOPSLA 2003. *ACM SIGPLAN Conference on Object-Oriented Programming, Systems, Languages, and Applications*, Anaheim, CA, November 2003. ACM SIGPLAN Notices 38(11), ACM Press. doi: 10.1145/949305. (pages 503, 505, 506, 519, 521 and 537)

OOPSLA 2004. *ACM SIGPLAN Conference on Object-Oriented Programming, Systems, Languages, and Applications*, Vancouver, Canada, October 2004. ACM SIGPLAN Notices 39(10), ACM Press. doi: 10.1145/1028976. (pages 501, 504, 519, 522 and 537)

OOPSLA 2005. *ACM SIGPLAN Conference on Object-Oriented Programming, Systems, Languages, and Applications*, San Diego, CA, October 2005. ACM SIGPLAN Notices 40(10), ACM Press. doi: 10.1145/1094811. (pages 518, 521 and 544)

OOPSLA 2012. *ACM SIGPLAN Conference on Object-Oriented Programming, Systems, Languages, and Applications*, Tuscon, AZ, October 2012. ACM Press. (pages 528 and 537)

Yoav Ossia, Ori Ben-Yitzhak, Irit Goft, Elliot K. Kolodner, Victor Leikehman and Avi Owshanko. A parallel, incremental and concurrent GC for servers. In PLDI 2002, pages 129–140. doi: 10.1145/512529.512546. (pages 300, 301, 304, 312 and 325)

Yoav Ossia, Ori Ben-Yitzhak and Marc Segal. Mostly concurrent compaction for mark-sweep GC. In ISMM 2004, pages 25–36. doi: 10.1145/1029873.1029877. (pages 346 and 385)

Ivor P. Page and Jeff Hagins. Improving the performance of buddy systems. *IEEE Transactions on Computers*, C-35(5):441–447, May 1986. doi: 10.1109/TC.1986.1676786. (page 101)

Krzysztof Palacz, Jan Vitek, Grzegorz Czajkowski and Laurent Daynès. Incommunicado: efficient communication for isolates. In *ACM SIGPLAN Conference on Object-Oriented Programming, Systems, Languages, and Applications*, Portland, OR, October 1994, pages 262–274. ACM SIGPLAN Notices 29(10), ACM Press. doi: 10.1145/582419.582444. (page 113)

Stephen K. Park and Keith W. Miller. Random number generators: Good ones are hard to find. *Communications of the ACM*, 31(10):1192–1201, October 1988. doi: 10.1145/63039.6304. (page 206)

Harel Paz and Erez Petrank. Using prefetching to improve reference-counting garbage collectors. In *16th International Conference on Compiler Construction*, Braga, Portugal, March 2007, pages 48–63. Volume 4420 of *Lecture Notes in Computer Science*, Springer-Verlag. doi: 10.1007/978-3-540-71229-9_4. (page 69)

Harel Paz, David F. Bacon, Elliot K. Kolodner, Erez Petrank and V.T. Rajan. Efficient on-the-fly cycle collection. Technical Report CS–2003–10, Technion University, 2003. (page 416)

Harel Paz, Erez Petrank, David F. Bacon, Elliot K. Kolodner and V.T. Rajan. An efficient on-the-fly cycle collection. In CC 2005, pages 156–171. doi: 10.1007/978-3-540-31985-6_11. (page 416)

Harel Paz, Erez Petrank and Stephen M. Blackburn. Age-oriented concurrent garbage collection. In CC 2005, pages 121–136. doi: 10.1007/978-3-540-31985-6_9. (page 416)

Harel Paz, David F. Bacon, Elliot K. Kolodner, Erez Petrank and V.T. Rajan. An efficient on-the-fly cycle collection. *ACM Transactions on Programming Languages and Systems*, 29 (4):1–43, August 2007. doi: 10.1145/1255450.1255453. (pages 72, 416, 419 and 420)

E.J.H. Pepels, M.C.J.D. van Eekelen and M.J. Plasmeijer. A cyclic reference counting algorithm and its proof. Technical Report 88–10, Computing Science Department, University of Nijmegen, 1988. https://www.cs.ru.nl/~marko/research/pubs/1988/IR88-10CyclicProof-incl-fig.pdf. (page 71)

Taciano D. Perez, Marcelo V. Neves, Diego Medaglia, Pedro H.G. Monteiro and César A.F. De Rose. Orthogonal persistence in nonvolatile memory architectures: A persistent heap design and its implementation for a Java Virtual Machine. *Software: Practice and Experience*, 50(4):368–387, 2020. doi: 10.1002/spe.2781. (pages 478 and 480)

James L. Peterson and Theodore A. Norman. Buddy systems. *Communications of the ACM*, 20(6):421–431, 1977. doi: 10.1145/359605.359626. (page 101)

Erez Petrank and Elliot K. Kolodner. Parallel copying garbage collection using delayed allocation. *Parallel Processing Letters*, 14(2):271–286, June 2004. doi: 10.1142/S0129626404001878. (pages 300 and 304)

Erez Petrank and Dror Rawitz. The hardness of cache conscious data placement. In *Twenty-ninth Annual ACM SIGPLAN Symposium on Principles of Programming Languages*, Portland, OR, January 2002, pages 101–112. ACM SIGPLAN Notices 37(1), ACM Press. doi: 10.1145/503272.503283. (page 54)

Pekka P. Pirinen. Barrier techniques for incremental tracing. In ISMM 1998, pages 20–25. doi: 10.1145/286860.286863. (pages 23, 337, 338, 340 and 341)

Filip Pizlo. Introducing Riptide: WebKit's retreating wavefront concurrent garbage
    collector. Technical report, Apple, January 2017.
    `https://webkit.org/blog/7122/introducing-riptide-webkits-`
    `retreating-wavefront-concurrent-garbage-collector.` (pages 33, 122, 133,
    242 and 352)

Filip Pizlo and Jan Vitek. Memory management for real-time Java: State of the art. In *11th
    International Symposium on Object-Oriented Real-Time Distributed Computing*, Orlando,
    FL, 2008, pages 248–254. Volume 10499 of *Lecture Notes in Computer Science*,
    Springer-Verlag. doi: `10.1109/ISORC.2008.40.` (page 425)

Filip Pizlo, Daniel Frampton, Erez Petrank and Bjarne Steensgard. Stopless: A real-time
    garbage collector for multiprocessors. In ISMM 2007, pages 159–172.
    doi: `10.1145/1296907.1296927.` (pages 454, 455 and 460)

Filip Pizlo, Erez Petrank and Bjarne Steensgaard. A study of concurrent real-time garbage
    collectors. In PLDI 2008, pages 33–44. doi: `10.1145/1379022.1375587.` (pages 396,
    458 and 459)

Filip Pizlo, Lukasz Ziarek, Ethan Blanton, Petr Maj and Jan Vitek. High-level
    programming of embedded hard real-time devices. In *European Conference on Computer
    Systems (EuroSys)*, Paris, France, April 2010a, pages 69–82. ACM Press.
    doi: `10.1145/1755913.1755922.` (page 464)

Filip Pizlo, Lukasz Ziarek, Petr Maj, Antony L. Hosking, Ethan Blanton and Jan Vitek.
    Schism: Fragmentation-tolerant real-time garbage collection. In *ACM SIGPLAN
    Conference on Programming Language Design and Implementation*, Toronto, Canada, June
    2010b, pages 146–159. ACM SIGPLAN Notices 45(6), ACM Press.
    doi: `10.1145/1806596.1806615.` (pages 461, 462, 463 and 464)

PLDI 1988. *ACM SIGPLAN Conference on Programming Language Design and
    Implementation*, Atlanta, June 1988. ACM SIGPLAN Notices 23(7), ACM Press.
    doi: `10.1145/53990.` (pages 503 and 510)

PLDI 1991. *ACM SIGPLAN Conference on Programming Language Design and
    Implementation*, Toronto, Canada, June 1991. ACM SIGPLAN Notices 26(6), ACM Press.
    doi: `10.1145/113445.` (pages 508, 518 and 545)

PLDI 1992. *ACM SIGPLAN Conference on Programming Language Design and
    Implementation*, San Francisco, CA, June 1992. ACM SIGPLAN Notices 27(7), ACM
    Press. doi: `10.1145/143095.` (pages 502 and 514)

PLDI 1993. *ACM SIGPLAN Conference on Programming Language Design and
    Implementation*, Albuquerque, NM, June 1993. ACM SIGPLAN Notices 28(6), ACM
    Press. doi: `10.1145/155090.` (pages 505, 508, 515 and 531)

PLDI 1997. *ACM SIGPLAN Conference on Programming Language Design and
    Implementation*, Las Vegas, NV, June 1997. ACM SIGPLAN Notices 32(5), ACM Press.
    doi: `10.1145/258915.` (pages 511 and 514)

PLDI 1999. *ACM SIGPLAN Conference on Programming Language Design and
    Implementation*, Atlanta, GA, May 1999. ACM SIGPLAN Notices 34(5), ACM Press.
    doi: `10.1145/301618.` (pages 507, 511 and 541)

PLDI 2000. *ACM SIGPLAN Conference on Programming Language Design and Implementation*, Vancouver, Canada, June 2000. ACM SIGPLAN Notices 35(5), ACM Press. doi: 10.1145/349299. (pages 509, 514, 515 and 537)

PLDI 2001. *ACM SIGPLAN Conference on Programming Language Design and Implementation*, Snowbird, UT, June 2001. ACM SIGPLAN Notices 36(5), ACM Press. doi: 10.1145/378795. (pages 503, 504 and 510)

PLDI 2002. *ACM SIGPLAN Conference on Programming Language Design and Implementation*, Berlin, Germany, June 2002. ACM SIGPLAN Notices 37(5), ACM Press. doi: 10.1145/512529. (pages 506, 518 and 532)

PLDI 2006, Michael I. Schwartzbach and Thomas Ball, editors. *ACM SIGPLAN Conference on Programming Language Design and Implementation*, Ottawa, Canada, June 2006. ACM SIGPLAN Notices 41(6), ACM Press. doi: 10.1145/1133981. (pages 510, 526 and 543)

PLDI 2008, Rajiv Gupta and Saman P. Amarasinghe, editors. *ACM SIGPLAN Conference on Programming Language Design and Implementation*, Tucson, AZ, June 2008. ACM SIGPLAN Notices 43(6), ACM Press. doi: 10.1145/1375581. (pages 506 and 534)

PLDI 2021. *ACM SIGPLAN Conference on Programming Language Design and Implementation*, London, June 2021. ACM Press. (pages 502, 531 and 536)

POPL 1994. *21st Annual ACM SIGPLAN Symposium on Principles of Programming Languages*, Portland, OR, January 1994. ACM Press. doi: 10.1145/174675. (pages 514, 515 and 542)

POPL 2003. *30th Annual ACM SIGPLAN Symposium on Principles of Programming Languages*, New Orleans, LA, January 2003. ACM SIGPLAN Notices 38(1), ACM Press. doi: 10.1145/604131. (pages 504 and 507)

POS 1992, Antonio Albano and Ronald Morrison, editors. *5th International Workshop on Persistent Object Systems (September, 1992)*, San Miniato, Italy, 1992. Workshops in Computing, Springer. doi: 10.1007/978-1-4471-3209-7. (pages 539 and 546)

PPOPP 2018. *ACM SIGPLAN Symposium on Principles and Practice of Parallel Programming*, Vienna, February 2018. ACM Press. (pages 519 and 544)

Tony Printezis. Hot-Swapping between a Mark&Sweep and a Mark&Compact Garbage Collector in a Generational Environment. In JVM 2001. http://www.usenix.org/events/jvm01/printezis.html. (pages 6 and 45)

Tony Printezis. On measuring garbage collection responsiveness. *Science of Computer Programming*, 62(2):164–183, October 2006. doi: 10.1016/j.scico.2006.02.004. (pages 423, 424 and 464)

Tony Printezis and David Detlefs. A generational mostly-concurrent garbage collector. In ISMM 2000, pages 143–154. doi: 10.1145/362422.362480. (pages 26, 352 and 355)

Tony Printezis and Alex Garthwaite. Visualising the Train garbage collector. In ISMM 2002, pages 100–105. doi: 10.1145/512429.512436. (pages 24, 77 and 149)

Tony Printezis, Malcolm P. Atkinson, Laurent Daynès, Susan Spence and Pete Bailey. The design of a new persistent object store for PJama. In *2nd International Workshop on Persistence and Java (PJW2)*, Half Moon Bay, CA, August 1997. https://www.researchgate.net/publication/2355041_The_Design_of_

`a_new_Persistent_Object_Store_for_PJama/link/`
`0deec535ea2c722cce000000/download`. (page 477)

Feng Qian and Laurie Hendren. An adaptive, region-based allocator for Java. In ISMM
2002, pages 127–138. doi: `10.1145/512429.512446`. Sable Technical Report 2002–1
provides a longer version. (page 155)

Christian Queinnec, Barbara Beaudoing and Jean-Pierre Queille. Mark DURING sweep
rather than mark THEN sweep. In Eddy Odijk, Martin Rem and Jean-Claude Syre,
editors, *Parallel Architectures and Languages Europe (PARLE)*, Eindhoven, The
Netherlands, June 1989, pages 224–237. Volume 365 of *Lecture Notes in Computer Science*,
Springer-Verlag. doi: `10.1007/3540512845_42`. (page 354)

Pedro Ramalhete and Andreia Correia. Brief announcement: Hazard eras —
non-blocking memory reclamation. In *29th ACM Symposium on Parallelism in Algorithms
and Architectures*, Washington, DC, 2017, pages 367–369. ACM Press.
doi: `10.1145/3087556.3087588`. (page 422)

Alex Reinking, Ningning Xie, Leonardo de Moura and Daan Leijen. Perceus: Garbage
free reference counting with reuse. In PLDI 2021. doi: `0.1145/3453483.3454032`.
(page 62)

John H. Reppy. A high-performance garbage collector for Standard ML. Technical
memorandum, AT&T Bell Laboratories, Murray Hill, NJ, December 1993.
`http://www.smlnj.org/compiler-notes/93-tr-reppy.ps`. (pages 111, 127,
207 and 213)

Carl G. Ritson, Tomoharu Ugawa and Richard Jones. Exploring garbage collection with
Haswell hardware transactional memory. In ISMM 2014, pages 105–115.
doi: `10.1145/2602988.2602992`. (pages xxxiii, 286, 287 and 382)

Sven Gestegøard Robertz and Roger Henriksson. Time-triggered garbage collection:
Robust and adaptive real-time GC scheduling for embedded systems. In LCTES 2003,
pages 93–102. doi: `10.1145/780732.780745`. (page 464)

J.M. Robson. An estimate of the store size necessary for dynamic storage allocation.
Journal of the ACM, 18(3):416–423, July 1971. doi: `10.1145/321650.321658`. (page 33)

J.M. Robson. Bounds for some functions concerning dynamic storage allocation. *Journal of
the ACM*, 21(3):419–499, July 1974. doi: `10.1145/321832.321846`. (page 33)

J.M. Robson. A bounded storage algorithm for copying cyclic structures. *Communications
of the ACM*, 20(6):431–433, June 1977. doi: `10.1145/359605.359628`. (page 95)

J.M. Robson. Storage allocation is NP-hard. *Information Processing Letters*, 11(3):119–125,
November 1980. doi: `10.1016/0020-0190(80)90124-6`. (page 98)

Helena C.C.D. Rodrigues and Richard E. Jones. Cyclic distributed garbage collection with
group merger. In Eric Jul, editor, *12th European Conference on Object-Oriented
Programming*, Brussels, Belgium, July 1998, pages 249–273. Volume 1445 of *Lecture Notes
in Computer Science*, Springer-Verlag. doi: `10.1007/BFb0054095`. Also UKC Technical
report 17–97, December 1997. (page 62)

Paul Rovner. On adding garbage collection and runtime types to a strongly-typed, statically-checked, concurrent language. Technical Report CSL–84–7, Xerox PARC, Palo Alto, CA, July 1985. http://www.bitsavers.org/pdf/xerox/parc/techReports/CSL-84-7_On_Adding_Garbage_Collection_and_Runtime_Types_to_a_Strongly-Typed_Statically-Checked_Concurrent_Language.pdf. (page 4)

Erik Ruf. Effective synchronization removal for Java. In PLDI 2000, pages 208–218. doi: 10.1145/349299.349327. (page 151)

Narendran Sachindran and Eliot Moss. MarkCopy: Fast copying GC with less space overhead. In OOPSLA 2003, pages 326–343. doi: 10.1145/949305.949335. (pages 164, 165 and 169)

Narendran Sachindran, J. Eliot B. Moss and Emery D. Berger. MC^2: High-performance garbage collection for memory-constrained environments. In OOPSLA 2004, pages 81–98. doi: 10.1145/1028976.1028984. (pages 8, 164 and 169)

Konstantinos Sagonas and Jesper Wilhelmsson. Message analysis-guided allocation and low-pause incremental garbage collection in a concurrent language. In ISMM 2004, pages 1–12. doi: 10.1145/1029873.1029875. (page 152)

Konstantinos Sagonas and Jesper Wilhelmsson. Efficient memory management for concurrent programs that use message passing. *Science of Computer Programming*, 62(2): 98–121, October 2006. doi: 10.1016/j.scico.2006.02.006. (page 152)

Jon D. Salkild. Implementation and analysis of two reference counting algorithms. Master's thesis, University College, London, 1987. (page 71)

Patrick M. Sansom and Simon L. Peyton Jones. Generational garbage collection for Haskell. In John Hughes, editor, *Conference on Functional Programming and Computer Architecture*, Copenhagen, Denmark, June 1993, pages 106–116. ACM Press. doi: 10.1145/165180.165195. (page 119)

Kunal Sareen and Stephen M. Blackburn. Better understanding the costs and benefits of automatic memory management. In MPLR 2022. (pages 10, 32 and 83)

Jennifer B. Sartor and Lieven Eeckhout. Exploring multi-threaded Java application performance on multicore hardware. In OOPSLA 2012, pages 281–296. doi: 10.1145/2384616.2384638. (page 468)

Jennifer B. Sartor, Wim Heirman, Stephen M. Blackburn, Lieven Eeckhout and Kathryn S. McKinley. Cooperative cache scrubbing. In *Proceedings of the 23rd International Conference on Parallel Architectures and Compilation (PACT'14)*, 2014, pages 15–26. ACM Press. doi: 10.1145/2628071.2628083. (page 469)

Robert A. Saunders. The LISP system for the Q–32 computer. In E.C. Berkeley and Daniel G. Bobrow, editors, *The Programming Language LISP: Its Operation and Applications*, Cambridge, MA, 1974, pages 220–231. Information International, Inc. http://www.softwarepreservation.org/projects/LISP/book/III_LispBook_Apr66.pdf. (page 36)

Martin Schoeberl. Scheduling of hard real-time garbage collection. *Real-Time Systems*, 45 (3):176–213, 2010. doi: 10.1007/s11241-010-9095-4. (page 464)

Jacob Seligmann and Steffen Grarup. Incremental mature garbage collection using the Train Algorithm. In Oscar Nierstrasz, editor, *9th European Conference on Object-Oriented Programming*, øAarhus, Denmark, August 1995, pages 235–252. Volume 952 of *Lecture Notes in Computer Science*, Springer-Verlag. doi: `10.1007/3-540-49538-X_12`. (page 149)

Rifat Shahriyar. *High Performance Reference Counting and Conservative Garbage Collection*. PhD thesis, Australian National University, April 2015. `https://openresearch-repository.anu.edu.au/handle/1885/99879`. Code at https://github.com/rifatshahriyar/JikesRVM-3.1.4. (page 178)

Rifat Shahriyar, Stephen M. Blackburn and Daniel Frampton. Down for the count? Getting reference counting back in the ring. In ISMM 2012, pages 73–84. doi: `10.1145/2258996.2259008`. (pages 79 and 406)

Rifat Shahriyar, Stephen Michael Blackburn, Xi Yang and Kathryn S. McKinley. Taking off the gloves with reference counting Immix. In *ACM SIGPLAN Conference on Object-Oriented Programming, Systems, Languages, and Applications*, Indianapolis, IN, October 2013, pages 93–110. ACM Press. doi: `10.1145/2509136.2509527`. (pages 65, 405 and 407)

Rifat Shahriyar, Stephen M. Blackburn and Kathryn S. McKinley. Fast conservative garbage collection. In *ACM SIGPLAN Conference on Object-Oriented Programming, Systems, Languages, and Applications*, Portland, OR, October 2014, pages 121–139. ACM Press. doi: `10.1145/2660193.2660198`. (page 178)

Robert A. Shaw. *Empirical Analysis of a Lisp System*. PhD thesis, Stanford University, 1988. Technical Report CSL-TR-88-351. (pages 122, 125, 203 and 213)

Premkishore Shivakumar and Norman P. Jouppi. CACTI 3.0: An integrated cache timing, power, and area model. Technical Report 2001/2, Compaq Western Research Laboratory, August 2001. `https://www.hpl.hp.com/research/cacti/cacti3.pdf`. (page 466)

Yefim Shuf, Manish Gupta, Hubertus Franke, Andrew Appel and Jaswinder Pal Singh. Creating and preserving locality of Java applications at allocation and garbage collection times. In OOPSLA 2002, pages 13–25. doi: `10.1145/582419.582422`. (page 57)

Thomas Shull, Jian Huang and Josep Torrellas. AutoPersist: an easy-to-use Java NVM framework based on reachability. In *ACM SIGPLAN Conference on Programming Language Design and Implementation*, Phoeniz, AZ, June 2019a, pages 316–332. ACM Press. doi: `10.1145/3314221.3314608`. (pages 478 and 480)

Thomas Shull, Jian Huang and Josep Torrellas. QuickCheck: using speculation to reduce the overhead of checks in NVM frameworks. In Jennifer B. Sartor, Mayur Naik and Chris Rossbach, editors, *Proceedings of the 15th ACM SIGPLAN/SIGOPS International Conference on Virtual Execution Environments*, Providence, RI, USA, April 2019b, pages 137–151. ACM Press. doi: `10.1145/3313808.3313822`. (page 480)

Fridtjof Siebert. Eliminating external fragmentation in a non-moving garbage collector for Java. In *Compilers, Architecture, and Synthesis for Embedded Systems (CASES)*, San Jose, CA, November 2000, pages 9–17. ACM Press. doi: `10.1145/354880.354883`. (pages 433, 461 and 463)

Fridtjof Siebert. Limits of parallel marking collection. In ISMM 2008, pages 21–29. doi: 10.1145/1375634.1375638. (pages 292, 293 and 324)

Fridtjof Siebert. Concurrent, parallel, real-time garbage-collection. In ISMM 2010, pages 11–20. doi: 10.1145/1806651.1806654. (pages 296, 298, 299, 326, 433 and 461)

Fridtjof Siebert. Guaranteeing non-disruptiveness and real-time deadlines in an incremental garbage collector. In ISMM 1998, pages 130–137. doi: 10.1145/286860.286874. (pages 433 and 461)

Fridtjof Siebert. Hard real-time garbage collection in the Jamaica Virtual Machine. In *6th International Workshop on Real-Time Computing Systems and Applications (RTCSA)*, Hong Kong, 1999, pages 96–102. IEEE Press, IEEE Computer Society Press. doi: 10.1109/RTCSA.1999.811198. (page 193)

David Siegwart and Martin Hirzel. Improving locality with parallel hierarchical copying GC. In ISMM 2006, pages 52–63. doi: 10.1145/1133956.1133964. (pages 56, 312, 313 and 326)

Jeremy Singer, Gavin Brown, Mikel Lujan and Ian Watson. Towards intelligent analysis techniques for object pretenuring. In *ACM International Symposium on Principles and Practice of Programming in Java*, Lisbon, Portugal, September 2007a, pages 203–208. Volume 272 of *ACM International Conference Proceeding Series*. doi: 10.1145/1294325.1294353. (page 84)

Jeremy Singer, Gavin Brown, Ian Watson and John Cavazos. Intelligent selection of application-specific garbage collectors. In ISMM 2007, pages 91–102. doi: 10.1145/1296907.1296920. (page 6)

Vivek Singhal, Sheetal V. Kakkad and Paul R. Wilson. Texas: an efficient, portable persistent store. In POS 1992, pages 11–33. doi: 10.1007/978-1-4471-3209-7. (pages 219 and 477)

KC Sivaramakrishnan, Lukasz Ziarek and Suresh Jagannathan. Eliminating read barriers through procrastination and cleanliness. In ISMM 2012, pages 49–60. doi: 10.1145/2258996.2259005. (page 344)

Daniel Dominic Sleator and Robert Endre Tarjan. Self-adjusting binary search trees. *Journal of the ACM*, 32(3):562–686, July 1985. doi: 10.1145/3828.3835. (page 95)

Patrick Sobalvarro. A lifetime-based garbage collector for Lisp systems on general-purpose computers. Bachelor of Science thesis AITR-1417, MIT AI Lab, February 1988. doi: 1721.1/6795. (page 208)

Sunil Soman and Chandra Krintz. Efficient and general on-stack replacement for aggressive program specialization. In *International Conference on Software Engineering Research and Practice (SERP) & Conference on Programming Languages and Compilers, Volume 2*, Las Vegas, NV, June 2006, pages 925–932. CSREA Press. https://www.cs.ucsb.edu/~ckrintz/papers/osr.pdf. (page 201)

Sunil Soman, Chandra Krintz and David Bacon. Dynamic selection of application-specific garbage collectors. In ISMM 2004, pages 49–60. doi: 10.1145/1029873.1029880. (pages 6, 45 and 84)

Sunil Soman, Laurent Daynès and Chandra Krintz. Task-aware garbage collection in a multi-tasking virtual machine. In ISMM 2006, pages 64–73. doi: 10.1145/1133956.1133965. (page 113)

Sunil Soman, Chandra Krintz and Laurent Daynès. MTM^2: Scalable memory management for multi-tasking managed runtime environments. In Jan Vitek, editor, *22nd European Conference on Object-Oriented Programming*, Paphos, Cyprus, July 2008, pages 335–361. Volume 5142 of *Lecture Notes in Computer Science*, Springer-Verlag. doi: 10.1007/978-3-540-70592-5_15. (page 113)

Daniel Spoonhower, Guy Blelloch and Robert Harper. Using page residency to balance tradeoffs in tracing garbage collection. In VEE 2005, pages 57–67. doi: 10.1145/1064979.1064989. (pages 157, 158 and 162)

James W. Stamos. Static grouping of small objects to enhance performance of a paged virtual memory. *ACM Transactions on Computer Systems*, 2(3):155–180, May 1984. doi: 10.1145/190.194. (page 54)

James William Stamos. A large object-oriented virtual memory: Grouping strategies, measurements, and performance. Master's thesis, Department of Electrical Engineering and Computer Science, Massachusetts Institute of Technology, April 1982. doi: 1721.1/15807. (page 54)

Thomas A. Standish. *Data Structure Techniques*. Addison-Wesley, 1980. (pages 91 and 95)

Guy L. Steele. Multiprocessing compactifying garbage collection. *Communications of the ACM*, 18(9):495–508, September 1975. doi: 10.1145/361002.361005. (pages 245, 338, 339 and 359)

Guy L. Steele. Corrigendum: Multiprocessing compactifying garbage collection. *Communications of the ACM*, 19(6):354, June 1976. doi: 10.1145/360238.360247. (pages 165, 338, 339, 340, 342, 343, 349, 352 and 364)

Peter Steenkiste. *Lisp on a Reduced-Instruction-Set Processor: Characterization and Optimization*. PhD thesis, Stanford University, March 1987. Available as Technical Report CSL-TR-87-324. (page 29)

Peter Steenkiste. The impact of code density on instruction cache performance. In *16th Annual ACM/IEEE International Symposium on Computer Architecture*, Jerusalem, Israel, May 1989, pages 252–259. IEEE Press. doi: 10.1145/74925.74954. (page 84)

Peter Steenkiste and John Hennessy. Lisp on a reduced-instruction-set processor: Characterization and optimization. *IEEE Computer*, 21(7):34–45, July 1988. doi: 10.1109/2.67. (page 29)

Bjarne Steensgaard. Thread-specific heaps for multi-threaded programs. In ISMM 2000, pages 18–24. doi: 10.1145/362422.362432. (pages 113, 151, 152 and 169)

Darko Stefanović. *Properties of Age-Based Automatic Memory Reclamation Algorithms*. PhD thesis, University of Massachusetts, 1999. (pages 135 and 167)

Darko Stefanović and J. Eliot B. Moss. Characterisation of object behaviour in Standard ML of New Jersey. In *ACM Conference on LISP and Functional Programming*, Orlando, FL, June 1994, pages 43–54. ACM Press. doi: 10.1145/182409.182428. (page 119)

Darko Stefanović, Kathryn S. McKinley and J. Eliot B. Moss. Age-based garbage collection. In OOPSLA 1999, pages 370–381. doi: `10.1145/320384.320425`. (page 135)

Darko Stefanović, Matthew Hertz, Stephen Blackburn, Kathryn McKinley and J. Eliot Moss. Older-first garbage collection in practice: Evaluation in a Java virtual machine. In *Workshop on Memory System Performance*, Berlin, Germany, June 2002, pages 25–36. ACM SIGPLAN Notices 38(2 supplement), ACM Press. doi: `10.1145/773146.773042`. (page 136)

V. Stenning. On-the-fly garbage collection. Unpublished notes, cited by Gries [1977], 1976. (page 339)

C.J. Stephenson. New methods of dynamic storage allocation (fast fits). In *9th ACM SIGOPS Symposium on Operating Systems Principles*, Bretton Woods, NH, October 1983, pages 30–32. ACM SIGOPS Operating Systems Review 17(5), ACM Press. doi: `10.1145/800217.806613`. (page 95)

James M. Stichnoth, Guei-Yuan Lueh and Michal Cierniak. Support for garbage collection at every instruction in a Java compiler. In PLDI 1999, pages 118–127. doi: `10.1145/301618.301652`. (pages 190, 191, 192 and 199)

Isabella Stilkerich, Michael Strotz, Christoph Erhardt and Michael Stilkerich. RT-LAGC: Fragmentation-tolerant real-time memory management revisited. In *12th International Workshop on Java Technologies for Real-time and Embedded Systems (JTRES)*, Niagara Falls, NY, October 2014. ACM Press. doi: `10.1145/2661020.2661031`. (page 461)

Will R. Stoye, T.J.W. Clarke and Arthur C. Norman. Some practical methods for rapid combinator reduction. In LFP 1984, pages 159–166. doi: `10.1145/800055.802032`. (page 77)

Robert Strandh. An improvement to sliding garbage collection. In *Proceedings of ILC 2014 on 8th International Lisp Conference*, Montreal, QC, Canada, 2014, page 97–102. ACM Press. doi: `10.1145/2635648.2635655`. (page 46)

A. Straw, F. Mellender and S. Riegel. Object management in a persistent Smalltalk system. *Software: Practice and Experience*, 19(8):719–737, 1989. (page 477)

Sun Microsystems. *Memory Management in the Java HotSpot Virtual Machine*, April 2006. `http://www.oracle.com/technetwork/java/javase/memorymanagement-whitepaper-150215.pdf`. Technical White Paper. (page 46)

Herb Sutter. The free lunch is over: A fundamental turn toward concurrency in software. *Dr. Dobb's Journal*, 30(3), March 2005. `http://www.drdobbs.com/web-development/a-fundamental-turn-toward-concurrency-in/184405990`. (page 291)

M. Swanson. An improved portable copying garbage collector. OPnote 86–03, University of Utah, February 1986. (page 203)

M. Tadman. Fast-fit: A new hierarchical dynamic storage allocation technique. Master's thesis, University of California, Irvine, 1978. (page 95)

David Tarditi. Compact garbage collection tables. In ISMM 2000, pages 50–58. doi: `10.1145/362422.362437`. (pages 190, 191, 192 and 193)

Gil Tene, Balaji Iyengar and Michael Wolf. C4: The continuously concurrent compacting collector. In ISMM 2011, pages 79–88. doi: `10.1145/1993478.1993491`. (pages 341, 342, 386 and 395)

S.P. Thomas, W.T. Charnell, S. Darnell, B.A.A. Dias, P.J. Guthrie, J.P. Kramskoy, J.J. Sexton, M.J. Wynn, K. Rautenbach and W. Plummer. Low-contention grey object sets for concurrent, marking garbage collection. United States Patent 6925637, 1998. (pages 301 and 325)

Stephen P. Thomas. *The Pragmatics of Closure Reduction*. PhD thesis, The Computing Laboratory, University of Kent at Canterbury, October 1993. (page 181)

Stephen P. Thomas. Having your cake and eating it: Recursive depth-first copying garbage collection with no extra stack. Personal communication, May 1995a. (page 181)

Stephen P. Thomas. Garbage collection in shared-environment closure reducers: Space-efficient depth first copying using a tailored approach. *Information Processing Letters*, 56(1):1–7, October 1995b. doi: `10.1016/0020-0190(95)00131-U`. (page 181)

Stephen P. Thomas and Richard E. Jones. Garbage collection for shared environment closure reducers. Technical Report 31–94, University of Kent and University of Nottingham, December 1994. `http://www.cs.kent.ac.uk/pubs/1994/147/`. (pages 181 and 201)

Mads Tofte and Jean-Pierre Talpin. Implementation of the typed call-by-value λ-calculus using a stack of regions. In POPL 1994, pages 188–201. doi: `10.1145/174675.177855`. (pages xxx and 112)

Mads Tofte, Lars Birkedal, Martin Elsman and Niels Hallenberg. A retrospective on region-based memory management. *Higher-Order and Symbolic Computation*, 17(3): 245–265, September 2004. doi: `10.1023/B:LISP.0000029446.78563.a4`. (pages 156 and 169)

David A. Turner. A new implementation technique for applicative languages. *Software: Practice and Experience*, 9:31–49, January 1979. doi: `10.1002/spe.4380090105`. (page 71)

Katsuhiro Ueno, Atsushi Ohori and Toshiaki Otomo. An efficient non-moving garbage collector for functional languages. In *16th ACM SIGPLAN International Conference on Functional Programming*, Tokyo, Japan, September 2011, pages 196–208. ACM Press. doi: `10.1145/2034773.2034802`. (page 97)

Tomoharu Ugawa, Richard Jones and Carl G. Ritson. Reference object processing in on-the-fly garbage collection. In ISMM 2014, pages 59–69. doi: `10.1145/2602988.2602991`. (pages xxxiii, 237 and 239)

Tomoharu Ugawa, Tatsuya Abe and Toshiyuki Maeda. Model checking copy phases of concurrent copying garbage collection with various memory models. In *ACM SIGPLAN Conference on Object-Oriented Programming, Systems, Languages, and Applications*, Vancouver, October 2017, page 26. ACM Press. doi: `10.1145/3133877`. (page 83)

Tomoharu Ugawa, Carl G. Ritson and Richard E. Jones. Transactional Sapphire: Lessons in high-performance, on-the-fly garbage collection. *ACM Transactions on Programming Languages and Systems*, 40(4):15:1–15:56, December 2018. doi: `10.1145/3226225`. (pages xxxiii, 83, 287, 345, 358, 376, 382 and 404)

Tomoharu Ugawa, Stefan Marr and Richard E. Jones. Profile guided offline optimization of hidden class graphs for JavaScript VMs in embedded systems. In *Proceedings of the 14th ACM SIGPLAN International Workshop on Virtual Machines and Intermediate Languages*, 2022, page 11. ACM Press. doi: 10.1145/3563838.3567678. (page 242)

David M. Ungar. Generation scavenging: A non-disruptive high performance storage reclamation algorithm. In *ACM/SIGSOFT/SIGPLAN Software Engineering Symposium on Practical Software Development Environments*, Pittsburgh, PA, April 1984, pages 157–167. ACM SIGPLAN Notices 19(5), ACM Press. doi: 10.1145/800020.808261. (pages 67, 68, 109, 112, 122, 126 and 136)

David M. Ungar. *The Design and Evaluation of a High Performance Smalltalk System*. ACM distinguished dissertation 1986. MIT Press, 1986. (page 119)

David M. Ungar and Frank Jackson. Tenuring policies for generation-based storage reclamation. In *ACM SIGPLAN Conference on Object-Oriented Programming, Systems, Languages, and Applications*, San Diego, CA, November 1988, pages 1–17. ACM SIGPLAN Notices 23(11), ACM Press. doi: 10.1145/62083.62085. (pages 120, 122, 127, 129, 143, 144 and 146)

David M. Ungar and Frank Jackson. An adaptive tenuring policy for generation scavengers. *ACM Transactions on Programming Languages and Systems*, 14(1):1–27, 1992. doi: 10.1145/111186.116734. (pages 127, 129 and 144)

Maxime van Assche, Joël Goossens and Raymond R. Devillers. Joint garbage collection and hard real-time scheduling. *Journal of Embedded Computing*, 2(3–4):313–326, 2006. http://content.iospress.com/articles/journal-of-embedded-computing/jec00070. Also published in RTS'05 International Conference on Real-Time Systems, 2005. (page 464)

Martin Vechev. *Derivation and Evaluation of Concurrent Collectors*. PhD thesis, University of Cambridge, 2007. (pages 83 and 360)

Martin Vechev, David F. Bacon, Perry Cheng and David Grove. Derivation and evaluation of concurrent collectors. In Andrew P. Black, editor, *19th European Conference on Object-Oriented Programming*, Glasgow, Scotland, July 2005, pages 577–601. Volume 3586 of *Lecture Notes in Computer Science*, Springer-Verlag. doi: 10.1007/11531142_25. (pages 333 and 360)

Martin T. Vechev, Eran Yahav and David F. Bacon. Correctness-preserving derivation of concurrent garbage collection algorithms. In PLDI 2006, pages 341–353. doi: 10.1145/1133981.1134022. (pages 352 and 360)

Martin T. Vechev, Eran Yahav, David F. Bacon and Noam Rinetzky. CGCExplorer: A semi-automated search procedure for provably correct concurrent collectors. In Jeanne Ferrante and Kathryn S. McKinley, editors, *ACM SIGPLAN Conference on Programming Language Design and Implementation*, San Diego, CA, June 2007, pages 456–467. ACM SIGPLAN Notices 42(6), ACM Press. doi: 10.1145/1250734.1250787. (page 335)

VEE 2005, Michael Hind and Jan Vitek, editors. *1st ACM SIGPLAN/SIGOPS International Conference on Virtual Execution Environments*, Chicago, IL, June 2005. ACM Press. doi: 10.1145/1064979. (pages 511, 517 and 540)

José Manuel Velasco, David Atienza, Katzalin Olcoz, Francky Catthoor, Francisco Tirado and Jose Manuel Mendias. Energy characterization of garbage collectors for dynamic applications on embedded systems. In *International Workshop on Integrated Circuit and System Design, Power and Timing Modeling, Optimization and Simulation PATMOS 2005*, Leuven, Belgium, 2005, pages 69–78. (page 466)

Ronald Veldema and Michæl Philippsen. Iterative data-parallel mark&sweep on a GPU. In ISMM 2011, page 1–10. doi: `10.1145/1993478.1993480`. (pages 322 and 323)

David Vengerov. Modeling, analysis and throughput optimization of a generational garbage collector. In ISMM 2009, pages 1–9. doi: `10.1145/1542431.1542433`. (page 129)

Hans-Nikolai Vießmann, Artjoms Šinkarovs and Sven-Bodo Scholz. Extended memory reuse: An optimisation for reducing memory allocations. In *30th International Symposium on Implementation and Application of Functional Languages*, Lowell, MA, USA, 2018, pages 107–118. ACM Press. doi: `10.1145/3310232.3310242`. (page 62)

Jean Vuillemin. A unifying look at data structures. *Communications of the ACM*, 29(4): 229–239, April 1980. doi: `10.1145/358841.358852`. (page 95)

Michal Wegiel and Chandra Krintz. The mapping collector: Virtual memory support for generational, parallel, and concurrent compaction. In Susan J. Eggers and James R. Larus, editors, *13th International Conference on Architectural Support for Programming Languages and Operating Systems*, Seattle, WA, March 2008, pages 91–102. ACM SIGPLAN Notices 43(3), ACM Press. doi: `10.1145/1346281.1346294`. (page 113)

J. Weizenbaum. Recovery of reentrant list structures in SLIP. *Communications of the ACM*, 12(7):370–372, July 1969. doi: `10.1145/363156.363159`. (page 64)

Adam Welc, Suresh Jagannathan and Antony L. Hosking. Transactional monitors for concurrent objects. In Martin Odersky, editor, *18th European Conference on Object-Oriented Programming*, Oslo, Norway, June 2004, pages 519–542. Volume 3086 of *Lecture Notes in Computer Science*, Springer-Verlag. doi: `10.1007/978-3-540-24851-4_24`. (page 288)

Adam Welc, Suresh Jagannathan and Antony L. Hosking. Safe futures for Java. In OOPSLA 2005, pages 439–453. doi: `10.1145/1094811.1094845`. (page 288)

Haosen Wen, Joseph Izraelevitz, Wentao Cai, H. Alan Beadle and Michael L. Scott. Interval-based memory reclamation. In PPOPP 2018, pages 1–13. doi: `10.1145/3178487.3178488`. (page 422)

Sam Westrick, Rohan Yadav, Matthew Fluet and Umut A. Acar. Disentanglement in nested-parallel programs. In *46th Annual ACM SIGPLAN Symposium on Principles of Programming Languages*, January 2019. ACM Press. doi: `10.1145/3371115`. (page 154)

Derek White and Alex Garthwaite. The GC interface in the EVM. Technical Report SML TR–98–67, Sun Microsystems Laboratories, December 1998. `http://dl.acm.org/ft_gateway.cfm?id=974971&type=pdf`. (page 124)

Jon L. White. Address/memory management for a gigantic Lisp environment, or, GC Considered Harmful. In *LISP Conference*, Stanford University, CA, August 1980, pages 119–127. ACM Press. doi: `10.1145/800087.802797`. (pages 53 and 113)

Jon L. White. Three issues in objected-oriented garbage collection. In GC 1990. doi: `10.1145/319016.319042`. (page 145)

Seth J. White and David J. Dewitt. A performance study of alternative object faulting and pointer swizzling strategies. In *18th International Conference on Very Large Data Bases*, Vancouver, British Columbia, Canada, October 1992. (page 477)

Reinhard Wilhelm, Jakob Engblom, Andreas Ermedahl, Niklas Holsti, Stephan Thesing, David B. Whalley, Guillem Bernat, Christian Ferdinand, Reinhold Heckmann, Tulika Mitra, Frank Mueller, Isabelle Puaut, Peter P. Puschner, Jan Staschulat and Per Stenstrøm. The worst-case execution-time problem — overview of methods and survey of tools. *ACM Transactions on Embedded Computer Systems*, 7(3), April 2008. doi: `10.1145/1347375.1347389`. (page 464)

Jesper Wilhelmsson. *Efficient Memory Management for Message-Passing Concurrency — part I: Single-threaded execution*. Licentiate thesis, Uppsala University, May 2005. (page 152)

James A. Wilmore. A hierarchical bit-map format for the representation of IC mask data. In *Proceedings of the 17th Design Automation Conference*, New York, NY, USA, 1980, page 585–589. DAC '80, ACM Press. doi: `10.1145/800139.804590`. (page 97)

Paul R. Wilson. A simple bucket-brigade advancement mechanism for generation-based garbage collection. *ACM SIGPLAN Notices*, 24(5):38–46, May 1989. doi: `10.1145/66068.66070`. (page 122)

Paul R. Wilson. Uniprocessor garbage collection techniques. Technical report, University of Texas, January 1994. `https://www.cs.utexas.edu/ftp/garbage/bigsurv.ps`. Expanded version of the IWMM92 paper. (pages 3, 332, 334, 336 and 337)

Paul R. Wilson and Mark S. Johnstone. Real-time non-copying garbage collection. In GC 1993. `https://www.cs.utexas.edu/ftp/garbage/GC93/wilson.ps`. (page 145)

Paul R. Wilson and Thomas G. Moher. A card-marking scheme for controlling intergenerational references in generation-based garbage collection on stock hardware. *ACM SIGPLAN Notices*, 24(5):87–92, 1989a. doi: `10.1145/66068.66077`. (page 208)

Paul R. Wilson and Thomas G. Moher. Design of the opportunistic garbage collector. In *ACM SIGPLAN Conference on Object-Oriented Programming, Systems, Languages, and Applications*, New Orleans, LA, October 1989b, pages 23–35. ACM SIGPLAN Notices 24(10), ACM Press. doi: `10.1145/74877.74882`. (pages 122, 124, 126, 127 and 208)

Paul R. Wilson, Michael S. Lam and Thomas G. Moher. Effective "static-graph" reorganization to improve locality in garbage-collected systems. In PLDI 1991, pages 177–191. doi: `10.1145/113445.113461`. (pages 54, 55, 57 and 312)

Paul R. Wilson, Mark S. Johnstone, Michael Neely and David Boles. Dynamic storage allocation: A survey and critical review. In IWMM 1995, pages 1–116. doi: `10.1007/3-540-60368-9_19`. (pages 11 and 93)

Paul R. Wilson, Mark S. Johnstone, Michael Neely and David Boles. Memory allocation policies reconsidered. `https://www.cs.utexas.edu/ftp/garbage/submit/PUT_IT_HERE/frag.ps.gz`. Unpublished manuscript, 1995b. (page 101)

David S. Wise. The double buddy-system. Computer Science Technical Report TR79, Indiana University, Bloomington, IN, December 1978. `https://www.cs.indiana.edu/ftp/techreports/TR79.pdf`. (page 101)

David S. Wise. Stop-and-copy and one-bit reference counting. Computer Science Technical Report 360, Indiana University, March 1993a. `https://www.cs.indiana.edu/ftp/techreports/TR360.pdf`. See also Wise [1993b]. (page 77)

David S. Wise. Stop-and-copy and one-bit reference counting. *Information Processing Letters*, 46(5):243–249, July 1993b. doi: `10.1016/0020-0190(93)90103-G`. (page 546)

David S. Wise and Daniel P. Friedman. The one-bit reference count. *BIT*, 17(3):351–359, 1977. doi: `10.1007/BF01932156`. (page 77)

P. Tucker Withington. How real is "real time" garbage collection? In GC 1991. doi: `10.1145/143776.143792`. (pages 110 and 146)

Mario I. Wolczko and Ifor Williams. Multi-level garbage collection in a high-performance persistent object system. In POS 1992, pages 396–418. doi: `10.1007/978-1-4471-3209-7`. (page 114)

Ming Wu and Xiao-Feng Li. Task-pushing: a scalable parallel GC marking algorithm without synchronization operations. In *IEEE International Parallel and Distribution Processing Symposium (IPDPS)*, Long Beach, CA, March 2007, pages 1–10. doi: `10.1109/IPDPS.2007.370317`. (pages 304, 314 and 326)

Mingyu Wu, Ziming Zhao, Haoyu Li, Heting Li, Haibo Chen, Binyu Zang and Haibing Guan. Espresso: Brewing Java for more non-volatility with non-volatile memory. In Xipeng Shen, James Tuck, Ricardo Bianchini and Vivek Sarkar, editors, *23rd International Conference on Architectural Support for Programming Languages and Operating Systems*, Williamsburg, VA, March 2018, pages 70–83. ACM Press. doi: `10.1145/3173162.3173201`. (pages 478 and 480)

Mingyu Wu, Haibo Chen, Hao Zhu, Binyu Zang and Haibing Guan. GCPersist: An efficient GC-assisted lazy persistency framework for resilient Java applications on NVM. In Andrew Baumann and Baris Kasikci, editors, *16th ACM SIGPLAN/SIGOPS International Conference on Virtual Execution Environments*, Lausanne, Switzerland, March 2020a. ACM Press. doi: `10.1145/3381052.3381318`. (page 481)

Mingyu Wu, Ziming Zhao, Yanfei Yang, Haoyu Li, Haibo Chen, Binyu Zang, Haibing Guan, Sanhong Li, Chuansheng Lu and Tongbao Zhang. Platinum: A CPU-efficient concurrent garbage collector for tail-reduction of interactive services. In *2020 USENIX Annual Technical Conference (USENIX ATC 20)*, July 2020b, pages 159–172. USENIX Association. `https://www.usenix.org/conference/atc20/presentation/wu-mingyu`. (page 383)

Feng Xian, Witawas Srisa-an, C. Jia and Hong Jiang. AS-GC: An efficient generational garbage collector for Java application servers. In ECOOP 2007, pages 126–150. doi: `10.1007/978-3-540-73589-2_7`. (page 113)

Bochen Xu, J. Eliot B. Moss and Stephen M. Blackburn. A model checking framework for a new collector framework. In MPLR 2022. (page 83)

Albert Mingkun Yang and Tobias Wrigstad. Deep dive into ZGC: A modern garbage collector in OpenJDK. *ACM Transactions on Programming Languages and Systems*, 44(4): 1–34, 2022. doi: `10.1145/3538532`. (pages xxxiii, 83, 396 and 399)

Albert Mingkun Yang, Erik Österlund and Tobias Wrigstad. Improving program locality in the GC using hotness. In *ACM SIGPLAN Conference on Programming Language Design and Implementation*, London, June 2020. ACM Press. doi: `10.1145/3385412.3385977`. (page 398)

Ting Yang, Emery D. Berger, Matthew Hertz, Scott F. Kaplan and J. Eliot B. Moss. Autonomic heap sizing: Taking real memory into account. In ISMM 2004, pages 61–72. doi: `10.1145/1029873.1029881`. (page 221)

Xi Yang, Stephen M. Blackburn, Daniel Frampton, Jennifer B. Sartor and Kathryn S. McKinley. Why nothing matters: The impact of zeroing. In *ACM SIGPLAN Conference on Object-Oriented Programming, Systems, Languages, and Applications*, Portland, OR, October 2011, pages 307–324. ACM Press. doi: `10.1145/2048066.2048092`. (page 176)

Xi Yang, Stephen M. Blackburn, Daniel Frampton and Antony L. Hosking. Barriers reconsidered, friendlier still! In ISMM 2012, pages 37–48. doi: `10.1145/2258996.2259004`. (page 202)

Taiichi Yuasa. Real-time garbage collection on general-purpose machines. *Journal of Systems and Software*, 11(3):181–198, March 1990. doi: `10.1016/0164-1212(90)90084-Y`. (pages 338, 340, 341, 342, 349, 352, 358, 364, 407 and 426)

Karen Zee and Martin Rinard. Write barrier removal by static analysis. In OOPSLA 2002, pages 191–210. doi: `10.1145/582419.582439`. (pages 139, 149, 173 and 349)

Chengliang Zhang, Kirk Kelsey, Xipeng Shen, Chen Ding, Matthew Hertz and Mitsunori Ogihara. Program-level adaptive memory management. In ISMM 2006, pages 174–183. doi: `10.1145/1133956.1133979`. (page 222)

W. Zhao, K. Ramamritham and J.A. Stankovic. Scheduling tasks with resource requirements in hard real-time systems. *IEEE Transactions on Software Engineering*, SE-13 (5):564–577, May 1987. doi: `10.1109/TSE.1987.233201`. (page 464)

Wenyu Zhao, Steve Blackburn and Kathryn S. McKinley. Low-latency, high-throughput garbage collection. In *Proceedings of the 43rd ACM SIGPLAN Conference on Programming Language Design and Implementation*, San Diego, CA, June 2022a. ACM Press. doi: `10.1145/3519939.3523440`. (pages 65, 68, 79, 138, 205, 347, 368, 405 and 408)

Wenyu Zhao, Steve Blackburn and Kathryn S. McKinley. Low-latency, high-throughput garbage collection (extended version). arXiv:2210.17175v1, October 2022b. https://arxiv.org/abs/2210.17175v1. (pages 65, 68, 79, 138, 205, 368 and 405)

Benjamin Zorn. Barrier methods for garbage collection. Technical Report CU-CS-494-90, University of Colorado, Boulder, November 1990. `https://scholar.colorado.edu/concern/reports/47429970d`. (pages 131, 349 and 442)

Benjamin Zorn. The measured cost of conservative garbage collection. *Software: Practice and Experience*, 23:733–756, 1993. doi: `10.1002/spe.4380230704`. (page 122)

Benjamin G. Zorn. *Comparative Performance Evaluation of Garbage Collection Algorithms.* PhD thesis, University of California, Berkeley, March 1989. http://www.eecs.berkeley.edu/Pubs/TechRpts/1989/CSD-89-544.pdf. Technical Report UCB/CSD 89/544. (pages 11 and 119)

Index

Note: If an entry has particular defining occurrences, the page numbers appear in bold, such as **17**, and if it has occurrences deemed primary, their page numbers appear in italics, such as *53*. An entry 'X *see* Y, —' indicates to look under 'Y, X.'

Colophon

This book was set in Palatino (algorithms in Courier) with PDFLATEX (from the TEX Live 2022 distribution). The figures were drawn with Adobe Illustrator, versions CS3 to 26.5. We found the following packages to be useful: `helvet` (sans serif text, scaled to match body text), `courier` (algorithms), `mathpazo` (typesetting mathematics to match Palatino body text), `amssymb` and `amsmath` (mathematics), `comment` (comments), `paralist` (in-paragraph lists), `geometry` (page size), `crop` (crop marks), `textpos` (positioning of cover images), `xspace` (space suppression), `setspace` (line spacing), `fnbreak` (detect footnotes spread over more than one page), `afterpage` (page break control), `tabularx` (tabular material), `multicol` (multiple columns), `multirow` (multiple rows/columns in tables), `dcolumn` ("decimal points" in tables), `caption` and `subcaption` (captions), `graphicx` and `epstopdf` (graphics), `listings` (algorithm listings), `rotating` (rotate objects), `suffix` (define command variants), `xparse` (constructing macros with optional arguments), `glossaries` and `glossaries-extra` (glossaries), `makeidx`, `index` and `idxlayout` (index), `hyperref` (hyperlinks), `varioref` and `cleveref` (smarter references), and `natbib` (bibliography).

Printed in the United States
by Baker & Taylor Publisher Services